THE
SAILMAKER'S
APPRENTICE

THE
SAILMAKER'S APPRENTICE

A GUIDE FOR THE SELF-RELIANT SAILOR

EMILIANO MARINO

ILLUSTRATED BY

CHRISTINE ERIKSON

International Marine
Camden, Maine

To ALL THOSE in whose hearts, minds, and labors the time-honored arts and

traditions of sailmaking, rigging, and sailing endure.

International Marine/
Ragged Mountain Press
A Division of The McGraw·Hill Companies

10 9 8 7 6 5 4

Copyright © 1994 International Marine®, a division
of The McGraw-Hill Companies.

Library of Congress Cataloging-in-Publication Data

Marino, Emiliano.
   The sailmaker's apprentice / Emiliano Marino ;
illustrated by Christine Erikson.
      p.   cm.
   Includes bibliographical references and index.
   ISBN 0-07-157980-X (alk. paper)
   1. Sails. 2. Sails—Maintenance and repair.
   I. Title.
VM532.M22   1994
623.8'62—dc20   94-12493
                                             CIP

Questions regarding the content of this book
should be addressed to:

International Marine
   P.O. Box 220
   Camden, ME 04843

Questions regarding the ordering of this book
should be addressed to:

The McGraw-Hill Companies
   Customer Service Department
   P.O. Box 547
   Blacklick, OH 43004
   Retail Customers: 1-800-262-4729
   Bookstores: 1-800-722-4726

The Sailmaker's Apprentice is printed on acid-free
paper.

Printed by *Quebecor Printing, Fairfield, PA*
Design by *Amy Fischer*
Production and page layout by *Janet Robbins*
Edited by *Jonathan Eaton, DeAnna Lunden,*
Pamela Benner, Dorathy Chocensky

Contents

Tables

Preface

A LTHOUGH I BEGAN WORK on *The Sailmaker's Apprentice* sixteen years ago, it would be a mess o' galley whispers to suggest that its creation has been a concerted sixteen-year effort. Rather, it has been an intermittent process marked by setbacks, diversions, some lucky breaks, and much encouragement from family and friends. So fid out your earholes while I spin a bit of a yarn about the process.

I wrote the pieces of this book in pretty much the same sequence in which they now appear, although recently acquired facts, updates, and inspirations were inserted in later drafts of the manuscript. Portions of *The Sailmaker's Apprentice* are reprints of material originally published in *WoodenBoat* magazine under my adoptive name, Malcolm Wehncke. More recently, I became "the Sail Doctor" for a question-and-answer column in *Small Boat Journal* magazine. That column and other pieces reprinted here were published under the stage name and *nom de plume* Malcolm Howes. I then entered a whole new life by finding my birth parents, their families, and my biological heritage. I have since woven a new identity for myself that has incorporated not only my family heritages but also my chosen name, Emiliano Marino.

I remain one of the many sailors who sees sailing as a means of holding onto a natural interaction with the earth and its elements. There are sailmakers who still practice the old ways of building sails—ways that, comparatively speaking, placed humans in balance with nature. I invite you, my apprentice, to seek that balance too by taking up the needle and palm, and by ploughing the oceans of the earth under sail, hearing the wind, with wings you've made yourself with your own magic and your own hands.

Emiliano Marino
World Citizen

Acknowledgments

T O THE FOLLOWING INDIVIDUALS I wish to express my heartfelt appreciation and gratitude for their care, support, and contributions to my life as a sailor, sailmaker, and author.

In particular, I must thank: John Foster, friend and sailor, for his unswerving devotion to me and my projects; Grant Gambell, sailmaker, for his patience, good humor, and generous sharing of sailmaking expertise; Christine Erikson, the illustrator, for her impeccable skill in rendering the details of sails, sailing, and sailmaking so intimately that one can almost taste, feel, and smell the subject; Robin Lincoln, sailmaker, for her love, partnership, and dedication to the launching of our respective sailmaking careers; Jon Eaton, friend, editor, and sailor, for his faith and willingness to revitalize this project and for his patience and good humor while serving as editor, advisor, mediator, and salesman throughout a prolonged literary birth.

Amber
Abe Baggins
Tom Baker
Carl Barus
David N. Barus

Jane Garey Barus
Maxwell Barus
Pamela Benner
Lindy Brooking
Matt Brown
Paddy Bruce
Challenge Sailcloth, Inc. (Bob Bainbridge, Carter Clark, Terry Cronburg)
Francisco Chaves Saenz y Familia
Dorathy Chocensky
Eva
John T. Fallon
Amy Fischer
Carol Hasse
Brad Hunter
David Jackson
Senator Edward M. Kennedy
Roberto Laingelet
Richard Lebovitz
Sam and Susan Manning
Mariposa
Anne Maxtone-Graham
Paul Mitchell
Grace Niniane Moondog
Moses
Selkie O'Mira

Brad Pease
Mike Pease
Patricia Pease
The Phillip Garey Fund
Janet Robbins
Anne Seeley
David Seeley

Barry Spanier
Peter Spectre
Roger C. Taylor
Brion Toss
Jane Ellen Wehncke
John Wehncke
Jon Wilson

Introduction

THIS BOOK IS AN EXTENSION OF ME. I make no bones about my being a writer. I am not. An entertainer perhaps, but a writer no. A writer, a wordsmith, can make a literary creation concerning any subject whether it interests him or her personally or not. I can't do that. I need some source of inspiration. I doubt I could even set down any thoughts about sails and sailing, subjects of considerable interest to me, were it not that I am not merely recording dry fact and observation; I am recording much of my philosophy, my aspirations, and my heritage.

I do not offer this confession apologetically, nor is this book about me. I will endeavor not to trot out my personal preferences and beliefs so frequently as to harass, intimidate, or bore the reader. Nonetheless, the information, assertions, and perspectives of this book are all organized, discussed, explored, and illustrated in light of my personal outlook on sails, sailmaking, and sailing.

I had the extraordinary good fortune to be adopted at the age of five months by a family who, on my adoptive mother's side, were descendants of a long line of seafaring ancestors. From the union of Thomas Howes and Mary Burr, who arrived on what is now called Cape Cod, Massachusetts, in 1635, there came successive generations of Howes, many of whom were involved in the maritime trades. It was Captain Frederick Howes of Brewster, for instance, who invented the Howes Patented Close-reefing Topsail. His and other tops'l shortening arrangements, which divided the formerly single square-rigged tops'l into two smaller, handier sails, were quickly refined and almost overnight universally adopted by square-rigged vessels.

It was my great-great-great-grandfather Osborn Howes, son of a ship captain, and a captain himself by the age of twenty-two, who, with his brother-in-law Nathan Crowell, formed the renowned Howes and Crowell shipping firm of Boston in 1838.

The nautical heritage involving Osborn Howes and his eldest son, Isaiah, had a great influence upon me. This book's illustrator and I shared residence with the last surviving grandchild of Isaiah Howes. Howes family lore has enchanted me since my earliest recollections: sea stories passed down; early prints, paintings, and then photographs; tales of square-rigged merchant vessels sailing under the Howes and Crowell flag, with its red star on a white field; fantastic yarns of life at sea. A considerable part of my youth was spent in the house in which Osborn Howes was born. Still in the family's possession were antiques brought back from voyages to the Orient.

Howes ingenuity and skill under sail did not

The ship Osborne Howes.

The Howes close-reefing tops'l.

adapt well to the inexorable advance of steam-powered transport. The sun slowly set on the Howes and Crowell flag as it did on sail-driven freighters in general. Nonetheless, the twentieth-century Howes descendants carried on certain traditions of nautical competence with a passion.

I was taught to sail in handsome wooden boats on Bass River, Cape Cod. Auxiliary motors were disdained. Nautical prowess was esteemed both on the race course and in voyaging. Only in a dead calm, on an outgoing tide, with the gnats gnawing mercilessly would we even consider resorting to oar or paddle if it was at all possible to make the mooring under sail! And don't think we got a whole lot of sympathy when we arrived home late and festooned with gnat bites! Foolhardiness and blissful arrogance with respect to the elements and the capabilities of a boat were sternly discouraged. The skills of reefing, navigation, and marlinspike work were highly regarded. We learned weather lore and observed the tides. We were taught respect for our craft, how to sail in safety, how to properly stow gear and the boat, and how to care for sails.

Most of my feelings and many of my attitudes about sailboats and sailing were formed in this Bass River, Cape Cod, environment—a familial situation fostered and maintained primarily by my grandparents, both of whom were direct descendants of Osborn Howes. I am sure that my strong sense of appreciation for the fine lines and shapes of a well-proportioned hull and rig developed when I was a child. Unforgettable are the smells of varnish, hemp, manila line, wet cotton sailcloth, tarred marline, and salt water in a wooden bilge.

I remember distinctly being small enough to

crawl under the foredeck of an 18-foot Wianno Jr. in order to escape the cold spray coming in over the weather rail. There in my safe, dry "cabin" I could feel the motion of the hull as it plowed through the afternoon chop kicked up by the prevailing so'westerly breeze on Nantucket Sound. I could hear the slosh, whoosh, and churn of water rushing by a wooden hull. Back again in the sheltered waters of the river, that din would change to an inimitable gurgle, a sound made only by the gentle action of wavelets against wood.

Huddled down there alongside the stop bucket, bilge pump, spare oar, boathook, anchor, rode, and spare line, I could look aft and observe the handling of the boat: the raising and lowering of the centerboard, the trimming of sheets, the tiller steering. I was often cold and wet but never frightened. More sounds: the slat of sails, the soft patter of reef nettles, "Ready abooout! Hard aleee!" So many sensual delights and thrills! There is no taste comparable to that obtained by sucking the salt water out of a sopping wet lifejacket lacing. Nor is there any sound quite like that of a gong buoy clanging at sea. And where can one find a complete and utter contrast to rival that of finally putting up helm and running downwind; the change in motion, sounds, action, warmth, and spray?

In a couple of years I became too big to fit under the foredeck. Then there were the wild afternoons sitting astride the stemhead fitting, riding the plunging prow as the little sloop pitched and nosed through South Shore waves. I clutched the forestay firmly with both hands as water sloshed aft across the foredeck, over the coaming, and down the sidedecks. I was then, and still am, filled with awe when looking over the transom down onto the wake of a moving sailboat. I am enchanted and captivated by the smooth, powerful eddies of water as they well up from the depths.

From a small child launched into this nautical world, it was not long before I was at the helm. Now a sailor myself, I further developed an appreciation for the forces and happenings I'd formerly recognized only as feelings and perceptions. I began to give analytical thought to the harmony and inter-action of hull, rig, and sail, with each other and with wind and water. The forms, sounds, and smells became associated with functions. There would be many ways in the future to accomplish a particular nautical endeavor—preserve a spar, drop and weigh anchor, cleat a centerboard pendant, rig a boat, build a sail—but inevitably I'd find myself drawn back to the early sense of aesthetics and character with which I'd been imbued.

That is what sailing remains for me in great part: the feelings derived from the parts and from the whole. In addition to that, I delight in the mechanical challenge of sailing, the challenge of beating odds, of sailing the most efficient course, the thrill of making flawless, spectacular landings under sail in a crowded anchorage. And even more than that I obtain the greatest of pleasure and fulfillment from accomplishing something under sail, performing some task. I feel a greater sense of meaningful endeavor when I am sailing with a purpose beyond diversion and entertainment. I like few things better than the feel of powerful movement through the water, but I am not enthralled by the pursuit of speed for its own sake and none other.

Perhaps it was New England tradition, or maybe my own obstinacy, and surely my economic circumstances and passion for self-sufficiency that led me to prefer sailing as independently and self-reliantly as possible. I wanted to be able to handle and maintain everything on board my vessel myself—even build most of it. In the event there was something I had neither the time nor ability to do, I felt I should have a seagoing trade to barter for the necessary goods or services.

With that in mind, and the notion that a seafaring life offered freedom and a natural lifestyle, I set out for San Diego, California, in search of opportunities. There I had the good fortune to fall in with two sailor/sailmakers who were willing to take me on, first as a rigging associate and then as a sailmaking apprentice. This was providential not only from the standpoint that someone in the business of making sails was willing to work with me at all, but that their loft produced durable, reliable sails that voyaging sailors could maintain at sea. This was no hemp and pine tar place, but, utilizing contemporary materials, they were making seaworthy sails with traditional hand-finishing techniques. My heart, soul, and abilities fit in. Perhaps that's why they let me stay.

Not long thereafter I started my own sail loft in Costa Rica, undertaking sail and rigging work for all sorts of vessels from sailboards to square-riggers. I saw boats, sailors, and sails from all over the globe. I saw everything from the ancient and traditional in sail materials and sail construction to the latest and most modern. I saw craft that were the product of skilled design, manufacture, and

maintenance, and others that were absolute make-do, seat-of-the-pants nautical concoctions. I observed the most up-to-date nautical electronic know-how and I saw bungling dead reckoning by street map! And I came to know from my own experience and that of so many other sailors what works in a sail and what does not. Storm, calm, heat, cold, sun, corrosion, constant use, chafe, stress, time, and more stress all took their toll. Costa Rica was far enough from anyplace else sails were made that, by the time a sailboat would arrive at the popular Central American port of Puntarenas, the durability of its sails had been well tested. Things took on a new slant. What had formerly been an aesthetic, philosophical, and theoretical approach to sailmaking became also practical.

It did not take long to fetch up on an unhappy discovery. In the United States and in other parts of the world, the average undiscerning "cruising" sailor was consistently being sold sails of poor quality. It would be comparable to selling a sky-diver a parachute built to self-destruct in mid-descent! To extend the analogy: If the parachutist had the presence of mind to attempt a repair of his tattered brolly during the ensuing plummet, he'd find that the chute had been constructed of materials not normally found in the average skydiver's repair kit, with mechanical laborsaving techniques that could not be reworked. *Caveat nauticus!*

And that is really how this book began. In its early fetal life, it was a pamphlet entitled "The Sail-maker's Dozen," a consumer's guide to sail construction that I passed out to sailors who put in to Puntarenas. It was a polemic; I was enraged by the swindle. Some sailmakers' victims actually thought I must be a landshark strategically located there, post-"papagayo," to rake in the dolares repairing or replacing their sails—their *new sails*—which despite all the assurances and promises of the maker were now a wreck! These sails, upon which people's lives depended, were consistently falling apart in a predictable manner.

I am still, fifteen years later, angered by the hype and ethics of the production sailmaking industry, and I mourn the general loss of traditional skill and artistry in sailmaking. Furthermore, I deplore a wasteful, thrill-seeking, exploitative economy of sails and sailing, so lacking in foresight except where making a bigger and faster buck is concerned.

I do not wish to alienate you by my ranting and raving about the shortcomings of mass-production sailmaking and boatbuilding. Nor will I risk offending you with pusillanimous platitudes, the jargon of the overbearing traditionalist. Beauty is in the eye of the beholder. What people choose to spend their money on, even if they knowingly choose "economy" over safety, is their own business (as long as I am not aboard). Undiscerning and compulsive consumers will always find a sailmaker, or whoever, to sell them something at the "right price."

There are, fortunately, a few artisans in the business of making sails who, while working in synthetic materials too, nonetheless continue to employ time-honored sailmaking principles and techniques. These humans rely primarily on acquired knowledge, personal experience, and their own brains and memories to create a suit of sails. Some of these people may have business and money-making acumen as well, but they all are making sails the way they do because they inherited or adopted a personal interest in the skill, artistry, and aesthetics involved. If they had not, they surely would not persist in trying to survive by making sails in a manner that by modern lights is archaic, anachronistic, and obsolete.

Now, and in the years to come, every voyaging sailboat will require a manageable number of high-quality sails of versatile design and function, and made of materials compatible with those requisites. For these, for seaworthy daysailers, and for classic small boats with their time-honored rigs, the techniques of this book are of particular relevance.

I recognize that more of you will repair, alter, or reinforce sails than will make them. The making of sails, like sailing itself, is hard work. At the same time, sailmaking is an art from which one can derive considerable pleasure and fulfillment, not to mention seagoing self-reliance. It is my fervent desire that this book, with its unique holistic approach to the subject, will open doors of appreciation, creativity, and resourcefulness, for the practical and adventurous sailor as well as the aspiring sailmaker. It is all connected: the sailor, the purpose for sailing, conditions, hull type, rig type, sail type, sail shape, sail materials and construction. I urge you to follow the deductive path, apply reasoning to your own situation, and, most important, to enjoy the process. Take delight in the act as well as the accomplishment of meeting your seafaring and general sailing needs.

A Note on Gender

Despite the fact that sexism in the sailing world is still going strong, a growing number of nautical artisans are women. Rarely is the serious participation of women in nautical endeavors acknowledged, even though women are the equal of men under sail, and there are skilled, competent women in all the maritime trades including the making of sails.

The traditional language of the sea *is* archaic in this regard (so much for die-hard traditionalism!): It excludes women. Sailmaking and sail repair is not "women's work" by virtue of its involving sewing, any more than it is "men's work" by virtue of its being a business. Sailing is everyone's work!

I'm afraid I don't care for the substitution or insertion of the word "person" in order to neuter a term, and substituting the word "woman" to make "seawomanlike," for example, does not produce a term which the Bard would say flows trippingly over the tongue. Absent from this book unless literally appropriate will be such terms as seaman, seamanlike, man this and that, seamanship, seawomanship, and so forth. Rest assured: Sailing and sailmaking are equally domains of women.

1

A Ditty Bag Apprenticeship

S EE HOW SHE SCHOONS! Cutting a feather in a four-lower breeze, sails filling in powerful curves and pulling like the muscles of a draft horse with a heavy load; sails straining under the relentless force of the wind!

By moonrise, the wind's diminished to a whisper—hardly a ripple on the water as she ghosts slowly along under light sails; great cloth phantoms tranquilly billowing in the moonlight.

Or in an oily calm, the limp cloth slats and slams from side to side, awaiting the day when it might explode from its boltropes under the force of a howling gale and be lashed and beaten to useless shreds. Harmony and discord in the marriage of wind, wave, wood, and cloth.

Cloth is admirable for both what it is and what it *does*. First a fiber, spun into thread and woven into a workable, versatile, yet vulnerable fabric, cloth is made into sails, the soul and salvation of the sailing boat. Cloth is a remarkable material; it comes only as a long strip to begin with and is dynamic by nature. Someone has to cut and assemble the pieces, control or compensate for the cloth's instabilities, provide a means of attaching things to it, and, of course, maintain the finished article. No two ways about it, the ability to work with cloth, synthetic or natural, is fundamental to sailing.

The sailing ship's onboard ability to deal with the various elements upon which its survival depended was once an absolute necessity, and there were always men aboard capable of handling the various materials, not the least of whom was the sailmaker. He was not alone in working with canvas; even the greenest hand had to take up needle and palm when there was extensive work to be done. Seafaring people ashore, out of geographical or economic necessity, had no less a need to be self-sufficient in the manufacture and repair of the sails for the boats with which they earned their livelihood. Those Johnny Newcombes who'd assist the seagoing sailmaker were often initiated into the sailor's arts by the making of a ditty bag. Those small bags were sometimes elaborately and intricately finished, thus offering a means of self-expression and furnishing something to occupy idle hands and to keep the mind alive.

To launch you in your apprenticeship, we are going to teach you about the ditty bag, help you gather together the tools you will need to make a ditty bag (and to use on your own for making and maintaining your sails), and then teach you to make the ditty bag itself, using techniques that will prepare you for many other tasks related to sailmaking, repair, and maintenance.

The proposed ditty bag and its contents embody

all sorts of abstract things as well as being a handy receptacle. But the skills! That's what you're really after. Remember, it's not the bag alone. This ditty bag is a cloth article requiring all the basic sail- and canvaswork skills, and in this carefully handcrafted container are stored the very implements and materials used in its creation. All is then in readiness for sail- or canvaswork. You'll know every stitch! The economy of doing your own work should be apparent, and so too will be the practicality, because the tools are simple, portable, and relatively inexpensive.

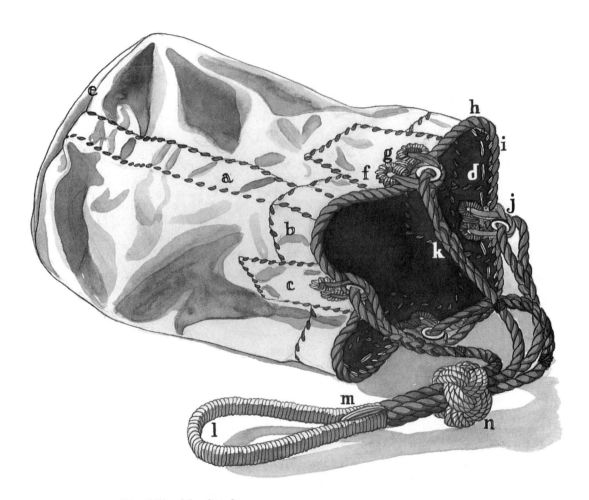

FIGURE 1-1. *The skills of the ditty bag.*
(a) Flat-stitched side seam
(b) Flat-stitched rolled tabling
(c) Flat-stitched reinforcement patches
(d) Sticking stitch
(e) Round stitch
(f) Worked eyelets
(g) Eyelet seizings
(h) Rope grommet
(i) Roping stitch
(j) Cringle and round thimble
(k) Sailmaker's eyesplice
(l) Marline serving
(m) Flat seizing
(n) Turk's head slider

The faint of heart might be heard to exclaim, "What about the sewing machine?" The sewing machine, in relation to this ditty bag, is like the relationship a motor has to the sails of a sailboat. It can substantially augment the ditty bag, but it is a poor substitute. There's no doubt about the time-saving capabilities of a sewing machine under favorable working conditions, but the sewing machine doesn't have the versatility, all-around capability, simplicity, and dependability of your hands, and the skills, techniques, and tools of this ditty bag apprenticeship.

With the fade-out of the fossil fuel–eating engine, the return of cloth sail power isn't going to come for free. Sails are going to become even more expensive than they are now. Obviously, it behooves prudent seafarers to cast an anchor to windward and not only concentrate on sails and sailing, but become capable of making and maintaining those wings upon which their boats will fly.

TOOLS

Plainly, it's time to introduce the tools, but only those required to make the ditty bag. Other tools of sailwork are introduced in Chapter 5.

Hands

First and foremost, meet your hands! Whether they be more dexterous on the left or right doesn't matter, except that most sailmaking instructions presume the worker to be right-handed. That's not an insurmountable obstacle. For a left-hander, there are two options: perform everything from the opposite point of view, or teach yourself to work righty—whichever comes more easily.

The Sailmaker's Palm

This is the indispensable tool with which the needle is pushed through the cloth. Waste not time nor money on the cheap models, or what is called a *sailor's palm,* as they are nearly use-

FIGURE 1-2 (PAGES 3–4). *Sailmaker's palms.*

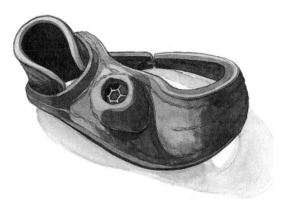

LEFT-HANDED ROPING PALM

ROPING EYE

SEAMING EYE

FIGURE 1-2. *(cont.)*

less and will not encourage you to sew. Seek instead a high-quality sailmaker's palm of finished leather and rawhide, a stout article firmly stitched.

There are two principal types of palms, both of which are essential, depending upon the job to be undertaken. The *seaming palm* is for sewing seams, tablings, and patching, and has an eye with small indentations to take the head of the smaller needles used in those and other finer operations. The *roping palm* is for the stouter work of sewing a boltrope to a sail, and has an eye with large indentations for the needles required in roping and other heavy work. In addition, the roping palm has a protective piece about the thumb hole so that a stitch can be hove home without the thread cutting the worker's hand.

Both palms are highly personal tools. Ideally, they are custom made for your hand only, or at least have been altered from a production version so that they are best suited to your hand and

sewing techniques. The "public palm," while better than nothing, is an abomination. Worse yet is the ham-handed nozzer's disrespectful attempt to cram his hand into someone's carefully fitted and broken-in palm.

Make the palm fit your hand. If it's too small to begin with, it's worthless to you anyway. A big palm can be reduced to some extent and the fit can be adjusted with the addition of leather padding. The palm and your hand become one. Fit it. Wet it. Work with it. Oil it. Then work more with it—and don't share!

Needles

Sail needles are triangular in section with the edges rounded so that the needle separates rather than severs the threads of the cloth as it enters and passes through. The thickness, or gauge, of the needle to be used depends upon the size of the thread

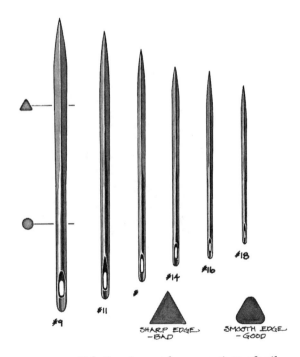

#18

#16

#14

#11

#9

SHARP EDGE
-BAD

SMOOTH EDGE
-GOOD

FIGURE 1-3. *Relative sizes and cross sections of sail needles. The No. 18 is 2¼ inches long; the No. 9, 4 inches.*

required in the sewing and the nature of the material sewn. Usually, the two requirements coincide, but not always. Synthetic sail twine, because of its great strength, can be smaller than cotton thread for a given application, but your needle should always be sized according to the cloth it has to penetrate. Matching the needle to the smaller thread may result in breakage.

Aboard ship there is use for *all* sizes. Therefore each size should be on hand, and it would be wise to have a few extra of the smaller or more frequently used needles. Sail needles in the smaller sizes break occasionally, and even the larger ones can be bent under the strain of heavy work.

Nothing makes sewing more tedious than a dull or dirty needle. Needles can be kept sharp with a razor hone or sharpening steel. Sail needles are wonderful little tools, but they will rust at the mere mention of the word moisture, especially at sea. Keep them oiled or greased and stored in an *airtight* container!

Knife

The knife is probably the most versatile tool in the bag. Within the realms of sail- and marlinspike work, it has many uses and can satisfactorily stand in for tools such as scissors and hole cutters.

Whether clasp or sheath knife, a blade with a rounded back, sheep's-foot point, and V-ground blade is best. Homemade or store-bought, the knife must be of good steel, kept clean, oiled, and sharp as a razor. This knife must never be asked to do anything but cut cloth, twine, or cordage.

Sailhook

The needle-sharp steel *sailhook* (also called a *stretching hook* or *bench hook*), with its swivel and 5- or 6-foot lanyard, facilitates various forms of sewing by holding the cloth in the desired manner so that tension can be applied and cloth layers kept in line, flat and immobilized. Sailhooks, bought or made, must be protected from rust just like needles and knives.

Fids

These come in an infinite variety and are used to expand, open, and ream things. They open the strands of a rope in splicing, or shape and smooth the inside of a handsewn ring. They make holes in cloth and stretch cringles prior to the insertion of

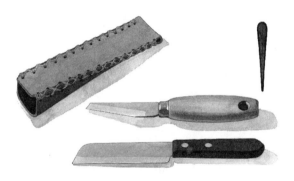

FIGURE 1-4. *Two ordinary knives adapted for sail- and canvaswork. The upper is a leatherworker's knife, the lower, a common kitchen knife with the tip ground to a sheep's-foot point.*

FIGURE 1-5. *The sailhook—the sailmaker's third hand. Note the scorpion stingerlike point with shoulders, which prevents the hook from goring the cloth with a large hole.*

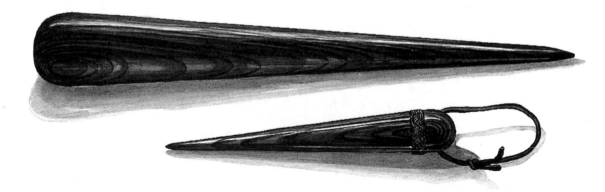

FIGURE 1-6. *Two fids of rosewood, ebony, lignum vitae, or a similar hardwood. The smaller is 12 inches long, the larger, 18 inches.*

FIGURE 1-7. *A traditional seam rubber carved from black locust.*

a round thimble. They are usually made of a hardwood such as lignum vitae, and one can get by with two of them, a small one and one that is moderately large.

Seam Rubber

Your own creation out of hardwood, this tool is for creasing cloth as well as smoothing stitches. The rounded knife back will serve, and really any hard smooth edge will do, but the seam rubber assures the job is done comfortably and consistently.

Mechanical Pencil

Notwithstanding the impression given by some sewing instructions, one can't expect to do all this clothwork without guidelines. Reference points are needed on the cloth. For marking the cloth, a mechanical pencil with a hard lead works best, and one becomes accustomed to the shape of this pencil and learns to make the appropriate allowances consistently. Lines and marks must be visible, but yet not smudge.

Push Pins and Awls

Push pins and awls come in handy for holding the cloth while it's laid out and marked. Many dozens of push pins would not be too many, but a half-dozen awls will suffice. They all rust, of course, and must be encased somehow.

Measuring Tape

Although there are successful ways of measuring without one, I recommend a 12-foot locking tape measure. It would seem as though you couldn't get along without it—but, of course, you can. It's possible to make do with all sorts of objects as units of measurement as long as you are consistent about it. Parts of the human body (your own) are the handiest objects: arm span, foot length, hand's breadth, and others. Those measuring devices are difficult to misplace, fairly immutable, and they don't rust!

In Addition

If you're planning on getting into canvaswork beyond making a ditty bag and occasional sail repair, you'll want to consider adding the following tools to those listed above:

- a 50-foot measuring tape
- heavy-duty scissors
- heavy-duty diagonal cutters for removing seizings, brass liners, and pressed-in grommets
- pliers for pulling needles stuck in heavy cloth
- an electric hotknife for cutting and sealing unhemmed synthetic cloth edges
- 50 feet of ¾-inch nylon webbing for drawing curves
- a chalkline
- a stitch or seam ripper

More than this we need not say until Chapter 5.

For a clearer idea of what all these tools are like, you might visit a sailmaker and ask to see these things. With luck, he or she will be happy to show you. Pay attention, as the sailmaker who doesn't use these tools regularly doesn't make the kind of sail *you* could easily work on either.

MATERIALS

While you're there, you could ask to see, and maybe purchase, the following materials without which no ditty bag would be complete.

Thread or Sail Twine

The type of thread or sail twine you need depends on the nature and stature of the work. Three-ply and seven-ply spun polyester will cover most needs. You can always quadruple it. The thread must be as strong and durable as the fabric. Linen thread is nearly unobtainable; you can find cotton twine in the form of heavy machine thread. Synthetic thread is strongest and most easily found. It may be used to sew natural fabric, but not generally the other way around.

If you have braided line or continuous filament three-strand polyester line, you've a source of sewing thread. Just cut a piece the appropriate length (remember it will be doubled through the needle) and unlay it down from strand to yarn to thread, and even to filament, to get the size twine desired. This source of twine is time-consuming but has the advantages of a wide range of thread and availability. It may be obtained at most boat shops, or, in an emergency, a length of sheet or halyard can be sacrificed.

Beeswax

Unless you are a glutton for punishment, you really can't sew with thread unless it's been waxed. Beeswax mixed with turpentine or pine tar makes thread more manageable and helps preserve natural fibers. With synthetic fiber, it helps hold the two threads together while you work. I don't recommend prewaxed thread; the spool is bulky and you always seem to need to wax the thread again anyway.

To prepare yourself for sail repair and maintenance, you should also gather together the following items:

Cloth

The cloth needed for sail repair is identical to that of which your sails are made. Now, whether you want to carry merely patching quantities or enough cloth for major surgery is a matter of personal preference. I'd be prepared to repair a sail torn from luff to leech. Cloth for more than that won't fit in a bag, or even a locker, but the prudent bluewater sailor might consider the possibility of having enough to make entirely new sails at some point when materials aren't within UPS range.

Seizing Line

Used in various parts of a sail, it is often heavy sail twine that has been redoubled for extra strength. Italian tarred hemp yacht marline, both light and heavy, has innumerable uses in marlinspike work, and of course there are synthetic alternatives.

Sail Hardware

Spares are needed for whatever hardware your sails and canvas goods use: thimbles, fasteners, slides, etc. That's not true in the case of a sail full of quick-throwaway hardware like squeeze-on hanks and spur-grommets. In that case, one must be prepared to replace *all* such things with sensible gear before they destroy the sail. Remember, no crimp-on or punch-in stuff; you don't have the tools to install it, and you can't reuse it.

Leather

On those parts of a sail where chafe is unavoidable, chafing gear, notably leather, has to be replaced. Leather's expensive, but not much is needed. A square foot or two of pliable, well-tanned or even oiled hide is sufficient. In the absence of leather, cloth can be used.

The materials you'll need to make the ditty bag are:

- 1 square yard of 13-ounce preshrunk, mildewproofed canvas
- 1 spool of three-ply spun polyester sail twine
- 1 ball of tarred hemp yacht marline

- 10 feet of ¼-inch-diameter manila line
- 4 round thimbles with ¼-inch score
- beeswax

Less salty equivalents to tarred hemp and manila are permissible. It's your call.

CUTTING, FOLDING, AND MARKING THE CLOTH

Do you have the cloth? The pins, pencil, knife or scissors, seam rubber, tape measure, and straightedge?

How's your work space? Roomy, warm, well-lighted, and tranquil, hopefully? The surface upon which you'll work should be clean, flat, and wooden, but not your prize floor or table. You'll be sticking pins in it.

Preparation is as important as anything. Relax. Concentrate. Each step in this kind of work is dependent upon the preceding one, and the final outcome and general ease of completion are greatly affected by thoroughness along the way.

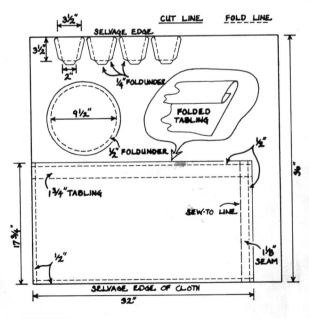

FIGURE 1-8.

Lay out the cloth as shown in Figure 1-8. It should be pinned out firmly, square, flat, and lying naturally without distortion. Draw the lines for the walls of the bag as indicated. Mark them dark and identify them as to their future use: fold, cut, or a reference sew-to line. The upper part of the bag, when folded over, will become a hem or tabling. The side seam and patches also get hemmed under—all exposed cut cloth must be hemmed in order to prevent unraveling. Both the bottom of the bag wall and the patches are cut from the piece of cloth in a way that utilizes the nonfraying *selvage.*

Next, with a compass, draw the sew-to line and the cut line of the bag bottom. Last to be drawn are the little trapezoidal reinforcement patches. Like any cloth added to a sail in the form of tablings or patches, it must be cut and placed with the same weave or cloth direction as the sailcloth beneath in order to give and take compatibly with the sail body. It should also be made of the same cloth when possible.

After you have cut your pieces, you'll find you have cloth left over. Save it. You might want to install pockets in the bag, or retread the seat of your pants someday.

Fold and rub down everything well. Then open up the top and bottom of the rectangular side piece and bend one end around to form a cylinder with

the hemmed end lying along the sew-to line (Figure 1-9). Flatten the cylinder now and pin it down firmly with the seam up and the cloth edges aligned. Every 3 inches or so *strike-up marks* should be drawn perpendicularly on both the upper and lower cloths across the *sew-to line.* The sew-to line guides in maintaining the alignment of the two cloths side to side, and the strike-up marks do the same for the cloths forward and backward.

SEWING

We'll begin with a few general rules:

1. Almost all sewing is done from one side of the cloth—the top side. Don't push the needle in one side, turn the work over, and then push the needle back through the other side. Imagine flip-flopping a large heavy sail enough times to sew a patch that way in the middle of the sail. I'll explain how to manage, in just a bit.
2. No knots! They are lumpy and chafe away. With very few exceptions, thread ends are sewn in.
3. No prepunched holes allowed. Your shoulder, arm, fingers, and the sewing palm are what push a clean, sharp needle through even the heaviest of canvas.

These things will take some getting used to, and for a time there's likely to be some hardship: sore back, sore hands, blisters, and bloodshed.

The Side Seam

Your tools and materials should be set up in advance and be accessible. A professional sits on a bench, with thread, wax, fids, etc. at one end.

Flat seaming will be your first step in sewing the bag. For a right-handed person, it is performed from right to left. The sailhook (your third hand) is tied to something firm off to the right, while the cloth is held in the left hand, pulling in opposition to the hook.

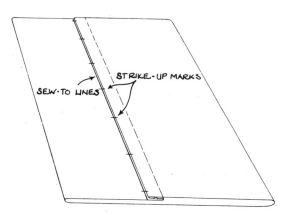

FIGURE 1-9.

Learn to hold the needle correctly from the beginning. The head of the needle should be held firmly with the ring finger against the eye of the seaming palm, and the thumb and index finger holding the needle down near the point (Figure 1-10). The palm and hand become one, and you will keep an almost constant grip on the needle until its final passage through the cloth. Don't insert the needle and then try to push it wobbling through the cloth with your fingers outstretched; you will probably break the needle and you won't have much directional control.

With good light in front of you, draw out a length of twine which, when doubled through a No. 16 needle, will equal just less than the distance from the work to your extended hand. A longer length of twine, although seeming to save time in making up thread, actually consumes more time since you have to let go of the needle to heave home the stitch. When your needle is threaded, pass the twine over the wax enough times to coat it thoroughly; the two pieces should stick together. The process of sewing the *flat stitch* twists the thread and can cause it to tangle. You can compensate for this in advance of sewing by working a right twist into the thread or, as you sew along, by turning the needle counterclockwise.

How do you keep from accidentally sewing the wall of the bag opposite the seam? When you sew, the needle is passed down through the folded cloth beneath the seam, then is withdrawn to the point where a sharp tick is heard, indicating that the needle is free of that layer of cloth and ready to pass back up through the upper cloth and the seam at hand. Cloth held across your lap, the upper cloth toward you, sailhook set, seam held in advance with another needle, if necessary, strike-up marks and the sew-to line matching, and your body turned slightly to the left, insert the needle into the lower cloth right alongside the edge of the upper cloth. When it's free from the layer you don't want to sew, change the angle of the needle so it comes back up again through the lower cloth and out the upper cloth, exiting far enough in from the upper cloth edge so that the twine will have a good hold, and slightly farther on down the seam than the point at which the needle entered. How far along and in depends on the nature of the work. The heavier the work, the farther apart the stitches. Ten to 12 stitches per needle length is a good guide. The twine is pulled on through, sufficiently taut to sink the twine slightly into the cloth, no more. Too much tension and it will pucker, especially on lightweight cloth.

If you are seaming synthetic cloth, you should keep in mind that Dacron has no woven selvage; the edge of the cloth has been cut and sealed with a hotknife. If you sew too close to this edge, the seal

FIGURE 1-10. *Holding the needle.*

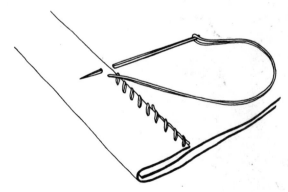

FIGURE 1-11. *The flat stitch.*

will break and the threads along the edge will unravel. In addition, Dacron is so tightly woven and stable that if your cloth gets puckered in sewing, it will stay that way. You will need to take extra care with your stitch tension to avoid puckering.

To begin the seam, anchor the tail end of the twine (an inch or so) with the first few stitches (see Figure 1-12; this is known as *oversewing*), and continue with stitches as consistent as possible with respect to size, angle, and tension. It takes some practice. Keep everything lined up and shift the sailhook along as you go. If you run out of twine, make up a new needleful and resume as shown. At the end of the seam, pass the needle back under the last four stitches.

Next, turn the bag inside out and sew the other side of the seam in the same manner. Wizards can dispense with sew-to lines and marks, but these references will help you keep the work straight. When the seam is done, go over your work with the seam rubber and rub the stitching and seam down flat.

The Tabling

With the bag turned back right side out, the top hem, or *rolled tabling*, is folded under and rubbed down, and the strike-up marks and sew-to line are drawn. The tabling is sewn in the same manner as the side seam, the only difference being that you can hold the cloth from both sides, thumb on top, fingers inside the bag, and there's no fear of sewing

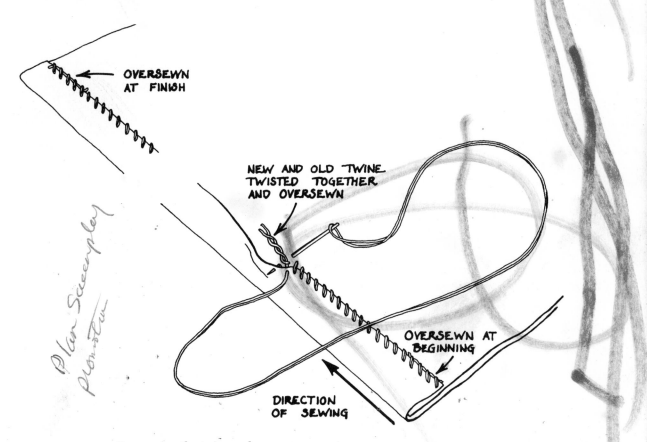

OVERSEWN AT FINISH

NEW AND OLD TWINE TWISTED TOGETHER AND OVERSEWN

OVERSEWN AT BEGINNING

DIRECTION OF SEWING

FIGURE 1-12. *Oversewing the twine ends.*

something besides the tabling (except your fingers).

Having circumsewn the bag, rub the tabling down as flat as possible, then divide and mark the circumference into quarters, avoiding the side seam. These quarter points are where the cringles will eventually be placed and, as in sailmaking, they need to have reinforcement patches.

The Patches

Patches provide extra strength through more layers; they are designed to distribute strain in the appropriate direction. Cut, fold under, and rub down the four little patches.

With the bag pinned down flat, pin down a patch so its centerline is on the quarter point mark and its top edge (which is the unfolded selvage edge) is flush with the top edge of the bag. Draw the sew-to lines (by tracing around the patch), and also the strike-up marks. Label the position and the patch, then repeat for the remaining patches.

Continuing with the same flat stitch you used for the side seam and the tabling, sew on each patch. You will be confronted with changes in

direction, some awkwardness in holding it, and the fraying of the patch corners. As you approach each corner, tuck it under with the needle's point and sew over it so that nothing is left to fray and look unsightly.

The Sticking Stitch

The next stitch, called the *sticking stitch*, is easy and is used in this case to anchor the layers of the tabling, bag, and patches so they don't shift around while the top edge of the bag is being roped. This stitch or a similar *running stitch* can also be used to run a strengthening *middle stitch* or *triple stitch* down the middle of a seam. Work from right to left about ¼ inch down from the edge of the bag. Make the stitches farther apart than when seaming, and do not pull them so tightly that the bag edge puckers.

The Round Stitch

The bag should be looking fairly natty by now, but of course it's not a bag yet, just a cylinder. But we're ready to make it into a bag now, by sewing in its bottom using the *round stitch*. This stitch has

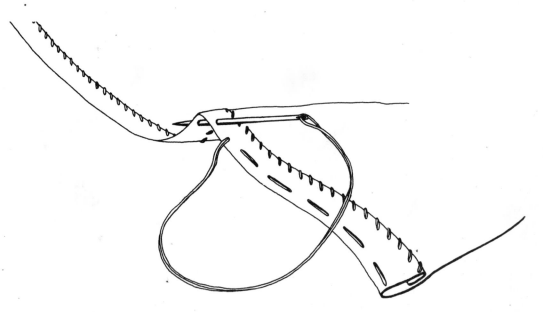

FIGURE 1-13. *The sticking stitch.*

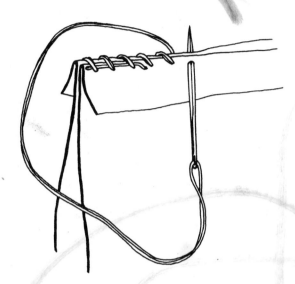

FIGURE 1-14. *The round stitch.*

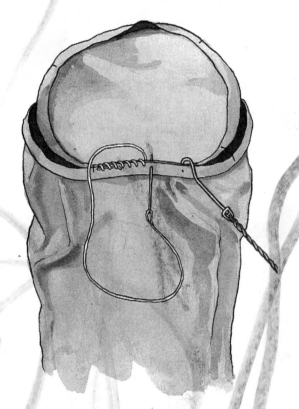

FIGURE 1-15. *Round seaming the bottom (bag inside out).*

numerous applications that generally involve some sort of seaming or oversewing. As a seaming stitch, it is very strong but leaves cut cloth edges exposed. That's all right though, on something like the inside of a bag. In the oversewing fashion, leech edges are stitched and cut edges are prevented from unraveling.

This stitch is sewn from left to right, with the sailhook on the right. Normally, this is one of the simplest of stitches, but sewing around in a circle makes it a little more difficult because you have to keep refolding and lining up as you go. Folding well in advance and having dark sew-to lines will help, as will marking quarter points on both the bottom and the lower edge of the bag cylinder.

With the bag inside out and the bottom placed with its folded hem out, hold the two with the lines matching and the bag bottom away from you. You will use the same thread and needle as in the previous work. Oversewing the thread end to begin, around you go evenly, 10 to 12 stitches per needle length, but with comparatively little tension. When the two layers are later spread open, you don't want a hard ridge remaining.

With the completion of this step, the bag may be likened to a sail that has been completed to the point of being ready for the "finishwork": roping, rings, hardware, and chafing gear.

This is a good point to stop, relax, reflect on what's been accomplished so far, and prepare for the work to come. How do you feel? So frustrated that you're ready to hoist a broom to the masthead and heave the palm overboard? Never let your mother say she had a "jibber." The ditty bag is for learning—it doesn't have to be a masterpiece.

Is your stitching correct and uniform? Are the seams, tablings, and patches flat and placed correctly? Does the bag seem strong? Emulation of the tried and true is the objective, but it doesn't have to be perfect the first time around.

For the finishwork to come, you'll need the roping palm, fids, the knife, an additional 8 feet of ¼-inch manila line, marline, wax, sail twine, and one sharp and one dulled No. 16 needle. You'll also need a mallet or block of wood to use in stretching the cringles, and if you want a Turk's head slider, you'll need 3 feet of braided cord.

Practicing in advance will help you make a neater bag, and studying the handwork on well-made sails will give you a standard of comparison for your work.

FINISHWORK

Rings

There are other means, but most frequently things are attached to sails through holes reinforced with metal or rope rings. Rope rings, called *grommets*, are laid up from a single strand of line, the size of which depends on the nature of the work.

The rings (or eyelets) on the ditty bag are small, so the rope grommets will be worked out of tarred marline as shown. Eight penny-size (O.D.) grommets will be needed, uniform in diameter and even in layup. Waxing the marline makes it more workable. This is where you first get to use the small fid, in forming and rounding the grommets. Note the terminating overhand knot, which has the two meeting strands worked into the lay together. Subsequent tucks may be made in a variety of ways, but in the case of these small grommets (which will be sewn in) it is not necessary to do the kind of finishing you'd do in a large unsewn rope grommet. One more tuck for each strand is sufficient.

Worked Eyelets

Now you are ready to sew the little grommets into the locations where the cringles will later be "stuck." Eyelets or anchor holes are used to distribute strain over a larger part of the sail, or bag, in this case. Their configuration might vary from a single eyelet to a complex multi-eyelet fanlike assembly in which all are joined so they work together to share the load. This ditty bag uses the configuration of two eyelets side by side.

The technique for sewing rings or eyelets is basically the same, regardless of the size of the ring. The grommets for the bag eyelets are placed on the patches so that their outer drawn circles will just meet at the centerline of the patch, and at the same time are ¼ inch down from the bag's upper edge. Draw circles both inside and outside the ring, taking care to make them round. Mark them so that you will know which ring belongs to which circle. Next, cut out the inner circles and draw identical outside circles on the other side of the cloth. These circles will guide you in sewing. Use the same size thread and needle as in the stitching. The grommet, being soft, might require fidding as you go to keep it round. Sew in all eight eyelets as follows:

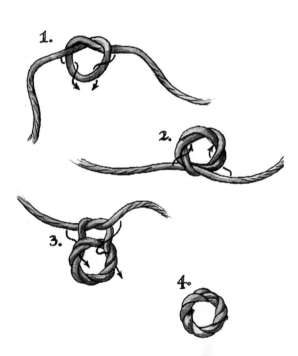

FIGURE 1-16. *A penny-size marline grommet. Begin with an overhand knot, tuck the ends as shown, tie a second overhand knot, tuck the ends once more, and trim.*

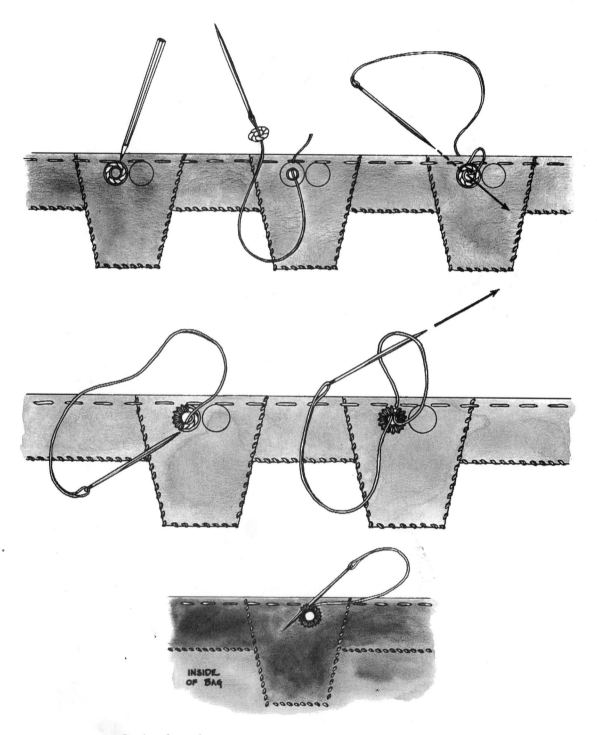

FIGURE 1-17. *Sewing the eyelets.*

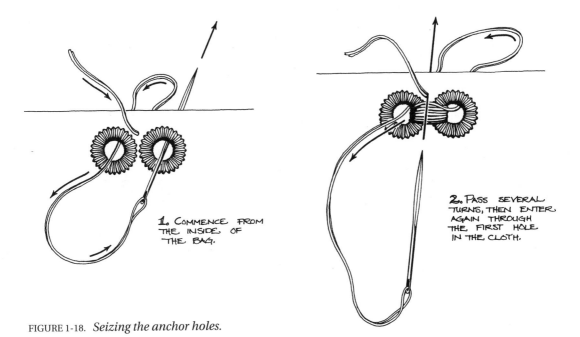

FIGURE 1-18. *Seizing the anchor holes.*

Sewing is always begun on the side away from the strain, so as to be less likely to pull out. Generally, this means on the side of the ring away from the center of a sail. In this bag it means at the top of the ring.

Holding the bag with the beginning point of the ring uppermost, push the needle through at that point, angling slightly ahead and outward, and pull the thread through, except for the last inch or so. Pass the needle back up through the hole in the bag and through the ring (or grommet), which has been placed into position. A stitch is then taken through the same spot you first sewed and then hove home; this holds the ring firmly against the cloth. The little thread tail is oversewn with the subsequent stitches. Working counterclockwise, you continue on around the ring. Even stitches that cover the ring are of sufficient tension to sink the ring into the cloth. You want stitches that radiate smoothly from the imagined center of the ring, crossing the ring on a perpendicular rather than pinwheeling obliquely across. Pinwheeling is controlled by the

relationship between where the needle enters and exits in a sequence of stitches. This is governed by the angle at which the needle is inserted and the space between the stitches. For these little rings, keep the stitches at least $1/16$ inch apart so that you do not weaken the cloth. It's a little tricky to develop a consistent technique, especially with rings of varying sizes, but once mastered it is not easily forgotten.

To finish, the thread is passed up through the last stitch prior to heaving it home. Finally, the thread is passed under the last three stitches on the back side and cut off. All the unraveling cloth in the hole should be covered, and the ring should be smoothed and rounded out with the fid.

Seizing the Eyelets   To further reinforce these four pairs of eyelets, each pair is seized together as shown in Figure 1-18, using the same thread. It is better to use many turns of a light thread than a few of a heavier one; if laid up with equal tension, all the parts will do their share.

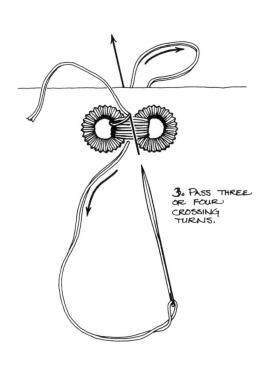

3. PASS THREE OR FOUR CROSSING TURNS.

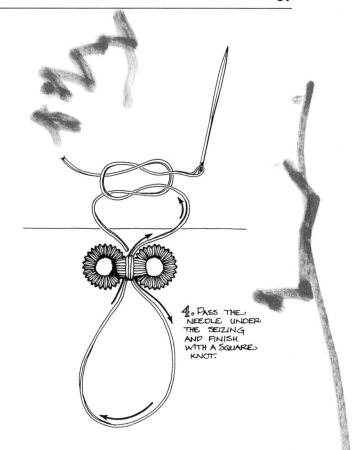

4. PASS THE NEEDLE UNDER THE SEIZING AND FINISH WITH A SQUARE KNOT.

The Rope Grommet

If we were making a sail and had the rings all worked and seized, we'd be at the point of roping its edges, which indeed we're about to do with the bag, except that the bag's "boltrope" is a rope grommet, which has to be made by you. Grommets are made up of a single strand of rope obtained by unlaying a length about 3½ times the circumference of the finished grommet (Figure 1-19).

Take your 10-foot piece of ¼-inch manila and unlay it into three strands, one of which you will use to fashion your rope grommet. The inner diameter of the grommet should be equal to the outer diameter of the bag lip.

Not quite as easy as it looks, the making of rope grommets requires careful laying up in order to get them the right size with an even lay and a well-faired splice. Rolling the final tucks underfoot will help in the fairing in. If the finished grommet takes on a per-sistent figure-eight shape, there's nothing to do but to try again. Notice that the way in which the strands are tucked maintains the three-strand configuration of the line; this is important for roping. Any fuzzy fibers jutting out from the successfully completed grommet can be singed away with a match.

Roping

Why bother? The edges of sails generally have to be reinforced so they won't overstretch and tear. Roping is the traditional method of providing this extra strength. In addition, fullness can be sewn into a sail to a certain extent by gathering slack cloth into the boltrope stitches. Furthermore, roping provides lateral reinforcement by helping withstand the strains imposed on all the rings at various points along a sail's perimeter. The art of roping involves not only the skill of sewing, but a perception of the relationship between the rope and cloth

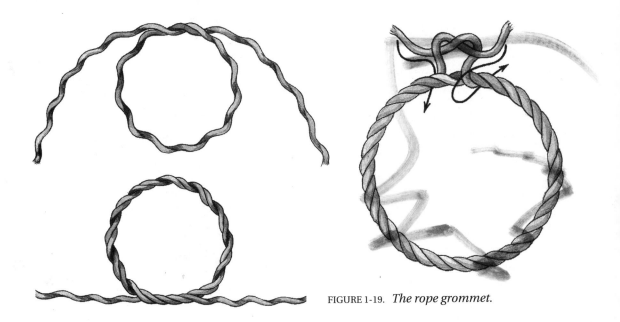

FIGURE 1-19. *The rope grommet.*

based on knowledge of their individual characteristics. This ability comes with experience and from a measure of intuition.

When a sail is roped, the rope is held closest to the worker and against the port side of the sail. On the ditty bag, it is held on the outside. Normally, a sew-to line is drawn on the rope to ensure its going on without twisting, and strike-up marks are made on both the sail and the rope so that the two have the desired relationship when sewn together. It

also helps to temporarily seize the rope to the sail at intervals. For the ditty bag, the rope grommet should be seized to the bag lip at quarter points and these seizings removed as you sew.

There are three ways of affecting how much cloth gets sewn to a given length of rope: First, bending the work away from you as you sew adds cloth. Bending it toward you makes for more rope and less cloth; this is undesirable since it is the rope that is supposed to be controlling the cloth.

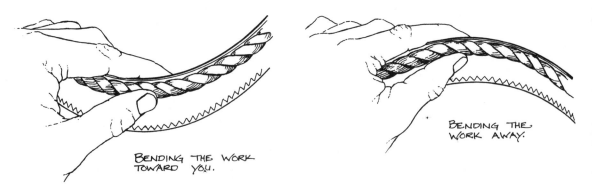

FIGURE 1-20. *Bending rope and cloth toward you gives slack rope. Bending the work away from you puts in slack cloth with tight roping.*

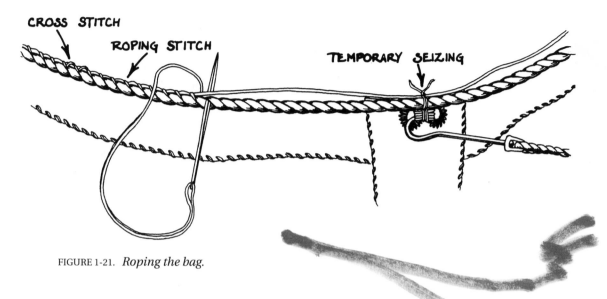

CROSS STITCH
ROPING STITCH
TEMPORARY SEIZING

FIGURE 1-21. *Roping the bag.*

Second, the amount of cloth taken up in each stitch can be varied. And third, how tightly the stitch is pulled or hove can be varied; the tighter the stitch, the more cloth is taken up as it is sunk between the rope strands.

A blunted needle (No. 16) with a suitable length of your twine (which is knotted at the end this time) is pushed cleanly between the rope strands and out through the cloth. Sewing from left to right, it is convenient in the roping of the bag to attach the sailhook in an eyelet off to the right. The basic roping stitch is augmented at all beginnings, ends, splices, cringles, seams, and places of additional strain with a cross-stitch, which crosses back over the strand just passed under, then under again, and out slightly farther along. When finished, the thread is knotted on the cloth side.

Cringles

With the completion of the roping, cringles and round thimbles may be *stuck* (installed) at each pair of eyelets. Cringles are laid up from a single strand of leftover boltrope. The initial size of the cringle is such that it must be stretched to permit the insertion of the round thimble, and so the subsequent shrinkage will inextricably hold it in place.

To start, take one strand of leftover boltrope at

least four times as long as the circumference of the finished cringle and lay it up carefully and tightly as shown (Figure 1-22), so that at the completion of the second step the open space between the top of the boltrope and the inside of the cringle should be half the diameter of your thimble. There are several ways of finishing off a cringle other than the one shown here. In one method the final strands are tucked over, one under two, as in the grommet, until they meet at the crown inside the cringle, where in a full-scale cringle on a sail they would be tied in an overhand knot and the ends left until after the fitting of the thimble, then cut off. The small size of these bag cringles makes the overhand knot optional.

Mark on the fid a point corresponding to the outer diameter of the thimble, and with the bag roping held up, drive the cringle down over the fid to the marked line and let it sit there for a few minutes. Then, with the thimble close at hand and your mallet ready, invert the fid and knock the cringle off. Now, like greased lightning, with the roping down, tap the thimble into position before the cringle shrinks up again. If you miss the boat and the cringle shrinks up before you can fit the thimble, refid the cringle and try again. The thimble should be so tightly held that you can't even

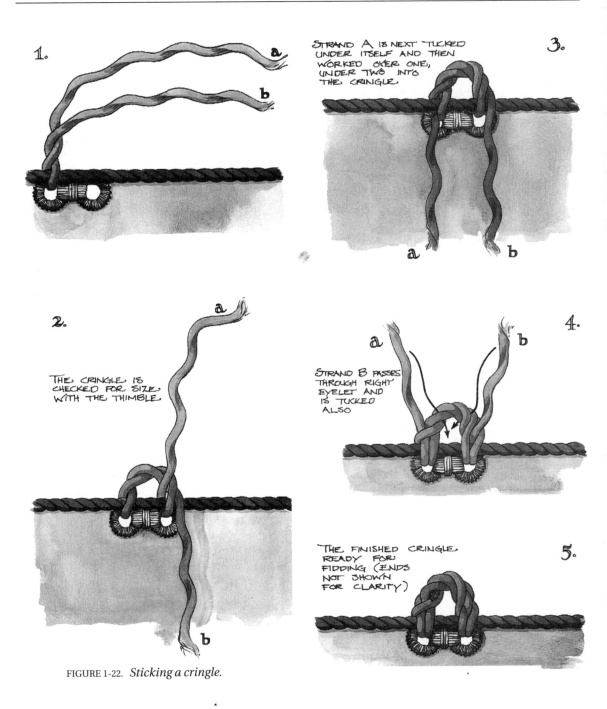

1.

2.

THE CRINGLE IS
CHECKED FOR SIZE
WITH THE THIMBLE

3.

STRAND A IS NEXT TUCKED
UNDER ITSELF AND THEN
WORKED OVER ONE,
UNDER TWO INTO
THE CRINGLE

4.

STRAND B PASSES
THROUGH RIGHT
EYELET AND
IS TUCKED
ALSO

5.

THE FINISHED CRINGLE
READY FOR
FIDDING (ENDS
NOT SHOWN
FOR CLARITY)

FIGURE 1-22. *Sticking a cringle.*

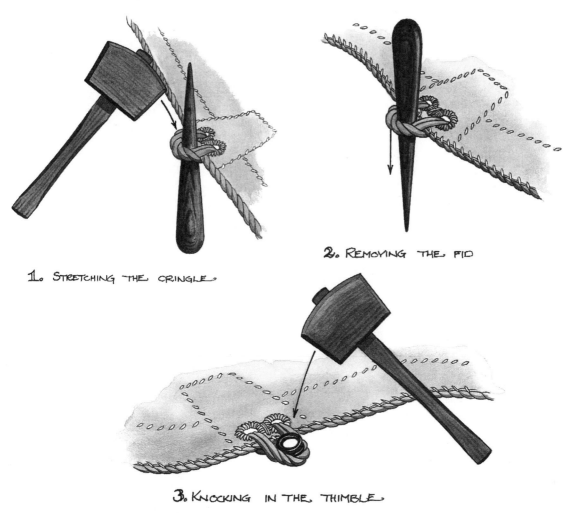

1. STRETCHING THE CRINGLE

2. REMOVING THE FID

3. KNOCKING IN THE THIMBLE

FIGURE 1-23. *Installing a thimble.*

rotate it. As in much of this kind of work, there are no surefire formulas and you will have to develop a feel for it.

Sailmaker's Eyesplice

The lanyard, formed of two pieces of line, must now be spliced to each cringle. The sailmaker's eyesplice is employed for two instructive reasons and one practical one. First, the tapering of strands is an important technique for terminating roping in a gradual manner and for fairing-in splices, particularly splices that will be sewn to a sail. Splices of this sort have the strands tucked with the lay so that the strands are worked in nearly imperceptibly and maintain the easily sewn three-strand configuration. Practically speaking, as far as the bag is concerned, the evenly tapered splice will enable the Turk's head slider to slide farther down.

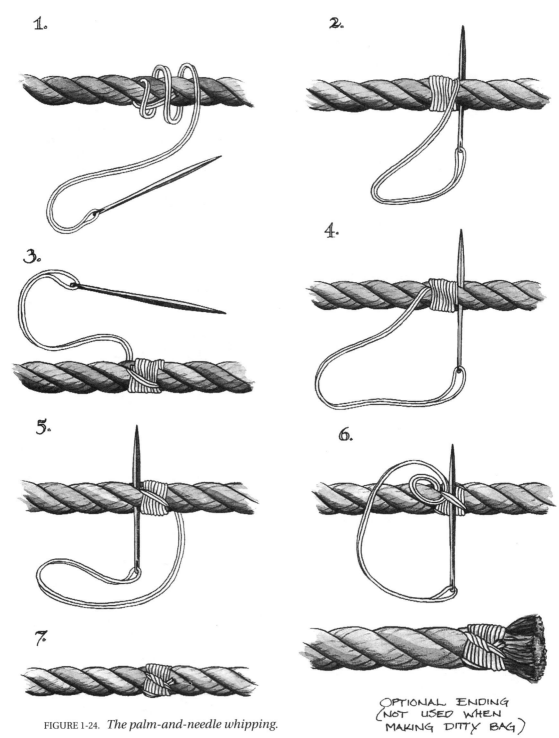

FIGURE 1-24. *The palm-and-needle whipping.*

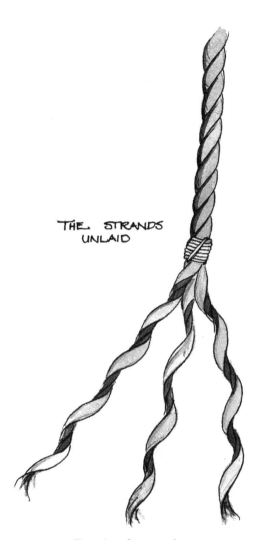

THE STRANDS
UNLAID

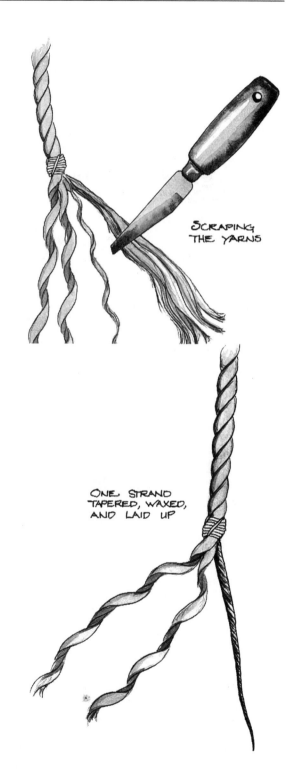

SCRAPING
THE YARNS

ONE STRAND
TAPERED, WAXED,
AND LAID UP

FIGURE 1-25. *Tapering the strands.*

Tapering Cut another 8-foot piece of line in half and whip all four ends 4 inches up as shown in Figure 1-24. Beginning with one of the ends, unlay the three strands. Taking one strand, unlay its yarns. Now, one yarn at a time, very carefully scrape the fibers down with the knife so that the yarn tapers gradually to nothing. Wax it, and twist it back up as it was. Repeat this technique with the remaining yarn as uniformly as possible. The yarns (text continued on page 27)

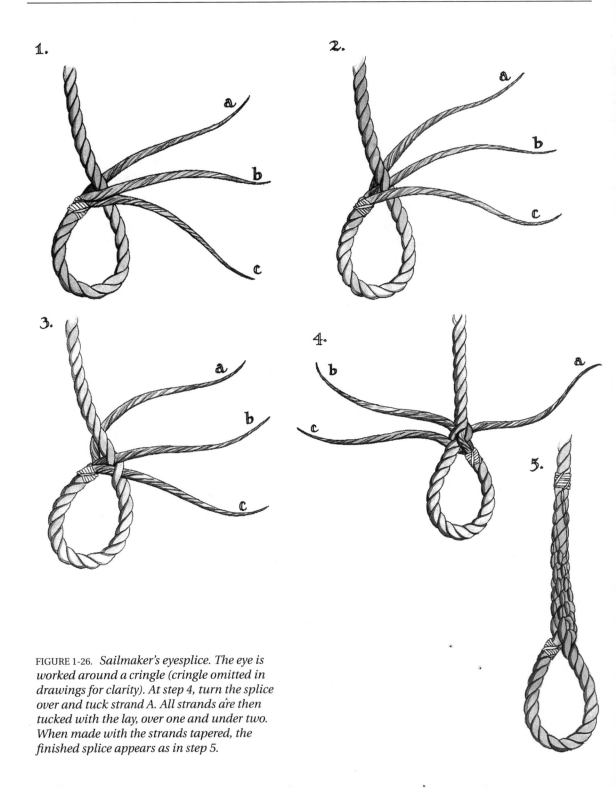

FIGURE 1-26. *Sailmaker's eyesplice. The eye is worked around a cringle (cringle omitted in drawings for clarity). At step 4, turn the splice over and tuck strand A. All strands are then tucked with the lay, over one and under two. When made with the strands tapered, the finished splice appears as in step 5.*

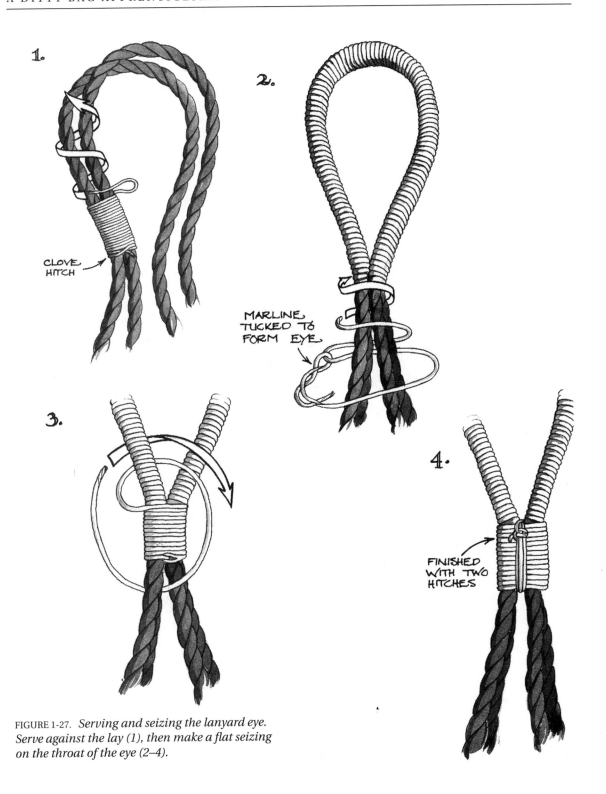

1.

CLOVE
HITCH

2.

MARLINE
TUCKED TO
FORM EYE.

3.

4.

FINISHED
WITH TWO
HITCHES

FIGURE 1-27. *Serving and seizing the lanyard eye.*
Serve against the lay (1), then make a flat seizing
on the throat of the eye (2–4).

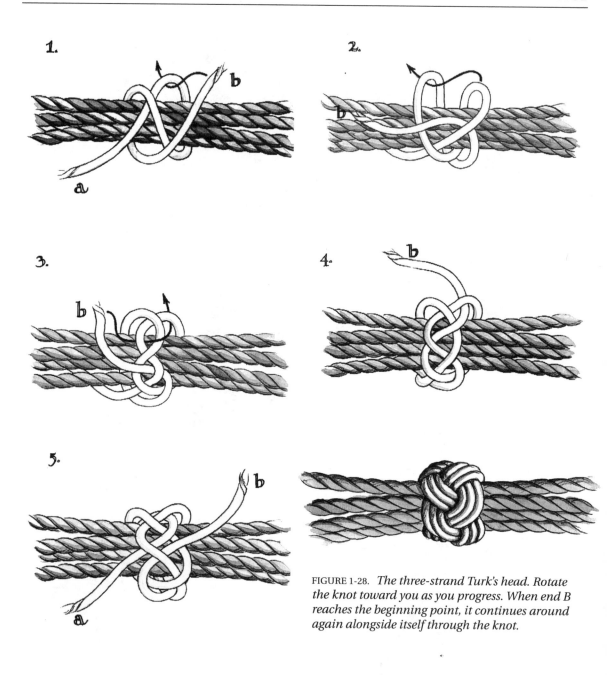

FIGURE 1-28. *The three-strand Turk's head. Rotate the knot toward you as you progress. When end B reaches the beginning point, it continues around again alongside itself through the knot.*

are then laid back up into a tapered strand and the whole process repeated with the two other strands. All four ends must be readied in this way before you begin splicing.

If it were a rattail to be roped to a sail, you'd lay the three strands back up into a tapered tail, which would then be sewn to the sail.

The splice is worked around the cringle as shown. Slightly unlaying the strand as tucks are taken will help in fairing them in well with the strands of the standing part. A small whipping will hold the very ends. Some accuracy is required so as to get lanyard legs of equal length.

Finishing the Lanyard

After splicing, the two legs are joined, middled, and a hand-size eye formed. The eye is served with marline and a flat seizing clapped on. Finally, a three-strand Turk's head, made from any light cord, makes a slider to close the bag.

There. The bag is done, ready to receive all the tools that made it and to store them inside for future use. Initials can be embroidered on the outside, pockets installed, whatever you like from here on out. It's your bag, they're your tools, and your hands brought the ditty bag to life. And if you think the bag was a lot of work, just think of how much more a sailmaker has to deal with. It is hard work bringing sails to life and keeping them seaworthy and dependable.

Wind, cloth, and self-reliance. You've begun.

2

Sailing, Hulls, and Sails

DAYSAILING IS RELATIVELY EASY on a sail. Adequate and reliable reefing should not be neglected, but generally light construction is advisable. I once built a suit of sails for an 18-foot Wianno Junior knockabout in a manner better suited to a 40-foot bluewater cruiser. The result was immortal sails that were useless in the usual daysailing conditions, and only came into their own in a gale. So as not to have made a complete waste of it, I took the boat out in a gale. The sails did fine, but the boat and I, and my terrified crew, had less than a delightful time.

And daysailing is supposed to be delightful. What's the point of going to all the fuss if it's no fun? Might as well have a powerboat. To maximize the happily entertaining side of daysailing, sails need appropriate construction and controls to permit their shape to be adjusted to prevailing conditions—usually in sheltered waters, with relatively light airs and fair weather. Daysailing sails should be easily bent on and removed, easily set, light and pleasant to handle, and as simple as possible.

At the opposite end of the spectrum, voyaging or cruising under sail imposes distinct requirements of its own. Limited stowage space means a small sail inventory, which in turn calls for versatile working sails. Each working sail, which is a compromise to some extent, can perform well in a wide range of conditions and will be augmented by a small inventory of light- and heavy-air auxiliary sails. A small inventory usually means one of each sail in the rig. A small crew necessitates manageable, easily handed sails—even with mechanical sail-handling gear, in the event the machinery fails. Depending on the extent of the voyage, the sails should be constructed with tools and techniques the voyaging sailor can use on board to effect repairs. Coincidentally, those techniques are also the most durable, resulting in less repair and maintenance in the first place.

Economy is of great importance to voyagers: economy in space, funds, fuel, and physical exertion. Sails play a big role in shipboard economy, and should be cost-effective in every respect to be of maximum benefit. The wind is free when it blows, but the harnessing of that energy has a price tag.

What does the voyager care about the look of a sail? Color is important, in that dark colors aren't so reflective of harsh sunlight. Yet light colors are more visible at night, and bright colors are more visible in fog, rain, and against a wave-tossed sea. Colors in general help sailcloth resist ultraviolet deterioration (while absorbing more heat). Gay color combinations provide identity and can lift the spirits on a dreary haul. Beyond color, the aesthetic appeal and reassurance of high-quality sailwork is a source of pride and comfort to the voyaging sailor. Cruising sails have to withstand prolonged exposure to the elements as well as long-term damp, dark, cold, wet, and hot storage.

These considerations are of greater or less importance depending on the length of the voyage. Bluewater sailing is the most demanding. Long, hard use of sails, infrequent ports of call, limited resources, lack of professional sail services, survival conditions, and fair weather punctuated by foul call for good sails indeed.

Coastal cruising imposes less stringent but similar sail requirements, depending on the coast, the sailor's budget, and the size of the boat. Gunkholing resembles daysailing in some respects, but in many ways is more akin to voyaging. Gunkholing sails, at least in temperate climates, won't receive nearly the beating from the sun that tropical or bluewater sails must withstand. Gunkhole to gunkhole is a small voyage, relatively sheltered, which is some justification for a light sail material but no reason to compromise strength and performance. A gunkholer has frequent need to sail off a lee shore, and a shoal-draft gunkholer may need multiple and reliable reefs in the working sails.

River and lake cruising runs the gamut. The Great Lakes resemble coastal cruising, but cruising a small lake or river is more like daysailing. The key factors are the length of the voyage, the conditions anticipated, and the location. There is no point in making a long-lasting, survival-oriented voyaging sail for a boat that's going on short, local camping voyages, but all purposeful voyages of any duration share basic considerations of economy. Ease of handling is of greater importance in the flukey, confined, unpredictable conditions found in sweetwater sailing.

Sails for classic boats deserve a little discussion. There is an aesthetic and functional conflict between the design, materials, aesthetics, and rig of a classic boat and contemporary sail materials and construction. On the other hand, the boat's cost and maintenance may be lowered and its performance enhanced if synthetic sails are bent. So choices must be made. To the purist, who is resigned to maintenance and may not be concerned about competition, putting a plastic sail on a wooden boat is heresy; only a natural-fiber sail will do. The look, feel, and sound of the sails must be consistent with the rest of the boat. The purists may not be making as big a sacrifice in performance as you might think, because their classic rigs work optimally with natural-fiber sails. The Chinese lug rig comes to mind. It can be argued that while sails have continued to evolve, the Chinese lug and other rigs reached their limits, and the imposition of one evolutionary entity upon another is dysfunctional, or at best ugly.

Many classic-boat owners don't give a hoot whether their sails are consistent in appearance with their boat, but there are many who do. The middle ground for these sailors is lower-maintenance (not maintenance-free), more stable synthetic sails that simulate the appearance and employ the sailmaking techniques of natural-fiber sails. This simulation is not merely cosmetic, but also more durable than off-the-rack synthetic sails, though the added strength is more often than not superfluous. Even the Coast Guard barque *Eagle* has dispensed with traditionally constructed and finished sails, and that's some test. All in all, unless authenticity is an absolute priority, the needs of the classic-boat owner might be best served by a traditionally made sail using synthetic materials.

WHERE ONE SAILS

The place and season of sailing have considerable bearing on the making of sails. In this chapter we merely outline the considerations; in later chapters we return to the materials and constructions these considerations demand.

Sails to be handed safely and comfortably in the cold must be soft, whether synthetic or natural. Natural fibers hold more water and will freeze more solidly if wet.

In an area of heavy and frequent rainfall, one must be concerned about the weight of wet sails when sailing and mildew when the sails are stowed.

Exposure to the sun—ultraviolet rays in particular—is detrimental to all sailcloth in all zones, but particularly in the tropics, where in a matter of months exposed cloth and stitching may be hazardously weakened. Ultraviolet deterioration is insidious, like the work of a powder beetle in the wooden legs of a chair. The chair looks and seems sound until you sit on it. Sun-rotten sailcloth to the undiscerning eye seems fine, too.

The choice of an appropriate material for tropical sailing is important, and so is the construction; some construction techniques fall apart faster in the sun than others. Sail fittings corrode faster in the tropics, and the high humidity and rainfall of the rainy season pose organic rot problems.

Of course, tempestuous regions of the globe call for stouter sails that can drive the boat in a lumpy sea but are not overpowering. Squally areas and known gauntlets like the Gulf of Tehuantepec in southern Mexico beg easily doused or reefed sails that may be quickly transformed for heavy going.

SAIL ALCHEMY

Q: *As a boatbuilder I am occasionally asked to convert a boat to sail. Is there a formula for determining small-boat sail area?*

A: No formula, but there is a ratio for small boats that suggests an appropriate sail area: Sail area (in square feet) divided by the displacement (including average crew and gear, in cubic feet—i.e., pounds divided by 64, the weight of a cubic foot of seawater) to the two-thirds power:

$$SA/Disp.^{2/3}$$

Figures range from a "low" 14 or less to a "high" 20+. The amount of sail a boat can safely carry depends on the stability provided by hull form, ballast (fixed, movable, and live), and ballast placement. Further considerations are the rig type, anticipated sailing conditions, intended use of the boat, and needs and abilities of the sailor. Successful, proven small-boat sail plans are a good guide for the sail and rig specifications of a conversion or new design.

Doldrums and calms are as detrimental to sails in their own way as any storm—perhaps more so. Slatting and slamming make for incessant chafe and brutal stress. These destructive forces can be countered by building a sail with some give and elasticity in its material, construction, and means of attachment.

Trade wind sailing, while tranquil in some respects, places strain on and exposes certain areas of the sail over extended periods of time. Chafe is the big troublemaker, and in anticipation of this, chafing gear should be built into a sail where it comes in contact with other parts of the boat.

No matter where or how you sail, try to anticipate the temperature, weather, and wind conditions you will encounter, and choose your sails accordingly. With appropriate materials and constructions, your sails will require less maintenance, will be easier and safer to handle, and will have a longer life expectancy.

ERGONOMICS

A sailor hampered by an infirmity has special needs in order to maximize his or her abilities, and a sailmaker needs to take this into account. A monoped, a blind sailor, a deaf sailor, a short sailor, a frail sailor—any relative diminishment of sail-handling ability can be compensated to some extent in the design and making of the sails. An infirm sailor might well be reluctant to make frequent sail changes on a heaving foredeck. A single forgiving sail with a wide wind range might be more appropriate. (Along these lines, within certain boat and rig types, I suggest there are novice, intermediate, and advanced sails appropriate for a particular sailor's intentions and ability.)

Sailors have all sorts of needs in relation to their bodies, minds, abilities, finances, and intentions. Sometimes sailors aren't aware of their needs, much less the implications for choosing Mr. and Mrs. Right Sail. But a sailor and sailmaker working together can create a safe, manageable, and successful sail.

THE HULL

It is imprudent to jump directly from ways of sailing into sail design and making. We should look at hull form first. It matters little that superb sails for a particular type of sailing have been created if they are then placed upon a hull designed and built for another kind of sailing altogether.

In this discussion, I borrow in part from Ted Brewer's book titled *Ted Brewer Explains Sailboat Design,* an excellent distillation of sailboat design considerations presented in clear, concise terms, with a necessary but not overwhelming analysis of technical data.

There are three basic hull shapes, the simplest being flat-bottomed hulls. The most basic of these is the scow or punt type, while skiffs, sharpies, and dories exemplify the remaining flat-bottomed types and are distinguished by their pointed bows. Of course there are scads of flat-bottomed designs, most of which are selected by a sailor for their shoal draft, carrying capacity, speed (sharpies), and seaworthiness (dories), among other reasons. What does this mean to the sailmaker? Some of these flat-bottomed boats are particularly weatherly, stable, and fast, and all will carry leeboards, centerboards, or daggerboards. Windward ability will be enhanced by a keel, but then the invaluable shoal draft is lost. So we see low sails of comparatively full shape. Generally used inshore, the sails on a flat-bottomed hull needn't be stoutly constructed, but efficient, functional reefs are essential to the safety of a capsizable hull.

The V-bottomed hull is seemingly a derivation of the flat-bottomed hull, modified for greater seaworthiness and carrying capacity. Sailwise these hulls may in general be distinguished from the flat-bottoms by their decrease in initial stability, necessitating a low rig, easily reefed. The type is fast and perhaps somewhat more weatherly in a chop than the flat bottoms.

On the whole, differences in sails for V-bottomed versus flat-bottomed hulls will depend on the boat and its use.

FINDING SAIL AREA

Q: *What are the formulas used to measure the reefed and full areas of a sail?*

A: Except in the estimation of sailcloth, sail area is usually calculated by the measurement of triangles, with the exclusion of roaches and hollows. For an extreme roach, calculus can be used, but it is nearly as accurate to break the area up into triangles and proceed geometrically. When a sail has a tack angle of greater or less than 90°, a measurement called the *luff perpendicular* (LP) serves as the height of the triangle; the luff is the base. Given a tack angle of 90°, the foot of the sail and the LP are the same.

The procedure for determining sail area will vary depending on what measurements are available and whether they are being obtained from a scale plan, from the sails themselves, or from measurements of the spars and rigging.

See also Figure 2-1, Figure 4-10, and Chapter 6.

A working skipjack, for example, required powerful, large, low sails to drag the oyster beds of Chesapeake Bay. It needed to work the wind sufficiently to enable crossing back and forth over the beds on close parallel courses for a clean sweep of the area. Reefing was essential for stability, given the hull type and the large expanse of canvas. Hard service and exposure to the elements called for sails as durable as the stout hulls they propelled, even with the installation of auxiliary engines.

The sails of a skipjack yacht, by contrast, need not be as powerful and are designed to maximize the speed and windward ability of the hull, minimize heeling, reduce weather helm, and permit some gleeful sailing in a fresh breeze before it is time to tuck in a reef.

This brings us to round-bottomed hulls. Ted Brewer prefers the term round-bilged to round-bottomed, because many round-bottomed hulls are actually quite flat in section (with little or no deadrise) but nonetheless have a distinct round turn to the bilge. Round-bilged hulls are of two basic varieties: the U-shaped section one sees in light-displacement craft from canoes to ultra-light ocean racers, and the Y-section generally reserved for moderate- to heavier-displacement boats. With some exceptions, the U-sectioned hulls are thrilling speed and sport sailers. Speed and weatherliness are likely the most significant aspects of this hull type, which influences sail design. Certainly it is a faster and more weatherly section than the previously mentioned forms;

depending on the flare of the topsides, it might or might not be as stable. Sails tend to be fast, tall, and light, though it is difficult to specify sail considerations when regarding the hull only in midsection.

A typical example is a state-of-the-art racing machine wanting only the fastest, lightest sails in a large inventory. The sails are designed purely for speed on various points of sail, and are usable in fairly narrow, specified wind ranges. Money is no object. The sails will be replaced by next season, and the boat sails locally in fair weather. A computer-assisted loft is close at hand, and the boat, a winner, is often asked to try new sails for promotional purposes. The sails have to *win* and at all times look the part. This boat in particular is on the squirrelly side, and with the sails cut with a minimum of tolerance with respect to variations in the wind's angle of incidence, the helm needs steadfast, concentrated attention.

The slower, more stable wineglass or Y-section can carry a more powerful sail, and what it may lack in speed is offset by its ability to carry sail successfully in rough weather. As always, it is difficult to generalize. Consider a wide-sectioned motorsailer for which sailing is important but not essential. Its stiff hull designed for comfort of habitation will sail primarily in fair and favorable breezes. The sails, offering auxiliary power and some dampening of roll, are heavily constructed. The owner, unconcerned about light-air sail performance, may choose moderately full sails of mechanical construction methods, which are mechanically stowed. The sails that will see heavy weather might be designed to be used fully unfurled—with the exception of the main and mizzen, which could be used for steadying and riding purposes in a three-quarter-furled position.

Of course, the capabilities and sail-carrying characteristics of a hull are described only in broadest generalities by its sectional shape. It is the overall form that distinguishes one boat from another, all the elements of which add up to particular sailing characteristics and thus certain sail considerations.

HELM BALANCE

One need not be an authority on the refinements of hull form and design, however, to appreciate the importance of helm balance. An understanding of this factor is essential to sailor and sailmaker. The following explanation is adapted, with thanks, from naval architect Dave Gerr's book *The Nature of Boats: Insights and Esoterica for the Nautically Obsessed* (International Marine, 1992). Helm balance or imbalance is a result of the relationship between the sidewards force generated by the rig and sails and the sidewards lift and resistance to leeway of the keel and underbody. It is a delicate

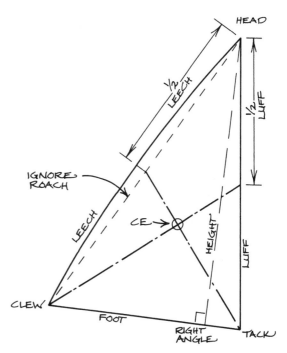

FIGURE 2-1. *Finding the center of effort (CE) of a Bermudan sail. Draw a line from a point halfway up the luff to the clew, and another line from the halfway point of the straight-line leech (ignoring roach) to the tack. The two lines intersect at the sail's center of effort. (The sail's area is approximately one-half the base times the height of the triangle. Often the luff is used as the base, as in Figure 4-10.)*

balance that can self-steer a boat, result in jibes and knockdowns, or help you off a lee shore. To state it another way, the balance of helm is a reflection of the relationship between the fore-and-aft center of effort of the sails and the *center of lateral resistance* (CLR) of the hull underbody. (Think of the CLR as a vertical line through a boat's underbody about which the boat pivots when it turns. A sideways force acting on the CLR would push the boat sideways without turning it.) Obtaining the optimal balance, one in which a boat will carry 3

to 4 degrees of weather helm and a definite but easily controlled sensation of resistance in the tiller or wheel, is rather like trying to juggle while standing on a skateboard. The quest is frustrated by the migrant nature of the centers. They move around and vary with boat speed, angle of heel, angle of attack and aero- and hydrodynamic shape.

In a proper relationship, the center of effort should *lead* the center of lateral plane by a distance generally regarded as a percentage of the load waterline length. The center of lateral resistance moves forward in a heeling boat (Figure 2-5), and without the appropriate lead, too much weather helm would result. How much lead is needed depends on several factors, and designers have their preferences according to rig and hull.

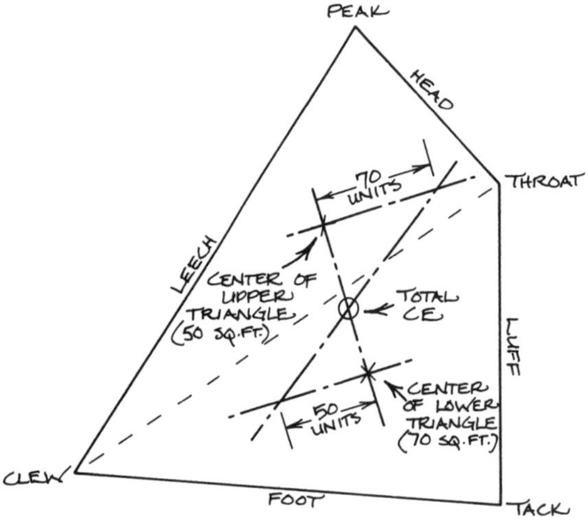

FIGURE 2-2. *Finding the center of a gaff sail. Divide the sail into two triangles with a line from clew to throat, then find the center of each triangle using the technique for a Bermudan sail. Next, draw a line connecting the two centers, then two perpendicular lines—one from the upper center toward the throat, and one from the lower center toward the clew. Measure from the upper center out along the perpendicular a distance proportional to the area of the lower triangle (say, 70⁄16 or 4⅜ inches if the lower triangle is 70 square feet in area). Measure along the lower perpendicular a distance proportional to the upper triangle (50⁄16 or 3⅛ inches if the upper triangle is 50 square feet). Connect these two points; this line crosses the line joining the two centers at the sail's overall center of effort.*

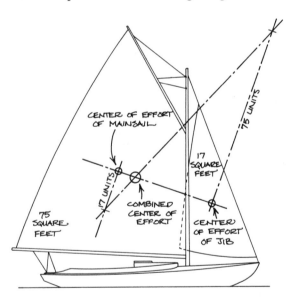

FIGURE 2-3. *Finding a boat's total center of effort. First find the centers of the individual sails, then draw a line through the mainsail and jib centers. Erect opposing perpendiculars as shown, measure along each a distance proportional to the size of the other sail, and connect these points with a line that crosses the line joining the two centers at the combined center of effort for the two sails. If this were a yawl, this combined center of effort could now be connected to the center of the mizzen to find the total center of effort for the boat.*

Once having determined an appropriate sail area and rig (the subject of the following chapter), modifications to hull or rig are made as necessary to obtain sufficient lead. Howard Chapelle describes early designs that actually incorporated "reverse lead," with the center of effort abaft the center of lateral resistance. More usual leads, according to Dave Gerr, are as follows: schooner, 7 to 12 percent; ketch, 11 to 14 percent; yawl, 12 to 15 percent; and sloop, 13 to 17 percent.

A wide hull with broad transom and hard bilges will become very asymmetrical about its fore-and-aft centerline (in a fish's-eye view) as it heels, giving it a strong weather helm indeed unless the effect is anticipated with generous lead. But a narrow boat with slack bilges that is not a whole lot beamier aft than forward will not show this tendency to nearly the same degree.

Further, a tall rig, when heeled, generates more weather helm than a short one, as you would

expect from Figure 2-5. Thus, a narrow, slack-bilged, double-ended sloop with a short rig might only need a 12-percent lead, rather than the 13 to 17 percent mentioned above.

No more immediate and impressive connection between sailors and the forces governing helm balance exists than in the demanding sailboards and St. Lawrence River skiffs, both of which are rudderless craft. How do you steer them? By manipulation of helm balance, constantly shifting centers of effort and lateral resistance. A boardsailor shifts both centers, but particularly that of the sail, fore and aft over a relatively fixed center of lateral resistance. On the St. Lawrence skiff, on the other hand, it is the fore-and-aft shifting of the sailor's weight that changes hull trim and center of lateral resistance beneath a relatively fixed center of effort. Windsurfing reduces the elements of sailing to the most basic, as the sailor assumes the role of the standing and running rigging and ballast while constantly shifting the centers of lateral resistance and effort in order to maneuver and perform. A windsurfer has merely to shift weight or tilt the sail a bit to change helm balance.

In general, to shorten lead you can (1) increase mast rake aft; (2) shorten a bowsprit and move the headstay aft; (3) move the mast; (4) move the centerboard forward; (5) increase the size of the mainsail relative to headsails; (6) add or enlarge a mizzen; (7) make the mainsail fuller and more powerful.

To lengthen lead, you can (1) plumb the mast or rake it forward; (2) add a longer bowsprit; (3) move the mast forward; (4) fit a smaller mainsail with a shorter boom; (5) shrink or remove the mizzen; (6) move the centerboard aft; (7) flatten the mainsail.

What's this got to do with making sails? Well, obviously rig type and placement and then sail type play a role in helm balance, as do the fullness and form of each sail. A sailmaker may be called upon to do anything from designing and balancing a hull/rig combination to adding reefs, altering a sail plan, or recutting sails in order to make a safe, comfortable, and efficient sailer.

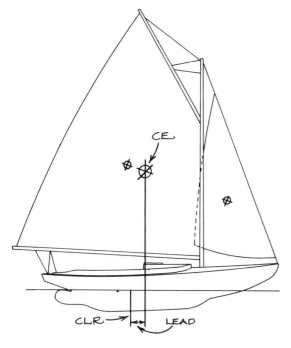

FIGURE 2-4. *Finding the lead. Lead divided by waterline length gives the percent of lead.*

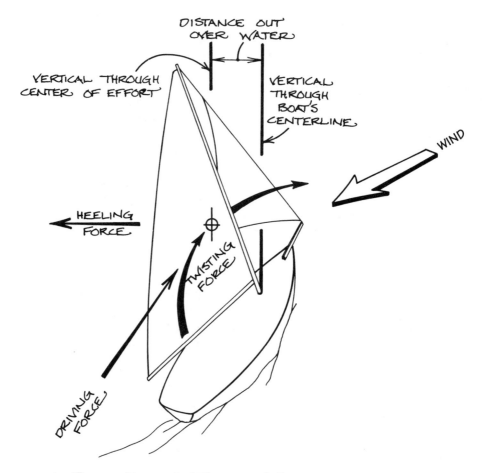

FIGURE 2-5. *A sailboat working upwind. The center of effort, out over the water, tries to twist the boat upwind, creating weather helm.*

A small amount of weather helm is desirable. One wants a boat to luff and round up into the wind to minimize the chances of capsize or knock-down, as well as to put the bow into the seas and wind if the helm should be abandoned. But positive weather helm has other, less obvious benefits: The rudder at a 1- to 4-degree angle of incidence generates lift, which assists the boat in windward performance. Windward ability is enhanced too in a stinky blow, as the boat's tendency to round up helps her constantly try to climb to windward.

Nowhere is this more apparent than when try-

ing to work your way off a lee shore in a snorter. That foolhardy escapade I mentioned in the beginning of this chapter with the 18-footer in a gale was testimony enough to this notion. In addition to overbuilding the sails, I had placed the reef in the mainsail too deeply. Reefed down, the boat did not carry sufficient weather helm to drive off the beach, especially with the centerboard up in the shallows, and I in fact wound up on the beach. Reef placement has everything to do with helm balance as the wind pipes up, a factor we'll explore in more depth later.

A balanced helm is less wearing on the sailor and is faster than severe weather helm, in which the excessive rudder required to hold the boat off the wind is a regular sea anchor. Lee helm is not only dangerous for its irascible tendency to jibe, but the rudder creates lift to leeward—the opposite of what one wants.

"Steering herself" means just that, of course: that once put on a particular course, the boat will continue on that course unless conditions or balance is changed. This usually refers to a neutral helm, but sometimes also to a helm that can be set (often lashed) to balance the boat's tendency to stray, after which the boat will maintain its course for prolonged periods. Some hulls are better suited to this than others, as are some rigs, sail plans, and sail shapes. These characteristics will enhance or impede wind-activated self-steering devices and make life harder or easier for an autopilot. You can't make a silk purse out of a sow's ear, but a sailmaker can, through sail combinations and shapes, improve a boat's tracking capabilities. It is worth knowing in advance whether the hull and rig type are predisposed to this desirable voyaging quality.

Helm balance and hull form are key factors in how or even whether a sailing vessel will weather a storm. This in turn dictates appropriate reef combinations and storm canvas. All boats, regardless of their ability in a gale, need to be prepared for heavy weather with stormsails and reefs, the only exceptions being pure fair-weather daysailers. Reefs balance sail areas, flatten sails, and keep boom ends from dipping in the water. Stormsails may be as much for stability and maintaining an attitude with respect to threatening seas as for sailing a course. The safest and most comfortable tactic for riding out a storm in a given hull dictates the best type and use of storm canvas.

Hulls are designed in anticipation of their use in certain sea conditions—some highly specific, like a punt, and some for conditions from oily calm to tempest. Sails are designed for sea conditions too, in that it takes more power to push any hull through rough water. Lumpy seas are generally accompanied by heavy airs and vice versa, but not necessarily; protected flat waters may still receive howling winds, and rough seas may outlast the winds that generated them.

The argument for fuller, more powerful sails for battling the chop has to be weighed against flattening for higher wind velocity and reduction of the angle of heel. And it depends on what point of sail you're on. Moving the greatest draft farther forward will increase drive at the expense of pointing high. Sails have to be able to do some of everything adequately.

Nonetheless, all else being equal you have rough-water sails and smooth-water sails, differentiated by fullness and draft positions. The only way to nail it down is to take a boat out on certain points of sail in certain wind speeds and try different sails under different sea conditions. Relatively speaking, as conditions get choppier the boat slows down, which moves the apparent wind aft and permits, within the limits of hull stability, a fuller, more powerful sail.

3

Rigs and Sails

IN THE EARLY DAYS of my apprenticeship I was unequivocally informed by one of my mentors that in order to be a good sailmaker one had also to be a knowledgeable rigger. I venture to say that truer words have never been spoken. An understanding of the principles, techniques, and materials of rigging is important to the sailmaker for three reasons. First and foremost, the rig type (gaff, marconi, sprit, etc.) and configuration (sloop, ketch, schooner, etc.) not only determine the number and profile of working sails, but will have a distinct bearing on the choice of sail materials and aerodynamic design—as different rigs have different sailing potential. Second, various rig and spar configurations respond differently to the stresses of sailing, and sails are built to take advantage of or compensate for rig dynamics. Last, the various rigs offer varied sail-handling techniques and means of bending sail.

A distinction must be made between rig type and rig configuration. Of a particular type there may be scads of configurations. Having selected an appropriate type, one then needs to come up with the configuration and then the size—that is, sail area. To further complicate matters, there are combinations of rig types to choose from in the attempt to gain the sailing advantages of more than one.

More has been written on the subject of rigs than you can shake a stick at, and I get the inescapable feeling that perhaps another presentation is like trying to improve on the mousetrap (which could stand some improvement, by the way). There are more rigs and even more combinations of them than would be practical to consider here, so what follows isn't all by any means. Even so, there is a lot of ground to cover. We begin by considering rig types, then sail types, then the combinations of rig and sail types in various rig configurations. On we go.

RIG TYPES

High-tech materials notwithstanding, contemporary sailmaking and rigging have their antecedents in and are descended from the vessels of the ancients; some acquaintance with these histories and traditions makes for a more well-rounded sailor/sailmaker. Furthermore, none of these rigs is extinct; a sailor may have occasion to use any of them, and a sailmaker will likely be called on to fashion any of the sails. Contrary to popular belief, even the oldest and rarest rigs have their redeeming qualities and are worthy of consideration in the right circumstances. We begin with one of the most ancient of rigs.

The Square Rig

When picturing the square rig, one's mind tends to jump immediately to the lofty maze of yards and masts gracing the hulls of 19th- and early 20th-century ocean carriers. These staghounds of the sea were of course the zenith of square rig development. But the basic rig type dates from the dawn of civilization and is characterized by a spar, called a *yard,* which is carried athwartships before a mast and from which is set a single quadrilateral sail not necessarily of equilateral proportions.

Various seafaring societies of antiquity, including the early Phoenician traders of the Mediterranean, utilized this rig, as did the Norse Vikings later. It was eventually superseded in small coastal and inshore vessels by the less demanding and more versatile fore-and-aft rigs, though many craft carried both rig types in order to exploit their respective virtues. The square rig as the primary rig came to be confined to large vessels and passage-making, where the winds were consistent and fairer.

Today the rig is seen on large training vessels, historic restorations and replicas, and charter vessels. The small-boat square rig is still alive on northern European replicas and descendants of the Norse boats, and it still ekes along in the form of courses and topsails on tradewind voyagers. I say "eke" because the rig does not get the promotion or attention lavished on various spinnaker lashups, so people miss out on a stout, manageable, powerful downwind rig alternative.

A yard may be stationary—that is, fixed to one height—or raised and lowered while still pivoting at the point of attachment to the mast. In its simplest form the square rig has merely a halyard with which to raise the yard and sail, port and starboard sheets

FIGURE 3-1. *Square rig.*

to each of the clews, and simple standing rigging consisting of a stay forward, a stay aft, and a shroud to each side. With increased size and better control of the sail's attitude—particularly in conjunction with other sails—comes a substantial increase in the complexity of standing and running rigging.

The square rig is primarily an off-wind sailer, and thus has greater support aft than forward or laterally. Mast, shrouds, and stays serve this purpose as well as permit the yards to pivot through a wide angle before the mast. Port and starboard braces control the fore-and-aft angle of the yard to the centerline and thus, along with the sheeting, the attitude of the sail to the wind. Bowlines too have some control in this manner. The sail's attitude is further controlled by port and starboard lifts with which the *cant*, or angle to the horizontal of the yard, is set.

The remaining running rigging lowers, stows, kills, or reefs the sail. Downhauls assist in dropping a yard underway. In order to spill the wind from a squaresail and render it ineffective, or to prepare for furling, the belly of the sail is hauled up to the yard by means of buntlines, which lift the middle or bunt of the sail. Clew garnets or clewlines gather in the clews, and leechlines gather the leeches. Squaresails may be reefed by gathering either the lower or upper portions of the sail; in the latter instance, reefing tackle brings the reef cringles up to the yard, where the reefed portions of the sail are lashed. Another way to reduce sail is to build a sail with removable sections called *bonnets* and *drabblers*. Elaborate square-rigged sail plans can eliminate entire sails to reduce area rather than risk lives by sending puny humans aloft to hand and reef a thundering squaresail.

So although the running rigging varies, there may be 21 or so strings to pull per sail! Squaresails are bent to yards either by lacing them directly to the spar or lashing them with rovings to a jackstay on the yard. For yachtwork, the yard may carry a track with an inhaul and outhaul system; the sail is bent on with slides and can be brought into the mast like a drape and then lashed while the yard remains aloft.

Because there is rarely anything frivolous about the use of the square rig, the sails require the highest standards of material and construction. Usually the sails remain uncovered, and the more sophisticated versions of the rig require chafe protection from all the handling lines.

The Lug Rig

The lug rig, at least in its Oriental form, may rival the square rig in age. It resembles the square rig in that a mast is crossed by a yard to which is bent a four-sided sail. From there, however, the rigs part company. The lug is a fore-and-aft rig with the yard peaked up, and the peaked-up portion abaft the mast is longer than the portion before. The yard and the sail of all lug rigs are raised and lowered and never left permanently standing. A lugsail may or may not carry a boom, and if boomed it may or may not be loose-footed.

The Chinese Lug Rig and the Balanced Lug Rig   I'm an ardent fan of the Chinese lug rig, and could go on at length about its virtues and eccentricities. Actually a type of balanced lug, the Chinese rig once towered in monstrous proportions above 300-foot vessels of trade and warfare. In the Orient, the rig endures on a smaller scale in virtually the same form it has had for thousands of years. It has been successfully adapted for Western craft and sailing purposes, both racing and voyaging. Thomas Colvin and his *Gazelle* and Blondie Hasler and his *Jester* have given the rig much exposure, and their designs are a tried-and-true blend of techniques.

The balanced lug rig is distinct from other lugs in that the foot of the sail is boomed, with the luff forward of the mast. The difference between the Chinese lug and the Western balanced lug lies in the several full-length battens in the perfectly flat Chinese sails, and in the wealth of sail adjustments and reef options afforded by all those strings.

All those strings! Not quite as many as a ship's squaresails, and yet despite the extra weight of battens more controllable, more easily reefed, and more versatile. The Chinese lug rig is the only fore-

FIGURE 3-2. *Chinese lug rig (left) and balanced lug rig.*

and-aft rig that can be adjusted to the point of virtually mimicking a square rig. In its original unstayed form, the rig permitted a bending of the mast like a tree in a breeze, thus spilling wind and providing a safety factor. Western adaptations with lighter masts and stiffer hulls have added shrouds and stays, which also permit the use of Western headsails and staysails.

The Chinese sail, shaped like an ear "listening for the wind," has a sheeting system in which the subdivisions of sheetlets permit complete leech control by tending the trim of most if not all of the battens. These sheetlets converge at a block called the *euphroe*, which in turn is attached to a master sheet. Sheetlets are set up in various configurations, depending on the desired set of the leech and twist of the sail. There can be port and starboard sheets or one system for both tacks, but if the latter is not led far enough aft, the auricular shape of the leech fouls the sheetlets in stays. Parrels hold each spar to the mast and are long enough that the

entire sail may be shifted quite a ways forward or aft, either with a parrel adjustment line or a tack downhaul. Few rigs have this wonderful sail and helm balancing capability, and few rigs are so handy when it comes to reefing. When the halyard is released on any point of sailing, the weight of the battens brings the sail down and nestles the reefed portion like a venetian blind in the lazylifts.

For the most durable arrangement, the sail is laced to the yard and boom as well as to the battens, which are external on boats of any size.

The shortcomings of the rig lie in the sail's inability to generate as much lift when sailing on the wind, or as much drag when sailing off the wind, as cambered sails. This is particularly true in light airs; and that sail, with all those sticks and gear, is heavy!

Nonetheless the rig is weatherly, and certainly powerful when squared off downwind. Sufficient halyard purchase can be applied to allow even the slightest sailor to raise a large sail.

No more ideal sail exists for the novice sail-maker than the Chinese lugsail, for its flatness precludes the ordinary concerns of designing and cutting to a particular three-dimensional form. No broadseaming, no tensioning, no round, no pleats—sit and collect dust, you computers! Cloth layout is simple. The emphasis when making a Chinese sail for any boat but a daysailer is on ruggedness and chafe protection. Therefore the sail is labor-intensive, especially when intended for *bona fide* seafaring. Compared to a Western-rig sail of the same area, there may be twice as many rings to sew, and unlike most yacht sails it will be hand roped all the way around. A large sail of such sturdy build would be an ambitious project for a novice—but a sail that, as long as it was strong, would be a success.

The Western balanced lug with its overlapping boom and sail tack, in comparison to the standing lug (see Figure 3-4), has seen considerable use as a recreational small-boat rig. The luff of the sail parallels the mast, and the balanced lug profile results in a more manageable sail than if the tack were at the mast—particularly downwind in a breeze. The boom is less likely to ride up, the peak less likely to twist off, and the boat is less likely to jibe over. In the unstayed rig, a single halyard raises a yard to which the sail is laced. Loose-footed or laced, the foot is bent to a boom with minimal sheeting. The high-peaked rig is weatherly and, as I said, a powerful, balanced downwind sail.

The balanced lug rig was adapted for canoes in the late 1800s with the addition of reefing battens, which, with an elaborate system of lines and miniblocks, made it possible to shorten sail quickly. Though these variations resembled the Chinese lug in flatness and battens, the handling was quite different, and of course they appeared only on very small craft.

There are various means of holding the yard and boom of the lugsail to the mast. The boom may use jaws, a becket and toggle, parrels, or a band on the mast. The yard may use a becket and toggle, a turn or bight of the halyard, one or more rope grommets, a sling, or parrels.

A balanced lugsail for daysailing and diversion will be a lightly constructed article. It is a relatively easy sail to design and build, particularly if, like the Chinese sail, it is flat with full-length reefing battens. Careful attention must be paid to the reinforcement of the luff of this and other lugsail types, as it is the leading edge that takes the strain of the upper yard and sail—the halyard's point of attachment being the fulcrum of the lever. The loose-footed Western balanced lugsail is easier to make than if the foot is laced, and also more receptive to sail-shaping adjustment.

With the yard and boom to port, the rig sets better on starboard tack. The sail on port tack is plastered against the mast, which obstructs the leeward airflow and, if the sail is loose-footed with any roach in the foot, crimps the foot. This in fact is a failing of all lugsails except the dipping lugsail and the standing lug when switched to the other side with each tack. It is not practical to dip a balanced lugsail; indeed, it is hardly practical to dip the dipping lugsail, but if you don't the whole sail will wind up aback and you'll promptly be awash. Anyway, an effort is made to offset the one-good-and-one-bad-tack problem on two-masted balanced lugs by setting each sail on the opposite side of its respective mast.

Note: If you really want to draw attention to the fact that there may be more of sod than salt in you, nothing identifies a greenhorn faster than the mispronunciation of nautical lingo. For example, a particular sail, say a main, is never referred to as a mainsail. It is always a mains'l. One more example: the top gallant sail. If you say even top gallants'l, you're a sap. T'gallants'l is the most you can get away with, but t'gants'l is better, and to be really reeking of pine tar it's gants'l. Now try studding sail. Studs'l? No, stuns'l.

The Dipping Lug Rig
A Northern development, the dipping lug is plainly a squaresail swung fore and aft and peaked up. Popular throughout Europe but seldom utilized in North America, the rig was nevertheless employed by New Orleans luggers. Still, having served successfully on working craft

up to 50 feet in a split-rig configuration, it is recommendable primarily for smaller vessels and is most appropriate for open-water sailing where frequent tacks are not necessary.

Though he considered it the most efficient sail of all, Pete Culler condemned the dipping lugsail as being rarely useful—partly due to the weight of the spar aloft but primarily because of the dangers and inconvenience inherent in having to shift tack and yard to leeward every time the boat is brought about.

The rig is simplicity itself, with no standing rigging and a single halyard, perhaps belayed to weather for mast support. A yard and a mast, with a tack pendant and a single sheet to the sail, complete the ensemble. The power of the dipping lug is unparalleled owing to its awesome shape and uncluttered leeward side. The rig is more weatherly than might be supposed, but being boomless, lacks downwind spread and leech control (making a disastrous jibe a great possibility). Depending on clew height, sheet and tack positions may be shifted to minimize this problem, or the clew can be poled out, as I have done with a sweep on numerous occasions.

The sail is easily dumped, and the halyard should be ready to let go at a moment's notice—as getting caught aback in any breeze at all would surely mean a capsize. For greater control at the risk of complicating matters with more strings, one can rig a line to swing the heel of the yard around abaft the mast, and a traveling tack pendant sys-

FIGURE 3-3. *A dipping lug ahead of but to leeward of a split lug.*

tem can be devised to move the tack abaft the mast and forward again to the new leeward rail when tacking.

The dipping lugsail is easily reefed, and multiple rows of reefs should be installed, because reefing a sail of such power is a necessity. The tendency for such a sail to develop its own powerful shape suggests that the sail be built with limited camber and with some compensation for the anticipated bend of the yard. The luff, of course, comes under great strain and should be adequately reinforced.

Numerous variations on the rig arose in various parts of Europe. The cant of the yard ranged from near horizontal to being peaked so high that the sail, tacked to the stemhead, was straight from tack to peak—and required additional peak halyard support.

When two-masted luggers carried a dipping lugsail, generally only the forwardmost of the two sails was dipped, the other being a standing lugsail. These split-rigged luggers are not to be confused with a single-masted variation on the dipping lug that I have heard of but have never actually seen: the split lug. This unicorn of the sailing world has all the power and eccentricity of the normal dipping lug, but with the added complication and benefits of two separate sails carried on the single yard. If the yard does not need to be dipped for tacking—and it would seem unnecessary—then this would be a big selling point of the rig. There may be some benefit too in windward ability from the aerodynamic interaction of the sails. (By the way, what are those two sails called: jib and main?)

The swing of the yard athwartship in the dipping lug rig would be limited by the luff of the sail, which is good for counteracting sail twist but presents a quandary for offwind work. It would be necessary either to shift the tack to weather or ease the tack pendant when turning off the wind, or else in effect the peak of the sail would be over-sheeted. There is not that much room to play around with if the sail is tacked to the stemhead and the mast fairly bisects the yard. Downwind you have the same problem with the luff and tack as you do with the leech and clew: no outboard

place to belay to. The split lug would certainly suffer from this.

Possibly more weatherly and certainly less confusing than a split lug would be the setting of a conventional jib forward of the normal dipping lugsail, as was often done. Nonetheless, I would like to give the split lugsail a try. The two sails would have to carry an equal number of reefs, but the luff of the headsail would be stouter than that of the main for yard support. The luff of the main would be fitted with eyelets for lacing to the mast or to the leech of the headsail. A system of latchings, as in bonnets and drabblers, might be used, too. For the contemporary look one could use a Delrin zipper. If the sails were shaped for maximum individual efficiency, the overall shape when they were both in use would have the contours of a miniature-golf course rather than a single, fair form. The mainsail and jib could be cut perfectly flat to avoid this, but then would not function as well when set independently.

The Standing Lug Rig   Devotees of any or all lug rigs are called "lugnuts," and in the adjectival form, one who is crazy about the rig is said to be lugnuts. I fully admit to being a raging lugnut in general, but when it comes to the standing lugsail I go particularly lugnuts. Distinguished from other lugs by a nondipping (usually) yard, a tack at the mast, and no battens, the standing lugsail may or may not carry a boom. The yard may be very high peaked, is held to the mast by any of a number of arrangements, and is raised by a single halyard. The power to peak up a standing lugsail best comes from a downhaul tack pendant setup. A higher peak improves windward ability but narrows the downwind spread of sail on a boomless rig. A whisker pole, sweep, or boathook can help compensate for this, though. This too is a powerful weatherly rig, despite the mast's disruption of leeward airflow on one tack. Dousing and reefing are easy, and brailing of the boomless lugs'l is of inordinate value. The sail is laced to the yard and can be laced to the boom (when it has one) or left loose-footed as in the contemporary Nutshell prams.

FIGURE 3-4. *Standing lug rig.*

The handsomest standing lugsails have a high-peaked yard, the length of which is artfully distributed forward and aft of the mast. If the yard's too high, it will be a top-heavy nuisance when being raised or lowered; too low, and there will be insufficient tension on the luff of the sail for it to set well. These principles apply to all lugsails.

The only reason for going to the trouble of dipping and transferring the yard is to improve airflow. Though late 19th-century racing models with extremely high peaked, nearly vertical yards demonstrated the weatherly and hotshot capabilities of the rig, I venture to say that if you want that kind of performance there are hotter rig types. Nonetheless, it's wonderful to be able to get the sail down when you want to, and the weight of the yard facilitates this; lowering some of the spar weight aloft when reefing is advantageous. When reefed the peak gets higher (depending on the sail plan) and sheet leads must be adjusted. The standing lug rig has been successful on both single- and two-masted craft from dinghy size to larger small craft. I am particularly fond of the double-lugsail rig of the merchant marine cutters of the late 1930s and early 1940s, and it is standing lugsails of these and similar proportions that I have adapted successfully to numerous craft, including sneakboxes, dories, semi-dories, skiffs, and canoes.

(The "lug foresail" on a schooner- or ketch-rigged boat is not a lug rig. In this case "lugged" means "overlapping"; the clew of the boomless foresail, which may take any of several forms, laps the luff of the after sail.)

The Gunter Rig

Bring the heel of the lug rig's yard abaft the mast while peaking the yard up to nearly vertical, and you have the spar configuration of a gunter rig. There is some question whether the yard should in fact be designated a gaff, as in certain aspects we now have the highest of high-peaked gaffs. To add to the confusion, the gunter rig is frequently indistinguishable from its variant, the sliding gunter rig, and indeed the two terms are often used interchangeably.

The sliding gunter rig historically does just that. The upper spar, which is held in the vertical position abaft the lower mast by a collar at its heel and another about one-third up that fetches up and stops sliding at the lower masthead, is in fact called the *topmast*. Much like the fidded topmast in larger rigs, the sliding gunter is sent up and down by means of the heelrope/halyard, but it takes its hounds with it wherever it goes.

The upper spar of the other gunter rig (which I think should be called a *folding gunter*) is hoisted from and lowered to a horizontal position for furling, though in some cases it assumes a vertical position when hoisted. Sounds gafflike to me. What distinguishes it from a high-peaked gaff, though, is not necessarily the height of the peak or the halyard arrangement, but rather the hoisting procedure. On some gaffers the peak is raised to as little as 15 degrees from the vertical, and some gunter rigs have gafflike double halyards while some gaffers (such as Pete Culler's Concordia sloop) have single halyards. But if in the proper setting of the sail the spar is first raised more or less horizontally and *then* peaked up, the spar is a gaff. If the spar is peaked up to the vertical first and then hoisted to its correct setting position, it is a yard, the true descendant of the lug rig's spar, and not a gaff that descended (or ascended, in a manner of speaking) from the sprit.

From a sail-setting standpoint, the gunter sail, though having four sides, is virtually three-sided. The gaff sail is always four-sided. The true sliding gunter has a peak angle of 0 degrees, the gunter from 5 to 10 degrees, and the gaff 15 to 45 degrees. The stresses upon the respective sail types are different, and the sails require different design and construction.

The sliding gunter was used on small naval ship's boats in the 16th century, where the sail was laced to the topmast or bent with robands, and lashed to hoops on the lower mast. The rig was boomless, enabling the sail to be furled to the mast after the topmast was lowered. Alternatively, a releasing mechanism could be contrived, or a sprit boom could be employed, or a conventional

FIGURE 3-5. *Gunter rig.*

GUNTER VERSUS SPRIT

Q: *My idea in this sail plan is to have a loose-footed gunter rig that would be as stowable as the sprit rig but less cumbersome, more aerodynamic, and prettier. What's your opinion of it?*

A: I basically like your sail plan but hope that you are aware that by departing from the inconveniences of the sprit rig you also leave behind its numerous virtues.

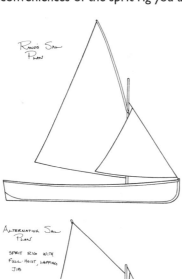

Rand's Sail Plan

Alternative Sail Plan

Sprit Rig with Full-Hoist, Lapping Jib

It is always debatable just where the gaff rig leaves off and the gunter begins. Your handsome curved spar seems to give the impression of a gunter while being at the same time a high-peaked gaffer. The Dutch, who have several successful variations on this form, would, I think, consider it a gaff.

The rig as a whole looks something like that of the Mirror Dinghy class, with a lilliputian genoa and no main boom. I'd prefer to see the jib set from the masthead with a longer luff, and just lapping the mast; you'll get greater visibility and better upwind performance. In order to *drive* a boat such as yours effectively, which is of greater benefit than trying to pinch as close to the wind as possible, the mains'l cannot really be sheeted in more tightly than over the quarter. Also, you have a mains'l-oriented rig; the little jib is there in great part, when going to weather, to help the main by guiding airflow. If the jib were to greatly overlap the main, there would be no space for air to pass between the two sails. If you sheeted the main in all the way to make sufficient space, the boat would tend to heel over and make leeway.

boom could be swung up to the mast with a topping lift and the whole bundle stowed. Conversely, the irons have sometimes been made releasable so that the topmast could be stowed on the boom.

Captain R. D. (Pete) Culler, a gunterphobe, relegated all gunters to a watery grave, feeling that it was difficult to get the sail to set well. It was not so much that Culler had nightmares about gunter, lug, and lateen rigs; rather, he was an ardent proponent of the sprit rig to the exclusion of all other small-boat possibilities. (Shortsighted as he may have been in this regard, I generally find Culler's notions utterly sensible. It was he who said "experience starts as soon as you begin," which applies to sailmaking as much as anything.)

Pete's sentiments about the rig notwithstanding, there is much to be said for the weatherly gunter. As reefs are taken, the spar weight and windage aloft decrease. The whole rig can be a handy, self-contained little bundle, and with a rotating mast it is safe and versatile, though it does not spread as much canvas as other rigs.

The "folding" gunter rig has some advantage over the sliding type. For one thing, a boom may be carried more practically. For another, the yard, while not perfectly vertical, can be longer—longer in fact than the boom—with its upper portions supported in part by a bridle and halyard. In the lower-peaked sails it is possible to alter sail shape and performance through gaff rig–like adjustments. This form also permits a curved yard—although I don't see why one couldn't produce a handsome and efficient curved topmast for the sliding version as long as the peak could twist off without the topmast binding in the sliding irons.

There are various methods for controlling the folding gunter's yard—parrels, jaws, or a car. Reefing the "folder" is not as easy, however. Either the attachment point of the halyard to the yard has to be shifted up, or (on bigger boats with bigger yards) throat and peak halyards must be employed, with the peak halyard attached to a bridle that is long enough to allow use of the halyard from full sail to deepest reef.

Sliding or otherwise, the gunter is a small-boat rig. It was attempted on a large scale by Sam Crocker on the schooner *Mahdee*, which originally carried a big jibheaded gunter-rigged mainsail. The havoc wreaked by a yard of those dimensions swinging wildly about when making sail was more than Sandy Moffat could endure, and a conventional Bermudan main was rigged as a substitute. Nevertheless, the gunter's devotees have every reason to extol its virtues and perpetuate its appropriate use.

The Sprit Rig

Although the sprit, once "spreet," rig was in common use among seafaring peoples of the Mediterranean in the early part of this millennium, a wave of ethnocentrism seems to have washed away any general recognition of Chinese use of the rig, which antedates their lugsail and perhaps is a predecessor to that seminal rig, and indigenous peoples of the Americas had employed the sprit rig in their canoes. I don't suppose it really matters who was the first to ship a sprit, but recognition of cultural variations on a rig type provides greater insights into the infinite possibilities of sail and rig and the incredible ingenuity of the ancient seafarers.

So simple and handy is the sprit rig in boats up to 20 feet or so that after Europeans reached the shores of the "New World" it became the most common small-boat rig in North America. Indeed, it endures there to this day, enjoying considerable popularity, though it has faded into obscurity in other places where it once dominated.

No standing rigging is required—or indeed wanted—in this rotating rig with its low center of effort, short mast, and sprit of approximately the same length. It is an economical and versatile rig. It carries maximum sail area for the least overall spar length; the peak of the four-sided sail is extended by the sprit, which is held to the mast and adjusted by means of an arrangement called a *snotter* or *heel tackle*. The rig is often used with no boom at all where sheeting permits; in other instances the sail is loose-footed, meaning that although a boom is present, the foot of the sail is attached to it only at the tack and clew. The loose-footed setup has

FIGURE 3-6A. *Sprit rig.*

advantages for downwind sailing, shape adjustment, and reefing, but the additional spar complicates things and prevents the use of the ever-handy brailing line (Figure 3-6B). A single halyard to the throat of the sail is an alternative to lashing the throat permanently to the masthead, and it facilitates reefing. In either case the sail is best laced to the mast; a nonbinding back-and-forth lacing style is used with a halyard, while a spiral lacing around the mast is favored when the throat is lashed. Alternatively, robands can be used for the lashed sail. The throat must be held close to the masthead either with a roband or a parrel; otherwise, the strain of the sprit will pull the corner away, distorting and spoiling the set of the sail.

There are various ways of rigging a snotter, but proper location on the mast is important. Too high a placement requires too much purchase to tension the head of the sail properly; too low, and the boat may foul the heel of the sprit when the sail is reefed. For good shape in a breeze, the sprit should place increased tension on the sail diagonally from tack to peak. A higher-peaked sail moves that diagonal farther forward in the sail, which is advisable for windward work.

The snotter should have sufficient power to increase sprit tension underway, but at the same time it should be possible to cast the thing off at a moment's notice and unship the sprit, even with the sail drawing. I don't know why, but little mention is made of the relationship between mast rotation, snotters, and sprit tension. Proponents of the rig rave about the ability to let go the sheet and let the sail stream before you as you run downwind onto a sandy beach. Detractors complain that on one tack the sail may set fine, but on the other the sprit's all out of adjustment. The problem is this: If the mast rotates from tack to tack, the snotter must turn with the mast. If it doesn't, the tension on the sprit will by turns increase and slacken. You have the same difficulty if the mast doesn't turn enough between tacks: The snotter may attempt to revolve about the spar, but this changes the relationship of sprit, mast, snotter, and sail, which should all turn as an ensemble. This alters the diagonal distance and cloth tension between tack and peak, and thus the set of the sail. Ideally, I think the mast should rotate freely. A round, tapered mast heel and leathered mast hole, all well greased with tallow, will help free the spar, as will metal bands. Any snotter that firmly encircles the mast is dependent on complete and smooth mast rotation for a balanced, smooth transition of sprit tension from tack to tack.

Despite the sprit's fouling the sail on one tack, it is nonetheless a weatherly rig, more so with a higher peak. But there are distinct proportions, which, if not fairly rigidly adhered to, will result in a rig of unfulfilled potential. Chapelle's *Small Sailing Craft* details many successful variations in addition to that shown here.

It is worth noting that the typical small-boat sprit is vulnerable in the spindle of its nose and the notch in the heel. Moreover, the sprit becomes unwieldy as it attains the dimensions required for sails over 85 square feet—a sailor begins to feel more like a knight with a lance trying to skewer that peak becket at full gallop. The rig is often split into mizzen and foresail, providing versatile sail combinations for light to moderate, moderate to blustery, and snorter breezes. A single reef is all that's required in the small boat's foresail or in a single sail. The sail may be shortened still further by unshipping the sprit—not a weatherly arrangement to be sure, but effective. If you're caught out in a real blow, you may choose to ride it out by dumping the setup overboard, making fast the sheet forward or aft, and riding to it as you would to a sea anchor. No other rig except the sprit or wishbone boom can brag of that last-ditch possibility. The sprit rig is often used with a jib, or in a split-rig combination with a sprit-boomed, jib-headed mizzen. Even in small boats it is possible to carry a topmast and set a topsail, as does the Norwegian *Rana* or the Albemarle Sound boat. This topmast, like the sliding gunter topmast, is abaft the lower masthead, and it might be workable to set a sprit topsail to a sliding gunter topmast. With a square-headed spritsail, sprit topsail, and jib, dousing the topsail and sending down the topmast

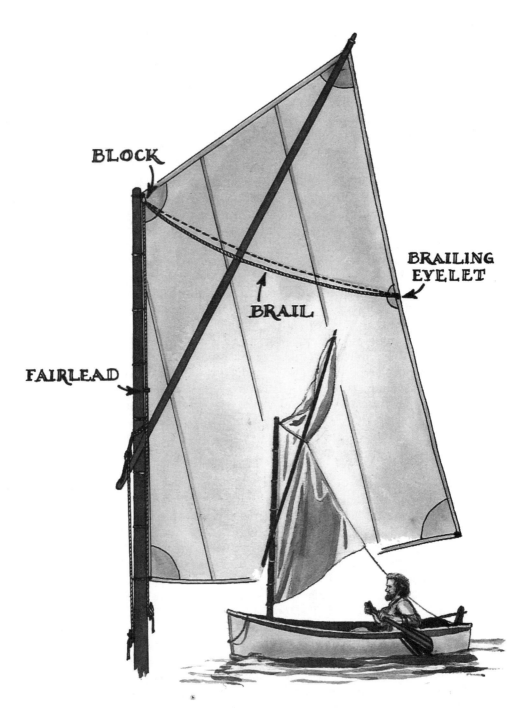

FIGURE 3-6B. *The brailing line is such sensible sail-handling gear for a boomless sprits'l or stand-ing lugs'l that I include a brailing eyelet in the leech as a standard feature of these sails.*

eliminates considerable sail area and reduces weight aloft. The jib is then struck, leaving reefing for last.

Sprit rigs of all sizes have a brail. This simple device makes so much sense there is no reason not to rig one. The light, slippery, nonkinking brailing line is dead-ended at the throat of the sail, led aft through a reinforced eyelet located in the leech (below the peak by a distance equal to the length of the sail's head), and from there forward again through a thimble or small block on the other side of the throat. It then goes down through a thimble fairlead at midluff, and then to a jam cleat on the mast at the tack or through another thimble on the tack and then aft to a jam cleat within reach of the helm. The latter method can impede mast rotation and spoil the set of a spritsail, but it makes the brail more accessible to the singlehander. For approaches, landings, and getting the sail out of the way while rowing, let go the sheet and haul on the brail. To sail again, cast off the brail and haul on the sheet.

The Chinese have a spritsail from which a valuable lesson can be learned: The sprit is a two-piece spar of socketed bamboo; the lower, shorter section could be removed for reefing, which I say beats lengthening the becket with a strop every which way. Maybe it's already been done, but I've never seen it, and if it can be made to work on a 35-foot bamboo sprit I'm sure our broomstick-size sprits can be adapted successfully. Maybe we should use bamboo—I haven't seen much of that either.

The Sprit-Boom Rig

The sprit-boom rig resembles the sprit rig in many ways, though it is distinctive in its manner of spreading a sail. It is the clew of this often triangular sail that is held out by the sprit boom, which crosses the mast and, like the sprit rig's spar, is supported and tensioned by means of a snotter or heel tackle. The other end of the sprit is shouldered and stuck through a clew becket. Depending on the height of the clew, mast rake, and length of foot, the sprit is angled to the mast to a greater or lesser

extent. The clew is always level with or lower than the sprit's forward end. The angle is important, as it serves to tension leech and foot respectively, and the tension should be distributed so that both edges set well.

The virtues of the sprit boom are many. The sail camber can be adjusted from flat as a dead frog in the summer, as you would want a mizzen, to a bulging belly. The light, simple spar is not only up out of head's way but is self-vanging, so that sheeting is for athwartships sail control only and need not serve the additional task of downwind leech tensioning. One result of this is that the jibe is tamed. Leech tension and sail twist are adjusted by sprit angle and tension.

Sprit-boom drawbacks include fouling the leeward side of the sail on one tack, so that really you get a sail of great shape on only one tack. Cambered sprits have been tried to offset this,

FIGURE 3-7. *Sprit-boom rig.*

with varying success. As in the sprit rig, synchro-nizing mast and snotter rotation is not always easy, and there are reefing complications. When you are reefing toward the mast (that is, sail area is reduced from the luff), one traditional arrange-ment requires dropping the sail. You must then tie in the reef, nettle by nettle, as you raise the sail again. The other traditional method is to haul on a reefing line that has been rove off through reef eyelets. This brings the sail forward to the mast—often with insufficient luff tension and inadequate reefed head and tack reinforcement in the sail. Simultaneously the sprit must be eased to allow the clew to come forward. It is possible to reef from the foot, which of course means wrestling with the sprit end and shifting the clew lashing.

The sharpie rig is a classic example of the sprit-boom rig with jibheaded sails. The sprit boom may be used in conjunction with other sail types, but not with the same sail-shaping capacity. One dodge for increasing sail size in the jibheaded rig while keeping the area low is to broaden the clew with a stick or club, either a T-shaped outer end of the sprit or a separate clew sparette attached to the sprit. It is even possible to have *two* sprit booms with clubs, one above the other, supporting a *very* broad clew.

Larger sprits are supported by a topping lift, which would facilitate reefing from the foot. The sail can then be bent to the mast by means of lac-ing or hoops, since a sail track would be smushed by the sprit boom.

Sails for a sprit-boom rig must be made with the rig's versatile shape adjustment capacity and its reefing techniques in mind. It is the foot of the sail that in great part prevents the boom from lift-ing, so this edge needs adequate reinforcement. It is quite important not to overlook the fact that in the unstayed jibheaded examples of the rig, you have in effect a long bow and arrow. The arrow is drawn aft by the snotter, the excess tension of which bends the mast, and sheeting in a breeze bends the whiplike mast further. The luff of the sail must be cut to accommodate this mast bend.

The Wishbone Rig

The wishbone rig is a natural development of the sprit boom, but while the sprit boom (with the exception of a few innovative contempor–ary designs such as those of Philip Bolger) has remained a classic boat rig, the wishbone is among the most avant-garde and may well take a speed-sailing record. Of course, it is the board-sailors among the daredevils, and the Freedoms and Nonesuches among the cruisers, who have so well exploited the virtues of the rig. The wishbone picks up where the sprit boom left off in that its camber permits the sail to assume an uninter-rupted airfoil shape on both tacks. The mast rota-tion/snotter conflict is eliminated; indeed, so is the snotter. Only an adjustable lift line supports the forward end of the wishbone, and the clew is outhauled.

On small boats, the sail is often held to the flex-ible spar by a sleeve open at the tack and closed at the head, which is slipped over the masthead to tack to the downhaul. There is no sheet for the boardsailor; the wishbone is a superb shape for grasping. It is not practical to reef a sleeved board-sail, but for that kind of sailing there is no need. (I did once install a reef in a windsurfer sail so that a lightweight novice could get used to the thing.) On small boats other than sailboards it is possible with sleeves or tracks to set up a functional reefing sys-tem as long as you have a halyard to support the head of the sail.

Most often a wishbone rig sports a three-sided sail, but even the boardsailers sport some wonder-ful forms that are truly four-sided sails; these are elaborated by full-length battens into bat- and butterfly-wing shapes, the purpose of which is to increase sail area and spill wind in a puff.

The attempt to adapt the aerodynamic advan-tages of a sleeved luff to big cruising sailboats was a dismal failure. Reefing was a nightmare and chafe a plague (as it is on all cloth pockets that have spars within). But dumping the sleeve in favor of a mast track not only put the rig back on the tracks but boosted its seaworthiness and appeal. The wishbone, now a hefty article, is

FIGURE 3-8. *Wishbone rig.*

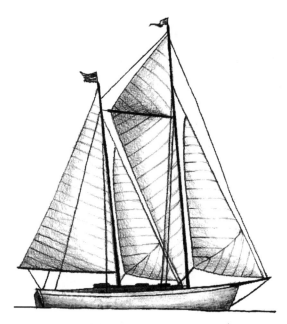

FIGURE 3-9. *Wishbone trys'l ketch.*

supported by a topping lift, and led within it internally are the clew and reef outhauls, which permit conventional slab-type reefing. The basket-like arrangement of lazyjack lines slung below the wishbone, into which the sail is dropped and furled, are extremely handy. (In one variation the boom was unshipped and the sail wrapped around the mast, but the wrapping time was an inconvenience and the sails deteriorated rapidly in the sun and weather.) And talk about mast bend—these whoppers curve like a fly rod with a 12-inch trout!

Wishbones and even half sprits can be used to spread sails set on a stay, too, with the same aerodynamic advantages. The forward end of the spar rides on the stay and is raised with the sail, necessitating a jackline in the luff but permitting more sheeting options. Outhaul tension not only offsets sag in the stay but can, with sufficient tension, bow the stay forward! This occurs because the outhaul, instead of pulling the clew aft, actually pushes the spar forward. Heavy wind pressure on leech and foot has the same effect. Though I have never

heard of a stay letting go on this account, I don't think it is a healthy situation. It does tend to flatten the sail as the wind pipes up, but not enough to prevent the sail from doing the tango cheek to cheek with the spar. Thus, the luff of the sail must be cut not for sagging but for bowing, and a chafe band must be installed to protect cloth from spar.

No discussion of the wishbone rig would be complete without mentioning the wishbone ketch rig, distinguished as it is by the wishbone-spread main trysail and carried most notably on Fritz Fenger's *Diablesse* and William Albert Robinson's *Svaap*. The "horse collar" rig, as it has been called, may employ a standing wishbone that stays aloft (though it can be swung down for storage against the mast), or one that is raised and lowered with the sail. Both types sheet to the mizzenmast. *Diablesse* carries a hoisted wishbone, the forward end of which has a gooseneck on a car traveling the same track as the sail's luff slides. The clew of the sail sets within the wishbone, lashing to its aft end. (It seems to lack adjustability once the sail is set.) A permanent topping lift sets and supports the slightly higher-than-horizontal cant of the spar. To lower, you let go the sheet, which runs to the mizzenmast head and down, and cast off the halyard. The descent of the gooseneck is checked at the appropriate point by a previously set up trip line; the wishbone's after end then swings down. Once the spar is under control, the trip line is let go and the whole spar slides down until the lower, after end is safely stowed in its "manger." There the spar is lashed and the sail furled and gasketed abaft the mast.

Diablesse's rig incorporates an athwartships horse and traveler at the lower end of the mizzen stay, thus permitting the sail to be tacked to leeward or to weather in order to give the sail more air on a reach or improved interaction with the mizzen when on the wind. This feature also helps keep the stay clear of the wishbone when lowering the spar close-hauled.

The design of a main trysail depends on whether the clew is lashed out or has an adjustable outhaul. One of the problems of this sail is that other than outhauling, downhauling, and increasing the luff tension, there is no way to support the foot and leech adequately. A flat sail with slack leech and foot will tend to fold at the wishbone, with the sail edges sagging to leeward, which is the same trouble gaff topsails run into. This is most likely a fault in the set of the sail, but it is a tendency the sailmaker should anticipate. After all, what is the benefit of a complicated rig (which this is) with enhanced windward capability if the main trysail, the crown jewel of the setup, sets like a dimestore kite?

While the wishbone rig can be highly successful when coupled with a Western yacht hull, Fritz Fenger employed it on a dhow-type hull and was particularly concerned about the highly complex juggling of centers and leads, which resulted in

the incomparable *Diablesse*. But the standing wishbone, at least, seems to be a big-boat rig at best, and even then should be dousable in a sneezer.

The Full-Batten Rig

Technically, it is hard to say whether the full-batten rig is a sail type, a spar type, or some of both. But since contemporary wishbone-rigged small-boat sails depend so heavily on full battens—battens running from luff to leech—for support, camber adjustment, and rigidity of form, it seems appropriate that full battens be the next topic of discussion.

The two major types of full batten are the rigid, nonadjustable type that provides profile support and reefing options to a fairly flat sail, and the flex-

FIGURE 3-10. *Contemporary full-batten mainsails.*

ible, adjustable type that imposes and supports sail camber. The classic full-batten sail is a representative of the first type; this is the Chinese lugsail, in which the heavy and inflexible battens are distinctly spars, to each of which separate sheets are attached. Rigid full battens have also been used on classic small-boat sails (perhaps most notably the batwing sails of sailing canoes, as described below), always with the same intent: to subdivide a sail into easily collapsed sections with an intricate system of reefing lines and small blocks, so that reefing could be accomplished smartly while underway by pulling a string from one cramped position in the boat—an obvious necessity for stability and accessibility.

When used on small daysailers, rigid full battens are often inserted in pockets built into the sails. This arrangement is unsuitable for bigger boats or harder use because the batten chafes from within, and anything rubbing against the pocket from without will eat through faster with the hard batten to press against inside. The seagoing Chinese sail has external battens and considerable chafing gear, and even then the sail has a hard time of it.

Flexible full battens found popularity first in small sport sails, multihulls, sailboards, and iceboats, but are now in vogue for big-boat racing and cruising. The rig has its virtues (including a stable aerodynamic form and great windward ability at high speeds), but economy and sail life are not among them.

In a small sport craft, the flexible full battens are adjustable and with the exception of catamarans are not part of a reefing system. Generally the sails aren't reefable. Larger trimarans, of course, have carried full-batten sails for decades, unencumbered by the rules restricting full battens from monohull competition.

Batten tension and thus the camber of a flexible full-batten sail is only adjustable ashore, with the sail lowered; this is one of the several drawbacks of the rig. The shape of the sail's leading edge cannot be altered underway except with mast bend; luff tension adjustments do not apply. Thus,

the full batten is not versatile, particularly with a rigid mast. This in itself would seem to make it inadvisable as a bluewater rig. Chafe and weight are further drawbacks, not wholly offset by quietness in stays and ease of reefing.

Unlike flat full-batten sails, the cambered variety are not easy to build. The battens are the skeleton of the sail, and if the sail's form is imperfect the skeleton will support and accentuate the imperfection. The cambered full-batten sail lends itself more to precise mathematical sail shaping and cutting techniques than to the traditional sailmaker's methods.

The Batwing Rig

The batwing rig is so named because it closely resembles the skeletal and membranous structure of the flying mammal. A thing of wonder and beauty, it is a combination of gunter and full-batten rigs that fans and folds out much the way a bat's wing does.

In the small-boat (typically canoe) rig, the yard and upper battens all radiate from a fitting that slides on the mast. It is this feature that distinguishes the batwing from other full-batten sails:

FIGURE 3-11. *Full battens in the batwing rig.*

the battens and the head of the sail meet at the luff. The lower, more horizontal battens are set up for reefing.

The true batwing is an easy sail to make—I daresay fun. Perhaps it is a little complicated in the laying out of the cloth, there being so many miters and little pieces, but what character! The main complication is the reefing system, which, as mentioned, is an intricate system of bee blocks and reefing pendants. Jibheaded sails with one or more full battens in the head supporting the roach are also said to be batwinged, as in the Erie boats described by Howard Chapelle. But these battens are built into and held aloft by the sail, whereas in the true batwing the yard and battens hold the sail aloft. Batwings of the Erie boat type are a cambered sail, although, when a single batten is used, it must be fairly rigid to support the roach, functioning more like a gaff with topsail. Still, it is an extremely simple unstayed small-boat rig, spreading nearly as much sail as a gaffer but without the weight and running rigging. It has a single halyard, a laced luff or slides, and standard reefing. It is a good light-air rig with so much area up high, but the gafflike batten without any "peaking ability" lacks the sail-shaping potential of a true gaff rig. Furthermore, the heavy batten will tend to sag off, which is good for spilling puffs but not for sail set and sail twist. A light, rigid, tubular batten might serve well in this rig.

The Gaff Rig

It is more than sentimentality that keeps this rig in continuing use. There is little doubt that the gaff rig is the single most versatile, efficient, manageable, safe, and seaworthy rig that has yet to sail the seven seas—and it epitomizes the seafaring philosophies of this book. Every other rig surpasses the gaffer in some specialized way, but no other rig combines so much potential and virtue.

No wonder, then, that from its presumed origin in 16th-century Netherlands (where it evolved from the sprit rig), the gaff rig went on to dominate commercial sail and yachting well into the 20th century. It remains unexcelled as a working rig, but the advent of steam and then internal-combustion engines spelled the decline of commercial sail in general. Among pleasure craft for yachting, racing, and cruising, modern trends have worked against the gaff rig. For windward speed and efficiency it was overhauled by the high-aspect jibheaded Bermudan rig, aided and abetted by fantastic advancements in sailcloth and design. Racing rules put the kibosh on big mainsails, while multipurpose downwind headsails made them superfluous. Simultaneously, in the pleasure-sailing world as elsewhere, industry made every attempt to standardize and homogenize production. The gaff rig was bypassed in the world of boatshow circuits and mass-produced formula pleasure craft. Moreover, the gaff-headed sail, even in the little pleasure daysailers, is an annoyance to the haul-it-up-and-go crowd who are just a snail's whisker away from buying an outboard runabout anyway. It takes time and skill to sail any boat well, but in a comparison of Bermudan versus gaff, the gaff rig takes more. There are more strings and more options, and you can't fake it so well in the gaff rig.

Thus, little effort has been made to apply design and material advancements to the rig. If the effort were made, the gaff rig might resume its rightful place of preeminence, which has been usurped by the less capable Bermudan rig.

The basic gaff-rig configuration was standardized in centuries of use. The gaff, to which the head of the sail is bent, is raised by two halyards, throat and peak, or possibly a single halyard rigged to perform both functions simultaneously. Though the gaff could be left standing aloft and the sail, if boomless, brailed up to the spars, there is no way to make a push-button roller-furling setup out of that. Thus, as mentioned, the gaff rig has a hard time competing with the Bermudan for pure ease of making and shortening sail.

There are gaff rigs for workboats and voyaging, racing and yachting, and daysailing. Each of these utilizes one or maybe all three of the basic gaff spar types. When what was originally called a *half sprit* became the gaff, the spar of moderate length was left standing aloft and the sail brailed up to the mast. Later two other forms developed. First came the short gaff, which, in its smallest form, was considered the "shoulder-of-mutton" rig and was raised and lowered. Finally the familiar long gaff, which offered more sail area and also was raised and lowered, came to the fore. Concurrent with these gaff developments came a transition from a boomless sail to a long, overhanging boom. The relatively long gaff and boom have maintained the most popularity, but all three gaff types have in common the throat and peak halyard; they may be stayed, may be boomed, and all have a sheet. From there on there are distinct differences.

Working and voyaging gaff rigs are distinguished by their ruggedness, means of sail attachment, sail-handling apparatus, and a generally lower gaff angle—30 to 45 degrees from the vertical. Spars, lines, and sail materials are stout, not only to handle strain but to endure chafe and abuse in a low rig where weight and windage are not critical. The sail is either laced, hooped, or parreled to its spars, and the peak and clew are lashed. The foot may be boomed, loose-footed, or boomless. (The first option is least suited to some working-craft needs, as the sail can neither be triced nor brailed. The only advantage it may have is for cruising, where, while sacrificing the sail-shaping

FIGURE 3-12. *Gaff-rigged schooner and Beetle Cat.*

benefits of the loose-footed arrangement, lacing the foot to the boom distributes strain more evenly, making the clew less vulnerable.) With all but the boomless rig, lazyjacks or lazylifts are a great advantage in sail handling. Once, having dropped sail, I missed a mooring, but was able to sail off a lee shore just by peaking up the sail while most of the sail remained nestled in the lazyjacks.

Working and voyaging gaffers, if they carry gaff topsails at all, usually have topmasts upon which the topsail is set while being sheeted to the outboard end of the gaff. The division of overall mast height into two spars facilitates finding trees of sufficient length and permits shortening the rig by housing or sending down the topmast in winter or in rough and windy places. Peak halyard tackle arrangements vary with length and weight of the gaff as well as with gaff height and sail-setting requirements. The more powerful the tackle (that is, the greater its number of parts), the slower the adjusting time and the greater the length of peak halyard required. It is these gaffers that most need a *gaff vang*—a line (or lines) that controls the athwartships trim of the gaff and offsets the spar's natural inclination to sag off to leeward and twist the sail excessively on all points of sailing. Not that a gaffer of this sort is necessarily going to have the most weatherly hull form; nonetheless, one of the principal hindrances to the rig's windward ability can be greatly offset with a gaff vang.

Clearly, the ruggedness of the working or voyaging gaff rig should be mirrored in the sail, materials, and construction. Expect greater exposure to the elements not only from year-round use but from uncovered storage, especially with a brailed, standing-gaff sail. The presence of a gaff vang permits a high/low distribution of relative fullness more similar to a jibheaded sail, as the head of the sail will not be twisted off so radically nor the boom trimmed in too far to compensate for that tendency. The traditionally constructed gaff sail of this type will have the cloths running up and down, parallel to the leech.

The yachting and racing gaff rig is a child of the seafaring version, but with an emphasis on speed,

weatherliness, and lightness. Of course, that's "light" relatively speaking, but I'm sure that were modern technology applied to the appropriate hull and rig there could be a very competitive gaff-rigged ultralight. But most gaff-rigged boats are heavy, and so are their rigs; only in comparison to their cumbersome progenitors do they seem refined. Nonetheless, the higher, more weatherly peak (15 to 30 degrees from the vertical), sometimes gunterlike in appearance, sets this version apart. Obviously such a height of peak would not work between the masts of a schooner with a spring stay. Also, too high a peak prohibits the setting of a gaff topsail.

If a topsail is set, it will likely be on the upper portion of a marconi-type polemast rather than a separate topmast. Jaws and saddles may still be used, but often the gaff gooseneck is a car that rides along the same track to which the luff of the sail is attached with slides. Both head and foot are also bent with slides, and adjustable peak and clew outhauls regulate sail edge tension.

Peak halyard systems vary widely, as do gaff lengths and even gaff shape, from the conventional straight gaff, to the elegantly arched, to outright curvaceous. Often in the racing gaff rig, lazyjacks, tricing lines, and even topping lifts are dispensed with in the interest of minimizing windage. Though the rig remains loose and elastic by contemporary standards, it is a tight fiddle in comparison with the workboat version; every possible sacrifice may be made in the interest of speed. So far, though, such developments still have not eliminated the sheer charm and beauty of the rig. Even with hollow aluminum spars to which the sail is bent by means of a sliding boltrope in a groove, the rig retains that inimitable charm.

It is usually class regulations or yacht aesthetics that rule out boomless or loose-footed sails, gaff vangs, or even boom vangs. Typically crosscut, the heavily roached sails are lightly constructed and shaped for speed, yet relatively versatile and adjustable. Gaff bend, both permanent and induced, becomes a major consideration in anticipating the cut of the sail. All edge tensions are adjustable. Competitive gaffers today, while having higher sail area-to-displacement ratios, nonetheless have lighter sails than voyagers.

A racing or yachting gaff sail is not a project for a beginning sailmaker. Even though the gaff rig is forgiving, a competitive gaff sail represents the ultimate in sailmaking refinement, with the most complexities and variables. Some of those refinements exist in other types of gaff sails, but small failures are not so noticeable. You can build a relatively shapeless, overbuilt voyaging sail out of easy-to-work materials, and its shortcomings won't interfere much with the use of the sail. But if you build a ho-hum racing gaff sail, you lose the race—it's that simple. The same is true of any racing sail, but with the gaff sail there's more to contend with. Although cotton is elastic enough to sometimes obscure your sailmaking blunders, it requires the utmost skill and experience to create a successfully competitive sail from cotton. Less skill is necessary to assemble a synthetic gaff sail, but the design subtleties can only come from much experience and many comparisons. Experience could be enhanced by electronically stored information, but as yet computers are not making patterns for gaff sails. I encourage any ambitious sailor to attempt making his or her own gaff sail, but not in the anticipation of its bringing home any silver.

Daysailing gaff rigs provide the greatest opportunity for the budding sailmaker. The sails are small, the materials are light, and the construction is undemanding—particularly in synthetics. Many of the sail-shaping concerns pertinent to voyaging and racing sails are applicable here as well, but no lives or races depend on the results. Visual embarrassment is probably the greatest misfortune that could befall the sailor of any unsuccessful homemade gaff sail; that and frustration with its performance. But it really doesn't matter; if you're out there doing what you want to do, "proper" is just a figment of some nautical snob's imagination.

In these small boats, not only is the sail easy as gaffers go, but so is the rig: one, maybe two halyards, and the mast unstayed or with simple shrouds. A topping lift and lazyjacks may be pre-

sent in bigger small boats. And the hardware is miniature—small jaws or car-and-track on the gaff, light lacing lines on boom and gaff with peak and clew lashings (and maybe masthoops on the luff), or slides, with peak and clew outhauls. If the sail is loose-footed or boomless, it is that much easier to make with some hope of pleasing results. The throat, as in all gaff sails, is still a mighty hurdle, but at least the tack is not so troublesome. Especially with these light sails, it is important to anticipate and compensate for gaff and boom bend. Peak halyard arrangements that concentrate peak support toward the center of the gaff are prone to greater bend; likewise with sheeting and boom bend.

Like the Chinese rig, the gaff rig has fabulous potential for craft of all sizes. But unlike junk sails, gaff sails also have tremendous competitive ability. It is a matter of knowing how to get the most out of the rig and sail. Despite the gaff rig's comparatively retarded state of development, time and again one hears of or observes a gaff-headed sailboat overhauling a Bermudan rig (maybe your own), even going to weather. Old gaffer, indeed.

The Bermudan Rig

Bermudan, Bermudian, marconi, jibheaded, sharpheaded, pointy-headed, or thimble-headed—call it what you will, why has this boomed, triangular sail abaft the mast become so popular? In its basic form—that is, mast, boom, sheet, and halyard—the answer lies in its simplicity and weatherliness. Early low-aspect triangular sails came to be called Bermud(i)an after their adaptation to a racing rig on the island of that name. The rig retained a low aspect until 20th-century advances in materials could permit rigs, sails, hulls, and ballast capable of sustaining the stresses of a high-aspect sail. In the meantime, the only way to add sail area was to add headsails, auxiliary sails, or more masts. More masts, of course, slowed things down to weather but did allow greater sail area with a low-aspect profile.

As a working and voyaging rig, and also for motorsailing, the low-aspect Bermudan rig has seen continued use up to the present, not only in small craft but also in larger boats—notably the

FIGURE 3-13. *Bermudan rig on a graceful 1930s-era racer.*

Chesapeake bugeye, skipjacks, and L. Francis Herreshoff and William Hand designs. Bermudan-type sails may alternatively be spread by sprit booms or carry flexible full battens. For stability and ease of handling, this rig is best when of relatively low aspect. Relative to what? Taking luff height to foot length as a ratio for quick comparison, you might see a ratio approaching 1:1 in an Alpha dory, a skipjack, or a traditional motorsailer; other than simplicity, such a low-aspect sail has little to offer that may not be found in other rigs. At the other extreme we find ratios of 4:1 or so in some modern racers with complex rigging systems. At this extreme, great aerodynamic efficiency is obtained at the expense of high stress on sail, rig, boat, and sailor.

In between there is a lot of room for wholesome design: 2:1 for a bugeye ketch, 3:1 for the Hinckley Bermuda 40, and other intermediate values for such diverse boats as L. Francis Herreshoff's *Nereia* and some of Ted Brewer's designs, all of which are seaworthy rigs that do not compromise too heavily the virtues of the Bermudan sail.

The Bermudan sail can be spread by a conventional boom with the entire foot of the sail attached, as is most common, or alternatively can be boomless or loose-footed. Both of the latter types are now seen principally in small daysailers but have some application in larger boats too. The loose-footed sail offers a great range of camber adjustment without interference from a spar as with the sprit boom. On the other hand the clew outhaul, which controls sail shape, may be more difficult to adjust underway than a snotter, and a conventional boom offers no self-vanging other than its own weight and sheeting. Larger boats, when unfettered by class regulations, can make effective use of the boomless or loose-footed Bermudan sail, though one must bear in mind that the entire strain of a high-stress corner in a particularly high-stress sail profile falls upon the clew.

Clearly, in order to support the taller and lighter mast of the Bermudan rig, new rigging techniques were required. It was some time before a high-aspect masthead rig was considered feasible and three-quarter and seven-eighths rigs with their struts, diamonds, and jumpers could give way to a tall but simple masthead system of shrouds, forestay, and backstay. Even so, flexible masts have allowed the fractional rig to retain some popularity in the interest of mainsail shaping and improved sail interaction.

Bermudan sloops with inboard single and double headsails are today the most pervasive rig configuration sailing the waters of sport entertainment and diversion. Split rigs, too, have tended to go Bermudan, which is mildly ironic given that 16th-century Dutch jibheaded cat schooners were overwhelmed by the greater sail area of the gaff rig. Schooners, ketches, and yawls may carry both Bermudan main and mizzens or a combination with some other rig type. The trend toward high aspect ratios has occurred as well in these rig configurations, reaching ribbonlike extremes in craft dedicated primarily to long-distance speed.

The high-aspect Bermudan rig has four inherent problems, three of which impede its forte, weatherliness, and the last of which compromises the seaworthiness of the sail. The first concern is heeling moment: The great heeling moment of the taller rig and sail makes for more leeway, more ballast, and/or greater weather helm, which is detrimental to windward performance. The second problem is mast turbulence. Numerous and novel attempts have been made to minimize or eliminate the loss of aerodynamic efficiency caused by the mast and the sail's leading edge. These have included several attempts to set the sail from a stay instead of the mast. Third, the terrific strain on the sail fabric at the leech causes cloth distortion, poor leech shape, and sail draft shifts, thus damaging a sail's drive and lift. New laminated fabrics and leech-oriented constructions that attempt to minimize this problem have been comparatively successful, but those materials and sailmaking techniques are not appropriate for anything but high-technology competitive sailing, which is where the high-aspect Bermudan sail belongs.

Concerning the seaworthiness of the sail: It is generally necessary in the higher-aspect Bermudan sail to provide greater area and improved leech form by means of headboard and roach. The roach, of course, must be supported by leech battens. Battens and headboards are undoubtedly the most self-destructive sail paraphernalia. Sails with this gear do not last long. Moderate- to low-aspect Bermudan sails have no competitive needs and may dispense with roach, battens, and headboards; a more durable sail is the result.

There is nothing simple about the Bermudan rig in its most competitive form, but on small daysailers it provides a high thrill-to-effort ratio. Sail may be shortened toward the luff, as in the sprit-boomed sharpie, or toward the foot as with other rigs. The Bermudan sail lends itself to rolling up along the luff on a wire either abaft or within the mast. In these systems one sacrifices sailing performance for ease of handling. Though the Bermudan sail can be laced or hooped, today in all but classic craft it is almost exclusively bent by sail slides on a track or by slides or a boltrope running in the slotted spar. Lazyjacks can be used effectively.

The Bermudan sail is more or less difficult to make depending on its intended use. More information on design and construction is available for the Bermudan sail (at least for dinghies and yachts) than for any other type, and there are countless examples close at hand for comparison. Kits are also available, and these eliminate all but the assembly portion of the sailmaking process.

Like the gaff sail, the jibheaded sail for voyaging and commercial use is a rugged article in which the best quality requires the skill and strength of hand-finishing techniques, but not necessarily flawless execution of those techniques. This is a reasonable and fairly forgiving project for the budding sailmaker, especially if the sail is boomless or loose-footed and the work is uncomplicated by any effort to build and support a big roach or construct a smooth-setting tack area. This is not to say that the standards of construction of working and voyaging sails are so lax that any crude assemblage will do, but there is more leeway than in the making of competitive sails.

The novice sailmaker cannot expect to build successful competitive Bermudan sails (except by luck), kit promotional materials notwithstanding. These sails require expensive, sophisticated materials and computerized analysis and design tech-

niques. For daysailing, however, the Bermudan rig offers the beginning sailmaker low stakes, light and inexpensive materials, a minimal demand on skills, and lots of latitude in the result. You'd have to make quite a botch of it to come up with a Bermudan sail that didn't work at all. The loose-footed or sprit-boom varieties are simplest, just as for voyagers, but even easier since they're smaller. If you must have a big roach, the problems of battens and headboard remain.

The first-time sailmaker should steer clear of full battens. Battens serve best in competition and high-performance sails, which are better left to high-tech sail manufacturers. Similarly, roller-furling Bermudan sails are not a good starting project.

When making a Bermudan sail, you must anticipate the bending of the boom, the type of clew outhaul, and interaction with other sails, as well as mast bend, halyard purchase, and leech control through sheeting and/or vanging. The luff must be cut in anticipation of bend in the mast and reinforced to withstand and balance the power of the halyard. If not, the sail will either be pulled apart or, at the other extreme, never be stretched taut. Sheeting and vanging help determine how large a roach a Bermudan leech might carry or what shape the leech will be if there is no roach. The power to exert a downward force on the boom, and thus the leech, controls sail twist and the vertical distribution of sail camber.

The Lateen Rig and the Settee Rig

Both the lateen rig and the settee rig are easily distinguished by their long, sometimes handsomely curved yards crossing the mast obliquely fore and aft. To the lateen yard a triangular sail is bent, but from the shorter settee yard a quadrilateral sail is hung, almost as though someone walked up to it with a scimitar and sliced off the tack. A Middle Eastern and Mediterranean rig of great antiquity, the lateen rig joins the Chinese rigs among the earliest fore-and-afters. Through the Middle Ages and after, many vessels of commerce, warfare, and exploration carried the rig exclusively; many others carried some combination of lateen, square rig, and headsails.

Now associated principally with the Indian Ocean traders called *dhows*, the lateen rig also featured prominently in the exploration and subsequent naval battles of North America's inland waters, such as the two-masted gundalows of the Lake Champlain region. The rig appeared as well in the late 19th-century seine boats of Apalachicola and St. George's Sound, Florida, and in the *feluccas* sailed by the Italian fishermen of San Francisco at about the same time.

Unlike earlier vessels, which had as many as three masts, the 19th-century North American lateeners had a single mast, no shrouds, a halyard for raising the yard, and an additional halyard for peaking the yard. At the heel of the yard is a tackle for greater control of this monstrous spar. Sailing the feluccas takes great skill, especially in the winds of San Francisco Bay, and capsizing is easy.

That the lateen rig, especially when coupled with the Middle Eastern dhow–type hull, is fast and weatherly is indisputable. It even has fantastic downwind capability as the yard is squared off and

the peak lowered, but there's the problem of controlling that terrific spar, and a jibe could be a nightmare. Reefing, when the sail is boomless, is accomplished along either luff or foot. Reefing up to the yard, or luff, is an arduous job necessitating the lowering of the yard; when reefed along the foot, the unwanted sail area is gathered in at the clew. Contemporary boomed lateen sails are not reefable. In the settee sail, the first reef ties up the lower portion of the sail to the heel of the yard. There being so many handier alternatives, these rigs find ready acceptance in the Western Hemisphere only among small boats, and only in some canoe rigs and boardsailers at that. Its vulnerability to capsize explains why it fell from favor for canoes, but has endured with the beamier and less tender Sunfish, still an immensely popular class. And there are other, similar boardboats splashing about with the lateen rig. Lateen sails of this sport type can be laced to boom and yard or, alternatively, bent with robands or even plastic clips. These small lateeners are as simple as can be: unstayed

FIGURE 3-14A. *Lateen rig on a Sunfish and a dhow.*

FIGURE 3-14B. *The settee sail has a short luff.*

mast, yard and boom of equal length, halyard and sheet, lacing or robands. Easy to set up, easy to sail (taking into account the swim factor), and a handy bundle of spars and sail to stow.

Notwithstanding that Sunfish are raced, the sport lateen sail is an excellent introductory sail project. Light, very cheap materials, minimal sewing and hardware, and no roach and battens all conspire to make it so. The only real way to go wrong is to underestimate the great amount the yard and boom will bend. A big lateen sail, on the other hand, is not a recommended beginner's project.

The Polynesian Claw Rig

One hears the word "exotic" used to describe anything uncommon, novel, or refined in a rig or high-tech sail fabric. To my way of thinking, you fetch up on a truer meaning of the word when considering the South Pacific claw rig. Now that's an exotic sail—a complete marvel and mystery! Yet it works so well, and it has Western applications for kayaks and even skate sails. It is also a thing of beauty and harmony.

For the kayaker, a variation on the claw sail couldn't be simpler to make. I am thrilled to see that kayaks are using the wind with this sail as well

as with spinnakers and in the Klepper rig. So often it seems that oar and paddle boats neglect such alternatives.

Anyway, if it will help you get there, put sails on it! Skateboards, bicycles, outboard motorboats, canoes, and kayaks are fair game. The kayak claw sail is V-shaped and is spread by two sticks tended by braces. Unlike the Polynesian rig, it has no mast; therefore, the V remains upright, whereas the claw sail with mast may be canted all over the place. The sail is held to the spar by either sleeves or lacing. With sleeves, no hardware is required. There are no seams either!

FIGURE 3-15A. *A pirogue with claw rig.*

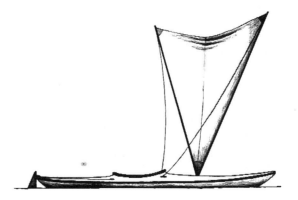

FIGURE 3-15B. *Claw rig variation on a kayak.*

SAIL TYPES

Next, we explore sail types categorized by function and use rather than by shape or construction.

WORKING SAILS

Working sails are all those sails fully set when a boat is sailing comfortably in wind conditions that, depending on the size of the boat and the point of sailing, may range from moderate to fresh. Lighter winds and offwind sailing require additional, or auxiliary, downwind and light-air sails. Heavy winds necessitate reefing and sail changes to smaller and stouter stormsails.

Following are some basic rig configurations with their respective assortments of working canvas:

- cat rig—single sail
- sloop rig—jib, mainsail
- double-headsail sloop—jib, staysail, mainsail
- cutter—jib, staysail, mainsail
- Bermudan ketch—jib, staysail, mainsail, mizzen
- cat ketch—mainsail, mizzen
- wishbone ketch—jib, main trysail, mizzen staysail, mizzen
- yawl—jib, staysail, mainsail, mizzen (jigger)
- cat schooner—foresail, mainsail
- two-masted schooner—jib, forestaysail (jumbo), foresail, mainsail
- staysail schooner—jib, forestaysail, main staysail, main topmast staysail, mainsail
- three-masted Chinese rig—foresail, mainsail, mizzen
- three-masted westernized Chinese rig—jib, jib topsail, jumbo, foresail, mainsail, mizzen

Working sails, though they have their ideal wind ranges, are often carried in both extremes. In light going they are augmented by other sails. In the rough and tumble they may be reefed and used further, or some may be used unreefed while others are taken in. Thus, these are multipurpose sails, and they require great aerodynamic versatility as well as the strength to hold up under the slatting of a calm and the pounding of a gale.

Headsails

This is our first opportunity to discuss headsails and staysails, which complement the various rigs mentioned earlier in the chapter. As working sails, these sails are usually triangular and may be hanked to a stay or set flying. They may be boomed or boomless. In small boats, short clubs make jibs self-tending. The sails are hoisted with a halyard and tacked directly or by means of a tack pendant to the appropriate location if boomless. They are tended with double sheets, or a single sheet if boomed or club-footed and self-tending. Club-footed sails hanked to a stay must either have luff jacklines or a way to slide the club forward, or they can't be lowered completely.

The height of clew depends on sail type, location, interaction with other sails, spar if any, and sheeting. Besides the restrictions of space, stay length, and fore-and-aft space for spars or tacking the sail, the peripheral measurements and shape of these sails depend on the sail area required to balance the working sail configuration and ensure ease of handling. A sailmaker's principal concerns are how much the luff will sag in the various wind ranges, how much power is on the halyard, what sails are affecting and being affected by the sail, its position in the rig, its angle of sheeting, and its means of attachment. Additionally, as in the case of fore staysails, staysails, and the jibs of single-headsail sloops, these sails must be built to withstand the stress of storm work and may require reefs.

(text continued on page 78)

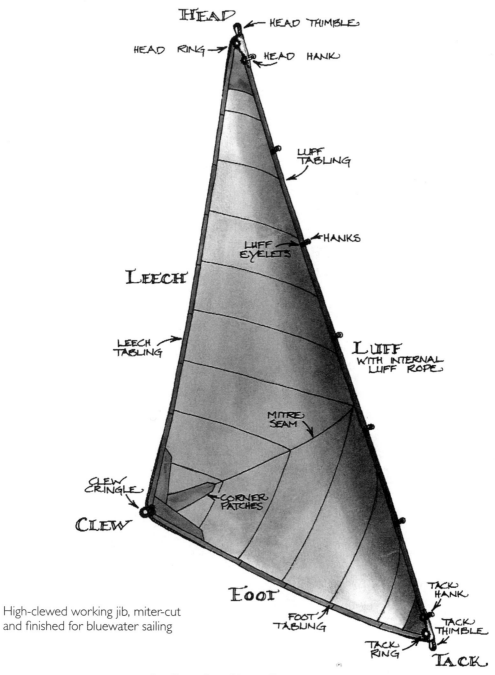

HEAD

HEAD THIMBLE

HEAD RING

HEAD HANK

LUFF TABLING

LUFF EYELETS

HANKS

LEECH

LUFF
WITH INTERNAL
LUFF ROPE

LEECH TABLING

MITRE SEAM

CLEW CRINGLE

CORNER PATCHES

CLEW

FOOT

TACK HANK

FOOT TABLING

TACK THIMBLE

TACK RING

TACK

High-clewed working jib, miter-cut
and finished for bluewater sailing

FIGURE 3-16 (PAGES 69–78). *A gallery of working sails.*

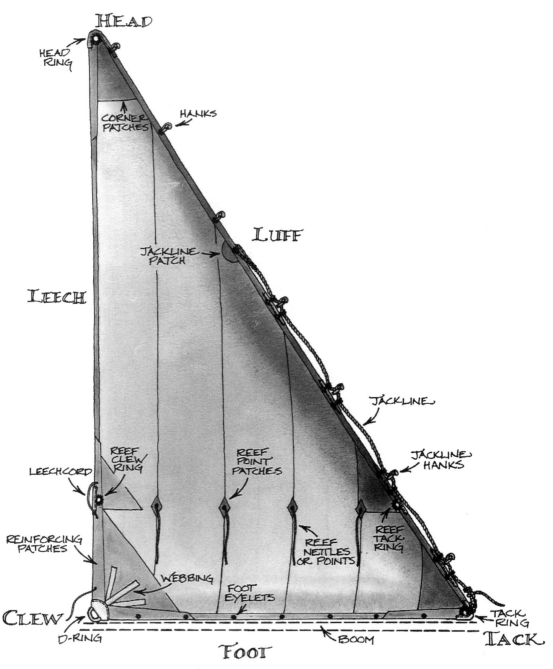

Working forestaysail—vertically cut, with reef
and jackline—a voyaging sail intended for use
also as a storms'l

FIGURE 3-16. *(cont.)*

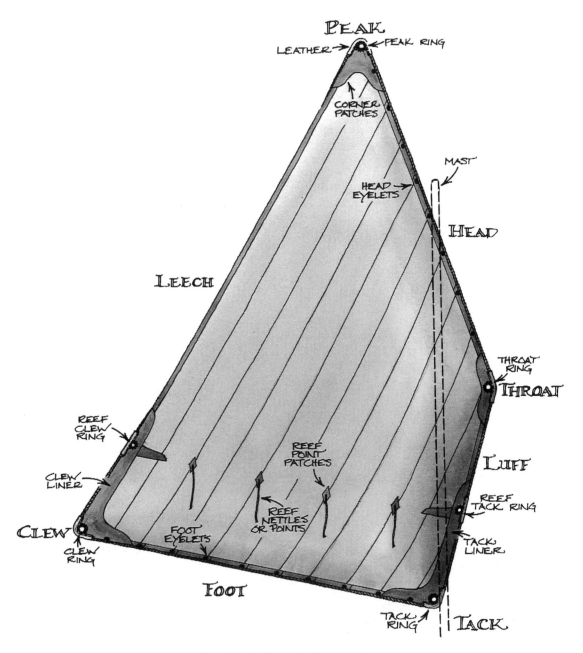

Standing lugs'l, vertically cut and
traditionally finished

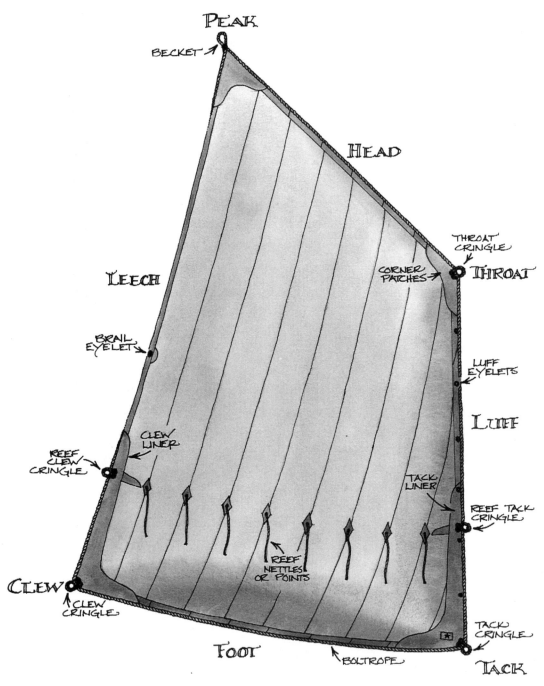

A vertically cut, traditionally finished sprits'l

FIGURE 3-16. *(cont.)*

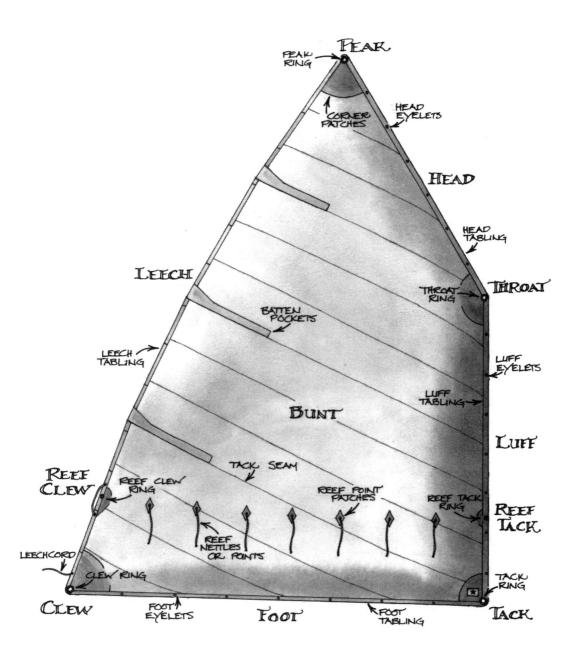

Crosscut gaff-headed sail, finished for daysailing

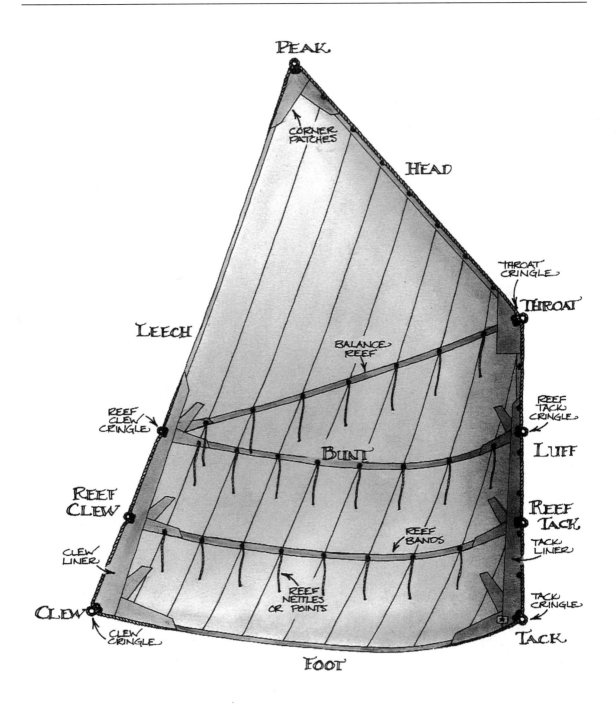

Loose-footed, gaff-headed voyaging sail with
traditional workboat finish

FIGURE 3-16. *(cont.)*

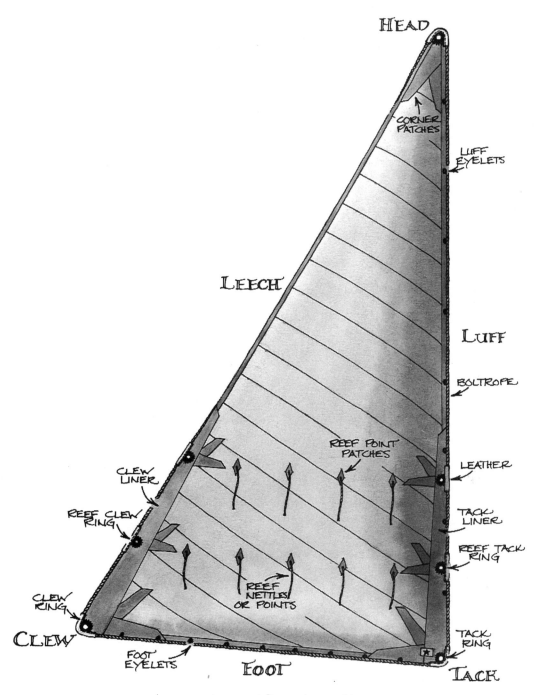

Low-aspect crosscut Bermudan working
mainsail, finished for voyaging

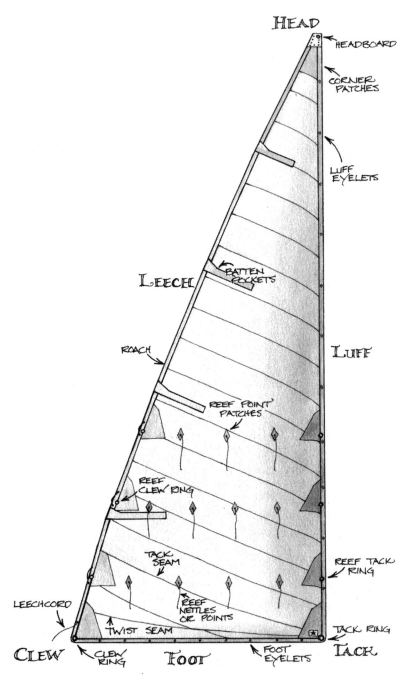

High-aspect crosscut Bermudan mainsail
finished for inshore sailing

FIGURE 3-16. *(cont.)*

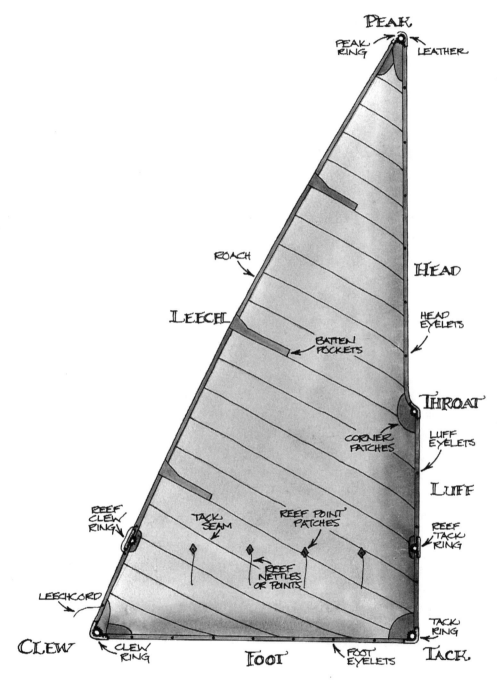

Crosscut gunter sail with light daysail finish

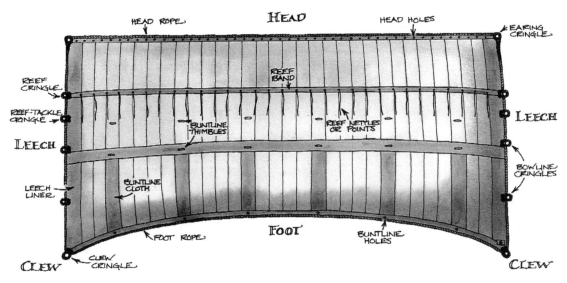

An ocean carrier's squares'l, traditionally finished

The club-footed mainstays'l of
the staysail schooner

FIGURE 3-16. *(cont.)*

AUXILIARY SAILS

Auxiliary sails are intended to provide safe and efficient sailing when either more and lighter canvas or less and heavier canvas is needed. Topsails, staysails, and light-air headsails are all auxiliary sails intended to add light-canvas sail area when the wind drops.

Topsails

Topsails are invariably set above another sail and vary with rig type and sail configuration. For example, a *square topsail* is carried before the fore topmast of a fore topsail schooner. *Gaff topsails* come in great variety over gaff sails, and may be flown from a pole mast or topmast. They may be just big enough to fill the space between gaff and topmast, or they may be spread and extended by a yard or jackyard. They may set half again the area of the sail below.

(text continued on page 86)

Square fore tops'l

Sprit-rigged tops'l

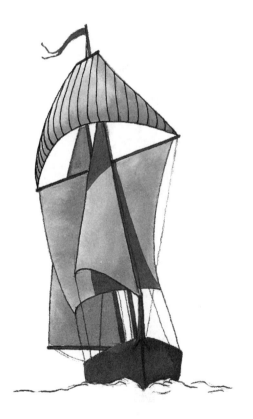

Raffee tops'l

Sprit tops'l

FIGURE 3-17 (PAGES 79–86). *A variety of topsails.*

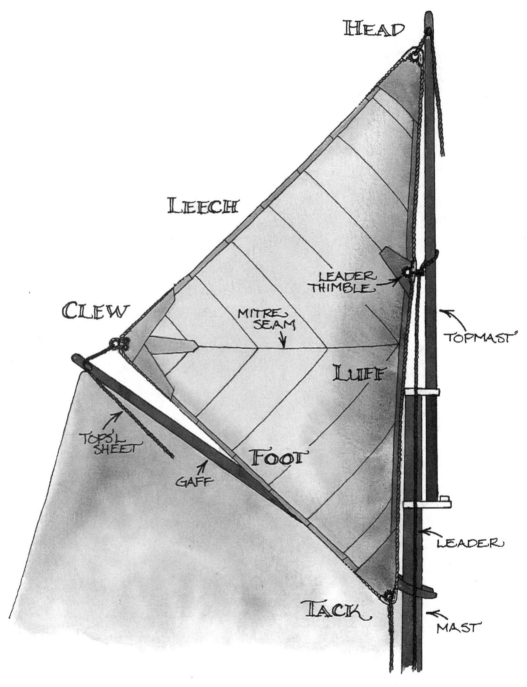

Gaff tops'l set on a jackline

FIGURE 3-17. *(cont.)*

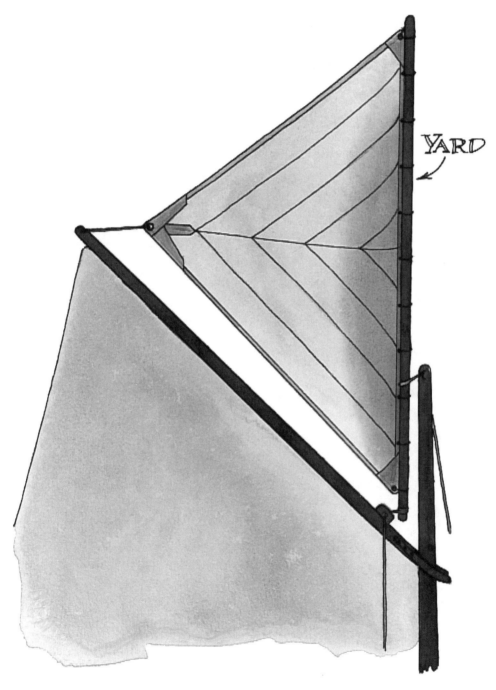

YARD

Cornish gaff tops'l

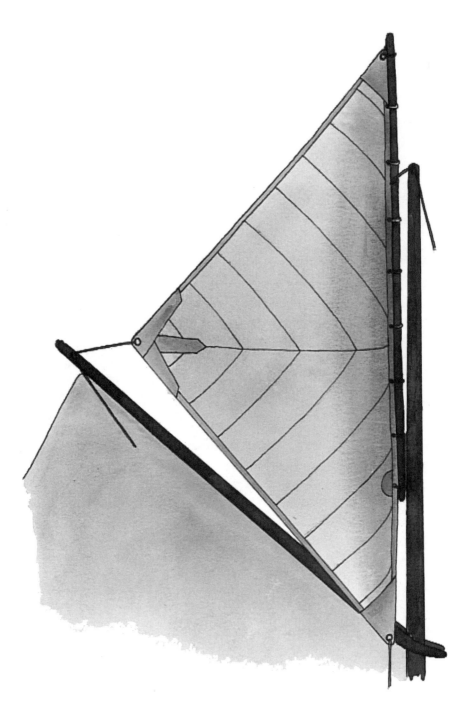

Gaff tops'l with yard

FIGURE 3-17. *(cont.)*

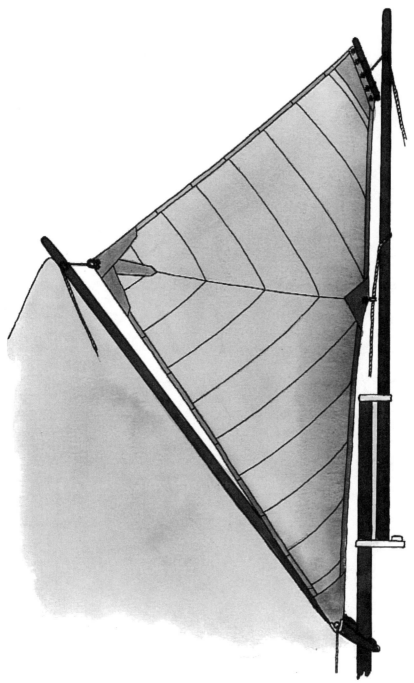

Gaff tops'l with head stick and jackline

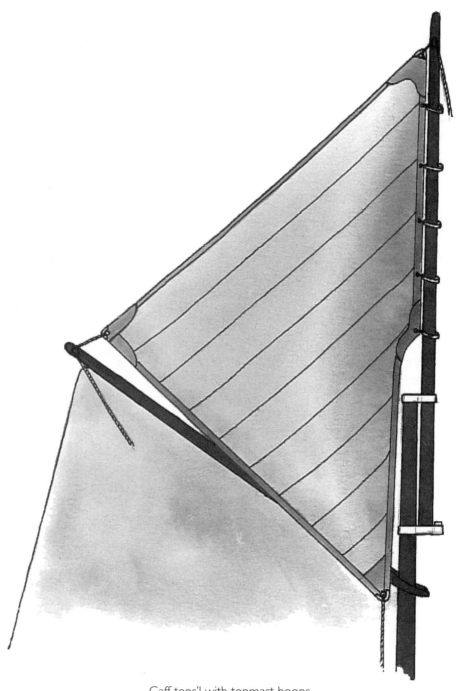

Gaff tops'l with topmast hoops

FIGURE 3-17. *(cont.)*

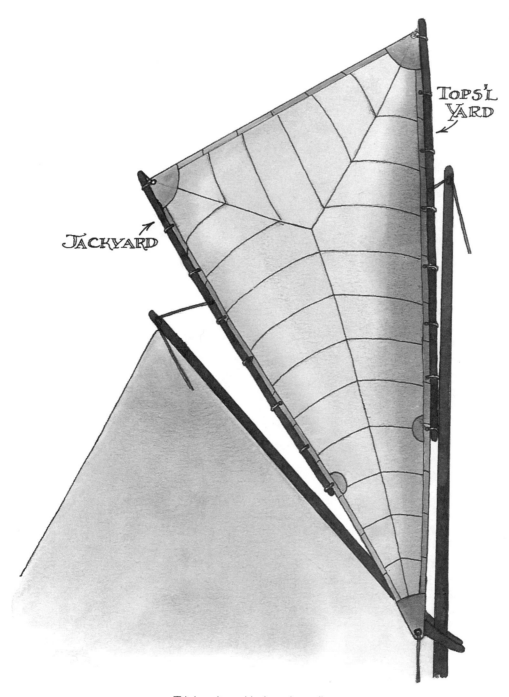

Triple-mitered jackyard tops'l

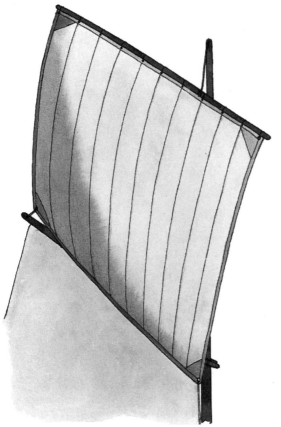

Yard tops'l set above gaff sail

FIGURE 3-17. *(cont.)*

Jib tops'l

A topsail set above a spritsail can be sheeted to the upper end of the sprit or, as with the Albemarle Sound boats, a standing topsail with independent yard and sheeting is brailed up to the *upper mast*.

Lateen topsails have been set above the low-aspect jibheaded Bermudan sail of Chesapeake racing log canoes, and both *sprit-rigged topsails* and quadrilateral *sprit-boomed topsails* can be set on Bermudan sloops. Topsails of these types are relatively flat and lightly constructed in comparison to working sails.

In certain multiheadsail craft, headsails carried outside and above the jib are called *topsails*. These are (commonly) a *jib topsail*, and above that (sometimes on racers) an even smaller *baby jib topsail*.

The *Yankee jib topsail*, so called because it was introduced as a racing sail on the J-boat *Yankee*, is distinguished by its high clew and long luff, which runs nearly the whole of the head or topmast stay. Long-luffed, high-clewed jibs are now referred to as *Yankees*, and racing sailors call their full-hoist high-clewed jibs *jibtops*. Though neither use of this sail is actually a topsail, Yankee or otherwise, that is the way nautical terminology sometimes evolves.

Staysails

There are the innumerable auxiliary staysails, ranging in number or complexity up to the nine or so staysails carried on a three-masted barque. They can be three-sided or four-sided (as in the case of a schooner's 'tween-mast staysails). A staysail may fill a gap in the sail plan unoccupied by any working sail, or it may replace and set in the same position as a smaller working sail, as in the case of a cutter's genoa staysail supplanting the working fore staysail.

Auxiliary staysails are set on the stays of the standing rigging, or on jackstays that are not an integral part of the mast support. Alternatively, auxiliary staysails can be set flying.

FIGURE 3-18. *Various staysails of a three-masted barque.*

For Sloops and Cutters   To begin with a rare exotic, the only *backstay staysail* or back staysail I've ever seen was carried by the ill-fated cutter *Seminole,* which was wrecked in New Zealand. A light downwind sail, it tacked to the rail, and its head was hauled aloft on a hank riding on the backstay. Its purpose was to increase manageable downwind sail area on a boat that carried no spinnaker, but I don't know how it performed.

Genoa staysails, spinnaker staysails, and *daisies* are all variations on a lapping fore staysail and are primarily for offwind work. On a spinnakerless cruiser, the genoa staysail is poled out on the opposite side from the genoa or drifter. The 110-percent spinnaker staysail and the smaller and lighter 85-percent daisy are reaching headsails set inside a reaching spinnaker.

A big-boat downwind race inventory includes a *blooper* (see Figure 3-28). This is a remarkably specialized staysail carried dead downwind on the opposite side from the spinnaker, not only provid-

FIGURE 3-19. *The rare back staysail.*

FIGURE 3-20. *A genoa staysail.*

FIGURE 3-21. *The mule—a main backstays'l of the ketch rig.*

ing resistance itself but sending wind into the spinnaker.

For Split Rigs   In addition to the capacity to carry the aforementioned sails, split rigs can carry staysails between the masts as well. The *mule* is a triangular sail rolled on or hanked to a stay or set flying in the space between the mainsail leech and the mizzenmast and sheeted to the mizzenmast head. Some ketch owners feel this is their reaching power sail and therefore merits the beast of burden title. Though doing little to offset the ketch's renowned weakness to windward, the mule fills a big hole in a low-aspect voyaging rig and adds great power even on a close reach. It is possible to rig a semiwishbone sprit boom for more efficient sheeting of a mule.

At least one ketch owner was able to improve windward performance substantially by carrying a *mizzen genoa staysail* in lieu of the mainsail, creating a "bald-headed staysail ketch." Chichester's *Gypsy Moth* carried a similar arrangement. The sail is tacked at boom level on the leeward side of the

mainmast and raised to the mizzenmast head on a wire luff. Cut as a conventional genoa, it is sheeted to the stern. The wishbone ketch *Vamarie* also set a mizzen genoa staysail.

Mizzen staysails set in the same location and are commonly used. These could be called *mizzen drifters* to distinguish them from mizzen genoas. A very powerful reaching sail, made of light cloth and set flying or on a jackstay, the mizzen staysail's tack can be moved anywhere from windward to leeward rail (usually windward), and it is sheeted to the mizzen boom or the stern. On ketches with main

FIGURE 3-22. *Mizzen staysail on a yawl.*

FIGURE 3-23. *Fisherman stays'l with yard on a Tancook Whaler.*

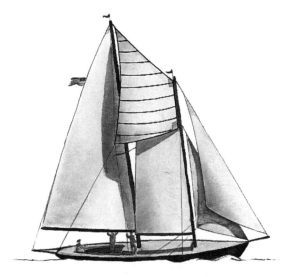

FIGURE 3-24. *Fisherman stays'l on a schooner yacht.*

backstays the luff of the mizzen staysail has a hard time of it, and chafing gear is essential for both stay and sail luff. Yawls, too, can make effective use of mizzen staysails, though in comparison to a ketch, a yawl's mizzen staysail is of much lower profile.

A schooner's reaching sail area is usually augmented by four-sided sails set between the foremast and the mainmast—the peak is raised to the mainmast top and the throat to the foremast top. The smallest of these, the *maintopmast staysail* (also called a *fisherman* for its commercial workboat origins), generally fills the space between masts above a gaff foresail. A powerful sail, it is the first sail added to the lower working sails. Tacked with a pendant a bit to leeward of the centerline, and sheeted to the stern, the sail is often set flying.

The fisherman is like the larger 'tween-mast staysails of a schooner in that they are set flying and controlled by four separate lines: peak halyard, throat halyard, sheet, and tack pendant. These sails are not usually tacked back and forth, and all the raising and lowering demands smart sail handling on the part of the crew. It is easy to lose a sail overboard. To combat this, I designed removable jackstays for Senator Edward Kennedy's *Mya* on which to hank and raise the fisherman. These stays on

either side of the foremast had to be releasable in order to get them out of the way of the fore gaff when cracked off, but ease of handling of the sail was immeasurably improved. The arrangement made it impossible to carry the fisherman to weather of the foresail, but this has not proven to be particularly detrimental, and the efficiency of sail handling and safety has far outweighed any drawbacks. With this setup the fisherman can be carried close-hauled effectively.

The *queen staysail* (now usually referred to as a *gollywobbler*) is a tremendous reaching sail of light construction set from the mainmast head, tacked to the foremast partner, and sheeted either to the quarter or the end of the main boom. Such a sail nearly doubles the working sail area and is the heavy-displacement schooner's lifesaver in light airs.

Rarely seen is the most colossal of schooner sails, essentially a gobblywobbler with the additional area of the foretriangle. It is hanked to the headstay and tacked to the bowsprit end. It's hard to say whether this is the King Kong of genoas or the Godzilla of gollies, but as far as I know, it made a brief splash in the racing schooners and was deemed too cumbersome. I believe, though, that a

FIGURE 3-25. *The gollywobbler—a large main stays'l of the schooner rig.*

FIGURE 3-26. *A genoa jib on a contemporary cruising sloop.*

small schooner or cat schooner might find a similar sail to be valuable, and indeed, Uffa Fox's cruising schooner *Black Rose* had one.

Auxiliary Light-Air Sails

Genoas I include genoas as auxiliary sails, although on many contemporary designs a genoa is definitely one of the working sails; indeed, the boat's performance may be designed around the use of the genoa as a working sail. Nonetheless, for traditional designs as well as for voyaging and cruising purposes, the genoa is properly an auxiliary sail.

The origin of the name is lost in an early-morning fog of raceboat terminology, but it is said to have been associated with the Italian city of that name. The *genny* is a large, low-clewed, often deck-to-masthead full-hoist jib, carried on the head- or forestay and lapping the mast or even the mainsail. Sloops, cutters, schooners, ketches, and yawls all may set genoas.

The rig and hull of a raceboat will be so designed that its genoas (it will have several sizes)

are the most frequently used headsail for windward work. It is the high-performance sail of the sloop rig and receives the most use and attention. If it is a roller-reefing type, it is the auxiliary and working headsail all in one.

The relative size of a genoa is given by the ratio, stated as a percentage, between its LP or *luff perpendicular* (the length of a straight line from its clew meeting the luff on a perpendicular) and the base of the foretriangle (stemhead to mast partners). A 170-percent genoa is a big one; a 110-percent is fairly small. Boats carrying multiple genoas label them numbers 1 (the largest), 2, 3, 4, and down to the *lapper*, at which point the headsail has a high clew and is more jib than genoa.

Deck-sweeping, low-cut genoas are mandatory for competitive sailing in order to maximize sail area and close off the space between deck and sail through which the higher air pressure could otherwise escape to leeward (see Chapter 4). For voyagers and economy-minded daysailers, however, the lower efficiency of a higher clewed, higher tacked genoa is offset by better visibility, no chafe on bow pulpit and lifelines, and a reduced likelihood of catching green seas coming over the bow. There is the additional advantage in a shorter luff genoa of raising or lowering the tack height in order to adjust the sheeting angle on a boat with a fixed turning block.

Oversized genoas do commonly commit suicide on bow pulpits, but this can be avoided with an appropriate cut of sail. An oversized genoa can be recut (see Chapter 6) or a sacrificial pulpit patch

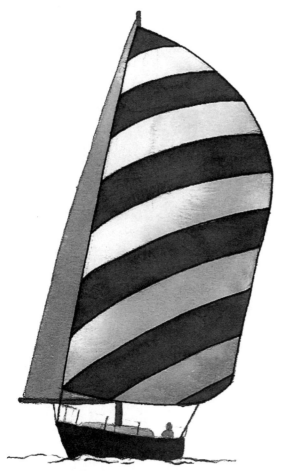

FIGURE 3-27. *A light-air drifter, or ghoster, on a modern cruiser.*

can be installed in way of the chafe. Of course, if the tack height of the sail can be raised, that is the first course of action.

Drifters *Drifters,* or *ghosters,* are big, full-cut, high-clewed, lightly constructed genoas designed for light-air reaching and light to moderate downwind work with a whisker pole or sheeted to the end of the boom. Though smaller and somewhat less powerful, a drifter hanked onto the headstay has advantages over a single-luff spinnaker set flying, in that it is much easier to jibe and take down. Made from gossamer-weight synthetic sailcloth, a drifter will stand when all other sails are slatting. Drifters can go to weather under the right mild conditions. These sails make a good choice for an amateur sailmaking project.

Auxiliary Downwind Sails

For extended downwind seaworthiness the square rig is unsurpassed, which is why voyagers sometimes carry a yard and course as an auxiliary downwind sail. Above that may be set a square topsail or, alternatively, a nearly triangular but four-sided *raffee* with a head stick (see Figure 3-17). *Sunrise,* a Jay Benford design, carries this arrangement and triangular stuns'ls to boot! Sometimes, but to no advantage that I can see, a raffee may be split into two triangular sails, port and starboard.

Spinnakers Spinnakers are the modern alternative, not only for running but reaching too, with flatter, narrower-shouldered chutes for the purpose. *Parachutes,* as they are sometimes called, are triangular sails of great symmetrical curvature set flying from the masthead and, with a system of sheets and guys, poled out to the windward side. Ketches and yawls can set mizzen spinnakers in addition.

A full spinnaker inventory ranging in size and sailcloth weight from large and light to smaller and relatively heavy (deceptively called a *storm spinnaker*) is essential for the contemporary competitive sailor, and a Grand Prix racing boat might carry
(text continued on page 94)

Downwind racing sail combination of
spinnaker and blooper

FIGURE 3-28. *Spinnakers.*

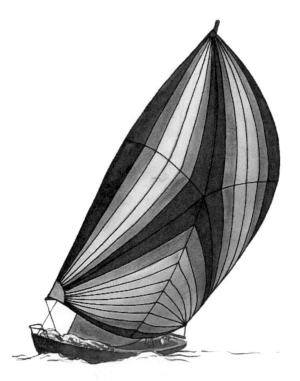

Star-cut reaching spinnaker on a
contemporary racer

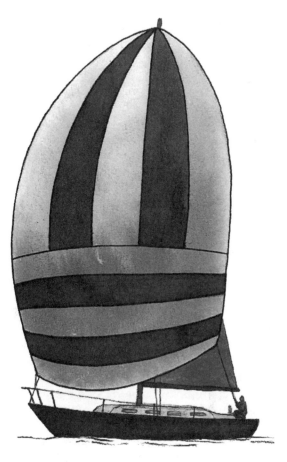

The contemporary single-luff spinnaker on a
cruising sloop

An improvised downwind spinnaker made
from a surplus parachute

up to five spinnakers. This type of sail is a colorful and effective means of enhancing downwind performance. Indeed, the contemporary Bermudan sail configuration with large headsails and very small mainsails is almost entirely dependent on the spinnaker for its downwind sailing capabilities.

Spinnakers are difficult sails to set, douse, and control, however. They require constant attention. More crewmembers, smart foredeck handling, and skill at the helm are necessary for smooth and effective spinnaker use.

It was the awareness of the spinnaker's inappropriateness for the small, shorthanded, noncompetitive cruiser that led to the rediscovery and development of the *single-luff spinnaker,* which was and still is available under a number of names, offering variations on the same theme. Poleless spinnaker, drifter reacher, flasher, cruising spinnaker, genniker—these are all sails larger than a drifter and fuller at the head and luff that are set flying. These sails are intended to enhance reaching and running while maintaining ease of handling, setting, and tacking with less gear and hardware. Various tube devices have been developed to facilitate the raising and dropping of sails of this type. Marketed under names such as Stasher, Squeezer, Shootscoot, and Strangler, all of these seem to work and are appropriate, I believe, for daysailing and coastal cruising.

Spinnakers and their mutations are at once good and bad choices for a beginning sailmaking project. The light, synthetic nylon materials are easy to handle and relatively inexpensive, but in the design and making these are extremely sophisticated sails. Some simple, basic cuts can be handled relatively easily by a novice and will yield satisfactory noncompetitive results, but the sails will disappoint if compared with contemporary styles.

Other downwind alternatives include twin jibs poled out from a single headstay or double headstays. These sails can, if required, be flopped over on top of each other (chafe! chafe!) for reaching. The twin rig developed and refined by Frederick Fenger comprises two separate staysails set flying and spread by two independent whisker poles. A successful innovation for improved self-steering downwind, this twin-jib configuration's advantages over the voyaging squaresail are less gear, less chafe, and less tendency to foul the standing rigging, all at the expense of maneuverability and self-steering on points of sailing other than downwind. In general the twin jibs are cut fairly flat to discourage collapsing if the boat should yaw wildly, and are of heavier material and construction than nonvoyaging downwind sails to stand up to stronger winds and extended use.

STORMSAILS

"Storm," in terms of sail stress, is not defined by cyclonic disturbances or barometric pressure. What counts is wind strength relative to the vessel involved, and a cruiser's ordeal is a "sweet and pleasant gale" for an ocean carrier. When the wind becomes too strong for the working sails—when the boat is overcanvased, heeling too much, out of control, carrying too much weather helm, going too fast, in danger of broaching or pitchpoling, headed the wrong way, or needs some steadying in the tumult—portions of the working sail area may be dropped altogether. The multisail split rigs lend themselves well to this means of sail reduction. Alternatively, rigs with fewer sails may reef down as well as drop sail. The smaller remaining sails and the deeper reefs of the larger working sails in effect serve as stormsails. Short of running off or riding it out under bare poles, the third heavy-weather canvasing alternative is to replace the working sails with stormsails of a size, design, and construction intended only for those severe rough conditions.

Returning to the first option—dousing certain working sails—the yawl rig is a good example. Once the mainsail is dropped, a snug jib and jigger configuration remains. The remaining sails in this and other rigs must be built to withstand the punishment they will receive.

Similarly, the reefed portions of sails receive intensified stresses. Reefs are part of a sailing boat's survival gear, and their construction within the sail as well as their system of handling should be rugged and dependable. A boat without reefs is like a car with a stuck accelerator and no brakes.

Reefed Sails

The two most common reefing systems are *slab reefing* (recently rechristened *jiffy reefing*) and *roller reefing*. Slab reefing usually takes area from the foot, with the exceptions of the sharpie rig, where the luff is taken in, and lateen-type sails and squares'ls, where reefs are taken to the yard. Roller reefing may take area from either the luff or the foot.

A well-designed, -built, and -maintained slab-reefing system is a seaworthy arrangement. The reef corner rings and reinforcements on all sails other than pure daysails should be as stout as those in the corners of a full sail. Reef points and patches should be no more than 18 inches apart and are *below* the straight line from reef clew to reef tack so that the big rings take the strain. Nettles (reef points) need to be long and easily tied. All corners need plenty of chafe protection.

Roller Reefing, Roller Furling

Well, here we go with the great debate! Is seaworthy roller reefing an oxymoron, or is it not? The "geriatric" rig, as former client and septuagenarian cruising sailor John "Mac" MacDonald, USN (retired), called his roller furler, has seen an incredible amount of development and improvement since Mac was twisting up his genoa on a wire attached to a spool in 1978. Roller-reefed sails now set better and handle more reliably, but they are also quite a bit more expensive. And they still have the same basic drawbacks:

- The sails suffer from exposure to the sun.
- In reefed positions the new unreinforced tack and head of the sail are overstrained.
- The clew, head, and tack rings are always in the sun.
- Sails rolled on or in spars suffer loss in area, because they are battenless; further, a mainsail rolling into the mast will need a high clew to avoid an ungainly lump at the bottom of the luff.
- Partially rolled sails don't set well.
- If left aloft there is great windage in the rolled-up sail.
- When reefed, the rolled-up portion of the sail causes turbulence on the leeward side on one tack.
- Head and tack rings twist out.
- The sheets are always in the sun.
- If a headsail system fails there is no backup, and you have to go up on the foredeck anyway.
- Some headsail systems are the mast's sole means of forward support. If the system fails, the mast will probably come down.
- If a roller-reefed sail of the luff-foil type sticks in the track—which, if torn and jammed, is what it will do—it becomes difficult to lower the sail.
- The sail eventually becomes distorted through stress problems.
- There is no means of setting a true stormsail.
- If the gear fails, the sail could unroll when you don't want it to, or refuse to roll up when you do want it to.

Now the pros:

- Everything can be done from the cockpit.
- The system can be power operated.
- One person can manage a big boat with large sail area.
- Less time can be spent handing and furling, more time drinking and cavorting.
- One sail does all: no stowage space needed.

With the meteoric rise in popularity of roller systems, sailmakers have assayed to overcome some of the drawbacks with:

- sails combining heavier with lighter cloths so that stormsail sections are stouter;
- reinforcements at reefed head and tack positions;

- sacrificial sun shields in the form of sewn edge covers or a self-adhering lamination of ultraviolet-resistant plastic on leech and foot;
- leeches and feet made of ultraviolet-resistant cloth;
- pads and doodads sewn in the luffs to take up extra cloth so that the sail does not become fuller as it is rolled up.

Of course the manufacturers of furling gear have expended considerable effort in making the gear as light, strong, corrosion resistant, and reliable as possible. But, though the longevity and functionality of the sails has improved greatly, every problem mentioned above still exists to a greater or lesser extent. I, for one, do not feel that roller-reefing is seaworthy.

On the other hand, for small-boat, inshore, daysail use, where the economics are different and the stakes are lower, there is a great deal to be said for a roller system. The inherent problems of the gear aren't of such great consequence in that type of sailing.

Only brief mention need be made of roller booms—that is, the reefing system that rolls the mainsail up around the boom itself. This system should be shunned at all costs. It is a sail killer and an ineffective technique that should not be tolerated even on daysailers.

True Stormsails

The last alternative for carrying on in heavy weather is to set substitute sails made for storm conditions. These are *survival sails*.

Typically, storm jibs are high-clewed, flat headsails of very heavy soft cloth with no seams striking the leech or foot. They may be equal to or less than half the area of the working jib or working forestaysail. Extra-stout hardware (especially the head hank, which could be doubled), extra-stout stitching, and strong reinforcements are needed. Tacked inboard, the sail is up out of the wash and free from chafe on anything. A large-boat storm jib is best roped all the way around.

A storm staysail, or a forestaysail for heavy-weather work, is the same size as the working

FIGURE 3-29. *Scotch-mitered storm jib set in combination with a gaff-headed trys'l.*

FIGURE 3-30. *Scotch-mitered, club-footed storm stays'l on a schooner yacht.*

FIGURE 3-31. *A vertically cut Swedish mains'l.*

FIGURE 3-32. *Scotch-mitered, jibheaded trys'l.*

forestaysail but more heavily constructed, possibly with a reef.

In the Bermudan rig, two types of stormsails can be carried abaft the mast. The first is a heavily reinforced, vertically cut, roachless jibheaded sail equal in area to the single-reefed main. Called a *Swedish mainsail* (for reasons that escape me), it is spread by the boom and is intended for prolonged heavy-weather sailing in which extended use of the reefed working mainsail would unnecessarily jeopardize that sail. It is a sort of intermediate stormsail with which the boat can sail on all points.

Less versatile and more rugged, but weatherly nonetheless, is the *storm trysail,* so named not for its tricornered shape (which it may not have) but because it is used when "lying atry" or heaving to. The storm trysail is laced, parreled, set up on a separate mast track, or even gated into the main track from its own side track. Boomless, it is sheeted to the quarters while the boom and furled mainsail are lashed down and stowed safely. The

FIGURE 3-33. *Vertically cut gaff trys'l.*

FIGURE 3-34. *A flat, vertically cut riding sail on a New England lobsterboat.*

clew is lower than the tack so that the tack will clear the working main, which is still bent at the mast. Its area is equal to or less than that of the triple-reefed main, to which it is a superior and safer alternative. No expense or effort is spared to make this survival sail a stout article; no seams strike the roped leech or foot. The prudent seafarer should have both a third reef in the main *and* a trysail when heavy weather comes on.

The gaff-headed trysail is more arduous to set up, but it serves the same function and has the same structural requirements as the jibheaded type. If given its own separate gaff, it could be ready to go with no need to unbend one sail and bend

FIGURE 3-35. *Flat, vertically cut steadying sail on a Pacific Northwest trawler.*

on another. But it seems to me that if you are going to go to the trouble of disconnecting the halyards anyway, it would be easier to set the peak halyard aside, lash down the gaff-headed sail, parrel on a jib-headed trysail, and raise it with the throat halyard—provided a sail of that size will balance the boat correctly.

The drawback for the amateur sailmaker when making stormsails for boats of 30 feet and up is the incredible strength and power required to sew the necessary materials. Large, expensive machines, great brawn and determination, or both are needed.

RIDING SAILS AND STEADYING SAILS

There are two other classes of sails which, though not intended for propulsion, are similar in form and construction to propulsive sails and are extremely useful as well as relatively easy to build. *Riding sails* are essentially rudders set aft to keep a boat, sail or power, head to wind while at anchor or mooring, while working, or while lying to a sea anchor. Cat-rigged, sloop-rigged, and split-rigged sailboats all may carry riding sails. Cut flat, they are intended to be left out in the weather and so are of stout construction. They may in fact be used as stormsails, either intentionally at sea or inadvertently when a gale catches an unoccupied boat at the mooring.

Steadying sails do just that, and are often employed by commercial power vessels and occasionally by pleasure craft. With or without wind, steadying sails set flat from light masts and cargo booms and stays to dampen roll. In commercial craft these sails get no respite from the elements, in addition to which they often are to leeward of exhaust pipes and charlie nobles and are slammed mercilessly from side to side when lying ahull to a windless seaway. That's their job, and therefore they should not be made of conventional sail materials. Commercially produced steadying sails are machine made of rubberized nylon fabric with nylon webbing all round.

Pleasure-craft steadying sails can be made of conventional sail fabric, though Dacron will not last long in the sun.

SAIL RIG CONFIGURATIONS

There are practical limits to the size of the sails a crew can manage, just as there are limits to the forces a single mast and its rigging can withstand. Thus, as boat size and sail area increase, at some point the sail area is divided up among a greater number of smaller, more manageable sails set upon an increased number of masts and stays. Dividing the rig this way makes each sail more manageable and the rig more versatile, but also more complicated and less weatherly. Windage increases, and several sails of lesser power do not perform as well as a few high-aspect ones. For many purposes, however, these drawbacks are minor.

The never-ending drive to develop better sail and rig configurations for every different set of requirements has led over the centuries to a rich diversity of sailing vessels, from dhows to clippers, from the seven-masted *Thomas W. Lawson* to catboats. The multitudes of rig and sail configurations are differentiated by their mast locations, the relative heights of the masts, and the rig type and sails set on each mast. A professional sailmaker should be familiar with the sailing characteristics of each configuration, and the interactions between sails in the rig at hand.

How do you know how much sail area a boat should have, and what is the best rig with which to carry it? There are formulas, of course, for estimating a successful working sail area for a boat from recommended sail area–displacement and sail area–LWL ratios. Ideally, if faced with these questions, you will have an existing sail plan to work from, a naval architect to advise you, a deep well of experience, or all three. When it comes to rig configuration, there is no "best" choice except what is best for you. There are many terrific books

Leg-o'-mutton cat rig

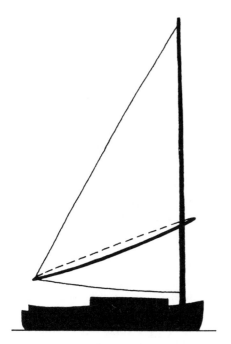

Wishbone cat rig

Single-mast gaff-sail cat rig

FIGURE 3-36. *Cat-rigged boats.*

with successful sail plans out there to help you decide, and there is no substitute for trying various rigs.

In the gallery that follows, we look at the basic sail and rig configurations from a sailor or sailmaker's point of view.

Cat Rig

The single-masted cat rig has definite sail-handling limitations, which confine it to small, inshore boats. Only in daredevil racers or with the easily reefed Chinese rig is this configuration permitted to have large sail area or to go to sea. The downfall of the once-popular catboat was a trend toward

dangerous overcanvasing; inevitable accidents resulted, giving the rig and boat a bad reputation. It is difficult for a seaworthy hull to find sufficient manageable area in a single sail. The Chinese rig offers one alternative, the Bermudan wishbone rig of the Nonesuches, another.

The single sail has to handle it all, from catspaw to snorter. For daysailing, at least one reef is advisable in smallish (100 square feet or less) sails. Two reefs are advisable in 100- to 300-square-foot sails, and three or more reefs in larger sails, depending on hull type and use.

The cat rig is often unstayed and, especially when coupled with a beamy, shallow hull, prone

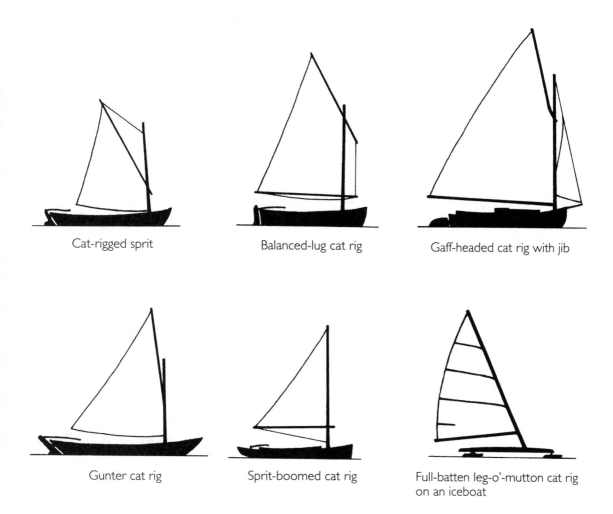

Cat-rigged sprit

Balanced-lug cat rig

Gaff-headed cat rig with jib

Gunter cat rig

Sprit-boomed cat rig

Full-batten leg-o'-mutton cat rig
on an iceboat

to generate weather helm. Sails must be forgiving, and should not exacerbate a helm problem by being too full aft with excessive roach. Their cut must anticipate the inevitable bend of the spars.

Sloop Rig

By moving the mast aft and adding a jib to the single mast, we transform the cat rig into the sloop rig. Weatherliness is improved, helm balance is more adjustable, and the size of the mainsail may be reduced proportionately. In some sloops it seems the mainsail is barely there at all, as headsails do the windward work and spinnakers pull the boat downwind. The sloop rig offers sufficiently man-

ageable power to take a seaworthy hull around the world, and has. The rig is unrivaled for its combination of efficiency and simplicity, and has become the most popular rig in yachting. Its stormsail-carrying capacity makes it a safer offshore rig than the cat. Although some small craft carry jibs with unstayed rigs, the jump from cat to sloop often entails a taller mast with shrouds, headstay, and, in the Bermudan type, a backstay.

One of the sailmaker's principal concerns with a sloop rig is to maximize its ability to go to weather by shaping the jib and mainsail to work together. The sails must generate as much lift and drive as possible with minimum drag and resistance. Some

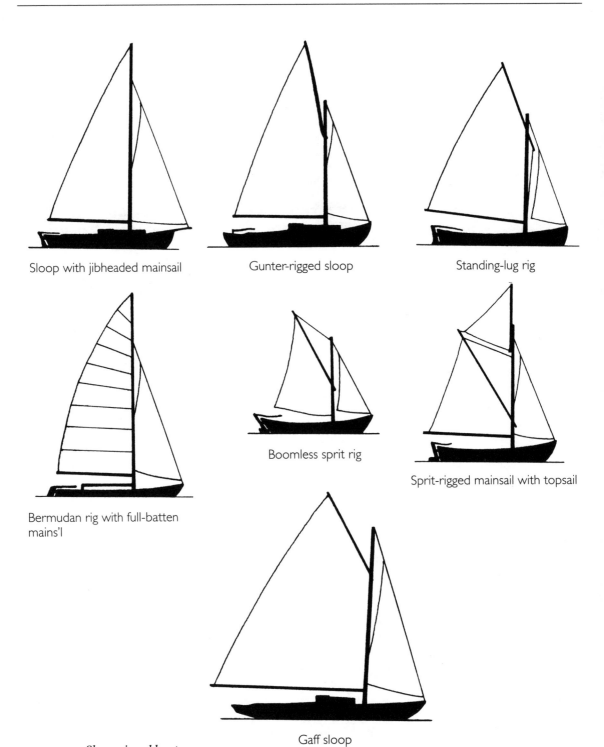

Sloop with jibheaded mainsail

Gunter-rigged sloop

Standing-lug rig

Bermudan rig with full-batten mains'l

Boomless sprit rig

Sprit-rigged mainsail with topsail

Gaff sloop

FIGURE 3-37. *Sloop-rigged boats.*

Gaff-rigged cutter

FIGURE 3-38. *Double-headsail rigs.*

Bermudan cutter

rig types and aspect ratios work toward those ends better than others. The high-aspect Bermudan sloop is the most weatherly, while the gaff sloop is the most powerful reacher. The sailmaker is also concerned with helm balance. The headsail-oriented sloop must change headsails and flatten and reef the mainsail when it blows on. The mainsail-oriented sloop must reef its bigger main safely and efficiently, as well as flatten the sail.

Double-Headsail, Single-masted Rigs

The addition of a forestay and a forestaysail creates the *double-headsail sloop*. The three working sails offer more options, including a safer inboard position for a storm jib. Now the interaction of three or more sails must be considered.

Differentiating between a double-headsail or cutter-rigged sloop and a true cutter can at times be difficult. The *cutter rig* is the last of the single-masted configurations, and is typified by its amidships mast, a bowsprit, and a jib and forestaysail. As sloops take on bowsprits and double headsails

they become harder to discern as sloops, but the primary indicator remains mast position, with the sloop's mast being farther forward than the cutter's.

The cutter rig has a large and loyal following among cruisers. Though slightly more complicated and somewhat less weatherly than a sloop rig, it is also handier. Once the most glorious and stupendous of racing rigs, spreading as much canvas on one boat as would be flown on a full-rigged ship, the cutter rig sees its greatest use now as a snug cruising, voyaging, or workboat rig in boats of 40 feet or under. Trimarans make efficient use of the low-aspect multiheadsail rig.

Double-masted Cat Rigs

The simplest of the double-masted rigs are the *cat ketches, cat schooners,* and *cat yawls.* These are cat rigs by virtue of the forward placement of the leading mast and the absence of headsails. They are differentiated one from the other by the relative height and placement of the two masts.

Cat ketches, such as the New Haven sharpie, Block Island cowhorn, and Freedom 42, have the

Sprit-boomed cat ketch rig

Wishbone Bermudan cat ketch

Gaff-headed cat ketch rig in a Block Island
cowhorn

Cat schooner with Bermudan main
and gaff foresail

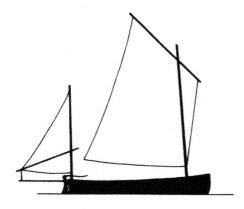

Cat yawl with sprit-boomed mizzen and
standing-lug main

FIGURE 3-39. *Double-masted rigs.*

after or mizzen mast a bit shorter or nearly equal in height to the mainmast and located forward of the rudderpost. Particularly when the two masts are of equal height, the sails can be referred to as mainsail and foresail, as in a schooner. Marvelously simple and efficient, a cat ketch is also weatherly and often has no standing rigging. As a small-boat rig it is extremely versatile, allowing various full sail and reefed combinations. The foresail may lap the main and be boomless, but the main invariably must be boomed. When the two sails are of equal area, both can be boomed and self-tending. Larger boats can carry this rig quite successfully, though the contemporary full-batten Bermudan sail employed by modern ketches is not as seaworthy as the rig. The interaction of the cat ketch's two sails is not complex, and the traditional sail types that have proven themselves in this rig configuration are good projects for the amateur sailmaker. Generally, too, the sails are small.

The cat schooner can be difficult to tell from the cat ketch, but it has both masts somewhat farther forward, and the mainmast is equal to or taller than the foremast. If the sails are not of equal size, the main is larger. A jaunty little example of the cat schooner, pictured opposite, is Commodore Monroe's *Junebug*, with Bermudan main and gaff foresail. Though not as weatherly perhaps as other cats, the cat schooner is a powerful reacher, and the multiple reefs in its sails are not there for looks! The foresail can lap the main or be boomed.

The cat yawl is a small-yacht rig, and it has graced numerous sailing canoes as well as N. G. Herreshoff's first boat, the beautiful *Clara*. The mizzenmast is stepped well aft, abaft the rudderpost, and the mizzen sail is a mere postage stamp in relation to the mainsail. The rig hopes to combine the simplicity of the single-masted cat rig with the versatility of two masts and the division of area and sail-balancing qualities of the yawl. As with the cat rig, a headsail may be added for weatherliness and light air, but with the mainmast in the eyes of the boat it remains a cat yawl. The mizzen is a rudder more than anything else, though in the canoes it adds much power.

Ketch

By moving the forward mast aft and adding headsails to a cat ketch, we alter the rig to a proper ketch, a rig configuration that has served well in commercial sail and continues as the most popular double-masted cruising rig. The ketch rig's windward shortcomings are more than offset by its phenomenal range of full- and reefed-sail combinations, making it safe even in fair-size boats, manageable by a small crew, and easily balanced.

The ketch rig's versatility is impressive even in smaller craft, which is why a small-boat sailor might choose the ketch rig even though a cutter or sloop offers better windward performance. Natural self-steering is a wonderful thing. The Bermudan ketch is the most common now, though nearly all rig types—including the Chinese lug, lateen, and South Seas claw rig—have been used on this form. The gaff ketch has been a highly successful and popular commercial (and later, yacht) rig in northern Europe; no one could fail to be impressed by the accomplishments of the gaff-ketch Colin Archer *Redningskoites*, or rescue boats. These boats, with their low-aspect gaff rigs and husky double-ended hulls—configurations so frowned upon today—routinely sailed in and out of the jaws of death under the most appalling conditions.

I have come to the conclusion that "efficiency" and "performance" are relative things, depending on what you're after, and a good deal of a boat's efficiency lies not in its design but in the sailor's skill and intuitive ability to make the boat do what's needed. In other words, *knowing* a rig goes a long way toward making it function efficiently.

A yawl's mizzen might constitute 10 percent of the working sail area, while a ketch's mizzen may account for 20 percent on up, sometimes almost equaling the mainsail in size. A relatively small ketch mizzen, however, offers some of the yawl's sail-combination versatility, which is an advantage. The ketch rig's balanced spread of working sail has encouraged innovators to use it with wishbone and staysail rigs as they tried to make a safe, handy boat handier and more weatherly. The ketch rig opens up a wonderful world of mizzen staysails,

Bermudan ketch

Trysail ketch with wishbone boom on trys'l

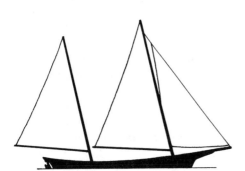

Leg-o'-mutton ketch

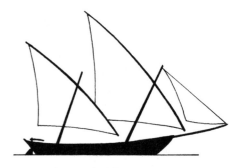

Lateen ketch

Gaff-headed ketch with topmasts and fore tops'l

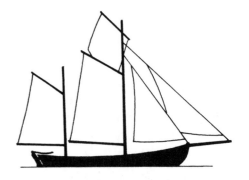

Gaff-headed ketch setting main gaff tops'l with yard

FIGURE 3-40. *Ketches.*

mules, and other auxiliary sails for reaching.

One of the advantages of the rig from a sailmaking perspective is that the performance lost by making seafaring sails is gained back by all its wonderful sail combinations—both working and auxiliary—all of which are reasonable projects for the self-sufficient sailor. This is not so true of the sloop rig, even though the sloop's sails may be smaller, lighter, and fewer.

Yawl

The *yawl* rig configuration features a short mizzenmast well aft, abaft the rudderpost. To fulfill its promise, as mentioned, it needs a mizzen of at least 10 percent of the working sail area. A puny little jigger tacked on the tail end of a sloop does not do the rig justice. Yawls range from the sprit-rigged Thames barges, to the classic Concordia yawl, to Joshua Slocum's *Spray* and its flotilla of reincarnations.

The yawl combines the weatherliness of the sloop with the handiness of the ketch. Its mizzen is not a power sail so much as a balancer, and setting as it does in the wake and downwash of a large mainsail, must be very flat indeed. Flat and stout, which is not to say clunky, it's a stormsail.

Compared with a ketch (except perhaps the ultra high aspect Bermudan oceanracing ketch or

Jibheaded yawl

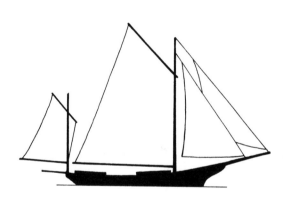

Gaff-headed yawl with standing-lug mizzen

Gaff-headed yawl

Yawl with jibheaded mizzen and gaff main

FIGURE 3-41. *Yawls.*

some cruising imitation thereof), the yawl's sails should be designed and cut for its greater weatherly potential and speed. Although a yawl can carry functional mizzen staysails with its shorter mizzenmast, they are smaller and only good up to a close reach. The yawl does not match the ketch in versatility of sail configurations.

Schooner

The *schooner* rig has two or more masts and headsails. A two-masted schooner typically carries the mainsail, the largest sail, on the tallest mast aft, preceded by the foresail on the shorter foremast and the forestaysail (jumbo) and jib, in that order.

However, some knockabout schooners (schooners with no bowsprit) set a single working headsail. In the three-masted *tern* schooners, the foresail, mainsail, and mizzen may be of equal size, though the mizzen (the aftmost sail) is usually bigger.

The schooner rig is noted for its ability to spread a tremendous amount of low sail area with a long main boom and bowsprit, in which configuration it is unbeatable as a reacher. From fishing to trading, at one time schooners engaged in every imaginable form of waterborne commerce, and in the 1920s the schooner was *the* racing and yachting rig.

Various adaptations have been made to improve

Stays'l schooner

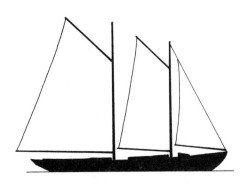
Baldheaded two-masted schooner

Gaff schooner with main topsail

Bermudan mainsail, gaff foresail with fisherman stays'l

FIGURE 3-42. *Schooners.*

the handling and weatherliness of the schooner rig, mostly involving the use of Bermudan, or jib-headed, sails. The Bermudan mainsail/gaff foresail configuration improved weatherliness somewhat, but more significantly it tamed the mainsail and did away with the main gaff topsail while still filling the between-mast space with a powerful sail, the gaff foresail, which could be carried alone when it really aired on.

The *staysail schooner* not only carries a jib-headed main, but fills the space between masts with a main staysail and a main topmast staysail. This is the most weatherly of schooner rigs and possibly the simplest, yet it retains many of the classic schooner rig virtues of seaworthiness, power, and storm-riding ability.

The schooner rig, though workable in miniature, is not really a small-boat configuration; however, schooners under 40 feet are not rare. One of the reasons the schooner rig seems incongruous on small boats is that it traditionally tends to utilize more complicated and heavier sparred rig and sail types—particularly the gaff rig. Thus, baby schooners often appear to be condensed coasters and give one that ship-in-a-bottle feeling. Basically, they sport an excessive amount of gear per foot of length and sailing accomplishment. *But,* the boats have character. Oh no, I've said it! "Character boats"

Two-masted Bermudan schooner

Foretops'l schooner

Fore and main tops'l schooner

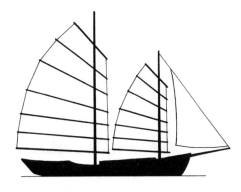

Chinese lug schooner

is a phrase that seems to relegate anything wooden, working, and curvaceous to a nautical museum, as if these boats are part of a scene to entertain tourists. I dislike the phrase, but there is no doubt that some rigs and boats have more character than others, and the schooner rig probably gets one of the highest readings on the audience applause meter. Just the word *sings:* s-c-h-o-o-n-e-r—"see how she schoons!"

Only feeble attempts have been made to update the two-masted schooner rig with Bermudan sails on main and foremast. The results are revolting aesthetically in comparison with the "character boats," but have the advantages of simplicity and ease of handling.

Among the schooner rig's great assets are its wonderful main topmast staysails—the fisherman and the gollywobbler. The ketch's mule may compare with the schooner's fisherman, but nothing the ketch can carry except possibly a combination of spinnaker and mizzen staysail can rival for sheer power the schooner's mighty gollywobbler.

Sailmaking for schooners is, I should think, a serious undertaking of great magnitude. The sails will probably be large, and regardless of their size they'll be sophisticated. You might say that the complications of the rig are reflected in the construction of the sails.

Big-Boat Rig Configurations

From schooners on up, sailmaking becomes an undertaking of large proportions not particularly

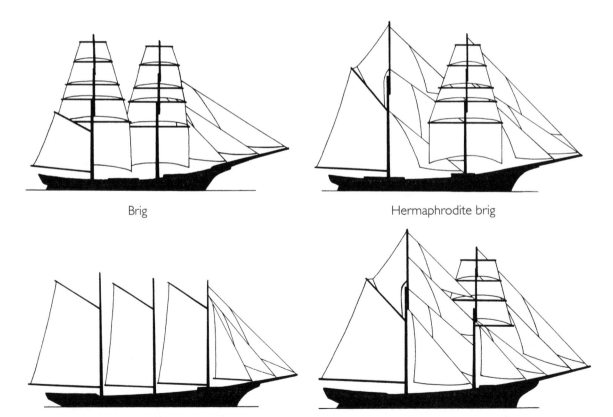

Brig

Hermaphrodite brig

Three-masted schooner, no topmasts

Two-masted schooner brig

FIGURE 3-43 *(PAGES 110–112)*. *Ship rigs.*

advisable for the amateur. But large vessels do offer the work and storage space for onboard sailmaking; indeed such vessels, as they did in the great age of sail, should have on board the materials, tools, and expertise to replace entire sails at sea if necessary. In the balance of this chapter we'll be content merely to identify some large-vessel rig configurations.

The true *brig* is a two-masted vessel, square rigged on both masts with fidded topgallant masts. Retaining the squaresail on the foremast but changing the main to a gaff rig topped by upper and lower square main topsails, with staysails between the masts, changes the rig to a proper *brigantine*. A *hermaphrodite brig* has no squaresails on the mainmast. There are numerous com-

binations of these two basic forms, collectively termed "jack-ass rigs," and heated discussions revolve around where a schooner leaves off and a brigantine begins.

The three-masted fore-and-aft schooner rig is still widely utilized even on comparatively small boats such as L. Francis Herreshoff's *Marco Polo,* a Bermudan variation. Used for racing, sail training, chartering, cruising, and even luxury liners, the multimasted staysail-rigged schooner takes the Bermudan schooner a step further, filling the spaces between masts and breaking the sail area up into more manageable bites. The advantages of this configuration are that a relatively small crew is required for a sizable boat, and it is easily balanced.

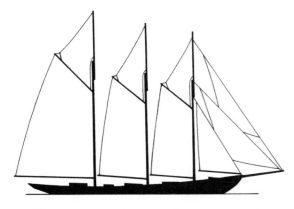

Three-masted schooner with topmasts and pointy-headed gaff topsails

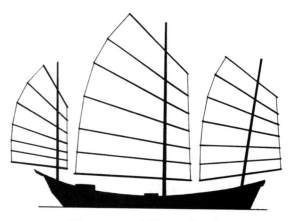

Three-masted Chinese lug rig

Full-rigged ship

Three-masted barque, or bark

Not as handy perhaps as the jibheaded schooner but still manageable with few hands, the three-masted Chinese rig features a small mizzen (a balancing sail) and a monstrous main that is nevertheless more manageable than the Western gaff rig. As an alternative to the square rig, the three-masted Chinese rig is certainly simpler and handier.

When all three masts are square rigged, the vessel is a *ship*. When there are three or more masts the mizzen or aftermost of which is fore-and-aft rigged while the rest are square rigged, it is a *barque* or *bark*. When all but the foremast alone is square rigged, it is a *barkentine*. The making of sails for vessels of this grandeur has become so specialized an undertaking that it is well beyond the scope of this book. The principles are the same, however.

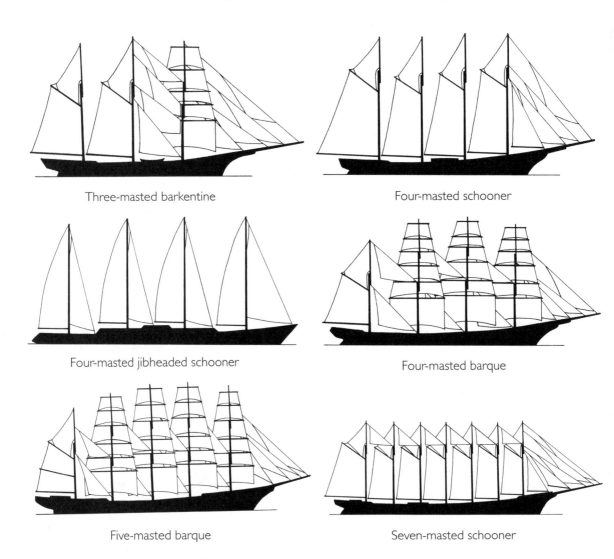

Three-masted barkentine

Four-masted schooner

Four-masted jibheaded schooner

Four-masted barque

Five-masted barque

Seven-masted schooner

FIGURE 3-43. *(cont.)*

4

Sail Shapes and Theory

HOW PROFOUND AN UNDERSTANDING of sail theory is necessary? A successful competitive sailor may not be an aerodynamicist, but will rely on a sailmaker who is (or a sailmaker who employs one). But the making of shapely, functional, seaworthy sails does not require a degree in aerodynamics nor even advanced knowledge of how a sail carries a boat into the wind, so long as you observe certain conventions of design and construction. Then why discuss sail theory at all? Because it does help when the time comes for you to make informed decisions about the design, making, function, and possible alteration of sails. Without the basic comparative criteria, a sailor can only rely on intuition when judging the success of sails in use. He or she won't have the vaguest notion how to repeat a sailmaking success, how to enhance a sail if some improvement can be made, or what to change if a sail is a flop.

I'll be the last to cast a jaundiced eye down a long and sneering nose at intuitive sailing and sailmaking. Each of us is imbued with a sense of harmony, proportion, and dimension—and as scientific as sailmaking has become, there is still, thank goodness, an artistic element. Of course, traditional materials and construction techniques with all their instabilities and incalculable properties grant much room for conjecture and experiment.

And even in the most scientific thinking about sails, there remain unresolved questions and disagreements about how sails work.

The proper setting, use, and trimming of a sail are all centrally important. Even the perfect sail can't possibly strut its stuff unless set correctly, and a sailmaker can't know the true results unless the sail's been used *as intended*. The low-technology voyager and even lower-tech small-boat sailor should know the elements of sail theory for a clearer understanding of the *potential* of their sails, so that those capabilities can be maximized and the drawbacks minimized or compensated for.

So, this chapter provides a basic, barebones introduction to the theory of sail. In later chapters we look at aspects of sail design in greater detail and with a more practical slant. I am not an aerodynamicist, nor need you be unless you wish to build ultra high performance sails, in which case you will need to get another book.

LIFT

We do not think of air—that gaseous combination of oxygen, nitrogen, and helium that surrounds us—as a tangible entity, but it is. It possesses mass, density, viscosity, and fluid motion. When it is surrounded by honey you can see a bubble of it move quite slowly. On the deck of a boat, we can only feel and hear it moving, and this lack of visual evidence is why air resists comprehension.

One has only to go for a stroll with an open umbrella on a windy day to experience what Daniel Bernoulli identified in 1738—the result of two different air pressures on either side of a curved object.

Holding an umbrella straight up and down so as to get the most rain protection and visibility ahead coincidentally trims it to an attitude relative to the wind such that air flowing over the curved surface must speed up in order to make that detour and still keep up with air passing below the brolly (Figure 4-1). Meanwhile, the air on the lower side actually slows down. The faster-moving air, which tends to follow the convex curve if the curve is not too extreme, has a lower pressure by virtue of its greater speed. With lower air pressure above and relatively higher pressure below, the umbrella is sucked upward, maybe resulting in an inverted bumber-chute. If the chute were strong enough and you were light enough, *you'd* be lifted, à la Mary Pop-

FIGURE 4-1. *The umbrella analogy is not exact, but it has the virtue of being familiar to everyone. We've all experienced the tendency of an umbrella, when perfectly trimmed, to soar upward. This is lift, the same force that moves sailboats to windward.*

pins! Lift—that's how birds soar, kites fly, airplanes stay aloft, and sails propel boats against the wind.

Lift is a measurable thing. Set an airfoil shape of certain dimensions at a particular angle of incidence, or attack, to a constant wind velocity, and you can calculate how much lift will be generated, where on the foil the center of effort of that force will be located, and in what direction tangential to the wind the force will be directed. Sails of course are unstable forms and are subject to varying wind velocities and to angles of incidence that vary both over time and with height above deck; thus the forces and directions are constantly shifting. Then there are the additional qualifiers and compromises of sea conditions, rig, and hull. Nothing is ideal or constant.

One variation on the concept of lift holds that while both leeward and windward flows actually travel fore to aft, the windward flow by virtue of its slower velocity seems to travel forward relative to the faster flow on the other side of the foil. The distinction *seems* unimportant when only one sail is under discussion, but it does affect the interpretation of sail interaction when more than one sail is considered, as we shall see.

SEPARATION, DRAG, AND EDGE VORTICES

But let's bring our umbrella analogy back to earth. Though the umbrella in Figure 4-1 may be held at the proper angle of attack to generate substantial lift, the airflow probably will not follow the cam-

FIGURE 4-2. *When the umbrella tilts too far backward, we experience drag, the same force that pushes a boat down a broad reach or run.*

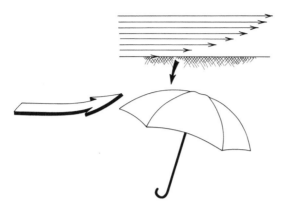

FIGURE 4-3. *When the airflow is attached to the umbrella (neither luffing nor stalling), the boundary layer is slowed by friction with the fabric. The steepness of the velocity gradient as one moves outward from the surface determines whether stalling is likely to occur.*

ber of the umbrella, because the curvature is too great. The flow detaches, or separates, and lift is lost. Further, if you let the umbrella tilt too far backward over your shoulder, its leading edge presents too wide an angle of attack to the wind. Now the detached flow is symptomatic of a stalled foil, like a mainsail close-hauled on a beam reach. The stalled area begins aft and commences forward as the angle of incidence increases. As the leading side of the umbrella rises to the wind and the aft edge lowers and stalls out, a new force—drag—takes over. This is readily perceived when an umbrella tries to leap out of your grip, but it is discernible in a boat only by excessive heel and leeway, speed loss, and helter-skelter telltales. Only when sailing off the wind (picture a spinnaker) is drag desirable.

On the other hand, when you tilt the umbrella

FIGURE 4-4. *Flow separation and turbulence. The umbrella at right, with its detached flow, is no longer lifting in the walker's hands.*

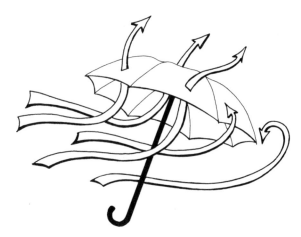

FIGURE 4-5. *Loss of lift due to pressure equalization around and through a porous fabric.*

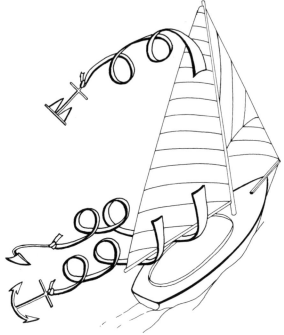

FIGURE 4-6. *Vortices created by airflow escaping under and around a sail. This energy-robbing turbulence is like dragging an anchor.*

forward to shield your face from a driving rain, the airflow is no longer divided by the leading edge, and instead pushes down on the top of the umbrella. This is analogous to a luffing sail.

When the umbrella is "full and drawing," the portion of the airflow closest to and most influenced by friction with the fabric actually adheres to it and travels with the umbrella. This is the *boundary layer*. Moving outward from this thin layer, the frictional influence diminishes by degrees to nothing at all. The relative speeds in the inner and outer strata of the boundary layer, and the amount of curvature the flow must negotiate, determine how likely separation is to occur.

As you walk ahead with the umbrella, the inner stratum of the boundary layer is actually moving against the flow, tending to divert and reverse adjacent strata. Eventually, as your own forward motion or the wind speed increases, this tendency causes a detaching, or separation, of the flow, with its resulting turbulence and lack of lift. A shallower umbrella will tolerate a higher wind speed before this separation occurs. On the other hand, at a lower wind speed, a humpier, more deeply cambered umbrella would generate greater lift.

There are other complications. The high-pressure air beneath the umbrella is not happy being separated from the low-pressure air above it, and tries to either sneak through the fabric or escape around the edges. In the latter process not only is lift lost through pressure equalization, but vortices are formed that dissipate energy and would retard the windward progress of a sailboat.

SAIL SHAPE

I once won a no-holds-barred race using an umbrella as a sail. Dead downwind it was very effective. The "hull" was an inflatable air mattress; the rudder, my flippers. But of course any bag will go downwind, though some will do it better than others. But to go upwind, the lift-generating capabilities of a bumberchute notwithstanding, a sail must have the proper form.

By a hundred million years ago, flying creatures had evolved wing forms to sustain themselves in the air. Refinements evolved depending on the kind of flying to be done—that is, speed, mobility, hovering, gliding. It is worth glancing briefly at the wing of a bird, which embodies a miraculous high-performance versatility and functionality that aeronautical engineers and sailmakers struggle to emulate.

Until recently it was thought by sailmakers that the form of a gull's wing was the most efficient shape for an upwind sail. This notion was shattered by wind-tunnel tests and the development of sail fabrics that lent themselves to building and retaining any shape, gull's wing or otherwise. The gull's-wing model that was appropriate for cotton sailcloth proved less so for more stable cloth.

By way of comparison, consider the artificial wing forms in Figure 4-8. Sometimes it is difficult to discern at what point sails leave off and become wings. Poetically and metaphorically, sails are often referred to as wings—and indeed, they function

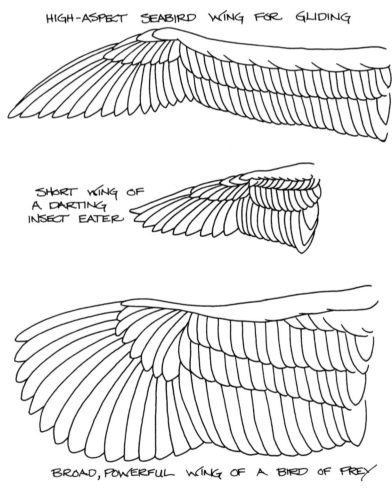

FIGURE 4-7. *Bird wings have evolved to meet the needs of power, speed, and maneuverability in flight.*

in the same medium, air—but they don't fly, and they are constructed differently and of different materials. More important, the way they propel a hull, which in part travels in another medium, water, is quite distinct from the way a wing lifts a plane. The important thing is that the aerodynamic qualities of wings are applicable to sails. It is no coincidence that so many aviators are sailors as well.

In order to discern, describe, and design sail and wing forms it is important to be familiar with the descriptive terminology. Sail *camber* is the curvature of the sail at any given section from luff to leech—often called *belly, flow,* or *fullness.* The

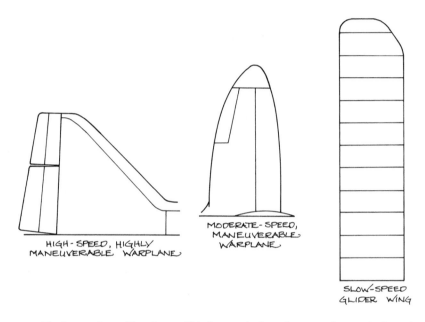

FIGURE 4-8. *Airplane wings, like those of birds, are designed to match certain functions.*

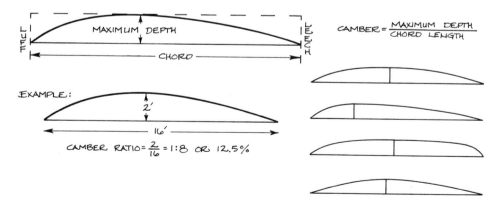

FIGURE 4-9. *Camber ratio is an important parameter of the shape of a sail section, but not the only one. At right are four very different curves, all with the same camber ratio.*

camber of a particular section is assessed relative to the straight-line chord length from the luff to the leech. Said another way, the degree or depth of camber is described as a ratio of depth to chord length and expressed as a fraction or percentage.

The height of a sail relative to its average (mean) width is called its *aspect ratio*, which in the case of a truly square squaresail is simply depth (height) divided by width. The at-a-glance method used to approximate the aspect ratio of fore-and-aft sails—Bermudan in particular—is to compare luff length with foot length. More accurately, however, for shapes other than rectangles, aspect ratio is determined by dividing the square of the height by the area.

When air flows around a cambered sail, as we have seen, two types of flow, *laminar* and *turbulent*, exist within the boundary layer. Laminar

flow is more efficient but also more difficult to obtain, there being so many obstacles and irregularities in a sail (stitching, cringles, etc.). Smoothness does make a difference in reducing friction and delaying separation, which is why an older cotton sail, smooth as a flannel shirt that has lost its nap, is faster than a new one, or in part why a synthetic sail, at least on smaller boats, is faster than a cotton sail. Delaying separation of

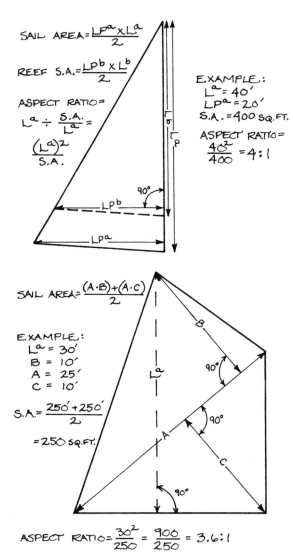

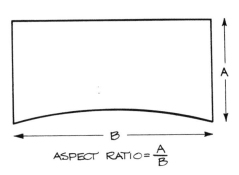

$$\text{ASPECT RATIO} = \frac{A}{B}$$

FIGURE 4-10. *The aspect ratio of a squaresail is easily calculated. More generally, a sail's height squared, divided by its area, yields the aspect ratio. Use luff length as height for a Bermudan sail. For a gaff sail, use a perpendicular line from the peak to the foot. To find the approximate area of a Bermudan sail, ignore roach and treat it as a triangle; use the luff (L^a) as the height and construct a perpendicular base (LP^a) from the clew, or use the foot as the base and drop a perpendicular height from the head (as in Figure 2-1). Treat a gaff sail as two triangles and find the area of each.*

SAIL SHAPING

Q: I've given much thought lately to making my own sails, but I'm in the dark when it comes to understanding the techniques for imparting three-dimensional form to a sail. What are the methods?

A: There are several ways of building shape that determine where and how much camber will be in a sail. Rarely is one technique used exclusively; some combination of methods is the norm, with the appropriate combination depending on the material used.

A sailcloth may be selected for its ability to stretch and elongate into a bellying form. *Bias elongation,* when properly anticipated and exploited, forms a pocket in the sail when tension is applied diagonally to the weave.

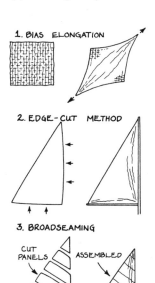

Naturally, if you make a convex curve of cloth along the perimeter of a sail conform to a straight spar or stay, the hump of cloth will be pushed into the sail, forming a bag. Alternatively, if that convex round is gathered up along a luff rope, wire, or tape, the effect is the same. These techniques are generally referred to as the *edge-cut* method.

Edge cutting is most appropriate for relatively soft, unstable, woven fabrics. The more stable the sailcloth, the more necessary it is to mold the sail by cutting the panels and pieces so that when assembled they create a somewhat static form. When such tailoring is performed in a limited manner at the seam ends of a conventionally cut sail, this method is called *seam tapering* or *broadseaming.* A typical noncompetition small-boat sail—especially of a classic type—will utilize all the techniques to some degree, with an emphasis on bias elongation and edge cutting. There will be a small amount of broadseaming to place and control the curvature.

Chapter 5 covers methods of sail shaping in more detail.

airflow is an important part of upwind sail performance.

Meanwhile, a trio of drag nasties are holding things back: *pressure drag,* created as the wind encounters sail and rig, particularly if any section of the sail is trimmed too closely; frictional *viscous drag;* and *induced drag.* The latter refers to those energy-robbing vortices escaping around the edges and corners of a sail.

Sail shape is further defined by the fore-and-aft position of deepest draft, known as the *draft position*—a point designated as a percentage of the chord length aft of the leading edge. The curved shapes forward and abaft the draft position—the *entry* and *exit*—are described as being relatively full or flat.

Within these parameters lie an infinite number of sail shapes. An awareness of the extremes provides some basis of comparison for more subtle forms.

Different forms under certain conditions maximize lift and minimize drag for going to weather,

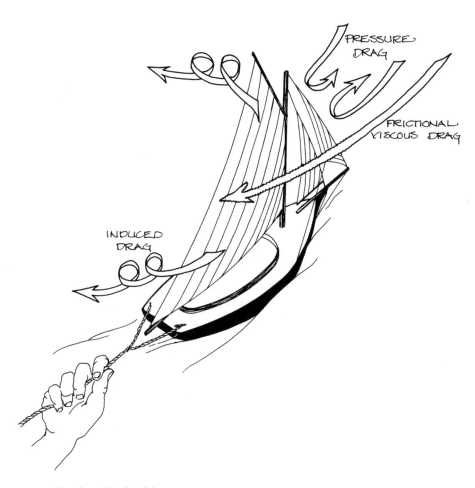

FIGURE 4-11. *The three kinds of drag.*

while others maximize drag for offwind sailing. Not only that, but different camber ratios and angles of entry are required at various heights up and down a sail because apparent wind velocity and angles will change with heights, especially under influence of other sails.

Intimidating as all this may sound, in practice such specificity of design and function is employed primarily by competition sailmakers and naval architects. And it *can* all be calculated much the same as for an airplane wing—with boat speed substituted for thrust. Of course, there are less-than-ideal gray areas where none of the forces involved are constant long enough to pin down; and there are limits to the number of alternative sails you can carry and set. Something is always amiss, something always being compromised.

Only at low wind speeds will an even airflow remain attached to a sail of deep camber. This is why fuller sails are used in lighter winds. Keeping the same camber and draft position as the wind picks up results in flow separation, perhaps overpowering the boat, and a loss of efficiency. In that instance a flatter sail would perform better.

Flat is faster and less powerful. Full is slower and more powerful.

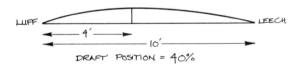

FIGURE 4-12. *Draft position is the location of deepest draft expressed as a percentage of the chord length from luff to leech.*

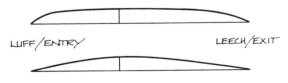

FIGURE 4-13. *Two curves of equal camber ratio and draft position, one with full entry and exit, the other, flat.*

SAIL TRIM

A sail's performance and the appropriateness of its aerodynamic shape are only as good as its trim—that is, its angle of attack to the apparent wind. Of course, the underbody, keel, and rudder design are of equal importance to the whole sailing effort. But considering only the relationship of the foil to the flow of wind, there exists a narrow range of 3 degrees or so in which the sail can function well aerodynamically. If oversheeted, flow separates, the sail stalls, pressure drag increases, and the boat makes leeway. If the sail is eased too far or the boat steered too close to the wind, the curvature collapses—the sail luffs and flaps like a flag—losing all lift and drive.

The angle of entry of a sail, its camber ratio, and its draft position all help govern the appropriate *angle of incidence* or *trim angle* at which the airflow may successfully approach and wend its way around the leeward side of the sail. A fuller leading edge—wider angle of entry—is more forgiving, providing a greater range within which the angle of incidence is neither too great nor too small, but the sail can't point as close to the wind as one with a narrower angle of entry.

A naval architect, knowing a hull and rig's windward abilities, will plan the sheeting base and trim angle of the sails accordingly. The sailmaker then provides the fastest, most weatherly and powerful compromise for the trim angle under the anticipated wind ranges, sea conditions, and boat speed.

As noted, aerodynamic conditions vary at different heights in a sail. In part, this is because parts of the sail twist off intentionally or uncontrollably, and thus have a different attitude to the wind. But just as importantly, the winds vary with height.

From the true wind speed and direction and the boat's speed and course a sailmaker arrives at the apparent wind speed and angle. The closer to the wind a boat sails and the faster it goes, the faster and farther forward the apparent wind will be. This is why, in the same breeze, you may freeze going to weather and fry going downwind, and it is also why fast boats such as trimarans and

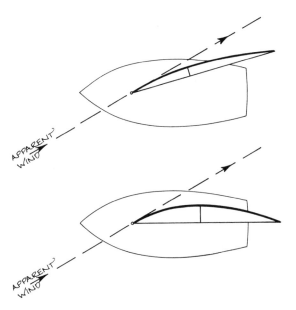

FIGURE 4-14. *The sail with greater camber must be trimmed closer to the apparent wind.*

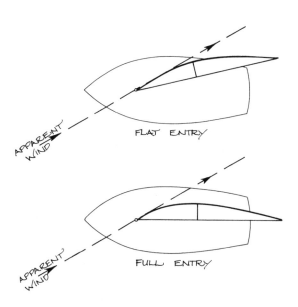

FIGURE 4-15. *Two sails with similar camber ratio and draft position experiencing a similar apparent wind angle. The sail with the fuller entry must be trimmed closer to the wind.*

FIGURE 4-16. *Leech twist in a gaff sail. The true wind is often stronger aloft, and the apparent wind angle therefore farther aft, so some twist may be desirable. Too much twist is to be avoided, however, except in the attempt to spill excess wind from the upper leech.*

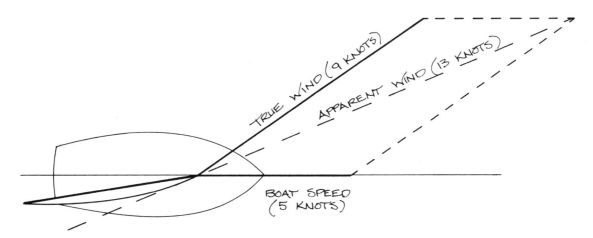

FIGURE 4-17. *To find the apparent wind angle and speed from true wind angle and speed and boat speed, construct a parallelogram with its sides proportional to the speed of the true wind and the boat. The diagonal will lie in the direction of, and its length will be proportional to, the apparent wind.*

iceboats are sheeted in tight even on a beam reach—their speed brings the apparent wind angle far forward.

The wind velocity may be greater aloft than alow due to what's called the *wind gradient,* a phenomenon that results from the wind closer to the water being slowed by friction, much as that in the boundary layer along the sail is slowed. As you reach a higher altitude the effect decreases and the wind increases. Clearly, if the true wind is greater aloft, the apparent wind angle will be somewhat wider, and this must be taken into account in the upper sections of a sail or in the overall shape of a sail set above another (such as a gaff topsail).

SAIL INTERACTION

The last ingredient to influence a design is the sail's interaction with one or several other sails. Aerodynamicists still debate how a single sail functions to propel a boat, let alone how two sails, one forward of and perhaps overlapping the other, func-

tion together to enhance windward performance. But there is no doubt that two sails working together produce more drive than the sum of their parts, and no one disagrees about how to set up the sails in relation to one another. There is an optimal range of fore-and-aft and athwartship proximity, and a coincidence of form; the after portion or leech of the jib should conform to the curvature of the mainsail.

Starting with the headsail and moving aft, each

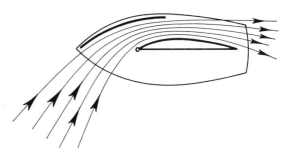

FIGURE 4-18. *The slot effect—one theory of sail interaction.*

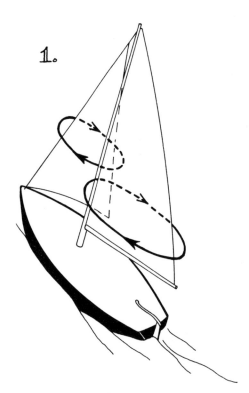

1.

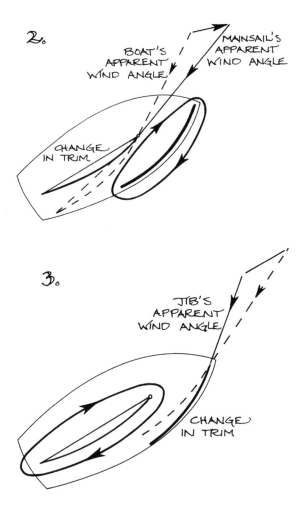

2.

3.

FIGURE 4-19. *The circulation theory of sail inter-action. (1) Air circulates around both jib and mainsail. (2) The relatively slower air on the windward side of the jib narrows the apparent wind angle to the mainsail and necessitates a flatter sail or sheeting closer to the centerline. (3) The faster airflow to leeward of the mainsail widens the apparent wind angle to the jib, permitting a fuller sail or wider trim angle.*

sail will operate in a narrower apparent wind angle. Thus it will be sheeted farther in and is likely to be flatter than the sail ahead of it.

In our efforts to explain how sails enhance each other's performance, we often speak of the *slot effect.* This interpretation—perhaps the most effective and easiest to comprehend while actually sailing—is that airflow deflected by the headsail is squeezed and sped up venturilike, and directed around the leeward side of the mainsail, thus narrowing the apparent wind angle and increasing the

mainsail's lift. The result is a faster boat sailing with a narrower overall apparent wind angle—closer to the wind. If the slot is too narrow, either because of inappropriate sail shaping or sheeting, it is said to be *crowded,* resulting in the airflow being directed toward rather than over the mainsail's lee surface, thus causing the leading edge to be back-winded or collapse. With restricted airflow in the slot, the air speed is decreased and the pressure increased; the suction is lost, and with equal pressure on both sides of the sail, it starts to flutter.

The "circulation" camp (Figure 4-19) interprets sail interaction according to the notion that, relatively speaking, air is circulating about the sail—the faster low-pressure air on the leeward side being called the *upwash,* and the slower high-pressure air on the weather side, the *downwash.* The downwash on the windward side of the headsail, because it is moving more slowly relative to boat speed, reduces the apparent wind angle at the mainsail. Unless this effect is relieved either by sheeting in the mainsail to the new apparent wind angle or by easing the headsail, air pressures around the mainsail's leading edge will equalize and backwinding will occur.

To substantiate this theory, proponents point out that reef nettles on the weather side don't stream aft as those on the leeward side do. Furthermore, if the slot effect were actually a venturi phenomenon involving flow constriction and speed increase, the headsail would be sucked into *that* low-pressure area!

By way of reassuring those who may now be wondering why anyone should carry a mainsail at all, it is opined that the mainsail becomes an extension of the headsail leech, and the flagging flow of the headsail leaps across and is rejuvenated by the fast-moving flow on the lee side of the mainsail. The result is an overall production of power commencing with the headsail luff and terminating with the mainsail leech.

Also, the apparent wind angle at the headsail widens as leeward wind speed increases relative to boat speed due to the influence of the mainsail. In effect, the main avails the jib of a continued lift.

I don't know that in practice either of these theories contradicts the other. Elements of the circulation theory, though entertaining, seem quibbling to me and at times contradictory. But regardless of the reason for the different apparent wind angles and speeds between sails, these differences need to be incorporated into sail designs or a loss of efficiency will result. This applies for split rigs as well as masthead sloops with overlapping headsails. Generally, each succeeding sail will be flatter than

TABLE 4-1.
ASPECT RATIO, SAIL MATERIALS, SAIL CONSTRUCTION
AND SAIL SHAPING OPTIONS

ASPECT RATIO / SAIL TYPE	RELATIVE STABILITY OF MATERIALS AND CONSTRUCTION	FLEXIBILITY AND OPTIONS ALTERING SAIL SHAPE
HIGH	STABLE	FEWER OPTIONS, LESS FLEXIBILITY
LOW	MODERATELY STABLE	MORE OPTIONS AND FLEXIBILITY
HIGH, BERMUDAN PROFILE	MOST STABLE	LEAST
LOW, BERMUDAN PROFILE	MODERATELY STABLE	
HIGH, FOUR-CORNERED PROFILE	MODERATELY STABLE	↓
LOW, FOUR-CORNERED PROFILE	LEAST STABLE	MOST

the one before. Very flat yawl mizzens are a good example.

SAIL MATERIALS AND CONSTRUCTION

With the aim of greater and greater performance in narrowly defined conditions, hull and rig configurations can be selected to the extreme of requiring an inflexible wing of a sail with no possibility of adjustment except to trim angle. Somewhat less radical but nonetheless highly specialized are laminate-fabric racing sails designed for particular wind ranges. Sail shape may be altered to suit within the range, but only within the range.

Still more moderate and less specialized are the sails of the middle-of-the-road sailors who want good performance, but not at the expense of all other considerations. They require fewer sails covering wider wind ranges, and thus need a greater degree of shape adjustment.

Last are those sails intended for extensive shape adjustment, sails that must do all—all speeds and points of sail—and may or may not be aided by auxiliary sails. Performancewise, these sails either tend to be jacks of all trades or are geared for certain kinds of sailing to the neglect of others.

In each rough category, as with birds' wings, there are sail profiles that are most successful for their tasks. To fulfill the potential of the profiles, certain sail materials and constructions are appropriate. Adaptable sailing calls for an adaptable rig, which in turn relies on a mutable sail and flexible, relatively unstable materials. The relationships set forth in Table 4-1 (page 127) will generally hold.

Some portion of planning of a sail involves the greater or lesser necessity of the sailor's manipulating sail shape to suit the conditions. In all but the most competitive sailing, the sail will be used on all points of sail, not just upwind where an ideal aerodynamic shape is appropriate. The problem with unstable materials is that every time the wind speed changes so do they, and so does the sail, usually for the worse—at least from an upwind aerodynamic point of view.

5

How Sails Are Made

O NE'S METHODOLOGY and philosophical approach to sailmaking can range from an intuitive, empirical, improvisational, and artistic stance to a refined, highly theoretical, technical, and scientific approach: sort of like the difference between dead reckoning and satellite navigation or the use of Loran. The two schools need not be mutually exclusive. In fact, in the end it is a judicious blend that will result in the best sailing, sailmaking, and sails.

This chapter presents background information regarding a commercial sailmaking environment and the general considerations, techniques, and procedures involved in making sails. Chapter 6, "Making Your Own Sails," applies this information to specific sails and amateur practice, skills, and needs. This is the do-it-yourself foundation course.

THE BUSINESS OF SAILMAKING

In the overall scheme of things, sailmaking is a small industry. Popular as sailing is, the manufacture of sails occupies a puny economic niche in this country's GNP—nothing alongside sugar or beef, for example. Sailmaking is highly competitive and in many respects quite centralized in terms of control of marketing trends. To compete successfully in the mainstream of the industry demands shrewd marketing, keeping up with trends, and skunking the competition with improvements aimed at one of three markets: racers, cruisers, or daysailors. The process tends to combine the interests of all groups and directs products toward them as if they all had the same needs. But there are middle-of-the-road sail lofts that, while offering some products and making concessions to the latest trends in order to stay afloat, do not try to compete on a large scale; they do so locally with small, slower production. Then there are the fringe specialists surviving in a specialty with a small, loyal clientele—local or mail order—usually with low overhead, low production, and unsophisticated technology of design and construction.

Where Are Sails Made?

Sails have not always been fabricated in the immaculate and comfortable sail lofts generally found today. The advent of sport sailing and the ensuing development of appropriate materials and aesthetics contributed substantially to changing what was formerly a harsh and unappealing work environment. Where cleanliness and precision are not required, sails can be lofted on the desert sand, as they are on the shores of the Nile, or on a frozen lake, as schooner sails were in Maine.

In days of old, indoor spaces were poorly lighted and inadequately heated. There often was no room to lay out a full sail, and the sails would be made in pieces. Sails made on board ship had to be pieced together within the confines of the sail locker or on deck. Ironically, mechanization and computers have brought state-of-the-art production sailmaking back into a similarly prefabricated piece-by-piece sail-construction procedure. Indoor commercial sailmaking, however, generally requires a floor space large enough to lay out sails of all dimensions. Forty feet by 60 feet of uninterrupted floor space would be ideal, although I've made do with less, and many lofts maintain a smaller space and periodically borrow or rent a big floor when the need arises. Having set up sail lofts in six different locations, I'll say that low-capital enterprises have a hard time finding suitable and affordable space. These days there is a hefty price tag on a square foot of rental space. Happily, sail lofts can be located in lofts and upper spaces that other businesses cannot utilize. A well-lighted, clean, warm space with an open, level, wooden, easily cleaned floor is preferable. A rest room is convenient and a view of the water is inspirational. For walk-in business, the closer to the boats the better. Proximity to and affiliation with other facets of the marine industry and maritime trades increases exposure, and complementary businesses pass clients along—chandleries, boatbuilding and storage facilities, rigging lofts, charter businesses, and so forth.

Who Works in a Sail Loft?

Sailmakers are often sailors, but sometimes, particularly in a departmentalized production setup, the people employed to construct sails don't know the sharp end of a boat from the dull end. You don't have to be an old salt to be skilled at any of the mechanical aspects of building a sail. As a minimum, a sail loft with one person for each division of the process, including sales, reception, and public relations, could have as few as six people. With high-volume production and auxiliary services such as canvaswork and sail cleaning, the crew may number a score or more—particularly at the

peak of the sailing season. In the opposite extreme, one or two people do everything year-round. The smallest of lofts often work in a feast-or-famine situation; at times it is all they can do to keep the wolf from the door—and then it doesn't take much to be swamped. The smaller lofts always walk an economic tightrope, and the sailmaker, while not discouraging work, must take care not to alienate clients by taking on more commitments than can be fulfilled. Extremely frustrated and unlikely to return is the sailor whose boat is waiting out on the mooring for a new sail as the short sailing season and vacation time tick past! Any financially solvent and profitable sailmaking enterprise will, of necessity, be highly organized regardless of the size of the operation. In the extremes, shops range from automated, rigid, impersonal, punch-clock factories to relaxed, personal workplaces with character and an atmosphere of camaraderie.

At one time women were seldom found working in sail lofts. Increasingly, though, women own, manage, and perform all aspects of the sailmaking process. The most expansive opportunities for women lie in small lofts dedicated to an enlightened clientele of less-competitive, less-biased sailors. It is possible, as women become more competitive in racing circles, that the making of their sails will fall under their control. Women sailmakers will then make money from women sailors. As it is now, in the competition and production lofts, women are generally employed as office help or work in the construction and assembly departments.

Sources of Materials

Synthetic-sailcloth manufacture is a mere pebble on the textile-industry beach, so specialized and refined are these fabrics. Only three or four mills actually produce the cloth; a handful of distributors then make further refinements to the cloth and market it. All lofts, big and small, must obtain their sailcloth from these few distributors—with the exception of some of the larger lofts that have their own cloth-finishing operation; they have the mills make up cloth to their own specifications. Even these big lofts, with their own brand-name sailcloth, rely on other distributors for fabric. Of course, high-volume enterprises have considerable influence over the characteristics of cloth available and are in the best position to benefit from bulk-rate pricing.

If the synthetic-sailcloth industry is a pebble, the natural-fiber sailcloth industry is but a grain of sand. In fact, true natural sailcloth is not manufactured on this continent and must be imported by the individual loft from extremely limited sources in Europe or purchased from another importer. Extensive detective work might turn up some sailcloth hidden away somewhere, left over from an old loft or remaining in a distributor's obsolete line. Of course, there are natural-fiber materials manufactured for purposes other than sailmaking that may be passable as sailcloth in certain instances. In this regard, as with marine fabrics in general, there are more manufacturers and mills and numerous distributors.

For materials, sail lofts go where price, quality, and service appeal to them. There is a tendency, though, to simplify things; thus the sailcloth distributors carry other marine fabrics as well as sail- and canvas-related hardware and tools. Limited applications and market, as well as exclusive importation and distribution contracts among manufacturers and distributors, have resulted in limited sail, tool, and hardware sources. Materials such as thread, tools such as sewing machines and canvas tools, and hardware with other applications are more readily available and are distributed by many firms. As we learned in Chapter 1, "A Ditty Bag Apprenticeship," several of the sailmaker's basic tools are unique items made by or for the artisan expressly for personal needs and use.

THE PRINCIPLES OF SAIL DESIGN

When a sail is designed, its two- and three-dimensional shape; its construction—that is, materials, hardware, and reinforcements; and its built-in sail-handling and shape-adjustment features should all be considered.

The desired two-dimensional shape is in part determined by requirements of additional sail area; aerodynamic attributes such as smooth leeches that minimize vortices, turbulence, and power loss by air pressure escaping around the sail edges; and the extent to which peripheral form affects sail handling and sail life.

The three-dimensional shape of a sail is determined by apparent wind speed, apparent wind angle, point of sail, trim, sea conditions, hull performance, stability, and rig type. In addition, the three-dimensional form of one sail is influenced by that sail's interaction with other sails. The sailor's needs also play a part, as does the availability of substitute sails: all else being equal, the jib on a boat with but one headsail for a wide range of wind conditions will likely have a different basic shape than a jib of the same dimensions on a boat carrying several jibs.

A sail's three-dimensional form may be disproportional, or asymmetrical, by design in order to achieve maximum performance in varying wind speeds and apparent wind angles in different parts of the sail. Though all these variables are real—and in the sole pursuit of performance they must be accounted for—in general, only approximations can be made, and the design process in regard to shape and performance is a mass of compromises. There is no right or wrong, just the appropriate set of compromises.

General design aspects are interrelated, of course, and all directly influence the selection of sailcloth. Here again there are trade-offs (see Table 5-1): aerodynamic efficiency and performance are achieved at the expense of nearly all other considerations except aesthetics (beauty being in the eye of the beholder and softness being in the hand of the stuffer). With synthetics, you might say that the design of the sail's shape starts back in the chemist's lab (or, in the case of natural materials, back in the plant), and continues on through the development of fiber, thread, weaving, and finishing. An understanding of sailcloth composition, design, and construction is necessary for informed sail shaping at the design table, on the loft floor, and on the water.

TABLE 5-1.

SAIL CLOTH TRADEOFFS

SAIL CLOTH	SHAPE RETENTION (POROSITY, STABILITY)	STRENGTH-TO-WEIGHT	AESTHETIC APPEAL (COLOR, FEEL, SMELL, ETC.)	DURABILITY	EASE OF HANDLING
COTTON	POOR	LOW	EXCELLENT	GOOD	GOOD (POOR WHEN WET)
FLAX	POOR	LOW	EXCELLENT	GOOD	GOOD
DURADON	FAIR	MED.-LOW	EXCELLENT	EXCELLENT	EXCELLENT
SOFT DACRON	GOOD	MEDIUM	GOOD	GOOD	GOOD/EXC.
FIRM DACRON	EXCELLENT	MED.-HIGH	POOR	FAIR	POOR
CRUISING LAMINATES	EXCELLENT	HIGH	POOR	FAIR	FAIR
RACING LAMINATES	EXCELLENT	VERY HIGH	POOR	POOR	FAIR

The preliminary designing of a sail entails working with and around the most elemental aspects of sailcloth, right down to the molecular structure of the fibers that in turn are transformed into yarns of greater or lesser size, twist, strength or tenacity, elasticity, and water absorption. These yarns are then woven into a fabric of a specified width. The yarns running the length of the fabric are called *warp;* those woven across are called *weft* or *fill.* The relationship of quantity of weft to warp yarns and the tightness of the weave highly influence the character of the cloth. The multitude of processes involved in refining and finishing sailcloth—heating, shrinking, *calendering* (heat pressing), impregnation, and coating the cloth—further render a sailcloth that is specialized and idiosyncratic. Variations in the process result in differing amounts of bias elongation, stretch, elasticity, porosity, and tear strength. Cloth then can be created not only for particular types of sailing, the rig, and the boat, but also for the sail type and cut, the wind range, and even for specific parts of a sail.

The area of greatest instability in sailcloth lies in *bias elongation,* the inherent tendency of woven

fabric to give when force is exerted diagonally to the direction of the weave. Within limits this "weakness" is not a failing, and it is this aspect of cloth behavior that plays such a major part in connection with sailcloth type and design and in the shaping of sails.

Ways of Putting Shape into a Sail

There are five basic means by which three-dimensional form is built into a sail: stretch, bias elongation, broadseaming and darts, molding or sculpting, and edge curves. Rarely is one technique used exclusively in a given sail; they are usually combined. Stretch and bias elongation are considered undesirable features of modern fabric, but in traditional sailmaking and noncompetitive sailing these aspects are an asset and a valuable tool.

Cloth Stretch—Elastic and Permanent   Clearly, with bound edges, if the body of the sail expands, some curvature will result. So the extent and distribution of cloth stretch in the given fabric must be exploited and controlled.

Natural fibers stretch more than synthetic

ones—permanent stretch, that is—and after a certain point have less recovery. Generally it is the force of the wind and the wear of weathering and use that encourage a fabric to stretch, but more than one cotton sail has been shaped in desperation by being strung up horizontally and loaded with wet sand! Synthetic fibers will elongate permanently to a small extent, especially if pushed by excessive strains. But generally it is the elasticity in synthetics that must be accounted for in producing sail shape. (Better-quality fibers of higher tenacity will have less give and faster recovery.) For example, if you're employing a lightweight fabric or a poor-quality material, you can count on the sail's being fuller as the wind picks up. It's all relative, of course, but it's one recourse in obtaining shape. Knowing the specifications of a cloth—that is, how much stretch there will be under a certain load—will give some indication as to the transformation the cloth will make. Frankly, in the realm of synthetics—with the exception of light, voluminous, off-wind sails—elasticity is not that serious a consideration. It is a factor in shape and performance of the sail, but not worth losing sleep over unless the sails are intended for competition.

On the other hand, with cotton, and especially with flax, there is much need of concern, since without planning, an unweatherly bag of a sail could result. Moreover, there is also the matter of shrinkage to contend with. For a rumpus room–built spritsail this is not so critical, but for a sail with any expectations of upwind performance, it is. Again, cloth weight and cloth quality have the biggest effect.

Bias Elongation

Bias elongation is a type of *cloth* stretch, with more or less elasticity, not to be confused with the permanent stretch and elasticity of the *fiber*. Bias elongation is the result of stress being placed diagonally upon a woven fabric.

Bias elongation in one portion of a sail, say the luff, forms a pocket that draws cloth from other parts of the sail. Thus, bias elongation can be intentionally induced to pull the draft position forward in a sail. Similarly, peaking up a gaff sail or spritsail creates a diagonal tension from peak to tack; cloth is drawn to that diagonal area. The wind then smooths it out to desirable sail curvature.

When bias elongation occurs in areas such as the clew and lower leech, it forms unwanted wrinkles. The sailmaker plans the cut of a sail in part

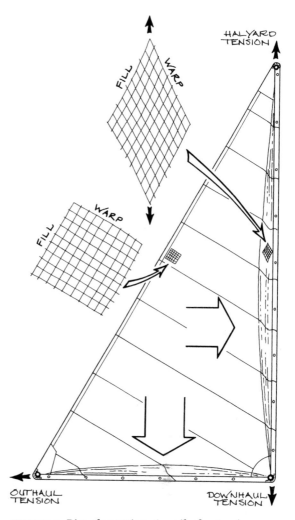

FIGURE 5-1. *Bias elongation. As sail edge tension distorts the weave of the sailcloth, cloth is drawn from within the sail toward that edge. Bias elongation is advantageous where intended, and a problem where unintended.*

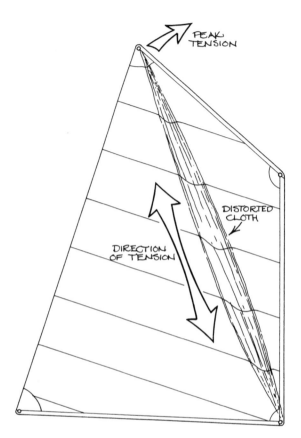

FIGURE 5-2. *Bias elongation in a gaff sail. The cloth tension provided by peaking up a gaffs'l draws extra cloth into the tensioned area. The wind will smooth this out to create the desired sail curvature. If the wind lightens, the peak must be lowered.*

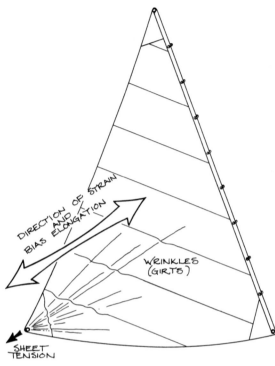

FIGURE 5-3. *Bias elongation wrinkles in the clew of a genoa. The wrinkled clews in genoas and other sails are the result of unwanted cloth distortion on the bias. If your genoa looks like this, you have either a hardware/reinforcement problem (perhaps curable) or a cloth problem (not much you can do).*

to minimize, or benefit from, bias elongation. Much of this will be anticipatory thinking and planning for sail controls—and for sailors who will make great use of bias elongation to change sail shape. The more versatile a sail is, the more bias elongation will be a factor in its design and use. Cloth selection will be based on a determined amount of bias elongation under a given amount of stress. Specifications available for synthetic sailcloths provide a clear indication of what elongation can be anticipated. Allowance must be made

for the increased permanent stretch of natural sailcloth along edges where the cloths are cut on the bias, or cut "on the gore" in traditional parlance. It might be thought that one could put something along the edge of a natural-fabric sail that does not stretch, and thereby prevent the sailcloth from stretching at all. It is, however, necessary to permit the sailcloth to stretch to the extent that it naturally would under the load along that side of the sail; if you don't, the edge will remain tight and the cloth within the sail will stretch. Thus

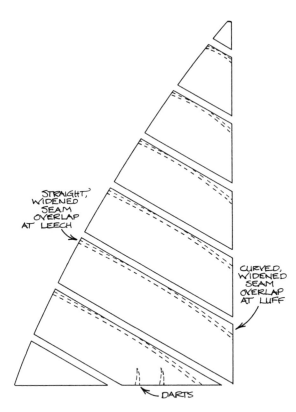

FIGURE 5-4. *Broadseams and darts. Widening the overlap of seam ends builds sail shape. A widened, straight overlap at the leech builds in a flat exit for the airflow; a widened, curved overlap at the luff builds in a curved entry. In synthetic cloth you may keep the seam width uniform by trimming away the excess cloth at the broadseams (upper dashed lines on each panel).*

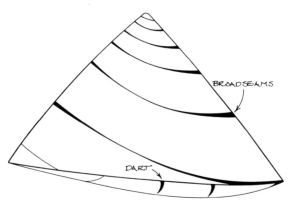

FIGURE 5-5. *Sail camber resulting from broadseaming and darts. Curved darts build a shelflike curvature into the foot of the sail. (Shaded areas in drawing represent seam overlap.)*

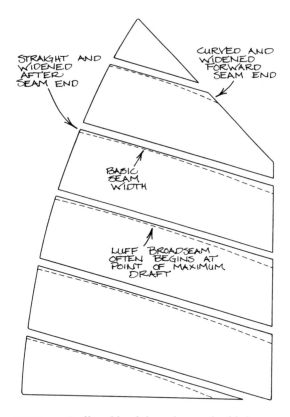

FIGURE 5-6. *Luff and leech broadseams build shape in a crosscut gaff-headed sail.*

you would lose the ability to control the sail's shape along that edge.

Broadseaming and Darts Broadseaming (tapering or tailoring) is one technique in controlling the stretch of bias-cut sail edges in natural-fiber sails. Just as important, it is a means of forming sail shape by widening the seam ends, which in effect adds cloth and creates curvature. Broadseaming puts in a certain amount of draft, but more impor-

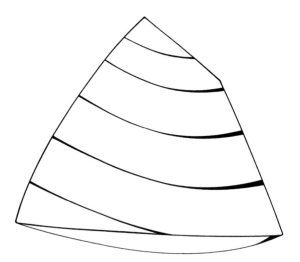

FIGURE 5-7. *Curvature built into a gaff-headed sail by broadseaming.*

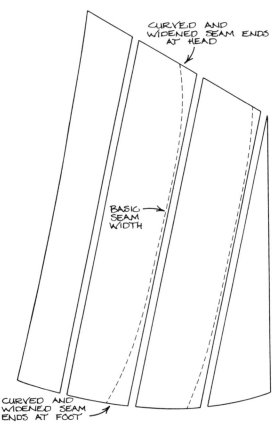

FIGURE 5-8. *Possible broadseaming configuration in a vertically cut loose-footed or boomless spritsail.*

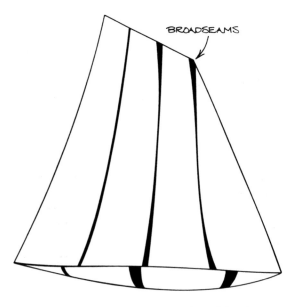

FIGURE 5-9. *Curvature in a spritsail resulting from broadseaming at head and foot.*

tant, in a crosscut sail, it is intended to control draft *placement*. Tightening the seams along unsupported edges may provide some curvature but also supports and assists that edge in standing in a breeze. Darts also provide shape and edge support.

The length and amount of broadseam are governed by the sail type, the intended sail shape, other shaping methods in the design, and the type of sailcloth. The more stable a synthetic sailcloth is, the more dependent on tailoring it will be for shape—thus wider broadseams.

Molded Sails Molding is an extension of broad-seaming, and denotes an extensive tailoring job in which a sail is sculpted of fairly stable materials. Cox Sails in the Northwest has been leaning in that direction for years now; they have constructed an ingenious wing form, and the sailcloth is laid over it and tailored to conform to the shape. This seems to work well for triangular sails. Similarly, computer programs now project a form and then determine the patterns of the cloth pieces required to create that form. This method of sailmaking is a natural outcome of sailcloth advances and economic interests. Unlike broadseaming, in which the straight edge of one panel is sewn with a curved overlap to the next panel, in molding the curved panel edges are joined by a seam of constant width, which for a firm cloth results in a smoother installation of curvature.

Any cut of sail—even the most traditional—can be molded. Molding is best employed, though, in cuts where draft position and control must be quite specific, and with materials that lend themselves to complex cloth patterns intended to align

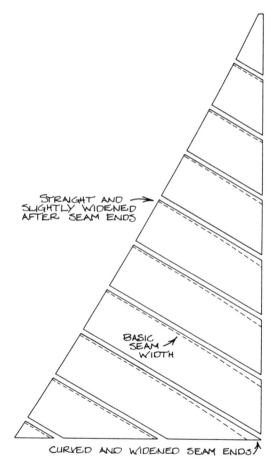

FIGURE 5-10. *Possible broadseaming configuration in a battenless Bermudan cruising mains'l. Since this sail will be built of softer cloth than the racing/ daysailing sail in Figure 5-4, it does not depend to the same extent on broadseaming for shape.*

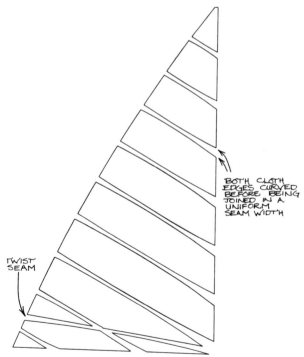

FIGURE 5-11. *The tailored and uniformly curved panels of a computer-generated racing sail mold in curvature while maintaining a uniform basic seam width.*

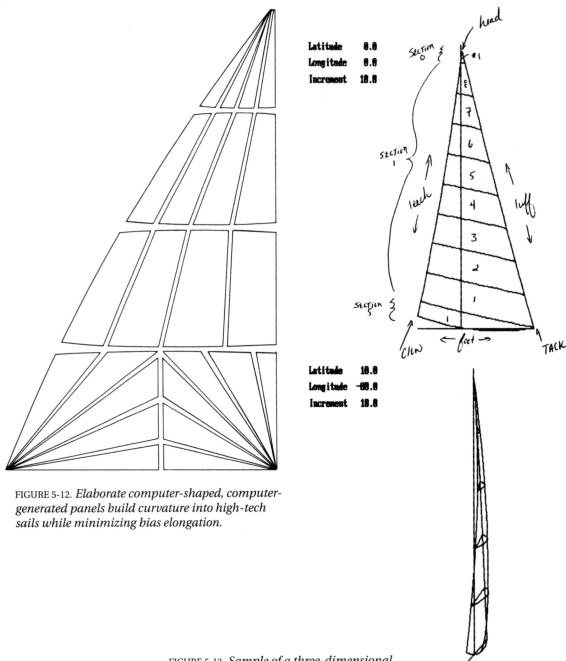

Latitude   0.0
Longitude   0.0
Increment   10.0

Latitude   10.0
Longitude   -60.0
Increment   10.0

FIGURE 5-12. *Elaborate computer-shaped, computer-generated panels build curvature into high-tech sails while minimizing bias elongation.*

FIGURE 5-13. *Sample of a three-dimensional computer printout, this one from Sailrite Kits. Computer design makes manipulation of sail-shape parameters easy. When the desired shape emerges, a pattern can be generated.*

warp and weft threads with directions of stress in the sail. When one thinks of molding, one thinks of the incredibly complex sail cuts seen on racers and even cruiser-racers.

Edge Curves Though broadseaming to some degree is virtually essential to impart curvature in a sail, *edge curves* are still needed to create draft, particularly in less stable fabrics. What are edge curves? They are the excess cloth outside the straight line from one corner to another that, when gathered up or pressed against a straight edge such as a spar or stay, is bunched into the body of the sail, allowing wind to create belly in the sail.

Clearly, only soft, flexible fabrics work well if this shaping technique is employed solely. In itself, edge curving does nothing to locate the curvature created, though the curvature will emanate from the sail edge where the round was cut. Draft placement will then be up to the wind and the sailor manipulating the sail.

Even if a sail's camber is to come from other

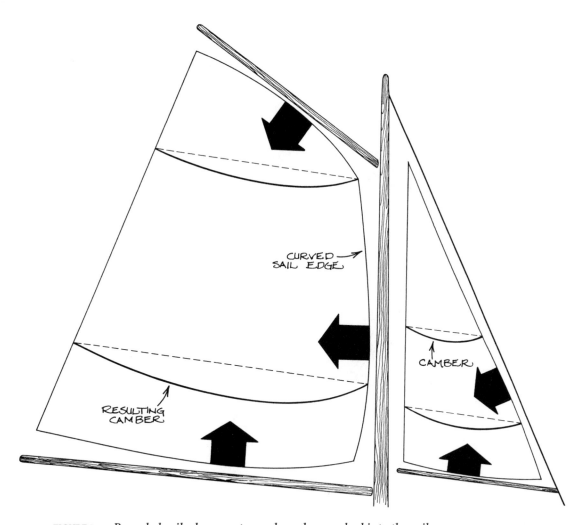

FIGURE 5-14. *Rounded sail edges create camber when pushed into the sail.*

means, edge curves are important. The flexing of a spar to which the sail is bent alternately reduces or increases sail camber, and whether these changes

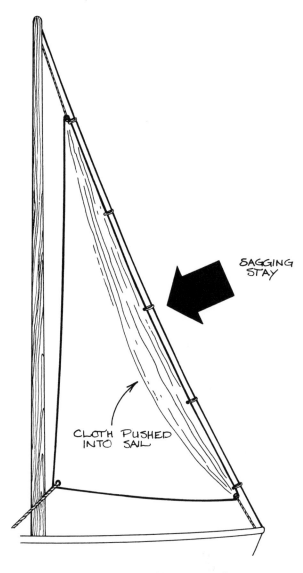

FIGURE 5-15. *The unavoidable sagging of a stay pushes cloth into a sail, which increases its camber. The sailmaker anticipates and either utilizes or compensates for this effect.*

occur intentionally or otherwise, allowances must be made in the extent and shaping of the sail's edge curves. Similarly, the inevitable sag of a stay, particularly as the wind increases, pushes cloth aft into the sail, making it fuller. To some extent this is desirable, but beyond a certain point it is detrimental to windward work, and the sail's luff must be cut to allow for an anticipated amount of stay sag.

Generally, if the sails are sails and not cloth-covered wings, some combination of these five techniques is used, with emphasis on some or others depending on materials, sail type, and use. For a seafaring, voyaging, and amateur sailmaking slant, the materials and sail types involved will rely most heavily on edge curves, bias elongation, and broadseaming, while taking into account stretch and elasticity of a particular fabric. There will be none of the cuts or materials appropriate for molded, computer-derived sails or wing-oriented constructions.

Sail Cuts

The *cut* of a sail refers not only to its two-dimensional form, but also to the manner in which the cloths, or panels, are laid out in the sail. The cloths are oriented so as to maximize strength and minimize stretch by placing either the warp or the weft—not the bias—parallel to the strain on an unsupported sail edge. Further considerations for sail strength and durability include running seams parallel to the strain, keeping seam ends from striking free sail edges, and planning the layout such that if a seam should let go, the sail is still usable. For these reasons, as well as material necessity, the traditional vertical or up-and-down cut was for millennia the prevalent cloth pattern in both transverse and fore-and-aft sails. The cloths in a squaresail are laid perpendicular to the head, and fore-and-aft boomed workboat sails have been cut with the cloths laid parallel to the leech. In the full-battened sails of the Orient, the cloths have been laid parallel to the luff.

Various miter cuts were developed in an attempt to control and limit stretch in the unsupported

(text continued on page 144)

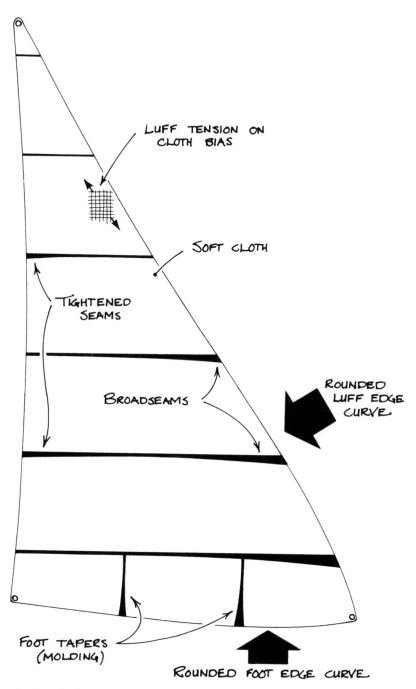

LUFF TENSION ON
CLOTH BIAS

SOFT CLOTH

TIGHTENED
SEAMS

BROADSEAMS

ROUNDED
LUFF EDGE
CURVE

FOOT TAPERS
(MOLDING)

ROUNDED FOOT EDGE CURVE

FIGURE 5-16. *Multiple sail-shaping methods utilized simultaneously (here in a club-footed stays'l) achieve a balanced, harmonious, versatile shape.*

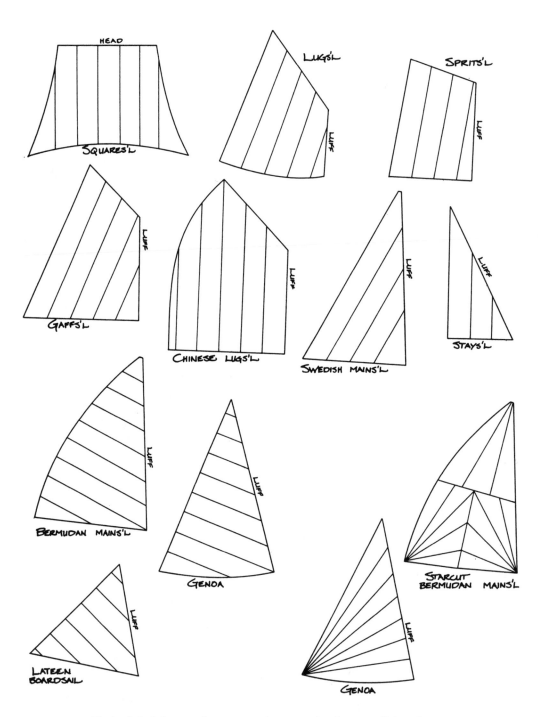

FIGURE 5-17. *Typical cloth layouts in constructions ranging from traditional to contemporary. These layouts either utilize bias elongation or attempt to minimize it.*

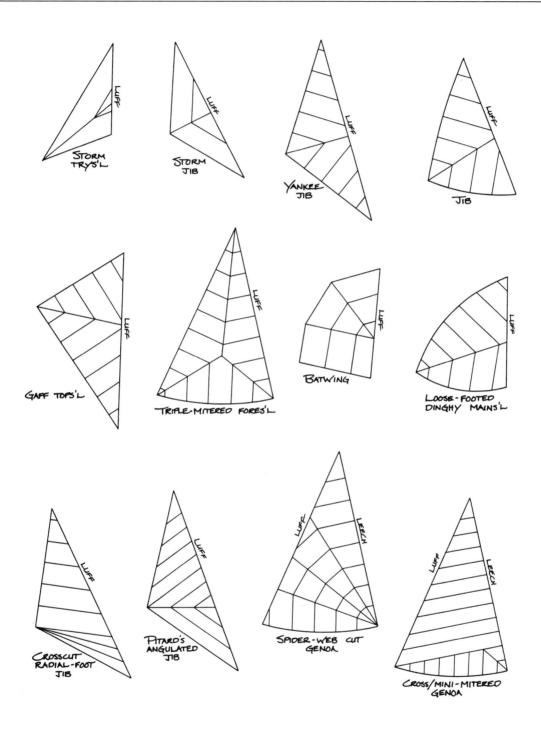

STORM TRYS'L

STORM JIB

YANKEE JIB

JIB

GAFF TOPS'L

TRIPLE-MITERED FORES'L

BATWING

LOOSE-FOOTED DINGHY MAINS'L

CROSSCUT RADIAL-FOOT JIB

PITARD'S ANGULATED JIB

SPIDER-WEB CUT GENOA

CROSS/MINI-MITERED GENOA

edges of boomless headsails. The Scotch miter survives today even with the use of synthetic sailcloths, since with the cloths running parallel to both leech and foot there are no seams striking an edge, which is important for a stormsail. The conventional miter, with cloth perpendicular to the straight-line leech and straight-line foot, though found on latter-day working craft, is a yachting convention, and one that has nearly become extinct in contemporary sailing. While the complicated and risky business of miter cutting a sail is essential in natural-fiber headsails—particularly genoas—stable synthetic cloths and economic considerations have essentially removed miter-cut sails from the scene.

The other principal consideration in the laying of the cloth is ease of broadseaming to create an airfoil shape. It was with this in mind and the idea of having the seams in the cloth running roughly parallel to and smoothly with the airflow, as well as the placement of leech strain upon the weft threads of the cloth, that N. G. Herreshoff in the 1890s developed the *cross-* or *horizontal-cut* sail. Suitable yacht-quality cotton fabrics made this possible and synthetics, in a sense, later made it obligatory.

The crosscut came to dominate sail construction—first in boomed yacht sails, then eventually in nearly all sails (with the exception of spinnakers in yachts, and of course seafaring craft around the world). Ironically, the introduction of laminated sailcloths, warp-oriented fabrics, and computer-

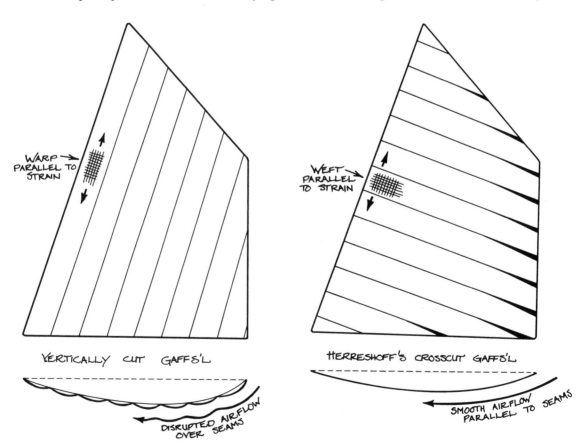

FIGURE 5-18. *Herreshoff's crosscut gaff sail reduced leech stretch, facilitated broadseaming, and produced a smoother surface in the direction of airflow.*

ized molding has brought back the vertical cut, with some variations.

Last there are the *radial cuts*—which are a synthetic-sailcloth innovation—often in multiples or combined with other cuts or partial cuts. The principle of radial construction—that of aligning warp with the fanned strain of sail corners—is sound stress distribution, but there are drawbacks:

- It is only practical with synthetics that can be cut, trimmed with a hotknife, and left unhemmed, or with very light synthetic fabrics that lend themselves to machine-folded seams.

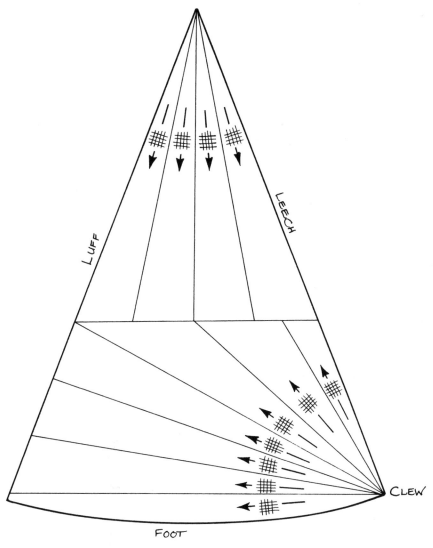

FIGURE 5-19. *This contemporary biradial genoa design aligns the warp of the cloth with the strain at head, clew, leech, and foot.*

- The more sophisticated radial patterns require complex calculations and cutting of patterns to build in a designed curvature.
- All those seams are a vulnerable aspect of this type of construction.

At one time the appearance of the Wizard of Bristol's crosscut sails was as novel as today's trend toward greater use of multiradial patterns in competitive sails and even in cruising and daysailing sails.

Although with a computer program or a kit anyone can obtain the pattern for a high-tech sail cut, the traditional cuts and their contemporary derivations lend themselves best to manual design and construction.

THE SAILMAKING PROCESS

The procedure of making sails can be broken down into several phases, with variations depending on the choice of construction techniques and the extent to which the process has been mechanized or automated. The following sequence is the traditional one, and the one an amateur would follow. This chapter presents a quick overview; the step-by-step details are in Chapter 6.

Sailmaking begins with the considerations set forth in Chapters 2 through 4: the type of sailing, the hull, the rig, the sail type, and the sail's interaction with and relationship to other sails. Peripheral measurements are then obtained either from a sail plan or from measuring the boat or the old sails.

In the design process all these factors are weighed in arriving at the desired two-dimensional, or peripheral, form (that is, the shape seen on an architect's sail plan) and the appropriate camber(s), draft placement, and distribution of curvature. Materials are selected and all construction requirements, techniques, measurements, reefs, reinforcements, and means of attachment are designated. All the materials and hardware are speci-

fied. All this is worked up in one or more scale plans that will later guide the full-size lofting.

Sails can be made in pattern pieces (rather than lofting them as a whole), such as was done in small lofts and on board ship and is now mimicked inside the circuits of a computer. But here we will loft the sail to its full-size dimensions, then assemble it from pieces laid over the full-scale plan, altered, and joined.

At this point the materials are gathered (at least the sailcloth) and any preparatory work the sailcloth may require is performed. In the case of natural-fiber materials the cloth may be aged, or dyed, and mildewproofed. Most certainly, unless the panels are quite narrow, it must be *bight,* or *false, seamed.* Depending on the woven cloth width and sail type, there may be from one to as many as three false seams sewn in per panel to minimize cloth stretch between actual seams.

Even with synthetic sailcloth—where no preservative coloring or false seaming is required—some preparation may be necessary if a cloth width narrower than commercially available is desired. Narrow synthetic cloth widths in Dacron are no longer regularly produced, though they can be special ordered for a cutting fee. Often the wide cloth is already in hand, so you must slit it down to the width you desire. There are aesthetic and tailoring reasons for using narrow cloths, as well as some shape-retention qualities when using softer fabrics.

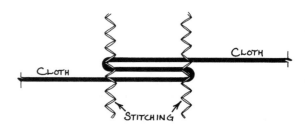

FIGURE 5-20. *A false seam in natural or very soft synthetic fabric will reduce stretch and may also enhance a sail's traditional appearance.*

FIGURE 5-21. *Peripheral measurements spiked out and twined off on the loft floor.*

Lofting

Lofting is nothing more than reproducing the sail design full size on a floor. First the endpoints (corners), the perimeters, and the edge curves, then the midpoints of each edge and the locations of deepest roach are marked. The miters, if any, are marked. The placement and direction of the cloths are marked out and reef row positions are designated. All these demarcations can be set off with spikes and string or drawn directly on the floor. (The wonderful shapes and curves of the sails lofted by the Herreshoff sailmakers can still be seen on the floor of what is now a T-shirt silk-screening company in Bristol, Rhode Island.)

Primary Layout

Over the lofted plan are laid the cloths of the sail, back and forth, overlapping by a determined seam width. Extra cloth is allowed at the panel ends for use as tablings and also to compensate for the cloth consumed by broadseaming. Each piece of the sail is marked as to location and relationship to its neighbors so that the pieces may be reassembled and sewn evenly. All the corners are marked, and the sail is ready to be sewn. With the plan entirely covered by cloth and the panels aligned, the broadseams are drawn and possibly trimmed.

Alternatively, the cloths can be stuck together with double-sided sticky tape while on the floor. Then the sail as a whole is aligned with the floor plan and the secondary layout (drawing of edge curves, marking of tablings, etc.) is begun, leaving the seaming and secondary machine work to be done at the same time. There is some advantage to doing this:

1. You get to see how smooth and fair a job you have done of broadseaming.
2. The sewing of the seams will be as even as the accuracy with which you stuck the seams together.

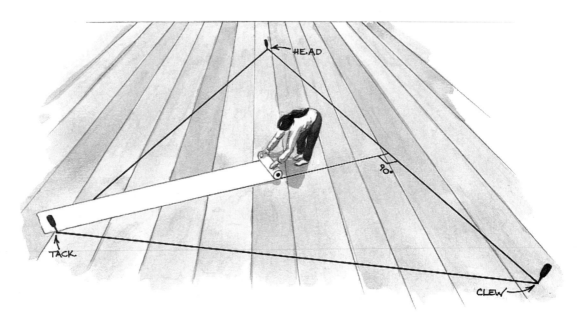

FIGURE 5-22. *In a crosscut sail the first panel, or cloth, is laid along the tack seam, which is the perpendicular from tack to leech.*

3. You need not roll up the individual cloths and make the extra trip to the sewing machine required to sew separate cloths accurately.
4. You have some advance indication of the shape and edge support you have tailored into the sail and can make corrections prior to trimming and sewing.

On the other hand:

1. You have the challenge of horsing the full sail through the machine as you seam it up, though on small or light sails this is not a problem.
2. You deny yourself the opportunity to learn how to really sew a seam.

Seaming

If the sail has not been prestuck, the next step is the *seaming*, in which the panels are taken cloth by cloth to the machine and sewn together. If the sail

is hand sewn, then it is better to piece it together with sticky tape or pins cloth by cloth as you assemble the sail. A full sail of prepinned cloths would be too unwieldy to handle. Seaming, even with a machine, is time-consuming, and the quality of the job will have a pronounced effect on the durability and appearance of the sail. Various contrivances exist to expedite and facilitate the job: special seaming machines, seam pullers, sliding tables, moving machines, and sunken floor-level seaming-machine pits, as well as cloth chutes and tables.

Secondary Layout

Once a sail is seamed up it is laid out over the plan and realigned with endpoints and cloth direction. It may be necessary to tension and smooth the seams in order to even out the stitch tension. The sail is pinned out as naturally as possible over the plan, the edge curves are drawn with long battens or tape, and tablings are marked and cut. It is

FIGURE 5-23. *Once the cloths are all laid out and either sticky-taped or sewn together with broadseams in place, all edge curves and tablings are drawn and cut. Here a leech curve with its tabling is being drawn. By resting the point of a compass against the batten and keeping the angle of compass to batten constant, you can trace lines parallel to the batten for the tabling and cut edge.*

always a thrill to finally cut the last edge; at that point the sail ceases to look like a bunch of strips sewn together.

The drawing of edge curves takes a good eye for form and fairness, the accuracy of which greatly affects the sail shape. Needless to say, a well-drawn curve may be lost in haphazard cutting.

Reefs are drawn. Corner patches are drawn and the pieces made up, and tablings are folded or rubbed under.

Finish Sewing

The sail is now taken back to the sewing machine or bench and all the added cloth reinforcements are sewn down. At this time any added reinforcements or sail controls, such as internal luff ropes or leech and foot cords, are installed. With the com-

pletion of this phase the sail is a whole entity in its finished form. There are no cut cloth edges left exposed, except for the extreme corners, which will be finished by hand.

Handwork

Handwork, or *finishwork,* both reinforces the sail and provides its means of attachment. All eyelets, corner rings, and cringles are installed. Luff ropes are spliced and seized. Boltropes are sewn. Reef points are installed and chafing gear is sewn. Hanks and slides are seized. It varies—some combination of these things: holes to attach things to the sail, edge reinforcements, and means of attaching sail to spar or wire. Much finishwork formerly done by hand is now done by machine.

I continually deceive myself by thinking that

when a sail is brought over for handwork it is almost done. Actually, depending on the sail, it may be less than half done, given all the labor that is required in finishing a sail by hand. By the time you get around to sewing that last leather and reef nettle, that sail is a pretty familiar—not to say tedious—article. What a joy to be folding it up at last and putting it in the bag!

Preservation

But we're not done yet, at least if it is a natural-fiber sail. For voyaging or working purposes the sail ought to be treated—dressed down with a preservative process to prevent organic rot and deterioration. Although sailcloth can be treated prior to making the sail, often it is left to treat the finished sail—boltrope, reinforcements, and all. More on this and the risks in Chapter 8, "Sail Care and Maintenance."

Bending Sail

The last task for the sailmaker is to bend sail and test it. Some lofts have test spars—indoors or out or both. Some sailmakers insist on bending their sails out on the water. This is by far the best approach. The sailmaker is then assured that the sails are bent correctly; adjustments can be made, and flaws and successes can be noted. Experience is acquired also, as the sailmaker profits from the continuity of involvement with the whole process and is not relying on secondhand information or feedback. Photographs can record the shapes. Bending sail on the water provides the opportunity for as much experimentation and exposure to various conditions as possible. I wish that more sailmakers actually handled their products. How often does a sailmaker test-sail a stormsail?

Followup

It is not unusual for a sail to be returned for alteration—perhaps immediately after an initial test sail, or later, as it takes time for some problems to reveal themselves. In competitive sailing, sails undergo repeated alteration, perhaps several times during a particular race series or season. A sail-maker must be reconciled to a certain amount of this and actually welcome the opportunity to correct and improve a sail. Minor alterations are one thing; major recuts may be nearly as time-consuming as building a whole new sail. Of course, even the most perfect and well-made sails receive routine maintenance, protection, and storage.

SAILMAKING MATERIALS

Sailmaking entails an aesthetic sense of proportion—bigger is not always better.

A timeline of major turning points in the making of sails would include the first cultivation of cotton, flax, and hemp; the discovery and use of bronze and iron for sail hardware; the evolution of the weaving loom; mechanization of weaving and ropemaking; the abolition of slavery; the development of wire rope; the invention of the sewing machine (first with treadles, then electrically powered); the advent of steam-driven shipping; the development of synthetic sailcloth and cordage; the use of computers in sail design and manufacture; and the development of laminated sailcloth materials. Meanwhile, in less than a century, the relatively unmechanized world of sail-dependent water-borne commerce, with its supportive sail-material industries, has been transformed into a highly centralized, mechanized, industrial economy with a very small but high-tech industry dedicated to the making of materials primarily for pleasure sailing.

Materials such as wool, cotton, flax, Orlon, linen, hemp, and manila have become obsolete in a very short period of time. It is disconcerting, to say the least, that synthetic sail materials developed within my lifetime—such as Dacron—are now considered "traditional." It has nothing to do with tradition and everything to do with marketing. Regardless, materials cease to be manufactured and gradually disappear. The trick now is to blend materials and techniques from different eras within the confines of budget, material availability, ease of construction, and material compatibility.

Except in the least valued of sails, it is false economy—not to mention dangerous—to use materials of inferior quality. At best, sailing performance and sail longevity suffer. At worst, there may be loss of life and vessel. This does not mean, however, that one is compelled to pay exorbitant prices for best-quality conventional materials. There are *unconventional* means of obtaining

DINGHY SAILCLOTH

Q: *I am building an 11-foot dinghy and its 75-square-foot sail. What sort of sailcloth do you suggest I use?*

A: The principal considerations are: availability, cost, your sailmaking skills, sail and rig type, intended use of the boat, and maintenance. Competitive and highly refined traditional sail construction—to mention two extremes—require costly materials—either synthetic or natural—and a high degree of skill and aptitude. The most convenient source of materials would be a sail loft that specializes in either of those kinds of sailmaking.

Is this your first shot at making a sail? Are you interested in exploring all facets of the art, or do you mostly just want to get the show on the water? Perfectly acceptable sails may be made from Tyvek, polyethylene tarps, London Fog raincoat material, bag nylon, or tent canvas—not to mention old sails. Tarp or Tyvek sails may be taped together and require no sewing. These are good materials for preliminary experimentation.

Typically, a noncompetitive cat dinghy rig—sprit, gunter, lug, or sprit boom—makes the best use of a sail that derives its shape from rig adjustments rather than a sail with a molded, comparatively fixed form. This means relatively soft, unstable, woven cloth. In the realm of manufactured sailcloth, your best bet is a soft 3.9-ounce Dacron available in colors from black to bubble gum. I know of no 4- to 5-ounce cotton sailcloth that has not been treated with toxic preservatives. Nonsailcloth cottons such as the rather heavy 10-ounce Vivatex, however, offer a durable, natural material that, with minimal expertise, expense, and labor, can be made into a functional and forgiving sail.

unconventional materials: affordable materials that are adequate, reliable, and functional, if not classic in appearance. These may be seconds, or scrounged, or adapted from nonnautical applications. Platt Monfort of Wiscasset, Maine, has made a splash by using Tyvek, a Du Pont (ironically the source of conventional sail fiber) building insulation material, as sail "cloth."

So, though it is often maintained that there is a "proper" way of making sails and rigging, and it is true that some conventions have withstood the test of time, there are also innovations that may be more easily accomplished at less cost and in less time, just as successfully.

There are five basic groups of materials of which sails are made, though not every sail will include all five. Sailcloth, sail twine/sewing thread, and hardware are certain; cordage of some sort is likely, but not essential; and wire rope now is least likely to be found. In addition many sails incorporate leather or webbing, and sometimes both.

Sailcloth

Dacron   The roots of contemporary sailcloth production extend far below the sail-loft floor; indeed, the sailcloth tree has its fine little root hairs in petroleum, from which E. I. Du Pont de Nemours & Co. derives the polymers, filaments, and films used in synthetic sails. Polyethylene tetraphthalate, a polyester called Dacron, has for the last 40 years been the mainstay of sailcloths, accompanied by nylon and now augmented by Mylar, Kevlar, and Spectra. What's manufactured in the United States as Dacron is produced around the globe in slight variations on the same formula under the names Teteron in Japan, Tergal in France, Terylene in Britain, Terital in Italy, Trevira and Diolen in Germany, and Terlenka in Holland. These are all registered trademarks, which means the monopolization and ownership of processes, filaments, and names. All U.S.-made Dacron sailcloth originates at one source of filaments: Du Pont.

Dacron, or any sail-fabric filament, is bundled, then twisted together, forming a yarn. The size,

strength, and character of a yarn are specified by *denier* (the weight in grams of 9,000 meters of yarn), twist per inch of yarn, break factor, moisture content, and photographic appearance. Yarns can be plied together for still greater strength.

The yarns next travel to the weaver to be woven into fabric in one of the two mills in the United States producing Dacron or nylon sailcloth. Up to this point, sailmakers can have some influence on the type of cloth available through the specification of yarn, denier, and tenacity. But now the particular qualities of a fabric are further defined by its construction—that is, the relationship of warp yarns to weft, or fill, yarns in relative number (quantity), denier, tenacity, and tension. Then there is the manner of the weaving, which dictates how tightly the yarns are packed together and the balance of crimp: the degree to which one set of yarns has to porpoise-dive over and under the other set of yarns. To a certain extent the greater crimp inherent in unbalanced constructions renders a fabric less stable on the bias. One cannot help but be awestruck by the power, speed, and quality controls in the production of this fabric—so tightly woven, in such great quantities, and under such rigid conditions is it produced.

Unless they happen to be doing the finishing of the sailcloth—which is the exception rather than the rule—sailmakers only have indirect influence up to this point on the nature of the fabric; they tell finishers and distributors what they are looking for and then the finishers and distributors, if it is economically worth their while, pass those desires on to the weaver in the form of construction specifications. You and I could say we want a particular construction, weight, and finish of fabric—but unless we can purchase several thousand yards, the finisher/distributor can't do it. None of the other cloth manufacturers are charitable institutions either, which is why you see the currently available fabrics and not others.

Untreated and unfinished Dacron fabric, though much more tightly woven and of different fiber characteristics, is not a whole lot more stable than a natural-fiber fabric. Duradon sailcloth in its finished form resembles unfinished Dacron sail-cloth in its stability.

So, the truck loaded with these greige goods rolls into any of the three sailcloth-finishing firms in the United States, or their equivalents in any other country. Now the finisher/distributor takes over with the finishing process, which renders a particular fabric into its final form and characteristics; it will then be marketed under various names and promotions. Finishing and distribution may occur in the same or separate locations. And the various finishers/distributors may have sailcloth finished to their specifications by other finishers/distributors and then market it under their own label and product name! These greige goods arrive at the finisher/distributor grungy with grease and lubricants from the weaving process. They look rather like your white sails might if you used them as truck tarps for a couple of years—impressive, especially compared with what they ultimately become.

Some shrinking and tightening occurs when the greige goods are scoured for several hours back and forth through a soap and hot-water solution. The cloth is then dried. But two basic steps in the ensuing process elevate this woven fabric into the realm of stability expected of woven synthetic sailcloth. The first is heat shrinkage, which locks warp and weft yarns even more tightly together. The second is impregnation and coating with resin, which fills any spaces and still further interlocks the weave. All this is done to minimize bias elongation, the major instability of any woven fabric.

If the fabric is to be dyed, it is done now with the cloth rolled up tightly about a holed cylinder through which the dye, under great pressure, is forced into the layers of cloth. Dyeing has no adverse effect on nylon, but because polyester fibers must be treated with strong chemicals in order to offer the color molecules a place to adhere, there is a reduction in fiber strength. Therefore tanbark-colored cloth, relatively speaking, has a lower strength-to-weight ratio than an undyed Dacron of otherwise identical characteristics. In the scheme of things, and given the type of sailing one is likely to be doing under tanbark sails, this is no big deal.

Again the cloth is dried over steamheated cans, and more shrinkage occurs in the drying. Once thoroughly dried, the cloth is ready for finishing.

THE RESINATION PROCESS. In the process of impregnation the cloth is passed through a trough of typically 20- to 30-percent melamine solution. The solution, which is chemically similar to the Dacron yarn, will later, when heated, form a tighter weave of greater stretch resistance.

In the subsequent process, a urethane resin is squeegeed over the cloth with a great steel knife. This coating fills all the spaces in the weave, smoothes the surface, and will, when heated, cement the fibers together. It is this step in particular that influences the "hand," or feel of softness, in the cloth—all according to the degree of resination. All the Dacron fabrics, even the softest of cruising cloths, have been resinated to some degree. The amount of resin has great influence on the pucker factor in sewing—more resin, less pucker, which is what you want. Unfortunately, that means the stuff that's easiest to handle as a sail is difficult to work with in the sailmaking.

Now, if you were to embark on the making of a sail and obtained a bolt of cloth, you'd notice not only that it is accompanied by disclaimers of responsibility (in case you should build yourself a winged suit and leap off the Eiffel Tower), but there is also a little tag that suggests some concern about formaldehyde in the cloth and its effect on your health. The formaldehyde is part of the resinating process—more resin, more formaldehyde. Emission levels are tested at the machines and proper curing is supposed to bring the levels down to a safe zone. Odor inhibitors are introduced to mask the smell, but it can be a scary cloud of fumes that emanates from a roll of cloth and up from the fabric as you try to build a sail—hence the little tag.

HEAT SETTING. Moving on at the finishing plant: The resinated cloth now undergoes the dramatic and essential process of heat setting. It is during this phase, as the cloth passes over drums heated to 400°F, that the resins are cured and the cloth experiences the greatest and final shrinkage—around 20 percent. Greige goods that started out about 47 inches wide will have shrunk, after heat setting, to close to 38 inches in width!

Next the cloth is given a Rolfing of sorts called a "button break," in which the fabric is passed over and under bumpy rollers to flex and stabilize the cloth.

Last, and very important, the fabric is *calendered*—that is, ironed between tremendous steel rollers that exert 50 tons of heated compression. This step flattens and tightens the weave and locks the fibers.

Before the cloth can be sold for sails it must be trimmed to the finished width, and typically a sew- to line is drawn an arbitrary seam width in from the selvages.

INSPECTION AND TESTING.   Now the cloth is inspected, graded, and tested. Fifteen yards of cloth are rolled out on a flat inspection table and checked for waviness along the edges and in the middle— and for straightness. This straightness factor is called *tracking,* and a cloth that arcs more than ⅛ inch is said to be "tracked" and of lesser quality. The frustrations of working with tracked cloth are explored in Chapter 6, "Making Your Own Sails."

The testing of all cloth, especially sailcloth, is a complex process in itself. There are many possible tests, but only a few are done routinely and the results passed on to the sailmaker. It is valuable to understand and be able to interpret the sailcloth specifications derived from these tests—leastways, it is good to know what works for your needs so

TABLE 5-2.

DACRON FINISHES AND SPECS (ADAPTED FROM CHALLENGE SAILCLOTH)

WEIGHT	DIAMOND SET DACRON	SUPER FIRM	FIRM	MEDIUM FIRM	MEDIUM	SOFT
4 OZ.	2-4	4-9	5-15	6-20	7-25	8-36
5 OZ.	2-4	3-7	3-10	3.5-15	3.5-20	3.5-28
6 OZ.	1.5-3.5	2-7	2-10	2-15	2-20	2.5-28
7 OZ.	1-3	1-7	1.5-10	2-15	2-20	2-28
8 OZ.		1-7	1-10	1-15	1.5-20	1.5-28
9 OZ.		1-7	1-10	1-15	1-20	1.5-28

NOTE: THE SECOND NUMBER IS THE BIAS, OR 45-DEGREE STRETCH AT 10 POUNDS OF LOAD. THE FIRST NUMBER IS THE FILL (90-DEGREE), OR IN THE CASE OF A VERTICAL FABRIC, THE WARP (0-DEGREE) STRETCH.

that you can specify or identify a cloth that will work to your satisfaction. Following are some of the tests and measurements that may be performed on sailcloth fabrics:

- *Porosity/air permeability test:* Measures the rate of airflow through a fabric. Valuable in determining how effective a sailcloth is in separating differing air pressures, and, conversely, how breathable a bag or cover fabric is. Rate of flow is measured in cubic feet of air per minute.
- *Water-resistance test:* The resistance of the fabric to the flow of water by capillary action.
- *Fabric width:* Measured as the perpendicular distance from selvage to selvage, to the nearest ¹⁄₁₆ inch.
- *Fabric bow:* Expressed as a percentage of the fabric width, this is the deviation of the weft (fill) threads measured to the nearest ¹⁄₁₆ inch from an imaginary line drawn perpendicularly from selvage to selvage. Any bow in sailcloth is important. For example, in a crosscut mainsail, those bowed weft threads, running parallel to the leech, would straighten out—elongate—under stress, thus messing up the set of the leech and causing the boom to sag. Duradon sailcloth often has a serious amount of bow to it that has to be allowed for in either the measurements or the cut of the sail.
- *Gauge:* This is the fabric thickness, expressed in thousandths of an inch.
- *Warp and weft count:* The count of the fabric is the number of warp *ends* or fill *picks* per inch of fabric. These specs reveal the tightness of the weave and, accompanied by information about the yarns, also indicate cloth strength in either direction or in relation to one another.
- *Tensile, or breaking, strength:* The measure of the ability of the fabric to resist rupture when tested under specified conditions.

- *Elongation:* The amount of stretch at break compared with the original length, expressed as a percentage.
- *Stretch-and-set test:* This test is designed to measure the initial elongation of a fabric sample under specified loading conditions, and the amount of retained elongation, or set, after removal of the load. These and related tests yield the cloth specs most readily available to the sailmaker and are the ones that reveal so much about how sailcloth will feel and behave.

Tests are conducted in three directions—warp, fill, and on the bias—with specified amounts of stress—usually 10 to 50 pounds in 10-pound increments on 16-inch-by-2-inch test samples of cloth. The resulting elongation is expressed in hundredths of an inch.

All these specs are revealing, but it is the bias spec that tells the most about whether a cloth is stable, and if so, whether that stability is attributable primarily to cloth construction and tight weaving or to resination. That in turn tells you whether a cloth is likely to feel like a pillowcase or a piece of sheet metal. The warp and fill specs reveal yarn quality, cloth construction, and quality of weaving, which translates into sail shape-holding ability under stress and over time.

A variation on this study is the *stress-strain test,* which applies a load (stress) to a material; the resultant stretch (strain) is measured in order to derive a ratio between the two, called the *modulus of elasticity.* A material with a high modulus of elasticity will elongate less than a material with a lower modulus of elasticity.

These tests also demonstrate the amount of what is called *recovery* in a fabric, which is the cloth's elastic ability to return from a degree of elongation after load has been removed.

Bainbridge/Aquabatten subjectively correlates bias specifications with cloth feel in the following manner:

very firm—under 10
firm—over 10, under 13
medium firm—over 13, under 18
soft—over 18
"Finn"—34–38

I personally would shift that scale so that "soft" was in the 34 to 38 range.

- *Flutter test and impact flutter test:* This is an extension of the stretch-and-set test and is conducted after a cloth sample has been given the kind of workout one could expect to give a sail over a reasonable time. A sample is whirled around at about 30 m.p.h. for 30 minutes at the end of a pole on an electric motor. Specifications are then designed as "after fatigue" or "after flutter" and reveal what the cloth will do under load after the resination has been broken in.
- *Tearing strength test:* Measures the force required to start and continue a tear under specified conditions. These tests are also conducted on warp and fill. Though the tests are conducted on the same machine, tearing strength is different from breaking, or tensile, strength. This is apparent in a sail where weak—say, sunrotten—material can have sufficient breaking strength to withstand a fair amount of wind if the sail is whole, but little or no tearing strength to resist being torn to shreds if punctured or already torn. A sail with little tearing strength can be torn apart by its own stitching holes and components!
- *Fabric weight:* The weight of fabric expressed as ounces per linear yard, ounces per given width, or pounds per yard. This becomes a little confusing, as what's called a "sailmaker's yard" in the United States measures 36 inches by 28½ inches, and

fabric weight for U.S.-made sailcloth refers to ounces per sailmaker's yard. All U.S. manufacturers list their sailcloths by this system. Elsewhere in the world sailcloth fabric weight is expressed in grams per square meter. In the United Kingdom sailcloth weight is designated in ounces per square yard.

- *Crimp:* The loss in straight-line length of a yarn when it is woven, expressed as a percentage of the final woven length.
- *Contraction:* The loss in straight-line length of a yarn when it is woven, expressed as a percentage of the length before weaving.
- *Abrasion tests:* Used to measure the resistance of fabric to wear. There are three tests:

1. flat abrasion—chafe abrading a fabric parallel to its surface;
2. flex abrasion—reciprocal folding and rubbing of a fabric;
3. edge abrasion—rubbing in one or all directions on the edge of a fabric.

This information is pertinent to the sailor/sailmaker who needs to utilize materials of high chafe resistance—or at least protect vulnerable fabrics from rigging chafe. Abrasion tests on sailcloth are performed particularly to determine the durability of the coating that has been applied for stability and ultraviolet resistance.

- *Sewability test:* Sewability is the characteristic of a fabric that allows it to be seamed at the full limit of performance of a high-speed sewing machine without weakening or degrading the fabric. Tests may also be conducted to determine the extent to which sewing causes a fabric to pucker.
- *Stiffness test:* The stiffness of a fabric is its resistance to bending when an external force is applied. Bias elongation specs give you some indication of this, but are not

conclusive. The nature of the cloth construction and weave can have a significant effect on the feel of the cloth: A warp-oriented cloth that specs out quite low can have a very different feel from an equally low-spec fill-oriented cloth. Manufacturers frequently forgo a stiffness test.

- *Wrinkle recovery test:* The ability of a fabric to recover from creasing and compression under controlled conditions. This is another test that would be useful but is generally not conducted on sailcloth because the results can be inferred from other tests: a low stretch spec indicates that a fabric wrinkles and stays wrinkled, at least if it's a heavily resinated fabric. Wrinkle recovery specs would indicate the care required in folding a sail, and also how smooth an aerodynamic surface would remain after a sail had been used and stored.

Fabrics may be tested still further for bursting strength, moisture content, thermal resistance, and UV resistance. This last concern is of great importance in estimating the durability of synthetic sail and cover cloths. Stretch and strength tests are conducted on samples of cloth that have been exposed to ultraviolet light in a lab—or left out in tropical sunlight—for a set period of time. The resistance of various fibers, dyes, and cloth weights to ultraviolet light and the effectiveness of UV protective screens and coatings are determined.

Nylon and Duradon Nylon and Duradon sailcloths go through a different but similar production process to that described for Dacron, and all the tests apply as well, though cloth specs are not routinely published.

Mylar, Kevlar, and Laminated Fabrics Laminated sail fabrics, which may be composites, woven substrates, scrims, and films, are a whole other realm worth a glance—partly to know what's available for the cruiser-racer or boardsailor, and partly because there's a move on to make laminates the dominant sail material.

Briefly, what are called *cruising laminates* combine the virtues of a low-stretch, bias-free, high strength-to-weight-ratio film, like Mylar, with the virtues of a highly tear-resistant woven substrate material, like Dacron, to make a relatively lightweight, stronger, more stable, high strength-to-weight fabric that is soft enough to be acceptable to the casual or nonracer who wants sail shape retention over a wide wind range—such as a roller-reefing headsail or a mainsail requires.

The trick in developing these expensive high-tech sandwiches has been to get the laminations to adhere to each other for a reasonable period of time. For this, what's called a *peel test* is conducted to measure the strength of the bond between a film and its substrate. In addition to the standard elongation specs based on stretch per given pounds of load, specs for laminates are computed based on pounds of load per 1 percent of elongation, which yields what is called the *efficiency coefficient.*

Natural-Fiber Sailcloth Isn't it amazing that in the same breath and within a mere five decades we can be talking about sailcloth technologies that are light-years apart? And cotton and flax sailcloth is still manufactured by the firm of Francis Webster and Son in Arbroath, Scotland! In certain respects the production of natural fabric is not all that different from the production of synthetics. Of course, the acquisition of the fiber is different, but it's still a matter of fiber and quality, yarns, design, cloth construction, and weaving techniques. It is true that cotton sailcloth woven too softly has poor shape-holding characteristics—even for cotton— yet, on the other hand, when woven too tightly cotton is unresponsive and lifeless.

The terminology is the same, but the finishing after weaving marks the greatest difference between the production of natural-fiber and synthetic sailcloth. Sizings and mildewproofing may be added, but there is no heating or coating and no trimming, since the edges are true woven selvages. Shrinkage does occur, particularly in preshrunk marine fabrics, but it is not nearly the percentage of heat-set Dacron, nor does it tighten the weave as dramatically. The cloth is calendered—and that's it, prior to conducting nearly all the same tests and inspections just described.

The Seafarer's Sailcloth   In the late 1940s one of the earliest synthetic fibers experimented with

for sails was Orlon. Nylon and Dacron quickly elbowed Orlon aside because it could not be heat shrunk and was three times stretchier than the softest Dacron. Orlon, in spun form, is the acrylic of which marine cover cloths are made; it thumbs its nose at ultraviolet light.

A practically invulnerable seafaring sailcloth—

STYLE	WEIGHT	FILL DENIER	PICKS/IN.	WARP DENIER	ENDS/IN.
ALL PURPOSE					
5170	4.0 oz.	300	63	150	104
5210	5.0 oz.	300	66	150	133
5260	6.0 oz.	495	48	250	117
5300	7.0 oz.	595	45	250	117
5340	8.0 oz.	750	44	250	133
5390	9.0 oz.	800	38	300	133
BLADE					
5155	3.5 oz.	180	75	130	114
5225	5.3 oz.	260	67	180	138
5255	6.7 oz.	500	49	250	117
5335	7.7 oz.	500	48	250	130
5375	8.7 oz.	750	42	300	132
5425	9.7 oz.	750	36	500	93
HIGH ASPECT					
5217	5.0 oz.	410	53	130	150
5277	6.3 oz.	410	58	180	140
5297	7.0 oz.	750	42	180	140
5327	7.7 oz.	750	44	260	108
5367	9.0 oz.	750	41	260	140
WARP					
5129	3.0 oz.	130	72	130	127
5219	5.0 oz.	180	76	180	163
5279	7.0 oz.	260	57	495	149
5389	9.0 oz.	410	54	750	61

TABLE 5-3A. *Sati/USA Dacron cloth constructions. The recommended uses for these cloth styles are listed in Tables 5-3B (page 159) and 5-3C (page 160). Other sailcloth manufacturers/distributors provide similar specification criteria.*

superior even to Duradon—could be produced of a tightly woven filament Orlon. Filament Orlon must be solution dyed in the yarn, but strength tests after six months' exposure in the tropics revealed that acrylic retained 95 percent of its strength, as opposed to Dacron's retaining only 25 percent.

In terms of the voyaging or workboat's sailing and economic needs, the virtues of an Orlon sail far outweigh the drawbacks—even the word *Orlon* has a rather pleasant singsong quality to it, for a synthetic. Anyway, it could be done. The problem

lies not in making the cloth; the big obstacle is the quantities necessary to make it economically feasible for a manufacturer to produce.

Sailcloth Types It would be an exercise in futility to attempt a presentation of all the various types of Dacron or nylon sailcloths available—not to mention the laminates. The various combinations of yarn, constructions, and finish are myriad, and every company has its own set of combinations. Not only is any combination possible, if you can

TABLE 5-3B.

DACRON CLOTH APPLICATIONS—MAINSAILS
(ADAPTED FROM SATI SAILCLOTH)

BOAT SIZE	TYPE	PANEL CONFIGURATION	HIGH-ASPECT	LOW-ASPECT
20'–26'	RACE	VERTICAL HORIZONTAL	5V 5M–6.3M	5V–6AP 5.3B–6B
	CRUISE	VERTICAL HORIZONTAL	5V–6AP 5AP–6AP–5.3B–6.3M	5AP–6AP 5.3B–6B–6AP
27'–32'	RACE	VERTICAL HORIZONTAL	7V 6.3M–7M	7V 6B–7.3B
	CRUISE	VERTICAL HORIZONTAL	6AP–7AP–7V 6.3M–7M–7AP	7B–7V–8AP 7AP–7.3B–7M
33'–38'	RACE	VERTICAL HORIZONTAL	7V–7AP 7M–7.7M	7V–8.4B 7.3B–8.4B–7AP–8AP
	CRUISE	VERTICAL HORIZONTAL	7V–7AP–7.3B 7AP–8AP–7M–7.7M	7V–9V 7.3B–8.4B–7AP–8AP
39'–45'	RACE	VERTICAL HORIZONTAL	9V 7.7M–9M	7.7M–9V–8AP 8.4B–9.7B
	CRUISE	VERTICAL HORIZONTAL	9V–9AP 8AP–9AP–9M	8AP–9AP–9V 8AP–9AP–8.4B–9.7B
46'–50'	RACE	VERTICAL HORIZONTAL	9V–5V(2-PLY) 9M–5M (2-PLY)	9V–5V(2-PLY) 9.7B–5B(2-PLY) 9M–5M (2-PLY)
	CRUISE	VERTICAL HORIZONTAL	9V–5V(2-PLY) 9AP–5AP(2-PLY)	9V–5V(2-PLY) 9.7B–6AP(2-PLY)

SYMBOLS: AP = ALL PURPOSE; V = VERTICAL/WARP; B = BLADE; M = MAIN (HIGH ASPECT, ALL PURPOSE). ALL CLOTH NUMBERS REFER TO WEIGHT IN U.S. OUNCES.

afford to have it made, but also, by the time you finish reading this book, probably some cloth will have fallen by the wayside and several "new" sailcloths will be on the market!

So saying, and evolution and planned obsolescence not withstanding, five major categories of Dacron sailcloth have been routinely used for a while now by cloth manufacturers and will likely continue to be used, at least while Dacron remains a major sailcloth. Although the sailcloth companies may use the same generic term for a type of cloth, there may be significant variations from one firm to another as to what the term represents. Nonetheless, these categories do indicate preferences for certain combinations of yarn quality, denier, yarn count, cloth construction, and finish.

- *All-purpose:* Usually means a relatively balanced but slightly fill-oriented construction, with no particular emphasis on tightness of weave or quality of yarn. In other words, it is not a performance fabric.

TABLE 5-3C.

DACRON CLOTH APPLICATIONS — HEADSAILS
(ADAPTED FROM SATI SAILCLOTH)

Boat Size	Type	Panel Configuration	#1	#2	#3
20'-26'	Race	Vertical Horizontal	3V 3.5B-4.8B	5V 4.8B-5.3B	5V 5.3B-5M
	Cruise	Vertical Horizontal	3V-5V 4AP-5AP-4.8B	5V-5AP 4.8B-5.3B-5AP	5V-5AP 5.3B-5AP
27-32	Race	Vertical Horizontal	5V 4.8B-5.3B	5V-6AP 6B	7V 6B-6.3M
	Cruise	Vertical Horizontal	5V-5AP-6AP 5.3B-6B-5AP-6AP	5V-6AP 6B-6AP	7V-7AP 6B-6AP
33'-38'	Race	Vertical Horizontal	7V 6B-7.3B	7V-7AP 7.3B-7AP	7V 7.3B-7M-7.7M
	Cruise	Vertical Horizontal	5V-7V 6B-7.3B-7AP	7V-7AP 7.3B-7AP	7V-7AP 7.3B-7AP
39'-45'	Race	Vertical Horizontal	7V 7.3B-8.4B	9V-8AP 84B	9V 8AP-8.4B-9M
	Cruise	Vertical Horizontal	7V 7.3B-7AP	9V-9AP 8.4B-8AP	9V-9AP 9AP-8.4B-9.7B
46'-50'	Race	Vertical Horizontal	7V-7AP 7.3B-8.4B	9V 9.7B-5M (2-PLY)	9V-5V(2-PLY) 9.7B-9M
	Cruise	Vertical Horizontal	7V-7AP 7.3B-7V	9V-5V(2-PLY) 9.7B-9AP-5AP(2-PLY)	9V-9AP-5V(2-PLY) 9AP-9.7B-6AP(2-PLY)

NOTE: #3 OR BLADE JIB SHOULD BE SIMILAR IN WEIGHT TO THE MAINSAIL. #1 = LARGEST GENOA. #3 = STORM SAIL. SYMBOLS ARE AS USED IN MAINSAIL CHART ABOVE.

It has more or less universal applications in terms of sail type and cut, and it may be lower in price. It is this designation of fabric that is often dyed or coated and sold as a colored or treated cloth with its own name, such as Tanbark or All-Purpose Colors or UV Sailcloth.

- *Blade:* Often indicates a slightly fill-oriented construction of higher-quality yarns, with a significant amount of resination for stability. It is appropriate for use in crosscut, low-aspect sails.
- *High-aspect:* Clearly represents a highly fill-oriented, unbalanced construction of high-tenacity yarns. It is tightly woven and will be heavily stabilized with resins. It is a performance fabric intended for use in high-aspect-ratio crosscut sails where there is high stress on the leech.
- *Genoa:* This is a fairly balanced construction, more dependent on high-quality yarns and a tight weave for its stability than on heavy resination. It is intended for use primarily in low-aspect headsails, where loading in traditional sail cuts requires balanced stress response. This type of construction—or close to it—is probably the most appropriate Dacron sailcloth available for gaff and other four-sided sails that depend on significant bias elongation and give for shape control.
- *Warp-oriented,* or *vertical-oriented:* These fabrics range from a balanced warp-and-fill denier to having slightly heavier warp yarns and a warp-oriented construction. The degree of finish—balanced denier, yet high warp count with heavy finish—yields a fabric of minimum pucker in sewing that may be used for either cruising or racing vertical cuts—such as for roller-furling sails—and in the various radial sail cuts and corner patches where the warp will be running parallel to the stress. Cruising laminates may also be warp-oriented in that the scrim or substrate fabric is stronger in the warp direction.

TABLE 5-4.

SAILCLOTH WIDTHS

CLOTH	AVAILABLE WIDTHS
DACRON	36", 48", 54", OR CUSTOM SLIT TO ANY WIDTH
NYLON	41", 54"
DURADON	24"
COTTON	36", 38", 53", 51"
VIVATEX COTTON	36"
COTTON NUMBER DUCK	36", 48", 60", 72"

Sailcloth Width An old-timer named Henry Brown, whose family had been making sails on the Chesapeake for three generations, once said to me that any sail with cloths wider than 24 inches looked like a bedsheet. He was right, of course, and it is incredible to think that in so short a time sails have gone from 9-inch bight-seamed panels to the 54-inch full-size bedsheet dimensions of the wide Dacron sailcloth available now. Aesthetics aside, wider cloth certainly offers the sailmaker economic advantages, but these widths only work well with contemporary cloth constructions and finishes, currently popular sail cuts and types, and contemporary sailmaking techniques. However, as the ever-optimistic prince of old-school sailmaking Grant Gambell points out, "These new wide cloths—if you can find one you like—can be slit in half, and there you are back to pretty near the old cotton cloth widths."

Sail Twine and Thread

The panels of a sail and all the sail's reinforcements are united by sewing. The thread used for the purpose when sewing by hand is called *sail twine;* it is generally made of the same fiber as the cloth or a compatible natural or synthetic fiber. So in the synthetic sail, twine will be either a polyester or nylon, and in the natural-fabric sail, cotton, linen, or hemp. It is acceptable to use synthetic twine on a natural sail, but generally not the other way around.

Commercial sail twine comes in spools, is sold by weight (ounces and pounds), and is gauged by the number of *plies*—that is, threads within the twine—which may range from three to seven. Natural-fiber twine is waxed before sewing, which serves to unite the plies and to preserve the fiber. Synthetics do not require waxing for preservation, but waxing does hold the twine together and ease sewing; thus, both natural and synthetic twines are available prewaxed. Though many love the stuff, I have always found prewaxed twine to be an annoyance: the twine doesn't hold together as it should, and I find myself having to wax it anyway—which results in a time-consuming and less effective twine.

Buying twine in spools is neat and convenient, but inevitably one requires twine of a size larger and stronger than commercially available. For years I never used commercial twine, much less prewaxed stuff. I always took rope—three-strand or braided—and broke it down to the size and length

needed. Continuous-filament polyester works best, but other types of line work too. Although I now use spool twine for seaming and small worked holes, I still use unlaid three-strand rope for large seizings, sewing big rings, and large boltropes. Breaking down line is less time-consuming than doubling and redoubling lighter spool twine.

A complete twine inventory would include three-, five-, and seven-ply spool twine as well as the twine available from ⅝-inch three-strand line and ½-inch braided line. The seaming and secondary sewing may not be done by hand, but all the finishwork that involves sewing or seizing will be, and it is for this work that sail twine will be required.

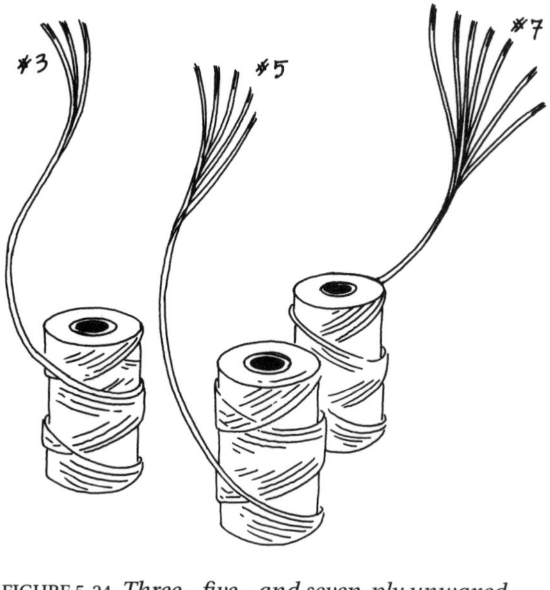

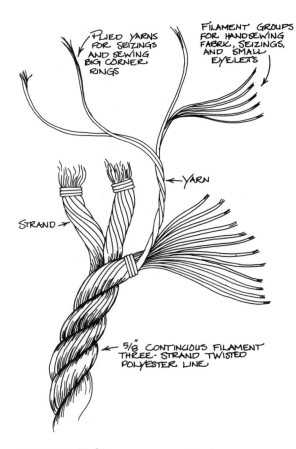

FIGURE 5-24. *Three-, five-, and seven-ply unwaxed polyester sail twine.*

FIGURE 5-25. *Making your own sail twine.*

TABLE 5-5.

SAIL TWINE SIZES AND APPLICATIONS

TWINE TYPE AND SIZE	USES	NEEDLE SIZE	LENGTH OF DOUBLED TWINE
#3 SPUN POLYESTER	• SEAMING — UP TO 13OZ. CANVAS OR DURADON — UP TO 9OZ. DACRON	#16 - #14	ARM LENGTH
	• LIGHT SEIZINGS, WHIPPINGS AND LASHINGS	#15 - #14	
	• LIGHT HAND ROPING, UP TO ¼"	#16 - #14	
	• FINISHING FINELY TAPERED RAT-TAILS	#17 - #15	
	• HANDSEWN PATCHES AND REPAIRS	#16 - #14	
4 CORD WAXED LINEN	• HANDSTITCHING OF MEDIUM-WEIGHT NATURAL FIBER CLOTH • NATURAL FIBER ROPING, ¼" - ⅜" • LIGHT SEIZINGS, WHIPPINGS	#14	ARM LENGTH
#5 SPUN POLYESTER	• SEAMING — HEAVY CLOTH • SMALL WORKED HOLES — EYELETS AND ANCHOR HOLES • MIDSIZE ROPING — ¼" - ⅜" • MIDSIZE WHIPPINGS AND SEIZINGS • LEATHER CHAFE GEAR — DAYSAILS AND LIGHT CRUISERS	#14	ARM LENGTH
6 CORD WAXED LINEN	• SEAMING OF HEAVY COTTON AND FLAX • NATURAL FIBER ROPING, ⅜" - ½" • SEIZINGS, WHIPPINGS, AND LASHINGS • HAND SEWING OF HEAVY LEATHER GOODS	#12	ARM LENGTH
#7 SPUN POLYESTER	• #3 - #9 HANDSEWN RINGS (DOUBLED TWINE)	#15 - #12	3' - 5'
	• #10 - #15 HANDSEWN RINGS (QUADRUPLED)	#10	6' - 8' (LENGTH QUADRUPLED)
	• VOYAGING SAIL WHIPPINGS AND LASHINGS, SEIZINGS	#12 - #11	4' - 6'
	• SEAMING VERY HEAVY FABRIC • ROPING, ½" - 9/16" • LEATHER CHAFE GEAR — LARGE BOAT	#13 - #12	ARM LENGTH
	• SEIZING SMALL HANKS — #0 - #1	#14	4'+
8-12 CORD WAXED LINEN	• EXTRA-HEAVY NATURAL FIBER SAIL AND LEATHER WORK	#11 - #10	
A SINGLE "PLIED YARN" OF ⅝" LINE	• #9 - #15 HANDSEWN RINGS (DOUBLED) • CORNER RING SEIZINGS - VOYAGING SAILS • SEIZING JIB HANKS — #2 - #6	#12 - #11	6' - 10'
	• ROPING LARGE COMMERCIAL SAILS - ⅝"+ • COMMERCIAL AND VOYAGING SAIL ANCHOR HOLES	#12 - #11 - #10	ARM LENGTH OR GREATER

TABLE 5-6.

MACHINE THREAD USES

* THREAD SIZE/TYPE	NEEDLE SIZE (METRIC) (SINGER)		CLOTH WEIGHT/TYPE	TYPICAL SAIL OR CANVAS PROJECT
#30 POLYESTER 46 COTTON	#80	#12	.75-1.5 oz. NYLON	DRIFTERS, SPINNAKERS, MIZZENSTAYS'LS, GOLLY-WOBBLERS, ETC.
#46 POLYESTER 40 COTTON	#90	#14	1.5 oz. NYLON 2-4 oz. DACRON LIGHT COTTON	DRIFTERS, LIGHT-AIR AUXILIARY SAILS, DINGHY SAILS
#69/24 POLYESTER 24/4 COTTON	#100	#16	5-7 oz. DACRON 13 oz. VIVATEX COTTON 4 oz. NYLON	DAYSAILING MAINS AND HEADS'LS, MID-RANGE CRUISING AUX. SAILS, LIGHT-DUTY BAGS AND SAIL COVERS, TABLINGS AND PATCHES OF SMALL DAYSAILS
#92/16 POLYESTER 16/4 COTTON	#110	#18	6-9 oz. DACRON NYLON WEBBING 13 oz. VIVATEX COTTON 14 oz. DURADON ACRYLIC COVER CLOTH	SMALL-BOAT STORMSAILS, INSHORE CRUISING AND VOYAGING WORKING SAILS, GENERAL CANVASWORK, MID-RANGE VOYAGING AND WORKING SAILS, LARGE-BOAT AUX. SAILS
#138/12 POLYESTER 12/4 COTTON	#120	#19	7-10 oz. DACRON NYLON/POLYESTER WEBBING 16.5 oz. DURADON	VOYAGING AND WORKING SAILS, STORMSAILS, SAIL-CORNER REINFORCEMENT, MACHINE ROPING
#207/10 POLYESTER 10/4 COTTON	#140	#22	12-14 oz. DACRON 14-18.5 oz. DURADON	LARGE WORKING AND VOYAGING SAILS, CORNER REINFORCEMENTS, AWNINGS AND COVERS, STORMSAILS, EXTRA CHAFE RESISTANCE
#346 POLYESTER	#200	#25	#4 COTTON DUCK HERCULON 18.5-22 oz. DURADON 14-16 oz. DACRON	HEAVY VOYAGING AND COMMERCIAL SAILS, COMMERCIAL STEADYING SAILS, COMMERCIAL CANVASWORK, EXTRA CHAFE RESISTANCE, HEAVY WEBBING REINFORCEMENT

*THE SECOND OF TWO NUMBERS IN A THREAD SIZE DESIGNATION, OFTEN SEEN IN CATALOGS, IS A CARRYOVER FROM EARLY COTTON THREAD DESIGNATIONS. NOTE THAT MORE THAN ONE WEIGHT OF THREAD MAY BE USED WITHIN THE SAME SAIL. THICK CORNERS AND HEAVY REINFORCEMENT REQUIRE HEAVIER THREAD THAN DO SEAMS.

There are distinct advantages to sewing a sail entirely by hand, but saving time is not one of them. Alternatively, sewing machines can use several types of thread. Machine thread varies not only in fiber and construction, but also in size, finish, and color. To repeat, it is permissible to use synthetic thread on natural cloth, but not the opposite.

Machine thread is selected for the strength requirement of a particular part of the sail and must be compatible with the machine. Generally it all goes together: heavy-stress sail, big machine, heavy threads. Machine thread is identified by any of various numbering systems that reflect the stature of the thread.

Sailmaking polyester machine thread ranges from a gossamer #30 to a near stringlike #346 and is available in a rainbow of colors. Number 30 through #138 cover the making of most sails for boats up to 50 feet using cloth weights ranging from half-ounce drifter-nylon to 10-ounce Dacron stormsail material. Bigger boats require more heavily constructed sails and, in turn, heavier thread and bigger sewing machines.

Machine thread is twisted—laid up by twist—either to the right or to the left. Most synthetic sail thread now is right twist. It is important that the twist of the thread be compatible with the sewing machine—mismatched thread can result in poor-quality stitching or malfunction. Synthetic machine thread is also finished with silicon to facilitate its passage through and around thread guides in the machine and through the cloth. A certain amount of reduced friction is important, but when there's too much lubricant, the oil will leach out into the sailcloth. It causes no harm, but the stain looks horrid.

Machine thread may be treated, too, for ultraviolet light resistance. Although it is the stitching of the sail that will fail due to ultraviolet exposure long before the sailcloth itself, I've been told that the UV-treated thread, a recent development, has not significantly prolonged stitch life. It has been my experience, however, that a colored thread will outlast an undyed one in terms of ultraviolet-light resistance.

Machine thread is sold on tubes by the ounce or pound and, with a guesstimated 40 yards of thread per yard of cloth in a sail, must not be overlooked as one of the cost-producing components of the sail—as much as $12 in a 300-square-foot genoa, for example. To compound matters—or more correctly, double them—a sewing machine sews with two threads at a time, an upper thread and a lower bobbin thread, which are interlocked in the stitching process. Therefore two sources of thread, or two spools, are required for any efficiency of sewing—one to feed the top, the other for winding bobbins. The amount of thread available on a single spool might be more than enough to sew an entire sail, but it would take an inordinate amount of time to stop to rewind bobbins. Alternatively, prewound bobbins can be obtained, though not necessarily in every thread type or bobbin size. So, in situations where bobbins are wound as the machine sews, two spools of thread are required for each size and thread type, and a minimum of two bobbins are needed for each type in order to have one in use while the other is winding. I have found that a supply of white, brown, and blue thread has met nearly every need, with the exception of various colors that have arisen in motley canvaswork. A shipboard or personal machine-thread inventory would include only two spools of each size thread needed to maintain one's own sails and canvas articles.

Sail Hardware

Sail hardware falls into one of four categories: a means of attaching something to a sail, a way of attaching a sail to something else, some sort of support, or a type of sail-shaping mechanism. All metal sail hardware, except in large craft, is now of brass, bronze, stainless steel, or aluminum (racing hardware excepted). Nonmetallic hardware can be plastic, fiberglass, or wood.

Reinforced Holes in Sails Lashings, sheets, halyards, lacings, and reef points are all attached directly or indirectly to a sail through reinforced holes in the sail, and the area around the hole has extra cloth reinforcement. Prior to the use of metal reinforcements and hardware in sails, holes were strengthened with rope grommets, and corners had served cringles for earings. To this day it is often preferable to reinforce eyelets and anchor holes with a soft rope grommet rather than a metal ring so that the hole will have the same qualities as the cloth and be more flexible.

This is as good a time as any to hash out the pros and cons of handsewn rings versus the hydraulically pressed rings common today. To question which is stronger is like trying to compare a football player and a ballet dancer. Certainly a metal ring of sufficient size and breaking strength installed under sufficient pressure in sufficient layers of heavy sailcloth has an overall initial failure strength far above anything that might be hand sewn into such material. Sheer holding power is

not the primary determinant of effectiveness, however. What is important is the compatibility of the fitting with the medium in which it is installed. In other words, what good is a superstrong link in a weak chain? Furthermore, the strong link and its qualities in relationship to the other links probably produces a weaker overall chain than if the chain links were all similar.

So it is with sail reinforcements. Rigid, inflexible, high-strength fittings have their place in sails of similar overall construction, particularly in production-oriented, limited-use sail types (overlooking the wasteful aspects). But in the appropriate medium, handsewn corner rings provide more strength, not to mention ease of replacement, and are reusable. The question is mostly moot, since commercial sailmaking hasn't the time anymore for hand sewing rings of any size. The inimitable

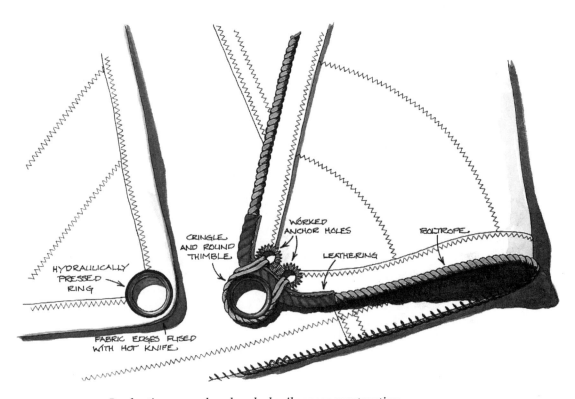

FIGURE 5-26. *Production versus handworked sail corner construction.*

Mr. Cox of Cox Molded Sails in the Northwest informally pitted his distinctive handsewn rings against a hydraulic sandwich ring by installing the two rings in the same piece of cloth. He then lashed one to a tree, the other to the bumper of his truck. Off he drove. It was the hydraulic doughnut that let go. Mind you, it's not usually the doughnut that fails—it's the cloth on the stressed side of the ring.

Brad Hunter of Gambell and Hunter Sailmakers did a similar test with a come-along. This time the handsewn ring was the loser. I don't think either of these tests is conclusive—we're comparing apples to oranges. The thing to do is know the strengths and holding power of the two methods *in their respective appropriate installations,* and then judge economics, ease of repair, and so forth.

In eyelets and small holes, there is no question that a handsewn ring is more durable than a spur grommet. For daysailing or racing, spur grommets are of adequate strength and sufficiently long lived, but for any sort of voyaging or extended sail life the strength of handsewn rings is preferable.

Brass rings and stainless steel rings for hand-worked holes range in size from ⅜-inch outer diameter to a little less than 3¼ inches and are numbered from #3 to #15. A #3 ½-inch ring is a typical eyelet size. A #15 is a monstrous thing such as you'd find in the corner of a large-boat sail. These rings are sewn in and the stitches subsequently protected by a brass liner or turnover that is inserted from one side and then splayed over with a setting die. Sometimes two liners are installed, one from either side. In the absence of liners, leather will, for a time, protect the stitching. A small loft would require a full range of setting dies,

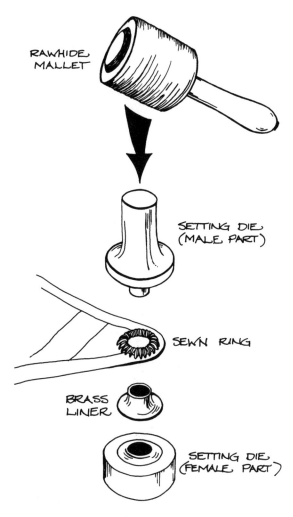

RAWHIDE MALLET

SETTING DIE (MALE PART)

SEWN RING

BRASS LINER

SETTING DIE (FEMALE PART)

FIGURE 5-27. *Setting a liner.*

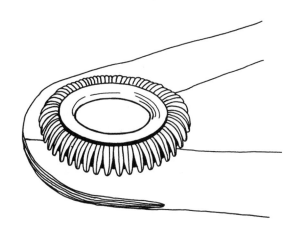

FIGURE 5-28. *A handsewn corner ring with liner installed. The corner will be oversewn, roped, and leathered. Sometimes, as pictured elsewhere in this book, short stitches alternate with longer ones, which helps keep some separation between stitch holes.*

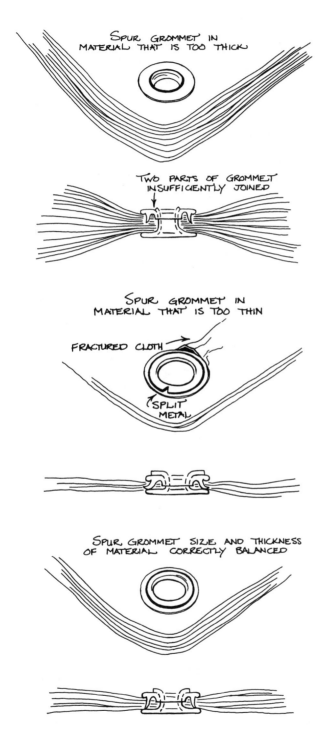

FIGURE 5-29. *Spur grommet installation problems.*

though #15s would collect some dust. On board a cruiser or for a personal inventory, only the sizes of rings used on board or used most frequently, and those sizes next larger, would be required.

Spur grommets are appropriate for the eyelets of nonseafaring sails. These are two-part fittings that are installed with a setting die. Care must be taken to match the spur grommet to the stress requirements and also to correctly cut the hole in the appropriate thicknesses of cloth. If the cloth is too thin, the grommet will cut through it. If the cloth is too thick, the sides of the grommet will not be mated together. Spur grommets range in size from a shoe eyelet, 5/16 inch, to a whopping 2 inches, and are identified in a range from #000 to #8. The #000s serve well as model-sail corner rings or eyelets in very small boat sails. The big ones work well for tarpaulins and awnings. Generally a small shop is covered by having #0, #1, #2, and #4 spur grommets. A voyaging boat or personal inventory would do well to have the same, or at least the middle two sizes.

Sail Perimeter Hardware   Hardware for corner attachment around the perimeter of a sail includes round thimbles and D-rings. But why have these things, if you can use a hole in the sail? The answer lies partly in tradition. Before the advent of hardware suitable for reinforcing large, worked holes, the cringle (see Figure 5-30, page 170), and subsequently the cringle and round thimble, dominated for corner attachment. But this approach is still recommendable, as it is compatible with seafaring sail constructions and materials.

The tools and materials are inexpensive, readily available, and reusable. Moreover, external attachments chafe less and are more appropriate for the wear and tear of shackles and spar hardware. Many machine-finished sails now employ exterior hardware affixed to the sail by machine-sewn webbing, often an efficient and effective means of attaching hardware.

Commercial round thimbles of bronze and stainless steel, and even galvanized, are available from ¾ inch up to 2 inches outer diameter. The size of the thimble to be used depends on strength requirements, what must pass through it, and the size of the boltrope employed.

Only a loft doing the most traditional of work would be sticking cringles, and in that event would have all sizes, even larger galvanized iron ones for big boats.

A small rope cringle and round thimble serve well

TABLE 5-7.

HOLE CUTTER AND DIE SIZES

Cutter Size (inches)	Use	Application
1/4	#0 SPURS, SMALL GROMMETS	EYELETS ON BAGS AND SAILS
9/32	#0 SPURS, SMALL GROMMETS	EYELETS ON BAGS AND SAILS
3/8	#1 SPURS, GROMMETS	EYELETS ON BAGS AND SAILS
7/16	#2 SPURS, #3 RINGS, GROMMETS	EYELETS ON LARGE SAILS, HEAVIER CANVASWORK
1/2	#4 SPURS, #4 RINGS	SMALL DAYSAIL CORNERS, CANVASWORK, VOYAGING EYELETS
5/8	#5 SPURS, #5 RINGS	HANDSEWN DAYSAIL CORNERS, VOYAGING EYELETS
3/4	#6 SPURS, #6 RINGS	SMALL HANDSEWN VOYAGING CORNERS
7/8	#7 SPURS, #7 RINGS	LIGHT HANDSEWN AUX. SAIL CORNERS, HEAVY CANVAS CORNERS
1	#8 SPURS, #8 RINGS	LIGHT HANDSEWN AUX. SAIL CORNERS, HEAVY CANVAS CORNERS
1 1/8	#9 HANDSEWN RINGS	MEDIUM VOYAGING CORNER RINGS, LARGE DAYSAIL CORNER RINGS, WORKBOAT EYELETS
1 1/4	#10 HANDSEWN RINGS	MIDSIZE VOYAGING BOAT CORNER RINGS
1 1/2	#11 HANDSEWN RINGS	LARGE VOYAGING BOAT CORNER RINGS, STORMS'LS
2	#15 HANDSEWN RINGS	EXTRA-LARGE VOYAGING AND WORKBOAT CORNER RINGS

NOTE: SETTING DIE NUMBERS ALWAYS MATCH THE NUMBERS OF THE RINGS OR SPURS WITH WHICH THEY'RE USED. E.G., USE A #0 SPUR DIE WITH A #0 SPUR GROMMET, A #3 DIE ON THE LINER OF A #3 HANDSEWN RING, OR A #8 SPUR DIE WITH A #8 SPUR GROMMET.

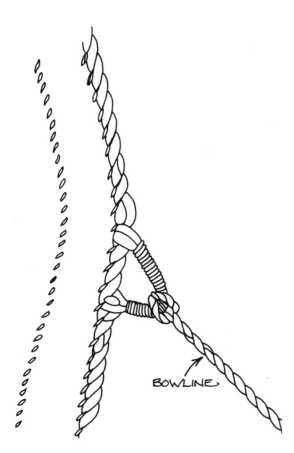

FIGURE 5-30. *A cringle in its earliest form, with no associated hardware. Shown here is a leech cringle stuck in the boltrope of a squaresail for attaching a bowline (a line led forward to flatten the leading edge of the sail). Figure 5-26 shows a more evolved cringle with hardware.*

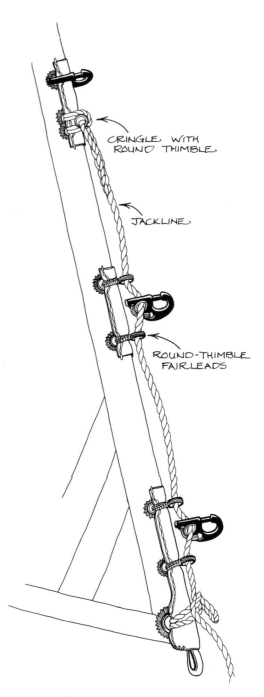

to anchor the upper end of a jackline (Figure 5-31). Generally, when a jackline is anchored to a single eyelet in the luff of a sail, there is an unfair lead and a torquing strain on the anchor point in the sail. The use of a cringle and round thimble brings the entire jackline into alignment with the luff of the sail. The size of the round thimble depends on the stoutness of the sail, the offset required to bring the lead of the jackline into alignment with other jackline fairleads, and the clearance between the luff and the spar or stay to which the sail is bent.

FIGURE 5-31. *A cringle with round thimble anchors the upper end of a jackline in proper alignment with the luff and fairleads.*

On board a bluewater cruiser, it would be prudent to have a couple of round thimbles and some three-strand line for cringles, as it is such a convenient seagoing means of effecting a repair or jury-rigging with available tools and materials.

D-Rings D-rings serve the same functions as round thimbles but are much more specialized,

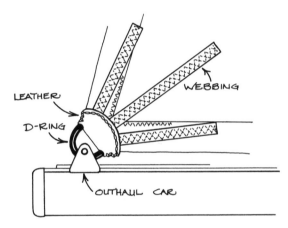

FIGURE 5-32. *Use of a D-ring and webbing. This seaworthy contemporary solution is easy to install and distributes strain evenly.*

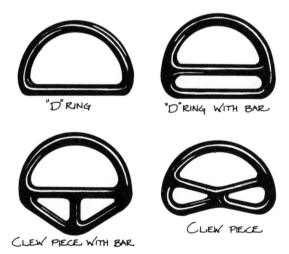

FIGURE 5-33. *Commercially available stainless steel D-rings.*

and there are designs for various corners and specific uses.

The simplest D-ring is a straightforward D shape—fine for straps perhaps, but prone to capsize under the torque and oblique strain of sheeting and outhauling when used in the clew of a sail. Consequently, there is a range of D-rings with inner crossbar configurations that provide stability of installation and isolate a shackle or fitting from the material holding the D-ring to the sail.

Marvelous corners of great strength and durability can be made with D-rings, and though contemporary materials are used—stainless steel, nylon webbing, braided line—the result is not all that far removed from the spectacle earings of old-

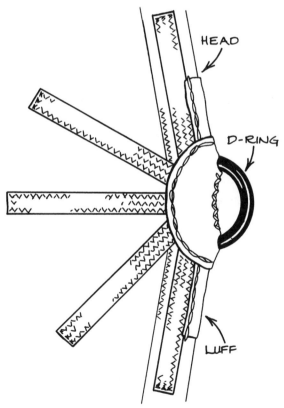

FIGURE 5-34. *A clew-piece D-ring (see Figure 5-33) in the throat of a fisherman staysail. Braided luff and head ropes are spliced to the D-ring.*

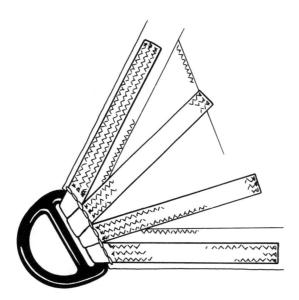

FIGURE 5-35. *A D-ring (with bar) in the clew of a genoa. (Leather not yet installed.)*

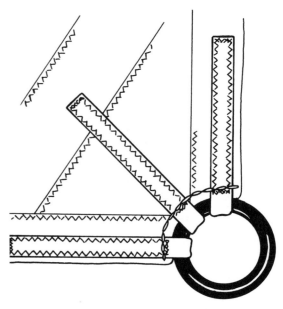

FIGURE 5-36. *Circular ring with webbing in the tack of a Bermudan sail. Leathering is frequently omitted in production sailmaking.*

time squaresails and gaff sails. D-ring installation can be done effectively by hand or machine and is perhaps an easier shipboard project than sticking a cringle, as no boltrope is required. Another advantage of D-rings is that they spread out strain more evenly than when force is applied by a halyard, lashing, etc. to a simple hole in the sail, resulting in a flatter-setting corner.

Hardware for Bending Sails to Spars   Bending sails to spars or wire requires another line of hardware. There are three types of slides: internal slides that run within an external track on the spar; external slides that also run on a track on the spar; and slug slides that run within a groove in the spar.

We have Nathanael G. Herreshoff to thank for the development of external slides, which now range from the nickel silver–plated brass ⅝-inch-track slides to 1¼-inch-track cast bronze types. There are foot slides and luff slides, though luff slides may be used on any edge. Clearly the heavy bronze slides are much stronger bluewater gear,

and are certainly worth placing at corners of high strain in any sizable boat's sail.

A sensible but very expensive arrangement is the external track with slides within. For this there are bronze slides, but Delrin slides, of two sizes, are more readily available.

The third category of slides includes all those that run inside the groove of a slotted spar. At one time these were wooden toggles, and sailors handy with a pocket knife or a lathe could fashion their own, either as a regular source or a jury rig. In contrast, the stainless steel, plastic, and composite slides now available have a bail that extends out through and beyond the slot so that the lashing or sail-attaching hardware does not come in contact with the spar. The bail receives a tremendous amount of shearing strain, which is why plastic bails often fail.

The largest all-metal slug slides are used in the corners of sails that have rope edges rather than slides running in the spar slot (see Figure 6-92, page 364). This added precaution is valuable, as unreinforced rope-in-slot arrangements come adrift at the sail corners. These hefty slugs could be used along the entire sail edge, but only when great strength is paramount and the cumulative weight of the slides is not a problem.

There are other slide configurations as well as other hardware for attaching a sail to a mast, but the three types described above are what a small loft will likely utilize and what one is likely to have on a boat. The weaker types, if you should persist in using them, often need replacement, especially if they are held to the sail with shackles (a no-no, by the way). A generous supply of replacements should be in the sail locker.

The stronger types, properly seized, rarely fail but might fall overboard, so it is best to have some extras just in case.

Hardware for Bending Sails to Wire Scads of schemes have been devised for holding sails to a stay. Generally the fittings are termed *hanks,* from the early wooden and wrought-iron varieties down to modern brass, bronze, and stainless steel hardware. With the transition from workboat to yachting sails came hanks permanently affixed to the sail rather than the stay.

The piston-type jib hank is seized to luff eyelets of the sail and is available in sizes ranging from a cute ¾-inch-long #0 to a stout 6-inch-long #6 heavy bronze. A variation on this type for jacklines is available (though increasingly less so).

For a time, small-boat sails utilized a galvanized variation on the common spring-gated boat snap. Though they chafed the sail and corroded, and the spring would fail, these were marvelous in that they could be clipped on swiftly and removed with only one hand. Wichard, of France, which for a long time offered a line of lifeline clips, has expanded its line to include an expensive stainless steel spring-bail gate-type hank that is sewn to a sail and permits expeditious one-handed bending and unbending. Unfortunately, these sewn-on hanks are decreasing in availability. They are available, if at all, only in medium and large sizes suitable for larger boats. They are exceedingly strong—

perhaps too strong: at least with soft-metal hanks the normal abrasion that occurs between the hank and stay is suffered by the hank and not the stay!

Most commonly used now are squeezed or pressed-on types of piston hank that require no seizing. For high-volume production work these are advantageous, and in some instances perhaps they really are appropriate—say in daysailing, or in any situation where strength, longevity, and ease of replacement are not important. Otherwise, this type of hank has no place on a well-found seaworthy sail. They are destructive to the sail and are not reusable.

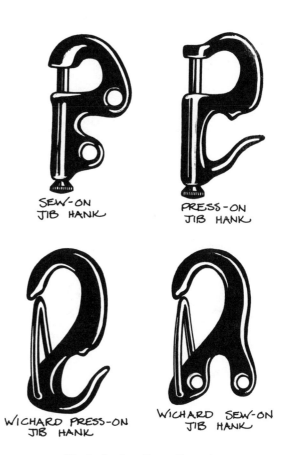

FIGURE 5-37. *Hanks for bending sail to wire. Available in brass or stainless steel. Other variations in design and materials (including plastic) exist for jacklines and sportsailing.*

Generally a sail loft will need hanks only in sizes ranging from #0 through #4. The appropriate size depends on the sail size and the size of the wire on which it is set. The only combination you will never get is a small hank on a large sail on a large-diameter stay.

Naturally, in a personal kit, you carry the same hanks your sails do—and for extended voyages, at least a dozen. Even if you have a roller-furling headsail setup, it is prudent to carry some headsail hanks—you may want to make a conversion.

Support Hardware   There are more kinds of commercially manufactured support hardware than you can shake a stick at. Life was simpler indeed when support hardware, principally battens and headboards, was wooden.

BATTENS.   Sail battens are the splints, in effect, that support the freestanding roach of sailcloth outside the straight-line leech. They also serve to maintain a flat and fair exit to the leech. If the battens are left out, the roach, unsupported, pops and snaps like a flag. Full-length battens not only support a leech profile, but also maintain the desired sail camber if they are of the pretensioned, adjustable, flexible type. The rigid full-length battens such as one finds in Chinese lugsails and canoe rigs are in certain respects additional spars rather than a component of the sail. But it's a fine line of distinction; some of the problems faced by the sailmaker are the same no matter the batten length.

Battens are available in wide variety and are distinguished by their material, construction, cross-sectional shape, thickness, rigidity, and length. The goal is to achieve the best leech support with the least weight. Length is governed by class rules or the size of the roach. Flexibility, a certain amount of which is advisable for sail curvature, varies with length among other factors. A batten can be uniformly thick or tapered, with more flexibility at its

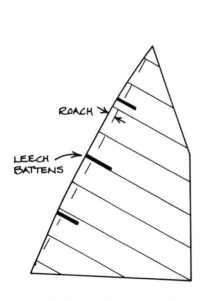

Gaff-headed pleasure sailer

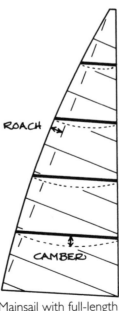

Mainsail with full-length battens

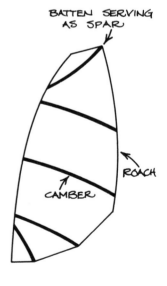

Boardboat sail with full-length battens

FIGURE 5-38. *Assorted contemporary uses of sail battens.*

FIGURE 5-39. *Full-length battens in a balanced lugsail.*

forward end. A tapered batten, while more vulnerable, conforms better to variable leech camber.

Ash wooden battens, tapered or untapered, are light, resilient, inexpensive, easily made—and they float! But they are relatively stiff and, if unvarnished, will mildew and warp when furled up in a wet sail.

Fiberglass battens, both laminated and pultruded, offer great strength and warp-free uniformity. They cost more but are readily found in chandleries and sail lofts in a broad range of sizes and flexibility. Untapered laminated fiberglass battens come in three somewhat subjective grades of relative stiffness: softest, intermediate, and stiffest. With the predictable flexibility of laminates, the degree of flex and its location can be built into the batten. Even custom battens can be obtained. The flexibility of the untapered pultruded battens ranges from wet noodle to ossified; the thicker and wider in section, the stiffer. Look to thinness for flexibility and width for strength.

The correct flexibility depends on size of roach, batten location, sail shape, and wind strength. Small roaches, upper battens, greater sail curvature, and light winds call for a relatively limber and lighter batten. A sail may carry a soft batten up high, an intermediate one at midleech, and a stiff one low—any of many combinations, mixing pultruded and laminated battens.

It is easier in the absence of racing regulations and influences to design a roach and batten ensemble that will set well and still provide additional sail area. It is no longer necessary to design around a specified batten length and number of battens, pushing the limits in order to maximize sail area. A moderate roach with battens of more than adequate length will provide performance and a good set of sail.

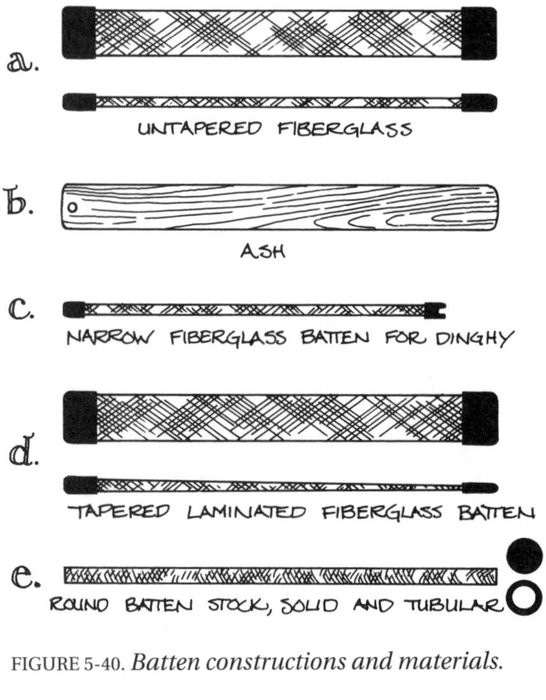

FIGURE 5-41. *Cross-sectional shapes of untapered pultruded fiberglass battens. These are manufactured in long lengths and cut to fit by the retailer or sailmaker.*

a. UNTAPERED FIBERGLASS

b. ASH

c. NARROW FIBERGLASS BATTEN FOR DINGHY

d. TAPERED LAMINATED FIBERGLASS BATTEN

e. ROUND BATTEN STOCK, SOLID AND TUBULAR

FIGURE 5-40. *Batten constructions and materials.*

Of the four batten construction types—wooden, laminated fiberglass, pultruded fiberglass, and round—a minimal loft inventory should include untapered laminated types in moderate lengths, thicknesses, and widths, as well as some pultruded stock in light and heavy ranges. With this supply most needs can be met, and no money is invested in more esoteric varieties. Yes, I am afraid that wooden battens are not a popular item—but ash battens are light, inexpensive, and easily made, which is good because they are so easily broken or damaged. And besides, I fear that the ghost of Hervey Garrett Smith would haunt me if I even so much as pointed a fiberglass batten at a cotton sail!

Naturally, any boat sporting roach and battens should have spare battens on board of the same size and type. And sporting is the word for the kind of sailing that would have battens in a sail, in view of all the destructiveness, headache, and expense they entail. Still, there's no denying their performance advantage.

HEADBOARDS AND CLEWBOARDS. Headboards and clewboards were at one time actually boards—and if you're desperate or feeling creative, you can make your own wooden ones of mahogany. Varnished, they are handsome indeed, though on a snow-white Dacron sail they have an inconsistent earthiness about them. Anyway, these devices, wooden or aluminum, afford the opportunity of obtaining extra sail area within limited spar length or edge measurements. On a high-aspect-ratio mainsail this is important. If you went to a point at the peak and had no roach, it would be a noodle of a sail indeed. Skipjack sails have headboards too, as do Bahamian craft. In the case of the skipjacks, this is a means of shortening a sail that has stretched out too long on the hoist; maybe the rea-

TABLE 5-8.
SAIL BATTEN TYPES AND APPLICATIONS

MATERIAL AND CONSTRUCTION	DIMENSIONS (INCHES)	TYPICAL USES
ROUND FIBERGLASS	1/4 – 5/16	DINGHIES, BOARDSAILERS
ASH PULTRUDED FIBERGLASS	1 × 1/8 3/8 – 5/8 × 1/8	SMALL DINGHIES
TAPER LAMINATED FIBERGLASS (STIFF)	3/8	DINGHIES, BOARDSAILERS
TAPER LAMINATED FIBERGLASS (STIFF) ROUND FIBERGLASS ASH	5/8 5/16 – 1/2 1 1/2 × 3/16	LARGE DINGHIES, MULTIHULLS, LIGHT-DISPLACEMENT KEELBOATS, DAYSAILERS (UNDER 30 FEET)
PULTRUDED FIBERGLASS TAPER LAMINATED FIBERGLASS ROUND FIBERGLASS ASH	1 – 1 3/16 1 1/4 1/2 – 5/8 2 × 3/16	LARGE DINGHIES, DAYSAILERS, SMALL CRUISERS
PULTRUDED FIBERGLASS TAPER LAMINATED FIBERGLASS ROUND FIBERGLASS	1 5/8 – 2 1 1/2 1/2 – 13/16	HEAVY-DISPLACEMENT CRUISERS
TAPER LAMINATED FIBERGLASS ASH	2 2 1/2 × 3/8	LARGE CRAFT (50 FEET AND UP)

son is the same in the Bahamian craft, but I believe the whacking headboards on these craft, which are almost sparlike in stature and length, are there to increase sail area. These Bahamian craft, by the way, hold the title for grandiose foot skirt in a mainsail.

Headboards are installed either internally or externally. The internal varieties, even the aluminum ones, are now seldom seen—not because they are mostly within the corner patches at the head of the sail, but because they are so labor-intensive to install, require some skill to replace properly, and are employed in conjunction with other forms of compatible and equally anachronistic sail construction, principally external roping. For a traditional appearance in headboards, the internal type is *de rigueur*. In addition, if battens and headboard are to be compatible with an expectation of extended sail life, the internal type is more durable and does less harm to the sail.

Externally mounted headboards are a two-piece sandwich, the head of the sail being the filling.

Made of anodized aluminum, or plastic in the dinghy sizes, these pieces are riveted together through the sail, making an initially strong and easily installed unit. It is easier to obtain a flat, wrinkle-free head area in the sail. But, as with any hard, metal edge firmly pressed against flexible cloth, the cloth eventually fractures where cloth and metal meet. This is the problem with headboards and hydraulic rings both: they have great fundamental strength but an overall weakness in that their rigidity leads to failure of the flexible medium in or on which they are installed. This notion of compatibility of materials is one of the fundamentals of seaworthy sailmaking. Rather than being riveted, the external headboards can be hand sewn if the holes in the metal or plastic are beveled so as to minimize chafe to the twine. The advantage to this is primarily the saving on a rivet tool, and it is a repair option.

Headboard size is determined, if not by class rules, by the size of the sail and desired roach. There is a point at which a headboard begins to be

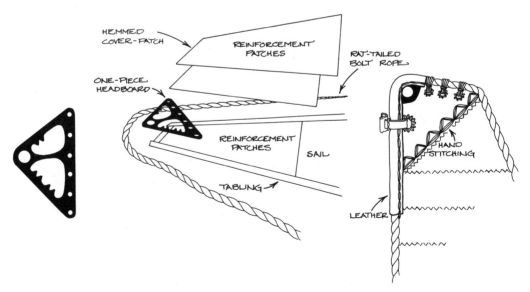

FIGURE 5-42. *Internal cast-aluminum headboard installation. First, reinforcement patches and then tablings are sewn to the sail. The hemmed cover patch and additional patch layers are next sewn to the sail as a separate group, thus forming a pocket of balanced construction into which the headboard is inserted, sewn, and seized.*

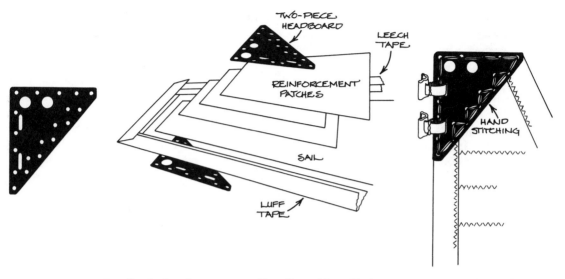

FIGURE 5-43. *Anodized-aluminum external headboard installation. Rivets are usually substituted for hand stitching in production sails.*

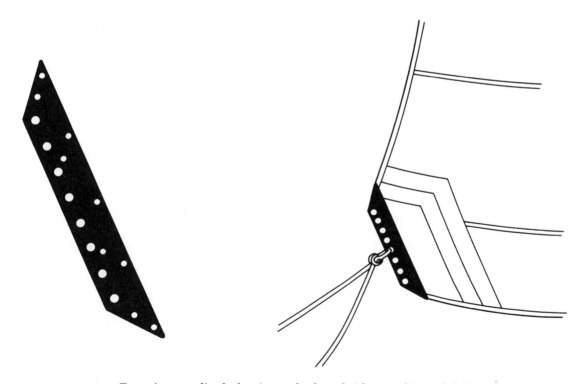

FIGURE 5-44. *Two-piece anodized-aluminum clewboard. Often used in multihull sportsailers.*

a small gaff and will not support itself unless the point of halyard attachment is moved aft, which takes the tension out of alignment with the luff.

Cordage

Several aspects of a sail's construction involve cordage of some type, particularly if the sail is of traditional design. It is rope, in traditional construction, that maintains a sail's peripheral integrity. With contemporary construction tech-

niques and synthetic cloths, this is not invariably so, but until comparatively recent times, the rope reinforcement of sails of all sizes was essential.

The external or internal ropes in the perimeter of a sail may be installed on one edge or all edges, and serve a number of interrelated functions. Roping is (1) a governor that limits the extent to which an edge can be pulled, under tension, keeping the majority of strain on the rope rather than the sail-cloth; (2) provides reinforcement and chafe protec-

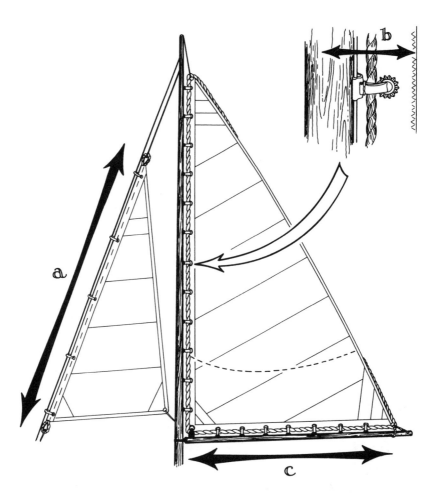

FIGURE 5-45. *Internal and external roping. (A) An internal luff rope permits elasticity while preventing overstretching. (B) External roping provides lateral reinforcement and chafe protection, permits and controls stretch, and (C) gathers a rounded sail edge into the sail for additional curvature.*

tion; (3) limits cloth elongation along the edge; (4) keeps the sail edge taut and smooth under lesser tensions; (5) offers a linear surface along which to gather cloth rounds and push that cloth into the body of the sail, thus imparting camber; and (6) when sewn externally to one side of the sail, enables sailors to tell by feel what side of the sail they are handling.

Natural-fiber cordage for the roping of natural-fiber sails is best made of tarred hemp but can also be manila or cotton. None of these is easily obtained except in Europe, a situation that may oblige even the most pure-blooded traditionalist to use synthetic line on a natural-fiber sail. One alternative is a type of three-strand boltrope, which,

though synthetic, has a natural appearance. Roblon and Hempex are both polypropylene soft-laid line developed for the running rigging of the "character boat" market. The line does not look like hemp, but at least it does not have the stark, sterile whiteness of undyed polyester. It is, however, quite mushy, difficult to sew, stretchy, and unpleasant to splice.

Alternatively—and somewhat messily and unpredictably—one can dye one's own spun polyester (Dacron) or Dacron/polypropylene composite boltrope. I have had some great successes and horrendous failures at this, utilizing various proportions of turpentine and pine tar. There may be some UV resistance imparted by this process, and the line

SEWN TO SAIL

or

OVERHAND KNOT

PALM & NEEDLE WHIPPING

FIGURE 5-46. *Alternative reef nettle installations.*

looks and smells wonderful. I have always done this by the sail, rather than, say, a whole coil at a time. Of course, if it is a cotton sail to be subsequently dyed or dressed down with preservative, there is no need to fuss with predyeing a polyester boltrope.

Even on a white synthetic sail, the contrast in color of a tarred boltrope looks rather snazzy.

When sewn externally to the edge of a sail, a boltrope should preferably be of three-strand, right-laid construction, though four-strand can be

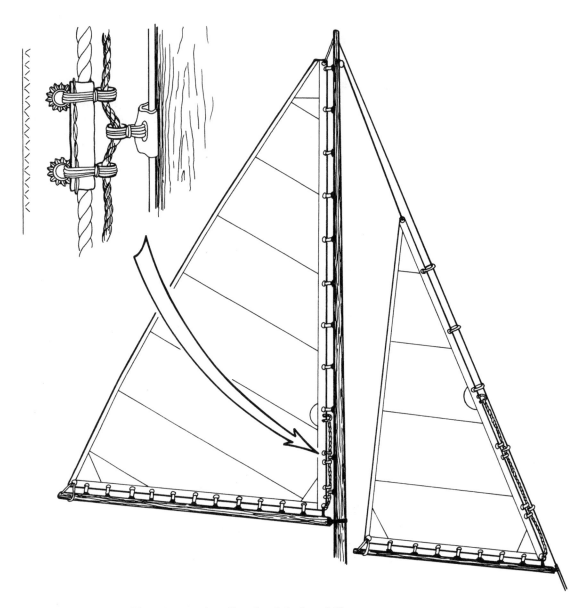

FIGURE 5-47. *Jacklines in a mainsail and a club-footed jib.*

TABLE 5-9.

BRAIDED DACRON LEECHCORD SIZES AND APPLICATIONS

DIAMETER (INCHES)	SYSTEM	APPLICATIONS
3/64 1/16	NO. 40 NO. 50	LEECH AND FOOT CORDS OF DRIFTERS AND LIGHT AUX. SAILS — DINGHY SAILS — LIGHT SEIZINGS AND LASHINGS — SMALL KNOTS AND HITCHINGS
5/64	NO. 205	LEECH AND FOOT CORDS OF SMALL AND MIDSIZE BOAT SAILS — MODERATELY HEAVY SEIZINGS, LASHINGS, AND HITCHINGS
1/8 5/32	NO. 505 —	LEECH AND FOOT CORDS OF STORM SAILS AND LARGE BOAT SAILS — HEAVY SEIZINGS, LASHINGS, AND HITCHINGS — SMALL BOAT LACELINES, REEF NETTLES, AND LUFF ROPES.

NOTE: BOAT SIZE IS A CONTINUUM WITH NO READY DEMARCATIONS, BUT FOR PRESENT PURPOSES WE CAN ASSUME THAT ANY BOAT OF LESS THAN 30 FEET, UNLESS HEAVILY CONSTRUCTED, IS A SMALL BOAT; A BOAT OF 30 TO 40 FEET, UNLESS VERY LIGHTLY CONSTRUCTED, IS A MIDSIZE BOAT; AND ANY BOAT GREATER THAN 40 FEET, UNLESS VERY LIGHTLY CONSTRUCTED, IS A LARGE BOAT. ADMITTEDLY THESE DEMARCATIONS ARE ARBITRARY AND LEAVE ROOM FOR DEBATE IN PARTICULAR CASES, BUT WE MUST START SOMEWHERE.

used. Internal roping can be either three-strand or braided synthetic line. Though nylon or even polypropylene can be used, polyester is best. Some elasticity is desirable, but significant permanent elongation is to be avoided in the internal roping of synthetic sails. If the rope elongates too much, it will no longer serve its purpose.

The diameter of the line used in roping depends on the strength required and, in part, on aesthetics. Synthetic line is so strong for its diameter and weight that a boltrope of adequate strength often looks skimpy and inappropriate. Moreover, if it is a small-diameter external boltrope, it will require comparatively more stitches to sew.

Installing roping of any sort in a sail is a demanding task, as a sailmaker attempts to find a balance between the qualities of the sailcloth, the rope, the strain, and aesthetics. There are so many variables! This imprecision, as well as the time required, is why this type of reinforcement (even the internal type) is now seldom done. We will return to this subject in Chapter 6, "Making Your Own Sails."

Other cordage in a sail includes the light line of which reef points are made. While braided cord is workable for very small nettles, three-strand line that holds a slipped reef knot and a whipping or backsplice is preferable. It would be a huge sail that employed reef nettles larger than ⅜ inch in diameter.

Leech and foot cords are tensioning lines that run within the tablings of the freestanding edges of a sail. Tensioned, they minimize edge flutter and sag as well as alter sail shape. The best material is a nonstretch braided line of a size compatible with the strain. Generally, the lighter the weight the better, except that the smaller-diameter line will chafe through the sail more easily. Keep in mind, too, that a sailor needs to grab and haul on that line.

It is also a sailmaker's task to install jacklines in the lower luffs of boomed sails with tack angles of less than 90 degrees. The jackline is essential to raising and lowering the sail as well as protecting the cloth from excessive strain. When a jackline is used in conjunction with a luff rope, it is kept somewhat smaller in diameter and strength; this way, while the jackline is under sufficient tension to pull the sail luff forward, it is the luff rope that takes the primary strain.

To stock a spool of 600 feet or more of each fiber and size (³⁄₁₆ inch to ⅝ inch) of three-strand line required in boltroping, nettles, and jacklines can mean a considerable investment for a small loft. Fortunately, in braided luff rope, three sizes—⁵⁄₁₆, ⅜, and ½ inch—cover nearly all applications and sail sizes.

The larger leech lines double well as small (⅛ to ³⁄₁₆ inch) headsail luff ropes. The smaller diameters of polyester braided leech line are only obtainable by the spool, and a full range of these for light sails and drifters should be maintained.

Obviously, a full cordage inventory is an expensive proposition, especially since some sizes will be used infrequently. With close proximity to a supportive chandlery, it is possible to obtain line in the lengths required for individual jobs. This, of course, costs somewhat more per foot, but you can include it in the sail price.

It should be apparent by now that all those who maintain their own sails should have in the locker replacement material for every component. This entails a few more items than what comes in a typical kit. For bluewater voyaging, the locker might hold enough materials to make an entire new sail, or even a whole suit! Fortunately, the running rigging of a vessel is often identical to the sail's cordage, and thus spare supplies can do double duty.

Wire

Sailmakers felt blessed when wire rope became available in sizes and constructions appropriate for reinforcing sail edges, and in particular the luffs of yacht sails. The wire rope was stronger and stretched far less than hemp boltrope. But no one who has ever handed a wire-roped squaresail or watched the luff of a yacht sail corrode, stain, and turn to dust will claim a fondness for wire in sails.

In the days of cotton sails, galvanized wire had to be parceled and served. In the scheme of things, at the time, there was nothing excessive about the labor involved, and the greater control over the luff offset the decrease in longevity as the wire inevitably corroded.

I am not enthusiastic about putting wire in a headsail. With virtually stretch-free braided luff rope available and the greater versatility of a sail with an elastic luff, it seems unnecessary to endure the problems inherent in wire luffs. Even plastic-coated 7 x 19 stainless steel constructions are prone to corrosion and awkward handling. In addition, I like the components of a sail to be as similar and compatible as possible. Spare rope for jury rigs is something a sailor is likely to have on hand, whereas ³⁄₁₆-inch plastic-coated wire is less likely—unless one wants to dismantle the lifelines. And wire is much harder to work.

Nonetheless, in some instances wire makes sense. Light-air auxiliary sails, particularly ones set flying, such as mizzen staysails, have no need of elasticity in the luff, and the luff of the sail doubles as a stay. For sails that are raised by a wire halyard, and in stormsails where constant high luff tension is desired, wire-rope luffs are appropriate. I'd maintain, though, that for several reasons it would be better to eliminate the wire altogether, halyards and all.

Wire is also used for the tack and head pendants

on a headsail, ensuring that a sail with wire halyards is tacked at the right height and the wire portion of a rope-tailed wire halyard makes turns around the halyard winch.

Nicopressing eyes in wire-rope luffs is tolerable, but splicing is better, and you're still a greenhorn until you can make a neat splice in a wire-rope luff reef tack eye.

Even with plastic-coated wire, the ends and splices must be parceled and served, if for no other reason than to fill the score of a thimble big enough to accommodate shackles and fittings.

A wire luff of stiff 6 x 7 construction is used in the type of roller-furling sail that employs a spool at the tack and a head swivel riding on a stay. It's an unmanageable snake and one of the *worst* forms of furling headsail arrangement for boat performance, sailors' comfort, and sailmaking. Dealing with the wire luff in this type of roller-furling sail is reminiscent of wrestling with the wire-roped squaresails and gaff sails in days of yore.

Stainless steel seizing wire and even shackles have been used extensively to unite and bind sail to luff wire and thimbles. Wire is fast and strong in a way, but it is difficult to lay up wire seizing turns evenly so that strain is evenly distributed. Thus, some parts must bear more strain than they can stand and so fail. And wire is inflexible and corrodes. Perhaps the inflexibility of a shackle is desirable when uniting wire thimbles with peak and tack rings in a roller-furling sail.

If you were to consult any sail-hardware catalog or, for that matter, look in at a typical production sail loft, you would find a fair number of sail components—plastic, metal, and cloth—not mentioned here. All these items I consider to be either superfluous or intended for a different sort of sailing and sailmaking than we're talking about here. There is no doubt that certain items, such as adhesive-backed colored cloth for numbers and insignias, are a boon, but one can make do without them. Furthermore, adhesive-backed material is only temporary, and for any permanence must be sewn down anyway.

Which reminds me of the time I was removing a large insignia that had rotted in the sun—as that light cloth is prone to do. It was a miserable job trying to remove the old pieces of insignia from the sail and, worse yet, getting the petrified stickum off. But incredibly, there, entombed between sail and insignia for several years, was the corpse of a common housefly! It was quite well preserved, which, I suppose, suggests that adhesive-backed insignia cloth could be used as high-priced flypaper by those with an archival bent.

Leather

Leather is somewhat of a loner, not belonging to any group. It just *is*—and must be, too, for a sail to hold up for long. The chafing gear on a sail is generally leather simply because sailcloth or webbing do not work as well.

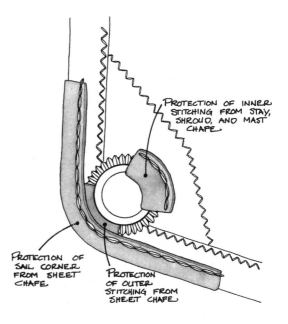

FIGURE 5-48. *Leather locations in the clew of an overlapping headsail. On a mainsail, leather should be added at all corners (including reef tacks and clews) and at other likely chafe locations such as from a topping lift. See also Figures 5-26, 5-31, 5-32, 5-34, 5-42, 5-47, among others.*

Leather is pliable, noncorrosive, sewable, and compatible with other sail materials. It is not indestructible, of course, and if not respectfully maintained, it will rot. It is there to protect the sail and be replaced when the time comes.

Leather is the processed skin of an animal—for sailmaking purposes, either cow- or elk hide. Elk hide, prized for its longevity in a marine environment and for its malleable nature, is a rare commodity indeed. It is better, I think, to let those elks that remain walk the earth, rather than sew their hides to sails. I have used deerskin on very refined small sails, but it is cowhide that is principally available, sold by the hide or half hide and the square foot. The belly portions of the hide are the most supple. The leather used in chafing gear is chrome- or oil-tanned and dyed.

The thickness of leather is specified in an ounce-per-square-foot system, 1 ounce translating into approximately $\frac{1}{64}$ inch of thickness. Leathers for sailwork range in gauge from 2- to 8-ounce, with 4-ounce being the most useful. Leather is one of the few sail components that is available from sources other than central sail-supply distributors, and a greater variety of leather of better quality at less cost can be obtained through leather distributors.

Lofts and amateur sailmakers alike would do well to have both the 4-ounce chrome-tanned leather and a heavier 8-ounce oil-tanned latigo. These are available in various colors and stiffnesses. For chafing gear on sails, an ability to conform to curves is important.

On board ship, leather has innumerable uses, not only as chafing gear in rigging and on oars and anchor rodes, but also in bags, containers for sheets and winch handles, and knife lanyards. A half hide of the two types previously mentioned would be the minimum for seagoing preparedness.

Webbing

There is one last sail material, my unbounded praise and advocacy of which may forestall your condemning me entirely as an antisynthetic and romantic cynic. Webbing, flat or tubular, a woven strip of polyester or nylon, is a material of incredible versatility and value in the making of a sail. It is strong, elastic, and highly compatible with other sail materials and components. And so many uses!—slide seizings, corner ring attachment and reinforcement, leech cord exits, batten pocket ends, reef ties, sail corner reinforcement, thimble-to-ring seizings, chafing gear, not to mention sail stops and lashing and lacing. Moreover, it can be stowed on board for any number of future uses. Wonderfully, this same webbing in sufficient length can be used as a portable alternative to battens for drawing the peripheral edge curves while lofting a sail. It takes a cool hand and a keen eye to fair a 40-foot compound curve with webbing—but it can be done, and that with the same roll of webbing that will later be built into the sail.

I have had some success with cotton webbing, too, and wondered why it was not used more extensively in the past. One reason, besides its variable shrinkage and stretch, is that cotton webbing, unlike synthetic, cannot be cut with a hotknife and left unbound. The cotton webbing must be oversewn to prevent its unraveling.

Flat webbing ranges in width from a thin ribbon to a wide belt. One-half-, $\frac{3}{4}$-, 1-, $1\frac{1}{2}$-, and 2-inch are the sizes in nylon, and the sizes most frequently used in a sail loft. It is the $\frac{3}{4}$-inch that works best as tape for drawing edge curves and doing most seizings. One-inch tubular polyester webbing does larger seizings and ring reinforcement. The larger webbing sizes serve as chafing gear and reinforcement. It would be valuable to have on board the four smaller nylon sizes, and $\frac{3}{4}$- and 1-inch widths in spun polyester tubular webbing for gaskets and lashings.

Flat nylon webbing has two idiosyncrasies of which you should be forewarned: First, it tends to shrink somewhat—both when it is sewn and then later as it becomes weathered and salty in use. If the webbing has been sewn to the sail for corner reinforcement, the result can be considerable puckering of the sailcloth. Second is nylon webbing's habit when first exposed to sunlight of turning bright urine-yellow. This I discovered to my horror after delivering and bending a fancy new sail with webbing slide seizings and returning the next day to find my work of pride looking as though a pack of male dogs had come by and lifted their legs on it! The yellow had leached out into every portion of the furled sail with which the webbing had lain in contact. I was grief stricken. But, mysteriously as the coloration came, it soon departed. I wondered where the yellow went, and can only conclude that rain and weather washed it away. I still don't know for sure. I first thought that the webbing had reacted to the formaldehyde in the sailcloth, but the cloth manufacturer refused to discuss the matter. Maybe there had been a

chemical reaction and sunlight bleached out the yellow. In any case, don't be alarmed at the initial yellowing of nylon webbing in a new sail; the stains should disappear.

THE PRESERVATION OF SAILCLOTH AND SAILS

Since the dawn of sailing, sailors have tried every means possible to prevent or at least delay nature's inexorable and inevitable deterioration and destruction of sails. Even today, with the most sophisticated synthetics, the battle is still fought (see Chapter 8)—primarily against corrosion and ultraviolet light, which wreak havoc in the molecular chains of synthetic cloth. With cotton and flax, it is not only the ravages of a marine environment and sunlight that prey on sails, but also organic rot.

Dressings of all descriptions have been used throughout history and around the planet, but the basic ingredient used as a preservative for natural-fiber sails is tannic acid, or tannin, found in barks, nutshells, and plant parts. This is the same material used in the preservation of leather and fishnets. Natural-fiber cloth may be treated prior to construction of the sail, during the building process, or long after the sail is complete and has been broken in for some period of time. (A year's use must pass before a traditional flax Norwegian squaresail is considered ready for barking.)

Dyeing and dressing sails is a rewarding and extensive undertaking that results in a handsome sail of great longevity. It is quite time-consuming and requires materials, tools, and facilities not readily available. One can make do, though, for a personal project—but it would be ill advised to undertake the barking of sails as a commercial endeavor, although it is still done routinely in parts of Europe.

I have used mangrove-bark formulas, tea, pine tar and turpentine, canvas paint and turpentine, and such for barking. Probably the most notable job was the dressing of a lugsail with a canvas paint–

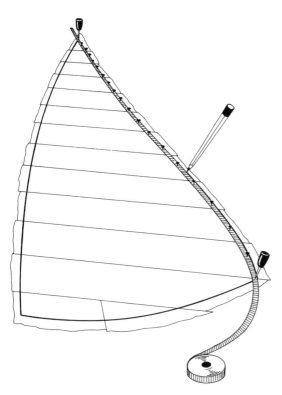

FIGURE 5-49. *Versatile nylon webbing being used in place of a batten for lofting. A more common use of webbing is shown in Figures 5-32, 5-34, 5-35, and 5-36.*

turpentine goop. My loft at the time was upstairs in the old ballroom of the Anacortes, Washington, municipal building. In the evening, after I had left the sail to dry, there was much to-do: the folk dance club, with whom I shared the floor space, had to cancel their weekly romp—the fuming sail was so powerful. Meanwhile, down below in the town offices, a town clerk doing some yeoman after-hours drudgery found that not even the intervening stout flooring and walls could keep the pungent aroma of the sail from bringing tears to his eyes. Fearing a conflagration, the dutiful clerk summoned Anacortes's fire brigade. The men in trucks of red arrived in the odiferous arena and promptly stuffed the sail into a plastic bag and confiscated it.

You can imagine my surprise when I arrived in the shop the following morning to find the sail gone without a trace. A grimacing town official related the events of the night, whereupon I went off to the fire department to recover the sail. A night spent crumpled in a plastic bag gave the sail a distinctive tie-dyed appearance. Needless to say, future sail dyeings in the shop were forbidden. This event did nothing to bolster an already faltering relationship with my municipal landlord, but I learned some lessons, among which was that sail barking must be done outdoors or in a well-ventilated space, neighbor-free.

There are a variety of unnatural preservative formulas for natural fibers. Unfortunately, the cotton sailcloth available now has been treated in advance with pentachlorophenol. An alternative, a cotton not originally intended as sailcloth, is Vivatex, which has been treated with arsenic. Pete Culler espoused clear Cuprinol, which I have used; also pine tar and kerosene, which I am told causes more deterioration than it prevents.

Last, there is the mineral spirits–based commercial tarp preservative Canvac, which I have used to prolong the life of cotton boat covers and suggest would work well on heavy natural-fiber sails. It can be obtained clear and colorless or in various shades that can impart a pleasing hue to the sail. Some treatments, such as Canvac and other petroleum product–based solutions, offer water repellency as well as mildew resistance.

These are the basic goals: mildew resistance, weather resistance, water repellency, and aesthetic appearance. The preservation of synthetic sailcloth and cordage is primarily a consideration of ultraviolet resistance, not aesthetics. These materials undergo both dyeing and UV treatment when they are manufactured and finished. The only exception—as noted—is the tarring of spun polyester boltrope, which can be done quite simply. Dyed polyester sailcloth of various colors does have some ultraviolet resistance, but it is the process of urethane coating that adds a temporary, general UV resistance.

The only other way to protect synthetic sails and stitching is with a cover material, which serves as a screen. This, of course, is not a treatment—it is protective lamination, and a procedure that is workable for limited areas on one side of a sail, such as the edges of roller-furling sails. It is not a technique for full sail protection.

THE TOOLS OF THE SAILMAKER

Sails can be designed and made with but a few crude tools or, alternatively, with a vast array of sophisticated electronic devices. What is presented here is somewhat more than the absolute minimum, but an inventory within the needs and means of a small loft or interested amateur. The basic goal is to combine economy, portability, and ease of production. At the same time, there is a concern for human-oriented experience and creativity, with as much self-reliance and independence as possible. The following tool inventory doesn't take much in the way of money, but it does take some character and appreciation for hand tools. If the list should start to seem daunting to you, remember that it is possible (given enough time) to build sails using only the tools discussed in

Chapter 1 plus the few design and lofting tools mentioned below.

Design Tools

It is not essential that a sail be designed in advance. It is beneficial to have a record for future reference, and in complex designs, a plan aids immeasurably as a procedural guide, especially if more than one person is involved in the lofting of the sail. Nonetheless, real seat-of-the-pants work has you making it up as you go, which on simple, repetitive work involving no precision is all that's necessary. In fact, that is why empirical and intuitive

sailmakers are hard-pressed to explain how things are done; they have no formulas—they just do what looks and feels right.

The following tools are helpful in making a scale design plan: an architect's scale, a compass with extension, a protractor, a French curve, a flexible curve, a straightedge, a pocket calculator, and a mechanical pencil and eraser.

Clearly, for precision and ease of drawing, good tools are better. The calculator is a wonderful aid for many sailmaking calculations. Several of the functions on the more sophisticated calculators are of value, but the basic arithmetical functions

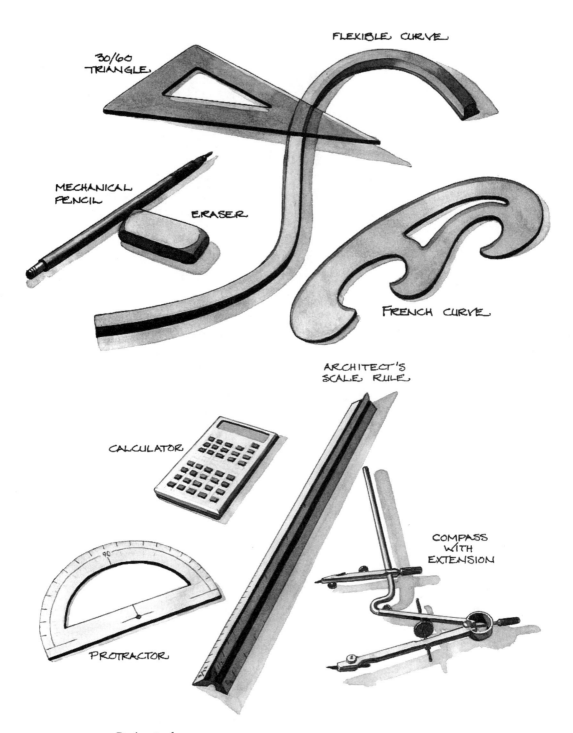

FLEXIBLE CURVE

30/60 TRIANGLE

MECHANICAL PENCIL

ERASER

FRENCH CURVE

ARCHITECT'S SCALE RULE

CALCULATOR

COMPASS WITH EXTENSION

PROTRACTOR

FIGURE 5-50. *Design tools.*

suffice. Any old hard-lead pencil will do, but a mechanical pencil always has the same point size.

Lofting Tools

Pins and spikes—4-inch scratch-awls, the contemporary substitute for the traditional sail pricker—are used to designate or locate endpoints for the corners of a lofted sail. In this position, the spikes provide firm fittings around which string is stretched and against which battens are sprung. A rubber mallet is useful for setting the spikes, especially in a hardwood floor. Lofting requires a minimum of 8 to 12 spikes. Moreover, the tips inevitably are broken as you inadvertently trip over the spikes (which is quite painful), so you need spares. The same 100- or 50-foot tape measures and 12-foot roll tape are used in the lofting as are used in the measuring of the boat. A minimum of two tapes are required, and one must be sure to allow for the ¼ inch or so lost in the placement of the spike in the end fitting of the tape measure.

Pins are needed to spring battens into a curve, retain lofting twine, and hold the cloth down in the layout process.

I like plain old thumbtacks for marking midpoints, because the cloth laid over them remains fairly flat. Masking tape or duct tape works, too,

for holding the twine in a rough curve to indicate the finished edge of the sail. Then, too, thumbtacks can be left in the floor until the sail's been through the final layout.

I prefer ⅝- or ¾-inch aluminum pushpins for the remainder of the pinning. Other types of pins are available, but they are not as durable. In addition, one can liven up a dull day by making dandy blow darts out of the aluminum type! Whether you use them as projectiles or only to pin up sail plans, at least 100 to 200 are needed for a moderate-size sail.

Lofting Twine   The twine must be long enough to circumscribe the sail or several sails individually lofted side by side. Nylon seine twine works well—so does cotton, as long as it is *elastic* and about ¹⁄₁₆ inch to ⅛ inch in diameter.

Lofting Battens and Tape   Battens enable a sailmaker to make fair curves about the edges of a sail. They are also used to draw out broadseams and delineate reef rows. The principal desirable qualities are fairness, straightness, flexibility, length, and width. Battens can be wooden (long-grain spruce), aluminum extrusions, or pultruded fiberglass. Naturally, one can't draw a fair curve

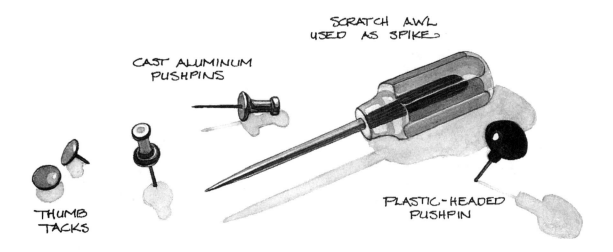

SCRATCH AWL USED AS SPIKE

CAST ALUMINUM PUSHPINS

PLASTIC-HEADED PUSHPIN

THUMB TACKS

with a lumpy, warped stick. The batten must be flexible enough to take a compound curve, but not be a squirming wet noodle. The natural resilience of the batten is often relied on to develop a fair and handsome curve.

It is convenient if the battens are of a length and width to match the sail. In terms of width, this means that the battens are the same width as leech and foot tablings—for example, ¾ inch, 1 inch, or 1¼ inches. Then a batten can be laid out to mark two lines at once and is useful in scoring the folded cloth edges. Great, long battens are impractical unless you have a large space in which you loft big sails on a regular basis. Somehow it often works out that either the sail edge is slightly longer than your longest batten, or the room is slightly smaller than your shortest batten. Joining two or more battens of about 20 feet each covers most situations. Three 20-footers and a 10-footer are all I've ever needed.

The alternative to straight battens is tape, which is indeed like using a wet noodle to draw a curve. The advantages are economy, portability, and ease of accommodating any size sail in any size lofting space. Nylon or cotton webbing in a ¾-inch width works well and comes in a roll. It takes much skill and patience to successfully lay out a fair curve by this very time-consuming method. Nearly every inch of the curve must be meticulously pinned out, but once you've "thrown the tape" a few times, you'll have a better feel than most for the ingredients of a fair curve.

Incidentals Only after years of dinking around with improvised means of drawing tablings did I become aware how easy a compass makes that sort of job. The little dime-store drawing compasses work, but the big wooden ones normally used on classroom blackboards enable you to draw standing up. The compass, of course, can be used for drawing large circles as well as parallel lines, and must be adapted from chalk and rubber tips to pencil and metal points. You only get a parallel line if you hold the compass at a consistent angle as you draw along the side of the batten.

Also of importance are a 4-foot metal straight-edge, a carpenter's square, and, for certain types of canvaswork, a chalkline.

Hotknife

Though the hotknife has numerous other applications in the cutting of synthetic cloth, such as repairs, patches, and cutting numbers, this tool can be used in the broadseaming of synthetic sails to trim away the extra cloth in the taper, which results in a uniform seam width without that telltale look of a widening broadseam. It takes a swift and steady hand to use a hotknife neatly. Unless an electrical current–regulating device is attached, the barrel and tip of the hotknife become red-hot. It is a dangerous tool to use and it's easy to burn yourself, the tool's own electric cord, or the sail.

A butane-fueled portable hotknife with variable heat and replaceable tips is now available. It seems ideal for shipboard use. It should be noted that as the polyester fiber is melted in the hotknifing process, noxious and toxic fumes and gases are given off that are not fit for human respiration— one should use a hotknife in a well-ventilated area. To use an electric hotknife effectively, you must have a light extension cord of 12 feet or so and a sheet-metal, stainless steel, or aluminum backplate against which to do the cutting. Cotton sails, of course, have no use for a hotknife, and synthetic

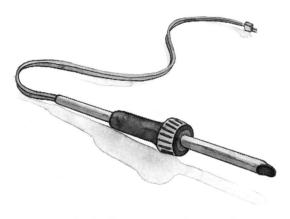

FIGURE 5-52. *Hotknife. A separate heat regulator is sold as an accessory.*

sails don't have to either. In fact, you can make a synthetic sail with no hotknifed edges at all other than the selvage of the cloth. For durability, hemmed edges are better than hotknifed ones.

Scissors

Working with cloth, you would of course presume that scissors are essential. In fact, it is possible to do with skill and a sailmaker's knife everything that can be done with scissors—if you have to. Otherwise, you can't beat a razor-sharp pair of 10-inch #1225 Wiss shears. Less expensive and less durable, cloth scissors of the department-store variety will work for light sails. I prefer to dedicate different scissors to different uses—cloth scissors for cloth, utility scissors for leather and general use, and thread nippers for the sewing machine. Not only are the respective scissors designed with these uses in mind, but their edges stay sharp longer when the scissors are segregated.

Here, I think, is the first tool mentioned that is not either-handed. If you are left-handed and not already trained beyond recall to use right-handed scissors, by all means obtain a left-handed pair.

Sewing Machines

The topic of sewing machines could fill a book itself. We must consider the machines themselves, and how they are powered. The choice of machine depends on the toughness and frequency of the work and where the work is to be performed. Sewing machines seem to have distinct personalities and minds of their own. Sailmaking sewing machines function in a few mechanical configurations, but no two machines—even of the same model—are identical. Every one requires its own settings, tuning, and adjustment for efficient performance, and I have yet to know a competent, affordable, and likable sewing machine repair person who is near enough to repair a machine in time

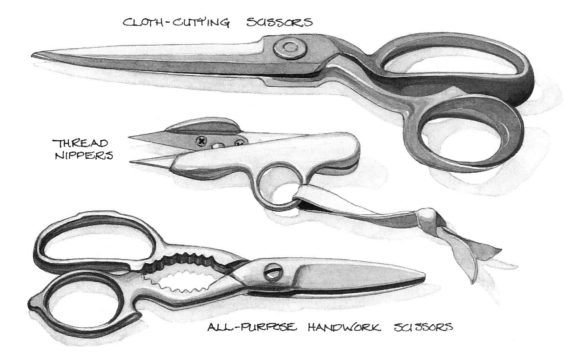

FIGURE 5-53. *Scissors.*

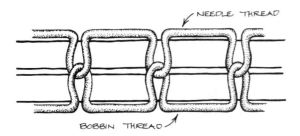

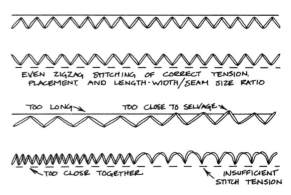

FIGURE 5-54. *Sectional view through two cloths joined with a locking sewing machine stitch.*

FIGURE 5-56. *Correct and incorrect zigzag stitching.*

FIGURE 5-55. *Straight stitching.*

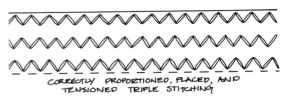

FIGURE 5-57. *Triple stitching as found in the seams of a large-boat or voyaging sail.*

FIGURE 5-58. *The three-step zigzag stitch is a wide, strong configuration. One row suffices in the seams of light-air sails.*

to prevent gross interruption and delay of the job. It behooves the small-time pro or amateur who expects to depend on a machine for any extended time to learn the principles of design, function, maintenance, basic adjustment, and troubleshooting. There probably is something mystical about all this, but mostly it is a matter of systematic diagnosis and remedy. There is often quite a bit of experimentation involved.

The sewing machine creates a locking stitch—interlocking a thread from below the sewn material with a thread above the material. Three locking stitch patterns have sailmaking applications. The most basic is the straight stitch—a straight-line series in which the length of the stitch (distance between needle entries) can be varied. The straight stitch is not advisable in anything but production sails for daysailing, cotton sails, and canvaswork.

The zigzag stitch is the most-used stitch in sailmaking. It has several advantages: it can oversew an edge to prevent fraying, the stitch configuration is somewhat elastic, and it can be taken out easily with a seam ripper. Most important, the holes in the cloth are not so close together as in a straight

line, and thus are less prone to tearing. The length and bite (width) of the zigzag stitch are variable. Generally, the zigs and zags meet one another at slightly less than 90 degrees.

The last stitch is really a combination of the first two. In this configuration, a series of two to four straight stitches are taken in a zigzag pattern. Logically, this is the most expensive stitch to acquire, as it necessitates the adaptation of the zigzag machine with a cam-controlled mechanism that determines the stitch configuration. There is the cost of the additional mechanism and then the cost of the cam. However, it is a powerful, versatile stitch most appropriate in situations where a wide, long stitch configuration is needed. Often a machine that is having trouble sewing a basic zigzag in a thick heavy spot will sew a "three-step" stitch quite well.

Selecting a Machine   The weight of the work and the frequency of sewing, of course, have everything to do with the power and ruggedness of the machine required. But also, heavy sails require bigger thread, for which a larger needle is used, and thus a bigger machine. Any of the ordinary home sewing machines will sew synthetic cloth up to 4 ounces in four layers or less, and though they are not as efficient as industrial models, I have made and repaired numerous sails on such machines.

For more layers or heavier cloth, industrial-grade machines capable of more power, more momentum, and larger needle/thread sizes are a necessity. Boing! This, in the used market, puts you at $800 to $1,000 a whack, and maybe $1,500 or more new, for the basic models.

Here are some general-purpose zigzag models that are appropriate for shop or boat:

- The Singer Model 107W1 or 107W3, with a wide stitch width, is the ancient workhorse of the industry. It will take from #30 to #138 thread, does not have reverse, and has a comparatively small 9-inch throat. These machines are probably the least expensive to obtain, used.
- The Pfaff Model #138, though discontinued, is one of the finest general-purpose machines obtainable, with reverse and an adequate (10-inch) throat. These machines can be set up to sew anything from ½-ounce spinnaker nylon with #30 thread to 14 layers of 9-ounce Dacron cloth with #138 thread! Expensive both new and used, they can be adapted to cams and the three-step stitch.
- The Bernina Model #217 is another machine of high cost and quality,

comparable to the Pfaff 138, except that certain models are capable of a much wider stitch width. This machine is not quite as versatile in the heavy end; it sews best up through #92 thread with a #120 needle and is capable of, but not preferable for, 9-ounce-and-up work.

- The Goliath of sewing machines is the Adler 266-1, which sews with thread sizes of #138 and up. The needles are like roofing nails, and these thumpers start at a no-nonsense $9,000. This machine has reverse, can be adapted to cams, and is a model you never want to have to heft around a shop, much less in and out of a boat locker. For large sails, thick corners, and stormsails, it is ideal.

There exist many more brands and models of industrial machines that do what these machines do and more: double-needle machines; walking feet; seam pullers; great, wide-throat machines; specialty machines for every occasion. It would seem as though there is an attachment to enable sewing machines to do everything from monogram hankies to peel apples. There are several specialty attachments that facilitate sailmaking procedures but are not essential: seam folders for light

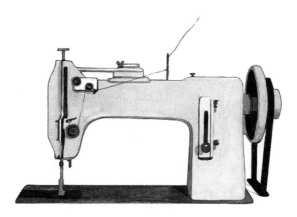

FIGURE 5-59. *The Adler #166-1 ultraheavy zigzag sewing machine, now the 266-1. Used model 166-1 machines cost around $5,500.*

nylon work, such as spinnakers and drifters; roping presser feet for machine-sewing boltrope to a sail; tape folders for canvas and upholstery work; and several more. It is best to have particular machines permanently set up with a specific attachment and function, rather than to be continually converting one machine from one task to another.

All these machines have appropriate applications and, in a production setup, speed the process. It is possible in a small shop to manage with one high-quality, versatile machine, such as any of the three mentioned. There is much downtime, however, readjusting the machine every time you change thread size significantly. The preferred small-time setup would be three machines—one for the light ranges of sailcloth, one intermediate, and the big daddy. The do-it-yourselfer will get by with one.

Power   The strength and efficiency of these machines is enhanced and augmented by the manner in which they are powered, as well as their mounting and the means by which their functions are controlled.

The motion to run the machine can be supplied by hand crank, foot treadle, or electric motor. In terms of the power inherent in momentum, heavy handwheels on the head of a sewing machine enable it to slog along through the thicker going. These larger handwheels also give you something to turn the machine with slowly in starting up or doing one or two slow stitches.

Hand cranks and treadles are wonderful for a boat or anyplace that is not electrified. A hand-crank setup is really a two-person arrangement, as two hands are needed for guiding the work. There is only the weight of the handwheel for momentum, but the machine is marvelously compact. A treadle stand, on the other hand, takes up more space. Sewing machines have been treadle powered for a century, but it takes a difficult-to-find, industrial-type treadle stand with a heavy flywheel to make this system work effectively with an industrial machine sewing heavy sailcloth. I have made sails of 8-ounce material quite acceptably with a Pfaff 138 set on a treadle stand. I have seen at least two arrangements where treadle stands were built into voyaging boats. In one, the stand supported the table in the main salon. In the other, the treadle was built into a locker in the forecastle.

Generally, the electric motor supplying power in an industrial setup is a ⅓- or ½-horsepower motor with a clutch mechanism so that the motor, always turning, can be gradually engaged and immediately

TABLE 5-10.
SEWING MACHINE NEEDLE SIZES *

SEWING MACHINE	NEEDLE SYSTEM	USUAL NEEDLE SIZES
PFAFF 138	130/135 × 5/438	80-120
SINGER 107 W1 AND 107 W3	135 × 7	80-120
ADLER 266-1	328	140-230
BERNINA 217	287 WKH	70-125
BROTHER TZ1-B652	K6 × 95/287 WKH	80-140

* SEE ALSO TABLE 5-6

disengaged. Domestic models and light portable machines have small variable-speed motors.

You can have any sort of table or stand you like, as long as it is sturdy, adjustable in height, and allows adequate work surface for the job. A standard tabletop measures 20 by 47 inches.

Four other features of the sewing machine/ stand ensemble are important:

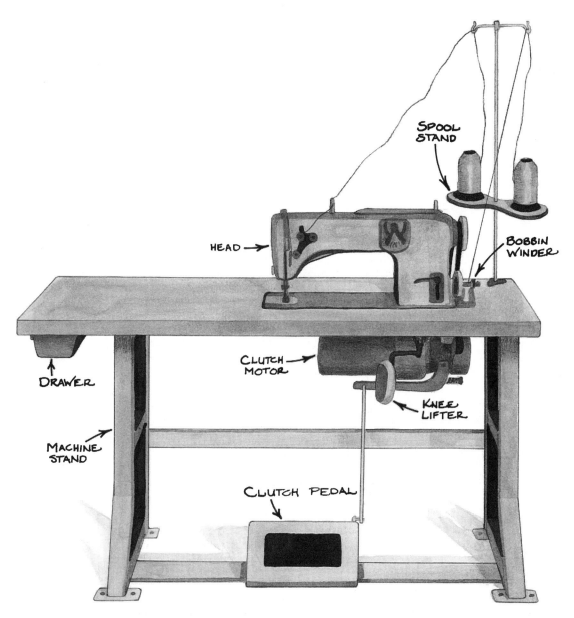

FIGURE 5-60. *A Bernina #217 with work station.*

1. An automatic bobbin-winding device that runs off the same drive belt as the machine.
2. A knee-operated presser foot lifting lever.
3. An adjustable light with a cool bulb, preferably wired so that the motor doesn't have to be running for the light to be on.
4. A stable thread stand to carry the reservoirs of thread for top thread and bobbin.

There are as many mounting arrangements as there are machines: flush with the floor, suspended from the ceiling, on wheels, sliding tables, and sliding machines.

Sewing machines are designed to run up to a maximum number of x stitches per minute. The relationship between the speed the machine turns, the number of stitches per minute, and the speed of the motor or drive is governed by the size of the pulley in the handwheel and the pulley on the motor. A larger pulley on the motor will turn more slowly with greater power. Rarely, in a small-time sailmaking operation, is a sewing machine run at its rated speed capacity. It is difficult to sew accurately at high speeds; furthermore, the needle heats up and breaks the thread.

Speaking of high-speed sewing, there are some hazards involved in machine sewing. A considerable amount of thread dust is generated; it is possible to sew your fingers; and if the needle shatters against the baseplate, little pieces of metal shoot out in all directions. (It is prudent to wear protective eyewear, though no one does.)

In recognition of the need for a portable, zigzag, semi-industrial machine for voyagers, two have been developed: the Reed Sailmaker and the Brother TZ1-B652, modified by Sailrite. Both have roughly the same features—self-contained, with hand crank and small electric motor, reverse, 9-inch throat, and bobbin winder—and both sell for under $2,000. They are rated to sew at about 2,000 stitches per minute.

The Brother machine has an incredible 12-millimeter stitch width capability, and seems a more rugged machine, with a two-speed drive. Both machines are certainly capable of sewing

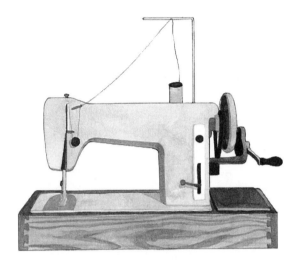

FIGURE 5-61. *The Brother TZ1-B652 modified for portability and hand-cranked power.*

multiple layers of 7-ounce cloth. Sailrite claims the Brother will sew 16 layers of 8-ounce in low gear, and I can personally vouch for the Brother's ability to sew 12 layers of 9-ounce Dacron with V-138 thread! In my experience it is a powerful, versatile machine and should be considered along with the previously mentioned industrial models as a small-loft workhorse when placed on an industrial stand with an industrial motor.

Hand Tools

Sailmaker's Palm   With this indispensable tool, a human hand can push a needle through heavy cloth. Waste neither time nor money on the cheap models, or what is called a *sailor's palm,* as they are nearly useless and will not encourage you to sew. Seek instead a high-quality sailmaker's palm of finished leather and rawhide, a stout article firmly stitched.

The two principal types of palms are both essential, depending on the job to be undertaken. The *seaming palm* is for sewing seams and tablings, and for patching, and has an eye with small indentations to take the head of the smaller needles used in those and other fine-scale operations. The *roping palm* is for the stouter work of sewing a boltrope to a sail; its eye has the larger indentations needed for the needles required in heavy work. In addition, the roping palm has a protective piece about the thumbhole so that a stitch can be hove home without the thread cutting the worker's hand.

Both palms are highly personal tools. Ideally, they are custom made for your hand only, or at least have been adapted to your hand and sewing techniques. The best commercially made palms are those imported from William Smith Company in England. (You can, of course, make your own,

FIGURE 5-62. *Sailmaker's palms.*

as described by sailmaker Brad Hunter in the April 1980 issue of *Small Boat Journal.)* I've said this earlier, but it is worth repeating here: The "public palm," while better than nothing, is an abomination. Worse yet is the ham-handed nozzer's disrespectful attempt to cram his hand into someone else's carefully fitted and broken-in palm. Make the palm fit your hand. If it's too small to begin with, it's worthless to you. A big palm can be reduced to some extent, and the fit can be adjusted with the addition of leather padding. The palm and your hand become one. Fit it. Wet it. Work with it. Oil it. Then work with it some more—and don't share!

Needles   Sail needles are triangular in section, with rounded edges so that the needle separates rather than severs the threads of the cloth as it passes through. The thickness, or *gauge,* of the needle to be used depends on the size of the thread required in the sewing and the nature of the material sewn. Usually the two requirements coincide, but not always. Synthetic sail twine, because of its great strength, can be smaller than the equivalent cotton thread for a given application, but your needle should always be sized according to the cloth it has to penetrate. Matching the needle to the smaller thread may result in the needle's breaking.

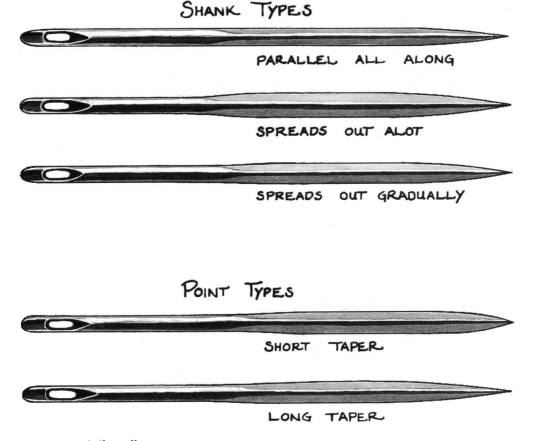

FIGURE 5-63. *Sail needles.*

While always retaining the basic triangular form, sail needles vary not only in length but also in proportion and taper. These subtle variations make a distinct difference in their use. A long, gradually tapered needle is more vulnerable but requires less effort to push through several layers of cloth. A blunter, thick-shouldered point is better suited to roping and seizing.

A needle of nearly straight body and shank passes easily; it works best with smaller twine. However, due to its relatively fragile nature, it is only appropriate for seaming and light sailwork.

A wider triangular body is for the heavier work of reinforcement. It may be designed or can be adapted for roping. The curvature of the upholsterylike roping needle facilitates the motion of passing through cloth and rope when the needle is held low. Standard short-tapered sail needles have blunt points to permit clear passage of the needle between the strands of boltrope.

It is important that the edges of the triangular tapered point be rounded and smooth so as to pass with minimal resistance and friction and not cut the cloth. And nothing makes sewing more tedious than a dull or dirty needle. Needles can be kept sharp and shapely with a razor hone or sharpening steel.

Aboard ship there is use for all sizes and types of sail needles; therefore, each size should be on hand, and it would be wise to have a few extra of the smaller or more frequently used needles. Sail needles in the smaller sizes break occasionally, and even the larger ones can be bent under the strain of

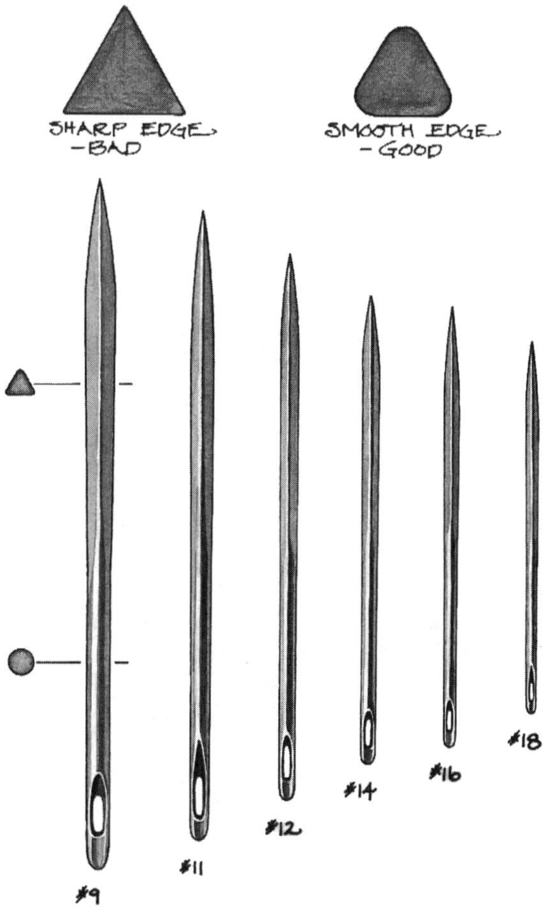

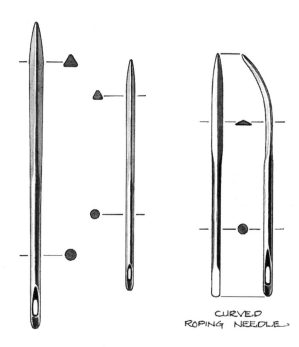

SHARP EDGE — BAD

SMOOTH EDGE — GOOD

#18

#16

#14

#12

#11

#9

CURVED ROPING NEEDLE

FIGURE 5-64A. *Relative sizes and cross sections of sail needles. The #9 is 4 inches long. Smooth edges are wanted, because sharp edges cut cloth.*

FIGURE 5-64B. *Sail needles used for roping want a short taper and blunt point.*

heavy work. Sail needles are wonderful little tools, but they will rust at the mere mention of the word moisture, especially at sea. Keep them oiled or greased and store them in an *airtight* container!

Knife   The sailmaker's knife is probably the most versatile tool in the inventory. Within the realms of sail and marlinspike work, it has many uses, and it can satisfactorily stand in for such other tools as scissors and hole cutters. Whether clasp or sheath knife, a V-ground blade with a rounded back and sheep's-foot point is best. Homemade or store-bought, a knife must be of good steel and kept clean, oiled, and sharp as a razor. This knife must never be asked to do anything but cut cloth, twine, or cordage.

Sailhook   The needle-sharp steel sailhook (also called a *stretching hook* or *bench hook*), with its swivel and 5- or 6-foot lanyard, facilitates various forms of sewing by holding the cloth in the desired manner so that tension can be applied and cloth layers kept in line, flat, and immobilized. Sailhooks, bought or made, must be protected from rust, like needles and knives. A store-bought sailhook must be altered so that it will work satisfactorily: the point needs to be ground down to a narrow needle projecting from a distinct shoulder so that the hook will remain in the cloth but not pull through, resulting in torn cloth and a big hole.

Fids   Fids come in an infinite variety and are used to expand, open, and ream: for instance, to open

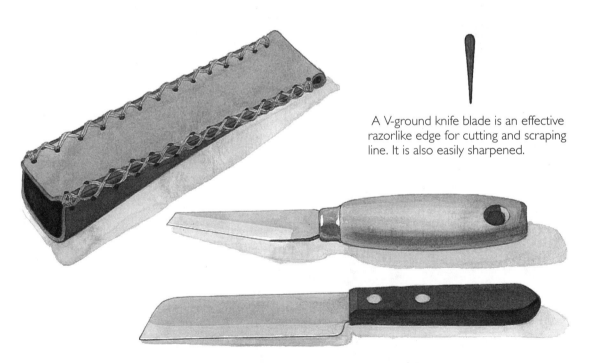

A V-ground knife blade is an effective razorlike edge for cutting and scraping line. It is also easily sharpened.

FIGURE 5-65. *Two ordinary knives adapted for sail- and canvaswork. The upper is a leatherworker's knife; the lower, a common kitchen knife with the tip ground to a sheep's-foot point. Both have a V-ground blade. The latigo leather sheath fits in the screwdriver pocket of a pair of coveralls to carry knife or scissors.*

the strands of a rope in splicing or to shape and smooth out the inside of a handsewn ring. They make holes in cloth and stretch cringles prior to the insertion of a round thimble. They are usually made of a hardwood such as lignum vitae. One can get by with two of them, a small one and one that is moderately large. There are numerous commercially made fids available for splicing. For sailwork, the trowel-like *Swedish fid* has served me well in two sizes, a 10-inch, and a 6-inch for smaller work. They are not hard to make—I have even adapted a mountain-climbing piton for this purpose.

FIGURE 5-66. *The bench, or sail, hook—the sailmaker's third hand—secures the work while seaming or roping. The lanyard is ¼-inch line about 4 feet long. Note the scorpion stinger-like point with shoulders, which prevents the hook from goring the cloth with a large hole.*

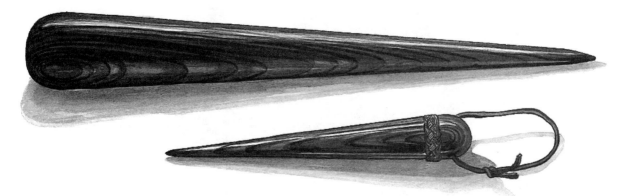

FIGURE 5-67. *These two wooden fids are made of rosewood and ebony and are 18 and 12 inches long, respectively. The ebony fid is adorned with a Turk's head tied into a score turned in the fid.*

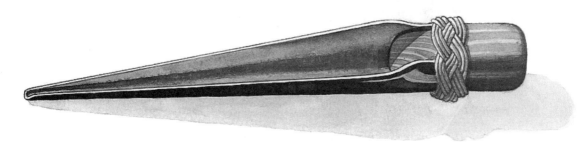

FIGURE 5-68. *The Swedish fid, an invaluable aid in splicing three-strand line, is commercially available in 10½- and 7-inch sizes. The smaller size serves up to ½-inch line.*

FIGURE 5-69. *Two-part fids driven through a hole in a board make a quick job of setting a round thimble into a cringle. The six smaller fids shown here are turned out of locust; they set thimbles from ¾-inch to 2-inch diameter. The big one-piece fid, called a set fid, is made of cherry wood and is used for large cringle and grommet work.*

Much ropework, either on or connected with sails, involves braided sheets and core line. Special essential tools are required for splicing this sort of line. Yacht chandleries and fishing-supply stores carry splicing kits, or they can be obtained from the manufacturer of the line.

There is a universal tool that obviates the need of a set of fids and a pushing tool. The separate aluminum fids do corrode, and it is wise to have ¼-inch through ½-inch sizes.

More Fids   No, this is not an assortment of dunce caps and devices for inflicting pain upon recalcitrant students! (Figure 5-69) The pointed items are all fids. These go beyond the basic assortment of fids mentioned above, but they make specialized tasks much easier. The largest, called a *set fid*, is a one-piece fid, 2 feet or more high and 6

inches or more in diameter at the base, that sits on the floor. This very traditional item is used for stretching larger rope cringles and rope grommets. The smaller ones each have two parts—the fid itself and the base—and are used for installing round thimbles in cringles. These devices so radically ease the slam-bam process of installing a round thimble (described in Chapter 1) that, if there is any anticipation of sticking cringles on a regular basis, it would be foolish not to have fids of this type in the sizes you will be using. This set incorporates ¾-inch, 1-inch, 1¼-inch, 1½-inch, and 2-inch round thimbles. The 2-incher would be a valuable cruising boat's tool.

I got the idea for two-part fids from the late Franz Schattauer, a sailmaker in Seattle, who had a carefully machined set made of steel; the fid portion actually screws into the base. My locust fids were turned

FIGURE 5-70. *Top: A traditional seam rubber carved out of black locust. Middle: A dulled barrel-knife blade used to score and crease sailcloth. Bottom: A wooden butter knife used as a creaser.*

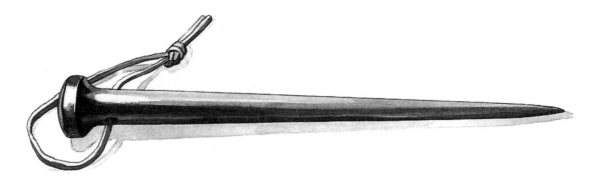

FIGURE 5-71. *Steel marlinspikes, available in several sizes, are essential for splicing wire but also serve in the removal of squeeze-on hanks. Twelve inches is a good all-purpose length.*

on a lathe, and the base is merely a socket. It is possible to dispense with a separate base and merely drive the cringle down the fid and over the thimble, which sits on a stump or on the floor. The problem with this method is that the cringle can only be driven down the fid on one side at a time; thus, when you make the final blow the cringle comes down onto the thimble on only one side, and you risk the cringle shrinking before you can complete the job. To avoid this, I created a holed plank that permits driving the fid down through the cringle (instead of the cringle down over the fid), which is stretched uniformly all the way around. With the final whack and installation, the fid portion of the tool falls through to the floor. It is a dandy system that usually results in a snug fit and offers leeway in the tightness and size with which the cringle is laid up.

Seam Rubber   A seam rubber can be your own creation out of hardwood (see Figure 5-70). This tool is for creasing cloth as well as smoothing and evening stitches. A rounded knife back will serve, and really any hard edge will do, but the seam rubber assures that the job will be done comfortably and consistently.

Steel Marlinspikes   Big and small, marlinspikes are not only useful for wire work and heaving seizings tight but also work well for removing ring liners and pressed-on-type jib hanks.

Rigger's Vise   For the wire splicing a sailmaker is likely to perform, a small portable rigger's vise is valuable but not essential. Any shop doing traditional rigging work as well as sailmaking will certainly have a small portable vise, and a larger vise as well.

Nicopress Tool   A Nicopress tool and Nicopress sleeves are the quick and dirty alternative to splicing. In *limited* circumstances this method of forming a wire eye is acceptable. If you're putting light luff wires in drifters or mizzen staysails on a regular basis, for example, you can save some time this way. Though the eyes are not as strong or durable as a splice, they will last as long as the sails. You will use only ¼-inch or smaller wire in Nicopress sleeves, so it is not necessary to obtain the larger tool. The small, portable, bolt-and-nut-type Nicopress tool is less expensive and covers four sizes, but it is more time-consuming to operate and requires the use of additional wrenches. The large lever-action-type tools are quite costly, handle only one or two sizes, and are cumbersome, but they crimp that sleeve right down to the necessary degree in one fell swoop.

Wire Cutters   Wire rope can be cut with a cold chisel or hacksaw, but a good pair of cable cutters, though more expensive, can do a cleaner and perhaps faster job. A small pair would be handy in any ditty bag, but both large and small cutters are important tools to have aboard a voyaging boat or in the sail loft, where wire-rope work crops up not only in building sails, but also in standing and running rigging and in lifelines. An offshore sailor would do well to have a large emergency pair of cutters, should it ever be necessary to cut away the rig after a dismasting.

I am sure there are many worthy brands of cable cutters out there, but I have found Felco cutters, which come in four sizes—$\frac{3}{16}$, $\frac{1}{4}$, $\frac{3}{8}$, and $\frac{5}{8}$ inch—to be of excellent quality. It is the blades, which are replaceable in all but the smallest cutter, that make these tools so expensive.

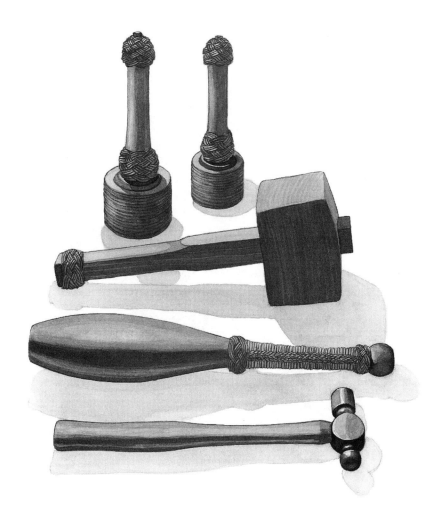

FIGURE 5-72. *Various beaters, pounders, persuaders, and tappers. Top to bottom: Five- and 3-pound rawhide mallets for driving hole cutters and setting brass liners in handsewn rings. A wooden mallet for driving cringles down a fid. A wooden bowling pin for fairing splices in line. A light ballpeen hammer for fairing ring liners and other odd jobs.*

FIGURE 5-73. *"Jack the merciless seam ripper"*
removes stitches and makes accidental cuts in your
sail with equal ease.

Seam Ripper   Be careful! This valuable little
devil will cut you or your sail as easily as it will
stitching (see Figure 5-73). A sharp, pointed knife
will serve for removing stitching, but a carefully
directed and controlled seam ripper does the job,
especially with zigzag stitching, much faster. The
tool itself is not very strong and is easily broken if
used for other purposes.

Mallets   Speaking of thumping and whacking—
stretching cringles, knocking round thimbles,
pounding splices, driving spikes, setting liners and
spur grommets, and cutting holes all require persuaders in the form of a specialized mallet. I use a
common wooden woodworker's mallet for cringles
and thimbles (see Figure 5-72). A candlestick bowling pin convinces splices that they ought to lie
smooth and fair. Cutting holes with cutters and setting liners demand great force that will not harm
the metal tool that is struck. Lead-weighted
rawhide mallets serve this purpose; they are available in weights of 1, 3, 5, and 10 pounds. A
3-pounder is fine for working on everything
through #10 rings. Number 11 rings and up require
a 5-pounder. A lightweight ballpeen hammer
smoothes out ring liners and works well as a lever
to make the final heaves on the strands of a cringle
after setting a round thimble.

Cutters   Prior to sewing in eyelets and corner
rings, or setting a spur grommet, a hole of the correct size must be cut in the sail. This can be done

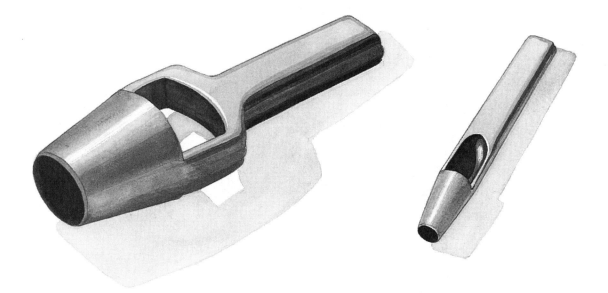

FIGURE 5-74. *Appropriately sized hole cutters make quick and accurate holes in a sail prior*
to sewing rings or setting spur grommets.

with a knife, scissors, or a stabber, but it is quickly, cleanly, and accurately accomplished with a hole cutter—either side-hole cutter or arch type. The hole cutters listed in Table 5-7 (page 169) make up an extensive working inventory.

For shipboard use, only those sizes pertaining to rings and spur grommets in use on board are needed. For a minimum small-boat and light canvas inventory, I suggest the following basic hole cutters: $\frac{9}{32}$-inch, $\frac{7}{16}$-inch, $\frac{3}{8}$-inch, $\frac{1}{2}$-inch, $\frac{7}{8}$-inch.

For a voyaging inventory and cruising canvas-work, it would be wise to have $\frac{9}{32}$-inch, $\frac{7}{16}$-inch, $\frac{1}{2}$-inch, and 1 $\frac{1}{8}$-inch.

Setting Dies Spur grommets and the liners for handsewn rings must be set with a two-part setting die: spindle and base. Hand-worked eyelets and corner rings depend on brass or stainless steel liners, not so much for strength as for chafe protection. Clearly, setting dies are needed for all spur grommets and rings. Cutters and dies go together. Thus, a complete, complementary inventory to the

FIGURE 5-75. *Two-part setting dies are required to turn over and set the brass or stainless steel liners that protect the stitching of a handsewn eyelet or corner ring.*

FIGURE 5-76. *A two-part setting die is also required to install the two halves of a spur grommet into a sail.*

previously listed cutters is advisable. A small-boat voyager needs these dies: #0 spur grommet die; #1 spur grommet die; #3 liner die; #4 spur grommet die; #4 liner die; and #7 liner die. A larger voyager should have these: #0 spur grommet die; #2 spur grommet die; #3 liner die; #4 spur grommet die and liner die, and #10 liner die.

Sailmaker's Bench

Here is the throne of traditional sailmaking. On this item, a complete sail can be assembled and finished. This particular pine bench (Figure 5-77) was taken from a design a Captain Dolf duplicated from the sail loft of H. H. Hamblin & Son at T Wharf in old Boston. Bruce Bingham published the plans in his *Sailor's Sketchbook*. My longer version was made for me by Bill Jackson of the famous Freya Boatworks in trade for a monogrammed ditty bag of the type presented in Chapter 1.

Ideally, a sail bench is designed around the stature and needs of the sailmaker. It must be the correct height, so that the lap as one sits on the bench is parallel to the floor. For a right-hander,

the tools and storage are on the right end; the opposite for a left-hander. There are nearly as many variations on sail benches as there are sailmakers. Some have drawers or storage compartments. My bench is stoutly made and stable. It is a long 6 feet to permit plenty of room for sliding along on a seam or rope. It has a backed edge that keeps me and the tools from falling off. Spools of twine are stored on removable spindles. A pad is drilled with holes for housing fids. The bench hook can be made fast to a strap eye at the end of the bench. A cut and whipped piece of 1-inch manila line made fast with bronze screws cordons off a section of the bench. This "cow pasture" has corralled within it the majority of hand tools. The line also serves as a storage place for needles. Mounted on the back side of the bench is a 2-foot piece of ½-inch hemp boltrope with a series of cringles that hold several more tools. Clearly visible are many of the hand tools mentioned earlier. In addition, there is a grease horn in which needles can be stored. Primarily, this is a storage vessel for tallow used in slicking down cringle fids or for helping a

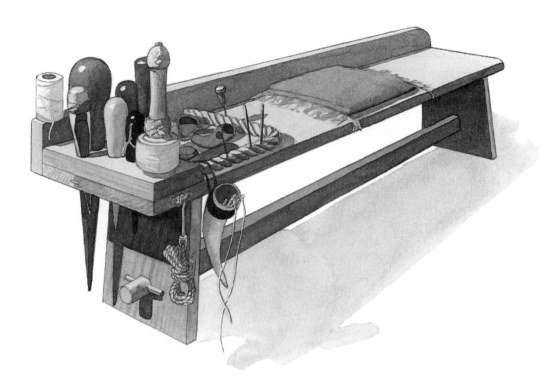

FIGURE 5-77. *Not just a seat, the sailmaker's bench is an ergonomic tool custom-built to facilitate all aspects of sewing and finishing a sail by hand. All tools and materials on this pinewood right-hander's bench are within reach, and a soft pad upon which to sit hopefully forestalls having to consult a proctologist! Note the locations of various other tools described in this chapter.*

needle get through heavy going. Last, there is a seat pad for comfort and to help in sliding back and forth. Some sailmakers prefer a doughnut form; others use no pad at all.

For roping it is convenient to have the bench hook tied off at a height above bench level. For this, some sailmakers have a permanent post built into the end of the bench. I attach an oak stave to the bench leg with a C-clamp. A handsome, well-organized bench is a utilitarian thing of pride and beauty and truly the hub of traditional sailmaking.

The Handwork Stump

When you weigh anchor and relocate a sail loft, especially at a great distance, there are some tools and furniture you just can't take along. Consequently, for every new shop, I've had to come up with a new handwork stump. Actually, it's an exciting adventure creating this essential piece of sailmaking equipment that serves as a solid surface on which to cut holes, set liners, and otherwise pound, slam, and roll parts of a sail during the finishing process.

Clean, dry, salt-free, dense wood is best, since the stump is not only used for pounding and persuading, but also spikes and pins are often pushed into it when doing ropework. I've used oak blocks, pine stumps, old pilings, and driftwood stumps. The important things are that the stump be dense and heavy so that the force of the blow goes into the work rather than the floor; that there be a protective nylon cutting pad on the stump so that tools, particularly cutters, are not marred or dulled; that the stump be cloth-covered if there is any likelihood of its transferring grunge onto the sail; and that it be the right height.

The right height is that which ensures that when the mallet strikes, its handle is roughly parallel to the floor, thus transferring maximum power and accuracy from the swing. My present handwork stump is an oak log 27 inches by 12 inches sur-

mounted by a commercially made nylon cutting pad 10 inches square.

Auxiliary Tools

A few auxiliary tools make life easier.

Soldering Gun   The Wen "quick-hot" soldering gun is used primarily for the hand sewing of synthetics, to melt a little globule at the end of the twine instead of making a knot, or to seal cut edges of webbing or cloth. This brand is the only one I

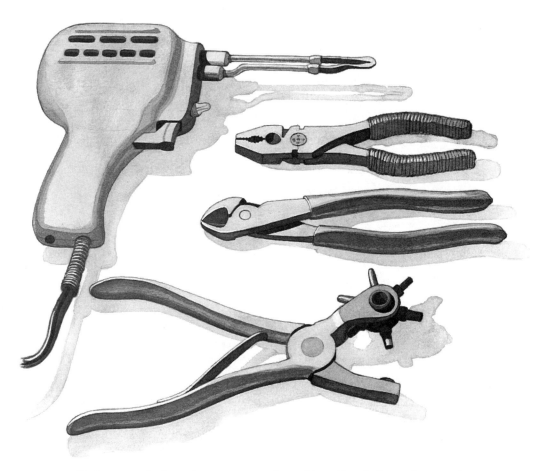

FIGURE 5-78. *Various unsalty but advantageous tools used in sailwork. Top to bottom: An electric rapid-heating soldering gun for cutting synthetic line or sail twine. Pliers—any pliers will do. (These are stock pliers from a Mercedes Benz tool kit, and the handles have been served.) Diagonal cutters. A revolving leather punch.*

know of that heats up fast enough. Rope-cutting blades are also available for it. For safety's sake and accessibility, and to prevent damage to the hot gun, it is suspended above the sail bench with a counterweighted system of line and two blocks. Three #15 brass rings provide just the right amount of weight at the other end. With a snap hook on the hot-gun end of the line, the tool can be easily removed when necessary.

The hot gun has two drawbacks in addition to its consumption of electricity. First, it fosters a tendency to be lazy and melt synthetics that should best be left soft, oversewn, or hemmed. Furthermore, a brittle globule as a knot substitute can easily disintegrate and fail. Second, the use of the hot gun produces clouds of acrid fumes injurious to eyes and lungs—proper ventilation is imperative.

Leather Punches All sorts of leatherwork requires accurate holes, for which a revolving leather punch is an excellent tool. There are both formed-metal and cast-metal types. The cast variety is stouter and has replaceable hole cutters.

Pliers and Cutters Pliers are essential for, among a zillion other things, pulling needles through recalcitrant material. They work well, too, for heaving cringle strands. Diagonal cutters and pruning shears are wonderful cordage and twine cutters. Moreover, diagonal cutters are the tool for removing spur grommets and working with seizing wire.

Handy Billy Making and checking sails involves imitating the sail-edge tensions found on board under sail. For setting up small-boat sails, an unassisted individual can exert sufficient power by hauling and swigging a line rove off through a single block—an approximation of the small-boat halyard, outhaul, or downhaul. But larger sails with multipurchase halyards or winches require a large application of force if they are to be properly tensioned in the loft. Several passes of a line can gain sufficient mechanical advantage, but blocks and sheaves make for less friction and offer consistent and even tension.

A handy billy or luff tackle of 3-to-1 advantage will cover most situations. An additional tackle will be required for setting up an internal luff rope or wire—one tackle is for stretching the rope or wire, the other for stretching the luff of the sail. My second tackle is a double-purchase, twin fiddle-block arrangement. The handy billy needs plenty of scope in a ½-inch easy-grip, slip-free knotable line. Any store-bought tackle will do, but it can't possibly compare with the grandeur and saltiness of the lignum vitae handy billy described in Brion Toss's recipe in *WoodenBoat* magazine's issue No. 41. Pictured here is the prototype for that instructional piece. I received it in trade for a duffel bag of Mr. Toss's own design. (It was a bag within a bag, a

FIGURE 5-79. *Mr. Knot's lignum vitae handy billy—incorporating a fiddle block, a single block with double becket, and ½-inch line—is a light top burton with many uses besides setting up the proper tension in the luff rope of a sail.*

laundry bag with its own separate compartment to isolate the itinerant rigger's pine tar-and-tallow–saturated work clothes from his formal evening attire.)

Swivel snaps on a handy billy prevent the sail and tackle from twisting.

Stitch Heaver The T-shaped stitch heaver is a traditional tool of great antiquity. Perhaps of equal or greater value to the contemporary sailmaker

working in synthetics is the small socket in the end with which a sticky needle can be coaxed through the cloth in a spot too confined for the sewing palm.

Serving Board There is available an assortment of specialized tools for traditional wire work, but for the sailmaker's limited use of wire, a serving board is all that will be required for the service of wire eyes, small grommets, strops, and splices.

6

Making Your Own Sails

MAKING A SAIL IS NOT a task to undertake lightly. It can be very rewarding and enjoyable, but if done well it is a terrific amount of work—some sails more than others. Large sails, those of 100 square feet or more, become arduous by virtue of their size and weight and the energy involved. Even smaller sails of heavy construction take time and muscle. At least one-third of the work required to make a sail involves preparation—designing, gathering tools, organizing work space, obtaining materials—without which the cutting and sewing can't even begin.

The appropriate design and *cut* (construction) of the sail may come to you in any number of ways. At one extreme you may be replacing an old one, which you have as a tangible reference; the other extreme is inventing a sail for an unbuilt boat in the process of design. This chapter assumes that you know what type of sail you'll be making and understand its relationship to the boat and the type of sailing to be done. So the first step is to determine the sail's peripheral straight-line dimensions, from which all other refinements of design will follow.

OBTAINING MEASUREMENTS

Measuring an Existing Sail

What can be simpler than having for duplication an old sail that you know fit and served well? Nothing, really. Except that a used sail in need of replacement probably yields elongated measurements; thus, if you were to duplicate those dimensions, particularly in a sail of natural-fiber cloth and reinforcement, the new sail could easily stretch beyond the limits of spars or stay. So allowances must be made. However, the old sail is a fine reference, maybe the only reference.

An excellent space for measuring an old sail is a clean, flat, wooden floor into which spikes can be driven. Ideally, this same space will be used to loft the new sail. For one thing, you know the sail fits in the room, and for another, it is possible, though not advisable, to go for a quick-and-dirty approach: Design and loft the sail right there on the floor by tracing the old sail! You've been forewarned of the dangers of elongated measurements, but if you know there is room to spare in the rig, tracing is okay.

Why not measure a sail edge by edge in a smaller space? This tempting approach excuses you from finding a place large enough to lay out the sail, but edge measurements taken in this way are likely to be inaccurate. Furthermore, this approach hinders, if it does not prevent, valuable detail measurements, and you miss the diagonal measurements that are essential for a four-sided sail.

Measuring a used sail can be a tricky business. On the one hand the sail's edges will have elongated, but on the other hand the sail's tape, rope, or wire reinforcements will, unless pulled to their working tensions, yield too-short measurements. You must take care, then, to spike the sail out to its fully tensioned dimensions, balancing the tension between edges so that the sail is not distorted in one direction or another. I start with the edge that is subject to the most tension and is therefore most heavily reinforced (generally the luff) and spike that out, often with the aid of a handy billy.

If a sail is old and dilapidated enough, the reinforcement may be shot or removable. Removing the reinforcement, though time-consuming, will reveal the sail's measurements (or at least its *elongated* measurements) without your having to exert much tension—but it also denies you information that might help you decide what types of reinforcement and amounts of tension you wish to build into the new sail. Large *girts* (stretched and distorted spots) of cloth in the body of the sail indicate misplacement of corners or improper and unbalanced tensioning. An excessively rounded leech suggests insufficient luff tension.

It is safer and more accurate to measure to the vertex of a corner, where the two edges would have met if extended, rather than to some part of the actual corner that has been altered with trimming and hardware. The headboards of Bermudan mainsails are an exception; assuming the new sail is to have a headboard also, the truncated corner should be measured as a fourth "side" to the sail.

The peripheral measurements alone (and diagonals on a quadrilateral sail) will provide sufficient information with which to draw another similar sail on paper. But one can and should take this opportunity also to measure and note every detail of the sail for future inclusion in or adaptation to the new sail. This also provides a check on your measurements, any errors in which might not otherwise have revealed themselves until too late, as when raising the new sail. It can give you a sinking feeling, I can tell you.

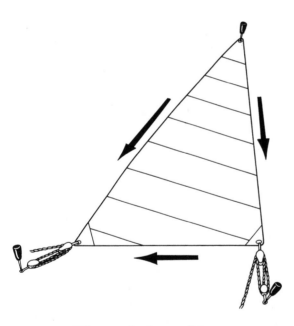

FIGURE 6-1. *When tensioning a sail for measurement, the sequence to follow depends on the type of sail. For a Bermudan mainsail or a headsail, first spike the head, then tension the luff, and finally pull the clew to tension foot and leech as shown. For a fixed-footed gaff sail, spike the throat and tension the luff, then the foot, then pull on the peak to tension leech and head. For a boomless or loose-footed sprit, lug, or gaff sail, spike the throat and tension the luff, then the head, then pull on the clew to tension the leech and foot.*

(text continued on page 220)

TABLE 6-1.
TYPICAL PROPORTIONS OF SELECTED SAIL TYPES

SAIL TYPE	LUFF	LEECH	FOOT	HEAD	DIAGONAL (PEAK TO TACK)	DIAGONAL (THROAT TO CLEW)
BERMUDAN (LOW ASPECT)	1.0	1.120	.620			
BERMUDAN (HIGH ASPECT)	1.0	1.071	.0411			
GAFF (LOW PEAK)	1.0	1.186	.799	.403	1.293	1.175
GAFF (HIGH PEAK)	1.0	2.232	1.666	1.096	2.064	1.838
LUG (HIGH PEAK STANDING)	1.0	2.328	1.582	1.45	2.340	1.846
LUG (CHINESE)	1.0	1.523	.976	.594	1.547	1.333
SPRITS'L (HIGH PEAK)	1.0	1.365	.944	.666	1.555	1.222
SPRITS'L (LOW PEAK)	1.0	1.393	.939	.727	1.525	1.333
STORM TRYS'L (JIB-HEADED)	1.0	1.240	.639			
STORM JIB	1.0	.770	.427			
GENOA	1.0	1.085	.594			
YANKEE	1.0	.708	.459			
DRIFTER	1.0	.952	.618			
MIZZENSTAYS'L	1.0	.802	1.298			
NORWEGIAN SQUARES'L (FORECOURSE)		1.727	1.345	1.0	(1.909)	(1.909)
JIB	1.0	.861	.394			
STEADYING SAIL	1.0	1.35	.925			

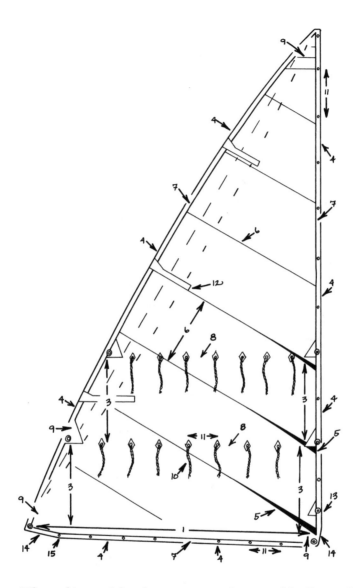

FIGURE 6-2. *When taking peripheral measurements from an old sail several other measurements and features may be recorded:*

1. *Luff perpendicular of sails with a tack angle less or greater than 90 degrees*
2. *Diagonals of four-sided sails*
3. *Depth of reefs at tack and clew*
4. *Edge-curve depth and distribution*
5. *Length, breadth, and placement of broadseaming*
6. *Cloth width and seam overlap*
7. *Tabling type, width, and location*

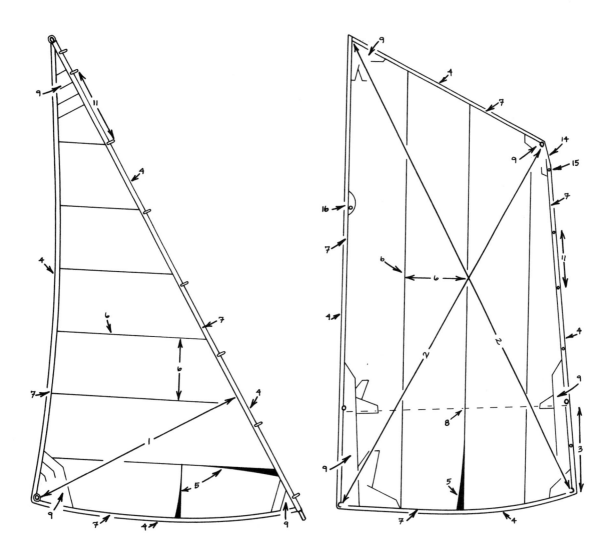

8. *Depth of reef curve*
9. *Number and spacing of corner-patch layers*
10. *Number and length of reef nettles*
11. *Spacing between reef, luff, foot, or head eyelets*
12. *Length, width, and placement of batten pockets*
13. *Cunningham hole or flattening reef location*
14. *Length and depth of offset at tack, clew, or throat*
15. *Location of clew slide, throat slide, tack slide*
16. *Location of brailing eyelet*

Measure and note the following:

- luff perpendicular
- diagonals on quadrilateral sails
- reef placements
- distribution, placement, and magnitude of roaches or rounds and hollows
- placement, length, and width of broadseams
- seam and cloth widths
- tabling sizes
- cloth type and weight
- corner patch sizes
- reef eyelet positions and spacing
- other ring and eyelet placement and type
- batten lengths and placement
- handling and adjustment features: brailing eyelets, cunningham hole, etc.
- offsets or cutbacks of sail corners to match spar hardware

Notes can be taken on every other detail of the sail: stitching, hardware, lines, slides, hanks, insignias, etc. Even if the sail is not drawn later—and it usually is—this information will be useful in gathering materials.

A scale plan of the old sail can be drawn and detailed as the information is recorded, or drawn later. This same plan can be used as a design for lofting the new sail, then or later, if no change is to be made in the measurements to allow for aging and elongation.

Measuring a Boat

Frequently, a sailmaker has only the boat and rigging from which to determine the measurements of a sail. Most working sail measurements can be obtained by measuring spars and stays. Some cannot, as portions of the area the sail is to fill (such as a high clew position) are simply not within reach. In such cases one can only measure the rig and spars and use this information to draw a scale sail plan of the boat, from which the dimensions of the sail can be determined. Drawing a sail plan is perhaps a good idea anyway, for reasons we will explore later.

Measuring on board a completed boat is actually the most successful approach to designing a sail because, assuming you measure accurately, all the variables are at hand and can be recorded. If no one makes a change in the rig, the sail will fit. Stock sail plans rarely are as accurate. With small rigs, it may be more practical and accurate to lay the spars out on the ground in their working relationship to one another. Estimations will have to be made for sheeting positions on the boat and heights above deck, however. An advantage to onboard measuring is that, with an assistant holding the measuring tapes in position (see Figure 6-3), you can, at a distance, study the profile of the sail at full scale in relation to the boat.

In either case, you will need two or three measuring tapes of sufficient length (50 feet plus), a small pocket tape measure (8 feet), some strong twine, a clipboard, a pencil, and paper. It really must be windless. Measuring with the tape slatting about is a nightmare.

Headsails (Jibs, Genoas, Drifters, Yankees—if the clew is within reach—and Staysails) The first measurement taken is the luff along the stay. Seize a shackle or jib hank to the end of the tape. With the hank or shackle clipped to and riding on the stay, attach the appropriate halyard and—very important—a downhaul of stout line. It is risky to rely on the tape for pulling the halyard down once measurements have been taken; the shackle tends to jam on the stay. Also, a heavy downhaul allows firm tension on the halyard with both halyard and downhaul belayed, so that there's little slop in the tape, particularly if there is a breeze or a roll to the boat.

Hoist the tape to the height desired. How far depends on the type of sail, obstructions (jumpers), and sheeting hardware. Maximum luff length, with adjustable track sheeting or a club foot, would have the head of the sail backed off at the masthead just enough to allow for sail stretch and obstructions on the mast. For a full-hoist sail, I raise the tape to the sheave or block, then back off 1 foot plus 1 inch for every 10 feet of stay length.

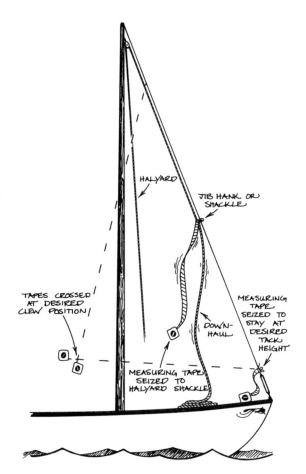

FIGURE 6-3. *Measuring for a heads'l (or any stay-set sail): Locate clew in close-hauled position, taking into account sheeting angle, sheet blocks, shrouds, and visibility under the sail.*

When measuring for a boomless sail that sheets to a fixed block, it is advisable to shorten the luff another 12 to 18 inches so that tack height can be adjusted with a tack pendant; this permits variations in sheeting angle.

The tack position is designated next. It should be high enough off the deck so that the foot of the sail will clear the bow pulpit and lifelines on all points of sail. This practice is wise not only for longer sail life but also for visibility and keeping water out of the sail. It also protects the tack of the

sail from chafe on the turnbuckle, and allows a hank to be placed right down low. The tack is often lower, however—sometimes even fixed right on deck. In any case, mark, measure, and record the luff length from head to tack position. Seize a second tape to the tack position and carry both tapes aft to the desired clew position and height, and record the respective measurements at the intersection of the tapes.

Genoas and drifters go outside the shrouds and can have clews that are high enough to be sheeted to the boom end if desired. The limits of how far aft the sail's clew can be taken are established by the type of sail, its relationship to other sails in use at the time, and the available fairlead for sheeting. Plans of similar sails on other boats of the same rig will show approximately where the clew should be for working jibs and staysails. Genoas and drifters offer more leeway in that, since they lap the mast anyway, your choices are simply between big and bigger, and you are limited only by shrouds, spreaders, and sheeting opportunities—the transom being the end of the line. A working genoa of 150 percent is standard, but if the sheeting block is fixed it may restrict the genoa to a smaller size. A drifter, ideally, should be as large as possible, with its sheet led well aft.

You will notice that the tapes, when measuring these sails, are bent around the shroud in a way that the sail never will be. Furthermore, in use, the sail's clew will actually sit forward of the measured position. Although measuring in this way does not precisely reflect the appearance and set of the sail, if the tapes are evenly tensioned and the profile is observed and checked from a distance, the resulting sail will fit without worry about its being too large. If it is not possible to reach the clew position, even with a stepladder, the only resort is a sail plan. Note stay diameter, height of turnbuckle and lower end fitting, and size requirements of halyard and tack shackles. Will chafe patches be required at tack or spreader ends?

Club-footed jibs and staysails are initially measured as above, but with allowance only at the head for elasticity and elongation (the tack being fixed).

Top the club up to its working centerline position, clear of stanchions.

With a pedestal or other loose-footed club staysail, locate the tack above the stay turnbuckle so the rounded foot of the sail will chafe less on the club when tacking. If the sail is loose-footed, measure its foot and leech to 2 inches shy of the maximum outhauled or lashed position. Allow an additional 1 inch for every 2 feet of foot length on laced or tracked feet. Note outhaul, track, and tack hardware sizes to ensure compatibility with the sail. Measure also the height of the outhaul car pin and the tack gooseneck pin above the spar.

Bermudan Main and Mizzen Prepare the rig for measurement by raising the gooseneck to its highest position, topping the boom to clear all obstructions and hang no lower than parallel to the waterline. (You will likely find that the boom looks best when kicked up slightly, 3 degrees or so on a plumb mast.) Stabilize the boom with sheet and preventers. Seize a sail slide to a 50-foot tape measure, attach the main halyard and a downhaul, raise to the masthead sheave, then ease the halyard 6 inches in 20- to 30-foot luffs of 6.5- to 7.25-ounce cloth, 9 inches in 20- to 30-foot luffs of less than 6.5-ounce cloth, 9 inches in most 30- to 40-foot luffs, and 12 inches in most 40- to 50-foot luffs.

With a fixed tack, it would be wise to deduct another 1 inch per 10 feet. Better too short than too long! Measure to ½ inch above the level of the boom or its track. Gooseneck configurations abound, and the type of fitting, with its various tack positions, should be noted so that your luff and foot measurements can allow for gooseneck offsets and so that the sail corner hardware is sized and located appropriately. If the tack fitting of a fixed gooseneck is below the track level of the boom, measurement to that lower level would result in a gross misalignment. Similarly, if the tack fitting is well aft of the mast, to neglect that offset will result in a misfit.

With a second tape measure lashed ½ inch aft of the mast, measure the boom out to the outhaul car or lashing. From the maximum position, deduct 1½ inches for 10 feet of foot length, 2½ inches for 15 feet of foot length, or 3½ inches for 20 feet of foot length. Done? Now, just to be safe, deduct an additional 1 inch for every 10 feet of foot length.

Measure from the head of the sail down to this same clew position, with minimal sag in the tape. Measure the offsets of tack and outhaul fittings. Sight up the mast and along the boom, and note any curvature or irregularities and their locations in order to cut the sail edges to compensate, as well as to avoid placement of slides at a bump or hollow. Sheet down hard with fractional rigs to note masthead bend. Check backstay and topping lift clearance if the sail is to have a headboard.

Reef Measurement Measure placement of the reef clew pendant cheek blocks on the boom aft from the mast. On double-headsail rigs, lower the halyard with the attached tape and measure from the intersection of the mast and forestay to the tack position, in order to place the head of a reefed sail at this advantageously strong point. (Hopefully, the existing reef clew cheek block was sited with this in mind.)

Note the track or slot size, the halyard shackle size, and likely areas of chafe: shrouds, lazyjacks, topping lift, or running backstays.

Odd Mains Variations on jibheaded or Bermudan-shaped mains require basically the same measuring process, with changes in foot and clew designation.

LOOSE-FOOTED. In this instance, usually a small sail, the boom should be topped to its working position, with tack and clew positions at least 1 inch above the boom level to permit the sweep of the foot roach to pass from side to side of the boom when tacking. As with the loose-footed club staysail, aft allowance of at least 2 inches must be made for elongation and outhaul adjustment.

BOOMLESS. With sheeting position(s) known, the measurement process is similar to that of a boomless headsail, combined with the luff-measuring procedure of the conventional Bermudan main.

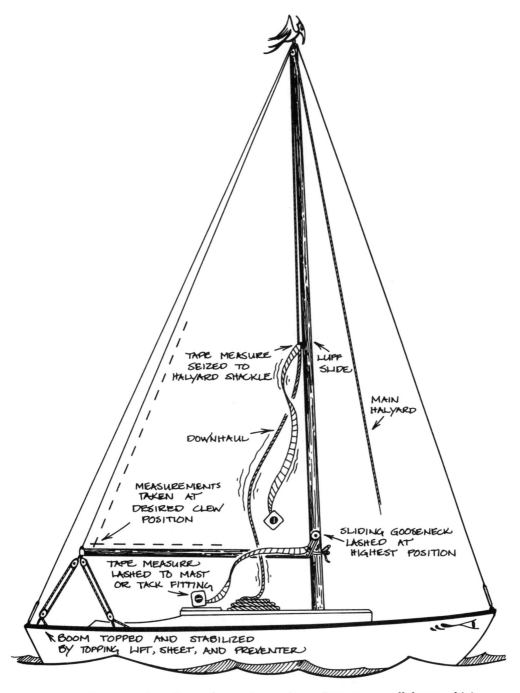

FIGURE 6-4. *Measuring for a Bermudan main or mizzen. Better too small than too big! Allowances must be made on luff and foot for elasticity and elongation. Visitations by prehistoric birds during the measurement process are portents of good luck.*

ROLLER-FURLING. Luff measurements are taken as in the conventional Bermudan main, except that the extrusion or wire is the straight line of the luff, rather than a track on the mast. In most instances, the sail is set loose-footed to a boom kicked up sufficiently to prevent the rolled-up foot from piling up at the very bottom of the furling gear. The boom, if long enough, may not be topped very high, but the clew is surely raised such that a straight-line tack angle of 86 degrees or less is created.

The measurement of the leech and foot presents no more difficulty than that of a boomless headsail or mainsail. Simply intersect the two tapes at the desired location—this time, above the boom at its working height, allowances being made for outhauling and sheeting angle, since there is no clew lashing. The tack is predetermined by the furling gear, although this type of sail can be set on a pendant. The tape is hoisted to the desired position on the furling gear swivel.

SPRIT BOOM AND WISHBONE BOOM. Measure these sail types with a combination of the procedures for the Bermudan main and the loose-footed variation. The tack is fixed and the foot rises to a high clew, with allowance for outhauling. The type of luff attachment determines the point of measurement at the mast. With a luff sleeve around the mast, measurements are still taken from the after side of the mast; the mast circumference is noted and the sleeve later constructed accordingly. Spar bend must be accounted for to get an idea how much the mast will bow with snotter or outhaul tension. Note also the snotter position on the mast so that you will not locate eyelets there.

Gaff Mainsail and Gaff Mizzen The principles of measuring Bermudan mains apply as well to gaff sails, with the additional considerations of another edge, spar, and corner, more likelihood of chafe, and a greater variety of sail attachments with their associated offsets. Three long tapes will be needed.

Gaff mainsail proportions vary widely, but the following proportions, though arbitrarily selected, are fairly typical:

Luff: 1
Leech: 1.73
Head: .833
Foot: 1.02
Tack angle: 86°–87°
Height of peak: 42° (angle of gaff with mast) to
   30° (or higher still in pleasure craft)

With the luff as the primary measurement, it is important to make sure that from an established tack position (set at the highest downhaul position) the gaff jaws will ride comfortably below the lower shrouds with enough room to spare for stretching of the luff. Further, the type of tack, throat, and luff attachment fittings and their working distance from the after side of the mast are crucial. Ideally, they would all be in vertical alignment, but that is rarely the case. If the alignment is off, it works best to measure from the position of the means of attachment to the mast (hoops, slides, etc.), and later deduct the appropriate offsets (cutbacks) from foot and head measurements.

To facilitate measurement, two vangs must be bent to the gaff end to center the spar athwartships and hold the peak down. Firmly seize a tape to the appropriate outhauled peak position on the gaff, allowing 1 inch for every 5 feet of head length for future stretch. Measure the head to the throat fitting and to the forwardmost luff position, if there is a difference. Depending on the type of jaws or saddle fitting at the throat, the aftward offset of the throat fitting from the extended line of the luff will be greater with the gaff peaked to its working angle. Therefore, the offset must be measured with the gaff set up. This can be done accurately enough with the spar within reach from the deck. Now to the measuring:

Step 1: With tapes affixed to the peak and the aligned throat position (a throat downhaul will be

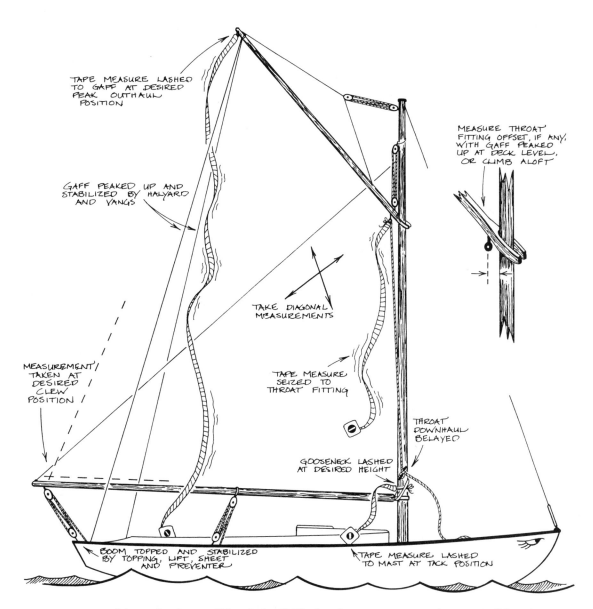

TAPE MEASURE LASHED TO GAFF AT DESIRED PEAK OUTHAUL POSITION

MEASURE THROAT FITTING OFFSET, IF ANY, WITH GAFF PEAKED UP AT DECK LEVEL, OR CLIMB ALOFT

GAFF PEAKED UP AND STABILIZED BY HALYARD AND VANGS

TAKE DIAGONAL MEASUREMENTS

MEASUREMENT TAKEN AT DESIRED CLEW POSITION

TAPE MEASURE SEIZED TO THROAT FITTING

THROAT DOWNHAUL BELAYED

GOOSENECK LASHED AT DESIRED HEIGHT

BOOM TOPPED AND STABILIZED BY TOPPING LIFT, SHEET AND PREVENTER

TAPE MEASURE LASHED TO MAST AT TACK POSITION

FIGURE 6-5. *Measuring for a gaff-headed sail. The head measurement and amount of throat offset are taken first, with the gaff set within reach of the deck. The gaff is then raised to its working height and angle for the remaining measurements. Allowance is made for elasticity and elongation.*

needed), hoist the gaff to its working height and angle. To allow for luff stretch, make sure the throat is well below the intersection of the mast and shrouds. Tension and belay the halyards, vangs, and downhaul to stabilize the gaff.

Step 2: Lift and top the boom to its highest working position; secure it with lifts, sheet, preventers, and lashings. From a distance, observe the profile of the sail.

Step 3: Measure the luff from the throat to a predetermined tack position above the boom.

Step 4: Attach a third tape to the tack point. Take the foot measurement from the tack point to a predetermined clew point (with allowances for elasticity and stretch). Measurements to the reef clew blocks can also be taken at this time.

Step 5: Measure from the peak to the clew point.

Step 6: With the edges of the sails measured, the next step is to take diagonal measurements to designate the form of the sail. Measure from peak to tack and from clew to throat.

Follow-up: Check the spars for curvature and flexibility. Light gaffs with a centrally placed peak halyard attachment will bend more. Note bumps and hollows in the track. Measure offsets in corner hardware and lashings. There should be consistency among throat, tack, and luff attachments so that if one portion of the sail is permitted to revolve about the after side of the mast, the rest of the sail can respond similarly. For example, if gaff jaws are used on a sail whose luff is bent to a mast track, the sail's throat eyelet and upper luff are unduly stressed when the gaff sags off. Avoid this configuration if possible, or alleviate its ill effects with a jackline on the upper luff, as discussed elsewhere.

The measurement of boomless and loose-footed gaff mains can easily be deduced from this procedure and from the discussion of the measurement of jibheaded mainsails.

Lugsails or Spritsails   Lugsails and spritsails can be measured on site in much the same manner as a gaff sail, with no concern for luff offsets, but it is generally more practical to measure the spars of relatively small rigs by laying them on the ground in their working positions or doing the whole process on paper.

A possible exception is the voyaging Chinese lugsail, which should be measured on board as a gaff sail. The principal differences in the measurement of the Chinese lugsail are the projection of the forward end of the boom and yard ahead of the mast, and the large leech roach produced by the individual battens in the sail. The allowance for this roach and the measurements between battens will later be worked out on paper.

Gunter Sails   The Crocker schooner *Privateer*, when first sailing as the *Mahdee*, carried a great whacking topmast at the head of a large gunter-rigged mainsail. Such a hefty gunter rig would be measured in much the same manner as a gaff rig. Here there is likely to be considerable offset at the throat to accommodate the heel of the topmast. Most likely this can be measured with the topmast peaked up at deck level to its intended vertical attitude. If not, that's what ratlines are for; aloft wi' ye!

All three forms of the gunter rig—sliding, folding, and "internal"—are usually dinghy sails and, like the lugs and sprits, can best be measured by laying the spars on the ground. Careful attention must be paid to the throat cutback in the sliding and folding types. The "internal" gunter has no throat at all, but one must reproduce the form of the curved topmast. To accurately reproduce the curve of such spars as this and the Dutch gaff, I think it almost better to measure and plan as if the sail were larger, with straight edges; then later, in the drawing of edge curves on the already seamed sail, trace the curve of the spar.

Squaresails   Rarely are squaresails square. They are usually trapezoidal in form. The head of a squaresail is bent to a yard, which must be set and belayed in its working position for measurement.

The foot of the sail can be clewed out to a yard below or to positions on deck. In either event, these positions must be set in preparation for measurement.

Since the trapezoid is symmetrical, each edge can be measured, or the trapezoid can be divided in half so that it is only necessary to measure one or the other side of the sail. From that the perimeter of the whole sail can be deduced. Even if you measure the entire length from yardarm to yardarm at the head of the sail, it is wise to determine the center point and measure out from there as well in order to ensure symmetry when laying out the sail. First, measure the head of the sail from earing lashing to earing lashing, then the foot of the sail from clew point to clew point. Next, measure the depth of the sail from the center point of the head to the center point of the foot. Last, measure the leech from earing lashing to clew point.

Generally the foot of a squaresail is hollowed in order to provide clearance on deck if the sail is set low or to clear stays, as with topsails and other squaresails set above courses. The location of these obstructions and heights must be determined in order to establish how much hollow there will be in the foot of the squaresail. This hollow will be drawn on paper, thus completing the profile of the sail.

For squaresails that are tacked and sheeted on deck or to the rails, such as the squaresails of Norwegian-type boats, the tack and sheeting positions must be determined and set up in conjunction with the position of the yard prior to measurement. To measure the leech of this type of squaresail, the tape is led from the lashed earing position on the yardarm down to the sheeted clew position as well as from the opposite lashed earing position at the yardarm down to the forward tack position. It is likely that these measurements will not yield a symmetrical trapezoid and adjustments will have to be made later on paper to achieve symmetry. If so, it is better to shorten rather than lengthen a measurement so that the sail will be smaller rather than larger for a particular position.

Measurements should also be taken from the opposite earing diagonally down to the clew posi-

tion. Since the sail is going to be symmetrical, it is only necessary to take one diagonal measurement. (If the sail is asymmetrical, which occasionally occurs, then it is necessary to take both diagonal measurements.)

Mizzen Staysails Set flying or on a jackstay from the head of a yawl or ketch mizzenmast, tacked at the aft lower main shroud or just abaft the mainmast, mizzen staysails are light reaching auxiliary sails and in many respects can be looked on as "mizzen drifters" in terms of measurement procedure and their high-clewed sheeting to mizzen booms.

Refer to the section on headsail measurement and proceed with tape and a downhaul, using the downhaul as a substitute for the luff of the hoisted sail. Seize the tape and one end of the downhaul to the mizzen staysail halyard, and hoist. Then lower the halyard somewhat from its maximum position to allow for sail stretch and elasticity.

Belay the lower end of the downhaul to the deck fitting for the tack pendant, and attach a second tape at the sail's tack height position, high enough for the foot to clear the deck and obstructions.

Tension and belay the halyard.

Lead the tapes aft outside the mizzen shrouds to the appropriate point of the clew position above and 1 foot forward of the wung-out mizzen boom end for offwind sheeting. Take measurements from the point at which the tapes intersect.

Note the likelihood of chafe on the main backstay when the sail's tack position is inboard. Chafe protection on backstay, sail, or both may be necessary.

Storm Jibs If the clew position can be reached, storm jibs can be measured on board. The intention is to have a high-clewed, high-tacked sail of about one-third the working jib area, set and sheeted conveniently well inboard. The sail should lap neither stay nor mast and be as low as possible without catching the seas. Measure in the same manner as a headsail.

Trysail (Gaff- or Jibheaded)　Measure a main trysail in the same manner as a boomless mainsail. It should be sheeted to the quarters, with its clew position above the stowed boom and its tack position above the furled mainsail. The head of a jibheaded trysail would best coincide with the intersection of the mast and forestay on a double-headsail rig. If the trysail is bent on an independent luff track or with parrels, measure accordingly. A gaff-headed trysail would best have an independent gaff and a luff bent on with parrels.

Swedish Mainsail　Measure in the same manner as a Bermudan main with the clew at reef clew cheek block position.

Other Sails　All other types of sails (such as the batwing) are best measured with spars laid on the ground, extrapolating from the above procedures, or designed on paper. The latter might be either a homemade sail plan with notations or a formal rigging and sail plan.

Obtaining Measurements from a Sail Plan

We should begin by establishing the difference between a *sail plan* and a *sail design*. The former is the overall above-water profile of the boat's hull, rig, and sails, while the latter refers to the shape, materials, construction, and measurements of an individual sail. Like existing sails or an existing rig, a sail plan can be a source—though a less desirable one—of the measurements needed for a sail design.

In some ways, although it is much more work initially, a homemade sail plan (if accurately drawn) is better than a commercially produced plan, being more likely to ensure a well-fitting sail. All dimensions and particulars of the boat are available, and you have firsthand knowledge of the details. A homemade plan is a useful though not essential byproduct when you have a rig to measure.

A stock sail plan as seen in sailing magazines or catalogs is a treacherous source of measurements,

particularly if you have never studied the boat. The scale and details are often too small to tell clearly what's happening. Then, of course, the boat, after construction and use, rarely conforms to the sail plan in every respect. If you're having a boat built, make every effort to head off deviations during the construction process, or to be aware of changes.

Often a large-scale naval architect's plan is all one has to work with, with no chance for verification until the sail is bent. In such nerve-racking instances, a sailmaker must be resigned to the inevitability of sail and rigging adjustments after the sail is made.

To take measurements from a sail plan you will need an architect's rule, a 3-foot straightedge, a compass, a pencil, and a calculator. The rest is self-evident. Obtain plans that are as large in scale as possible. Avoid enlargements with odd scales. Obtain, if possible, photographs of the boat, both close-ups and distant views. Use the naval architect's sail plan and measurements as a reference, but remember to make allowances for elasticity and stretch. Remember also that the sails shown may never have been measured on board, and that you may be planning sails that were never considered for the boat before. It is better to err on the small side rather than push dimensions to the maximum allowed on the drawn plan.

Sail plans are a two-dimensional profile. With a deck plan, trim angles and certain measurements can be checked, but a sail made to the measurements of the two-dimensional profile, particularly boomless sails, will in actual use occupy quite a different fore-and-aft space.

Naval architects indicate or omit all manner of sail cuts, hardware, cloth specifications, and reinforcements. Often their ideas are fanciful.

Creating your own sail plan or including a new form of sail in an established rig and plan is not a daunting project. You merely employ the naval architect's process of weighing all the variables. You want a configuration that is balanced, aesthetically pleasing, and functional. For a single additional sail or variation, measurements can be obtained on the boat or on paper. The measuring process is the same in either case, and within given size and handling restrictions, the only limitation is your imagination—especially if you abandon the conventions of Western rig and sail types!

DESIGNING A SAIL

There are five fundamental aspects to designing a sail:

1. the sail type—that is, its two-dimensional profile;
2. the materials, cloth and cordage in particular;
3. the three-dimensional, flying shape of the sail;
4. the construction plan;
5. subordinate features for reefing, sail handling, sail support, and sail shape.

The information for the sail type, materials, edge measurements, and diagonal measurements has been collected, and now it is time to specify the remaining design features and draw the sail in a two-dimensional scaled plan, which will later be lofted full-size on the floor. Refer to Chapter 5 for the appropriate tools. The creation of a three-dimensional shape is predicated on knowledge of the various techniques of building form in a sail. It is this aspect of design that tends to preoccupy the would-be sailmaker. Refined and technical as the process has become, there is still no precise for-mulaic answer to the question "How do you build a particularly shaped sail in a traditional manner?" It is for this reason that the prospect of a computer-generated sail shape is so tempting.

In the absence of a computer-generated pattern, what we have instead is a collection of guidelines, rules of thumb, and formulas with which to create a sail-design scale plan that depicts visually and numerically the sail's desired construc-tions. The scale plan should be no smaller than ³⁄₁₆ inch to 1 foot, and for any sort of detailed illustration, ¾ inch to 1 foot or larger is best. The accom-panying sample plans are a guide to quantity and

placement of information and techniques of illus-tration.

Preparing a Design Plan Prior to Drawing It

Have at hand the necessary tools (see Chapter 5).

Step 1: Identify the sail by type, owner, boat name, date, and fee, if for hire.

Step 2: List the appropriate peripheral mea-surements, as well as diagonals, luff perpendicu-lars, and area. These are the measurements you obtained as described earlier in the chapter, with the appropriate allowances for stretch and elastic-ity. Further shortening of the measurements beyond those specified earlier are in order if the sail is to be built from natural fibers or stretchy synthetics such as Duradon. There are no surefire formulas here. All cloths and ropes and their con-structions vary; moreover, how they are used is an important factor. Anywhere a woven cloth strikes the edge of a sail at a diagonal, there is a greater degree of elongation. Gray areas arise when a sail-maker combines natural-fiber fabrics of great stretch with reinforcement of very little stretch, say a cotton sail with a polyester boltrope. The approach then, in order to allow the cotton to move naturally, could be to cut the sail with short measurements to allow for the stretch of the cotton and then rope the edges slackly so that when the rope reached its fully stretched length (minimal though it is) the cotton would be stretched too. Another and simpler way to go about it is to bag the notion of permitting the cloth to go much of any-where and cut the edges to allow only for the elas-ticity of the synthetic reinforcement. Or, a judi-cious balance can be achieved.

In any event, with the use of synthetic rein-forcement, reduction of edge measurements on natural-fiber sails is not nearly as critical. Never-theless, here are some guidelines: Small-boat cot-ton sails with synthetic reinforcement need no extra edge reduction beyond that required for the elasticity of the reinforcement. Boats of, say, 18 to

35 feet with synthetically reinforced cotton sails need the edges reduced 1 inch per 8 feet of sail edge length. Large voyaging and commercial vessels with synthetically reinforced cotton or Duradon sails need the edge measurements reduced ½ inch per 1 foot of sail edge length. Finally, natural-fiber sails with natural-fiber reinforcement should have their edges reduced approx-

imately 3 inches per 10 feet of length. This allowance should be doubled for very large sails and for edges cut on the cross, or bias.

The reduced measurements, if any, should be drawn in the plan, or you can draw the full measurements and later loft to the reduced measurements, if you wish to see and work with a drawing that reflects the intended fully stretched appearance.

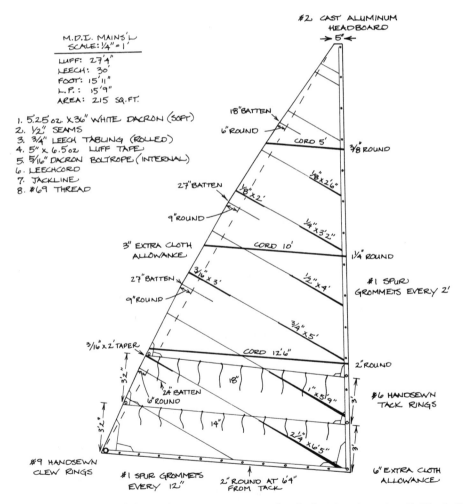

FIGURE 6-6. *Sample sail design for a Mount Desert Island–class boat's mainsail. The luff and foot curves have not been drawn. Note the broadseam measurements, and that the reef rows are straight.*

Step 3: List in detail the type, dimensions, and quantities of materials used in the sail, both cloth and cordage. How much sailcloth do you need? The amount of cloth required to build the sail will be at least the area of the sail plus additional yardage for seam overlaps, reinforcement, tablings, bands, and patches. Obviously, a sail with narrow cloth and more seams or with false seams or wider seams will use more yardage. Additionally, large and heavy multiple layers of reinforcement in the corners, even efficiently cut, will use a great deal of fabric. Just a corner patch on a mainsail for a 40-foot voyaging boat can use over 3 yards of cloth. In a sail with three reefs, that's

(text continued on page 237)

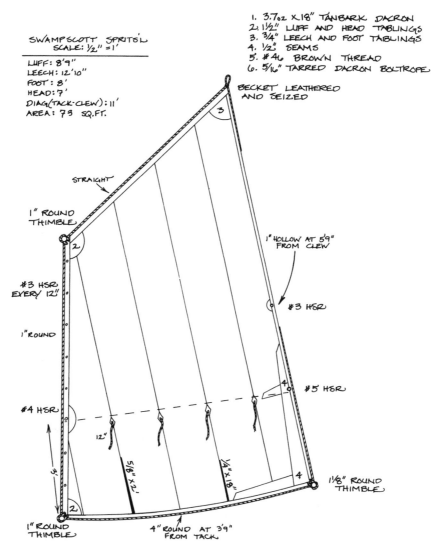

FIGURE 6-7. *Sample design of a Swampscott dory sprits'l. "HSR" means handsewn ring. The numbers in the corners refer to the number of layers in the corner patches.*

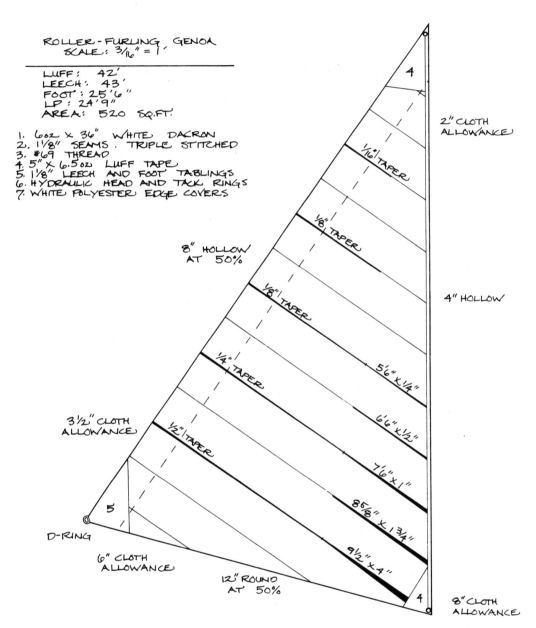

ROLLER - FURLING GENOA
SCALE: 3/16" = 1'

LUFF: 42'
LEECH: 43'
FOOT: 25'6"
LP: 24'9"
AREA: 520 SQ.FT.

1. 6oz × 36" WHITE DACRON
2. 1⅛" SEAMS. TRIPLE STITCHED
3. #69 THREAD
4. 5" × 6.5oz LUFF TAPE
5. 1⅛" LEECH AND FOOT TABLINGS
6. HYDRAULIC HEAD AND TACK RINGS
7. WHITE POLYESTER EDGE COVERS

4

2" CLOTH ALLOWANCE

1/16" TAPER

⅛" TAPER

8" HOLLOW AT 50%

⅛" TAPER

4" HOLLOW

¼" TAPER

5'6" × ¼"

6'6" × ½"

3½" CLOTH ALLOWANCE

½" TAPER

7'6" × 1"

8⅝" × 1¾"

5

9½" × 4"

D-RING

6" CLOTH ALLOWANCE

12" ROUND AT 50%

4

8" CLOTH ALLOWANCE

FIGURE 6-8. *Sample quick-and-dirty sail-design sketch for the roller-furling genoa of an Offshore 40. Note that no edge curves have been drawn. A guess has been made as to where the leech edge cover will go, but the only way to know for sure is to roll the sail up and mark the exposed areas on leech and foot as in Figure 6-90.*

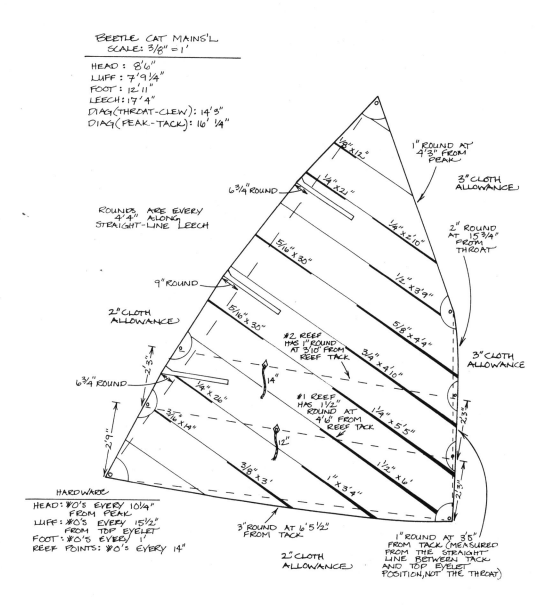

BEETLE CAT MAINS'L
SCALE: 3/8" = 1'

HEAD: 8'6"
LUFF: 7'9 1/4"
FOOT: 12'11"
LEECH: 17'4"
DIAG (THROAT-CLEW): 14'3"
DIAG (PEAK-TACK): 16' 1/4"

1" ROUND AT 4'3" FROM PEAK
3" CLOTH ALLOWANCE
2" ROUND AT 15 3/4" FROM THROAT

1/8" X 12"
6 3/4" ROUND
1/4" X 2'
1/4" X 2'10"
1/2" X 3'9"

ROUNDS ARE EVERY 4'4" ALONG STRAIGHT-LINE LEECH

5/16" X 30"
9" ROUND
5/8" X 4'4"
3" CLOTH ALLOWANCE

2" CLOTH ALLOWANCE
5/16" X 30"
#2 REEF HAS 1" ROUND AT 3'10" FROM REEF TACK
3/4" X 4'10"

6 3/4" ROUND
2'3"
1/4" X 26"
14"
#1 REEF HAS 1 1/2" ROUND AT 4'6" FROM REEF TACK
1/4" X 5'5"
2'3"

2'9"
3/16" X 14"
12"
1 1/2" X 6'

HARDWARE
HEAD: O'S EVERY 10 1/4" FROM PEAK
LUFF: O'S EVERY 15 1/2" FROM TOP EYELET
FOOT: O'S EVERY 1'
REEF POINTS: O'S EVERY 14"

3/8" X 3'
1" X 3'4"
1 1/2" X 6'
2'3"

3" ROUND AT 6'5 1/2" FROM TACK

1" ROUND AT 3'5" FROM TACK (MEASURED FROM THE STRAIGHT LINE BETWEEN TACK AND TOP EYELET POSITION, NOT THE THROAT)

2" CLOTH ALLOWANCE

FIGURE 6-9. *A detailed working sail-design plan for a Beetle Cat mainsail. Additional designations might have been included, such as #4 spur grommet corner rings and 1/8-inch hollows between each of the battens along the leech. Note the second reef, which is a seldom seen but valuable addition to a Beetle Cat sail.*

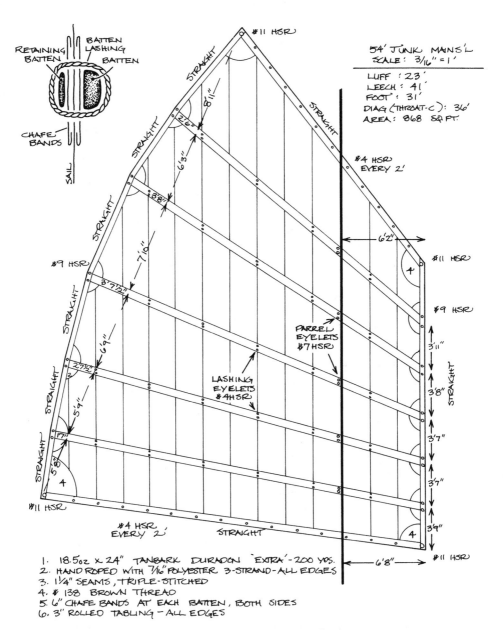

FIGURE 6-10. *Sail-design plan of a Chinese lugs'l—Thomas Colvin's 54-foot junk, Luk-Chin. The voyaging Chinese lugs'l is very labor-intensive with all its rings, roping, and chafe protection, but being completely flat with no edge curves or broadseams, it is the easiest type of sail to make. In contrast with other fore-and-aft sails, the cloths run parallel to the luff.*

TABLE 6-2.
SUGGESTED CLOTH USES

BOAT/SAILS	CLOTH TYPE	CLOTH WEIGHT (OUNCES)	CHARACTERISTICS
TRADITIONALLY CUT DINGHY SAILS UNDER 100 SQ.FT.	COTTON	4.25	WHITE, 36"
		6.10	WHITE OR TANBARK, 53"
	DACRON	3.9	SOFT—MED. FIRM; WHITE, TANBARK OR COLORS; 18"/36"
"QUICK-AND-DIRTY" SAILS UNDER 100 SQ.FT.	FLEET BOAT DACRON	3	FIRM; RED, WHITE, OR BLUE; 38½"
	TYVEK	—	WHITE, GRAY
	POLYETHYLENE TARP	—	BLUE, ORANGE
	NYLON	4.5	VARIOUS COLORS
	COTTON DRILL	7	WHITE, 48"
DAYSAILERS AND SMALL WORKING SAILBOATS			
WORKING SAILS	DACRON	4.5–6	SOFT—MED. FIRM, 18"/36"
	VIVATEX COTTON	10.10	WHITE OR KHAKI, 36"
	PRESHRUNK ARMY DUCK	8.98	WHITE OR KHAKI, 31"
DRIFTERS AND LIGHT AUX. SAILS	NYLON	.5	VARIOUS COLORS, 41"
GENOA	DACRON	2.2–3.9	MED. FIRM, COLORS, 36"
MIDSIZE INSHORE AND DAYSAIL CRAFT			
WORKING SAILS	DACRON	6–7	SOFT—MED. FIRM, 36"
	VIVATEX COTTON	10.10	WHITE OR KHAKI, 36"
	DURADON LIGHT	14	WHITE OR TANBARK, 24"
	PRESHRUNK ARMY DUCK	11.23	WHITE OR KHAKI, 31"
MIDSIZE INSHORE CRUISER AND DAYSAILER AUX. SAILS			
GENOA	DACRON	3.9–5	MED. FIRM, COLORS, 36"
DRIFTERS AND LT. AUX. SAILS	NYLON	0.75–1.5	COLORS, 41"/54"
STORMSAILS	DACRON	7+	SOFT, 36"

(CONT. NEXT PAGE)

Suggested Cloth Uses (cont. from previous page)

Boat/Sails	Cloth Type	Cloth Weight (Ounces)	Characteristics
Midsize Offshore Voyagers			
Working Sails	Dacron	7-9	Soft-Med Firm, 36"
	Duradon Light	14	White, Tanbark, 24"
	Cotton	13	White, 36"
Storms'ls	Dacron	9+	Soft, 36"
	Duradon Standard	16.5	White, Tanbark, 24"
Drifters and Light Aux. Sails	Nylon	1.5	Ripstop, Colors 41"/54"
Genoa	Dacron	5-6.5	Med. Firm, 36"
Large Offshore Voyagers			
Working Sails	Dacron	9-12	Soft-Med. Firm 36"/48"/54"
	Duradon Standard	16.5	White, Tanbark, 24"
	Cotton	14-16	
Storms'ls	Duradon Extra	18.5	White, Tanbark, 24"
	Dacron	10+	Soft, 36"/48"
Light Aux. Sails	Nylon	2.2	Force 9, Colors, 41"
	Dacron	2.2-39-4.5	Colors, 36"
	Duradon Light	14	White, Tanbark, 24"
	Cotton	7-13	
Genoa	Dacron	7-8	Med. Firm, 36"/48"
	Duradon Light	14	White, Tanbark, 24"
Large Commercial Vessels			
Working Sails	Dacron	12+	Soft, 36"/48"/54"
	Duradon Extra	18.5	White, Tanbark, 24"
	Cotton	#4-#2	22"-27"
Storms'ls	Dacron	14	Soft, 36"/48"/54"
	Duradon Heavy	22	White, Tanbark, 24"
	Cotton	#2-#0	22"
Light Aux. Sails	Dacron	8-9	Soft, 36"/48"/54"
	Duradon Standard	16	24"
	Vivatex Cotton	13	36"

potentially over 20 yards of cloth in corner patches alone.

Here are some rules of thumb for estimating cloth yardage:

1. General formula for any cloth width or material:

$$\text{Yardage} = \text{Sail area (sq ft)} \div \frac{\text{cloth width (in)} + 45\%}{4}$$

2. General formula for lightly reinforced sails of 36-inch cloth without large roaches:

    (a) Sail area (sq ft) ÷ 6
    (b) Sail area (sq ft) × .167

3. Lightly reinforced mainsails with roaches of 36-inch cloth: Sail area (sq ft) × .18
4. Light nylon auxiliary sails of 41-inch cloth: Sail area (sq ft) × .13
5. Heavily reinforced voyaging mainsails with multiple reefs, of 36-inch cloth: Sail area (sq ft) ÷ 4

6. Heavily reinforced Scotch-miter-cut stormsails of 54-inch cloth: Sail area (sq ft) ÷ 4.

You may have estimated the cloth before beginning this plan, but the quantity should be listed anyway for later comparison with the amount actually used.

Having reached this point, you might think you are ready to draw the sail, but you are not, quite. All the other materials must be accounted for, as described in the pages that follow.

Cordage Requirements   At least in terms of handsewn boltrope selection, life was simpler prior to the advent of synthetics. One had a choice of twisted natural or twisted natural, and then if you wanted the best, only tarred hemp. Now there are many possibilities in both synthetic and natural-fiber cordage. Briefly, for the most traditional, strongest, and most serviceable external boltrope construction, three-strand line is best. Synthetic line can be used with cotton cloth, but not the other way 'round. For the greatest strength and

(text continued on page 240)

TABLE 6-3.
SUGGESTED SEAM WIDTHS

BOAT SIZE / SAIL TYPE	SEAM WIDTH
VERY SMALL BOATS AND SAILS UNDER 100 SQ.FT.	½"
DAYSAILER / WORKING SAILS	½" - ¾"
MIDSIZE-BOAT WORKING SAILS; SMALL- TO MIDSIZE-BOAT TRIPLE-STITCHED SAILS; LIGHT NYLON AUXILIARY SAILS	⅞"
MIDSIZE VOYAGING CRAFT STORMS'LS	1"
LARGE-BOAT WORKING SAILS, TRIPLE-STITCHED	1" - 1¼" - 1½"
COMMERCIAL SAILS; EXTRA-HEAVY STORM SAILS; HANDSEWN VOYAGING SAILS	1½" - 2"

TABLE 6-4.   SUGGESTED BOLTROPE/LUFF ROPE

SAIL OR BOAT	HANDSEWN BOLTROPE	INTERNAL LUFF ROPE
TRADITIONAL SMALL-BOAT MAINS'LS AND JIBS UNDER 100 SQ.FT., COTTON	1/4", 5/16" POLY 3X 1/4" (6MM) H-R 3X 1/4" MANILA 3X 1/4" TARRED HEMP 3X	
TRADITIONAL SMALL-BOAT MAINS'LS AND JIBS UNDER 100 SQ.FT., DACRON	1/4", 5/16" POLY 3X 1/4" (6MM) H-R 3X	
SMALL-BOAT MAINS'LS UNDER 200 SQ.FT., DAYSAILS, DACRON	5/16" POLY 3X	
SMALL-BOAT HEADS'LS, DACRON	5/16" POLY 3X	3/16"-5/16" DBP 1/4", 5/16" POLY 3X
MIDSIZE-BOAT MAINSAILS AND JIBS, COTTON	3/8"-7/16" POLY 3X 3/8"-7/16" MULTI 3X 1/2" TH 7/16" (10MM) H-R 3X	
MIDSIZE-BOAT MAINSAILS, DACRON OR DURADON	3/8"-7/16" POLY 3X 3/8"-7/16" MULTI 3X 7/16" (10MM) H-R 3X	5/16"-3/8 DBP 3/8"-7/16" POLY 3X
MIDSIZE-BOAT HEADS'LS DACRON AND DURADON	SAME AS ABOVE	5/16"-3/8" DBP 3/8"-7/16" POLY 3X
LARGE-BOAT MAINSAILS AND JIBS, COTTON	1/2"-5/8" POLY 3X 1/2"-5/8" MULTI 3X 1/2"-5/8" MANILA 3X 1/2" (12MM) H-R 3X 1/2"-5/8" TH 3X	
LARGE-BOAT MAINS'LS, DACRON OR DURADON	1/2"-5/8" POLY 3X 1/2"-5/8" MULTI 3X 1/2" (12MM) HR 3X	1/2" DBP 1/2" POLY 3X
LARGE-BOAT HEADS'LS, DACRON OR DURADON	SAME AS ABOVE	SAME AS ABOVE
COMMERCIAL VESSELS, COTTON, DACRON, OR DURADON	3/4"-1" MULTI 3X " POLY 3X " ROBLON 3X " MANILA 3X	5/8" DBP

KEY: POLY 3X = SPUN POLYESTER THREE-STRAND; MULTI 3X = MULTILINE POLYESTER-POLYPROPYLENE THREE-STRAND; TH 3X = TARRED HEMP THREE-STRAND; H-R 3X = HARDY HEMP OR ROBLON SPUNFLEX POLYPROPYLENE THREE-STRAND; DBP = DOUBLE-BRAID POLYESTER

Sizes, Materials, and Constructions

Internal Boltrope	External Machine-Sewn Boltrope	Internal Machine-Sewn Boltrope
5/16" NYLON 3x 5/16" DBP 5/16" POLY 3x	5/16" NYLON 3x	5/16" NYLON 3x
3/8" NYLON 3x 5/16"–3/8" DBP 3/8" POLY 3x	3/8" NYLON 3x 3/8" POLY 3x	3/8" NYLON 3x 3/8" POLY 3x
	1/2" NYLON 3x	

least elongation in an internal luff rope or boltrope, synthetic braid construction is best, though three-strand is certainly usable. (Synthetic braid is not appropriate for an external rope because it cannot be sewn.)

Consistent with natural-fiber sails, in reverse order of preference, is the use of cotton, manila, hemp, or tarred hemp line. For the hand roping of any sail, again in reverse order, synthetic three-strand line can be polypropylene, nylon, filament polyester, spun polyester, or polyester polypropylene composite. For machine roping, I use nylon line. For the synthetic double-braid lines, use polyester. The size of the line selected depends on the strain the line will bear and the amount of elasticity desired, as well as, to some extent, the desired appearance.

The amount of boltrope on hand should well exceed the length specified for the edges to be roped. The rope "shortens" as it is sewn, and much line is taken up rounding corners and in splices. Additionally, some line may be needed for cringles or pendants.

Since I obtain line by the spool, I often use it right off the reel or lay a piece out along the sail's edge, with an eyeballed amount to spare. This approach has its anxious moments—better to have some extra, though additional lengths can be spliced on.

Follow these guidelines for determining cordage requirements:

Braided or three-strand luff rope in headsails or internal roping of mainsails, etc.: If not sewn, the length of the edge(s) plus the sum of the lengths of the two patches at each end. Handsewn boltrope requires an amount equal to the edges to be roped, plus 15 percent. Don't forget to include extra line for splices, rattails, and cringles.

Nettles: Cordage for knotted nettles equals the length of a nettle plus two overhand knots times the number of nettles.

Sewn Nettles: Cordage equals the length of the nettle times the number of nettles.

Note that with deeper reefs, the nettles must be longer for secure tying. Therefore, there will be as many nettle lengths to calculate as there are rows of reefs. If nettles are to be backspliced, additional line is needed for each nettle (two times the length of the splice plus 2 inches). If the reef must also be

TABLE 6-5.
SUGGESTED REEF-POINT SPECIFICATIONS

BOAT	FINISHED LENGTH PER SIDE (INCHES)		DIAMETER (INCHES)	MATERIAL
	1ST REEF	2ND REEF		
SMALL CRAFT UNDER 20 FT.	10-12	12-14	1/8 - 3/16	COTTON, SPUN POLYESTER
MIDSIZE CRAFT 20-35 FT.	12-18	16-24	3/16 - 5/16	SPUN POLYESTER
LARGE, HEAVY CRAFT	18-24	24-30	5/16 - 1/2	SPUN POLYESTER
COMMERCIAL CRAFT	30+	FIRST REEF LENGTH PLUS 6 INCHES	1/2 - 5/8	SPUN POLYESTER, MANILA

led around the boom, much greater nettle length will be required. One can experiment, or check a similar boat.

Luff Wire for Headsails and Staysails In the luffs of light-air auxiliary sails set flying with a sail area under 300 square feet, use ⅛-inch diameter plastic-coated stainless steel 7 x 19 wire. For sails between 300 and 500 square feet, use 3⁄16-inch plastic-coated stainless steel 7 x 19 wire. The length needed is the length of the luff plus 1 inch for each inch of edge curve in the luff (i.e., the maximum perpendicular distance from a rounded or hollowed luff to the straight line connecting tack and head of sail), with an additional 3 feet for end splices and fittings.

Luff Tape for the Edges of Synthetic Sails The length needed is the length of the taped edge

plus 2 feet. An additional amount is needed if the edges of corner patches are to be reinforced. You will need the sum of all taped corner patch edges plus 6 inches per edge. Sometimes it is appropriate to reinforce intersecting sail edges with a single tape folded around a corner. On other occasions— because tape widths or weights change, or the corner is too sharp to permit a continuous tape, or it is desirable to tension the tapes independently— separate tapes are used but are purchased according to the totals needed. Tapes from the distributor generally come in 70- to 110-yard rolls, but can be purchased cut to order.

The tape width needed is based on the sail type and use. The widest production-cut tape is 6 inches (3 inches when doubled). Don't forget that the tape will be folded in half or even fourths and that specified width anticipates a narrower (usually half) luff-tape width. Wider tapes are used

TABLE 6-6.
COMMERCIALLY AVAILABLE DACRON LUFF TAPES

CLOTH WEIGHT (OUNCES)	WIDTHS (INCHES)	USES
3.9	3⁄4–5	SMALL DACRON SAILS, LIGHT TABLINGS
5	1–6	SMALL-BOAT LUFFS AND TABLINGS, NYLON AUXILIARY SAIL LUFFS
6	1–6	SMALL-BOAT LUFFS AND TABLINGS, LIGHT CRUISING AUXILIARY SAIL LUFFS
6	3–4	TANBARK COLOR FOR TRADITIONAL DACRON OR DURADON SAILS OF SMALL BOATS
7	2½–6	MIDSIZE-BOAT LUFFS AND TABLINGS
8	3–5	LARGE BOATS, VOYAGING SAILS, STORMS'L REINFORCEMENT
9	2–6	WORKING AND STORMS'LS OF LARGE, HEAVY CRAFT

(a) when eyelets are placed along the edge, (b) along edges under greater tension, (c) on large sails of heavy boats, (d) on stormsails, and (e) in the reinforcement of corner-patch edges, because they can be tapered from maximum width down to 1 inch or so for a gradual transmission of strain.

For Dacron sails, selecting a tape cloth weight is relatively easy: You need a weight equal to or greater than that of the sailcloth itself. It is preferable, but not essential, to have a similar finish to that of the sail. In application, wide tapes tend to be heavy tapes, which is why mass-produced tapes come in heavy-wide and light-narrow specifications. Nylon sails can be reinforced with nylon tape or light-narrow Dacron tape. In either case, the tape is always at least twice as heavy as the nylon sailcloth, for the simple reason that the tape is under a great longitudinal strain. Duradon sails can be taped with Dacron for speedier construction. Since there are only four, relatively heavy cloth weights of Duradon, appropriate tape selection is easy.

Luff tapes for grooved headstay systems are commercially available in two constructions: 5-inch-wide, 6.5-ounce Dacron tape or Teflon tape. They are stitched through and behind the primary rope and have a 1/8-inch backup cord sewn in.

TABLE 6-7.
LUFF TAPE SIZES FOR GROOVED HEADSTAYS

HEADSTAY SYSTEM	PRIMARY ROPE						
	GEMINI	1/8 INCH	5/32 INCH	3/16 INCH	7/32 INCH	1/4 INCH	9/32 INCH
CRUISING DESIGN REEFER				4 - 12			18 - 22
FURLEX				61A-65A, 60B-66B	61C-64C	61D-63D	
HARKEN				0, 1, 2, 3			
HEADFOIL			20	30, 40	50, 60		
HOOD GEMINI	8, 12, 16				14A, 20A		20C
HOOD SEAFURL		NEW 'A'		ALL OTHERS		OLD 'B'	OLD 'C'
HYDE STREAMSTAY			8	9		10, 12	16
SCHAEFER				2000			
PROFURL				ALL			
RECKMANN	R1, R2			R3, R4			
TUFF LUFF			1205	1706 2206			
NEW TWINSTAY/ DYNAFURL		8, 12		18, 24 30, 48			

NOTE: ALWAYS TRY A PIECE OF LUFF TAPE IN ALL GROOVES OF FOIL SYSTEM IF POSSIBLE, TO ASSURE CORRECT MATCH OF LUFF TAPE TO SYSTEM.
NOTE: THIS TABLE ADAPTED FROM AQUABATTEN HARDWARE, INC.

Machine Thread Note the thread type, size, and color on your sail-design plan. There is a limited assortment of appropriate thread from which to choose, both in terms of material—Dacron or cotton—and sizes, as indicated in Table 5-6, page 164. Colors, however, abound, and aesthetics aside, for inspection purposes there is a visual advantage in contrasting colors. Colored thread will hold up longer in the sun than its undyed counterpart, too. Traditionally, white cotton sails are often sewn with brown thread on the seams and white thread on the reinforcements. Except for rare eccentric color combinations, I have used only natural-color (i.e., white) and red-brown thread in sails.

Simply put, the greater the anticipated strain, the bigger and heavier the sail, and the greater the severity of the storms for which a sail is constructed, the heavier the thread (see Table 5-6). In voyaging sails, I sew the reinforcements with a thread one size heavier than that of the seams.

Hand Sewing Twine I generally do not note on a plan the size of the twine to be used for hand sewing reinforcements and hardware. I do note it, however, if the sail is to be entirely hand sewn. It is good, in any case, to specify your needs. I have always found a spool of sail twine or a 15-foot hank of three-strand line to yield more than enough twine for several sails' worth of finishwork.

There are more materials in the sail, but I generally leave their designation for later listing.

Tablings Next, list tabling styles and widths for parts of the sail not reinforced with tape. If there will be no tape at all, such as in the traditionally built sail with cut tablings, the widths for all edges should be specified. The required width is a function of strain and sail size. Tablings (other than the precut Dacron luff tapes) are always made of the cloth used in the sail, so there is no need to specify cloth types, weights, etc.

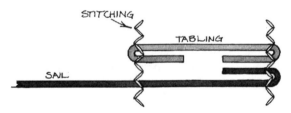

Traditional "cut" tablings maintain cloth direction along a curved or diagonally cut sail edge.

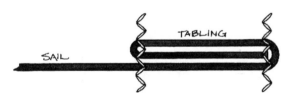

A "rolled" tabling is fast and durable but does not maintain cloth direction. Moreover, a hollowed sail edge will be tight; a rounded edge, floppy.

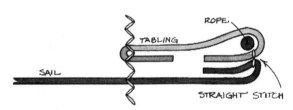

To install a wire in the luff of a sail with a cut tabling the tabling and sail are first straight-stitched together.

FIGURE 6-11(PAGES 243–244). *Various ways of finishing the edges of a sail with cloth—known as tablings.*

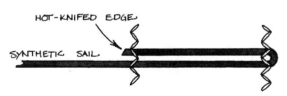

Hotknifing, folding over, and sewing the sail edge is a fast production technique that saves cloth and weight.

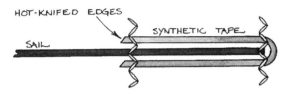

Taping the edge of a sail provides greater longitudinal strength and can save much labor.

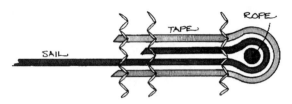

Great additional strength as well as an extra cloth layer may be obtained in the luff of a heads'l by folding the sail within the luff tape and around the luff rope.

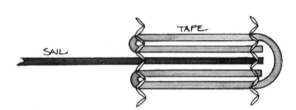

Quartering an edge tape eliminates hotknifed edges, makes the tape narrower, and adds two more layers of cloth for the installation of eyelets.

Cut tablings maintain cloth direction, especially around curves, but require much more time and material than rolled tablings, which do not follow curves as easily but form a strong, hemmed edge. Tapes, as discussed previously, are fast to install, distribute strain well, may fray unless folded under, are expensive, and do not conform to dramatic curvature.

Drawing the Sail Design

At last you are ready to lightly draw the straight-line perimeter of the sail, using scale-rule and compass. I generally try to orient the sail to the bottom of the page as it will eventually be oriented to the waterline of the boat, though sometimes all the written specifications make that impossible.

All reinforcements and hardware will be sewn to the same side of the sail. Traditionally, all hand-sewn boltrope is sewn to the port, or left, side of a fore-and-aft sail and on the aft side of a squaresail. Therefore, sails that are hand roped are drawn port side up; I usually draw any other sail star-

board side up, unless the sail will not fit in the available lofting space that way. It is very confusing to loft a sail port side up from a drawing of the opposite view.

Headboards   For mainsails with headboards, include the headboard's top-edge measurement, drawing the line aft at right angles from the top of the luff.

Designing the Leech of a Sail with Roach and Battens   This section applies to battened mains, mizzens, and headsails, such as conventional day-sail and nonvoyaging mains; fully battened Bermudan sails; jibs and staysails with small leech roaches; sportsails and boardsails; and fully battened lug and batwing sails. There are no other Western working sails with rounded leeches.

The roach must be supported by battens, and it is their length and strength on which the size and distribution of roach depends.

The amount of roach, if batten length is not

Table 6-8.
Tabling Sizes and Applications

Sail Size	Sail Edge	Tabling Type	Tabling Width (inches)
Small-Boat Sails under 100 sq. ft.	Luff	Cut	1½
	Foot	Cut	1½
		Rolled	3/4
	Leech	Cut	5/8
		Rolled	3/4
	Head	Cut	1½
Small-Boat Sails 100–200 sq. ft.	Luff	Cut	2
	Foot	Cut	2
		Rolled	1
	Leech	Cut	2
		Rolled	1
	Head	Cut	2
Storms'ls under 200 sq. ft.	Luff	Cut	3–4
	Foot	Cut	1¼–2
		Rolled	1⅛–1½
	Leech	Cut	2
		Rolled	1⅛–2
Sails 200–300 sq. ft.	Luff	Cut	2½–3
	Foot	Cut	2½–3
		Rolled	1–1⅛
	Leech	Cut	2
		Rolled	1–1⅛
	Head	Cut	2½–3
Light Nylon Aux. Sails 200+ sq. ft.	Leech and Foot	Rolled	1
Working Sails 300+ sq. ft. Heavy-Boat Storms'ls	Luff	Cut	3+
	Foot	Cut	3+
		Rolled	1¼–1½–2
	Leech	Cut	2+
		Rolled	1¼–2
	Head	Cut	3+

TABLE 6-9.
HEADBOARD SIZES AND APPLICATIONS

TYPE	SIZE (INCHES)	LUFF LENGTH (FEET)	BOAT TYPE
EXTERNAL TWO-PART ANODIZED ALUMINUM	3 – 4 1/2	18 – 20	DAYSAILER
	5 1/2 – 6	20 – 30	MIDSIZE BOAT
	6 – 8 1/2	30+	LARGE BOAT
INTERNAL CAST ALUMINUM	3 1/2 – 4 1/2 (#00 – #1)	18 – 20	TRADITIONAL DINGHY
	5 1/4 – 6 1/2 (#2 – #3)	20 – 30	TRADITIONAL MIDSIZE BOAT
	8 1/2 – 11 (#4 – #5)	30+	LARGE TRADITIONAL JIBHEADED BOAT

TABLE 6-10.
CONVENTIONAL BATTEN ALLOCATIONS

BOAT SIZE	LEECH LENGTH (FEET)	NUMBER OF BATTENS
DINGHIES	12 OR LESS	2 BATTENS
UP TO 25'	12 TO 25	3 BATTENS
OVER 25'	OVER 25	4 BATTENS

can afford the gear, there is much to be said for a fully battened sail. Among its other advantages, it leaves you no worries about hinged or hooked leeches. It is also quiet in stays and easy to douse and reef. Fully battened boardsails utilize extensive roach support on a small scale. The variety of leech shapes in these sails is limitless. Even with the restrictions of the marconi rig's backstay, full battens can add an additional 8 percent to the sail area in an advantageous, lofty position.

But back to conventional battens and the old-fashioned Western yacht roach: in nonlapping jibs and staysails, minimal roach can be supported by as few as two battens, which divide the leech into three equal sections. On sails set abaft the mast, the leeches are supported by three or four battens, usually dividing the leech into four or five equal sections. The general rule of thumb for determining conventional batten length is to allow a minimum of 3 inches of length for every 1 inch of roach depth.

If you are building a class sail and wish to conform to the rules, batten lengths and thus roach

restricted by racing regulations, is influenced by sailcloth type, rig constrictions (such as backstay), aspect ratio, balance of sail area and helm, and aesthetics. Stiff cloth can better support a large roach. The absence of a backstay allows great leeway in roach extension. Without a great deal of sheeting and vanging power, it is difficult to prevent hinging and excessive leech twist in a high-aspect sail with conventional battens and a big roach. It is best to be conservative.

Conventional batten lengths and roaches make sense for daysailing. If you must have a battened Bermudan mainsail for cruising, however, and you

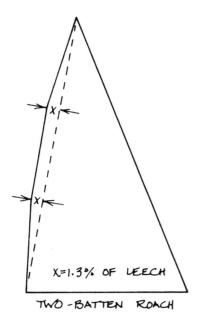

X=1.3% OF LEECH

TWO-BATTEN ROACH

The typical small roach found in headsails and sails with short leech measurements.

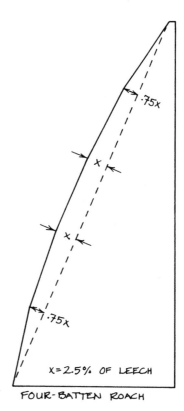

.75x

X

.75x

X=2.5% OF LEECH

FOUR-BATTEN ROACH

Leech roach for high-aspect sail on medium to large boat.

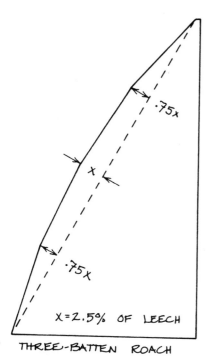

.75x

X

.75x

X=2.5% OF LEECH

THREE-BATTEN ROACH

Common small-boat mains'l leech roach.

FIGURE 6-12 (PAGES 247–249). *Various forms of leech roach. Curve distributions and proportions vary according to sail size and type.*

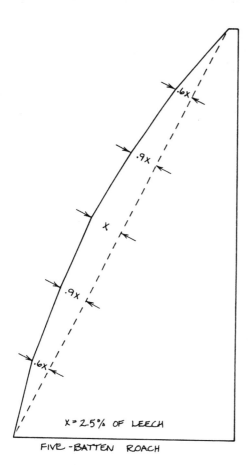

X = 2.5% OF LEECH

FIVE - BATTEN ROACH

The leech roach of large-boat sails requires great support and an even distribution of curvature.

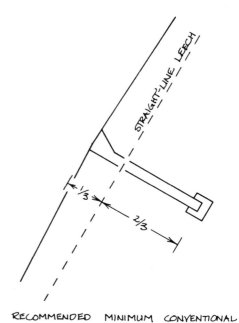

RECOMMENDED MINIMUM CONVENTIONAL
BATTEN LENGTH
BATTEN = 3 X DEPTH OF ROACH

"Minimum" means minimum! A hinged leech will be the result of pushing roach size in relation to batten length, especially with heavy battens, soft cloth, and a light boom with no vang.

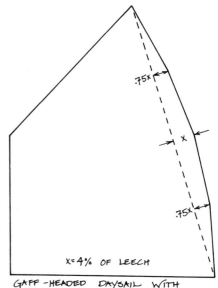

X = 4% OF LEECH

GAFF - HEADED DAYSAIL WITH
LARGE ROACH AND BATTENS

Wianno and Beetle Cat mains'ls carry great roach in a relatively short leech.

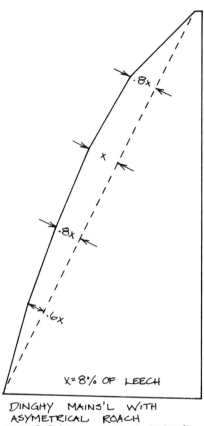

.8x

x

.8x

.6x

X = 8% OF LEECH

DINGHY MAINS'L WITH
ASYMETRICAL ROACH
DISTRIBUTION AND EXCESSIVE
DEPTH OF ROACH/BATTEN LENGTH

A whacking asymmetrical speed hump crowds extra sail area into a dinghy sail limited by spar length. A moderate variation would offer a little extra sail area in a schooner fores'l.

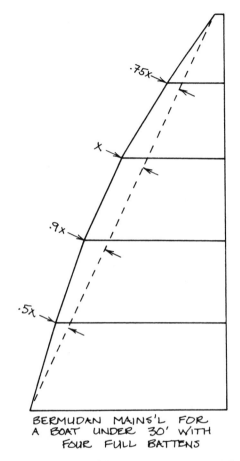

.75x

x

.9x

.5x

BERMUDAN MAINS'L FOR
A BOAT UNDER 30' WITH
FOUR FULL BATTENS

Contemporary full-battens can support a large asymmetrical roach in a high-aspect sail.

sizes will be dictated. Usually leech roach is symmetrically distributed above and below the midleech point. Fully battened sails—including contemporary sails, Chinese lugsails, and batwings—are able to support a wide range of asymmetrical forms, often with much area added above the midpoint.

Contemporary flexible full battens are placed horizontally and parallel to the foot. Though capable of extending a leech considerably, they serve more as a shaping skeleton. In contrast, the rigid battens of the Chinese and batwing sails are actually spars, capable of supporting great leech curvature.

Following the considerations above and the accompanying illustrations, draw the roached leech from head or peak to clew.

Designating the Cut of a Sail When natural-fiber cloth is used, panels must be parallel or per-

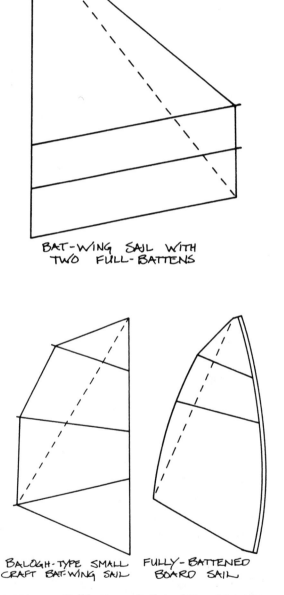

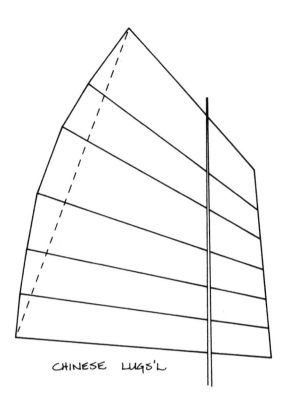

BAT-WING SAIL WITH
TWO FULL-BATTENS

CHINESE LUGS'L

BALOGH-TYPE SMALL   FULLY-BATTENED
CRAFT BAT-WING SAIL   BOARD SAIL

FIGURE 6-13. *Full battens—both traditional (rigid) and contemporary (flexible)—can support a wide assortment of leech shapes, offering great additional sail area.*

pendicular to the leech and foot of a fore-and-aft sail, or to the head and foot of a squaresail. The exception is the Chinese lugsail, which, by virtue of its battens, is traditionally cut with cloths parallel to the luff. The same orientations hold for soft woven synthetics except in such places as the foot of a Yankee jib, where one might choose a radial cut. The choice of cloth layout depends on sail type, appearance, proportions, desired strength, and ease of tailoring.

The vertical- and Scotch-miter cuts are rare now, except in classic boat sails, and the advent of stabilized, resinated fabrics has all but eliminated miter-cut sails. These cuts are still necessary in natural-fiber sails and have great benefits in soft working-sail synthetics, where strength and traditional appearance are desired.

It's basically quite simple: the cloths run perpendicular (cross- or horizontal cut) or parallel (vertical or up-and-down cut) to the leech, as in

Figure 6-7. In a boomless or loose-footed sail with a clew angle of much greater than 90 degrees (such as a high-clewed working jib), or much less than 90 degrees (such as a low-aspect genoa) the sail is mitered with cloths running perpendicular to the leech and foot, or Scotch-mitered (parallel to the leech and foot). The exceptions are headsails utilizing firm, stable synthetics, where the cloths may strike the foot diagonally. But cloths (except for Chinese lugsails and squaresails) always run parallel or perpendicular to the leech of a sail. Once a cut has been selected, the placement of the first cloth must be determined in order to draw the seams in the plan. In fact, the first cloth drawn at this time will also be the first cloth laid out on the fully lofted plan. There is a degree of imprecision here: As the small scale precludes drawing an actual seam width, a pencil line must represent the approximate seam position.

The first cloth drawn in a *vertically cut sail* is the leech cloth. The first seam is drawn parallel to the straight-line leech, separated from it by one cloth width minus allowance for tablings and extra cloth for shrinkage and, if applicable, broadseaming. The remaining seams are drawn a full cloth width apart, proceeding forward until the sail is filled. False seams, when appropriate, are also drawn in. The first seam can be closer to the leech if it facilitates the placement of seams in other parts of the sail; for example, in order to better locate seams in the foot or perhaps at the throat of a gaff sail, for shaping and support with broadseams. The vertical cut is not compatible with conventional leech roach and battens.

The first cloth of a *crosscut sail* is laid along the tack seam, which is the seam from the tack intersecting the leech at 90 degrees. The remaining cloths are drawn a cloth's width apart above the tack seam, and then below to the foot. When false-seamed material is used, all seams are drawn.

Sometimes the first seam does not strike the tack, but rather is offset so that one or more seams strike the leech at or near batten locations, where they provide additional support with proper broadseaming. But it is preferable to have the tack

seam of a crosscut sail strike on or near the tack, because broadening that seam is the best way to create or tailor shape in a spot where edge curves have little effect.

In a *miter-cut sail*, the first seam drawn is actually called "the last seam." This is the *miter seam*, which bisects the clew angle formed by the straight-line foot and leech; it is so named because it is the final seam sewn, which then joins together seamed-up upper and lower portions of the sail.

The placement of the first cloth in a miter-cut sail is a little tricky: In *Scotch-mitered sails*, it is best to consider the foot first, as any roach in the foot will necessitate an allowance in addition to that needed for tabling, shrinkage, and, if applicable, broadseaming. (I can think of no instance where

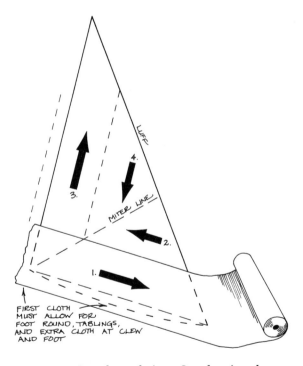

FIGURE 6-14. *In order to design a Scotch-mitered storms'l, voyaging sail, or workboat heads'l, the position of the first cloth must be determined in relation to the round in the foot of the sail. Also shown here is the direction and order in which the cloths will be laid out on the full-size lofted plan.*

the leech would have roach in a sail of this cut.) You start with the edge having the greatest convex curve so that in the subsequent layout of cloth, the upper and lower panel seams meet on the miter seam.

In order to draw this, you need to know how much round to place in the foot. Edge curves will be discussed shortly, but the maximum depth of foot rounds in sails of this type should not exceed 3 percent of the foot length.

You can, with a flexible curve, draw the sweep of the foot if you wish, or just leave it straight while drawing in the first cloth seam, which will end at the luff and the miter seam. The remaining seams are now drawn parallel to that one, a cloth's width apart, until the area below the miter is filled.

The seams of the upper portion of the sail can now be drawn, commencing with the leech cloth and the seam running parallel to the straight-line leech. Make sure this seam strikes the seam of the first foot panel at the miter.

In a conventional miter-cut sail, the first cloth laid or drawn has its seam perpendicular to the straight-line foot and a cloth's width in, minus the tabling width and cloth allowances, from the clew. It is important to make the extra cloth allowance at the clew; otherwise, there will be no cloth for tablings right at the corner.

The next cloth is parallel to that one, and on toward the luff. Continuing with the portion of the sail above the miter, the first cloth is at the clew, perpendicular to the straight-line leech, with the same overlap and distance from the clew as the first cloth on the foot. Drawn accurately, the seams should meet exactly along the miter. Follow on up the leech with the remaining cloths.

The *radial-foot sail* is the next cut to consider. In boomless and loose-footed Dacron sails with a clew angle greater than 90 degrees—a Yankee jib, for example—labor can be saved by fanning out the lower cloths around the clew. There are additional benefits: cloth direction radiating from the clew area along the foot is roughly in line with the strain, and the increased number of seams striking the lower luff offer broadseaming possibilities

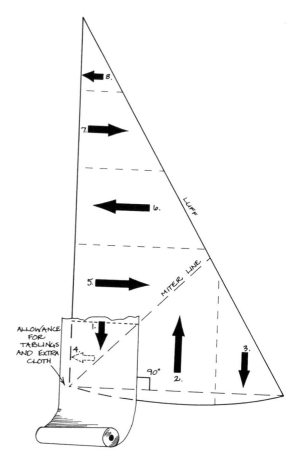

FIGURE 6-15. *In order to draw the seams of a conventional miter cut on a sail design, it is necessary to establish the placement of the first cloth in relation to allowances required for tablings and the extra cloth taken up by stitching and broadseams. Shown here also is the order in which the cloths will be laid out over the full-size lofted plan.*

not found in the conventional miter cut. On the other hand, since no seams strike the foot, you lose the potential for broadseams there to help support roach. To draw the sail, begin as previously described for crosscut sails, with the first seam perpendicular to the leech, but running from the clew to the luff rather than from some point on the leech to the tack. Frankly, though this procedure saves

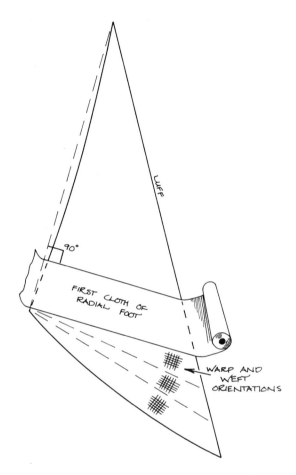

FIGURE 6-16. *Before you can draw the seams of a high-clewed heads'l with a radial foot, it is necessary to position the first cloth, the lower edge of which strikes the straight-line leech slightly above the clew on a perpendicular.*

labor, I've noticed no great improvement in the set of the foot of a sail cut in this manner. Moreover, on a traditional boat where you often find high-clewed headsails, the radial foot looks out of place. The working jib of a multihull, with firm cloth, would be an excellent use of this cut.

There are numerous other ways to lay out cloth. In the traditional cloths, they are all variations on the miter, cross-, and vertical cuts. In contempo-

rary fabrics, they are mostly variations on radial patterns. I have provided the basic patterns, which will serve all but racers and high-tech sailors.

Leech Curve The next thing to consider is edge curves, or those that have not already been drawn. It is not absolutely necessary to actually draw all the curves; in fact, in very small-scale designs it's pointless, as the curves can't be drawn accurately enough to reveal much. But if the scale of the plan permits it, drawing the edge curves is a good idea. Even if they are not too accurate, you'll get a feel for the shape of the edge and the whole sail, plus, if you're doing a suit of sails, the roaches can complement one another in form and function. I frequently make the foot curves in headsails to match one another. Whether drawn or not, amount and placement of curves should be written on the plan alongside the corresponding sail edge.

You've already drawn a roached leech, if that was intended. Rarely will a leech be perfectly straight, so if yours is not roached, it's probably concave. How much of a concave curve there is depends on the type of sail, the winds it will be used in, and the relationship between that sail and the one immediately abaft it. The worst that too much hollow can do is look bizarre and make a ribbon out of the peak of a high-aspect sail. Too little hollow could flutter, or it could crowd the next sail. The rule of thumb is to hollow a leech 1 inch per 6 feet of length, and to place the maximum depth at 45 percent of the leech length above the clew. Headsails, especially those set flying or on saggy stays, should have greater hollow, particularly in the upper leech.

Squaresail leeches, which ultimately set straight or hollowed, may start out with rounded edge curves prior to roping or stretching, but only if the cloth is soft. No Dacron currently available is sufficiently giving to turn a rounded edge into a straight or hollow leech. Therefore, the edges of a Dacron squaresail can be drawn straight.

Once you draw the leech hollow, all of the seams that were drawn to strike the straight-line leech will project beyond the concave curve and must be

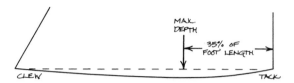

Fine ends combined with moderate round and forward distribution of curvature are advisable for firm synthetic cloths in cat-rigged mains'ls.

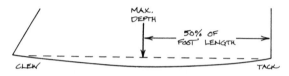

Fine ends combined with moderate round centrally located are advisable for firm synthetic cloths in rigs with large overlapping heads'ls.

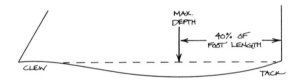

Foot curve with moderately deep and forward distribution of curvature is useful with soft fabrics. Hollow in the aft end tends to flatten the clew in natural fibers.

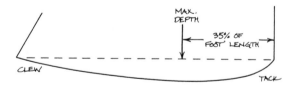

An exaggerated foot curve of great depth and forward distribution works well only in extremely soft and mutable fabrics—for example, a light cotton gaff sail.

FIGURE 6-17. *A few of the possible foot curves in a fixed-footed, boomed sail. Drawing the edge curves in small-scale sail designs is often impractical. Drawing edge curves on paper, however, is good practice for future lofting.*

erased, along with the straight-line edge, if the drawing is to look correct.

Foot Curve   Foot curves are drawn for one of two reasons: to put curvature in the lower portion of a fixed-footed, boomed sail, as in a conventional mainsail, or to add area or a pleasing profile to a boomless or loose-footed, boomed sail. Headsails are an obvious example of the latter, and the Bahamian mainsail is a radical one.

Rarely, the foot of a sail will be perfectly straight, as in Chinese lugsails or batwing sails, in which all edges except the leech are straight, and even the leech is straight between battens! What joy! It is also rare for the foot of a sail to be hollow; the exceptions are squaresails and other transverse sails, in which the foot is always hollowed to a lesser or greater degree, and sails in which the foot forms an extreme angle to the waterline, such as main trysails and gaff topsails. In these instances, the leech-hollow rule of thumb applies: 1 inch per 6 feet of straight-line edge length, with the hollow placed in the center.

A good compromise to incorporate moderate camber when drawing the foot curve of a *fixed-footed boomed sail* is to allow 2 to 3 inches of round for every 10 feet of foot length and, in general, to place the maximum depth of round at about 45 percent of the foot length aft of the tack. But it is really too simple to say that if you add *x* amount of round to the foot of a boomed sail, it will result in a specific camber ratio at boom level. Camber in this powerful area of the sail is certainly desirable, and the edge-curve method can give you a great deal of it in natural or soft synthetic fabric. But problems arise when you seek great curvature with stiff synthetics, particularly tightly woven and finished Dacron, as there is no way to gather all that edge curve along a straight edge without its becoming a wrinkly bag. Moreover, the fullness tends to blow up into midsail as the wind increases. Only with great outhaul tension can that shape be held low. One conventional solution for racing mainsails is a tailored or constructed foot shelf, but while this is a great way to get extreme camber down low in a stiff synthetic sail, it is difficult to construct and impossible to flatten except with a flattening reef or zipper. The formula above yields a moderate, versatile sail camber—somewhat less than ideal for low wind speeds but serviceable over a broad range of winds. This camber is easy to design and build, and its effectiveness can be enhanced with various sail-shaping techniques. With sufficient elasticity in the foot reinforcement, for example, the outhaul can be eased to make the foot area fuller in light winds.

In stiffer fabric, or instances where I want a more stable and sculpted shape to the foot, I will broaden certain seams that strike the foot; or cut tapers; or cut a *twist*, or *speed, seam*, as described later in this chapter. Folding and stitching one or more darts is also an acceptable technique in soft-fabric daysails.

Remember that bias elongation and broad-seams add fullness, and thus may reduce the amount of foot round needed. On the other hand, boom bend (as in a light boom sheeted from its

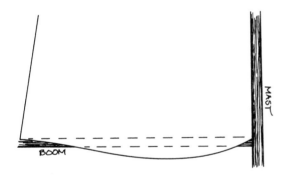

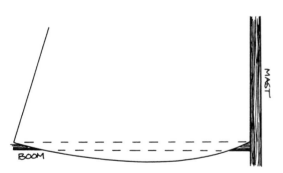

A moderate roach of slight forward distribution is a relatively easy, pleasing, all-purpose foot curve.

FIGURE 6-18A. *Three possible variations of the foot curve on a loose-footed, boomed sail. Much additional sail area as well as distinctive grace and beauty can be obtained with carefully proportioned foot roach in sails of this type.*

A profound sweep with a forward distribution of curvature and a recurve to the after section yields a traditional look of much elegance to a sprits'l or lugs'l.

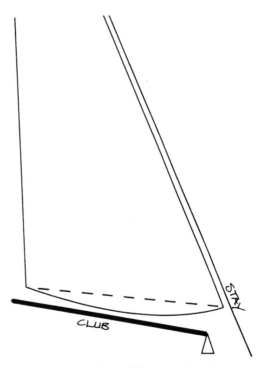

Club-footed stays'ls and jibs set well with moderate foot curves centrally located.

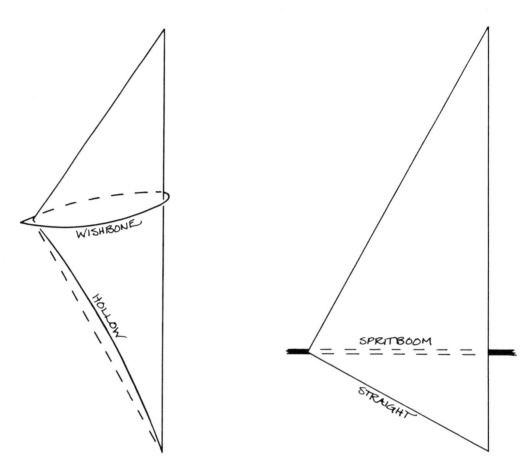

The foot curves of wishbone trys'ls and gaff tops'ls are best hollowed, with the maximum depth centered, in order to minimize edge flutter.

The foot curve of a sprit-boomed sail is actually straight, as it is the reinforcement in the foot that serves as a vang to prevent the clew from lifting. Camber is induced in the lower sail by adjusting either a snotter or a clew outhaul.

FIGURE 6-18B. *Other foot curves.*

midpoint, like that of a Sunfish) will flatten the lower portion of the sail, and you may wish to anticipate this with additional foot round.

The maximum foot round in a boomed sail should be at the point where the deepest draft is desired—usually between 35 and 50 percent of the foot length aft of the tack. The remaining curve distribution is shaped primarily by two critical locations: (1) Too abrupt a transition from tack to foot round will result in too much fullness up for-

ward and the likelihood, except in very forgiving fabric, that the cloth will not smooth out properly in the tack area. Therefore, I gradually bring the curve out from the tack and fair it into the deepest point, keeping as much round forward as I dare. This curve mirrors the sort of camber form you'd like to see along the boom. (2) The after 25 percent or so of the foot curve is much flatter, faired in and tapering back to the clew, more or less depending on the draft position. It is possible to introduce here a reverse curve with hollow in order to help flatten the clew area, a technique that works best in natural or elastic fabrics. I have had the best success in general with a very straight, fair taper in this area. Hollowing the clew area of the foot results in a dramatic hardspot in firm synthetics.

For *loose-footed boomed sails*—mains, club-footed staysails, and wishbone sails—we rely on outhaul adjustment to provide camber, while foot round adds area and enhances appearance. The primary limitations, when not restricted by one-design class rules, are practicality and a means of support.

Excess roach in the foot chafes on the boom and is hard to tack. It blocks visibility and is difficult to support. Battens can be added, as in wishbone boardsails; short battens can even be used to support a large foot roach in a dinghy sail. But generally, too large a roach should be avoided, for the reasons stated or because the added area is not advisable in such sails as a forestaysail that is doubling as a stormsail.

There is a dramatic sweep to loose-footed sails set abaft a mast, the deepest part of which may hang below the boom; the point of maximum curvature is usually 35 to 45 percent of the foot length aft of the tack, with an emphasis on the forward section. Both ends of the curve are drawn to facilitate the sail's passage from one side of the boom to the other. The after section can look quite graceful with a slight reverse curve, which also prevents the sail from hanging up on the boom when tacking. Any further difficulty can be alleviated by raising the clew and tack lashings.

A minimal roach of up to 3 percent of the foot length will stand unassisted, though this depends on wind strength, sheet lead, the angle at which panels strike the foot of the sail, the stiffness of the cloth, and the type of foot tabling. Stiffer cloth can support a bigger roach. With soft cloth, one must rely more on broadseams, edge-reinforcement tension, or a foot cord to help the roach stand. Outhauling only serves to crease the roach. Therefore, big roaches go well with the perpendicular seams

of vertical and miter cuts, which can be tightened for support.

All the same restrictions concerning foot roach on loose-footed boomed sails apply to *boomless sails* as well, except that boom chafe and interference are not factors. In the case of headsails and staysails, however, there may be lifelines and pulpits to clear, as well as the sailor's head. The means of support of foot roach are also similar. When vertical seams are not available, however, as in a crosscut Dacron genoa, foot roach support is often achieved by cutting seams in from the foot and widening them; these I refer to as *foot tapers*. (More on that when we plan the broadseaming.) The installation of a foot cord and/or tensioned tablings (reinforcement) will support a great sweep to the foot.

With certain exceptions, the foot round of a boomless sail is centered symmetrically about a maximum point 50 percent aft of the tack. I have strayed from this guideline to complement the asymmetrical foot roach distribution of other sails on a boat, or in instances when, with a short foot on a sail of high aspect ratio, the clew angle would be too wide, the after portion of the roach unsupported, and the general appearance unsightly. I then give the foot a sweep similar to that of a loose-footed boomed mainsail, with more round forward than aft. If the amount of round is negligible, of course, its appearance will be affected by its distribution.

The amount of hollow in the foot of a *square-sail* can be expressed as 4 to 6 inches per 20 feet of straight-line foot, the curve being symmetrically drawn about the midpoint. Additionally, greater hollow may be necessary in courses to clear deck features, in upper squaresails to clear stays, and generally for visibility.

No matter what kind of sail you are designing, consider whether camber is going to be induced or withdrawn by other means as well as by foot round, and make allowances. For example, stretchy cloth and broadseams will make a sail fuller, and a bendy mast will make a sail flatter. Any round now drawn on the foot can be filled out

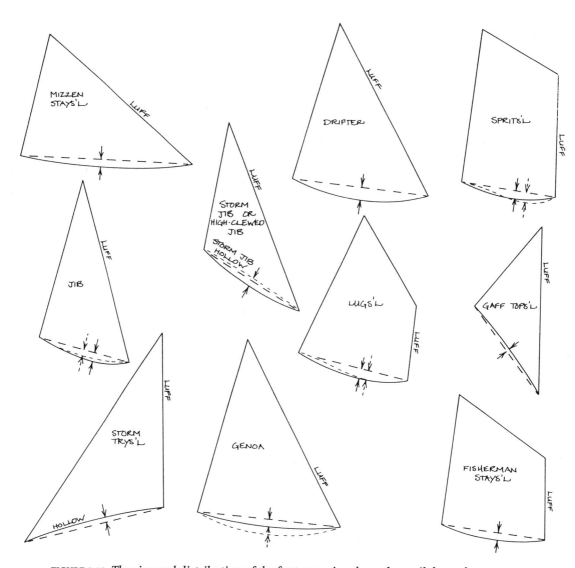

FIGURE 6-19. *The size and distribution of the foot curve in a boomless sail depends on many factors: the type and cut of the sail, the sailcloth, expected wind range, aesthetics, and the relationship with other sails.*

on the sail drawing with "cloth" by extending the seams.

Luff Curve We'll consider first the luff of a sail *set on a spar.* Only when the sail is intended to be perfectly flat (Chinese lug, batwing, riding sails, steady-

ing sails), or if edge curves are not being utilized for camber formation, is the luff drawn straight. Simply put, the amount of cloth added outside the straight-line luff at any given point is a percentage of chord length, luff to leech, which, when pushed into the sail, will result in the desired camber.

Procedure

1. Determine how much camber you want (see Chapter 4).
2. Divide the luff into quarters.
3. Measure and record the luff-to-leech chord length at each of the three quarter points.
4. Using the table in Figure 6-21, calculate the amount of round. As with foot round, consider whether camber is going to be induced or withdrawn by other means as well, and make allowances. Again, broadseams and stretchy cloth will make a sail fuller, and a bendy mast will make a sail flatter. Do not neglect offsets.
5. Measure forward perpendicularly from the straight-line luff and mark the added cloth at each height.

Note 1: I cut loose-footed wishbone sprit boom sails quite flat (little additional luff round), as camber is needed mainly just to shape the entry of the sail, not the sail itself.

Note 2: The gaff or lugsail with a proportionately short luff and long foot will not accommodate large amounts of round in the lower luff to make a full sail there. It is better to rely on broadseaming to let fullness into these areas.

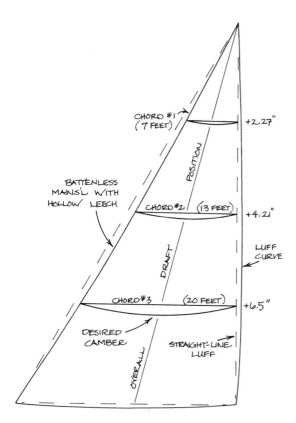

FIGURE 6-20. *To calculate the desirable amount of camber-inducing round in the luff of a sail set on a mast, a percentage of the chord length at each of three heights in the sail is added as cloth outside the straight-line luff. In this example the desired camber ratio is 10 percent and the percentage of chord length to be added is therefore 2.7 percent (see Figure 6-21).*

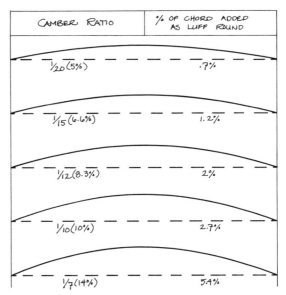

CAMBER RATIO	% OF CHORD ADDED AS LUFF ROUND
1/20 (5%)	.7%
1/15 (6.6%)	1.2%
1/12 (8.3%)	2%
1/10 (10%)	2.7%
1/7 (14%)	5.4%

FIGURE 6-21. *A range of camber ratios—very flat to very full—produced by adding a percentage of chord length as extra cloth to the luff of a sail. Cambers in between those shown may be interpolated. Generally a sailmaker does not rely on edge curves alone to produce camber; a smaller percentage of chord length might be employed if another means, such as broadseaming, is also being used to create sail shape.*

6. Connect these marks in a fair curve from head to tack. You may find, however, that the marks refuse to be connected by a single fair sweep without S curves. Furthermore, there is the problem of fairing the lower quarter with the tack offset in a Bermudan sail, and fairing both the upper and lower quarters with throat cutback and tack offset, if any, in a four-sided sail. The problems are addressed beginning on page 291.

A fair luff curve on a Bermudan sail usually requires cheating; that is, you wind up extending or shrinking the round at each height to bring the curve into fairness. I like to start the curve back into the tack about one-eighth of the way up the luff from the tack. This is necessary unless the cloth is very forgiving, because too much extra cloth in the tack area will not work in or smooth out.

The luff curve on a four-sided sail tends to be more nearly symmetrical about the midpoint, because of the need to fair the curve into the endpoints of throat and tack. The tack offset starts at the first slide up from the tack, and the throat offset begins at the slide closest to the throat.

A sail set on a stay or flying (jibs, staysails, drifters, mules, etc.) is usually triangular, and the luff is the longest edge. Exceptions are the main staysails of the schooner rig—fisherman and gollywobblers, for example—which, unless bent to a track, as in staysail schooners, have similar luff curves to triangular sails.

The process for calculating the amount of round is basically the same as that for a sail set on a spar, but the fun comes with compensating for the sag of the stay or luff. With a slacker stay or weaker halyard power, greater compensation must be made. Therefore, you now subtract from the round the amount you expect the luff or stay to sag at each quarter point. The rule of thumb is to anticipate 1 inch of sag per 10 feet of luff length, and subtract the full amount of this from the round at the midluff point. Subtract 75 percent of that amount at the quarter points. The result, when drawn in an averaged-out fair curve, is a long S. Depending on

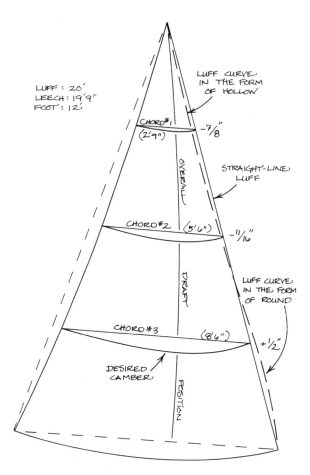

FIGURE 6-22. *Calculating the needed amount of camber-inducing round in the luff of a stay-set sail. We begin by adding a percentage of the chord length as in Figure 6-20, but then must make a deduction to compensate for stay sag, which itself induces camber. As a rule of thumb, 1 inch is deducted for every 10 feet of stay length—a bit more or less depending on rig tune. Generally the full allowance is deducted only at midluff, with three-quarters that amount deducted at the top and bottom chords, though you may want a greater allowance up high to compensate greater sag there. In this example, the desired camber ratio is 8.3 percent (draft position 35 percent aft of luff), so 2 percent of the chord length is added at the luff (see Figure 6-21). At chord #2, $1^{5}/_{16}$ inches is added for round, but 2 inches is deducted to compensate for sag, for a net deduction of $^{11}/_{16}$ inch.*

the desired camber of the sail and the anticipated sag, especially in the heavy wind ranges, the luff curve may fall entirely inside the straight-line luff! It is important not to have too extreme a contrast between the hollow of the upper section and the round of the lower section, or the luff will not set well and it will be difficult to fair the curve into head and tack.

If anything, I try to err on the side of shallowness of camber, with emphasis on hollowing the head and adding little round down low. The reason for this is that the sag tends to concentrate up high as the wind picks up, and in high-clewed, high-aspect headsails, you don't want to be building great draft into the short-chord-length sections below the clew. Depending on the cut of the sail, it is possible to create some camber in the lower sections through broadseaming; then it is even

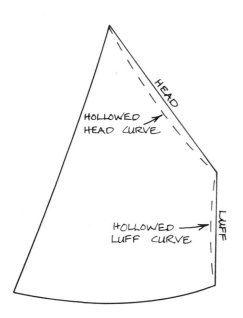

FIGURE 6-23. *The head and luff of a fisherman stays'l will sag under the force of the wind. If the sail is to be flat, you must anticipate and compensate for the sag. A gollywobbler, on the other hand, being a reaching sail, would benefit from the voluminous, full power imparted by sagging edges.*

less warranted to add fullness with the luff curve down low.

The result of cutting a luff perfectly straight, particularly in high-aspect, low-clewed sails, is that the head of the sail sets fuller than the lower section. This becomes more pronounced as the wind increases, with the draft blowing aft in the upper sections and the upper leech flapping.

The luffs of *four-sided sails set flying or on a jackstay*—such as fisherman staysails and various lugsails (except Chinese)—also sag, and greater or lesser allowance must be made. These sails tend to sag in midluff; therefore, the luff curve, which may still be concave, is still nearly symmetrical above and below the midpoint, unlike on the three-sided sails, which have an asymmetrical dramatic change in curve distribution after sag allowance has been made.

While we're on the subject of fishermen and the like, and since we're headed for the head curve of four-sided sails: The head of a main staysail of this type should be treated like the luff of a headsail in that it sags considerably. In order to cut a fisherman with any expectation of weatherly use, the head must be hollowed. With a gollywobbler it is not so critical, because as a reaching light-air sail it can be much fuller with great benefit.

Head Curve (Gaff, Lug, and Spritsails)   The shape and extent of the head curve is very much affected by whether or not the head is bent to a yard or a gaff; and if so, how much the spar will bend. The spritsail has no support in the head other than that provided by the tension in the reinforcement. The head, then, will tend to sag, if anything.

I have had the most success by making the head of a spritsail perfectly straight. The natural sag of the edge, and the shape induced by sprit tension on the diagonal from peak to tack, puts plenty of shape in the upper part of the sail, which is usually loose-footed or boomless. Only in a low-peaked sail, with no weatherly aspirations, would I put round, and then not much.

The head length of a gaff sail, gunter, or lugsail may vary greatly relative to the other edges, and

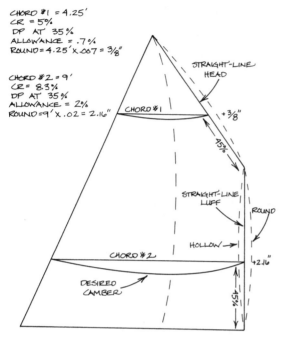

CHORD #1 = 4.25'
CR = 5%
DP AT 35%
ALLOWANCE = .7%
ROUND = 4.25' x .007 = 3/8"

CHORD #2 = 9'
CR = 8.3%
DP AT 35%
ALLOWANCE = 2%
ROUND = 9' x .02 = 2.16"

STRAIGHT-LINE HEAD

CHORD #1   +3/8"

45%

STRAIGHT-LINE LUFF

ROUND

HOLLOW →

CHORD #2   +2.16"

DESIRED CAMBER   45%

FIGURE 6-24. *When designing the head and luff curves of a four-sided sail bent to spars, such as a gaff sail, calculate the rounds as for a Bermudan mains'l. Add a percentage of the chord length outside the straight-line measurement, with the maximum round 45 percent of the edge length up from the tack or throat. The luff of a standing lugs'l may be cut slightly hollow to allow for sag. A smaller camber ratio is needed in the head of this sail to compensate for gaff sag.*

thus the head curve may be providing camber for anywhere from the upper two-thirds to the upper quarter of the sail (or even less, as in the stubby gaffs of the shoulder-of-mutton cowhorn sails, which are really just big headboards). Shorter spars permit less round, regardless of the chord length of the sail.

Gaffs and yards notoriously sag off to leeward—longer, heavier, and lower-peaked gaffs especially. The head of a four-sided sail, for that reason, should be flatter than the lower sections. With a high-peaked sail and vangs, gaff sag can almost be eliminated. A balance must be struck, taking all these variables into account and remembering that cloth stretch, bias elongation, and broadseams can also be used to provide camber. I generally design a rather modest amount of round, then, with its greatest depth about 45 percent of the head length up from the throat. The upper portion of the curve is quite straight; the lower portion has more curvature, but must fair gradually into the throat. Additional round must be made if spar bend is anticipated.

To determine the round, you can proceed in the same manner as for the luff, measuring chord lengths and calculating rounds according to the camber desired, or merely add 1 inch of round for every 10 feet of head length, placed at the 45-percent position. (Again, remember to allow for spar bend.)

Broadseaming and Tailoring   The next step is to indicate on the plan the placement and extent of broadseams and other forms of tailoring. I will discuss this edge by edge in relation to the sail. First, some general thoughts: Broadseaming is a useful means of developing shape in a sail or providing support; it is not the only means, by any means, and often it is not only unnecessary but also inadvisable. In some cuts, the seams do not strike an edge in such a manner as to make broadseaming effective. From the standpoint of camber formation and placement, broadseaming (or sculpting) is a necessity in cloth that is too stiff and stable to permit any other method of shaping. Beyond that, and in the cloths you are likely to use, the purpose of broadseaming is, yes, to offer some fullness; but more important, it is there to regulate the location and distribution of draft, shape of entry, and shape of exit. Generally, because stable fabrics rely on shaped panel edges for camber formation as well as placement, the broadseaming will be slightly wider than in soft cloth. Broadseams in natural fibers tailor shape but also inhibit excessive cloth stretch. Last, broadseaming and its opposite, the easing of seams, shape, support, or loosen the free edges of a sail while affecting camber and draft placement.

A small scale prohibits the actual drawing of the broadseams, but I do indicate their length and width. The full-size broadseams will be discussed and diagrammed during the lofting process.

BROADSEAMS ON THE LUFF. With a few exceptions, only *crosscut sails* lend themselves well to extensive broadseaming at the luff. This cut can most successfully utilize broadseaming to create and distribute draft, because its seams most nearly parallel the chords of the sail. The length of the seam taper is determined by the desired draft position. That is, the seam begins to widen at the intended point of maximum draft, and widens progressively further as it approaches the luff.

Using Table 6-11, plot the draft position in your sail at low, middle, and high chords (the ones used for determining luff and head round may work). You will notice that connecting these points does not make a fair curve. (This is because of the vari-able roach or hollow in the leech.) I juggle things a little in order to make the curve fair. Now, the point where this light, rough line of draft placement crosses each seam to be broadened is the point where the luff taper should begin. There is a school of thought that holds that broadseaming is only necessary in the lower two-thirds of the sail luff—that edge curves do the rest, that a midchord draft position up high is okay, and that the purpose of broadseaming is primarily to create entry shape and tack-area fullness. I have found that this approach sacrifices the opportunity to influence upper sail shape, although I admit that the short upper tapers are somewhat hard to draw.

The tack seam, or lowest luff seam, is always broadened, generally with double the standard allowance prescribed for that cloth type and taper length (see Table 6-12). Proceeding on up the luff, one could broaden every seam, but this is unnecessary. I usually go up about halfway in a Bermudan sail with 36-inch cloth, tapering each seam. I then taper every other seam, since the tapers

Table 6-11. Suggested Draft Positions for Initiating Luff Tapers

Sail	Percentage of Distance from Luff to Leech
Mains'ls (with headsails)	45-50 %
Single-Sail Rig	35-40%
Working Headsails	35-45%
Four-Sided Fore-and-Aft Sails	40 %
Mizzens	35%
Light-Air Auxiliary Sails	45-50%

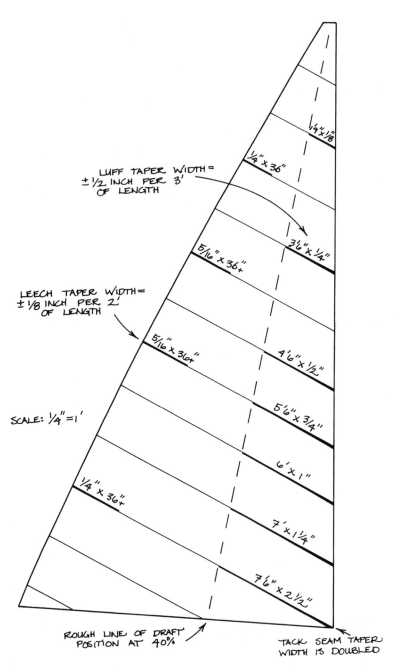

LUFF TAPER WIDTH = ± ½ INCH PER 3' OF LENGTH

⅛" × ⅛"

¼" × 36"

3'6" × ¼"

5/16" × 36+"

LEECH TAPER WIDTH = ± ⅛ INCH PER 2' OF LENGTH

5/16 × 36+"

4'6" × ½"

5'6" × ¾"

SCALE: ¼" = 1'

6' × 1"

¼" × 36+"

7' × 1¼"

7'6" × 2½"

ROUGH LINE OF DRAFT POSITION AT 40%

TACK SEAM TAPER WIDTH IS DOUBLED

FIGURE 6-25. *Luff and leech tapers (broadseams) in a sample Bermudan sail of soft Dacron. The designated draft position determines the length of the broadseam. The width of the broadseam at the luff is about ½ inch for every 3 feet of length. These curved luff tapers create entry shape as they establish draft position. The straight leech tapers are ±⅛ inch wide at the leech for every 2 feet of length, and serve to support and flatten the exit of the sail.*

TABLE 6-12.
LUFF TAPER (BROADSEAM) WIDTHS

CLOTH	WIDTH OF TAPER AT LUFF
SOFT DACRON, COTTON, DURADON	½" PER 3 FEET OF TAPER LENGTH
MEDIUM-FIRM DACRON	½" PER 2.5 FEET OF TAPER LENGTH
STIFF DACRON	½" PER 2 FEET OF TAPER LENGTH

NOTE: TACK SEAMS AND "TWIST" SEAMS RECEIVE APPROXIMATELY TWICE THE STANDARD TAPER WIDTH ALLOWANCE.

become progressively smaller. By the time I reach the upper quarter of the sail, there is no need to continue. A high-peaked, crosscut, four-sided sail is different; I continue the broadseaming right up past the throat as if the luff and head comprised one long leading edge, which they do.

On small sails, 100 square feet or less, with cloth narrower than 36 inches (say, 18 inches), it is all right to broadseam consecutive seams, but in large sails with narrow cloths, tapering that many consecutive seams would be too much work. Therefore, from the tack, every other seam should be tapered until the midpoint of the luff, and from there, every third or fourth seam.

Miter-cut sails offer limited luff-taper options. The miter seam itself can be broadened, particularly on a high-clewed sail, and the seams of the lower cloths in a Scotch-mitered sail can be broadened. Tapering a small number of seams in this manner can have only a limited effect, not enough to create an overall sail form, and if overdone they will merely make an isolated bulge. But they can assist in moderation.

The throat area of a *four-sided vertically cut sail* can be given a little shape if the seams are conveniently located. But care must be taken not to exaggerate these, as their only purpose is to make some curvature in the throat area, which will set poorly if too bulgy.

FOOT TAPERS.   Foot tapers for support and some shape are placed in the existing seams of vertically cut and mitered loose-footed or boomless sails, as well as crosscut boomed sails with fixed feet (such as the sail of a Beetle Cat). But crosscut loose-footed or boomless sails lack sufficient seams striking the foot to build shape and support this way; instead, they must employ additionally cut and tapered seams perpendicular to the foot.

In general, the tapers employed for support are placed in the vicinity of the greatest foot round; often only one or two such tapers are necessary. To create shape in the forward half of the foot and tack area, tapers are emphasized in that section.

I extend tapers up into a loose-footed or boomless sail approximately two to three times the local amount of foot round. On the fixed foot of a crosscut sail, I use the aft end of the tack seam taper as a reference, and terminate the foot tapers on the line descending from there to the clew. In a vertical cut, I begin with the seam closest to the draft position and extend the taper up until it strikes the line that bisects the included angle between the straight-line luff and foot (the tack angle). The remaining tapers are distributed around that and get progressively shorter toward the clew and tack. Foot tapers generally have a width of ⅛ inch for every 1 inch of round.

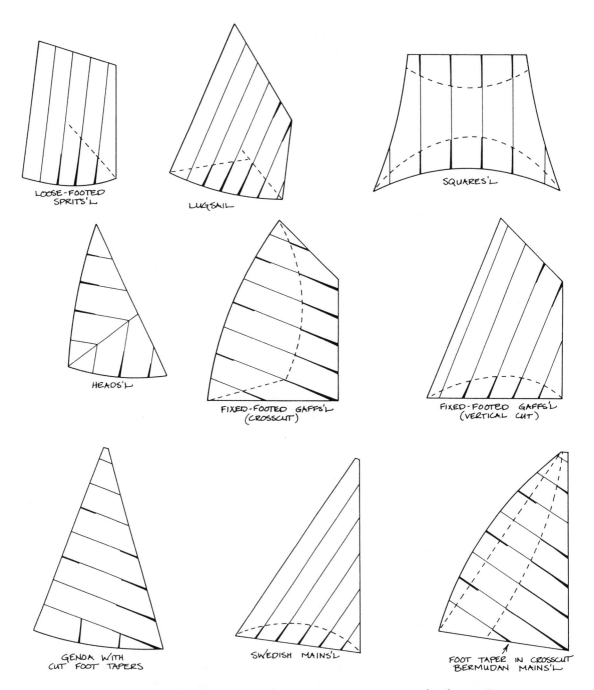

LOOSE-FOOTED
SPRITS'L

LUGSAIL

SQUARES'L

HEADS'L

FIXED-FOOTED GAFFS'L
(CROSSCUT)

FIXED-FOOTED GAFFS'L
(VERTICAL CUT)

GENOA WITH
CUT FOOT TAPERS

SWEDISH MAINS'L

FOOT TAPER IN CROSSCUT
BERMUDAN MAINS'L

FIGURE 6-26. *The use of broadseaming or foot tapers in various cuts and sail types. Foot tapers may be used to support foot roach in a boomless or loose-footed sail, or to provide camber along the foot of a boomed, fixed-footed sail. Foot tapers are usually curved.*

LEECH TAPERS AND SEAM EASINGS. Leech tapers are the easiest to draw and deal with, because they are short and perfectly straight. Obviously, mitered and crosscut sails are the only ones on which leech tapers can be employed. In the extreme, if connected to the luff tapers of a crosscut sail or if numerous and broad enough, leech tapers can create camber and locate draft position. For our purposes, they are intended mainly to provide leech support and a flat exit to the sail, plus a little draft. Never, except in large-boat sails, will leech tapers exceed ½ inch in width; they are generally between ⅛ inch and ¼ inch wide with a taper length of 2 to 4 feet. These measurements are only a rough guideline, however. The fact is, I make these tapers diminish to nothing as gradually as possible, so that there is a completely smooth and fair transition to the underlying seam width. So they are as long as they are long, as determined by their width. And the width, along with number and location, depends on what is being supported: greater roach, heavy conventional battens, heavy tablings, reef patches, and hardware.

Following are some rules for leech tapers:

- Place tapers to support battens and hardware.
- Increase taper width in midleech and areas of greatest roach.
- Tapers at conventional battens should exceed the batten length by at least one-half.
- Tapers of fully battened sails (not Chinese lugsails) should meet luff tapers and can, in fact, be drawn later, when lofting, at the same time as the luff tapers and with the same batten.
- Hollow leeches have taper lengths of approximately 10 percent of the chord length.
- Space tapers at every other seam, or farther apart, depending on the support needed and the cloth width. Close grouping may be warranted in areas of great leech weight, such as reef clews.

Due to shrinkage, stretch, and cloth alignment, it is advisable to ease the leech seams of cotton sails in order to avoid a tight or hooked leech. These easings, which take the same straight gradual form as tapers, but in reverse (that is, they narrow rather than broaden the seams), are placed at each batten or, in the case of a hollow leech, where battens would have been placed had they been needed.

Drawing in Reefs Reefs are not merely a straight line of nettles with big rings at each end. To function well, they must not only be placed correctly but also designed and constructed along certain guidelines. By reefing you are making, in effect, a new foot or, in some sails, a new head or luff for the sail. The design requirements are very similar to those for the unreefed edge, with some additional factors to be considered, not least of which are harsh sea conditions.

On a small-scale plan, I draw the reef in as if it were straight across at the predetermined height. If you absolutely have to guess how deep a reef to draw, refer to the following rule of thumb: The first reef row reduces the sail area by 30 percent. The next row would be placed above that at a distance roughly equal to the distance from the tack to the first reef tack. Otherwise, go with plans or experience.

At the very least, the placement of the reef eyelets should be specified, and you should indicate whether you plan to reinforce the eyelets with individual reef-point patches or with a reef band or bands. Eyelets should be no farther than 2 feet apart, even on large boats. On sails of 100 square feet or less, I place them every 12 to 14 inches. Try to have a measurement and a spacing that avoids disproportionate gaps at the forward and after ends of the reef row. The seams on a vertically cut sail provide convenient spacing.

The choice of bands versus patches is based on strength and convenience. On a large, heavy, working mainsail, for example, the strength is needed, and it may be easier to sew one continuous band with a machine than to horse the sail around a myriad of separate patches. Bands add longitudinal strength to the reef, as well as hold the bunt of the sail together in a vertical cut. Bands are the same width as the foot tabling and are either straight or cut to a curve from extra cloth along the foot of the sail. Individual patches, usually diamonds or squares, are sized as shown later in this chapter. But I have known creative hotknifers to cut reef-point patches of Dacron in the form of everything from hearts to daisies. A poker-playing sailor might alternate hearts, clubs, spades, and diamonds! They all work.

You can draw only the rough reef, or you can be more detailed; regardless, the following requirements must be observed.

Romeo's Reef Rules

- On boomed sails with fixed foot, the corner rings must be positioned above the straight-line reef row so that they take the primary strain. A good guide is to start and end the row of eyelets a ring's diameter below the corner ring. If the rings are of different sizes, use the larger measurement of the two. Otherwise, place eyelets 1 to 2 inches below corner rings on small sails and 2 to 3 inches below corner rings on large sails.
- On boomed sails, always kick the leech end of the reef up to prevent the boom's sagging when a reef is taken. Each reef is progressively kicked up a little farther. The leech end of the first row of reefs would be kicked up at least 3 inches for small boats, 6 inches for boats in the 25- to 45-foot range, and 12 to 18 inches on larger craft.
- Quite simply, the reef row on a boomed sail with fixed foot can be perfectly straight, the idea being that in heavy winds you want a flat sail anyway; otherwise, the reef curve is drawn reminiscent of the foot curve, with the maximum depth at the draft position. I do provide for proportionately less camber, allowing 1 inch of round per 10 feet of reef length.

- Loose-footed and boomless reef rows run parallel to the foot curve, except in instances where the sail profile is altered to a radically different shape, such as in the transformation of a low-clewed sail to a high-clewed one in the reefing process.
- On sails reefed to the luff (sharpie sails), the reef curve can be parallel to the luff curve, or straight.
- Reefs taken to the head or foot of squaresails are straight.
- Reefs in contemporary full-battened sails are straight.
- Trip reefs and balance reefs, as well as odd reefing configurations in headsails, are straight.

Designing Corner Patches, Other Reinforcements, and Chafe Patches

The form and construction of corner patches directly influence the strength of a corner, the security of corner hardware, the set of the sail, and the sail's overall appearance. In terms of size and thickness, it is better to err on the large side, but overbuilt patches add weight, use up cloth, and look too imposing.

Patch design has changed as radically as sail fabric, but outside of certain conventions, it still provides an opportunity for creativity. Here are some of the conventions:

- The cloth direction in patches is the same as that in the surrounding sail.
- All corner patches of voyaging sails and any natural-fiber sail should be hemmed.
- The outer edge of the cover patch (the topmost layer of the patch) should be at least 1 inch long for every foot of sail edge to which it is applied.
- The peak, clews, and reef clews of voyaging sails and heavy-displacement-boat sails should have at least five patch layers; the tacks and throat, no fewer than four layers. Small boats and daysailers can reduce the number of patches to four in the peak and clews and three in the throat and tacks.

- Size increments: In order to transfer the strain gradually from the point of maximum stress out to the unreinforced cloth of the sail body, it is necessary that the patch layers have sufficient difference in size. Their perimeters should be no closer than 1 inch in small daysailers, on up through 3 inches apart on large boats and 6 inches or more where very large patches with great elasticity are used, as in voyaging drifters and auxiliary sails. The second largest layer is put on first, followed by successively smaller layers until the last, which is the largest. (Patch construction is illustrated in several places in this book.)

- Corner patches must distribute the strain in the correct direction.

It is amazing how traditional natural-fiber sails withstand so much strain with such small patches. There are two reasons for this miracle: The durability of traditional materials derives in great part from their elasticity, resilience, and absorption of shock. In addition, traditionally made sails are supported and bound by rope or wire, which takes most of the strain. Increasingly,

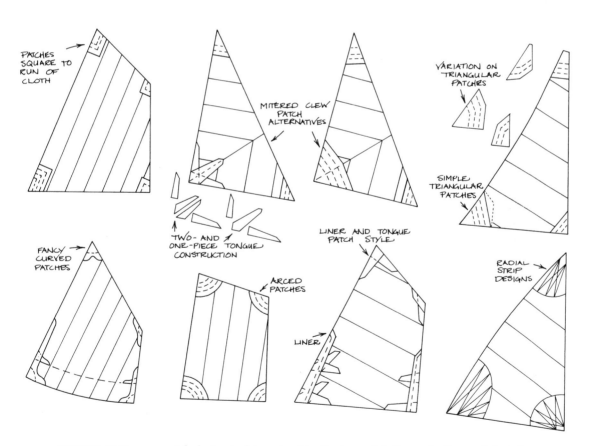

FIGURE 6-27. *Corner-patch design is determined by the type of cloth, aesthetics, and time. In all but the radial cuts, the cloth direction of the patches should match that of the sail. Nothing looks more ridiculous than a classic boat with sails finished to contemporary aesthetic standards.*

with the use of rigid synthetic fabrics, the emphasis has been on the sailcloth itself sustaining the stress. With little absorption and elasticity, either the fabric itself must provide the brute strength or there is insufficient strength to withstand the load. This is why you find large corner patches in unroped soft Dacron sails and mammoth radial-strip patches in hard-finished Dacron and laminate fabric sails.

Early workboat patches were simply kept square to the cloth in design, and for an antique but functional appearance, this approach is still quite satisfactory. With the advent of miter cuts and yacht sails, a method had to be created for dealing with the diverse cloth directions in a mitered corner. Hence, the traditional upper-and-lower-and-tongue corner patch of a mitered sail, as shown in Figure 6-27. This very traditional pattern does work with Dacron and looks best with the old-time miter cut, but much labor can be saved and a strong patch constructed by using a one-piece, multiple-layer corner patch. On an unroped, firm-cloth sail, cloth direction can be alternated between patch layers or laid all the same. For simplicity in Dacron, nothing beats merely crossing the corner with a triangular patch.

Traditional patching often united clews and tacks with reef clews and tacks using long liner patches, and these lent themselves to creative elaborations of shape. Soft materials lend themselves to curved patch edges and some very distinctive results, but stiff resinated synthetics do not hem well in a curve and therefore negate this approach. In light synthetic daysails, however, inventive patch shapes can be cut with a hotknife.

On your sail drawing, roughly draw in the corner patches and designate the number of layers. From this you get a feel for the overall appearance of the sail and the aesthetic relationship between patches in different parts of the sail. Clearly, style and proportions should be consistent throughout the sail.

Other reinforcements include chafe bands and batten chafe bands, brailing eyelet patches, chafe patches at hanks, jackline-anchor patches, cunningham-hole patches, and trip-reef patches.

Cloth Allowances   It is important when laying out cloth over a lofted plan to allow a certain amount outside the perimeter of the finished edge, for the following reasons:

- Some is needed for tablings.
- The initial rough curve set out by string will change when drawn with a batten.
- To some degree the fabric may shrink or pucker in the seaming.
- The process of broadseaming takes up cloth.
- Natural-fiber and hygroscopic materials change dimensions with humidity.

In addition to the obvious allowance for tablings, other special allowances are made:

- In extra-reinforced synthetic sails with internal boltropes: slightly less than half the tape width is allowed beyond the finished edge to make a foldover and additional cloth layer around the rope.
- On a sail with reef bands, these are cut from extra cloth along the foot to ensure correct cloth direction.
- Where long liner patches are desired along the luff or leech of a crosscut sail, they are cut from those edges.

If in doubt, it's better to allow too much extra cloth outside the sail than too little.

Guidelines: Broadseams both shorten an edge and pull it in toward the middle of the sail. Curved and wider broadseams take up more cloth. Add to the length of a foot or head (on a four-sided sail) at least the sum of all broadseam widths on that edge, adding the cloth at the forward end of the edge. Then move the entire edge outward with a cloth allowance (in addition to that for tablings, etc.) at least twice the amount expected in round.

To the lower end of leech or luff, add no less

TABLE 6-13.
ROUGH GUIDE TO CORNER HARDWARE SELECTION

SAIL SIZE AND TYPE	HARDWARE OPTIONS	LOCATION
NO-FRILLS SAILS UNDER 40 SQ.FT.	#1 SPUR GROMMETS	ALL CORNERS
FINELY FINISHED SAILS UNDER 40 SQ.FT.	#3 (1/2") HSR, 3/4" C+RT	ALL CORNERS
NO-FRILLS SAILS 40-100 SQ.FT., OPTION #1	#2 SPUR GROMMETS	TACKS, THROAT
	#4 SPUR GROMMETS	CLEWS, PEAK
NO-FRILLS SAILS 40-100 SQ.FT., OPTION #2	#2 SPUR GROMMETS	TACKS, THROAT
	#4 (5/8") HSR	CLEWS, PEAK
FINELY FINISHED SAILS 40-100 SQ.FT.	#4 HSR, 1" C+RT	TACKS, THROAT
	#5-#6 HSR, 1 1/8" C+RT	CLEWS, PEAK
NO-FRILLS DAYSAILS 100-200 SQ.FT.	#6 SPUR GROMMETS	ALL CORNERS
SMALL-DAYSAILER AND CRUISER WORKING SAILS 100-200 SQ.FT.	#5-#6 HSR, 1 1/8" C+RT	TACKS, THROAT, PEAK
	#6-#7 HSR, 1 1/4" C+RT, #2 DR	CLEWS
SMALL-BOAT STORMS'LS UNDER 7 OZ. DACRON	#7-#9 HSR, 1 1/2"-1 3/4" C+RT	TACK, THROAT
	#9 HSR, 1 3/4"-2" C+RT #3-#4 DR	CLEWS, PEAK
MIDSIZE-BOAT STORMS'LS 7OZ. DACRON OR DURADON; STEADYING SAILS	#9-#10 HSR, 2" C+RT	TACKS, THROAT
	#10-#11 HSR, 2" C+RT, #4 DR	CLEWS, PEAK
MIDSIZE-BOAT WORKING SAILS AND AUX. SAILS OF 200-350 SQ.FT.	#9-#10 HSR, 2" C+RT	TACKS, THROAT
	#10-#11 HSR, 2" C+RT, #5-#6 DR	CLEWS, PEAK
LARGE-BOAT WORKING SAILS; COMMERCIAL STEADYING SAILS	#10-#11 HSR, 3" C+RT	TACKS, THROAT
	#11-#15 HSR, 3" C+RT, #6-#7 DR	CLEWS, PEAK
CHINESE LUGS'L UNDER 300 SQ.FT.	#7 HSR	BATTEN END RINGS
CHINESE LUGS'L 300+ SQ.FT.	#9 HSR	BATTEN END RINGS
LIGHT-AIR NYLON AUX. SAILS UNDER 300 SQ.FT.	#7-#9 HSR	TACKS, PEAK
	#9-#10 HSR, #2-#4 DR	CLEWS
LIGHT-AIR NYLON AUX. SAILS OVER 300 SQ.FT.	#9 HSR	TACKS, PEAK
	#10-#11 HSR, #4-#6 DR	CLEWS

KEY: HSR = HANDSEWN RING; C+RT = CRINGLE AND ROUND THIMBLE
DR = D-RING

than the sum of all broadseam widths. Add to the edge allowance at least twice the round measurement at any given point. To this must be added some for the contraction of sewing, especially hand sewing or machine sewing of soft cloth.

I use the peak of the sail as the static point of reference—everything else is expected to shift some. Hopefully, enough cloth is allowed so that after seaming, the sail will line up and cover the loft plan, including full edge curves, tablings, bands, foldovers, and patches.

Selection, Designation, and Placement of Hardware   Though hard to imagine, it is possible to build a sail with no metal in it at all—no metallic means of attachment fastened to the sail, even! Except in terms of chafe protection, there is much to be said for an approach of such elasticity. But the usual practice, with some exceptions (one being the headboards in some Bermudan mainsails), is that all big corners will have rings, or a cringle and round thimble, or a D-ring.

The choice of hardware style depends on the size, type, and use of the sail and the location on the sail (see Table 6-13). Places of greater strain, such as a clew, will have heavier hardware. Some-

times more than one type is used in a sail—for example, handsewn rings at each corner but a rope cringle and round thimble at the tack of a boomed mainsail when the gooseneck tack pin is recessed; or a handsewn ring at each corner of a gaff sail, except the throat, where there is a cringle and round thimble, for the same reason; or a handsewn ring at the tack and head of a headsail, but a D-ring at the clew for chafe reduction and ease of machine installation. Cringles and round thimbles can only be stuck on edges with roping.

D-rings can be installed by hand with webbing, or by machine, which, in anything but a small sail, requires a powerful sewing machine. Cringles and round thimbles are the next step above the metal-free approach, and are the saltiest looking. They also require the fewest store-bought tools to install.

Headboard Selection   The style of headboard depends on the amount of work you want to do and how classic an appearance you wish to have. The internal sewn type does chafe less and is appropriate for roped Bermudan sails. The external riveted type can be hand sewn rather than riveted, and can work with roped—machine-roped

TABLE 6-14.
CAST BRONZE HEAD THIMBLE APPLICATIONS

Size	Overall Length (inches)	Score Diameter (inches)	Application
#1	1 1/4	1/8	Small boat wire-and rope-luff sails
#2	1 1/2	3/16	
#3	1 3/4	1/4	Light auxiliary sails under 300 sq.ft.
#4	2	5/16	
#5	2 1/4	3/8	Midsize boat rope-luff working sails; light aux. sails over 300 sq.ft.
#6	2 1/2	7/16	
#7	2 3/4	1/2	Large-boat sails; midsize boat storms'ls
#8	3 1/4	5/8	

and hand-roped—and unroped sails. Sizes are shown in Table 6-9, page 246.

Rope or Wire Headsail Luffs The ends of rope or wire luffs in headsails and staysails, and other sails set flying, have thimbles in them—cast bronze or stainless steel thimbles are best. Thimble size, particularly the *score* (groove), depends on the diameter of the rope or wire and whether the eye will be served over or leathered. Some thought must be given to the size of what's going to attach to the thimble.

Eyelets Eyelets are all the little holes through which everything else on a sail is attached. They may be rope grommets, spur grommets, or small handsewn brass rings. Simple rope-grommet eyelets are appropriate in classical sails. Spur grommets are viable for daysailers and small cruisers.

Voyagers, traditional sails, and stormsails should have handsewn eyelets (worked holes). Internally roped edges that run in a slotted spar, of course, have no eyelets at all.

Reef eyelets should be placed every 2 feet or less; foot eyelets, every 12 to 18 inches; head eyelets, every 12 to 14 inches; luff eyelets on a spar, every 12 to 24 inches; luff eyelets on a stay, every 24 to 36 inches.

Generally, it is advisable to space eyelets evenly along the edge of a sail. In sails set on wire, they should be spaced as close to the luff ends as possible, depending on how low a headsail is tacked. The first eyelet may have to be high enough up to clear a turnbuckle and stay end fitting. I often place two eyelets at the head to accommodate two hanks or two slides for greater strength. I do the same at the clew of a fixed-foot boomed sail if there is room. Often the outhaul and track arrangement on

TABLE 6-15. EYELET SELECTION

Size #/Type	Inside Diameter (inches)	Use
000 SG	5/16	L,F,H,R eyelets for very small dinghy sails
00 SG	1/4	
0 SG	9/32	L,F,H,R eyelets for daysails under 100 sq.ft.
1 SG	3/8	L,F,H,R eyelets for daysails 100-300 sq.ft.
2 SG	7/16	
0 HSR	1/4	R eyelets for traditional dinghy sail under 100 sq.ft.
3 HSR	1/2	L,F,H,R eyelets for traditional and cruising sailboats under 45 ft.
4 HSR	5/8	L,F,H,R eyelets for boats over 45 ft. and storms'ls of boats under 45 ft.; peak and tack eyelets
5 HSR	3/4	
6-9 HSR	7/8 - 1 1/4	L,F,H eyelets for large commercial craft

Key: SG- Spur Grommet
HSR- Handsewn Ring
L - Luff
F - Foot
H - Head
R - Reef point

a boom requires a considerable inboard placement of the clew eyelet.

Note: Eyelets on the luff of a spar-bent sail with reefs must be spaced above and below the reef tack ring so that the ring can be brought down for lashing when a reef is taken. In other words, the eyelets immediately above and below the reef tack ring must be far enough from it that the ring can be pulled down past the accumulated luff slides or hoops to reach the tack hook or lashing position at the gooseneck.

Jacklines and Additional Eyelets

Any boomed sail with a tack angle significantly smaller than 90 degrees must have a releasable outhaul to permit the clew to move forward, or else a jackline to permit the luff to move aft when the sail is lowered. Otherwise, reefing produces a distorted, deformed sail, and often the inability to drop sail, because the distance from clew to luff along the luff perpendicular is actually smaller than the foot length.

Jackline eyelets are the same size as the other luff eyelets and are placed in pairs 3 to 6 inches apart, with each pair centered about the placement appropriate for a single eyelet, probably every 3 feet in a club-footed staysail or every 2 feet in a boomed mainsail.

The jackline extends up the luff twice the distance from the tack to the luff perpendicular. The anchor hole to which the jackline is spliced is placed just below the next luff eyelet above that measurement; it should be a strong ring or a cringle and round thimble. The jackline itself is lighter than the luff rope and must be considered in the cordage quantity.

The Chinese lugsail has more eyelets and rings than a shark has teeth. Not only are there the head and foot eyelets along the boom and yard, but also with external battens there are pairs of eyelets equally spaced along the battens for the lashings. Small daysails of this type can employ rigid battens in pockets. In fact, quick work can be made of the assembly process by running seams along at batten positions with enough seam width to serve as the batten pocket. This is clearly not a bluewater

approach. The external Chinese battens are actually a heavy batten on one side of the sail and a retaining batten on the other side, with the sail and chafe bands in between. The retainer not only increases seizing strength but also provides chafe protection from sheetlets, lazyjacks, etc.

In a vertically cut sail, the double eyelets along the battens are placed at every seam, though with 36-inch cloth I go every 18 inches. Duradon is an excellent, though costly, junk sailcloth, and its 24-inch width gives a good, natural eyelet spacing. Use

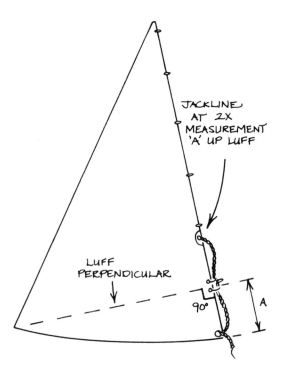

FIGURE 6-28. *You know the sail needs a jackline if the tack angle is greater or less than 90 degrees and the clew is fixed—such as in a club-footed stays'l. Failure to install a jackline could result in severe cloth distortion or inability to lower the sail. Why? Because the distance from the clew to the luff above and below the LP is greater than the length of the LP; thus, the movement of the sail at the LP is restricted.*

the eyelet sizes of head and foot as a guide to size. There is something to be said for using spur grommets in terms of chafe, but I'd only use them in small junk sails or daysails. There are double rings at the forward and after ends of the batten in a Chinese sail. Through these are lashed the batten and sheetlets, parrels, and blocks. They, therefore, should be of larger size than the batten eyelets but need not be as large as the big corner rings.

The biggest shortcoming I find in contemporary sailmaker's use and adaptations of traditional techniques is poor sense of proportion, both aesthetically and in choice of materials. There is the notion that bigger, wider, heavier, and multiple layering produces security in a sail, which, up to a point, is true. Then there must be a balance of proportion within the elements of the sail. I have never seen a well-proportioned sail fail, except by accident. One must develop an eye for what looks right and obtain security through balance and interdependence rather than brute strength.

Gaff Topsails   All sail types have variations, but I segregate pointy-headed gaff and sprit topsails because the variations are so distinctive as to prohibit generalization. (Several variations are illustrated in Chapter 3.) First of all, in types other than the yard topsail with full luff spar, are we considering a four-sided sail, à la the gunter, or is it a three-sided sail with a two-part luff? I think you'd have to say it is a four-sided sail, and it will take diagonal measurements to draw it. Furthermore, the upper and lower leading edges require different edge curves. Of course, the lug topsail is virtually a balanced lugsail, so there is no confusion there.

The leech and foot curves of gaff and sprit topsails follow the same rules as other loose-footed or boomless sails, though the foot roach, if any, should be minimal. The sails can be cut either vertically or mitered.

The upper luff or head eyelets are spaced according to the means of attachment: laced or hooped to a spar, every 12 to 18 inches; or set on a jackline, every 2 to 3 feet. The edge curve will vary according to attachment also. Fixed to a spar, the

standard chord-length-determined round is added, with the awareness that the topsail needs to be quite flat. (If set on a stay, the sag must be allowed for in the luff curve.)

The lower luff is often cut back a ways to clear mast doublings, halyard blocks, and gear. This may take anything from a straight angle aft from the throat to a great notch at the throat, depending on the height at which the sail is set and the clearance required. Designing this feature requires either a sail plan or accurate measurements of the rig. In either event, the edge curve of the lower luff is not intended to provide camber.

Means of Attachment   The last thing to be specified on your design plan is the means of attachment, or bending sail, with a note about how and with what the hanks or slides, if they are used at all, will be affixed to the sail. The appropriate types of hardware have been discussed in Chapter 5. The size used depends on sail use, rig type, existing boat hardware, and stay dimensions. Standard jib hanks and luff slides can be adapted for use on a jackline by seizing round thimbles to them. Note that different edges of the sail might have different sizes or even types of attachment.

LOFTING AND SEAMING THE SAIL

If you've skipped to this section without having made a plan, you may or may not have irrevocably oversalted the casserole. Many have been the times when a sail type was so familiar I just went straight to lofting, measurements in hand. This generally is not advisable, however, without considerable experience. The making of the plan in many ways has done in reduction what will now be done full size, so that in a sense the plan was a practice run. It is analogous to building a model of a boat before building the boat itself. Moreover, there may be unexplained elements in the lofting that presume the prior experience of having drawn the plan. Plus, you'll get mighty sick of my saying, "Refer to your plan" over and over if you haven't got one!

I once said, in a fit of perfectionism, that each step in the making of a sail is an opportunity to mess it up. Rather than intimidate yourself with such self-imposed anxiety, it is wise, as you begin this phase, to keep in mind that each step depends on the preceding one, so it pays to take care as you go so that you are not struggling to compensate for past carelessness.

Your Working Conditions

So, after reading all those criteria outlined in Chapter 5 for the preferred loft space and tools, where have you ended up doing this—in the forecastle or the rumpus room? Using a bent coat hanger for a lofting batten? That's okay, and it brings up the point that it is certainly possible to make sails in pieces in a long enough, narrow space. If you are precise about it, you could make the whole sail and never see it fully outstretched until sailing time. This, in fact, is not far from how sails were made on board ship in days of yore, and how computer-cut sails are now created. But it's far preferable to have enough space to lay out the whole sail with some room to spare around the perimeter for walking, rolling the cloth, and extending battens. Oh, yes, another thing about the process of lofting and layout—a whole step, the second layout, can be saved if double-sided sticky tape is used. On the other hand, it is sometimes easier and more convenient to sew the individual pieces together rather than heave the whole sail through a machine in order to sew each seam. More on this as we go along.

Lofting the Perimeter

The overall procedure for lofting, layout, and sewing is similar for all sails (variations will be specified). Let's get started.

Step 1: With tapes and spikes, *spike out the corner points of the sail.* I often orient the sail to the

boards on a planked floor as a straight-line reference and to avoid distractions, then angle the spikes out.

- Include the fourth corner of the headboard in a Bermudan sail of that type.
- Don't forget to utilize any reductions you made in measurements to compensate for anticipated stretch.
- Save offsets and cutbacks for later.

Step 2: *Stretch the lofting string tightly around the spikes.*

- Start at the tack with crosscut sails and at the clew for all other sails.
- Work your way around, edge by edge. Make off the string firmly on the same spike at which you started.

Step 3: *Widen narrow corners.* Sail area and corner width are added within a given edge measurement by widening the corner at the endpoint an amount equal to the outer diameter of the ring that will go there plus two times the thickness of the ring. Typically, this occurs at the head of pointy-headed sails, and sometimes the tack on a very high clewed headsail.

Procedure: Place the ring along the luff string while spiking the leech string out a sufficient distance to make room for the ring (see Figure 6-29). When you're done, the string turns a square corner at the top of the luff, then turns into the leech around the spike just added. The corner ring, in effect, is serving somewhat the same function as a headboard. The string will stretch enough to permit the corner widening.

Step 4: *Measure to and mark the mid- and quarter points.*

Procedure: Measure along each edge to the midpoint, then measure out or in for round or hollow, at right angles to the string, and put in a thumbtack.

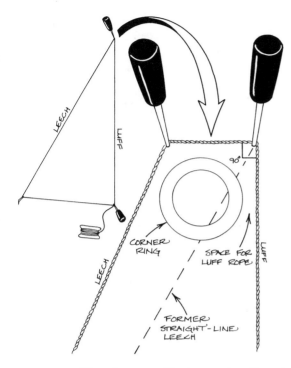

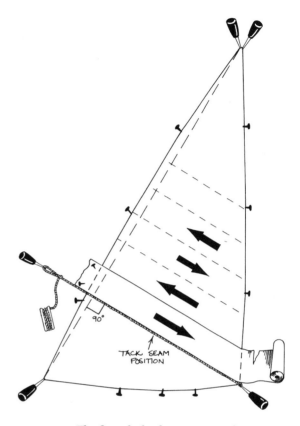

FIGURE 6-29. *Though not as effective as a headboard, additional sail area can be obtained by widening the head of a narrow sail to accommodate the corner ring. This also widens a high-aspect, narrow sail with a hollow leech—and improves the set of the sail. This technique may be used to widen any narrow corner, such as the tack of a narrow, high-clewed storm jib.*

- On leeches with roach, find the batten locations and measure out at each.
- For hollow leeches, designate the midpoint—on a crosscut sail, much cloth can be saved by laying cloth to the curve rather than the straight-line edge. For a vertically cut sail, the leech cloth is laid overlapping the straight-line leech, with additional cloth allowances.
- Quarter points are best measured for accuracy, but on edges other than roached leeches they can be eyeballed and marked roughly.

FIGURE 6-30. *The first cloth of a crosscut sail— Bermudan or otherwise—is laid out along the upper side of the tack seam, which is the perpendicular from tack to leech. Extra cloth is allowed outside the lofting string for tablings, a cloth reduction due to broadseams, and sewing. If you're lucky, the floor and the cloth will be straight enough to permit an even back-and-forth layout of the upper sail (arrows). Then, commencing at the lower side of the tack seam, lay out the lower portion of the sail.*

Step 5: *Pull the string out or in around the mid-point pins.* If quarter points have not already been measured, eyeball them and tack out the string to the rough finished-edge form. (Alternatively, use masking tape to avoid having to lay out cloth over the tacks.) I'm not too particular here. Edge curves are carefully drawn later. The important thing is to make sure that the rounds are sufficiently allowed for.

You now have an impression of the full-size sail.

Step 6: *Prepare to lay out the first cloth.*

- *Crosscut sail:* Attach a string to the tack spike, then run it out beyond and at right angles to the straight-line leech (see Figure 6-30).
- *Vertically cut sail:* Using more of the lofting twine, set up a string outside the tabling and

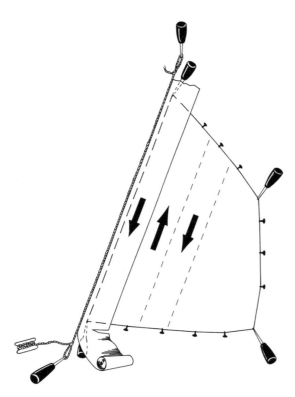

FIGURE 6-31. *The first cloth of a vertically cut fore-and-aft sail is laid out along the leech, with at least enough allowance for tablings. Subsequent cloths are laid back and forth with even seam widths over the whole plan, and extra cloth is allowed outside the lofting string for tablings and for cloth reduction due to broadseams and sewing.*

cloth-allowance distance and parallel to the straight-line leech (see Figure 6-31).

- *Mitered sail:* Bisect the included angle of the straight-line clew with a string from the clew spike out beyond the luff. For a Scotch-mitered sail, set up another string parallel to the foot and (after turning at a spike) the leech, outside the round and the tabling and cloth allowances.
- *Chinese lugsail:* Set up an additional string parallel to the luff, outside the cloth allowance.
- The first cloth in a squaresail is laid in the center, perpendicular to the head.

Step 7: *Mark all the end- and midpoints* with either masking tape or easily read marker on the floor—label the corners to avoid later confusion.

Laying Out the Cloth

At this point the bolt of cloth must be readied. If the cloth was to be bight seamed, this should already have been done (see Chapter 5). If you are sticky-taping the seams, this can be done on the floor while the sail is over the plan, or by taking pieces up and sticking them together later, as they are sewn. The first technique is the easiest and will be described later.

Roll out the first panel. On a crosscut sail, lay the first panel along the upper side of the string from leech to tack. On a vertically cut sail, lay it along the string parallel to the leech. In a Scotch-mitered sail, lay the first cloth along the string parallel to the foot, and on a cross-mitered sail, lay it perpendicular to the straight-line foot next to the clew. On a Chinese lugsail, lay out the first cloth along the string at the luff.

As you lay out a panel, place a pin anywhere in the middle of the cloth to anchor it. Then roll the cloth out to the other edge or to the miter, where you measure for sufficient overlap (at least a seam's width at a miter, and enough for tabling and other cloth allowances at an edge). Take a deep breath, and cut the cloth parallel to the edge or miter string.

Here, if cloth of any appreciable length has been rolled out, you may fetch up on the bane of the sailmaker's existence: poor tracking. That is, the cloth, laid flat, forms an arc. Poor hotknifing, poor weaving or finishing—whatever the cause, it is as annoying as a lumpy floor.

A curved floor, by the way, will show up as curved edges in the cloth. If you attempt to join all this presailmaker curvature, you are actually building the curve of the warped cloth or the rolling floor into your sail. Natural fibers can accommodate this with little effect—Dacron cannot. Do not try to tension or straighten grossly curved cloth. The result will be a tight edge on the hollow side and a rum-pled edge on the convex side. These will then be sewn to the next panel edges, which will have the opposite tension. The result will be a combination of tight and puckered seams.

To deal with excess tracking of the cloth:

1. Send the stuff back to the lummox who made it.
2. Lay the cloth back and forth across the plan as usual, but do not straighten the edges; rather, sew alternating elliptical- and hourglass-shaped seams (see Figure 6-32).
3. Roll the cloth out all the same way so the curves match up. This entails a considerable waste of cloth.

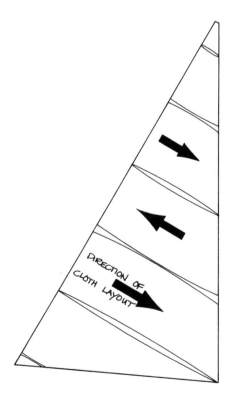

FIGURE 6-32. *Curved cloth is said to be "tracked." Laying out tracked cloth back and forth over a plan results in alternating elliptical- and hourglass-shaped seams. It is extremely difficult to make accurate broadseams—or any seams, for that matter—with tracked cloth. Send it back.*

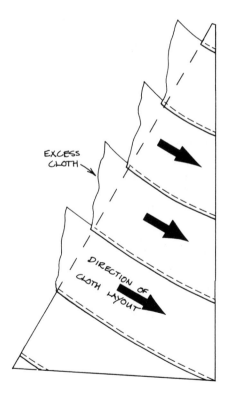

FIGURE 6-33. *Alternatively, tracked cloth can be laid out all in the same direction. This results in consistent seam widths but makes broadseaming difficult and wastes material. Unless you're absolutely stuck with the stuff, send it back!*

Short of returning the goods, I'd go with the ellipses and hourglasses, if they're not too extreme. In bad cases, lay the cloths all the same way, but make sure you have enough cloth!

All you can do about a wavy floor is try to plan things so that the cloths run with the waves.

If all has gone well, align your first panel straight and evenly and naturally, with pins every 3 feet or so.

What seam width have you selected? If there is no commercially installed sew-to line, or if there is and the seam is too narrow, go along the cloth edge with a tape measure or some seam-width gauge, and mark the seam width every 3 feet or less.

If sticky-taping, tape up the seam, leaving the paper backing on the upper side until the sail is all laid out.

Turn the roll of cloth and lay out the second cloth in the opposite direction, allowing the correct amount in seam overlap and cloth allowance outside the sail. Cut, align, and pin this panel.

Proceed to cover the rest of the sail. Fore-and-aft vertically cut sails—both Western sails and Chinese lugsails—are the only cuts in which the entire sail can be covered by proceeding in one direction from the first cloth. With all other cuts (except a crosscut sail with a clew angle of 90 degrees), one portion of the sail will be covered, then a second portion follows in the opposite direction.

To cover the second portion of the crosscut sail below the first cloth (that is, below the tack seam), follow the same alternating procedure as described, but once each cloth is aligned and pinned out, place its edge *beneath* the edge of the preceding cloth so that all the seams overlap in the same direction. The upper section in a mitered sail is done the same as the lower section below. The first cloth laid is the one striking the clew, either parallel or perpendicular to the straight-line leech.

In the layout, you may encounter flaws in the weave, finish, or trimming. Dysfunctional or unsightly sections should be removed and the remaining piece or pieces of cloth saved for subsequent shorter panels or for patch material.

Cutting Special Seams

Part of the layout process is to set up any cut cloth, such as foot tapers, radial foot, twist seams, or miters. All of these techniques, with the exception of finishing a miter seam, are methods of tailoring synthetics and will call for the first use of the hotknife. Setting up the *miter seam* is simply a matter of measuring one-half seam width on either side of the string bisecting the clew angle, then trimming the overlap of the upper and lower sections (see Figure 6-34). Usually, I have the lower panels on top. Measure one-half seam width above the string and draw a line. (Here, for natural fibers, a hem, folded under, of slightly less than one-half the seam width is allowed.) Then cut off the remainder. With synthetics, the extra cloth is removed by hotknifing right along the straight line. Great care must be taken to cut straight without going off the backplate onto the cloth below. Hemmed or cut, that finished edge is laid back down and a sew-to line and strike-up marks drawn before removing the miter string and finishing the miter edge of the upper panels in the same fashion. Sticky tape can now be applied if the sail is fairly small. Otherwise, it is easier to stick the miter seam together later, after each of the upper and lower groups has been sewn.

To prepare the lower panels of a crosscut sail for cutting *foot tapers,* draw the seams (both edges) at the determined position perpendicular to the straight-line foot (see Figure 6-35). (The curved sew-to line of the taper will be drawn later.) At each seam, hotknife the edge closest to the tack. Slide the cloth from the tack over to the correct position of seam overlap while in alignment with the other seams. (It may help to have drawn a clearly visible sew-to line on the tack seam.) Pin in place, and install sticky tape. Sticky tape is recommended here, even if the rest of the sail is not stuck up, so as to minimize the number of pieces floating around and facilitate the sometimes tricky broadseaming. Cut foot tapers are not compatible with cut tablings or reef bands, because the material you're cutting now is the cloth from which tablings or reef bands could otherwise have been constructed.

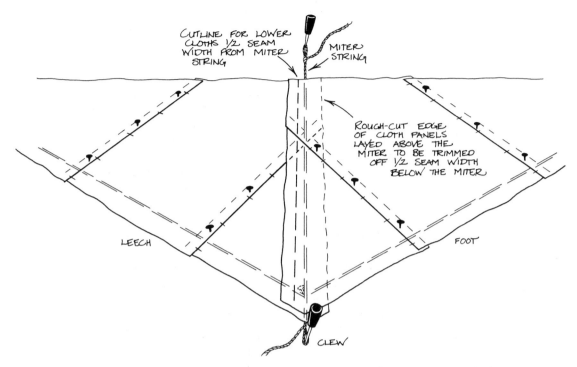

FIGURE 6-34. *After the cloths above and below the miter line of a mitered sail are laid out, the panels that strike the miter must be hotknifed or hemmed into a miter seam. This last seam is sometimes wider than the others for strength in a storms'l, and can even be broadseamed at the luff. Double-sided sticky tape greatly eases this phase of construction. Be careful with the hotknife; it is easy to slip and burn a hole in the sail.*

A *twist*, or *speed, seam,* is cut into the foot area of a fixed-footed boomed sail in order to tailor camber into sailcloths of firm synthetics that are not conducive to other camber-formation techniques. After seaming up or sticky-taping the lower cloths of the sail together, a seam is drawn and cut (hotknifed) from the lower leech to the tack just below the tack seam. The twist seam strikes the leech anywhere from 6 to 12 inches or more up from the clew, depending on the size of the sail. The seam is actually drawn and broadened in the same manner as the tack seam, with 1½ to 2 times the broadseam allowance normal for that type of cloth, and with the taper com-

mencing at the desired draft position. Of course, a twist seam will require extra cloth, and this must be allowed for in the layout. The twist seam is only one of several options for shaping a foot and may be looked on as a means not only of creating camber but also of regulating its position in the sail.

Radial Foot Unlike the preceding cuts, this one does not come after the full layout of cloth. Rather, it is needed to complete the layout below the first cloth laid from leech to luff. Figure 6-16 shows the seam layout and desired warp and weft orientations in the panels of a radial foot.

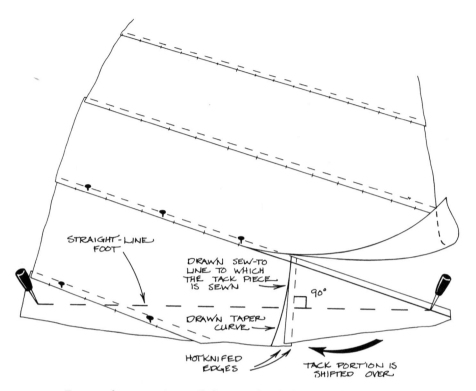

FIGURE 6-35. *To put a foot taper in a sail, first cut the cloth with a hotknife, perpendicular to the straight-line foot at the desired location. Then shift the tack piece a seam's width toward the clew, draw the curve of the taper, and sticky-tape the cloth or sew it together. If a foot taper crosses a seam, it is necessary to sticky-tape or sew that seam prior to cutting the foot taper.*

Marking the Panels

Step 1: *Mark and label all the corners and mid-points* on the sail, as well as the batten points on a roached leech.

Step 2: Refer to your design plan. *Mark the inner ends of all broadseams* and the point where the outer end of each seam crosses the lofting string. Write the width of the taper at this same point.

Step 3: *Check all alignment and seam widths for uniformity,* then take up the lofting string.

Step 4: Here's where the sticky-tapists and the purists start to part company. *Return to each seam.*

If you're a purist, draw sew-to lines and place strike-up marks every 3 to 4 inches. Or, remove sticky-tape backing and stick the seams together. In either case, work only on the untapered portions of the seams.

Step 5: *Draw broadseams.* The shape of the curve drawn, and thus the form of the broadseam, will very much determine the form of curvature in that portion of the sail. This type of broadseaming sews the straight bottom edge of one panel to a curved sew-to line on the upper edge of the panel below it. (Alternatively, in a computer-designed sail, two curved edges are sewn together.) You are in effect drawing camber, but in the special case of luff tapers in a panel a crosscut sail, you are more importantly designating fore-and-aft draft location, as mentioned previously. In this instance, too abrupt and wide a taper will result not only in a very rounded entry but also in a draft position farther forward than desired.

Foot tapers in panel seams, if too wide and abrupt, will cause a loose foot to hook or a fixed foot to be overly shelflike. The taper must be fair and diminish gradually into the general seam width. Any flaws in the transition will show up as rumples and hardspots.

Leech tapers are straight. At the finished edge, measure the taper width perpendicularly from the edge of the upper cloth. Put a pin in at that point. Now, lay a straightedge of sufficient length against the pin and upper cloth edge and draw a new sew-

to line. The seam will be wider at the after end than at the forward end. The taper will fair into the original sew-to line at the forward end.

Luff and Head Tapers of a Crosscut Sail

The luff and head tapers are curved according to the shape you want the forward part of the sail to have. Starting with the tack seam at the finished luff edge, measure the taper width perpendicularly from the overlapping edge of the upper cloth, and mark this point on the lower cloth. Place a long flexible batten along the seam, with its upper edge abutting the upper cloth selvage. Place a pin, or several pins, along the upper edge

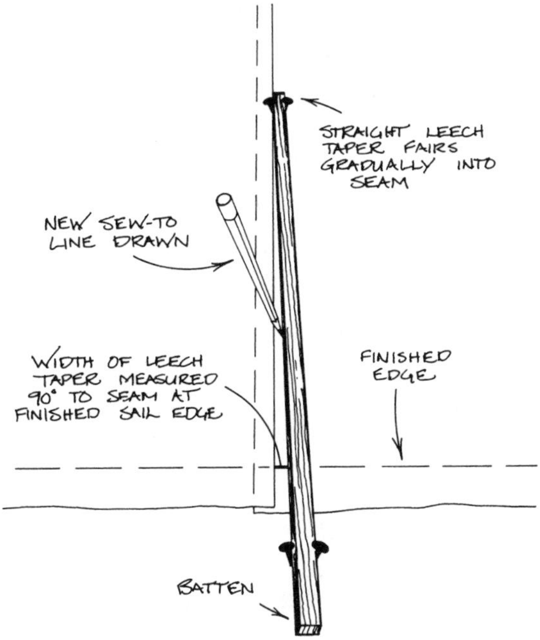

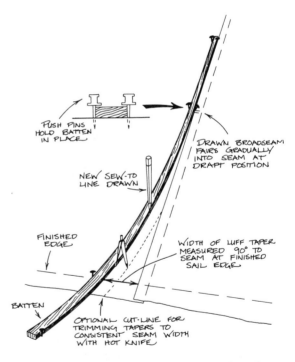

FIGURE 6-36. *Leech tapers can often be drawn by eye as long as the taper is straight, not too long, and diminishes to nothing in the seam. Too abrupt a transition will create a hooked leech. In contrast to Dacron, cotton leech seams are narrowed or eased rather than broadened and tightened.*

FIGURE 6-37A. *Drawing a fair luff taper or broadseam takes an eye for form, fairness, and symmetry. It is important that the curvature of the taper not be so great that the draft position is shifted farther forward than intended, and the entry becomes too full. Hotknifing tapers down to the overall seam width is necessary only in very firm cloth or for looks.*

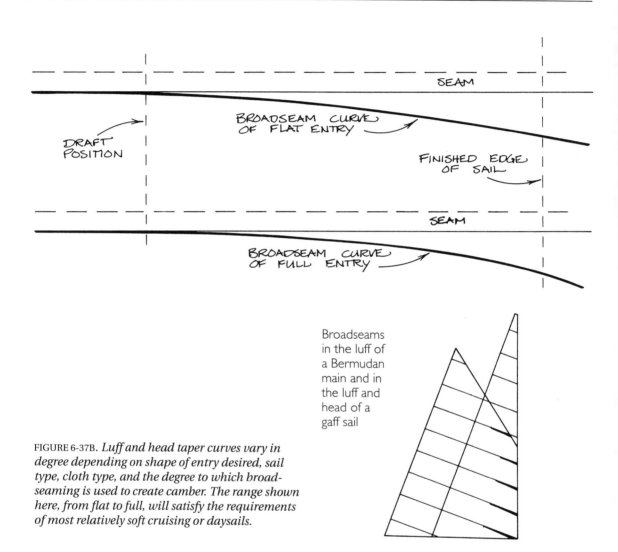

SEAM

BROADSEAM CURVE
OF FLAT ENTRY

DRAFT
POSITION

FINISHED EDGE
OF SAIL

SEAM

BROADSEAM CURVE
OF FULL ENTRY

Broadseams
in the luff of
a Bermudan
main and in
the luff and
head of a
gaff sail

FIGURE 6-37B. *Luff and head taper curves vary in degree depending on shape of entry desired, sail type, cloth type, and the degree to which broadseaming is used to create camber. The range shown here, from flat to full, will satisfy the requirements of most relatively soft cruising or daysails.*

of the batten at the draft point, or after end of the taper; then place a pin on the lower edge of the batten at the same point. (Allow for the width of the pencil sew-to line.) Spring the batten down until its upper edge passes the measured mark. Place a pin on each side of the batten at the mark. Sight down the batten while continuing to spring the curve from the forward end. Pin the batten in place when the desired curve is obtained. Draw the new sew-to line along the upper edge of the batten.

Option: At this point it may be aesthetically or functionally warranted with synthetics to draw a new "selvage" a seam's width up from the sew-to line of the taper in anticipation of later trimming the extra cloth with a hotknife. A small compass works well. This is only necessary in very wide tapers, say at the tack. Otherwise, it is mostly a means of maintaining visual uniformity of seam width—an option not available in the broadseams of natural fibers, and inadvisable in Duradon. Once you have established a form for the curve of your taper, try to make the succeeding tapers as similar as possible. Patterns can be made for this kind of work, if it is to be done repeatedly. Otherwise, this is really your first big chance to eyeball curves with your own unique sense of distribution and proportion.

You will notice as you work your way up the luff through progressively smaller tapers that it becomes increasingly difficult to see the curve of the taper and fair it into the seam.

Cut Foot Tapers in a Crosscut Sail The procedure for drawing cut foot tapers (that is, foot tapers that are not in panel seams) is the same as that for luff tapers, but in loose-footed or boomless sails the purpose and thus the shape of the curve are quite different. The desire is to shape and support the foot. I tend to make the lower end of the taper flare a little more, especially since, compared with

luff tapers, these are usually much shorter in relation to their width. Sometimes a thinner, more flexible batten is required.

In pursuit of sail curvature, foot tapers forward of the midpoint are more rounded, while those nearer the clew tend to be flatter. Foot tapers in the seams of a vertically cut sail are drawn in the same manner and placed for the same purpose.

Trimming and Sewing the Seams

If you'd planned on trimming your broadseams in order to maintain a pleasing uniformity of seam width, now is the time. If you're working with a synthetic, simply cut with a hotknife as described and pictured elsewhere. Sticky tape, if you're using it, will have to be shifted aside.

Here's where the sticky-tapists and the purists really part company. *Tapists,* take up all the pins and proceed with sticking together the broad-

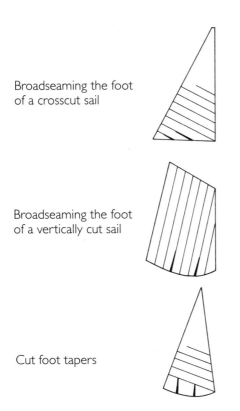

Broadseaming the foot of a crosscut sail

Broadseaming the foot of a vertically cut sail

Cut foot tapers

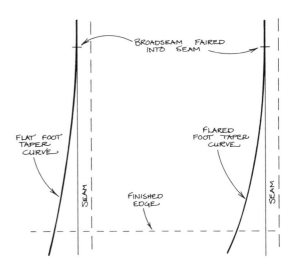

FIGURE 6-38. *Foot taper curves vary depending on their use—that is, support or camber—their fore-and-aft location in the sail, the type of sailcloth, and the type of sail. Excessive flare will hook the foot of a boomless or loose-footed sail. The farther aft in the sail the taper is located, the smaller and flatter it should be. The foot tapers in a sail of great foot roach must not flare excessively.*

seams while removing the sticky-tape backing. Proceed from the narrow end out. This is tricky; care must be taken to stick the seam overlap together smoothly right along the sew-to line. It is more difficult with stiff material on greater curves. Straight tapers are duck soup. It often helps to roll up the upper layer, then remove the tape backing section by section as you unroll the cloth along the sew-to line. The roll of cloth gives you something to hold onto. Pushing the cloth in toward the middle of the sail also helps in the alignment.

Here is the tapist's big advantage, and one of the big arguments for sticking everything together: You can now see the shape you have tailored and the fairness of your work, before sewing it all together. If you are unhappy with it, you can take it apart and stick it again, redraw it, flatten it, flare it, fair it, or whatever it needs. Wide, untrimmed broadseams will need two rows of sticky tape for smooth sewing later on.

Once everything is securely stuck together, I take the added precaution of stapling the seam ends. By sticking the sail together, you also have advance notice of whether your sail is failing to cover the plan as a result of insufficient cloth allowance for broadseams.

There, now you tapists can skip ahead to drawing the sail edges.

Nontapists, label each cloth panel and seam so that it is clear what order they are in. They should be labeled consecutively from left to right at the edge or seam ends at which you start sewing. Machine sewing has the work accumulate to the left as cloths are joined. In hand seaming, the finished work accumulates in front of you. A miter seam, as mentioned, is sewn last, with the larger portion of the sail to the left of the machine or in front of the hand seamer.

Therefore, on a crosscut sail constructed starboard-side up, it is preferable to number the seam ends along the leech from clew to peak. There is another valuable reason for this: The big luff broadseams have no strike-up marks; thus, it would be very inaccurate to start sewing from the luff. (Sticky tape makes sewing possible from either end.)

I usually start sewing the seams of a vertically cut sail at the leech; thus seam end numbers start at the peak and work down, or forward.

Insofar as possible, choose your starting point so as to avoid starting with a broadseam. Sometimes it is unavoidable, as in leech tapers, in which case you can start on the untapered middle portion of the seam where there are strike-up marks. Sew to the luff, then turn the sail around and go back over the leech taper. Often leech tapers are so narrow and fine they can be sewn up directly.

Having completed the numbering, take up the cloths, panel by panel. Sew them together, first one side of the seam, then the other. Then add a third row of stitching for voyaging sails. Proper zigzag stitching is shown in Chapter 5 and discussed below.

Machine Seaming   When seaming by machine, making all those marks and sew-to lines match up while still having an accurately placed, uniform stitch is an art. Without the aid of tape or mechanical contrivances, like seam pullers and walking presser feet, it is a matter of bringing the two cloths together accurately along the sew-to line while aligning the seam edge with the path of the needle for correct placement, *and* having the layers of cloth flow through the machine both in unison and at the same rate that the machine is operating. Yi! Complicating this herculean endeavor are the feed dogs (little teeth in the bed of the machine that pull the cloth through), which haul the bottom layer at one rate while the upper layer's passage is being retarded by friction with the presser foot. Moreover, the machine does not sew at a constant rate—it varies with how fast you power it—and the cloth has its own peculiar qualities of slipperiness and elasticity. The most challenging part is to compensate consistently for the relative flow of the top and bottom layers so that the strike-up marks line up. This entails some form of slowing the bottom layer, speeding up the top layer, or doing both simultaneously.

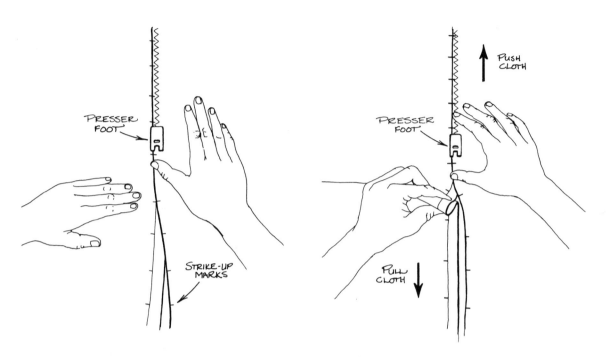

FIGURE 6-39. *Machine seaming techniques. To compensate for differing upper and lower cloth feed rates, match strike-up marks by maintaining a forward pressure on the upper cloth with the right hand while holding back the lower cloth with the left hand. Alternatively, the lower cloth can be gripped to retard its pace through the machine. You will develop your own technique; much depends on the machine, the sewing setup, and the cloth.*

Care must be taken, when sewing portions where there are no strike-up marks, to maintain the same balance between top and bottom layers. Natural fibers and Duradon are more forgiving than Dacron or nylon; with the latter two, uneven tensions and straying from the sew-to line may not be obvious, but they are there to stay. If you are intolerably off, the best thing is to tear out the messed-up stitches, oversew the end of the good stitching by an inch or so, and have at it again.

Natural-fiber and soft synthetic sails are traditionally machine seamed with the zigzag stitch moving back and forth over the selvage. In any fabric of great elasticity—cotton, flax, Duradon, or nylon—this produces sufficient strength. Dacron seams, on the other hand, are strongest when sewn with the full stitch in the seam, close to the edge but not so close as to fracture the hotknifed seal. The argument for oversewing the selvage in Dacron is to contain unraveling cloth edges, but I opt for keeping the full stitch in the seam.

The zigzag stitch is the stitch of choice in seams, but the three-step zigzag, which is a three-stitch straight stitch in a zigzag pattern, is exceedingly strong and can fill a narrow seam with one row of stitching. Both stitch types are illustrated in Chapter 5.

Machine adjustment for thread tension is very important, not only to the quality of the stitching but also to the success of the seaming. I do not propose to discuss sewing machine use in depth, but there are a few observations with which one can head off gross frustrations. Of course, have the correct thread and needle size for the job (see Table 5-10, page 196).

Have sufficient presser-foot tension downward to prevent the cloth from lifting on the upstroke of the needle and to keep the work from skidding around. When relative tension between the top and bottom thread is out of balance, one tends to tighten only the looser of the two. For fine adjustments this is okay; but unless the whole stitch is hopelessly loose, it is better to ease the tension of the overtight thread than to tighten the loose one. Otherwise you may overtighten and may eventually run out of adjustment. The overtensioned stitch itself may look correct, but the tension tends to pucker the cloth and break the thread.

I always sew with the bobbin thread slightly visible from the top. I have too many times sewn for miles only to discover when I turned the sail over that the underside was a mess. It is often difficult to pull the bobbin thread up through resinated, tightly woven fabric. A larger needle may help, or a lighter bobbin thread.

Take your time, and use tables and chutes to ease and support the work. If you become aggravated, take a break. Sewing machines can ruin your day.

Keep an eye out for having run out of bobbin thread. With experience, you can hear the change in the noise of the machine. Otherwise, if missed, you can poke a lot of needless holes in the sail. Find some other visual reference for alignment than the dancing needle. It is very hard on the eyes. Generally, lighter and less tightly woven fabrics require less overall thread tension, relatively speaking. In fact, anything but the lightest tension on drifter-weight nylon will result in a very puckered stitch and seam.

When you finish this step, you will know why production lofts have sliding tables and sewing machines built into the floor! I place sheets or cloth on the floor around the machine where the cloth will be dragging, to avoid grunge. Have good illumination of the sewing area.

Check the sewing of seams and broadseams for fairness and accuracy. Any problems found are more easily resewn now than later. Note, too, how puckered the seams are from the sewing. Usually with softer fabrics it will be necessary to lay the sail out, put tension on each seam, and give them a vigorous rubdown with a seam rubber. I have even left a sail's seams tensioned overnight to stretch them out. Hand seaming always needs rubbing, but often so does machine sewing. Clearly, if you cut the finished edges of a sail that's all puckered up from sewing, when the seams stretch out the edge curves will distort.

Hand Seaming   If you are actually hand seaming, you are eligible to join SWEAT—the Society of Workers in Early Arts and Trades—and have my hearty support. The ditty bag apprenticeship of Chapter 1, brief as it was, gave you a feel for this work to come. Lengthy time spent at this work really demands an efficient and comfortable setup. At least approximate the functions of the sailmaker's bench with some kind of bench, a strong place to tie off the bench hook, good access to wax and twine, good light, and elbow room.

Seaming is seaming. You follow the sew-to line and match up the marks. In this work it may help to pin the seam together every 2 to 3 feet or so with an old sail needle. There are sewing techniques for gathering or advancing the upper cloth that must be employed to counteract any tendency for the top layer to slide ahead of or behind the strike-up marks. Bending the cloth down gathers cloth—that is, puts in slack. Bending the cloth up does the opposite. Heaving the stitch ahead advances the upper layer; heaving back gathers slack cloth.

The work is in front of you across your lap; the upper cloth of the seam is folded around, beneath the lower cloth. Locate the fold so that enough of the upper cloth shows for a good handhold, against the bench-hook tension, but not so much as to move the seam beyond the reach of your thumb. The bench hook is belayed at bench height, with the hook in the cloth just outside your thigh. The body is turned slightly in the direction you are sewing. Use your whole upper body, not

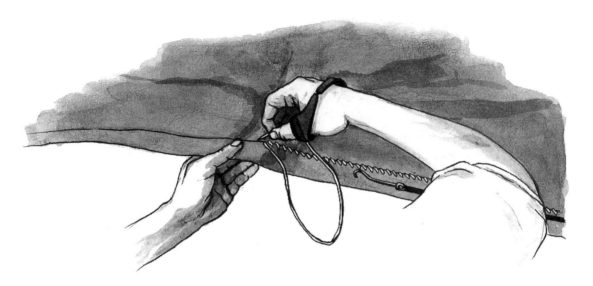

Walking down the seam with a flat stitch—the upper
cloth is folded underneath, and the seamer must be
careful not to sew together more than the two layers
in the seam.

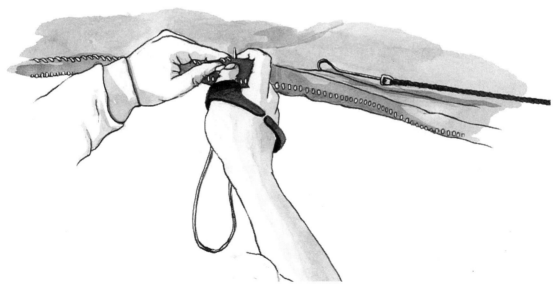

The round-stitch in seaming is advanced toward
the hook. This is a strong stitch, appropriate for
heavily built sails.

FIGURE 6-40. *Hand seaming.*

just the wrist. Making up twine lengths longer than your arm length is a waste of time. Counteract the act of twisting of the thread by rotating the needle as you sew.

Traditionally, the seams of Norwegian workboat sails are sewn with a round stitch, selvage to selvage. This is fast and strong and easy in elastic, natural fabric. It would work, too, with Duradon. It is not a seaming technique, however, that permits broadseaming.

To facilitate hand seaming, sew protective leather pads on your pantleg where the bench hook crosses it, heave the stitch only tight enough to slightly bed it into the fabric (Dacron won't permit much), fix yourself a soft cushion to sit on, and have lots of good music on hand.

Drawing the Sail's Edge Curves

Lay the rubbed-down sail over the plan. On all sails except Chinese lugsails, start by putting one spike in the head, then one in the clew, then the throat, then the tack. On Chinese sails, the tack is the first corner spiked down, then the throat, then the clew, and then the head. You will notice that even on perfectly flat, well-rubbed sails the marks on the sail will no longer correspond to those on the floor. If there has been broadseaming, there will be a great shift. The sail must be swung so that in its altered form the cloths still run in the same perpendicular or parallel relationship to the edge of orientation—perpendicular to the leech on a crosscut sail, for example. Do not pull or distort the sail when aligning it to the floor marks. Lifting the final corner and rapidly fanning it up and down will fill the sail with air, pulling cloth toward the middle and enabling you to see the camber. Otherwise, just the weight of the cloth will splay the sail out along the edges, causing inaccurate edge curves. I have even reversed a vacuum cleaner to inflate the sail from beneath.

With all corners spiked, further distribute the cloth of camber toward the middle of the sail so that the sail's edges are as flat as possible and can be pinned every 2 feet or so, with the pins placed well inside the straight-line edges (so as not to foul the lofting battens). A clean broom will help in pushing the cloth around.

Now, there's the chance that your cloth allowance was not sufficient and the sail does not cover the plan. If it's very close, perhaps a change of tabling style—for example, using tape—will help, or if it's a broadseam that caused the problem, some of them could be eased. Otherwise, there is nothing to do but make the sail a little smaller. (Sort of an early recut.) Locate all the midpoint marks on the floor; mark them on the sail.

Now comes an aspect of sailmaking that I truly enjoy—creating and sighting down those big, luscious curves. Get out your battens and take your time getting the fair curve you like. If L. Francis Herreshoff could take weeks on a sheerline, you can give the leech one half hour. Study the curve from both ends, down low—then stand on a chair. You can get a friend to make subtle changes in the batten while you observe. Set up a straight-line string for a reference, if necessary, and don't be too impatient or proud to bag it, unpin everything, and start the curve over.

In short lengths of great curvature, there is much tension in the batten, so the pinning out and removal of pins must be done with care. Spikes are needed at the endpoints, and sometimes at the midpoint and spring-lever points.

Procedure

- Unless the batten is being used for designating a tabling width, place it against the inside of the endpoint spikes. Hopefully, the batten length is sufficient for the curve but not too long for the work space. If the batten is too short, join two battens or otherwise contrive an extension. Locate the union, which will be an inflexible hardspot, at a flat point of the curve. If the batten is too long, you could cut it, find a bigger loft space, or draw the curves by pinning out tape of ¾-inch nylon webbing. Whether webbing or batten is employed to draw the curve, it is pulled or pushed at midpoint to the position of maximum curvature and firmly pinned in place. A radical curve may need some help by your springing the ends of the batten, then pinning the midcurve.

- Push or pull the batten to quarter points, if any. Often these don't lie in a fair position along the curve, but they are a reference. Compromise as necessary. From there it is a matter of springing, pulling, and pushing until the wonderful form reveals itself. Next, firmly pin the batten along its length and draw the finished edge. Then, with a compass, draw additional tabling fold and cut lines, if any. It is helpful to score the cloth along the batten with a dull metal edge to facilitate folding later.

- Cut tablings, if any, will be cut from the cloth edges, folded and hemmed under, and stitched onto the edges of the sail. When sewn to the sail, however, they will be shifted slightly along the sail edges from where they lay prior to cutting, so that the panel edge seams in the tablings will be offset from the panel edge seams in the body of the sail. (Sewing would be difficult if the seams were allowed to pile up on each other.) For that reason, cut tablings can be pictured as shifting around the edge of the sail clockwise for right-handed sewing, and the reverse for left-handed sewing. They are also shifted clockwise for machine sewing. Therefore, when you start drawing the edge curves of sails with cut tablings, you'll want to draw them in sequence around the sail. (It doesn't matter which edge you start with, as long as the right end of the curve extends beyond the endpoint, and the left end terminates at the endpoint.)

Offsets—Tack, Throat, and Clew Offsets (also called *cutbacks*) may or may not be part of your sail design. If they are, there are a couple of general considerations to deal with before we move on to more detail of the edge-by-edge curves. The manner in which an offset is incorporated depends on

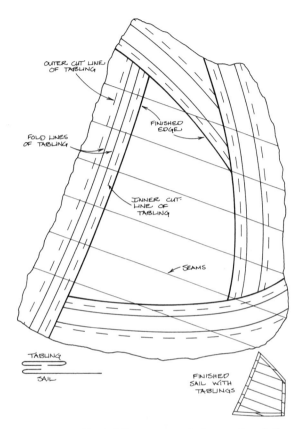

FIGURE 6-41. *Cut tablings are made from extra cloth around the perimeter of the sail for consistency of cloth direction between sail and tabling. The tablings are shifted 4 to 6 inches along the sail edges (clockwise in this case) to keep panel edge seams from piling up on top of each other. A sail lofted port side up would have everything done in reverse.*

the source of the measurements for your sail. If, for example, your measurements for a gaff sail were made on the boat with the gaff set up in its working position, you will have obtained a straight-line measurement from the throat-attachment hardware on the gaff (which could be several inches abaft the mast to make room for the gaff jaws) to the tack attachment point, and to this straight-line edge you will *add* a throat offset to move the upper portion of the luff into the mast. On the other

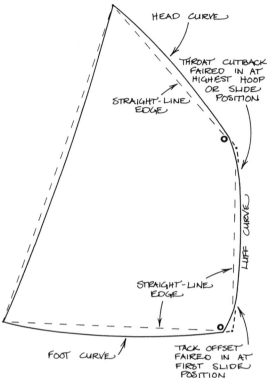

HEAD CURVE

THROAT CUTBACK
FAIRED IN AT
HIGHEST HOOP
OR SLIDE
POSITION

STRAIGHT-LINE
EDGE

LUFF CURVE

STRAIGHT-LINE
EDGE

FOOT CURVE

TACK OFFSET
FAIRED IN AT
FIRST SLIDE
POSITION

FIGURE 6-42. *Cutbacks, or offsets, are measured, drawn, and cut on the lofted sail after the edge curves have been drawn. Depending on its magnitude, an offset may be faired into the edge curve or depart abruptly from it.*

hand, if your measurements came from a sail plan, you may (depending on the hardware) need to *deduct* a throat offset to make room for the gaff jaws.

The easiest procedure for incorporating pronounced offsets requires that the original peripheral measurements and the lofting ignore them. Then, after the edge curves have been drawn, measurement for the offset is made and drawn in the appropriate place. An offset is sometimes drawn perfectly straight, say from the tack slide position down to the offset tack position. Often, though, an offset can be incorporated as a faired-in extension of the luff curve. In this instance it is possible to set up and draw the edge curve and offset simultaneously. Care must be taken when assigning the offset corner position to have the corner hardware—ring, D-ring, or round thimble—line up accurately with spar fittings.

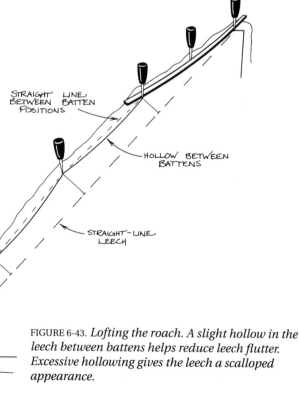

STRAIGHT LINE
BETWEEN BATTEN
POSITIONS

HOLLOW BETWEEN
BATTENS

STRAIGHT-LINE
LEECH

FIGURE 6-43. *Lofting the roach. A slight hollow in the leech between battens helps reduce leech flutter. Excessive hollowing gives the leech a scalloped appearance.*

Leeches with Roach Usually a roached leech with battens is not cut as a fair, continuous curve—it is segmented, so that you will be drawing sections. Most simply, these sections can be straight, but to minimize flutter between battens, a slight amount of hollow—⅛ inch to ½ inch—is centered between the endpoints of each section. The more hollow there is in a given length of section, the more segmented the leech will appear.

Hollow Leeches The only caution in drawing a hollow leech is to avoid neglecting the upper leech by making the curve too straight and flat there. If it is, the leech will be more likely to flutter in that upper area, and the lower leech and clew will seem to have been pulled out like taffy.

Luffs In general, the key to a successful luff curve is a smooth transition at the ends as well as in the middle of reverse curves. In all cases except when a taped luff is to be sewn with a sew-to line and strike-up marks, the innermost line drawn will be

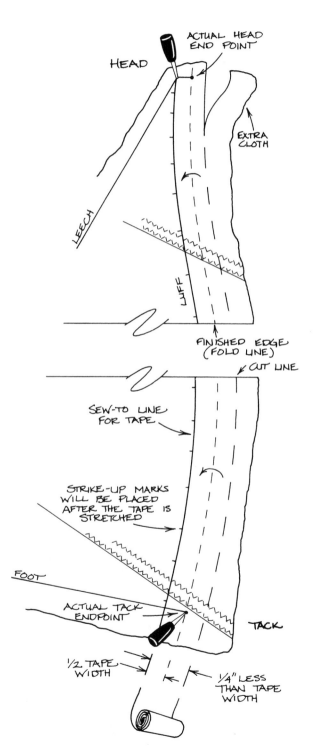

FIGURE 6-44. *There are two methods of installing a luff tape over a folded sail edge. In the first, shown here, draw a sew-to line with a batten and compass half the tape's width in from the finished edge. Then stretch and strike up the tape along that line. Make marks on the cloth at the outer edge of the tape, and use these as a reference for trimming off the excess cloth. Sew the tape to the sew-to line, then fold the tape and sail over and sew them down from the other side. (A luff rope, or a line with which to fish one through, is laid in at this time.)*

Alternatively, draw the finished luff curve, then move outward slightly less than half the width of the luff tape and draw the cut line. (To facilitate, lay a batten along the finished luff curve, and use a compass set to the proper width to draw the cut line.) Fold the edge under using the finished edge as the fold line, then stretch a prefolded tape over the edge and staple it into position with luff rope or feeder line in place. Then sew, as all those staples shred your hands and your sewing machine's paint job.

the finished edge, either cut or folded. If a luff tape is to be installed with a sew-to line and strike-up marks (as opposed to stapled), then the line drawn is the sew-to line and is half the luff tape width in from the finished edge. Measure this distance aft at both endpoints at right angles to the straight-line luff. Place spikes and batten in this position for drawing the sew-to line. The same procedure will be necessary at the foot and head if tapes *are* to be sewn in this unstapled way. The tape will be stretched and pinned to this curve and struck up.

Draw all tablings or cut lines according to tabling type.

The Foot　　The foot varies from sail type to sail type, so it is difficult to generalize.

- *Fixed to spar:* Care must be taken to keep the aft end flat and, while accentuating the forward curvature, still fair it gradually into the tack. If the edge is taped, draw the sew-to line one-half tape width in from the finished edge.
- *Loose-footed on boom:* This can be a very exciting curve to draw if it has a dramatic sweep to the forward part and becomes nearly hollow in the after part.
- *Boomless:* Draw all tablings or cut lines, as needed, and draw all reef bands designated with hems.

The Head　　When drawing the head of a quadrilateral sail, keep the ends flat, then draw the necessary cut, fold, and sew-to lines. The head of a fisherman taped with a foldover will be drawn like a taped luff with a foldover.

Drawing the Reef Rows

The line drawn for a reef band will be the upper sew-to line. It is continuous. When individual reef-point patches are used instead of a band, the horizontal axis of each patch will be drawn at its location, resulting in a discontinuous line. Remember to make the appropriate height allowance between the reef-point patches and the corner rings (the rings

are higher, and it is to their bottom edges that the measurements are made up from the foot). Prior to drawing the reef rows, it will be necessary to smooth out and pin down the middle of the sail. With much broadseaming the sail will be rumply beneath the batten. Try to smooth the sail around evenly.

It helps to lay a batten along the straight-line foot in order to assure the perpendicularity of your measurement up to the reef clew positions on the leech and the reef tack positions on the luff. For sails reefed to head or luff, the procedure here is basically the same except that one measures from a different edge.

Measure to the reef clew and tack positions on the finished edge, and place spikes there. Except for a perfectly straight reef row or a reef radically out of parallel with the foot, the curves of the reef rows will be shallower but otherwise similar to that of the foot. In *fixed-footed sails*, the reef curve is drawn to the depth and draft position desired—generally, fairly flat if not straight. In *boomless and loose-footed sails*, for uniformity, I measure up at several points along the foot to imitate its curve. Often it can be eyeballed. I'll set the battens up for two or three reefs at a time, adjusting each to achieve symmetry and similarity. Of course, the deepest reef can't be a chopped-off segment of the foot—it would be bulbous—but the reef curves can be made similar enough so as to look parallel with the foot and with each other.

The sew-to line for reef bands is drawn right along the batten after it's laid between the reef clew and tack ring positions and sprung to the desired curve. If not already delineated by the seams of a vertical cut, a mark can be made in each reef eyelet location. For individual patches, the batten is adjusted downward at least 1 inch from the corner rings as discussed earlier in the chapter, then sprung to the curve. Draw the horizontal axis for each patch, then draw the vertical axis of each diamond-shaped patch in the correct location. I draw this axis perpendicular to the batten; thus they are somewhat tripped around the curve. At the leech and again at the luff, draw a line along the batten to use as a reference for the corner patches.

Drawing Sew-To Lines for Chafe Bands and Batten Pockets

It is easier to build pockets for conventional battens (as opposed to full battens) if the lower edge of the pocket starts at the vertex of two leech sections and is perpendicular to the straight-line leech. The exception is any lower batten that will be tucked into the reefed sail. These battens can still be placed at vertices, but should run parallel to the foot.

Full battens of the contemporary variety, running parallel to the foot, have pockets that are centered on the leech vertices; therefore, the sew-to line is drawn half the pocket width below the vertex, then extended across the sail to the luff, paralleling the straight-line foot.

For Chinese sails, the positioning in relation to the leech vertices is the same—centered—but chafe bands for the battens are not always parallel to the foot. In traditional batwing sails, the first batten is parallel to the foot; the remaining battens are not.

Trimming the Perimeter of the Sail

Cut off the excess cloth (save any large pieces), trimming to the outside cut edge if a rolled tabling will be used; or to the cut edge outside the folded (finished) edge of a taped section with foldover; or to the finished edge of a taped section with no foldover. If you lofted the sail with cut tablings and/or bands (reef bands, chafe bands, etc.), trim the excess cloth outside the hem of the tabling or band. Label the tablings and bands in terms of the appropriate edge or corner for later installation. Next, cut them off along the cut lines. Roll them up for later. It is amazing the change a sail goes through at this point; it looks smaller and the edges look neat and curvaceous.

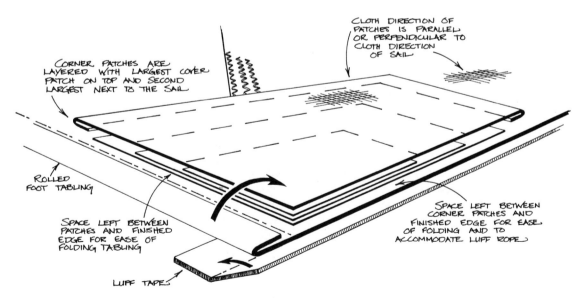

FIGURE 6-45. *A proven method of assembling corner patches for sewing to a sail. Stick the layers as shown one by one to the sail and each other, or assemble them into a unit with staples or stitching, then sew the unit layer by layer to the sail. Much control or many staples are needed to sew a flat patch. It is often necessary to draw the inner patch edges on the cover patch in order to see where to sew.*

Drawing Corner Patches

Corner patches can be drawn and cut elsewhere than on the sail, especially for repeated pattern work, but I generally draw all the patches, their layers, and the marks for hems on the sail itself. You will follow the design you have already created, or at least the same formulas. In regard to placement, the several layers of a corner patch make quite a thick piece for tablings and foldovers and tapes to bend around. Therefore, the group is set in somewhat from the edge, especially when there's an internal luff rope. This is done in order to make more room for the rope.

I occasionally find myself in a funk of indecision when it comes to making all the tongues and liners of traditional corner-patch designs look handsome on a sail full of reefs. If you go that route, take your time—the result is worth the effort.

Cutting Out Corner Patches

The corner patch outlines drawn on the sail serve as patterns for drawing and cutting the patches out of new cloth.

Procedure: Smooth and pin out the sail corner. Then, if the cloth is transparent, roll out the new cloth over the drawn patch, paralleling the cloth direction of the sail. Pin the new cloth. Mark the corners of the appropriate layer of the patch, which should be visible below. Draw the patch edges. (The largest patch will have hems on all exposed sides.) Remove the cloth from on top of the sail and cut out the patch. Repeat the process for the remaining layers, using the cloth as efficiently as possible. With a cloth of stable, balanced construction, it is permissible to swing the cloth direction 90 degrees between alternating layers of the patch for more efficient use. Label each patch as to corner and layer number.

If the cloth is not transparent, the process is the same, only slide the cloth *under* the sail. Then with a pricker, poke through at the patch corners, thus marking them, and remove the patch cloth, draw the patch, and cut it out. (I hope you find cutting corner patches a delight. For me it's the least excit-

ing part of building a sail. I don't know why.)

The traditional crosscut sail with liner patches utilizes extra cloth that is laid out with the rest of the sail at leech and luff for that purpose, with hems all around. Without this advance preparation, you may find that no matter which way you turn the cloth, it is not possible to make a large patch while maintaining proper cloth direction. In such instances, two or more cloths can be sewn together with the standard-size seam, thus producing sufficient patch cloth.

To maintain the cloth direction at a mitered clew of traditional patch design, the tongue is of two pieces, one reflecting the cloth direction above the miter, and one with the cloth direction below the miter. Only on the tongues of finely crafted cotton yacht sails do I see this as necessary. I generally choose the upper cloth direction and make the tongue of one piece, especially in synthetics. I discussed earlier the option of reinforcing the miter corner with full corner patches, which works well in Dacron. I either alternate the cloth direction or go with the direction above the miter.

Set the patches aside for later assembly and installation.

Fabricating Batten Pockets

There are three basic forms of batten pockets. The simplest is merely an open-ended slot with ties to retain the batten. Alternatively, there are two forms of side-access batten pockets, one with an open side, the other with a pocketed side. While the latter is better able to retain a batten, it is more work to make. All batten pockets need extra layers of cloth in the ends, and heavier sails need chafing strips and reinforcement patches at the ends. No matter what you do, though, eventually the batten will chafe through.

The conventional batten pockets of Dacron sails can be made quickly from Dacron tape of roughly the same cloth weight and finish as that of the sail. Likewise, though the cloth direction is inconsistent, the pockets for full-length battens are easily made out of tape.

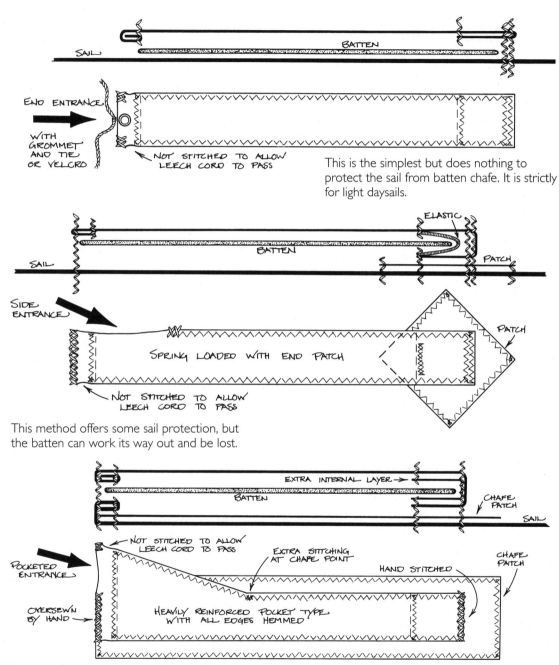

ENO ENTRANCE

WITH GROMMET AND TIE OR VELCRO

NOT STITCHED TO ALLOW LEECH CORD TO PASS

This is the simplest but does nothing to protect the sail from batten chafe. It is strictly for light daysails.

SIDE ENTRANCE

SPRING LOADED WITH END PATCH

NOT STITCHED TO ALLOW LEECH CORD TO PASS

This method offers some sail protection, but the batten can work its way out and be lost.

POCKETED ENTRANCE

OVERSEWN BY HAND

NOT STITCHED TO ALLOW LEECH CORD TO PASS

EXTRA STITCHING AT CHAFE POINT

HAND STITCHED

CHAFE PATCH

HEAVILY REINFORCED POCKET TYPE WITH ALL EDGES HEMMED

These sturdy pockets, designed to retain battens, meet the minimum requirements for serious sailing.

FIGURE 6-46. *Three methods of installing batten pockets.*

Fabricating Reef-Point Patches

Note the cloth direction at the reef points and transfer this to spare cloth. Draw and cut out the necessary number of patches. For small daysailers, one layer is sufficient; two layers will be needed for all others. The best patches are hemmed, but hotknifing of Dacron reef-point patches on inshore sails is acceptable. After all, the edges of the cloth panels are hotknifed, and so are edge tapes! Stick the double layers of diamonds together in advance, either with tape or by sewing.

Folding Tablings and Hems

Before heading to the machine or bench, all tablings and hems should be carefully creased, folded, and rubbed. Stay on your fold line, especially around dramatic curves. All the hems of cut tablings need to be folded, and tape should be folded in half lengthwise.

Seaming Sticky-taped Sails

Okay, you seam tapists, it's time to get sewing and catch up to everyone else! Read the section on "Trimming and Sewing the Seams," beginning on page 285. You don't have to worry about strike-up marks, but you do have to concern yourself with everything else other machine seamers do, plus you'll be feeding the whole sail through with each pass.

The sail is rolled up on either side of the seam being sewn, and the two rolls are held with clips. It will be easier to guide the sail if the stiffer and heavier roll is on your preferred side. That is, if you are right-handed, the sail is on your right and the heavier roll is in your right hand, and vice versa. Once you reach the point at which the balance of weight in the rolls is shifting over, turn the sail around and sew from the opposite end. If necessary, the whole sail can be turned the other side up to sew the second row of stitching. A third row of stitching down the center of a seam can be sewn with either side up. *(Note: sticky-taping handsewn seams is best done seam by seam as you sew [refer to the section on "Hand Seaming," page 288], so you have strike-up marks for reference.)*

The rolled-up sail needs support on both sides of the machine. Portable sewing machines work satisfactorily on the floor with light sails or sails under 300 square feet, but working this way is hard on your back and knees. Table-mounted machines can be extended by tables fore-and-aft, and this is fine until the weight and friction of heavier sails make it difficult to feed the sail through at a smooth pace. Perhaps it was the childhood pastime of constructing marble-chutes out of wooden building blocks that instilled in me a passion for constructing ramps for sliding the cloth downhill past a table-mounted sewing machine. It works well and is worth the effort when sewing a heavy sail. They are also fun to build.

FIGURE 6-47. *Let gravity help feed a large sticky-taped sail through the sewing machine. Building a temporary chute can be a fun challenge. Tables, boards, cloth—in the door, out the window, up the stairs, whatever it takes to get a big enough run on both sides of the machine. The less friction there is, and the fewer bumps, the more smoothly the cloth will slide.*

FIGURE 6-48. *Whether you construct a chute or not, seaming a sticky-taped sail requires feeding the rolled-up portions through the machine from an awkward sitting position. It is not easy to sew accurately if the sail is heavy. The person shown here is left-handed, and sits on what is for her, the better side. A right-hander would find it easier to sit on the other side. When I (a right-hander) use a portable machine on the floor, I place my left knee to the left of the sail, and my right leg over the sail with my foot on the other side. The sail then passes between my legs and through the machine, and my body and point of view are in line with the sewing rather than off to one side. In any position, especially on the floor, you're in for an aching back.*

INSTALLING CLOTH REINFORCEMENTS

If you've made it this far, congratulations. You have the body of the sail in front of you and all the cloth reinforcement pieces ready to install. You've earned a break, and you'll need it. The next round of sewing is a long one, and you'll be stitching through multiple layers. So get your breath.

Assembling Corner Patches

Unite corner-patch layers with staples, sticky tape, or stitching. Corner patches are installed on a sail in various ways, depending on their form or function and whether they are machine or hand sewn, and according to the type of tablings employed. Refer to Figure 6-45.

If you are hand sewing your sail, it will not be possible to sew very many layers of reinforcement at once. Therefore, the layers are divided into groups, half of which are sewn to the sail, and the other half to the cover layer of the corner patch. They are still in a sequential order of size when they are united by sewing the cover-patch group to the sail.

In contrast, machine-sewn patches are generally sewn as whole patch groups. When an internal headboard or clew piece is to be inserted between an equal number of cloth layers in the corner of the sail, however, the corner-patch layers are divided in half for installation regardless of sewing and tabling style.

Cut tablings change the construction approach if they are installed prior to the corner patches, or at least before the cover patches. When machine sewing sails with no inserted headboards or other hardware, cut tablings can be installed anytime. But you can see that flat stitching the tablings by hand through heavy corner patches would be difficult. In most instances involving rolled tablings and tape, the corner patches, bands, etc. are sewn first, the rolled tablings next, and the edge tapes last.

Sewing the Corner Patches

When I learned sailmaking, all sewing was done with strike-up marks and sew-to lines—no staples, glue, or sticky tape. But sewing corner patches without affixing them first is a challenge not worth wrestling on a one-shot project. And wrestle you do, trying to keep all those elusive layers lined up with each other and the sail while sewing evenly and accurately and keeping the patch flat! That is perhaps the most difficult part, to keep it all flat.

The inner layers of handsewn patches can be anchored with old sail needles until they are sewn with a running stitch or flat stitch along the edge. Even with staples or tape, a machine-sewn patch wants to buckle under the force of the presser foot. Much presser-foot tension is required, too, to hold down these thick sections. Spread hands and much use of the left forearm serve to control the cloth and keep the upper edges moving through flat. A

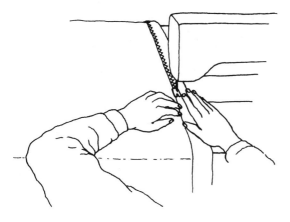

FIGURE 6-49. *Maximum control of the surrounding cloth is necessary when sewing tablings and corner patches to a sail. In order to get everything to feed through the machine, it often helps to use the whole forearm as well as the hands, at the same time leaning into the machine. Be careful not to burn your head on the sewing machine light!*

slower sewing pace may be needed to keep the needle from heating up to the point of melting the thread. Take care not to pull or push the cloth unduly, or the needle will bend and break on the baseplate. The thread and needle sizes are generally increased an increment for the sewing of heavy reinforcement.

The stitch size can be larger, and greater thread tension will be necessary for the thicker sewing. On cotton, Duradon, and hotknifed Dacron cover patches I oversew the inner (sailside) edges of the patch, but this is not necessary or advisable for hemmed nylon or hemmed Dacron cover patches.

For some reason, the reinforcements on machine-sewn cotton sails are traditionally sewn with white thread, in contrast to the red-brown of the seams. It is often difficult or impossible to see the inner edges of the bottom layers as you sew them. Sometimes the edges of the layer can be felt, but it is advisable to draw a line for reference. If the patches vary in complexity from one corner of

the sail to another, I suggest you sew the easiest corner first, probably the head. If the corner patch is too wide to fit in the throat of the machine, roll it up as much as necessary. You will soon see why commercial lofts working with stiff synthetics opt for prestuck, patterned patches sewn with heavy, large-throat machines!

At any rate, when you are done, you may find that the straight outside edges of the patch material overhang the finished edge of the sail. You needn't trim these until you are ready to install tablings.

Sewing Other Reinforcements

Other reinforcements include those that are placed under tablings—reef bands, chafe bands, jackline anchor patches, hank chafe patches, brailing eyelet patches—and even reef-point patches. I sometimes postpone this last chore—sewing reef-point patches—in the interest of not having the cut edges of the sail fray any further through all the lugging and hauling that will be going on.

Sewing reef bands on by hand is in one respect easier than by machine: The sail is merely doubled back under itself to the appropriate point, whereas the entire sail up to that same point must be rolled up in order to pass it through a machine. For me, sewing individual reef-point patches comes close to cutting corner patches in degree of excitement. Going round and round in the middle of a large sail is awkward by hand and downright ungainly by machine, the worst being with stiff cloth and a small-throat machine. I use a vertical strip of sticky tape to affix the patch to the sail, with the corners of the diamond aligned with the axis, then sew across horizontally to tack the diamond down. The sticky tape serves to keep the patch from rotating as you sew. Alternatively, a sew-to line and strike-up marks can be used. Take care to include the pointy little corners in your stitching. On light, small sails with good adhesion, all the patches can be stuck in advance with sticky tape, then sewn. Otherwise, it is best to have the patches on hand in a pile and install them one by one as you sew. Check to see that the cloth direction from patch to sail is correct.

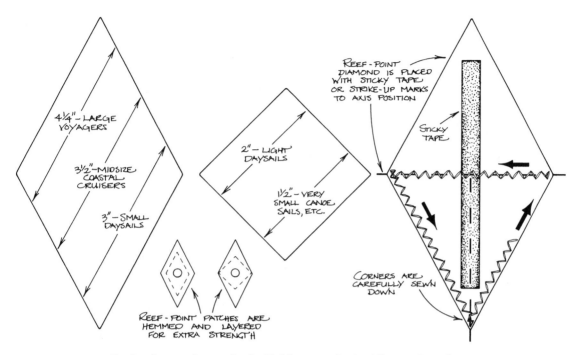

FIGURE 6-50. *Reef-point patches are hotknifed from synthetics (diamonds and squares are the standard shapes) unless extra durability is desired, in which case they are hemmed. I've seen reef points reinforced with hearts, clubs, spades, and circles; I'm not sure it matters as long as they are big enough and the cloth direction matches the sail. Sewing reef-point patches can be tedious, especially for a large sail with heavy cloth and a small machine. In such cases, reef bands are an easier alternative.*

Sewing the Tablings

All right, unless you have a sail with batten pockets, sewing the tablings is the last major step before finishwork. Of course, there are various options, depending on what sort of tabling you have chosen, which edge of the sail you are working on, and whether anything goes inside the tabling.

Rolled Tablings Rolled tablings (see Figure 6-11) are simply folded hems, and are commonly used on free edges even though they do not maintain the cloth direction of the adjoining sailcloth. (This is not so much of a disadvantage with stiff, heavily resinated fabrics.) Machine sewing the rolled tabling of a leech or foot is at its most basic a simple process of trimming patches and reinforcements, folding the rolled tabling over, then machine sewing two rows of stitching with the same thread and needle used in the patches. First the outer row, right along the sail edge, is sewn. Then the inner row is sewn along the inner edge of the tabling. Hold the tabling flat; counteract the tendency of the presser foot to push and pucker the tabling. Sew continuously around the portion of the sail that is edged with rolled tabling. To sew past a corner (such as the clew), you will need to cut away some material for a flat, easily sewn turn.

Installing a leech or foot cord is a matter of sewing the outer row of stitching, laying the cord inside the tabling, then sewing the inner edge of the tabling with the leech cord inside. But the second row of stitching is delayed until entrances and exits for the cord at the ends and at reefs have been anchored and reinforced.

LEECH & CORNER PATCH CONSTRUCTION

1. ROLLED TABLING

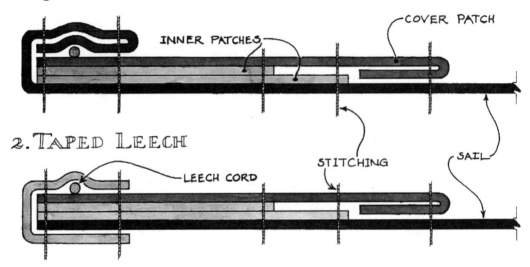

2. TAPED LEECH

FIGURE 6-51. *Sectional view of a corner patch along the leech of a sail. Both tabling types show a leech cord (a foot cord in a similarly tabled foot would look the same). Though not apparent in the drawing, the stitching should be zigzag. There would almost certainly be more patch layers than shown here in the head and clews of anything but a light daysail.*

FIGURE 6-52 (PAGES 303–304). *Nylon webbing is a good corner reinforcement and makes a strong, relatively chafe-free entry or exit location for a foot or leech cord. In Method #1, the webbing is not covered by liner pieces. The first line of stitching along the outer edge of the leech sews the webbing in place; then you lay in the leech cord while sewing the second row of stitching along the inner edge of tabling. At the head or anchored end, the cord is doubled back on itself and cut off. Once the second row of stitching is complete, take some machine or hand stitches in the doubled portion to anchor the cord. Alternatively, the cord can exit at the head to be spliced to a boltrope or belayed to the corner ring.*

Method #2 is similar except for the addition of liner pieces as additional reinforcement over the corner-patch edges. Leech-cord entrances and exits must also pass through appropriately placed spur grommets in the liner pieces, and all of this must be rove off before the second row of stitching in the tabling. After the leech tabling is completely sewn, you can staple the liners in place and sew them with one row of stitching, carefully avoiding the leech cord at the tapered ends of the liners. It makes a neat and impressive job. Various means of belaying the hauling end of the leech cord will be discussed later in the chapter, under "Finishwork."

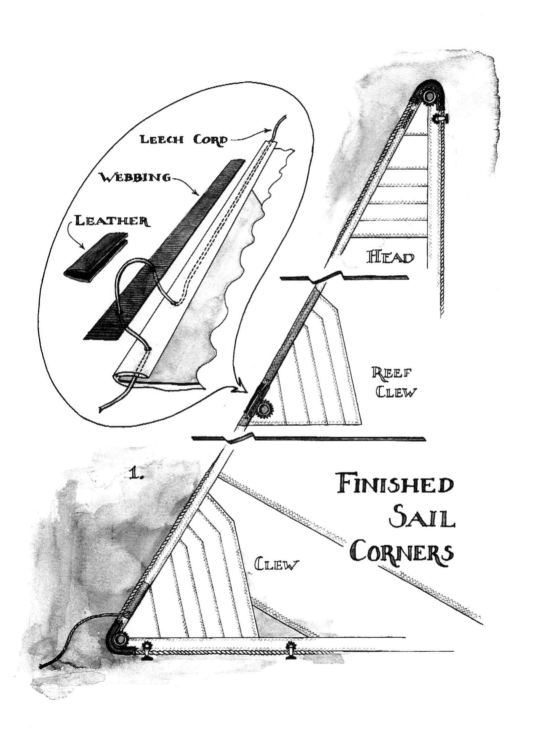

LEECH CORD

WEBBING

LEATHER

HEAD

REEF CLEW

1.

CLEW

FINISHED SAIL CORNERS

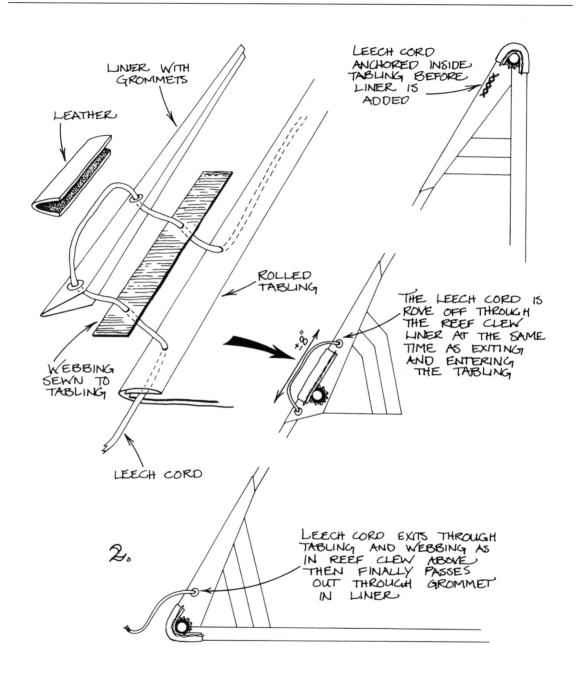

LINER WITH
GROMMETS

LEATHER

LEECH CORD
ANCHORED INSIDE
TABLING BEFORE
LINER IS
ADDED

ROLLED
TABLING

THE LEECH CORD IS
ROVE OFF THROUGH
THE REEF CLEW
LINER AT THE SAME
TIME AS EXITING
AND ENTERING
THE TABLING

WEBBING
SEWN TO
TABLING

+8"

LEECH CORD

2.

LEECH CORD EXITS THROUGH
TABLING AND WEBBING AS
IN REEF CLEW ABOVE
THEN FINALLY PASSES
OUT THROUGH GROMMET
IN LINER

FIGURE 6-52. *(cont.)*

There are many ways of accomplishing this. On all but natural-fiber sails, I use nylon webbing to provide a strong, chafe-free material for the entrances and exits. The webbing first has to be sewn down with the outer row of stitching. Then, if you are sewing on the port side of the sail, start your cord installation at the anchored end; if you are sewing on the starboard side of the sail, start at the exit end. The easiest way to anchor the end of the leech or foot cord is to double it back 6 to 8 inches within the tabling and either machine or hand sew it firmly in place. Alternatively, the cord can exit the tabling to be spliced into a boltrope. Entrances and exits in reef clews have to be rove off before the second row of stitching. I reeve cords through webbing and tabling with a #9 sail needle or a spike and small Swedish fid.

The same effect can be accomplished in natural-fiber sails by utilizing spur grommets or worked holes for the entrances and exits of the leech cord. This gives a more traditional appearance than webbing, but metal grommets tend to chafe the leech cord. In another peculiarity of natural-fiber sails, leech cords can exit on the side of the sail opposite the tabling to avoid having to deal with cover patches. When sewing the leech cord in, avoid sewing the cord itself (except where it's anchored), and leave at least 2 to 3 feet extra before cutting it off at the hauling, or working, end.

The installation of a leech or foot cord in synthetic sails can be complicated by the addition of a tape liner as corner-patch reinforcement. The tape liner is made up as described below and the exit position marked. Then a grommet or webbing is sewn to the liner at that position. The cord is then rove off through the tabling and liner as necessary.

Tape Liners

A convenient method for reinforcing the edges of corner patches of synthetic-cloth sails is with folded tape. We will discuss how to install these reinforcements now, before looking at other types of tablings, only because of their involvement with leech-cord installation. These *liners*, as I call them, are not actually sewn on until all tablings are finished. They could be cut from sailcloth, but if you have wide enough tape on hand it is faster to cut, fold, and trim it, staple it in position, and sew it down. These liners are a substitute for the roping that could be used as reinforcement in this area. Soft Dacron tape is best.

Extend the liner 6 to 8 inches beyond the corner patch; cut the tape to length and fold it lengthwise. With a hotknife, taper the folded tape down from its full folded width to just slightly wider than the edge tabling. Then bevel the narrow end as shown in Figure 6-52. Open the tape. As noted, liners through which leech or foot cords exit must have an appropriately placed grommet or nylon webbing patch for the cord to pass through. Position the liners by pinning the ends out firmly, then staple ½ inch in from the inner edge along the length of the liner every 2 inches or closer. The liners will not conform easily to very sharp curves; therefore, more closely spaced staples will be needed in such instances.

Untensioned Cut Tablings and Tapes

Though they are convenient, rolled tablings do not, by their nature, maintain consistent tension along a curved edge. Hollow edges will be tight; rounded edges, floppy. Thus, for curved edges, cut tablings (cut from the sailcloth being used; see Figure 6-11) or tapes (precut, commercially made strips of cloth) are used. Cut tablings maintain consistency of cloth direction and properties, and are the preferred choice for sails built labor-intensively from extremely soft synthetics or natural fibers. Tapes will not maintain cloth direction but are fast and easy, and are chosen when building a sail quickly from stable synthetics.

One has the opportunity to sew cut tablings and tape with more or less tension. On edges that are not receiving great strain or are not using edge curves to put camber in the sail, these tablings are sewn on evenly, or with only enough tension to have them lie flat and bend around the curve. The tabling can be laid against the finished edge and sewn as you go, or it can be tensioned—stapled every 4 inches or so—and then sewn. Leech and foot cords are installed as with rolled tablings.

Cut Tablings or Tapes with Tension Relax. We are primarily concerned here with tapes along the edges of synthetic sails that (1) have edge curves, (2) provide camber, and (3) have great rigging-induced edge tension. These tapes may or may not have ropes within or without (it is possible to place a wire or rope within a cut tabling). The business of stretching edge tapes is an often neglected and misunderstood aspect of the artistry involved in contemporary sailmaking. It is reminiscent of the art involved in hand roping. Though there aren't nearly as many variables involved, the principles are the same for gathering the round, if any, and providing a reinforcement that takes the majority of the anticipated strain before any tension falls on the sailcloth itself. (See Figure 6-44 for reference.) Clearly, if a luff tape were sewn evenly to a typical luff curve, as soon as the sail was hoisted, tension would fall on the cloth in the straight-line luff. The luff edge would be slack in comparison, and any degree of tension would distort the sail and eventually pull it apart. By contrast, picture an over-tensioned tape, one that is too short or too heavy for the power exerted on that edge. The edge will be tight but the cloth puckered and baggy. The key is to anticipate tension and consider whether or not the luff tape is solely responsible for gathering any edge curve. The goal is to set up just the right balance between cloth and tape tension (and rope tension, if there is rope within the tape). Both of the methods that I mentioned earlier for sewing these tensioned tapes—one with a sew-to line and strike-up marks, the other with staples—involve stretching the tape.

THE STRIKE-UP-MARK METHOD. It is possible to perform the following tensioning process at the time of drawing the initial sew-to line. Lay out the edge of the sail to be taped. If more than one edge is to be taped consecutively, start from the head in sails sewn on the starboard side, and from the clew or tack of sails sewn on the port side.

Note: You will notice that you have sewn corner patches over your sew-to line. The sew-to line can be redrawn from above if visible, or by flipping the sail

and poking holes through the patch with a pin along the sew-to line, thus reestablishing the line on the side on which you are about to sew the tape.

Pin down one end of the sail securely outside the sew-to line. From the other end of the edge, firmly stretch the sail, but not to the point of distortion or bias elongation, then pin that end. Place pins along the edge every couple of feet. Next, securely pin the tape at the outer end, right along the sew-to line, then roll the tape to the other endpoint of the edge. The next move is best done with an assistant to drive pins while you stretch the tape. How much do you stretch the tape? I do this by feel; if you pull the tape as far as you can before you start hauling yourself across the floor, you will do all right. Experiment. Make matching marks on sail and tape, then pull to see how much effort it takes to stretch the tape a certain distance. Think about a halyard, outhaul, sprit and snotter, or whatever is putting tension on that edge. Only on very light tapes used on straight edges subject to little strain is it possible to overdo the tape tension. If more strength, elasticity, or gathering ability is required than the tape can provide, two tapes should be laminated, or a rope added.

Heave on the tape, then quickly pin the hauling end quite securely, with the tape edge right at the sew-to line. From there, pin progressively smaller segments by halves, until the tape lies fairly along the sew-to line. Now, draw strike-up marks every 3 to 4 inches. Label the ends, and mark any corner that is to be turned and which corner it is. Take this opportunity, if the edge will have eyelets, to mark their locations as designated in your plan. Then remove the pins in the opposite order in which they were placed. Release the end pins while maintaining a firm grip on the tape.

To carry a tape around a corner, fold the tape to the correct angle around the corner while maintaining alignment of sew-to lines and marks on the edge just completed. Lay out the next edge, pin the tape at the corner just turned, and proceed as before. The tension on this new edge may be radically different; think about what strains and curves are involved before stretching the tape on succeeding sides.

Often now, sails are bent to spars or furling gear by rope inside a tape, which then runs in a slot. The rope, in this instance, is not so much a longitudinal

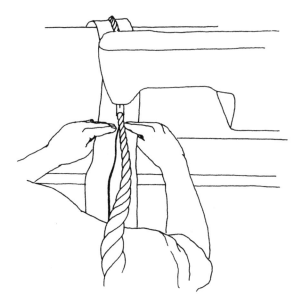

FIGURE 6-53. *Machine sewing ⁵⁄₁₆- or ³⁄₈-inch boltrope to a tape requires heavy thread, a heavy needle, and an industrial machine. A special, arced presser foot guides the rope and maintains alignment with the needle, which is centered on a maximum-length straight stitch. The tape is prefolded in half lengthwise to provide a centerline to sew the rope to, and to ease subsequent folding around the sail edge. You may want an assistant to pull from the other side, helping the tape and rope flow consistently through the machine. With the rope sewn on top of the tape, the machine's action tightens the rope relative to the tape—which is what you want. Later, on the sail, the rope will take the strain before the tape. Sewing the tape on top of the rope will reverse the effect, which could be useful for an internal rope that will run in a slotted spar or extrusion. Equip yourself with protective goggles and lots of patience, for broken needles and thread are frequent in this work.*

strengthener and governor of stretch as it is one long slug slide. Internal roping is stronger than an external rope. On the other hand, an external rope can be sewn so as to provide tension, but it is not advisable to have a tensioned machine-sewn rope inside the tape, as the tape will be too puckered to flow smoothly in a slot. Roping can be presewn to a tape by machine with a roping presser foot. To machine sew an internal boltrope to a tape, place the rope underneath the tape as you feed it through the machine. If the machine-sewn boltrope is to be external and without tension, merely flip the tape over when applying it to the sail. To create tension in a machine-sewn external boltrope, place the rope on top of the tape while sewing. The action of the feed dogs pulling the tape while the presser foot retards the flow of the rope will automatically make the rope shorter than the tape. By this method, there is no damage to the rope from the teeth of the feed dog. (Some chewing of the rope doesn't matter on an internally sewn rope slide.) Preroped tape is commercially available for slotted furling gear; it is simply attached and installed in the same manner as the folded and stapled tape liners described earlier. This is called *continuous luff-support tape,* and it is available with Teflon woven in to reduce friction in the slot of the spar.

The choice of whether to sew an internal rope or let it run unattached but tensioned within the tape is governed by whether the rope is destined to run in a slot or not. Presewn rope is already there on the tape as you lay and stretch the tape, but an unattached internal rope is added later. How much later depends on which method of tape installation is used, or whether the rope is to go around corners. Normally it is advisable, as the luff tape is sewn, to lay in a light line with which to later fish the boltrope through. With this technique you can fish the rope around corners, too—as for a boltrope along the foot, luff, and head of a gaff sail—but it will be necessary to cut a hole in the tape at the corner in order to fish the rope through edge by edge, corner to corner. The holes will be sewn over later.

Having tensioned and pinned on the tape, drawn the strike-up marks, and then unpinned the tape, take the sail and tape to the machine. Because the tape is so much shorter than the edge curve of the sail, the tape must be pulled quite forcefully while the cloth of the sail is pushed in order to match up the marks—especially at heavy

corner patches where the cloth is reluctant to gather.

Once one side of the tape is sewn, flip the sail over, bend the tape around, then sew the other side down. If the sail is insufficiently transparent to see the sew-to line through the fabric, then pinpricks along the sewn tape edge every 2 inches or so will give guidance enough. The boltrope (or twine with which to later fish the boltrope through) is laid in as the free-floating second side of the tape is sewn.

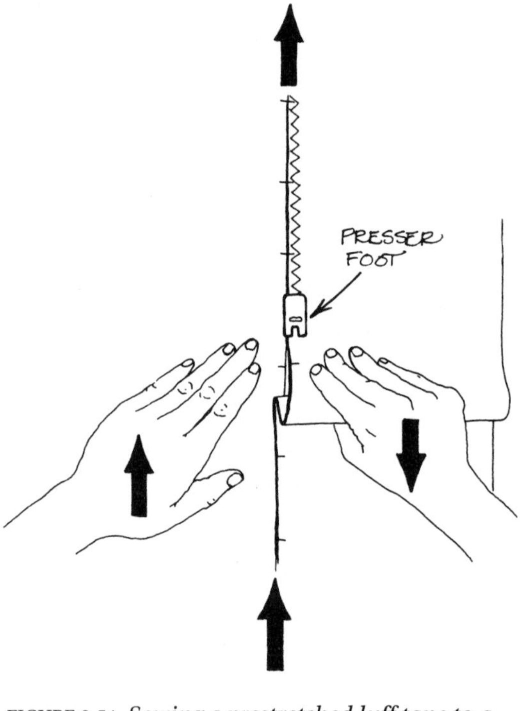

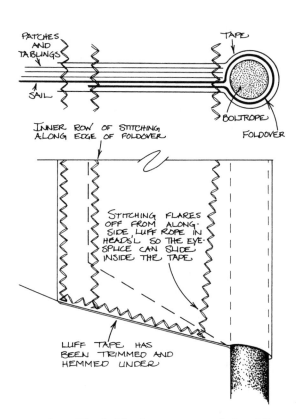

FIGURE 6-54. *Sewing a prestretched luff tape to a sew-to line and strike-up marks requires extra tensioning because the tape is shorter than the sail edge. The left hand pushes, the right pulls and guides, and the machine's action aids the process as both sail and tape pass through the machine. Even stitching and matching of the marks is important, and most difficult at the corner patches. Sew one side, fold the tape in half around the sail, then sew the other side, aligning the two tape edges on either side of the sail. Keep the stitching on the tape; oversewing the edge makes for a weak luff construction. Add other rows of stitching for greater reinforcement and to facilitate the sewing of eyelets (see Figure 6-55).*

FIGURE 6-55. *The finished appearance of a heads'l luff with foldover and luff rope. The line of stitching along the luff rope must flare off at head and tack so that the doubled rope at the base of the eye around the end thimble can fit inside the tape. The corner ring, which is sewn prior to finishing the luff rope, must be set back far enough to permit the ending (splice or seizing) of the rope to slide into the tape. A snug fit is best.*

The tape ends can be trimmed and hemmed under as they are sewn down or left to be cut off later and oversewn by hand. I generally add two more rows of stitching, the first ¼ inch inside the inner row already sewn along the tape edge, and a third row of zigzag as close as possible to the rope once it has been installed. If the rope (whether sewn or not) will serve in a slotted spar, a line of straight stitches of the longest stitch length possible is sewn with a zipper foot attachment right next to the rope. This is one of the few acceptable uses of straight stitching in a sail of this type. This stitch can also be sewn by hand.

THE STAPLE METHOD.   It is easier, whenever possible, to prefold tensioned tapes, stretch them, and staple them to the sail. There is one less row of stitching and no sew-to line and strike-up marks to worry about. There are a zillion staples on which to shred your fingers, though—not the last opportunity to bloody the sail! The procedure is basically a combination of the two processes of attaching untensioned tape tablings and attaching stretched tapes with a sew-to line.

Since the tape is prefolded, any rope can be installed in advance, whether it be loose or sewn onto the tape, internal or external. The exception to this is when a foldover extension of the sail edge is wrapped around the rope inside the tape. In that case, the rope is fished through after the tape has been sewn.

The sail edge is pinned out firmly, as previously described, and without distorting the cloth. In contrast to the last method, where the edge curve was left to stand, this time it is necessary, once the sailcloth is tensioned, to push any round into the sail—that is, to straighten the edge as much as possible. Pin the edge to this position, placing the pins back from the edge far enough to allow the tape to fit on. Fold any foldover along the finished edge. Place the folded tape over the edge of the sail at one end, and pin it firmly. If a rope is to be fished through the tape later, the pull-through twine must be placed in the tape at this time. You are now ready to stretch the tape as described earlier. Make sure that the crease

of the tape is right up against the finished edge of the sail. Stretch and firmly pin the tape at the opposite end. Now, with a stapler, proceed to staple the tape to the sail by halves until there are staples every 3 to 4 inches, about ½ inch back from the inner tape edge (so as not to be in the way of sewing). Take care to have the tape right up to the finished edge of the sail all along, and to avoid sewing through the twine within. If any eyelets are to be placed along this edge, this is a good opportunity to mark their locations, as indicated in your plan.

Caution! Before releasing the end of the tape, remove all of the pins holding the sail. There can be enough tension on the tape to tear the sail at the pins as the tape contracts. Pins removed, release the tape slowly. You can now see to what extent the tape has gathered the round, and any spot where the staples are too far apart. If you are going on to another edge with a continuation of the tape, fold the tape around the corner, pin, then repeat the stapling process, bearing in mind that the edge will possibly require a different amount of tension in the tape. As I said, usually you will be stretching any tape of 4-inch width or wider as much as you are able, by hand, there on the floor.

Trim and fold the ends of the tape, if desired, to conform to the corner of the sail; alternatively, trim the ends later and oversew them. Then sew the tape down along its inner edge. It is important not to oversew this edge, a place of great strain at slides and hanks. The perforation created by so doing can easily tear, resulting in the whole luff being torn off. Remove the staples. Fish through any rope, then sew the remaining rows of stitching as described above.

Sewing Batten Pockets

Batten pockets are simple to construct (see Figure 6-46 for reference). Some general notes on the process:

- The forward and after ends can be sewn by machine on daysails. Any other sails should have the ends oversewn by hand, with a cross-stitch.

- Nothing rumples the run of a leech like a poorly sewn batten pocket. Use sticky tape, or stay on the marks with no more stitch tension than necessary.
- Be careful not to sew through a leech cord at the after end of the pocket.

FINISHWORK

Whenever I reach this point in the making of a sail, I always heave a great sigh of relief, thinking that the majority of the work is done. On a tape-and-spur-grommet daysail, I am right. However, on a seafaring sail of any size or degree of strength, the work, in truth, may be less than half done.

The general process and sequence is this:

1. Install corner rings.
2. Install eyelets and D-rings.
3. Set up, install, and finish the roping.
4. Stick cringles.
5. Install headboards, clewboards, and batten hardware.
6. Whip and seize reef nettles.
7. Sew chafe protection.
8. Seize hanks, slides, and robands.
9. Finish details, such as batten pockets, flags, and leech-cord ties.

All the finishwork that needs to be done on a sail could be accomplished in a space the size of your main salon, your living room, or the deck of a moderate-size boat, with one exception: if there are any edges to stretch and roping to set up, a space longer than that edge will be needed. You must make do. I once set up the luff of a headsail by fastening it to a shed, running it in the back window of a house, through two rooms, then out a window in the front of the house, and then attaching the other end to the railing on the other side of the porch! Ideally, your original lofting space is available for doing the finishwork. If not, a much smaller space will suffice, with a trip outdoors, if necessary, to set up any roping.

Large Corner Rings

These are the rings installed at the clew, tack, reef corners, and often the head. On small daysails, no matter the fabric, #4 spur grommets will work. They are easily installed, with a few concerns: Make sure the grommet is no closer than ⅛ inch from any unroped edge. Along a hand-roped edge (external rope), they must be set back two-thirds of the rope's circumference from the sail's edge. They are located firmly alongside internal roping, but not so close as to cut the cloth when setting the grommet. Any other sails must have stronger rings or some other strong form of corner hardware such as D-rings, or cringles. There is the option, if you're not particular and want to save time, of taking your sail to a commercial loft where they'll wham in hydraulically pressed corner rings. But this could be a mistake if you don't have the appropriate cloth and patch construction. Worked holes, or hand-sewn rings, are sewn with basically the same technique used to sew the anchor holes of the ditty bag in Chapter 1. The differences lie in the size of the work and the relative inflexibility of a sewn brass ring, as opposed to a rope grommet. The ditty bag apprenticeship is insufficient preparation for sewing large corner rings. I suggest, if you have little experience, that you either sew a couple of practice rings or begin with the smaller eyelets (see below). There is no virtue in having too many stitches crowded together. In fact, such a ring is probably weaker than a ring with less than optimal stitch spacing.

Note: If your sail will have tensioned internal roping, read the roping section below to learn the proper sequence of corner ring installation.

Place the ring in the desired location, then draw

FIGURE 6-56. *Sewing corner rings is like sewing eyelets, as described in Chapter 1, except that the scale is much larger and much greater strength is required. The stitching should be as even as possible in both sides of the sail so that the corner remains flat and there is an even distribution of strain. It helps to draw guiding circles on both sides of the sail.*

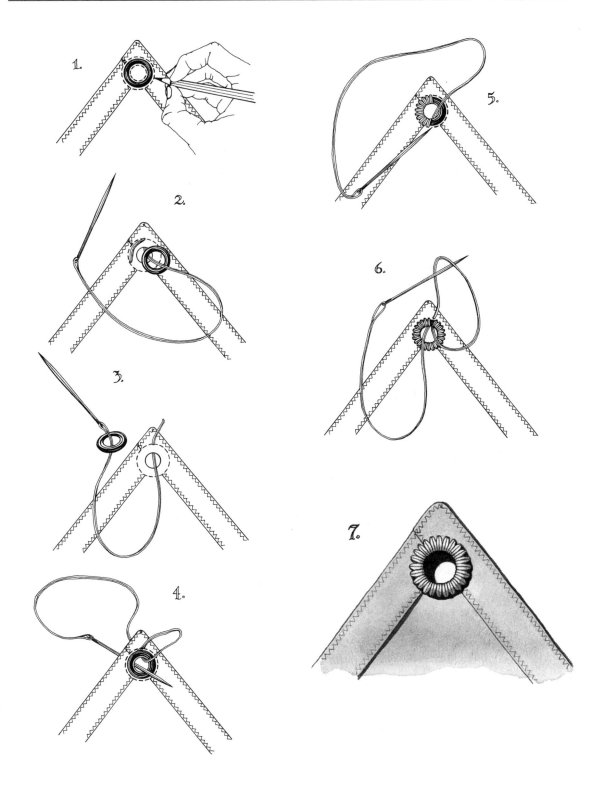

a dark pencil line inside and out. Cut out the center with a hole cutter or knife. It is better to cut the hole too small than too big.

Two types or sizes of twine will cover the full line of brass rings available. The #7, seven-strand spun polyester sail twine will serve for ring sizes 0 to 7, and a single, plied yarn from a ⅜-inch continuous-filament polyester three-strand line will sew ring sizes 8 to 15. The seven-ply twine can be doubled again for the larger rings. Many other sorts of twine are available that work. I have even seen rings sewn with polyester leech cord! Heavy cotton or flax twine is best for sewing rings in natural-fiber sails, but synthetic twine will work. Unlike the twine lengths preferred in seaming or roping, a needleful of twine long enough to sew a large ring without rethreading is much longer than an arm's span.

A minimum #14 needle size is necessary to sew seven-ply twine, and a #12 needle is needed for the heavy twine. But a larger needle may be necessary to avoid breakage in thick, heavy corners. A needle with a long, tapered point will pass with less effort through the thick stuff, but it is more easily bent.

Eyelets and corner rings are usually sewn with a single, even circle of stitches around the ring (Figure 6-56). But voyaging sailor Bernard Moitessier advocated a technique of alternating stitch lengths in and out so that the strain does not fall on a single line of perforations (Figure 6-57). This makes sense to me, and I recommend the technique on all corner rings of voyaging sails. I believe it is most important on the side of the ring where the strain falls, the side toward the middle of the sail. It takes no more time and skill, and will forestall the kind of cloth fracture that can occur at ring stitching. It is possible to miscalculate and run out of twine partway around the ring. As long as you are well past the area of strain, you can lay in a fresh needleful and finish. Otherwise, remove

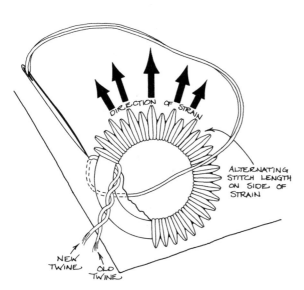

FIGURE 6-57. *Sometimes when sewing big rings you run out of twine. If this occurs anywhere on the strained side of the ring, you must remove the ring and start anew with a longer needleful of twine. Elsewhere, merely make up a new needleful of twine, twist the old and new ends together, and oversew them while continuing to sew the ring. This ring has been sewn with alternating stitch length on the side of strain, which helps to prevent the cloth from tearing.*

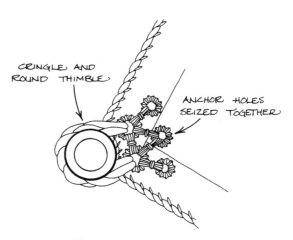

FIGURE 6-58. *The two primary anchor holes of a cringle and round thimble can be augmented in a variety of patterns that provide reinforcement in the direction of strain. Anchor holes can also be used to attach D-rings or enhance the strength of handsewn corner rings. The sewing and seizing of anchor holes is described in Chapter 1.*

the stitching and start again with a longer needle-ful of twine.

It is to combat the problem of stitch failure around a ring that a sailmaker sews reinforcing anchor holes in various configurations on the strain side of a ring. Another method is to sew webbing by hand or machine through the ring in the direction of the strain (Figure 5-32). These two reinforcing techniques may permit the use of a smaller, lighter corner ring, and can be employed in conjunction with the Moitessier method. A ring

sewn with the Moitessier method is exceedingly strong and only in large boats will there be need for augmentation with anchor holes or webbing.

Voyaging-boat corner rings, especially clews, have leather sewn on the side where lines or hardware are attached. Clew or reef rings of any sail that's going to be chafing on mast, stay, or topping

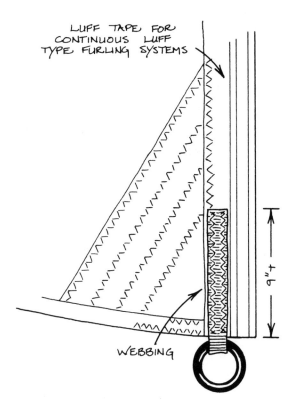

Handsewn or pressed-in corner rings do not work well in the head or tack of roller-furling sails. With a configuration of webbing and ring like this one, the sail will roll more tightly.

FIGURE 6-59. *Webbing provides a quick and effective corner attachment by hand or machine for a light-duty sail.*

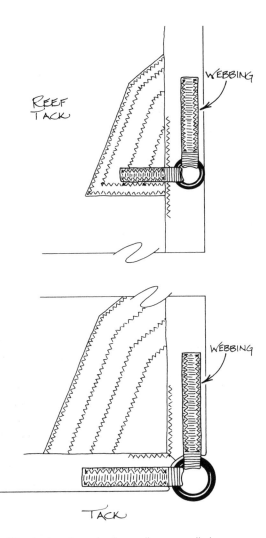

The tacks of production sails can easily be finished with webbing and ring, and this construction makes a good emergency repair or a user-friendly method for building a daysail.

lift have leather sewn over the stitching on the strain side of the ring. Many combinations of leather protection are possible in order to protect the ring and the edge simultaneously.

Eyelets and D-Rings

Eyelets are installed on the fixed edges of a sail, since they are always involved with the system of attaching the sail to its spar or stay. Loosely construed, even reef-point eyelets fall in this category. The outer rims of spur-grommet eyelets—whether for head, luff, or foot—should lie about $\frac{3}{16}$ to $\frac{1}{4}$ inch from the finished edge of an unroped sail. Alongside external hand roping, outer rims of the eyelets should be set back two-thirds of the boltrope diameter from the sail's edge. Spur grommets ought to be installed up close against a tensioned internal boltrope, but not so close as to cut the cloth or prevent the rope within from moving. Handsewn eyelets take the same positions as spur grommets. Again, the eyelets along the internal roping must be as close as possible to the rope, but not sewn into the rope!

Note: If your sail will have tensioned internal roping, read the roping section below to learn the proper sequence of eyelet installation.

Sewn reef eyelets are a challenge in that they are sewn without one's being able to see the underside. In addition, there is no freedom to move around for good sewing position as there is when sewing eyelets at the perimeter of a sail. Start sewing on the side toward which the reef is taken. It is not necessary to install liners in reef eyelets with sewn reef nettles, because there will be very little chafe on the eyelet stitching.

If the clew is unroped and is to have a D-ring, you can install the D-ring as soon as you finish hand sewing the anchor holes to which it will be seized. Alternatively, webbing—either machine or hand sewn—makes an exceedingly strong and fast method of affixing a D-ring to a corner. The corner is trimmed to the shape of the base of the D-ring, and its cut edge oversewn by hand. The webbing is first doubled, then rove through the D-ring, and then laid out on both sides of the sail, extending

inward along one of the paths of strain. The sandwich now has four layers of webbing (two per side) and 10 or more layers of cloth, making it quite a pile to stitch through! Sticky tape can be used to hold the webbing in alignment while machine sewing. Avoid tensioning the webbing, or the corner will be badly puckered. Since strain radiates into the sail from the clew, you will need, typically, four or more strips of webbing along different paths of strain (Figures 5-32, 5-35). Sew one, then on to the next.

A similar technique is used at the tack and head of a roller-furling sail to enable the sail to roll without twisting out a corner ring. It is very simple. The webbing is doubled, rove through a ring, and sewn on parallel to the luff. Then, when the sail is rolled up, the ring is not embedded in and trying to rend the sailcloth. This technique has recently come into use as a tack and reef-tack fitting in production sails of nonrolling type. An arc of the same radius as the ring is hotknifed out of the tack, and doubled webbing is run through the ring and sewn along the foot and luff (see Figure 6-59).

Roping

All roping, except internal continuous luff rope, is intended to be the ultimate governor of how far, under an anticipated strain, a sail's edge will be permitted to stretch. Hand roping with natural-fiber rope on a natural-fiber sail is the most complex form, because there are so many variables to both the rope and the cloth. Experience is required to sew a boltrope so that ultimately, when both cloth and rope reach their finished, elongated lengths, all will be in balance. Even prior to the advent of synthetics, a sailmaker was loath to generalize about how much rope was sewn to a given length of sail. These days, with so little natural-fiber rope being manufactured and that to inconsistent standards, it is even harder to be specific. I have no formula myself and only sew by feel, judging the relationship between the cloth and the rope to be about right based on past experience, known qualities of the materials, anticipated strain, and the type of sail edge. You know, for instance, that

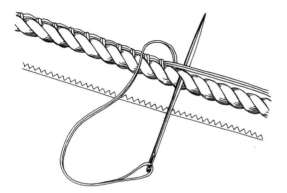

Passing the needle through at a right angle to the cloth, with a strand's width between stitches, puts little or no slack into the cloth and is useful when a loose rope is required—for example, in a leech or the roached foot of a loose-footed sail.

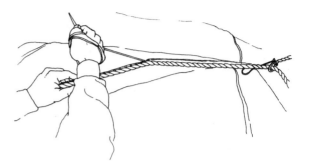

Heaving back on the stitch gathers cloth, especially when you also bend the work away from you and angle the needle ahead. Here the left hand must bend the work and keep the gathered cloth from slipping.

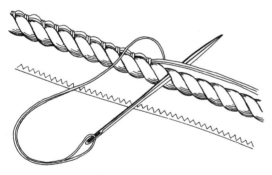

Angling the needle ahead gathers more cloth along a given length of rope. This is especially useful in soft cloth when there is much round to gather and much rope stretch to compensate.

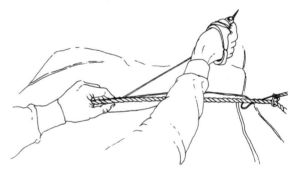

Heaving ahead on the stitch sinks the twine between the strands of the boltrope and pulls the cloth along. To sew a slack rope, bend the work toward you, use small stitches, and heave them forward. Even when sewing a tight rope, I often heave ahead first to bed the stitch, then haul back to gather cloth for the next stitch.

FIGURE 6-60. *Sewing a boltrope. As described in Chapter 1, one way to slacken the cloth and sew a tight boltrope is to bend the work away from you. Here are some other useful variations on the sewing technique.*

at the very least the rope must be shorter than the straight-line finished edge of a sail edge with round bent up against a spar, and that the length of the round has to be gathered in the rope. This is calculable, roughly, but it is easier, given all the uncertainty, to put the boltrope under the kind of strain expected; place next to it the sail edge, also hauled out firmly (this is very much the same process as setting up a tensioned luff tape), then seize the rope to the sail at every eyelet or every 12 inches. When the whole is slacked off, it will be seen that

(text continued on page 323)

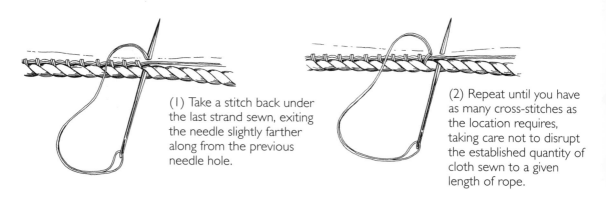

(1) Take a stitch back under the last strand sewn, exiting the needle slightly farther along from the previous needle hole.

(2) Repeat until you have as many cross-stitches as the location requires, taking care not to disrupt the established quantity of cloth sewn to a given length of rope.

FIGURE 6-61. *When you hand rope a sail, cross-stitching is necessary at all corners, eyelets, splices, rings, and twine ends, and at the seam ends of voyaging sails.*

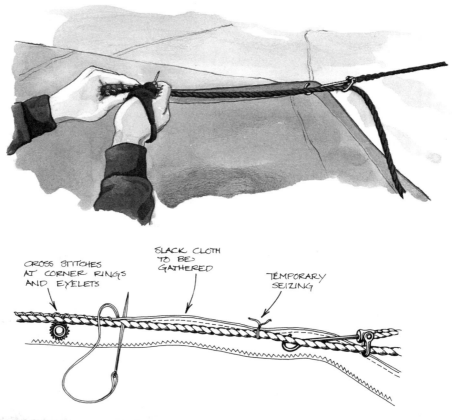

CROSS STITCHES AT CORNER RINGS AND EYELETS

SLACK CLOTH TO BE GATHERED

TEMPORARY SEIZING

FIGURE 6-62. *Overall views of hand roping. The left hand grips both cloth and rope where the stitch is taken, while your shoulder and body push the needle through. The bench hook leads off high, and a shackle helps to keep the rope in position. A left-handed roper would set up everything in reverse, but would still sew from left to right.*

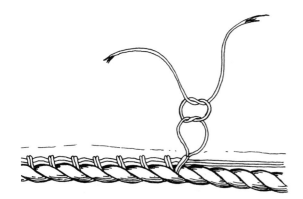

(1) Near the end of the twine, take a cross-stitch back one strand as shown. Cut off the needle, and square-knot the ends of the doubled twine firmly against the cloth.

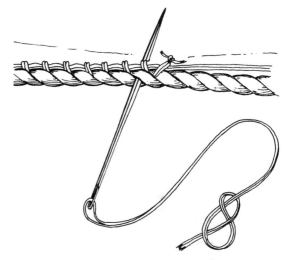

(2) Make up a new needleful of twine, and throw a figure-eight knot in the end. For the first stitch, back up yet another strand.

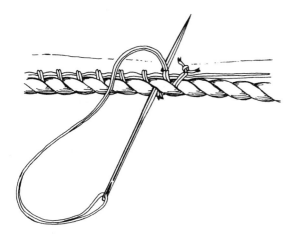

(3) Pull the figure-eight knot up to the cloth, then take a cross-stitch at that strand.

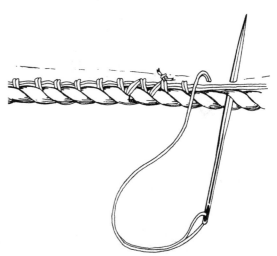

(4) Resume roping as before, passing over the final cross-stitch of the preceding needleful of twine, then on, taking all due precaution not to lose rope alignment and tension.

FIGURE 6-63. *The workboat style of stopping and starting when you run out of roping twine involves knots and cross-stitching. Take care not to lose the continuity of the roping.*

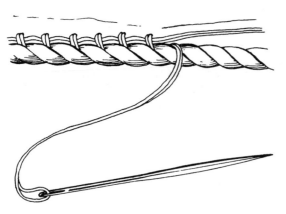

(1) After the last possible stitch, either cut off the needle and pull the twine back out, or pass the needle through the next strand of rope and then cut the twine.

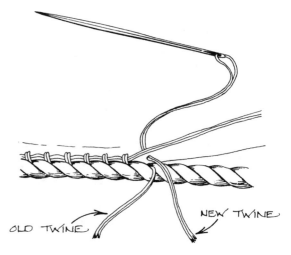

OLD TWINE   NEW TWINE

(2) Make up a new needleful of twine, then pass the needle through the sail where the next stitch is to be taken.

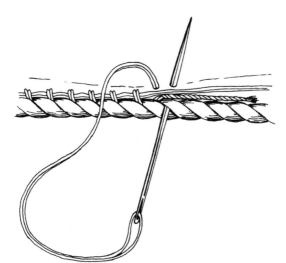

(3) Twist the ends of the old and new twine tightly together for at least 1½ inches, and lay them between the rope and sail.

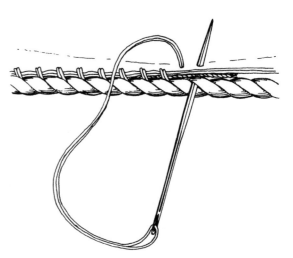

(4) Continue roping as before. Everyone will wonder how you managed to rope an entire sail with only one piece of twine.

FIGURE 6-64. *An alternative method for starting a new needleful of twine while roping. This technique, suitable for yacht- or daysails, is more elegant than the workboat technique shown in Figure 6-63, though not as strong.*

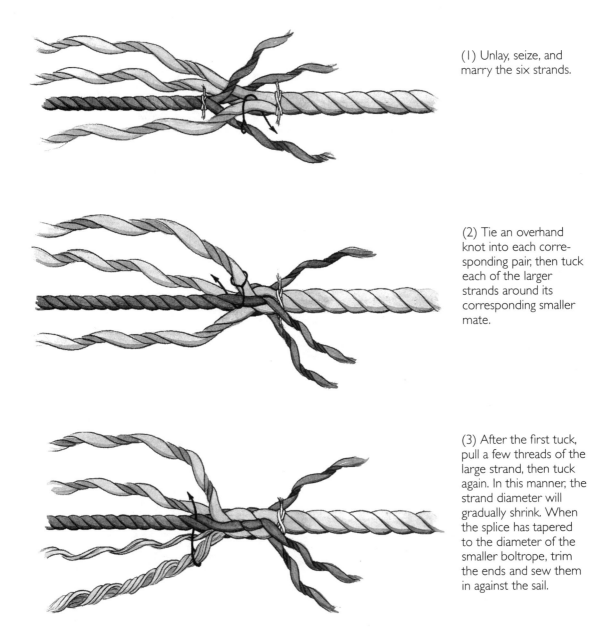

(1) Unlay, seize, and marry the six strands.

(2) Tie an overhand knot into each corresponding pair, then tuck each of the larger strands around its corresponding smaller mate.

(3) After the first tuck, pull a few threads of the large strand, then tuck again. In this manner, the strand diameter will gradually shrink. When the splice has tapered to the diameter of the smaller boltrope, trim the ends and sew them in against the sail.

FIGURE 6-65 (PAGES 319–320). *The tapered splice is a sailmaker's shortsplice, used to join two boltropes of different diameters. This may occur at the head and clew of the mainsail with roping on all edges, or where leech and foot ropes meet the heavily roped clew of a loose-footed sail.*

(4) Now tuck the small strands into the larger rope, beat the splice, trim the ends, and cross-stitch the splice to the sail.

FIGURE 6-65. *(cont.)*

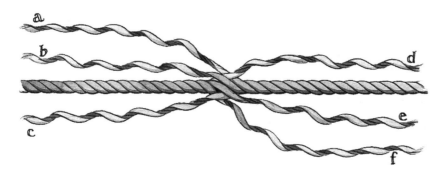

(1) Unlay each of the six strands to half the length of the splice, and marry the ends as shown.

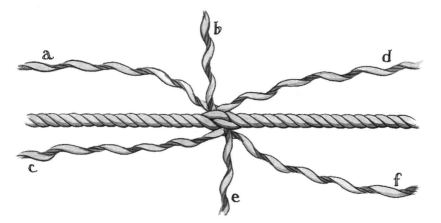

(2) Tie an overhand knot in strands B and E. These strands will be left and finished there, in the center of the splice.

FIGURE 6-66. *A long splice is useful to replace a section of torn boltrope or to save the day when you run out of boltrope before the job's done. In most ropework a long splice should be at least a fathom long for maximum strength, but since the boltrope will be sewn, a splice there can be as short as 4 feet.*

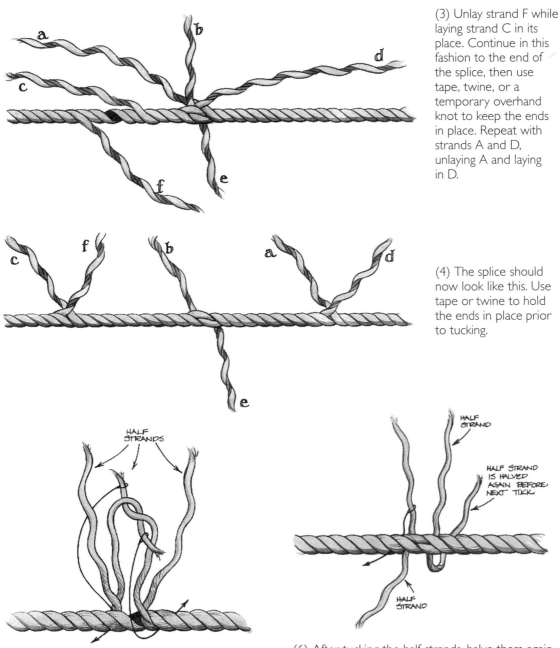

(3) Unlay strand F while laying strand C in its place. Continue in this fashion to the end of the splice, then use tape, twine, or a temporary overhand knot to keep the ends in place. Repeat with strands A and D, unlaying A and laying in D.

(4) The splice should now look like this. Use tape or twine to hold the ends in place prior to tucking.

(5) At each of the three locations, halve both meeting strands. Join two of the halves together with an overhand knot, leaving the other two halves where they are. Then make a tuck as shown with the halves exiting the overhand knot.

(6) After tucking the half-strands, halve them again, then tuck again. Repeat until the strand diminishes to nothing. All strand ends, hopefully, are on the side of the rope toward the sail. Beat the splice and trim all ends. A fair job will be almost indistinguishable from the unspliced rope.

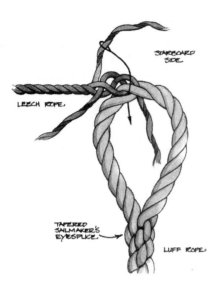

Working a leech rope into a head eyesplice.
(1) Tuck one strand of the leech rope under a single strand of the eye, then bring it back under itself and into the leech rope. Keep tucking it around itself into the leech rope. Tuck the other two strands of the leech rope into the eye.

(2) Make several tucks into the eyesplice so that the ends will be covered by the sail or head thimble. Then beat the splice, trim the ends, and sew the roping to the trimmed sail with cross-stitching. Finally, knock a thimble into the eyesplice.

Working a foot rope into a tack eyesplice.
(1) Tuck one strand of the foot rope under a strand of the eye, then back under itself and around. Pair the other two strands and tuck them under one strand of the eye.

(2) Make several more tucks into the eye, leaving the ends where they will be covered by the sail or the tack thimble. Then beat the splice, trim the ends, and sew the roping to the trimmed sail corner. Finally, knock a thimble into the tack eye.

FIGURE 6-67 (PAGE 322). *I first saw these splices worked in the head and tack of a flax storm staysail that had been hand sewn by Ratsey and Lapthorn prior to World War II. This method joins leech or foot roping of smaller diameter and lesser tension to a large luff or head rope. Both splices tuck into the crown of a sailmaker's eyesplice, as used in the lanyard of the ditty bag in Chapter 1. All tucks after the initial union are made sailmaker fashion—tapered and backed around a strand— so that the splice can be sewn to the sail.*

there is a consistent amount of extra cloth to be taken up between each seizing. You have only to do the sewing, taking out the seizings as you go. This method will work well enough for the following combinations: hemp line to cotton or flax cloth; polyester to cotton, flax, or Dacron; polyester to Duradon. There are instances of hollowed sail edges where roping is slack, or even great roaches where roping is slack. In these cases there is little, if any, cloth taken up in the roping.

The following sails should be hand roped: Duradon sails, cotton sails, stormsails, Chinese

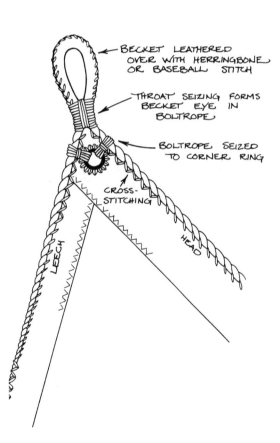

To make this very simple becket, splice or lay up a grommet, then seize the grommet to form two eyes. Cowhitch one eye through the corner ring to form the becket. (Note the rattailed end of the head rope, oversewn with round stitches on the upper leech.)

FIGURE 6-68. *Some sort of becket is required in the peak of a sprits'l to engage the nose of the sprit.*

This snazzy becket is made by seizing a leathered eye in the boltrope as it turns the corner of the peak. For extra reinforcement, seize the boltrope to a corner ring.

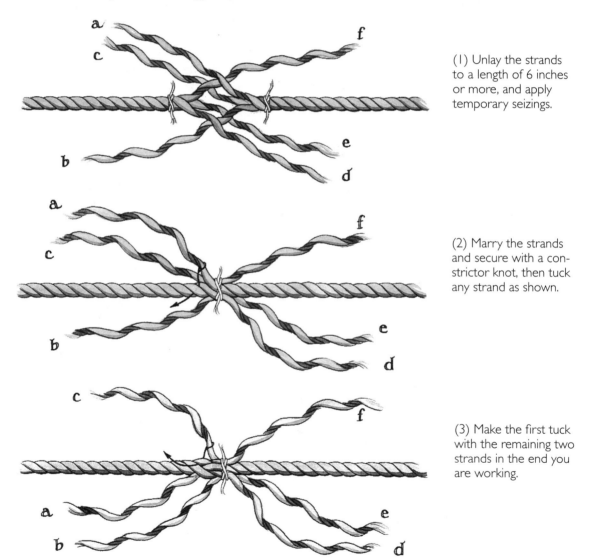

FIGURE 6-69A. *Except in workboat sails, all roping not spliced to itself should finish in a well-tapered rattail. The process of unlaying, scraping, and laying up the strands is described in the "Dittybag Apprenticeship" (Chapter 1). A well-made rattail diminishes fairly from boltrope diameter to nothing. It may be 6 to 9 inches long in ¼- to ⅜-inch rope, or 9 to 12 inches long in ⁷⁄₁₆-inch or bigger rope. Oversew the last inch or so with a round stitch.*

(1) Unlay the strands to a length of 6 inches or more, and apply temporary seizings.

(2) Marry the strands and secure with a constrictor knot, then tuck any strand as shown.

(3) Make the first tuck with the remaining two strands in the end you are working.

FIGURE 6-69B. *The common shortsplice may be used in a workboat finish to join the boltrope ends on sail roped all the way around.*

lugsails, voyaging sails, and any sail where traditional character is desired.

Externally machine-sewn three-strand boltrope can just be whipped and hotknifed off, but you make a handsomer and stronger job of it if you sew the rope tail around the corner by hand and rattail the end as you would a fully handsewn boltrope. Because one hand ropes from left to right and it is quite difficult to rope toward a fixed end (in this case, the stopping point of your machine sewing at the corner), you will probably want to turn the sail over so you can rope *away* from the corner. Alternatively, a tail can be sewn by hand right along the edge of the sail, starting from the end of the machine stitches with an overlap, in a manner that looks the same as the machine-sewn portion except the hand stitching is slightly visible. This technique also serves well in the repair of a

machine-sewn boltrope that has come adrift from the tape, so it's worth describing.

Unlike conventional handsewn roping, in which the boltrope is sewn *alongside* the edge of the sail (like a pencil resting on the flat of a ruler; see Figure 6-60), this technique mimics the machine-sewn appearance with the rope perched on the edge of the sail like a pencil balanced on the edge of a ruler. The sewing process differs too in that the needle passes over one strand and under two—rather than over two and under one—as a stitch is taken through the rope. To complete the stitch, pass the needle back through the sail about ⅛ inch in from the cloth edge; it should exit in line with the next groove of the rope, in correct placement to begin the next stitch.

This method entails working somewhat from above and behind the job, as well as flipping the

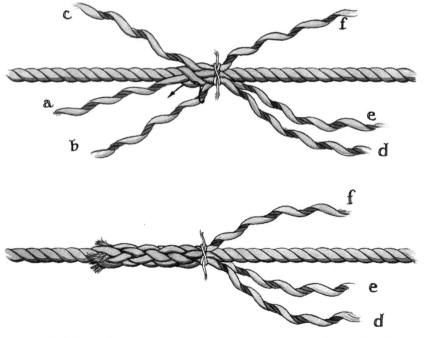

(4) Make at least four more tucks with the active strands.

(5) Release the constrictor knot, then turn your attention to the three strands that have so far been inactive. Tuck these as you did the others, draw up all strands tight, and smooth the splice with a mallet or by rolling it underfoot. Trim the strand ends, but not too close.

sail from side to side as stitches pass through rope and sail. For this reason it is not suited to extensive roping, but is worth the effort when finishing the corners of a machine-roped sail. The rattail ends are oversewn with round stitches for an inch or so, as in usual hand roping (see Figure 6-68).

A three-strand internal boltrope can be cut off at the ends once it has been tensioned, or it can be sewn and rattailed as with the external line. The braided internal boltrope of a spar-bent sail is cut off at the ends after tensioning and seizing.

Tensioning Internal Ropes in Sails Set on Spars

The basic procedure for setting internal rope tension on a spar-bent sail is to stretch the tape and the sailcloth along an edge to their working tension, stretch the rope to within a similar

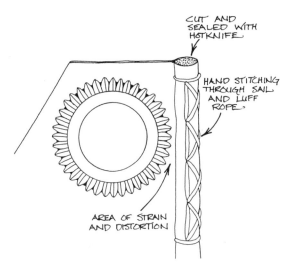

FIGURE 6-70. *One quick but inadvisable technique for finishing an internal luff rope is to sew through the sail and rope by hand. This anchors one end, then the sail and rope are tensioned and the other end of the luff rope is hand sewn in the same manner. The extra rope is cut off. The only connection between corner ring and luff rope in this method is the sail, which becomes distorted under load. A three-strand luff rope could, alternatively, be rattailed and hand roped around the corner, thus providing a little more support.*

load, and then cement the relationship between the sail and the rope by seizing the ends.

On a Bermudan sail this is quite simple. At most, there are two edges to stretch: luff and foot. You start by seizing the rope to the ring and cloth at the tack. (The seizing looks just like that shown for an external boltrope in Figure 6-76.) From there stretch one edge at a time—start with the luff. Your sail will be spiked out on the floor or strung out between eyebolts, trees, or anything that works (see Figure 6-74). How do you know how far to stretch the tape? First, get the wrinkles out from the tensioned tape, then pull until you get a moderate amount of bias elongation or pocketing along the edge. On a large sail you might need a handy billy, but this is unlikely, unless you strayed from my admonishments and have used this daysail-type construction in a big-boat sail. Once the sail is correctly tensioned, spike or tie off the end you've been hauling on.

To determine how much to stretch the rope, approximate the hauling power on the boat. If it will be just one crew swigging on the halyard, just swig on a line tensioning the rope as if the sail were being raised. If you have winches, use a tackle. Get the line taut by whatever means. Fix the line, then spike or temporarily seize through the sail and rope. Remove the spike or lashing that was tensioning the sail, then ease off on the rope. Seize through the rope and sail with a cross-stitch at the end and at the reef tacks (Figure 6-70). Repeat the process for the foot, with less tension, of course.

The problem with using this method on a gaff sail or other four-sided sail is that you must cut a hole at the throat or tack in order to be able to stretch the rope in the luff. This can be done, and the stretching process is otherwise the same as for a Bermudan sail; for this reason, however, this sort of reinforcement is not ideal on a four-sided sail.

Tensioning the Internal Luff Rope of a Sail Set on a Stay or Set Flying

There are three ways to set up the luff rope of sails set on a stay or set flying. The first two are inferior variations on the method previously described for the internal roping of

(1) Form the eye snugly around the thimble by sewing through the rope, then taking several turns around both standing part and end.

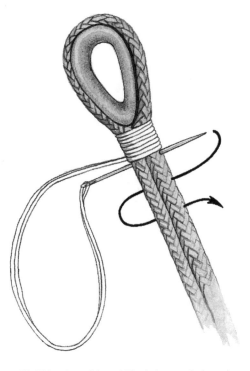

(2) Take firm, ⅜- to ½-inch-long stitches through the doubled rope.

FIGURE 6-71 (PAGES 327–328). *Finishing the luff rope of a sail set on a stay or set flying. It is possible to splice an eye in a three-strand luff rope, but with braided rope it is faster and more accurate to seize an eye and thimble. Double the rope around a heart thimble with at least 6 inches of overlap in light sails, 8 to 9 inches in heavy sails. There is room to play with in the first eye, but not in its counterpart at the opposite end. Use heavy sail twine. If the eye is to be leathered, do so prior to seizing.*

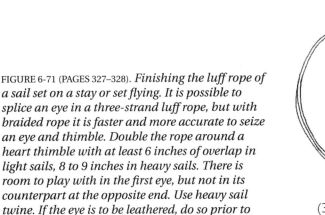

(3) At the lower end of the seizing, make several turns around both parts.

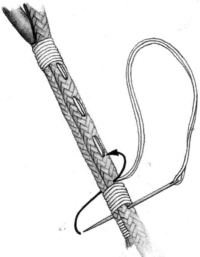

(4) Take stitches around the turns to anchor them, then stitch back up to the eye, using the same holes your needle made on the way down.

(5) Finally, take several stitches around the original turns at the throat of the eye, then tie or burn off the twine.

FIGURE 6-71. *(cont.)*

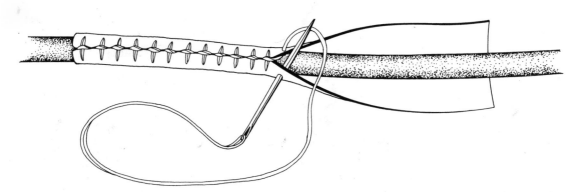

FIGURE 6-72. *To leather the eye of a luff rope or sprits'l becket, use supple leather and the herringbone stitch. Place the stitching on the inside of the eye of a luff rope, toward the thimble. Place the stitching on the outside of a sprits'l becket eye, away from the chafe of the sprit.*

spar-bent sails: The tensions are set up, and the ends are seized and either cut off or tailed around the corners and rattailed down. The superior voyaging method in effect has the luff rope with its end fittings taking the strain, and the sail corner rings are then seized to it. This is similar in many ways to the handsewn luff rope described on page 314.

It is an easy process but takes some time. After the corner rings have been sewn and their liners installed, a heart thimble is spliced or seized at one end of the luff rope (Figure 6-71). Splicing is easier to do with three-strand line, but with the braided line preferred for a voyaging luff rope, it is easier and faster to sew and seize the thimble in place. A splice, however, is stronger.

The eye can be leathered in advance, if desired (Figure 6-72). The corner is trimmed, then the seizing and eye are pulled down into the luff. The corner

rings, we hope, have been sewn so as to permit a snug but unrestricted fit. The trimmed edges of the sail are cross-stitched. The thimble now is seized to the corner ring with either twine or webbing. The area can be leathered now or later. Once the seizing is done, it is time to sew in all luff eyelets and reef tack rings, but don't install the liners yet.

To tension the luff rope, string up the sail horizontally, with its luff about waist-high off the ground. Firmly lash the completed end of the luff to a stationary point: a tree, an eyebolt, a window frame, etc. Attach a block or handy billy to another stationary point a sufficient distance away to pull the luff taut, plus 4 feet. Reeve off a hauling line, if necessary, and attach it to a temporary eye or bowline in the unfinished end of the luff rope. (On a small, light sail, there may be enough extra luff rope to obviate the need for a hauling line.) Haul

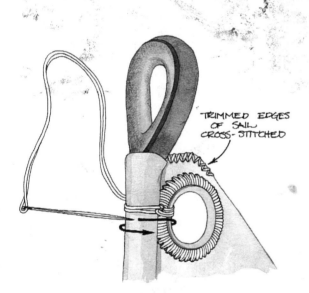

(1) Seize the corner ring to the luff rope with several turns of heavy twine.

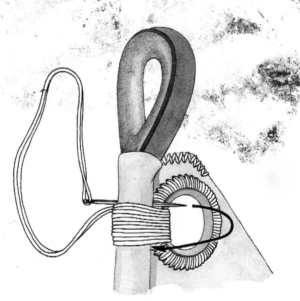

(2) Pass at least two crossing turns around the seizing, and heave them home firmly.

FIGURE 6-73 (PAGES 329–330). *Seizing the luff rope and thimble to the corner ring. First slide the seized or spliced portion of the luff rope into the luff tape, heaving from the other end as necessary. Turn the thimble at right angles to the sail to prevent chafe to the eye. Trim and cross-stitch the sail edges.*

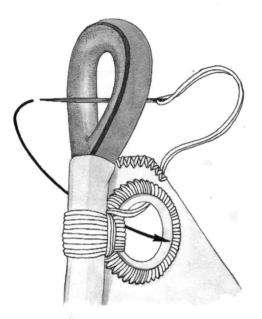

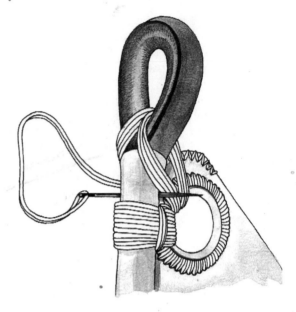

(3) Pass the twine repeatedly back and forth through thimble and ring.

(4) Take crossing turns around this seizing and heave them firmly home.

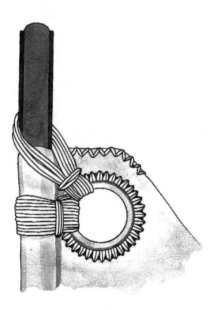

(5) Tie or burn off the twine, leaving the finished seizings to be leathered.

FIGURE 6-73. (*cont.*)

(6) Alternatives. You can seize with webbing, and/or you can turn the thimble parallel with the sail if desired for a wire luff. You can use a separate piece of webbing for each of the two seizings, or one continuous piece. Firmly stitch both seizings with heavy twine.

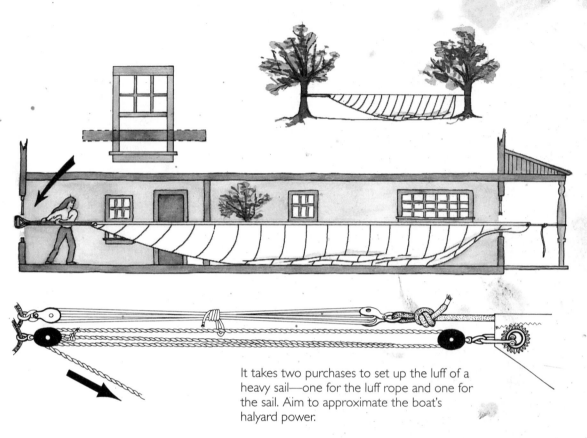

It takes two purchases to set up the luff of a heavy sail—one for the luff rope and one for the sail. Aim to approximate the boat's halyard power.

FIGURE 6-74. *Where does a loftless sailmaker set up tension on an internal luff rope? Between two obliging trees on a fair, windless day, or in the house, making judicious use of whatever doors, windows, and fixtures offer a long enough run and strong places of attachment. Ideally, you want enough width to spread out the tensioned sail and have a look at its shape and camber.*

the luff rope tight. Fix another hauling line or purchase between the unseized corner ring of the sail and the purchase point, and tension the sail. This is a very interesting stage in the process. First of all, when you tension the sail you will immediately see whether you inadvertently caught the luff rope with the stitching of an eyelet. If you have, you must discover which eyelet and carefully cut the problem stitch, then resew the eyelet later. This is why the setting of eyelet liners is left until after the stretching of the luff rope. The next thing you will see very clearly is the change in the tape and sailcloth as you apply tension. Moreover, with the luff

"halyard" made off, you can pull out the clew and observe the shape of the sail.

As tension is applied to sail and tape, the luff rope will go slack, and its tension must be freshened. I set the two up in relation to one another so that, with the hauling power on the boat, the rope will be taut and the luff tape firmly stretched, with the sail exhibiting a good pocket of bias elongation. Play with it. You will be amazed at what a difference a little change in tension makes. Notice, too, that more sag in the rope puts more belly in the sail, and that your luff curve straightens under these tensions.

(text continued on page 334)

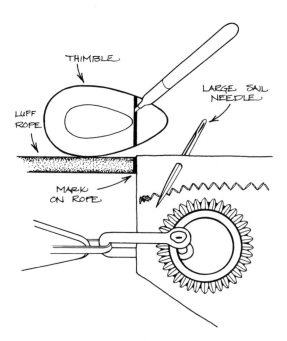

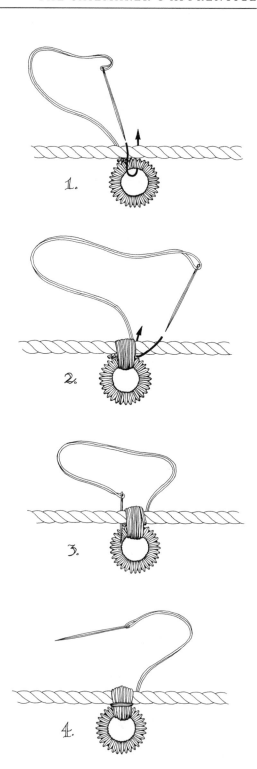

FIGURE 6-75. *Once you achieve the desired tension in sail and luff rope, lock them together temporarily with a sail needle or two, mark the rope, and ease and remove the sail and luff rope tackles. Gather the sail back along the luff rope to expose your mark and permit you to seize the eye and thimble into the rope. The mark on the rope should align with the inner throat of the thimble. When the seizing is done, slide the sail back over it, then seize the thimble to the corner ring, and apply leather as before.*

FIGURE 6-76 (RIGHT). *Seize corner rings to a handsewn boltrope before installing liners in the rings. Using heavy twine, make enough turns to fill the side of the ring toward the boltrope, then put two crossing turns around the seizing before tying or burning off the twine. Fid out the ring, being careful not to cut the seizing when you set the liner. Finally, leather over the seizing.*

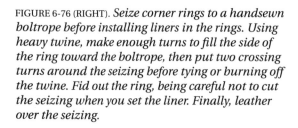

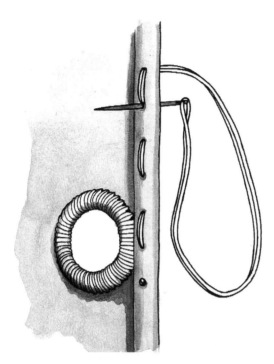

(1) Take ⅜-inch stitches through the sail and rope with heavy twine, stitching 6 inches up from the ring, then back down.

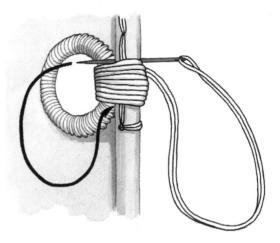

(2) Seize the ring with several turns, then cinch up the seizing with two crossing turns.

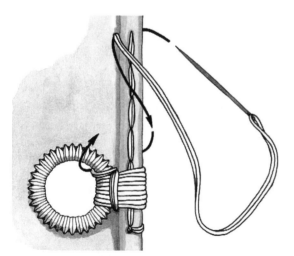

(3) Make an upper seizing by crisscrossing over the sail edge, through the ring and through the sail.

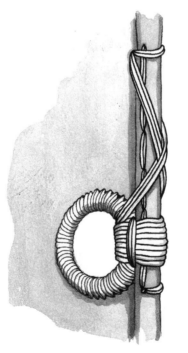

(4) The finished seizing looks like this. You may leather it over, including the inside of the corner ring if it is well fidded out and the ring liner permits.

FIGURE 6-77. *After setting up and finishing the luff of a sail with internal luff rope, you must seize any reef tack rings to the luff rope prior to installing a liner in the ring.*

Once the desired relationship between the sail and rope is set, push one or two #11 needles through the sail and rope at the corner to lock them. Mark the trimmed edge of the sail on the rope, release the sail, then release the luff rope from tension.

All that remains is to seize in another thimble, and leather it over.

Seizing Reef Tacks   It is important to understand that in a sail where roping is the primary reinforcement, reef tack rings should be fixed in some manner to the rope. A cringle grabs the rope adequately, but a ring alongside has no connection to the rope other than the cloth. With a rope luff, the reef tack ring is seized firmly to the rope. It is not so simple in a wire luff; there a reef tack fitting must be Nicopressed or, better yet, spliced into the wire.

INSTALLING A WIRE ROPE LUFF.   Frankly, given the types of line available now, I can see only limited call for a wire luff, and that in the luff of a sail set flying, or a stormsail, or a drifter. Such sails are not likely to be reefable, and therefore will not entail the reef-tack work just described. Cotton yacht headsails all went to wire towards the end, and the subsequent synthetic headsails generally had wire luffs until the advent of taping and stable synthetic line.

Anyway, in working sails where strength is desired, with no elasticity in the luff, wire luffs are best used in conjunction with wire halyards. There are three approaches to the wire-luff setup: (1) the most forgiving one is to make up wire in excess of the tensioned luff length so that there will be extra wire to use as the sail stretches; (2) a length of wire is calculated—the untensioned straight-line luff length plus 3 percent, or plus 1 inch for every 1 inch of round or hollow—then made up and fished through the sail, which is then set up to the wire length without allowance for future stretch; or (3) luff and wire can be set up in the same manner as a tensioned internal rope luff—a temporary eye will be made in the wire for tensioning pur-

poses. Any of these will work. The first method is the most advisable for natural fibers and Duradon.

Once a luff wire is set up and the ends of the sail are seized to it, there is no place for the extra wire to go when the sail contracts but to snake up inside the luff of a sail.

Bernard Moitessier once said that life's too short to take the time to splice wire. For the most part I disagree. However, when it comes to the light 7×19 wire rope recommended for the luffs of light auxiliary sails set flying, it really is all right to make eyes with Nicopress sleeves. Nicopress sleeves do not have the handsome taper of a well-tucked, well-faired eyesplice, but they and the luff wire will hold up as long as the rest of the sail.

Of course the large or heavy sails of voyaging craft with wire luffs should have spliced eyes. For that purpose, or if you must have splices no matter what, I refer you to the inimitable Brion Toss's squid-taming formula: the Liverpool Eyesplice (*SAIL* magazine, November 1983, or *The Rigger's Apprentice,* International Marine, 1985, 1992).

For the taped-luff synthetic sail, it is not necessary to do all the hitching, seizing, and stitching that was formerly done to keep the wire evenly distributed along the luff of a natural-fiber sail. I suggest vinyl-coated stainless steel wire, such as the wire used in lifelines, $3/16$ to $1/4$ inch. The Nicopressed eye can be served or the vinyl coating slid back over the eye before Nicopressing. The thimbles of wire-roped luffs are seized with the eye in the same plane as the sail's corner ring, as in Figure 6-73(6), not turned 90 degrees as in Figure 6-73(1–5). The setup procedure is the same as for a tensioned internal rope luff.

It is necessary to seize the sail to the wire every 2 to 3 feet on wire-luff roller-furling sails. (This type of wire, by the way, can be heavier and of a less flexible construction than that described above. Generally 6×7 or 7×7 stainless steel wire rope is used; it ought to be Nicopressed rather than spliced because there is so much torquing stress on the wire as the sail is rolled in and out.) The seizings ensure that the whole luff of the sail will turn as the wire rotates. Usually, a hand or machine sticking stitch is also required to keep the wire in place right along the leading edge. I can't think of anyone still opting for that style of gear, except for owners of small sportsailers, catamarans, and the like.

Sticking Rope Cringles

Cringles have numerous advantages in voyaging and traditional sails as alternatives to D-rings or large corner rings (see Chapter 8). If you are using cringles, they can be stuck in place as roping progresses, or after all roping has been done. When individual corners are separately roped, the cringles are stuck on completion of the corner. I find it more efficient to work through a particular job in one sitting—I am all set up for it and in the mode—rather than a little here and a little there.

It is not uncommon to see the boltrope leathered beneath a cringle. This does provide added protection and looks sharp. It also serves to fill the score of a large round thimble in a cringle, but it is not really necessary for chafe protection. (Norwegian squaresails traditionally have no hardware and no chafe protection at all.)

The process of sticking cringles is described in Chapter 1. There is not much to add for these larger cringles, except that there are numerous ways to lay up a cringle, and also different forms if the cringle is worked into the boltrope instead of anchor holes. The cringle is an extremely useful fitting that a self-reliant sailor would do well to understand, regardless of the overall construction of the sail. It is inexpensive, easily worked, and will serve in emergencies; it can be made from available materials and has many unnautical applications as well. Besides, nothing looks saltier.

Installing Headboards, Clewboards, and Full-Length Batten Hardware

Headboards and clewboards are designed to be riveted, but two-piece anodized aluminum headboards are easily hand sewn. I have had success, too, covering the two sides with adhesive-backed cloth to mask their ugliness. Rivet if you want, and if you have the tools. Otherwise, (a) bevel the outer edges of the holes to minimize chafe, (b) cover

the outside of the pieces with cloth, if desired, (c) sticky-tape the pieces in position opposite one another on both sides of the sail, and (d) stitch through all the holes with heavy twine and needle.

Batten end protectors and combination end-protector luff slides are screwed in place at the forward ends of contemporary full-length battens.

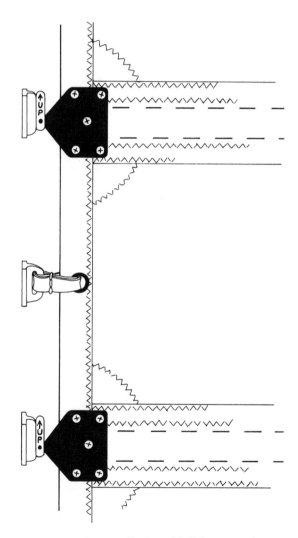

FIGURE 6-78. *The installation of full-batten end fittings is a simple job with an awl and a screwdriver. All luff fittings and slides must be equidistant from the sail edge.*

Reef Nettles

There are few things more important to the safety and well-being of a sailing vessel than the ability to shorten sail quickly and efficiently when the wind comes on to blow. Seafarer-like preparedness dictates that all downhauls and reefing tackles be rove off and ready to go before setting sail.

Reef points, or *nettles*—a row of short lines between the reef tack and clew—are needed to tie up the reefed portion of the sail. These individual nettles should be permanently attached to the sail. The nettles at a single point on either side of the sail are usually one piece of line passed through a hole in the sail and middled. Of course, the hole should be a worked hole—a handsewn ring or an eyelet.

For strength, the reef eyelets must be sewn into more than just one layer of cloth. On a sail cut up and down, the reef eyelets can be sewn into each seam. Another means of reinforcing a row of reef eyelets is to sew a reef band across the sail. Alternatively, a separate reinforcement patch can be sewn at each reef-nettle location.

What sort of line makes a good reef nettle? Any line will do—three-strand or braid, natural or synthetic fiber—as long as it is strong enough for the job and will hold a slipped reef knot.

Of great importance is that the nettles be long enough to go around a hastily gathered sail, with enough line remaining to adequately tie a slipped reef knot under obscure and rough conditions. The deeper the reef, the longer the nettles. The only way to know the proper length for sure is to take a

(2) Cinch up the crown knot and proceed to tuck the strands over one, under one.

(1) Start by unlaying 2 to 3 inches of line, and tie a crown knot.

FIGURE 6-79. *A backsplice is a secure way to finish a three-strand nettle, but takes more line than a whipping.*

(3) Thump and roll the splice after tucking each strand three times, then trim the ends, leaving ½ inch.

dry run at the mooring and see how much line you actually need.

I prefer three-strand line for nettles, because the nettle ends can take a palm-and-needle whipping. Or alternatively, a backsplice can be worked on the nettle end if the line is small enough so that the backsplice made from the line will fit through the worked hole in the sail.

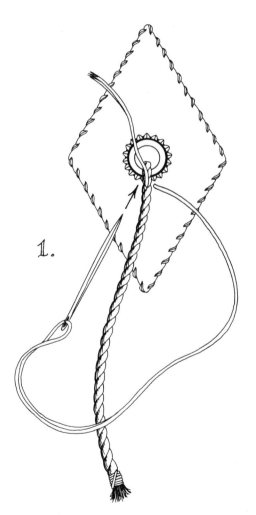

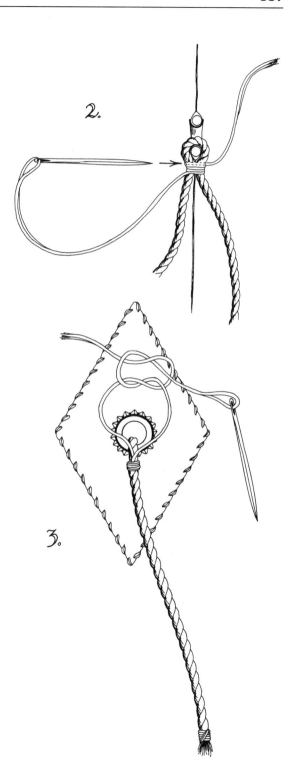

FIGURE 6-80. *Reef nettles on a voyaging sail are better seized than knotted. An even more secure method than that shown here is to make crossing turns in the form of half hitches around the seizing, between sail and nettle, on one or both sides.*

The nettles should be prepared in advance, and once cut to the desired length, the ends should be whipped in the manner described in Chapter 1, "Ditty Bag Apprenticeship." Or, as I just mentioned, if the line is suitable, the nettle ends can be back-spliced. This preparation is so time-consuming that there is a great temptation to use synthetic line and just melt the ends. But synthetic line, if just melted off, will eventually break apart and come unlaid, while the hard knob at the end is noisy in a breeze and possibly harmful when it slaps against the sail.

Now with all the nettle ends prepared, there are various ways of affixing the nettles to the sail. The least desirable way is merely to knot the line on either side of the reef eyelet. For one thing, such a knot uses up a considerable amount of the line, and for another there is more chafe and a greater likelihood of uneven strain distribution. Moreover, the knot eventually becomes so tight that it is often necessary to cut the line in order to remove the nettle from the sail.

I sew all reef nettles to the sail. A minimum of line is used; there is no chafe to the eyelet; the tension is evenly distributed; and the nettle is firmly and permanently attached to the sail. Sewing is simple but requires time and patience.

Here's how it's done: Middle the line, mark the center dividing the two nettles, and reeve the line through the hole in the sail. Place the mark at the bottom of the reef eyelet on the inside of the hole, ensuring that exactly half the line is on either side of the sail. Bind the nettle around the lower side of the eyelet.

Now, with an arm's length of light twine doubled and waxed through a #14 needle, pass the needle through the nettle on the upper side of the sail and out through the nettle on the other side (see Figure 6-80). This pass should be taken just below the stitching of the eyelet and pulled through with a couple of inches of twine left remaining. It will probably be necessary to turn the sail over in order to be sure that everything is lined up for accuracy in passing the needle back the other way through the sail.

Next pass the needle back up through the sail just to one side or the other of the nettles. Figure 6-80 shows both this and the following step, where again on the upper side you cross over the upper nettle and pass the needle down through the sail alongside the nettles. These turns encircling the nettles on both sides of the sail pass through the sail just below the stitching of the eyelet, and when they are hove taut, they should firmly hold the nettle centered and doubled through the reef eyelet.

Continue with half a dozen or so good, tight, evenly tensioned turns passed through the same holes on each side of the nettles. On large sails, extra strength can be obtained by cinching the seizing up tightly on both sides of the sail with a few crossing turns. To end, come up from below through the original stitch going through the nettles. The twine ends are then tied off in a square knot and cut.

To avoid damaging the sail, every effort should be made to tie reef nettles with equal tension and distribute the load evenly. There's nothing more salty than a well-tucked reef, and nothing makes a sail look more finished and seaworthy than neat rows of uniform reef nettles.

Leather Chafe Protection

All corners of voyaging sails should be leathered, and hank positions and jackline attachment locations should be also. The stitching of all but the lightest leather is taken firmly with five-ply twine; stitches are no more than ⅜ inch long. They should not be so tight as to pucker the cloth.

FIGURE 6-81 (PAGES 339–340). *All corners of voyaging sails should be leathered for chafe protection. These patterns cover most instances; other variations can be deduced from the basic types. Leather is generally sewn with five- or seven-ply twine. Take care not to heave the stitches too tight or make them much longer than ½ inch, or the sail will be puckered.*

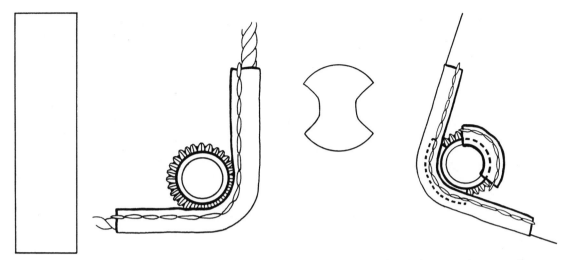

The outer stitching of corner rings must be protected, as must the inside stitching on the corner ring of an overlapping headsail.

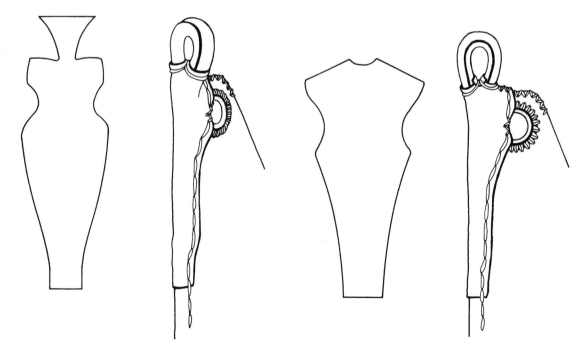

Leathering the head of a headsail that has its thimble perpendicular to the sail.

Leathering the head of a headsail in which the thimble is parallel with the sail.

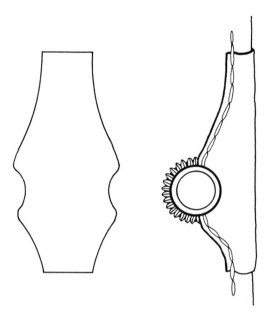

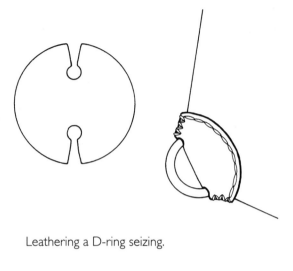

Leathering a D-ring seizing.

Leathering a reef tack seizing. This approach works only if there is room for the ring liner over the seizing and leathering.

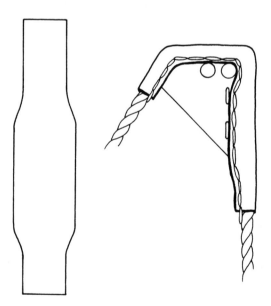

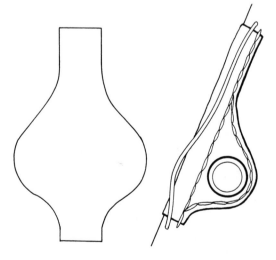

Leathering a headboard's boltrope and seizings.

Leathering a reef clew. Here the stitching of the ring is entirely covered, but this only works when there is room for the ring liner over the leather. Sew the outer edges first, then cut the hole and stitch around it.

FIGURE 6-81. (*cont.*)

Seizing Hanks, Slides, and Robands

The manner in which sails are bent to spars is of great importance in the prevention of harm coming to the sail by chafe. Hardware and metal fittings at sail corners and along the head, luff, or foot may be strong, but they are mercilessly destructive to these parts of a sail if either inappropriate in the first place or improperly installed. In a rubbing contest between cloth and metal, metal always wins.

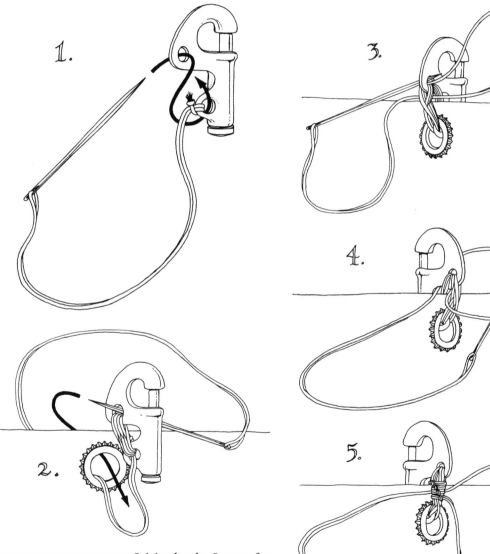

FIGURE 6-82 (PAGES 341–342). *Seizing hanks. See text for a step-by-step description. Remember: Don't give chafe a chance. Isolate hanks from the sail with a sound seizing.*

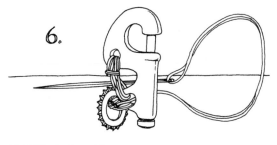

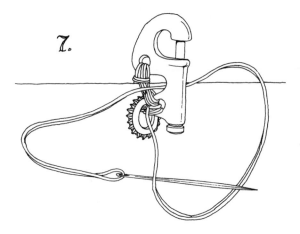

FIGURE 6-82. (*cont.*)

Material that is compatible with cloth and cordage is needed—material that does no harm to the sail, and if chafed through itself, can be easily and inexpensively replaced.

Hardware can be attached with strings—big or little strings, meaning seizing, lashing, or lacing.

Using these in sail attachment requires time, knowledge, and care on the part of a sailmaker. Naturally there is some degree of elasticity and stretch, which sailwise is the bane of the speed sailor's existence. But with correct use of strings, particularly synthetic ones, stretch can be kept to a minimum.

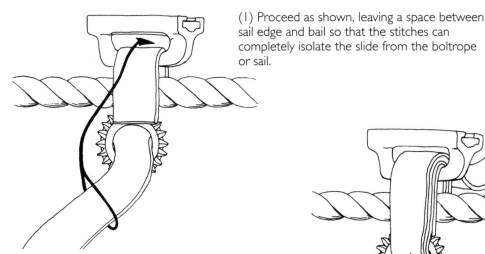

(1) Proceed as shown, leaving a space between sail edge and bail so that the stitches can completely isolate the slide from the boltrope or sail.

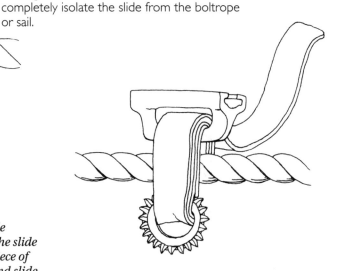

FIGURE 6-83. *Webbing makes a strong, durable seizing for a sail slide, provided the bail of the slide is big enough to accommodate it. Reeve a piece of webbing at least three times through ring and slide to gauge the length needed per slide. Measure and cut as many pieces as needed.*

(2) Lay up the turns of webbing with even tension.

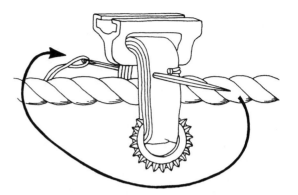

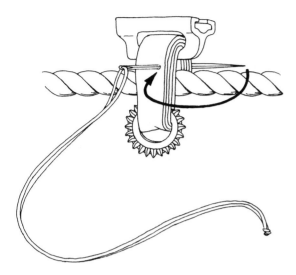

(4) Take another stitch through the hole made by the first stitch, then make a stitch to the left of center. Make a turn around the edge of the webbing as shown by the arrow.

(3) Take your first stitch through the webbing to the right of center, then take a turn around the edge of the webbing.

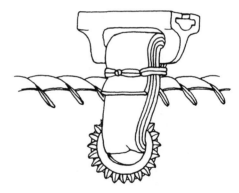

(6) Burn or knot the twine ends. For heavy sails, double the stitching.

(5) Take another stitch through the left-of-center hole, then pass the needle once more through the hole right of center.

In working and voyaging sails, the emphasis is on durability, reliability, and less expense.

Clews, tacks, throats, and peaks do well to be lashed. Hardware, slides, and mast hoops need to be seized. Lacing, as a means of attaching a sail to a spar, eliminates any hardware coming in contact with the sail. I suggest you ban all shackles and squeeze-on metal hardware from your sails. Learn knots, lashings, seizings, and lacing techniques instead.

Figure 6-82 shows a method for seizing hanks that I learned from Paul Mitchell of San Diego, who got it from Barry Spanier, and where he got it, I don't know. It seems to be a good method, reliable and sensible.

"Into" piston hanks, named for their inventor, range in size from #0 (about 1¼ inches long), to #4 (about 4 inches long). The size and length of twine required for seizing hanks and the gauge sail needle used depend on the hank size. The size of the hank, in turn, depends on the sail, its size and use, and the diameter of the wire on which the sail is to

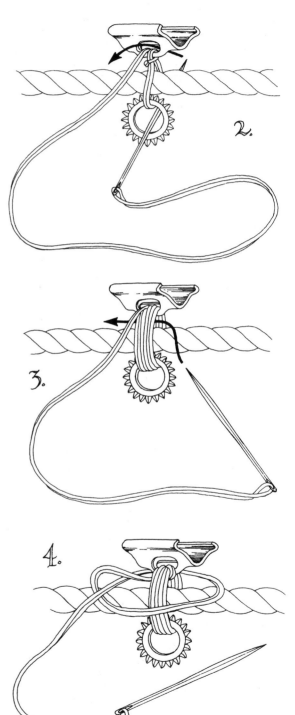

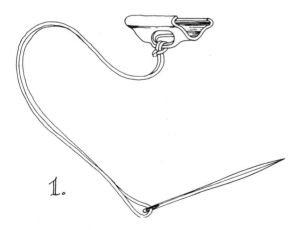

FIGURE 6-84. *When you don't have webbing or the bails of the slides are too small for it, heavy twine is a fast, readily available alternative. Seven-ply or heavier polyester twine, well waxed, is best. All slides must be isolated equidistant from the sail. Places of great strain, such as the head and clew of a mainsail, need extra-heavy slide seizings and even two slides within a few inches of each other.*

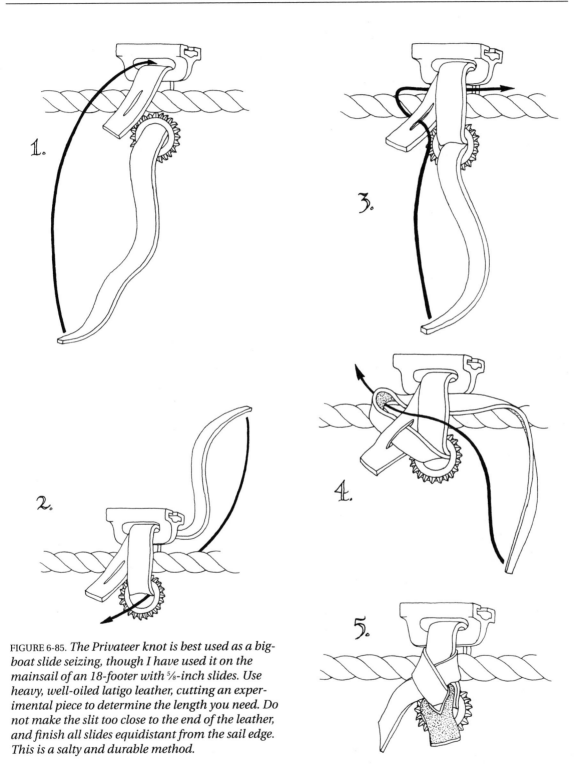

FIGURE 6-85. *The Privateer knot is best used as a big-boat slide seizing, though I have used it on the mainsail of an 18-footer with ⅝-inch slides. Use heavy, well-oiled latigo leather, cutting an experimental piece to determine the length you need. Do not make the slit too close to the end of the leather, and finish all slides equidistant from the sail edge. This is a salty and durable method.*

A roband bent to an eyelet with a round throat seizing.

A roband bent to an eyelet with a cowhitch.

FIGURE 6-86. *Robands are an inexpensive, easily replaced means of bending sail to a spar. There are many ways to affix a roband to a sail; the four shown here vary in complexity from simple knots to seizing and woodworking. The rope's resistance to chafe and weather is more important than its strength, since there is not all that much strain placed on a roband. The cordage must be able to hold a square knot on the opposite side of the spar.*

The foot stopper knot. After middling the roband through the sail's eyelet, each end is passed through the lay of the other end, close to the sail.

be bent. Among the hanks on a particular sail, those that are to receive extra strain, such as at tack and head, could stand stouter seizings. A well-worked hank seizing is not only a proud and handsome accomplishment but a source of security and reassurance as well.

One's arm span of doubled #7 polyester twine, waxed, and a #14 needle will serve for seizing the middle range of hanks (#1 and #2). The roping

palm is preferable for this operation, as it has an eye designed for large needles, and the thumb stall is an invaluable asset in heaving the turns as tightly as possible. The knotted twine is passed through itself and cowhitched to the lower eye of a serviceable hank. With the hank held facing away, at least five turns are taken in a figure-eight fashion, with the needle entering the eyes of the hank, passing left to right. Each turn should be

A roband bent to an eyelet with a foot stopper knot.

A roband with toggle and eyesplice bent to an eyelet with a clove hitch.

firmly hove home. This step terminates with the twine coming out of the lower eye. This completes what I'll call the inner seizing.

On which side of the sail are you going to seize the hanks? It makes a difference. It depends on your dexterity and where you're safest and most comfortable bending the sail. Having chosen, though, make sure that as you progress from one hank to the next you keep to the desired side.

Place the hank on the eyelet location, facing you on the selected side of the sail. Pass the needle through the eyelet and proceed to pass a minimum of seven turns in a figure-eight manner, back and forth through the worked ring on the other side of the sail, thus forming an "outer" seizing. This time the needle enters both eyes of the hank, passing from right to left.

Finishing the preceding step with the twine left coming through the upper eye, the next impor-

tant step of covering the upper horn of the hank with twine is begun by turning the sail over, so that the hank is on the opposite side. From right to left, the needle is now passed through the space between the inner and the outer seizing, between the hank and sail edge. Then back through the eye for at least another go-round until the metal is covered with twine. These turns require some heaving to get them settled in correctly. This step ends with the twine coming out of the left side as you look at the work in hand.

Now a half hitch is taken, as shown, about both the inner and the outer seizing. Cinch this down as if your life depended on it.

The outer seizing is next served down with a French hitching–like series of half hitches, each hitch aligned and firm. Passing the needle from right to left between the outer seizing and the sail will be tight, and care must be taken to harm neither seizing, sail, nor worked ring. Dulling the

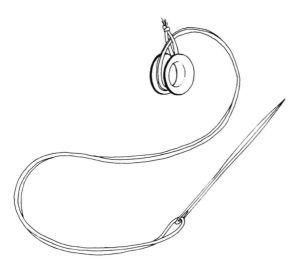

(1) Knot a needleful of twine and cowhitch it to the round thimble.

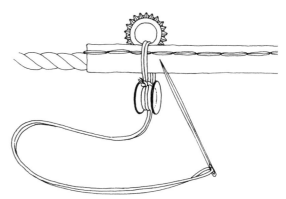

(2) Position the thimble close to the leathered jackline eyelet, and make sufficient even passes of twine through the eyelet to fill the score of the thimble.

FIGURE 6-87. *Seizing jackline thimbles to sail eyelets. The seizing must be strong, must isolate the thimble from the sail, and must align all the thimbles equidistant from the sail edge. Use heavy, well-waxed twine.*

needle in advance will help. Hitch all the way down, as close to the lower hank eye as possible from that side of the sail. Pass the needle through the worked ring and turn the sail back over so that the hank is toward you again.

In this next step, the lower horn of the hank will be prevented from chafing the sail by means of a couple of turns around it just as with the upper horn. The needle is passed through the lower eye from left to right, then back under the inner seiz-

ing. The same care must be taken as before not to harm sail, ring, or seizing.

To finish, two half hitches are cinched up as tightly as possible about the inner and outer seizings, further tightening the whole job and isolating the hank from the sail. Last, the twine may be cut off, knotted, or melted. The end result should be a snug, rock-hard seizing, with the hank firmly held more or less perpendicular to the sail's edge.

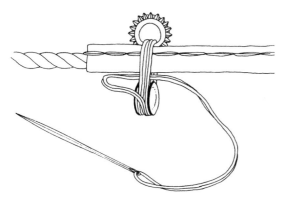

(3) Pass the needle between sail and thimble preparatory to taking a half hitch crossing turn.

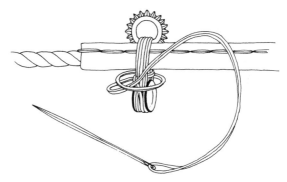

(4) For a simple finish, make two half-hitch crossing turns around the seizing, heave them as tight as possible, and burn or knot the end. For an even tighter and more wonderful job, make a single half-hitch crossing turn, heave it tight, and get ready to do some French hitching.

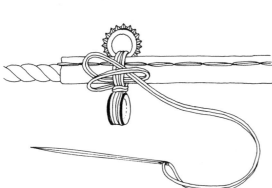

(5) Make a series of half hitches through the seizing, starting at the thimble, marching through the eyelet as the half hitches pile on top of each other, and continuing down the opposite leg of the seizing until you reach the thimble again.

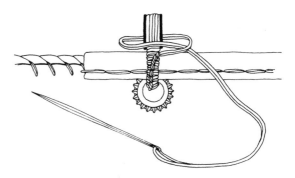

(6) Finish your French hitching with one last half hitch around the whole seizing, then burn or knot-off the twine.

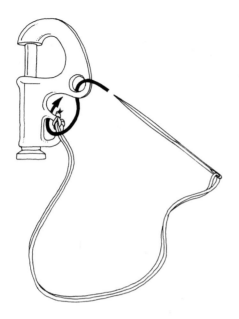

(1) Pass several crossed turns of heavy waxed twine between the eyes of the hank.

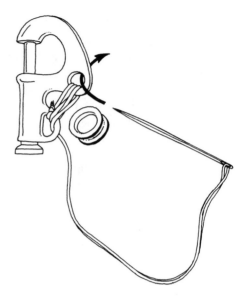

(2) Place the thimble in the crotch and make several crossed turns over it, cinching it in.

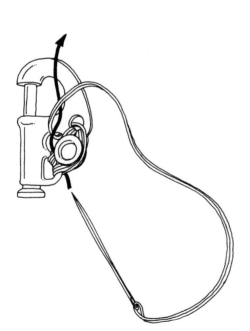

(3) Make a half hitch around the upper portion of the seizing and heave it forcefully.

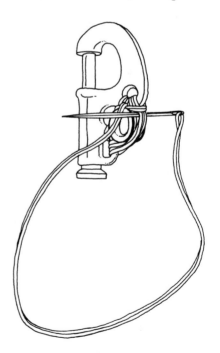

(4) Start a series of half hitches down the outer seizing, picking up only the outermost turns of twine around the thimble's score.

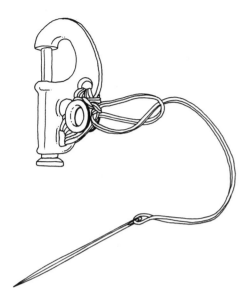

(5) French hitch right down to the bottom of the seizing.

FIGURE 6-88. *Cast jackline hanks can be difficult to obtain, but standard hanks can be converted for use on a jackline by seizing on a round thimble. Though it is not essential, you can pound the thimble into the hollow between the eyes of the hank.*

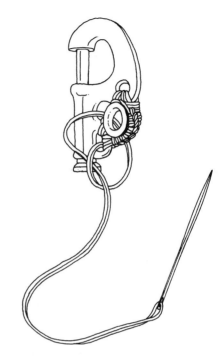

(6) Finish with two tightly hove half hitches around the lower portion of the seizing, then burn or knot-off the twine.

Of course a slide seizing must be strong, but in addition, it should firmly isolate the slide from the sail, with all slides equidistant from the edge of the sail. The choice of material depends on what's available that will not chafe the sail. Webbing is ideal; twine is fine; and sailcloth will work. The accompanying illustrations include the Privateer seizing (Figure 6-85) for its salty simplicity. I have used it on small sails, but it is better for attaching large-boat bronze slides with heavy latigo leather. I first encountered this aboard Bob Goss's schooner *Privateer* (formerly *Mahdee*) where it had been in use for several years. He'd devised and adapted the technique; thus the name.

Finish Details

Hand-finishing Batten Pockets　On batten pockets of any sail other than the lightest of daysails, it is best to hand sew the ends with a cross-stitch (see Figure 6-46). Full batten end protectors and adjusters that can be riveted in place can also be installed with hand stitching.

Leech and Foot Cords　Clam- and jam-type cleats for belaying leech and foot cords are easily riveted or hand sewn in place, and they are viable choices for racing and inshore work. In long-term use they tend to chafe through the leech cord. Moreover, a lapping headsail clew needs a protec-

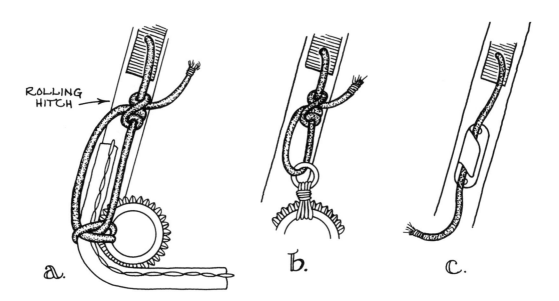

FIGURE 6-89. *Leech and foot cords are oft-abused sail-handling devices. They are no sub-stitute for halyard tension, sheeting, or vanging, but as a last resort can take out that last bit of flutter. Here are three ways to belay a leech cord, the goals being ease of installation and adjustment. (A) Belay to a strong corner ring. (B) Belay to a small brass ring, which in turn is seized through the sail around the corner ring. (C) Belay to a clam cleat that is sewn or riveted to the sail. When used on an overlapping headsail clew, this method requires that a flap be sewn over the cleat to prevent it from snagging during tacks.*

tive flap to keep the plastic cleat and leech cord from snagging other lines and wires.

Alternative techniques are twin button cleats of leather, or eyelets in the sail. The strongest method I know of that results in the least chafing is to tie the cord off through the corner ring. This can be made adjustable with a rolling hitch, though it is not as instantaneous as a clam cleat. Clams are an attractive alternative at reef clews, where it is diffi-cult to haul out enough cord to tie off. Another approach, which also eliminates the hazard of for-getting to release the cord when shaking out the reef, is to dead-end the leech cord at the clew, pass it over a turning block in the head, and run the hauling end down the luff. I imagine some-thing similar could be rigged for a gaff-headed sail as well.

Flag or Pennant Sewn to the Leech of a Sail
Nothing demanding about this. The flag can be sewn directly to the sail or seized to eyelets, making sure that the flag is not compressing the leech. A flag with a luff length of more than 12 inches should be seized in the middle, too. It is best to locate a pennant high, or in a position of good leech support.

WHEW! Put it in the bag.

CHECKING OUT YOUR SAIL

Some commercial lofts have test spars. You have a handy billy, spikes, trees, and your own boat. On many occasions, I have taken the spars of small sails, particularly spritsails (where the lines are all belayed to the spars), and set the whole rig up indoors. From this you learn whether the sail fits the spars and whether the edge tensions have been set up correctly. Setting up a sail on the horizontal, as was briefly done when installing the luff rope, reveals edge tension problems, sewing errors, and some indication of sail shape and edge support.

Gravity, of course, will not have the same effect on a sail lashed out horizontally as the wind will have on a sail in use. But gross flaws can be caught. Naturally, any soft or natural fabric is going to take time to break in and reach its final shape. For that matter, a natural-fiber sail will need a gradual break-in period of at least three mild-weather sailings before full tension is placed on the boltrope and cloth. Duradon takes several outings with a good breeze to work out the wrinkles. It takes some time, too, for the stitching in soft Dacron to settle in, and for the seams to stretch out. Therefore, when looking at the sail, don't panic immediately if it looks rumply. Aeolus will likely smooth out all or most of that.

The rough shape of the sail including camber and draft position will be discernible, but if the edges are sagging excessively or there is insufficient tension placed on the edge, the sail will be fuller than designed. The weight of slides and hanks adds to this phenomenon. Stretching a string or holding a straightedge over chord positions will help in visualizing curvature if there are no draft stripes attached to the sail.

Do not be alarmed if a large, roached, loose foot curls downward. If a small foot curve flops down, the foot tapers need tightening a tad. A leech with battens should certainly support itself, and contemporary full battens should also support the sail's camber.

Nothing can be ascertained about a sail if the diagonal and edge tensions are not set up as they will be in use on the boat. Therefore, the sail must be lashed or spiked out, not merely held out by you and some assistants.

If all is well, take down the sail, fold it properly, and stow it in a bag. Generally, sails are folded along the foot, but this method leaves hanks and slides inside the folded sail to chafe and cut stitching. Alternatively, a sail can be folded parallel to the luff for chafe protection.

SAIL ALTERATIONS AND ADJUSTMENTS

Recutting a Used Sail

There is much money and time to be saved by altering an inexpensive used sail to fit your boat. There are varying degrees of recut, ranging from the alteration of an edge to fit a spar to using some portion of good cloth for a new sail of significantly different proportions—perhaps even of a different type or cut. In both instances, the used sail must pass a survey so as to be economically and functionally acceptable (see "Surveying a Used Sail" in Chapter 10). When salvaging cloth from a used sail, what you're after is a sail with sound cloth, good seams, and sound stitching over enough area to cut out your sail with the cloth running in the correct direction (see Chapter 5). A used sail with shape built in will have to be studied carefully, especially if the broadened seams have been trimmed. Unless proper adjustment is made, you will end up with that shape someplace in your sail, and trimmed broadseams can't be let out again to be resewn.

Initially, the work is done on paper, similar to the design process described early in this chapter. Draw the used sail out to scale, including panel formation. If the sail has discernibly broadened seams, or you know where the draft has been placed, mark the placement on the plan. Next, place a paper scale cutout of the new sail, with its panels, on top of the plan. Simply move the cutout around until it occupies the best position. Sometimes more than one sail can be gotten out of a big used sail. Don't forget to allow for tablings and bands. It may work out that old reef rows will serve in your new sail; maybe not. The process of cutting out the sail, then, is similar to this paper-on-paper technique, except that you loft the new sail right on top of the old one.

First, remove all the edge reinforcement on the old sail. This serves two purposes: It facilitates flattening out the sail, and it gets hardware out of the way of lofting battens. Save all the reusable hardware, even corner rings!

It is fastest to loft the new sail right on top of the old one, but complications arise if alterations in broadseams are necessary. Without taking apart whole seams, it will be possible only to install the equivalent of foot tapers in the form of darts, a technique possible but not advisable in stiff Dacron. If changing luff broadseams is necessary, do a rough lofting, as you would a new sail with unseamed cloths, and leave the required cloth allowances if the seams will be broadened. Obviously, to ease them, no extra cloth will be needed. Unpick only as much of the seam as you need to change. Draw the new sew-to lines. It is fastest to sticky-tape the seams back together, leaving their sewing for later, and proceed with the formal lofting of edge curves, etc. From there, the process is the same as that for a new sail.

Reroping

There are many reasons for a hand-roped sail needing reroping, and the extent of the job can range from reroping a short section to redoing the whole sail. Short sections may be damaged or be inconsistently sewn in comparison with the rest of the edge; a whole edge or sail may be improperly roped—rope too large or too light, too tight or too slack. It is easiest to resew a short section by stringing up the edge under tension, then restitching the section right there in place. Old stitch holes can be reused. If the section was poorly roped, unpicking the section, then sewing it while the sail is stretched, will assure you of an even reroping. If passing the needle through the taut line is too difficult, the line can be struck up and seized, then sewn at a bench.

Reroping a whole sail or complete side would be done in the same way as if one were roping the sail for the first time, by drawing a sew-to line on the new boltrope, then stretching the sail edge and rope. The two are seized together at 1-foot intervals before being sewn. I don't recommend attempting to rope back into an already-sewn section of rope. The chances of the rope's twisting and tightening are so great that by the time you reach the sewn portion of the rope, things will be quite a mess. It would be better to rerope the whole sail. Repairs of handsewn boltrope are discussed in Chapter 9, and the restitching of machine-sewn boltrope is covered earlier in this chapter.

Changes in Luff Rope or Wire

So often, the internal roping in a sail is either the incorrect length or an inappropriate strength or elasticity. If the size is off, there is nothing to do but replace the whole thing. Rather than pick apart miles of stitching and multitudes of eyelets, it is simpler, when the rope can't be slid out and another fished through, to cut the whole edge off along the tabling, thus reducing the size of the sail somewhat but retaining the luff curve to which a new tape can easily be sewn. If the edge of the sail is baggy despite your having hauled the rope as tight as you are able, it is a sign that the rope is too short. A luff wire with extra length on it merely needs restretching, adjustment, and seizing.

If a rope or wire is just slightly short, there could be enough extra around the thimble to extend it at one or both ends. Usually, though, if the rope is too short, the choices are possibly to splice in an extension (with the splice clear of luff eyelets), or to replace the whole thing. Alternatively, if you are dealing with a short but elastic luff rope, you could increase the rig's hauling power, and perhaps you should. In the event that the rope is too long, indicated by the sail's receiving too much tension while the rope remains slack and sagging, it is simply a matter of freeing one end of the luff rope and then proceeding through the luff-rope setup process, which should be concluded by cutting off the extra rope. Wire of excessive length can be freed at the peak, then the sail's luff set up correctly with an extended seizing from the wire's head thimble to the sail's head ring.

Taper and Broadseam Adjustment

There is a big difference between tapers that provide edge support and those that create camber. The former are far easier to alter. They are generally shorter and straighter, and, most important, they are located in relatively uncomplicated parts of the sail when it comes to preparation and taking the seams apart. The leech tapers of a crosscut fore-and-aft sail are the easiest to alter in that they are small, straight, and have not already been trimmed. These tapers are eased or tightened only slightly to relieve a hooked or sagging leech. Only in instances where one particular location needs help would the adjustment be concentrated in one seam, say to support a reef clew; otherwise, it is better to make small adjustments in several seams, equidistantly spaced along the edge. A tremendous difference can be made by $\frac{1}{16}$ inch greater or lesser overlap in four to six seams along a leech. Changing the foot tapers of boomless and loose-footed sails is, again, a simple operation, but it can be complicated by having to rerope the foot of a sail. Generally, one is trying to remedy a hooked or floppy foot. Note first whether there is excessive roach in the foot and whether outhauls and sheeting are correctly adjusted. Clearly, a foot with no tapers at all that flops to leeward needs support, as described earlier in this chapter, particularly seam tapers in the area of maximum roach. But if there is a problem, it usually lies in the curve of the taper, not in the amount of overlap: too abrupt a flaring of the taper puts the roach on a hinge. Thus, to relieve hooking, the curve should be flattened, with less flare down low. To remedy a floppy foot, the seam tapers can be broadened another $\frac{1}{8}$ inch or so, and the curve made more pronounced.

Luff tapers on a crosscut fore-and-aft sail are by far the most difficult to alter, as it is necessary to remove all the luff eyelets and reinforcement to start with, then unpick and redraw the seams (as described earlier in this chapter). The need to make these adjustments arises from dissatisfaction with draft placement or shape of entry. A pattern-cut sail does not lend itself to this sort of adjustment—it is too difficult to see what has been done before, and both sides of the seam may have been trimmed. The easiest sails to alter are those on which you can see untrimmed broadseams; and then, when the seam is unpicked, you are back at flat, straight cloth panels to work with.

Essentially, unless it is but one or two offending seams that need adjustment, the project is identical to broadseaming the luff of a new sail. The only difference is that the portion from the draft position aft is already sewn. With these, as in all taper adjustments, it is best to sticky-tape them back together: first, to ensure even tension of layers; second, to check out the new shape in advance of sewing; and third, to permit the immediate redrawing and cutting of the edge curve that will be necessary if any major changes have been made. In order to make the entry of a sail fuller, the broadseams have to be widened. As a result of doing this, you will find that the luff is now shorter and the luff curve will have to be slightly flatter.

Installing a Reef in a Used Sail

This is a very common job—so many production sails are made with no reefs or only one in anticipation of the boat's being a fair-weather sailer prone to motoring. Any working sail and some auxiliary sails can be reefed. Do not overlook the possibility of putting reefs in headsails.

Reefs are not just stuck in a sail at any old depth. They reduce sail a specified amount to achieve control and balance of helm under specific conditions, wind ranges, and sail combinations. Some study of the correct position of the reef(s) is the first requirement. Without a sail plan or some experiential reference, the sail plans of similar boats can be used as a guide. Successive reefs are often, but not always, placed equidistant from one another.

Reefs are survival gear and as such should be built as strong as the rest of the sail and designed for easy and speedy use. Most reefs are parallel to the foot of the sail, or the luff, as in sharpies. But they can be on the diagonal, as in the boomless lateen rig or the balance reef of a gaff sail. Diagonal reefs provide an alternative sail profile while at the same time reducing area. Often in these instances one corner, such as a tack, will serve for both full-sail tack and the reef tack. The diagonal reef makes a single sail quite versatile.

Procedure

- Lay the sail out fully tensioned and as flat as possible.
- Locate the reef endpoints with some kick-up to the after end of a boomed sail. (See reef-location discussion earlier in this chapter.) Pin out the reef area as smooth as possible.
- With spikes at the reef clew and reef tack endpoints, spring a batten to the desired curvature of the row of reef points. *Note: Boomed, fixed-footed sails must have the eyelets below the straight-line reef. The curve will be straight or shallow, with its deepest part 40 to 45 percent aft. The curve on a boomless or loose-footed sail will be the same as the foot curve.*
- Mark reef-point locations, as evenly spaced as possible and a maximum of 2 feet apart.
- If more than one row of reefs is to be installed, it is convenient for ease of measurement to set them all up at the same time. Comparisons can be made.
- Remove battens, and draw reef clew and tack patches.
- Cut out and assemble all patches.
- Prepare the sail by unpicking and lifting leech and luff reinforcements in way of the new reef clew and tack.
- Sew all patches in place.
- Resew leech and luff tablings. This may necessitate rereeving a leech cord with exits and entrances at each reef clew (as described earlier in the chapter).
- Install corner rings, eyelets, reef nettles, and leather as described earlier.

Converting a Sail to or from Roller-Furling

Converting a conventionally hanked sail to any of the extruded-slot roller-furling systems is extremely simple, and entails only a slight loss of the original sail area. First, make sure your sail has the appropriate tack angle (less than 85 degrees), is relatively flat (little camber), and is a good compromise in cloth weight—that is, light enough to be of some use in light airs, but strong and heavy enough to hold shape and integrity in moderate winds. Many strategies have been devised to make roller-furling sails as effective and versatile as possible: graduated cloth weights, reef-position corner patches, luff systems to counteract the tendency of the rolling to push camber into the reefed sail configurations. The only one of these innovations that is appropriate to a home conversion would be the addition of reef-position corner patches. And those, if not already known, would have to be designated under sail after some experimentation once the sail's luff has been converted.

Procedure

1. It is easiest to use commercially made luff tapes intended for furling systems. The size and type of tape depend on the size of the sail and the brand of furling gear. Furling gear manufacturers specify the size of rope, and the tape width of prepared tape is sized accordingly. Purchase the tape in the desired straight-line length of luff. (See Table 6-7.)
2. With the luff of the sail spread out, remove the old luff tape, eyelets, corner rings, rope, and all by simply cutting along the very inner edge of the luff tabling.
3. The remainder of the tape installation process is the same as any stretched-edge tape (see the method using staples earlier in this chapter). It is to be hoped that the former luff curve will serve in the converted system; if not, the luff curve must be redrawn. Tension and spike out the luff.
4. Place the tape over the cut edge of the sail

with the edge flush against the innermost of the two ropes within the tape. Pin the tape firmly to the floor at the head.

5. Stretch the tape as taut as possible. Pin at the tack.
6. Staple the tape to the sail, dividing the intervals in half down to a spacing of 3 inches apart. Alternatively, pins and double-sided sticky tape can be used. Make sure the tape is flush against the cut edge of the sail all the way along.
7. *Important:* Remove all the luff pins from the sail before releasing one end or the other of the tape; otherwise, the contraction of the luff tape will tear the sail at the pins!
8. Fold and trim the tack and head with a hotknife. Sew the tape with two to three rows of zigzag stitching.
9. Middle 2 to 3 feet of double-thickness, 1-inch-wide flat polyester webbing and reeve it through a stainless steel ring of 1 to 1½ inches outer diameter. Sew the two equal-length tails of webbing to both sides of the sail simultaneously (four layers of webbing in all) alongside the innermost rope of the tape. (See Figure 6-59 for reference.)
10. By hand, oversew with light twine the cut edge between the inner and outer rope ends to protect against chafe.

Converting a continuous-luff roller-furling sail to a conventional hanked luff is a matter of cutting off the furling-type luff tape, then proceeding as you would in the building of a luff in a new sail. A real quick and dirty job can be made of it by slapping eyelets and hanks into the furling luff. This is not recommended for anything but a beater of a sail, and a fair-weather one at that. It's not worth bothering with anything but spur grommets and squeeze-on hanks in this instance.

Installing Edge Covers on Roller-Furling Sails

Unless you plan on using a sock to protect your roller-furling sail from ultraviolet light, you can kiss that sail good-bye if it has no edge covers. Even if the cloth and thread are coated with UV inhibitors, the sail will not last long. It is easier to install covers on a new, unwrinkled sail, but used sails, if not too creased, present no great difficulty. Edge covers are essential, but they are ugly, and until recently, if they were at all UV resistant, they were quite heavy.

For a long time sailmakers grappled with the problem of not having a suitable, lightweight edge-cover material for small-boat roller-furling sails. For that matter, the cover material available for heavy sails wasn't all that wonderful either. With the advent of UV-resistant adhesive-backed film, I thought not only that the lightweight edge-cover problem was solved but also that anyone, with some patience, could now install an edge cover. The stuff had all the attractiveness of Saran Wrap on the sail, and it was like working with flypaper, but it seemed to need no sewing, blocked the sun, could cover areas that cloth covers couldn't, and was easily patched.

It was these appealing features that caused me to persuade a trusting client to give the UV film a try—only to have her discover en route to the Caribbean that the film immediately started peeling off the sail, was easily torn, constantly needed repair, and somehow managed to permanently wrinkle the sail into a sticky wudge! The informative postcard I received about these developments was friendly, but I felt like a turd anyway.

So use the UV film if you want, but alternatively, a light 2-ounce, UV-coated, adhesive-backed Dacron cover cloth is available that seems to be a great improvement on the film and is obtainable in white and blue. Being adhesive-backed, this material still has the problem of stickiness oozing out around the edges, but in any case it is a reasonable option for the home sailmaker with a light roller-furling sail. This material is not recommended for cruising and constant heavy use. It is more for light, seasonal sailing. For heavy sails and ones that demand some durability of the edge cover, a heavier UV-coated Dacron or the standard acrylic edge-cover material is preferable.

For installing nonadhesive cloth covers, the eas-

iest approach is to sew a long strip along the leech
and another on the foot; therefore enough cloth
must be obtained to cover both lengths. Cloth
could be saved by making up the edge covers from
numerous short cloths running perpendicular to
the straight-line foot and leech, but this involves
much more work. Long strips parallel to the sail
edges do waste cloth, but the time saved is worth it.
The more pronounced the leech hollow and foot
round, the greater the wastage will be. (When
designing a new roller-furling sail, edge curves,
particularly in the foot, are kept to a minimum.)

Procedure

1. Roll up the sail as it will be on the boat—
   correct side out—and mark with a pencil the
   overlaps along the entire length.
2. Unroll, spike, and pin out the sail as flat as
   possible.
3. Set up a taut string in a straight line parallel to
   the straight-line leech and 2 inches in from
   the deepest overlap mark made.
4. Roll out the cover cloth along the string, from
   head to clew, and pin it securely along string
   and leech. Cut the end, leaving material for
   hemming under at head and clew.
5. Set up the taut string parallel to the straight-
   line foot, 2 inches in or up from the overlap
   marks at clew and tack.
6. Roll out the cover cloth parallel and along the
   string, starting at the clew, but only overlapping the leech cloth by 1½ inches.
7. Pin the cloth securely along the string and
   foot. Cut the end of the cloth at the tack,
   allowing enough extra to be hemmed under
   along the luff.
8. Along both leech and foot, trim off extra cloth,
   leaving the tabling's width to be hemmed
   under.
9. Firmly sticky-tape or staple the covers to the
   sail along inner and outer edges, with the
   leech cover overlapping the foot cover. Trim
   and hem under around the corner rings. Have
   the outer edge of the cover protrude slightly

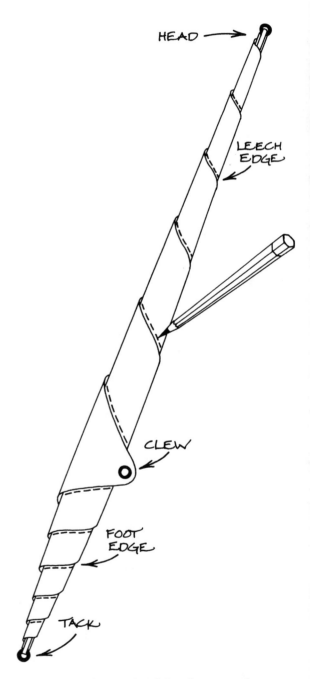

FIGURE 6-90. *To be certain of the edge-cover placement on a roller-furling sail, roll the sail up and
mark it along luff and foot. The cover must extend
at least 3 inches into the sail.*

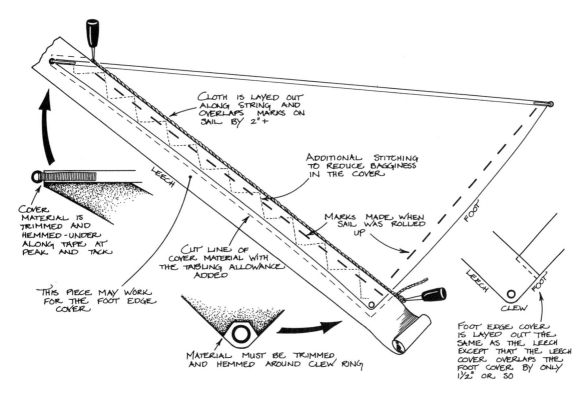

FIGURE 6-91. *Laying out a roller-furling sail for the installation of edge covers. You can lay out one edge at a time if space is limited, but it's important that the edge be laid out as it will naturally set in use on the boat.*

past the edge of the sail for maximum protection.

10. Last, draw a long zigzag line across and along both edge covers. Sew the cover down with heavy thread and a zigzag stitch along the zigzag line. This will minimize bagging of the cover cloth. Avoid sewing the leech and foot cords.

Installing Adhesive-backed Edge Covers

Anyone who has assayed to lay contact paper on cupboard shelves has some idea what you're in for with this project! But don't let that deter you—just make sure you have a couple of extra yards of the material on hand for the inevitable foul-up. It's still easier than sewing an acrylic cover.

Preparation: Are you going to work your way around following the edge curve, or go along a straight inner line as described for one-piece cloth covers? The first method can be done in a small space, pinning the sail edge out, section by section, on a piece of plywood. Then the material is laid out in manageable 6-foot sections. (Even if the entire sail were pinned out, the cover might still be applied in 6-foot sections.) The sail edge must be pinned out fairly, as it will be the line along which the film is laid. The straighter the edge is to begin with, the easier this is, particularly along the foot, where it is awkward to work along any round even with short, 6-foot sections.

The second method requires full layout space; a steady hand could roll the adhesive-backed material along the whole edge in one piece. Regardless of the method, the sail must be clean and pinned out perfectly flat—new, unused sails probably lend themselves better to this process and stand a better chance of permanent adhesion. For the best possible adhesion, the sail and the work space must be dry, warm, and clean. Every free-floating dog hair and potato chip crumb for miles around will be drawn to this stuff! Once this goo sticks to itself, forget it; cut a new piece.

Procedure, Short-Section Technique

1. Cut sufficient 6-foot lengths of the cover material to cover the length of the leech. *Caution:* Make sure you are mounting the cover on the correct side of the sail!
2. Pin out the head and upper 8 feet of the leech in a straight line, to the width of the material.
3. Pin a section of the material with the backing in place along the leech. Mark and trim around the head shape, and trim the outer edge flush with the leech.
4. Roll the piece up. Separate the cloth from the backing at the head and roll it out, pulling the backing out from underneath. Maintain even tension across the roll.
5. Smooth it out lightly with your hand, then firmly with stockinged feet.
6. Lift the sail, pin out the next section, and repeat with a ⅜- to ½-inch overlap—because the sail edge is curved, the overlap will be wedge-shaped. Mark where the overlap begins to ensure alignment with the sail edge during rollout. The edges of sails are often not fair curves, and it is easy to misalign the material. Small deviations are okay, as the edge is later covered with an edge tape of the cover cloth. Inevitably, there are bloops and wrinkles that are inconspicuous when smoothed out.
7. On reaching the clew and tack, trim the cover material to fit closely around the hardware before removing the backing.

Procedure, Full-Layout Method

1. Spike and pin out the full sail.

2. Determine the area to be covered (as described for nonadhesive cover cloths) and draw the layout line 4 inches in from the overlap marks.
3. Trim the end of the film to the shape of the head of the sail. Work down the leech.
4. Trim off the excess or, possibly, fold it around the sail.
5. Proceed as for steps 4 and 5 under "Short-Section Technique," above.
6. Finally, section by section, with the full sail edge suspended in the air, adhere the edge tape made of cover cloth over the sail edge. This serves to help hold down the outer edge of the cover and fully protect the sail edge from the sun. Save any extra material for patches and places of chafe, such as pulpit and spreader patches.

The adhesive-backed edge covers of sails receiving heavy use, particularly those that chafe on stays, mast, or shrouds, should be stitched by machine along the edges of the cover material.

Altering Sail Camber

Here we are concerned with changing the camber ratio—the depth of curvature divided by the chord length—which measures how flat or full a sail is either in general or at a specific height. Draft position, shape of entry, and shape of exit are related considerations, the alterations of which are discussed elsewhere in this chapter.

Broadseaming has become the primary means of forming camber in firm synthetic fabrics. A molded sail of this type is really a fixed and unalterable form. Sails on which the camber can be adjusted are made of relatively soft fabrics, with curvature being created by edge curves, limited broadseaming, and bias elongation. It is generally easier to flatten an excessively full sail than it is to give greater camber to a sail of insufficient curvature.

Flattening a Sail   First check to see whether the edge tensions are correctly balanced with the hauling power on the boat. If the sail's reinforcements are too short, tight, or strong, this will show up as a baggy sail along with other symptoms such as crow's feet at the hanks or slides. Reroping, lengthening the luff wire or rope, or replacing a luff tape with a lighter tape of less tension, will correct this fault and enable a flatter sail, but does not alter the sail's built-in shape. Be sure, too, that the problem is not one of excessive edge length for the spar or stay. This situation is rectified by a different sort of recut, as discussed elsewhere.

Clearly, if a sail is deriving its overly full shape from excessive edge curves, those curves can be recut with less round, or so as to redistribute curvature to push less cloth into the sail. If one part of the sail is disproportionately full, the section of edge curve governing that area should be reduced.

The only problems arise in deciding how to deal with rings and eyelets. The sail has to be disassembled back to the stage of fabrication at which its original edge curves were drawn. Handsewn rings can be removed and the edge recut without reducing the size of the sail, but to recut the edge curve of a sail with hydraulically pressed rings, the whole edge tape must be cut off as when converting to roller furling (see above).

If broadseaming has played a major role in the fullness of a sail, it may be discovered on taking everything apart that there is little edge curve to reduce.

Do not overlook the fact that a sail's camber can depend heavily on the curvature of the wire or spar on which it is set. If a stay sags excessively, or a spar is not bent enough, the sail will be fuller. You could recut the sail to compensate, and perhaps that is necessary, but the problem may be resolved by adjusting stay tension or spar bend.

How much should you reduce an edge curve? You could calculate this photographically or visually by estimating the camber of the sail in relation to its chord length when full and drawing. If the present round results in too much fullness, it can then be deduced how much less would yield the desired camber. Alternatively, given the chord lengths and quarter points, you can estimate what

you think the round *should* be for the camber desired (see the section on sail design earlier in this chapter). Last, you can judge intuitively based on how excessively full the sail is in relation to the present edge curve.

To check the present edge curve, all tensioned reinforcement must be removed. The sail is then laid out flat, lying as naturally as possible. If any other edges are tensioned, they must be set up in the spiking out; otherwise, the edge you are working on will be bowed or distorted.

Pin the old curve out fairly, then stretch a string taut to designate the straight-line edge. Thus revealed is the offending lump, or even a lack of hollow in a stay-set sail or one that is set flying. The rest of the procedure is one of drawing, trimming, reinforcing, and finishing the edge as in a new sail. Note that it may not be worthwhile going to great lengths to reinstall a seafarer's construction, though if the sail doesn't merit a quality reconstruction, it probably wasn't worth the time and energy of a recut in the first place.

Making a Sail Fuller Camber cannot be increased without shortening edge measurements in some way (unless, in the case of a cotton sail, you resort to the expedient of loading the horizontally strung-out sail full of wet sand!). Widening broadseams will shorten the edge of a sail unless extra cloth is added, and redrawing and recutting edge curves for increased round will likewise shorten the straight-line edge.

As I pointed out in the above section on flattening a sail, do check to see that the overly flat set of the sail is not a rig or sail-handling problem. Excessive sail-flattening spar bend or stay tension can be reduced. Outhaul tensions can be eased. It is possible that the flatness of a sail is a construction fault in that the hand roping is slack, the taping is of insufficient tension, or the luff rope or wire is too long. This fault will be revealed by excessive bias elongation and a pocket along the edge of the sail. In this event, the edge reinforcement can be removed and reset for proper balance.

Much labor can be saved, when only a moderate increase in camber is required, by increas–ing the width of broadseams at the freestanding edges of the sail, leech or foot—or at least, on those edges with minimal reinforcement to remove and replace. Foot seams can be broadened, and foot tapers or darts can be added.

WIDENING LEECH SEAMS OF A CROSSCUT OR MITER-CUT SAIL.   The taper begins at the draft position, then gradually widens aft. It must be quite flat, if not straight, since you are not only building camber but also creating the shape of the exit. Depending on how much of the sail needs renovation, the emphasis may be on tapers in one location or evenly distributed along the whole leech. Any seam adjustment will require later redrawing of the edge curve. Seams can be adjusted anywhere, and darts cut or folded as necessary.

EDGE RECUTTING.   Recutting edges to increase camber is a major project. Because there are so many less-arduous alternatives for imparting fullness, it should be a last resort. All reinforcements must be removed and the endpoints moved in, thus reducing sail area. It may be possible to increase the broadseaming somewhat along that edge at the same time, thus creating some fullness with less need to rely upon edge curve change and consequent loss of sail area.

Shortening a Sail Edge

Shortening an edge of a sail, either to adapt a pre-owned sail or because your sail is too long for spar or stay, can be either quick or almost as time-consuming as building a new sail. An alteration will be more or less complicated depending on which edge of a sail you are working. Some sail area will inevitably be lost, but this may be partly your intention.

The four major considerations are:

1. The angle at which the cloths will strike the recut edge, and the resulting effect on bias elongation and sail shape along that edge.

2. The correlation between the unrecut sail's shape and broadseaming and the recut sail's new dimensions. Adjustments in broadseaming may be necessary.
3. The removal and replacement of edge and corner reinforcements and hardware.
4. Redrawing and cutting new edge covers.

Each of the above considerations has been discussed in the process of building a new sail or altering sail camber, so you have the information you need to do the work. But the attempt may not be advisable if the work is too extensive. Remember, when you change one edge of a sail, you alter at least one other edge in the process.

Adding a Clew Slide to a Sail

Frequently, on production sails having an internal boltrope that slides in a slotted spar, there is no reinforcement at the corners of great stress—the clew in particular. All the strain not absorbed by the outhaul, and all the chafe, fall on two layers of tape between the boltrope and sail. It's a weak point that could be strengthened by a good lashing through the clew ring and around the boom, or alternatively, by the installation of a clew slide. The latter is a simple conversion—many types of slides are available, from light plastic to massive stainless steel. The slide must be strong enough and of correct size to slide smoothly in a slot, and it must be attached in alignment with the boltrope.

Procedure

1. Cross-stitch through the bolt rope to prevent its tension from going slack.
2. Merely hotknife or cut away sufficient area below the clew ring to fit the slide.
3. Oversew the cut portions by hand.
4. With nylon webbing, seize the slide to the clew ring.

Other corners of various sails could use the same treatment—the peak on a slotted gaff; the head of a Bermudan main on a slotted mast; even,

RECUTS AND SHORTCUTS

Q: A year ago I bought a Ranger 23 with a full inventory of headsails but only one main. A local sailmaker informed me that a second main with two reefs would cost $950, so I looked around for a second-hand mainsail and bought one from a larger boat for $10 at a yard sale. Using the Ranger main as a template, I cut 25 inches off the foot of the larger sail, folded the new edge over a few times, and stitched it by hand. I left the original boltrope in the fold; it took me about eight hours. Then I cut about 7 inches off the leech end of the foot and faired it in with the curve of the leech so the foot would not be too long for the boom.

I have never done any sailwork before, but to my surprise, when I set sail, the sail fit like a glove! I know this was an unorthodox way to recut a sail, but it seemed to entail the least work. What is the proper way; how would a sailmaker do it?

A: Congratulations! You're a successful graduate of the self-taught quick-and-dirty school of sail alteration. For your work to have turned out so well you must have taken care to spike out the sail with sufficient tension on the edges so that it lay relatively flat and undistorted. You also must have done a careful job with the fairing of the leech and the cutting of the foot. Any problems in the end product would likely have been in the leech, due to an asymmetrical distribution of roach curve and batten support and a diagonal strain on the bias of the cloth.

A sail loft would first study the feasibility of utilizing the camber built into the old sail. Cutting a smaller sail out of a larger one of molded shape changes both the amount and location of draft unless the recut sail is retailored.

Every effort would be made to have the cloths run perpendicularly to the straight-line leech, thus keeping the strain parallel to the fill threads of the fabric. With that in mind, the route in your case would have been to cut a new leech from new head to new clew, shortening the luff and foot sufficiently to fit the spars. The procedure would be much like that for removing batten pockets as described in the accompanying text. The foot or luff might have to be cut a little shorter than would otherwise be desired in order to keep the cloth panels perpendicular to the leech. The loft would then rebuild the head, clew, and reef clews, install batten pockets and leech cord, and sew up the leech. It would be a major job requiring at least as many hours as your courageous effort (if done well) and costing a lot more than $10!

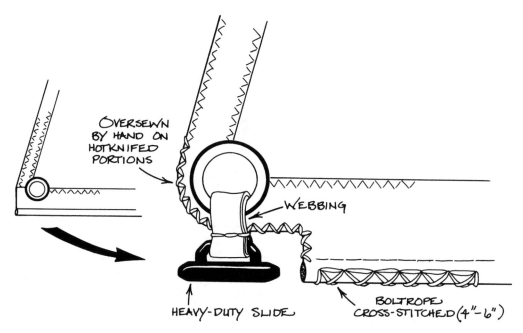

FIGURE 6-92. *The internal boltrope and edge tape are weak points in a sail bent to a slotted spar. A clew lashing would help take the strain. Alternatively, a heavy-duty slug slide seized to the clew ring will add much chafe-free reinforcement.*

if slides small enough can be found, the tack and head of roller-furling sails in slotted systems.

Removing Batten Pockets, or Dumping the Hump

What part of a sail do sailmakers and sailors find themselves repairing most frequently? Batten pockets! Does the mere mention of the word give you the cold collywobbles? Bluewater sailors, coastal cruisers, racers, and daysailors all have the same complaint: Battens are eating up their sails! Battens cause other problems too. They break and tear the sail. They fly out of the pocket and are lost overboard. They catch under spreaders and lazy-jacks. What are those sticks doing in the sail in the first place? Do they have to be there? Why?

Battens are splints of a sort that support the roach—the hump or convex curve outside the straight-line leech from peak to clew. This hump, in a typically jibheaded mainsail or mizzen, for exam-

ple, is also supported by a headboard at the top of the sail. Headboards also cause problems. They corrode, and their sharp edges can cut through the sail.

Battens and headboards are there primarily to permit greater sail area. More sail area hopefully means more speed. An adjustable leech form and sail afterbody are advisable for the most efficient sailing. Do you have to have the battens in? Take them out and see. A speed hump, unsupported, pops and snaps like a flag, resulting in worse damage than the battens cause and providing no extra speed. Does the roach requiring the battens and headboard have to be there? If you are a competitive sailor or want maximum sailing performance, yes; otherwise, no.

For the sailor whose primary concerns are safety, durability, and economy in a well-found sail, the leech can be cut straight or even with a certain amount of hollow or concave curve, thus eliminating the need for battens and headboard.

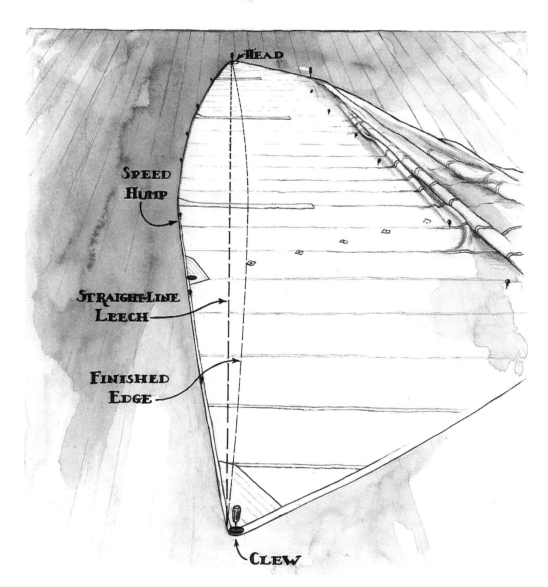

HEAD

SPEED HUMP

STRAIGHT-LINE LEECH

FINISHED EDGE

CLEW

FIGURE 6-93. *Once you dump the hump, you'll wonder why you put up with those battens as long as you did. Lay out the leech as naturally as possible so that the hollow cut into the leech remains a fair curve. With any luck you can reuse cloth, leech cord, and even rings, so that little in the way of materials need be purchased.*

If you are about to get a new sail, hallelujah! Simply make it clear that you want no roach. But legion are the sailors who possess what otherwise would be a seaworthy sail were it not for that troublesome speed hump. In that case, it's time to dump the hump! A professionally executed roachectomy can be quite costly; the larger the sail and the more reef clews to be relocated, the greater the expense. Any patient and determined person can recut a leech. You don't even have to have a sewing machine or a space big enough to spread out the whole sail.

Is a meticulous roachectomy always appropriate? Not always. If you find that the specifications for nonbattened leech construction outlined below differ from the construction of the rest of your sail (which is probable, since anyone building a sail with these seafaring techniques presumably wouldn't have put in battens and headboard in the first place), it would be prudent to decide whether you'd be merely putting a strong link in a weak chain. If so, refinishing most of the sail is in order; or else buying or making a new sail altogether would make better use of your resources. Occasionally, however, overall sail condition; lack of space, time, or materials; and batten loss can conspire to warrant a quick-and-dirty job.

Tools and Supplies for the Roachectomy

Floor space long enough to lay out the entire leech and wide enough to lay out the after third of the sail is essential. A clean, wooden-floored, well-lighted space is preferable.

Tools: #2 pencil, seam ripper, heavy scissors, electric hotknife (optional), stapler, sailmaker's palm and sail needles, bench hook, fids, knife, sewing machine capable of sewing multiple layers of your sail's cloth (optional), a length of twine longer than the leech, a length of ¾-inch nylon webbing or a flexible batten longer than the leech, eight scratch awls, and pushpins.

Materials: Sailcloth of the same weight, construction, and finish as the sail (enough to make

new corner patches if the cut-off material is insufficient), sewing machine thread the same as the sail's (if sewing by machine), sail twine, leech cord, brass rings and liners, leather, wax, sail tape of the same cloth weight as the sail and half as wide as the luff tabling (optional), and nylon webbing.

Preparation   Before laying out the sail, with a seam ripper, knife, and scissors, unpick the head and clew reinforcements (rope, tape, webbing). Lift the old reef clew patches, if reusable, and open up the tabling. A leech tape can possibly be salvaged. Taping the recut leech (even if some other type of tabling was formerly used) saves the time of folding and fairing in a new rolled tabling at head and clew, covers seam ends on a crosscut sail, and avoids a tight leech.

Remove battens and hardware and lift the portions of the batten pockets that will overlap the new leech. You may want to leave the head and clew as they are, either because they are perfectly sound or because the corner rings have been permanently pressed in.

Procedure

1. Spike and pin out the after third of the sail so that it lies smoothly and naturally. This may require putting some tension on the foot and head.
2. Find the endpoints of the new leech curve. In locating these points there are three interdependent major considerations: cloth direction, leech-curve fairness, and corner-ring size and position. The straight line between the two points should best parallel the weave of the sailcloth, and every effort should be made to fair the new leech into the head and clew. This will be influenced by the size of the corner rings, which should be at least as big as the old reef clew rings. Difficulties may arise in what was formerly a headboard area, particularly in a low-aspect sail. An oversized ring can be installed to fill some of the extra area at the head and permit

the best alignment of the leech. If necessary, the sail's edges can be shortened.

3. Place spikes at the endpoints and stretch twine taut between the two. This will be a reference in judging the fairness and shape of the leech curve.

4. At a point 45 percent or so of the leech length up from the clew, measure in from the straight line a distance of 1 inch for every 6 feet of straight-line leech, and mark.

5. With webbing or batten, set out a fair curve between the endpoints and through the maximum depth mark. With the spikes at the endpoints of the finished edge, it is a matter of preference whether you place the batten or webbing on one side of the spikes or the other. On the inside, it is easier to compare the curve with the twine. On the outside, a batten can be used for drawing the fold line of a rolled tabling.

6. Draw the finished edge and, if making a rolled tabling, the fold and cut lines. Make the new tabling at least as wide as the old.

7. Now, take a deep breath, relax, and whack that hump right off! Or rather, carefully cut along the finished edge for a tape, or cut on the outermost cut edge for a rolled tabling.

8. Fold new tabling or tape. Make new corner patches if necessary—five or six layers per corner for seafaring purposes, with the cloth direction paralleling the adjacent sailcloth.

9. Locate, staple, and sew the patches layered as described earlier in this chapter with one row of stitching per patch. Hem under the inner edges of the cover patches.

10. Trim corner patches and sew tabling or tape in anticipation of redrawing and refolding the tabling. A leech cord is installed at this time. Nylon webbing is an effective means of strengthening a corner patch and providing strong reinforcement for the entrance and exit of the cord without excessive chafe to the cord. It is necessary to reeve off the leech cord at the clews after having sewn down the outer finished edge but before sewing the inner row

of tabling stitching. Use a large sail needle for reeving. If a wider and stronger additional reinforcement tape is to be used, it should be made up in advance with the webbing sewn to it in the correct location and the cord rove off.

Finishwork   Sew in corner rings with reef clews located above the straight line of the reef eyelets, for strain. Obtain liner setting dies or have liners set in a sail loft. Anchor the upper end of the leech cord with hand stitches. Rerope the clew and head if the sail was roped. Hand sew leather chafe protection at each corner.

Postoperative Observations   Bend and raise sail. How does the leech set? What does it do when the wind comes on to blow, and on different points of sail? Try adjusting various sail-edge tensions. What happens to the leech? How does the boat sail? Any change in the helm?

You may have succeeded in cutting a fair and flat leech, maybe not. Are you getting depressed because tweaking and vanging don't relieve postoperative leechaches? Maybe some additional snips and tucks in the leech, as described elsewhere in this chapter, will help.

There are consistent aspects of sail construction, and to some extent what I've given you here is recipelike. However, in many ways, no two sails being the same, this is an adventure requiring creative thinking and resourcefulness. What you have here are general guidelines. You'll be making many decisions, comparisons, and analyses yourself. Follow through with this self-reliant, seafarerlike approach by saving the remaining pieces of the hump for future repairs. Inevitably, your sail will need some patching. But one thing's for sure, you'll never have to repair the batten pockets!

Foot Surgery

It is always painful to behold the set of an otherwise shapely headsail ruined because the foot and tack are scrunched by the bow pulpit and lifelines. If the tack height of such a sail cannot be raised to

LEECH FLUTTERS

Q: *I recently built a small Dacron spritsail for my Whitehall skiff. I cut the leech with an inch or so of roach and now it flutters noticeably. What can be done to correct this?*

A: First check for balanced sprit and luff tension. Excessive luff tension pulls camber forward, causing slackness in the leech. Lack of snotter tension causes an obvious girt from throat to clew. Try some adjustments while moving the sheet lead forward, thus putting more sheet tension on the after edge of the sail.

If there's no improvement and you have a crosscut sail (panels running perpendicular to the leech), you may tighten a couple of seams by overlapping the panels an additional ⅛ inch or so at the leech in the area of flutter. A light leechline rove off within the leech tabling, secured at the head, and exiting the clew permits tensioning, which can reduce flutter. But overtensioning a leechline is a poor substitute for proper sheet lead, sail trim, and rig adjustment.

To eliminate the problem altogether, recut the leech straight or with a ¾- to 1-inch hollow. Locate the deepest point of the hollow about 45 percent of the leech length up from the clew.

relieve this sail-eating situation, the foot can be recut in a relatively simple podiatric operation.

First of all, determine how much higher the tack must be in order for a foot with 3-percent roach to clear the pulpit and lifelines. The simplest foot surgery only requires removing a wedge of sail between the old clew and the new tack; but if the sail is terribly low clewed to begin with, it may be desirable or even necessary to whack off both the clew and the tack in order to get a functional and aesthetically pleasing height of clew to match the new tack height. The preparation, tools, and materials for foot surgery of this type are similar to those for leech surgery.

Preparation Before laying out the sail for drawing and cutting the new foot, it will be necessary to release any tension in the luff rope or luff wire. If the luff is only reinforced with luff tape, you may proceed directly to the next step; otherwise, the anchor sewing or seizing of the luff rope or wire must be removed and, in the case of a luff rope shorter than the luff of the sail, any thimble in the tack end must also be removed.

Now, if you are making a simple wedge-shaped recut, unpick and remove any reinforcement on the foot side of the clew, and open up the foot tabling for a good 6 feet or so. At this time the foot cord, if any, can be extracted from the old tabling. Note how it was installed, as that is a model for how you will reassemble the foot and

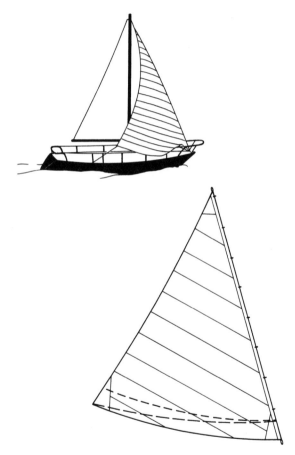

FIGURE 6-94. *How many times out on the water do you see a low-clewed, low-tacked genoa suffering the chafe of bow pulpit and lifelines? If the sail can't be tacked any higher, a foot recut can save its life. Much reuse of materials is possible. The most complicated aspect of this foot surgery is resetting the luff, but this is the same process as in a new sail. The lowest hank may need to be moved.*

foot cord. If you will be doing a complete foot recut, none of this unpicking and foot-cord extraction is necessary except to study the construction and reuse of materials.

Layout and Cutting Spike and pin out the sail. Preferably you have room enough to spread the whole sail; if not, at least the lower third should be flat, the cloth evenly tensioned, and all tension in the luff removed.

The new foot curve for either form of recut is now drawn. Quite likely the curve will be fair and evenly distributed either side of its maximum round at the midpoint. Furthermore, it will not be a roach of great depth. (In the wedge cut there wouldn't be cloth enough, and in both cuts it is necessary to limit the size of the roach so as not to have to monkey with foot tapers for support.) Keep the round less than 3 percent of the straight-line foot length.

Fairing the foot curve into the clew in the wedge cut is a little tricky because of all the creases in the old tabling, and, since the clew ring is still there, the curve cannot be faired into the actual vertex of foot and leech. The clew patches will have to be trimmed back to accommodate the new foot curve. Most likely you will be installing a rolled tabling, but a foot could also have a cut tabling or merely be taped. In any case, the fold, finish, and cut lines for the desired tabling are all drawn with batten and compass.

Reassembly The new tabling is folded and rubbed down after the curve has been cut. In the full foot cut, new clew and tack corner patches must be cut and installed—probably five to six layers in the clew and four to five layers in the tack. (It is possible, but unlikely, that the recut has left enough of the old corner patches to make this unnecessary.) For the wedge cut you will probably have to rebuild the tack completely. Hopefully the old tack patches are salvageable, or there might be enough usable cloth from a roachectomy.

You will notice that the luff tape is in the way of all this tack reconstruction. It must be struck up with sew-to marks for later reinstallation and then removed to at least 6 inches above where the new tack patches will end so that the patches and foot tabling can be installed. We have a little problem, too, with the leech cord, which, if the old clew is removed, must be extracted from the lower leech tabling and later rerove through the tabling and leech-cord exit of the new, rebuilt clew. Be careful not to accidentally snip off the leech cord when cutting the new foot curve!

All this leech- and foot-cord installation, exiting, anchoring, and belaying is discussed earlier in this chapter. Sew the new foot tabling and lower leech tabling, if necessary, while installing the foot cord and leech cord of the full foot recut. Now, all that remains prior to finishwork is to replace the luff tape to its original sew-to lines and marks.

Finishwork *At the clew:* For the full foot recut, it is now necessary to install reinforcements, corner hardware, chafing gear, leech-cord belaying system, and foot-cord anchor as if it were a new sail. For the wedge cut, one has only to replace reinforcements and chafing gear and anchor the foot cord.

At the tack: Both types of foot recut are now in the same boat—reinforcement, corner hardware, and foot-cord belaying system are installed as though for a new sail. Taped luffs are now home free except for trimming the corner and sewing on some leather for chafe protection, but everyone with a luff rope or wire is in for it. (I know I said this foot-surgery business was a simple operation, but if I'd let on in the beginning that maybe you were in for some hard sledding, you might never have begun this worthy sail-saving project!)

As in a new sail, the tensioned relationship between the sail and the wire or rope must be reestablished. This will entail stretching the luff of the sail and the wire or rope to their respective tensions in relation to one another and according to the halyard power on the boat, as discussed earlier in the chapter. An eye with the tack thimble can be seized or spliced into the rope or wire; then the thimble is seized to the corner ring, or the rope, sans eye, is merely stitched through the sail. The whole is then leathered over.

Depending on the new tack height and old hank spacing, it may be necessary to work a tack eyelet and seize a hank to it. Some sort of tack pendant will now be required. I suggest splicing on a rope pendant with a snap shackle. The snap shackle can be spliced on or the pendant left adjustable with a rolling hitch.

If after careful consideration you find this project too daunting or deem the sail unworthy of the time and effort—or you actually *like* having the extra sail area—sail life can be prolonged by installing chafing gear on the lifelines and a special form of chafe patch, called a *pulpit patch*, on the sail, the procedure for which is presented in Chapter 8, "Sail Care and Maintenance."

Many sodtrodders use phrases that actually have their origin in sailing and the sea. From the above sail-recutting operation we obviously get "to start out on a new (or the right) foot" as well as the commonly heard "to set off on a new tack." So there you are: off on a new foot and tack, out on the water. The most likely flaw to arise in the set of the new foot is flutter and sagging to leeward. First check that the sheeting angle is correct, then try a little foot-cord tension. If it takes scrunching up the foot of the sail like the mouth of a laundry bag to stop the flutter, you could leave it, or you could head back to the operating theater, where, hopefully, some adjustment of already existing foot tapers will provide the necessary support. In a vertical- or miter-cut sail, some of the seams can be broadened as described earlier in this chapter. As a last recourse, the foot curve can be recut with less round.

7

Sail Fittings: "Hardware" and "Software"

I N A CHAFE CONTEST between cloth and metal hardware, or between cloth and wood, the cloth always loses. Aside from sun deterioration and abuse, sails are most prone to die young from the ravages of hardware. The hardware is of three sorts: (1) that which is part of the sail—battens, for example; (2) that which is used as a means of attachment to the rig and is united with the sail—hanks, for example; and (3) that which is part of the running or standing rigging and is attached to the sail from without—say snapshackles or reefing hooks.

One could have a sail and rig with absolutely no metallic hardware if one chose, but generally hardware increases the strength, efficiency, and durability of a sail if used judiciously and appropriately. This is not rampant purist traditionalism—it's common sense. If the components of a sail are of compatible materials, they will work and age together rather than compete or self-destruct. Thus, if metal fittings must be attached to a sail, it makes sense to couple them with compatible and complementary metal fittings in the sail. But an even better solution is to isolate metal fittings from a sail with soft seizings; then the sail and the fitting will endure, and the seizing can be replaced.

So to balance strength and chafe resistance and maximize sail life and economy, a sailor makes use of hardware and sacrificial but strong software.

What follows are some common examples of the hardware that causes sail destruction, along with suggestions for substituting or adding software or less-destructive hardware to create a seaworthy, seafaring sail, means of attachment, and rig.

The notion of software flies in the face of contemporary sail gear, with its emphasis on high cost, speed of installation, and maintaining fixed sail shapes and rigid foils. But software can introduce great flexibility and elasticity, increasing shock absorption and adaptability. Moreover, given the incredible stability of synthetic fibers, use of software can be made with little sacrifice in sail performance. The goal is a cohesive ensemble of sail and rig working together.

Fittings Within Sails

- *Rings and eyelets:* All-metal rings and eyelets are compatible with firm, thick fabrics but not with voyaging materials or materials of much elasticity. Furthermore, they corrode. The traditional, softest, and most flexible alternative is rope grommets, used as eyelets or as anchor holes for cringles and round thimbles (see Figure 6-58). After that, there are hand-stitched eyelets (brass or stainless steel rings), which combine rigidity with elasticity and ease of replacement.

- *Thimbles:* Placing heart- or teardrop-shaped thimbles at the ends of luff ropes is sound practice, but the open ears at the throat of the split thimbles typically used in moorings chafe the seizing between the thimble and the sail corner ring. These thimbles can be pinched shut, the ears spread to accommodate the splice, and the throat leathered to minimize seizing chafe. The best alternative, though, is a cast, solid, heart-shaped thimble of bronze or stainless steel, filed smooth as necessary so as not to chafe the seizing.

- *Wire rope:* There was a time when wire rope was the only sort of luff reinforcement that could withstand the enormous strain of halyard winches without stretching inordinately. Then, there was no choice but to endure the corrosion, weight, ungainliness, and labor-intensiveness of wire luff ropes. Now, with few exceptions, a sail's strength, longevity, ease of handling, and versatility are best served by synthetic double-braid low-stretch luff ropes of polyester or Kevlar. I daresay even natural-fiber sails could utilize such ropes, though little experimentation has been done.

- *Wire seizings:* Stainless steel seizing wire might be used to retain slides, seize a luff-rope thimble to a corner ring, or affix a round thimble to anchor holes, among other things. These techniques are strong but cause much chafe, and it is difficult to lay up the turns of wire so the strain is evenly distributed. Moreover, there is no give, elasticity, or shock absorption. Alternatively, slides and thimbles can be seized with twine or webbing (see page 342), while round thimbles can be stuck with

cringles or even seized with heavy leech cord.

- *Headboards and clewboards:* Of necessity, these are hard and inflexible. They have to be to support the area they do. The alternatives are not to have them at all or to minimize the problems with certain variations. One option is to incorporate a large handsewn ring or a cringle and round thimble in place of a headboard in a Bermudan sail. I doubt that the clewboard in a go-fast sail is ever likely to be eliminated, as such equipment is generally part of a complete sail/rig package of compatible, go-fast orientation. It would be pointless to make the sail last longer than the rest of the boat. Internal headboards are easier on a sail than external sandwich-type headboards, but beveling and smoothing the edges of the latter will somewhat reduce wear. In either case, using webbing instead of shackles to seize slides will eliminate one source of chafe to the headboard.

  It is possible to revert to the days of yore by installing a wooden headboard. How strange it would look on a Dacron sail! But it can be strong, light, noncorrosive, and fairly kind to the sail.

- *Battens:* The chafe of battens, like that of headboards, can only be slowed, not eliminated, unless battens are dispensed with altogether, which entails recutting the leech of the sail (see page 364). There is no software alternative; one can only render battens less destructive with smoothing, beveling, and plastic endcaps. Simultaneously, the sail can be fortified with extra cloth, webbing, pads, and, in the case of full-length battens, plastic end protectors and sockets (which themselves have sharp, abrupt edges).

Fittings Seized to Sails

- *Hanks:* These are discussed on page 173. Jib hanks of the type crimped onto a sail, or any hanks in which metal or plastic is in constant contact with the sail, are extremely destructive. Plastic or leather chafing gear in way of these hanks is but brief postponement of the inevitable. The only durable alternative is to hand seize hanks with twine in a strong, consistent manner, which isolates the metal from the sail (see page 341).

- *Slides:* Plastic, metal, or composite sail slides don't in themselves cause much harm to a sail, unless they come in direct contact. It is the use of shackles to attach the slides to a sail that destroys both sail and slide. Seizing slides with webbing or twine completely eliminates this problem. In

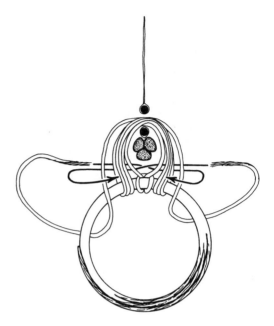

After repeated turns around the hoop and through the luff eyelet, cinch with crossing turns between sail and hoop.

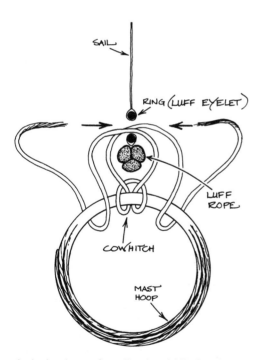

A single piece of marline is middled and cowhitched to the hoop. Then the ends are passed in opposite directions through the luff eyelet.

FIGURE 7-1. *Seizing a mast hoop.*

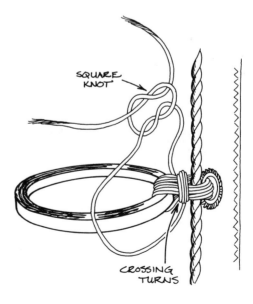

Finish the crossing turns with a square knot. The finished seizing isolates the hoop from the sail.

addition, the sail is quieter in stays, and there is some shock absorption.

- *Mast hoops:* Like slides, they don't harm a sail unless there is direct contact, which there generally is, unless the method of seizing separates hoop from slide. Alternatively, there are cast-bronze two-part fasteners available for small mast hoops. The female part is mounted on the wooden mast

hoop, and the male part is seized to the sail with twine. It is a common feature on Beetle Cats with mast hoops and greatly facilitates the bending and unbending of sail.

- *D-rings, cringles, and rings attached with webbing:* While handsewn corner rings do not directly cause chafe or reduce sail life, their use in the sail may bring secondary impacts. For example, even if only line

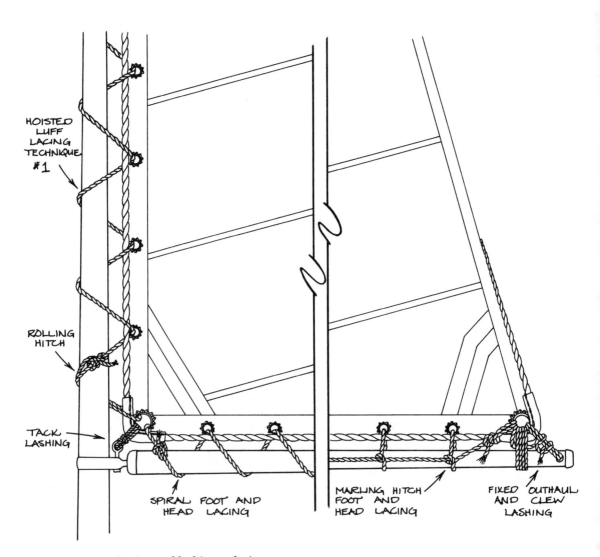

FIGURE 7-2. *Lacing and lashing techniques.*

passes through it, there is much chafe on the loaded side of a handsewn ring. Leather is a deterrent but doesn't last long, especially against metal shackles, pins, or hooks. Here we find the virtues of cringles and round thimbles, D-rings, and rings attached with webbing. They are easy to install, strong, and require no special tools, and they are outside the sail, offering the compatibility of metal to metal if such hardware is to be attached to the sail (see page 171 and Figure 6-58).

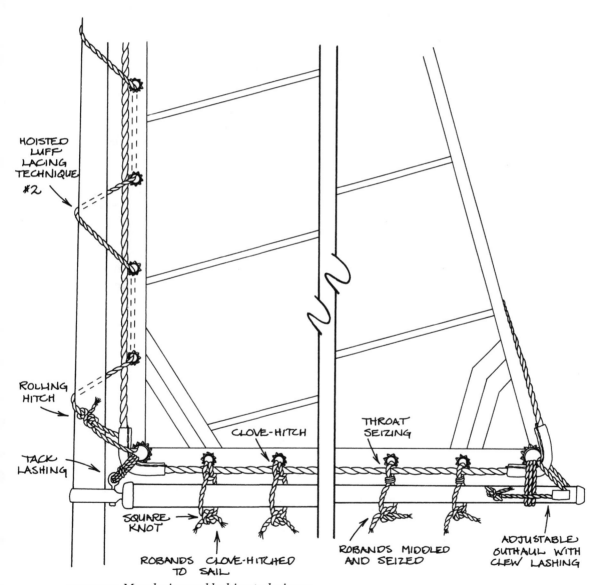

HOISTED
LUFF
LACING
TECHNIQUE
#2

ROLLING
HITCH

TACK
LASHING

CLOVE-HITCH

THROAT
SEIZING

SQUARE
KNOT

ROBANDS CLOVE-HITCHED
TO SAIL

ROBANDS MIDDLED
AND SEIZED

ADJUSTABLE
OUTHAUL WITH
CLEW LASHING

FIGURE 7-3. *More lacing and lashing techniques.*

Rigging Fittings

- *Outhaul cars and tack fittings:* These wreak havoc, particularly on sails with clew and tack rings. D-rings and round thimbles provide a means of separating a sail from rig fittings, if correct alignment can be maintained so that the clew, tack, and sail edge of a fixed-footed sail are all equidistant from the boom. The software alternative to this hardware is lashings of line. A tack or throat lashing is a fixed thing, whereas a clew lashing or gaff (or yard) peak lashing is often adjustable. A lashing can be in two parts—one around the spar, which takes the strain, and an outhaul for tension adjustment—or, where frequent adjustment is not required, the outhaul and lower lashing can be combined. It is important that the lashings maintain alignment of the sail edge.

- *Slotted spars:* These are fast and convenient in several ways, and they do make for very simple sailmaking (no eyelets, no slides, etc.), but sometimes their attendant chafe, grime, and awkwardness of reefing and furling are overridingly undesirable. To alleviate these problems, the sail can be made with or converted to eyelets and slug slides (seized with twine or webbing). The slides must run smoothly in the spar slot, and the bail of the slide must protrude far enough from the spar to permit three layers of webbing in the seizing. A conversion may require some extension or adjustment of end fittings on spar or sail to maintain sail edge alignment.

There is great economy, strength, and versatility in bending sail with robands, parrels, and/or lacing. There are many forms; see Figures 6-86 (for robands), 7-2, and 7-3 for a few ideas. While seldom seen on production boats, these techniques might be considered for a new boat, a refitting, or an emergency repair. Naturally, lacing of a hoisted luff will only serve on an unobstructed spar.

Other hardware sources of harm to a sail, such as spreader-end, pulpit, lifeline, and shroud chafe, are best alleviated by a change of sail configuration or position. The next best option is to simultaneously protect the sail with chafe patches while rendering the offending hardware less abrasive by means of a generous application of baggywrinkle or lamb's wool, tennis balls, or some store-bought antichafe system.

8

Sail Care and Maintenance

NATURAL-FIBER SAILS, as modern sailors are so quick to point out, are prone to rot. Numerous methods were developed in the past to protect and prolong the lives of cotton and flax sails, the vulnerability of which was well recognized. But with the age of synthetic sailcloths has come the erroneous notion that these fabrics are invulnerable and virtually maintenance-free. Not so. Sails, natural-fiber or synthetic, represent a sizable portion of the investment in any sailing vessel. Even throwaway production sails are costly items. It makes sense then, in many ways, to prolong the life of a sail by a regimen of care, maintenance, and storage.

Much of the harm that comes to sails is the result of abuse or neglect while underway. Sail life can be significantly prolonged by judicious use and adjustment of sails at sea. Flutter, slatting, slamming, flogging, and chafe must be minimized, if not eliminated. Abuse and neglect aside, a well-set sail lasts longer.

PREVENTIVE MAINTENANCE

It could easily have been a sailmaker who first coined the phrase, "A stitch in time saves nine," and an ounce of prevention is certainly worth a pound of cure when it comes to sail care. Stitching, both hand- and machine-sewn, is all that holds the pieces of a sail together. The failure of a weak or worn spot can cause vast lengths of otherwise sound stitching to let go in succession. Conduct a survey of your sails as described in Chapter 10.

In regard to stitching, check in particular the areas noted in Table 10-1. Stitching fatigues with strain, sunlight, chafe, age, and, in the case of cotton, rot. It is a good idea to resew the stitching at all visibly weak spots immediately, and throughout the sail at about its midlife. Repeated restitching in the same location weakens the sail; thus, new stitching should be shifted slightly to avail the thread of fresh cloth in which to take hold. A hand-sewn boltrope frequently needs restitching in isolated locations and eventually along its entire length. If the boltrope is sound, it is easier to resew while the rope is in place than to wait until it has come so adrift you essentially have a whole roping job to do.

The biggest problem in restitching handsewn rings is the removal of the old liner, which can be done, I find, with a marlinspike. Usually the same stitching holes can be reused. If not, the next size larger ring can be worked instead. If you see the loaded side of a ring giving way, reinforce the area with webbing or anchor holes and seizings, as illustrated in Chapters 5 and 6.

When you inspect a sail's attachment fittings, you should examine not only the hanks, slides, robands, etc., but also the seizing or equivalent that holds the fitting to the sail. Both periodically need replacement, though the hardware of a well-maintained, well-stored, and properly used sail will usually outlast the rest of the sail and can live on in yet another one.

Chafe in certain areas of a sail is inevitable, requiring chafing gear either on the sail or on the rig. These protections, if they do their job, need to be renewed periodically. On the sail, there is the leather chafing gear sewed to all corners and in way of jackline hanks. In addition, there are sacrificial cloth patches and bands that protect the sail from pulpits, spreader ends, lines, battens, and hanks. Chapter 7 offers alternatives to destructive sail hardware such as squeeze-on hanks and shackles. If you persist in using such items, you will have heaps of maintenance to do.

Installing a Spreader or Pulpit Patch

Ideally, installing spreader or pulpit patches is a type of *preventive* maintenance, but all too often one does not figure out that chafe protection is necessary until considerable harm has already come to the sail. Nonetheless, the sail can be repaired and then chafe-protection measures taken. At least in this catch-up method, it is clear which area of the sail needs protection. Spreader and pulpit patches are not repairs in themselves; they are sacrificial chafing gear added to the sail. Even if you've applied chafing gear to the spreader ends, lifelines, and pulpit, and even if you've changed your headsail's tack height, pulpit and/or spreader patches on the headsail may still be necessary.

If the sail is fairly new, there is really no accurate substitute for setting the sail and marking the locations of spreader and pulpit or lifeline chafe on the sail. Don't skimp. It is better to cover too much of the sail than too little. Moreover, if the sail is to be tacked at various heights in order to adjust

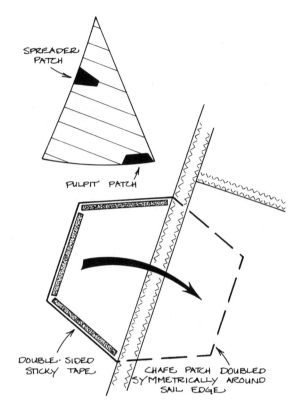

FIGURE 8-1. *Spreader and pulpit patches.*

sheeting angle, there will be more than one spreader-patch location—which may be covered by one large patch or multiple smaller ones.

Basically, applying this type of chafe patch is very similar to working a repair patch. At the same time, it is completely different because nothing is removed from the sail, and the patch—which is one piece—is folded in half, doubled around the leech or foot of the sail, and sewn to both sides of the sail. This way chafe protection is afforded to both sides and the very edge of the sail.

Procedure

1. Pin the area of the sail to be patched as evenly and as flat as possible. Measure the area to be covered and determine the form and

measurements of the appropriate-size patch. Don't forget that the patch will be doubled symmetrically around the edge of the sail. Spreader patches often have a triangular, pennantlike profile; pulpit patches are more of a stubby shape. It doesn't really matter what shape the patch is, as long as it covers the chafed area of the sail.

2. Draw and cut out the patch on sailcloth of the same material, weight, finish, and cloth direction as that of the sail. There is some leeway here, but it is important not to add any more weight than necessary to the edge of the sail. If the sailcloth is synthetic, the patch can be cut out with a hotknife, or cut and the edges sealed with a flame. Otherwise, the patch can be hemmed—so allow for a ½-inch hem all the way around in the drawing and cutting.

3. Fold all hems, if any, and apply double-sided sticky tape all the way around the perimeter of the inside of the patch. Fold the patch in half as it will be when applied to the sail.

4. Slide the folded patch over and under the edge of the sail in the correct location, and pin it in place.

5. Remove the backing of the sticky tape on that side of the patch and firmly adhere the patch to the sail.

6. Unpin the sail, flip it over, and repin it evenly and smoothly. Refold the patch over the sail and pin it in place exactly opposite its other half on the other side of the sail. Remove the backing on the sticky tape and firmly adhere it to the sail. For added security the patch can be stapled.

7. Sew around the inner perimeter of the patch, taking care not to sew through the leech cord or foot cord. Do not sew along the edge of the sail.

It is certainly possible, though a little more time-consuming and difficult, to apply a chafe patch without sticky tape, in which case sew-to lines and strike-up marks can be used and the patch sewn one side at a time. Alternatively, the patch could be stapled one side at a time and then sewn through all layers, as is done in the sticky-tape method.

Sail Cleaning and Washing

Sounding much like the *The Graduate*'s Mr. Robinson when he said to Benjamin the word of the future—"plastics"—a man who had made a fortune in the rug-cleaning industry once advised me in hushed tones, "sail cleaning!" His theory was that the big money was to be made not in making sails but in keeping them pretty and in good shape. It was to be a year-round service—pickup, cleaning, repair, storage, and delivery. The client need do nothing but sail and sign the check. He envisioned swimming pools used as cleaning vats, fleets of delivery trucks, and franchises.

It was a good idea, and he was right about the money. Many lofts incorporate cleaning into their services; some specialists have even set up operations along the lines of the rug-cleaning tycoon's idea, though I know of no service as comprehensive as he outlined. Those services that are available are costly—currently $1.50 to $2.00 per pound or 25 cents per square foot. To have a sail professionally cleaned is a serious matter. Cleaning a sail, in general, is a serious matter; for sails to last as long as the materials are capable under ordinary use, they must be cleaned and, in particular, rinsed regularly. It is not a matter of looking pretty—it is one of preservation and performance.

Certainly there are chemicals that break down natural and synthetic fibers, but the most consistent source of problems in a poorly maintained sail is salt saturation. This, combined with improper storage, spells the doom of any sail, regardless of the cloth type. Salt corrodes all hardware and fittings, not only destroying the hardware but also weakening the surrounding cloth. Just as important, salt adds weight and is hygroscopic, which in turn adds more weight and invites mildew, the blemisher of Dacron and the death of cotton.

Clearly there is much to be gained from merely rinsing your sails thoroughly with fresh water on a regular basis. Soaking in warm water will dissolve

SAIL CLEANING

Q: *It is time to clean my sails! I heard that it is safe to use a mild soap in a large laundromat washer. Do you agree with this?*

A: DON'T, whatever you do, throw the patient into a washing machine! The result will be a lifeless, weakened bag. I suggest a 24-hour soak in a large tub of fresh water with a mild detergent (e.g., Ivory Flakes, Amway, or Ecover), agitated periodically by hand with a paddle. Then scrub the spots with a moderately soft brush; make sure not to back the sail with anything abrasive, such as concrete. Flush the spot while continuing to scrub in a circular motion. Whatever cleaning agent you use, it is quite important to rinse these spots and the whole sail thoroughly. This method may not work for really recalcitrant grunge, particularly if the stain has had some time to work its way into the cloth fibers, but at least it is inexpensive and you can do no harm to the sail.

most caked salt, and mild scrubbing will remove the rest. Such devotion to salt-free sails will go a long way toward clean-looking sails, especially if the sails are thoroughly air dried and stored in a clean place. When it comes to dirt and stain removal, care must be taken not to harm either the sail or oneself in the process.

Increasing the level of alkalinity in Dacron and acidity in nylon renders both fabrics more vulnerable to their big nemesis, ultraviolet light. Excessive force in scrubbing removes ultraviolet-protective silicones and resins and breaks down stabilizing resin coatings. Here's an undeniable example of this: Take a swatch of sailcloth, crumple

it up awhile, then give it a whirl in a washing machine. No hand cleaning would normally produce such a limp rag but, little by little, that is the effect of violent scrubbing and agitation.

Various sail cleaners are available. A mild household soap and lukewarm water will serve well for all-purpose cleaning. The important thing is to thoroughly rinse the sail afterward in order to remove all traces of pH-altering cleaners. This method is safe for natural and synthetic materials.

There are specific sail-cleaning recipes in Jeremy Howard-Williams's *The Care and Repair of Sails*, which he borrowed from ICI Fibres. Personally, I've had great success with just a gentle soapy washing and occasional bleaching—and a sail would have to be mighty ugly before I'd go splashing around with any polysyllabic chemicals.

Sails are most likely to need bleaching because they've become mildewed—probably the most common stain to a sail, especially in warm climates. Mildew is merely discoloration to a synthetic sail, but marks the return to the earth for natural fibers. Bleach—sodium hypochlorite—lightens or removes mildew stains while serving temporarily as a fungicide. Howard-Williams suggests diluting a domestic bleach such as Clorox in a ratio of 1 part bleach to 10 parts cold water, or ½ cup to ½ gallon.

The mildewed area of the sail is first scrubbed lightly with a stiff brush to remove surface mildew—followed by two or more hours of soaking in the bleach bath. I knew a sail-cleaning company that soaked its synthetic sails for days. Frankly, the extra time didn't seem to make that much difference. Naturally there is a point with cotton where bleaching efforts become more deleterious than the humble but mighty mildew.

Bleaching is not advisable for nylon or colored fabrics, and of course, all sails must be thoroughly rinsed after bleaching.

SAIL STORAGE

It is of the utmost importance that sails be stored dry and salt-free. Moreover, the storage place should be dry, clean, cool, and ventilated. Natural fibers, especially, should be allowed good air circulation. The best care of sails used periodically and stowed on board for short periods is to furl or fold them when they're dry, cover or bag them, and leave them in a ventilated place—possibly on deck or down below. It should be shipboard routine to maintain dryness and protect all sails on board, even the seldom seen stormsails! Imagine the disappointment of going for the storm jib at the onset of a gale, only to find that the hanks have corroded shut!

Ashore, and in long-term storage, sails must be protected from rodents. I was once brought a sail that had been home to rats; it looked as if it had been used for shotgun target practice. In the event

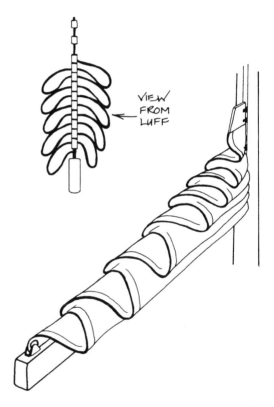

FIGURE 8-2. *Flaking a sail. Flaking a boomed sail is essential when the luff rope runs in a groove in the mast. It is optional with any other means of luff attachment. Flaking is most easily done by two people as the sail is lowered. The person on the leech hauls aft and folds while the person at the luff brings the sail down while folding bights in the sail. If there are slides, the slide is in the center of each fold. One person with six hands and great determination can flake a large sail alone. This is a good technique to use with heavily resinated, stiff fabrics.*

HAVE A BAKE SAIL!

Q: I have two areas of inquiry about the care of new sails:

1. *My Dacron sails are wrapped in a blue "Taylor-Made" tarp and kept in the attic or in the trunk of my car when not in use. The car and the attic get very hot in the summer. How will this prolonged exposure to high heat affect the sails?*
2. *To reduce friction in slotted spars, is it hazardous to a sail to spray the mast and boom with a heavy-duty silicone or something like WD-40? Is there another solution to the problem?*

A: Even the heat in your car's trunk during summer causes a certain degree of shrinkage in *nylon* sailcloth. If the sail has been stored wet, colored nylon will bleed—and bleed more and faster under the influence of heat.

Dacron has a melting point of 500°F and the finish on cloth has been cured at 400°F. Therefore, damage due to hot storage is unlikely. Shrinkage or resin finish deterioration *is* possible, however, in a poor-quality fabric if the processes of heatsetting and finishing have been inadequate.

Unless thoroughly rinsed and dried, a stored sail will undoubtedly contain salt, which attracts moisture and thus results in mildew and corrosion—especially in a warm, dark, unventilated space. In summation: Store nylon sails rinsed, dry, and cool . . . and to be safe, do the same with sails made of Dacron.

In regard to giving those sticky spars a squirt: The lubrication of slotted spars, while doing no physical harm to the sail (maybe to you, though, if you breathe that stuff), will surely stain the cloth and boltrope. A luff or foot rope should be correctly sized to run smoothly in the slot. You might consider having a smaller rope or a Teflon luff tape installed. Alternatively, you could convert the sail to eyelets and slug slides. In addition to easing the hoisting, dropping, and adjusting of the sail, this would have benefits in furling and reefing.

the storage place cannot be rid of rodents, it is wise to suspend the sails in their bags by a single line or wire from the rafters. Good air circulation is simultaneously afforded.

When it comes to the zealous care of sails, I know of no one who has gone to such exacting lengths as a devoted sailor I know in Osterville,

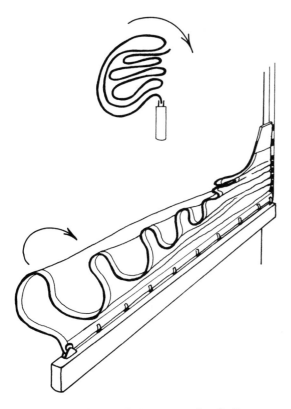

FIGURE 8-3. *Furling techniques. Another furling technique—"skinning the bunt." This works best with soft fabrics. (1) Remove battens. (2) Pull all folds (dog ears) of the luff to one side or the other. (3) Beginning at upper leech, haul leech aft and dump into belly of sail. (4) Continue this process, folding the sail into itself as you would bread dough. (5) When the foot is reached and the sail is gathered in like a tight sausage, roll the bundle on top of the boom and gasket it.*

Massachusetts. To ensure the well-being of his sizable investment in sail and canvas, he has set up within the major portion of his garage a sail locker that includes storage, cleaning, drying, and work facilities. It is a monument of devotion to sail preservation.

It is most unwise to furl and cover a wet cotton sail; the wet furling and covering of even a synthetic sail will result in mildew. Roller-furling sails, of course, are particularly prone to this neglect. At the earliest opportunity, the sails should be aired, without being left to whip about or slam. Part of the success of the sails' storage depends on the manner in which they are furled or folded. Wooden battens should always be removed from their pockets or they will surely warp. Any reefs tied in should be shaken out before a sail is stowed overnight.

How to Fold a Sail

An excellent test of teamwork and cooperation is the task of folding a sail correctly. Done most efficiently, it is a two-person job on any sail larger than a bedsheet. Two people who can fold a sail together can probably successfully engage in any other form of mutual undertaking. It's all a matter of coordination and balance of tension, like any dance, so that each folded panel is flat and of uniform width.

Often sails are folded parallel to the foot, but if the sail has a clew angle greater than 90 degrees this doesn't work. The sail can first be doubled close to the clew, then folded parallel either to the foot or the luff. There is some benefit to the latter method if the hanked headsail is to be transported or agitated after having been folded—the hanks will be on the outside of the folds, not chafing the cloth and stitching on the inside. It is true that folding heavily resinated fabrics will form permanent creases and break down the resin coatings. Such sails are best rolled and stowed in long tubular bags. Using care in folding, one can avoid creasing corner patches permanently. On soft cruising fabrics, there is no concern about creases.

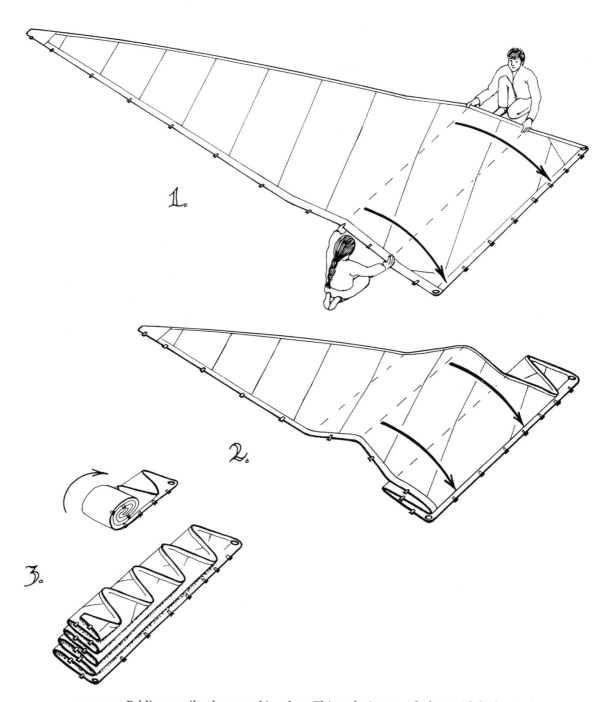

FIGURE 8-4. *Folding a sail to be stowed in a bag. This technique works best with little wind and plenty of room to spread out, and makes an effective prenuptial compatibility test. Fold toward the wind.*

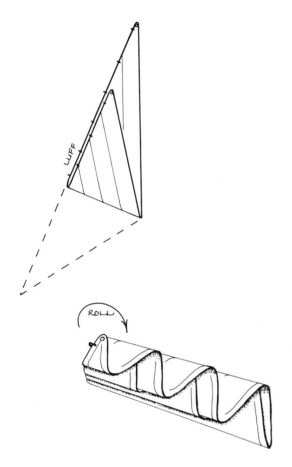

FIGURE 8-5. *Folding a headsail with a large clew angle. First double the sail as shown, then fold and roll as before.*

Sailbags and Sailcovers

The best-quality sailbags and sailcovers are made of treated cotton or acrylic cover cloth. The point of a cover is to contain and protect, and good sailbags and sailcovers are an investment in long sail life. It seems obvious that the single most important aspect of the sailcover is that it cover the whole sail! Frequently one sees a clew or a head peeking out. What use has a healthy bunt with a rotten head and clew? This is a common failing of many of the commercially made stowing and furling systems.

TANBARKING AND THE PRESERVATION OF SAILS

In Chapter 5, I related the tale of how I once dressed down a sail with such a volatile preservative liquor that the sail was confiscated in the middle of the night by the noble men in rubber of the Anacortes, Washington, fire brigade. The innocent cotton lugsail had been thoroughly paid over with a mixture of red canvas paint and turpentine—no wonder they confiscated it! Anyway, it was retrieved and is now, a decade later, still in perfect condition. So, you see, it makes great sense to preserve natural-fiber sails; there are various ways of going about it, some more natural and some more toxic than others.

There is the kind of waxy-feeling, paraffin-and-mineral spirits–based treatment available from the Buckeye Fabric Finishing Company, called Canvac,

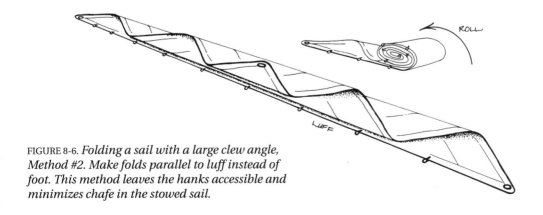

FIGURE 8-6. *Folding a sail with a large clew angle, Method #2. Make folds parallel to luff instead of foot. This method leaves the hanks accessible and minimizes chafe in the stowed sail.*

which is obtainable in colors and has zinc naph-thenate as its antifungal agent. I have used Canvac in its clear form on boat covers and found it to be easy to apply and a significant factor in extending the life of the cover. It does nothing to stiffen the cloth but does add some weight. Who, you might ask, in this world of Hinckleys, Pearsons, and Tartans, is treating sails with goop like Canvac? Actually, a significant number of the Maine Coast windjammer fleet do so—and, I suppose, many other natural-rag sailors who see their sails as an investment worth preserving to the bitter end.

In the tanning or barking of sails, it is tannic acid that serves to inhibit organic rot. This natural preservative can be found in blackberry bark, blue vervain, coltsfoot, sumac, oak, hemlock, mangrove, and tea. Of course, those canvases that come from the manufacturer already mildewproofed with tin, arsenic, or PCBs don't need any protection for a while. But eventually they will, so it does not make much sense to subject yourself to those poisons: If you want a natural-fiber sail, better to obtain untreated fabric and then bark it yourself when the sail is stretched out and ready.

Canvac is the most likely preservative agent these days, but in former times no-nonsense workboat formulas were used extensively on both fishnets and sails. Tanning recipes now are found only in vintage books in the dusty nautical corner of antique bookstores. Two such books are *Yacht Cruising*, by Claude Worth, and *Fishermen's Knots and Nets*, by Graumont and Wenstrom.

9

Sail Repair and Restoration

WHAT IS A SAIL REPAIR? It is helpful to maintain a distinction between small repairs and restorations or rebuilds, which are bigger jobs (see Chapter 10). These differentiations not only hint at the work, time, and money necessary to bring a sail back on line, they also help you anticipate required tools and materials; a ditty bag's worth of small-repair potential is quite different from a sail locker full of restorational capability.

Many sails and systems are built to self-destruct, but, strictly speaking, only neglect, catastrophe, or utter expiration should necessitate the restoration of a properly constructed, well-maintained, seaworthy sail. Well, if a sail is giving up the ghost at the end of a long life of reliable service, its time has come, and time and money put into repair and restoration are resources better devoted to making a new sail.

That does bring up the possibility, though, of having to "repair" a sail that should be given its last rites just to complete a voyage or a season. It is amazing how much wind a sail can hold as long as it is in one piece, no matter how far gone the material. The best chance of keeping the sail in use is to repair it with relatively tired materials so as not to create a stressful, strong link in a weak chain. If you've ever tried patching a well-worn pair of blue jeans, you know what I mean—the patch is fine, but

almost immediately the pants part all around it.

An ounce of prevention is worth a pound of cure. Here are some common examples and sources of damage that require repairs:

- burns from cigarette and pipe ashes
- fishhooks in wire standing and running rigging
- cotter pin ends
- battens
- pulpit and lifeline chafe
- improper reefing
- leech and foot flutter
- sun exposure
- poor maintenance
- rodents
- excessive wind strength
- motoring with the sails flogging about
- slatting and slamming
- improper storage
- spreader and shroud chafe
- chafe from rig components

DAMAGE ASSESSMENT

There are three categories of damage in a sail: damage to the cloth, damage to the stitching, and damage to the attachments. How do you determine what needs repair, and how quickly should the repair be made? It is obvious when damage is so extensive that the sail is unusable, or if the problem is conspicuously precarious (one sneeze and the sail blows), but how about pinholes or a stitch torn here and there?

It is true that the repair of many types of minor damage is not critical—indeed, the sail could live out the rest of its life chock-full of little dings, and most do. With regard to cloth damage, it was the rule of thumb in my apprenticeship that a hole too small to stick a pencil through is not worth patching. As it pertains to overall sail integrity, I think this is true; pinholes constitute no significant loss in strength. Moreover, a fully sewn patch must be big enough for seams and measure at least 1 inch along each edge.

Little holes are, however, places for something pointed to catch on, and they don't help the aerodynamic quality of the sail. Therefore, a herringboning or a protective piece of tape would be prudent. The need for an immediate cloth repair is determined as much by the location as by the extent of the tear. A larger hole can go for quite some time in the bunt of a sail—a place of minimal strain—whereas a small tear at a place of great strain, say a corner, the leech, or particularly the clew, demands immediate remedy. Of course, the weather is a great factor in what the sail will have to withstand. When in doubt, fix it.

Stitching damage is similar to cloth damage in that a single stitch torn here and there is of no great concern, especially on the seams of a vertically cut sail where the strain is parallel to the seams. Likewise, the location of stitching loss is important. If stitching has let go from stress, it is clearly in a place of great strain; if it has been chafed through, the location may not experience great cloth tension. Move quickly to restitch places of strain: corners, leeches, patches, and reinforcements. Again, when in doubt, fix it. Stitching tends to fail in a chain reaction. The destruction of one link puts unsupported strain on successive stitches, and they all go, even the sound stitches in good cloth.

Broken hardware, seizings, and attachments are obviously cause for immediate remedial action, no matter where they are. A similar chain-reaction potential exists as with stitching. Seizings, webbing, and the stitching of rings can last an amazingly long time in a state of disrepair, especially if located in places of little strain and only subjected to fair-weather sailing. It is a testimony to the longevity of software that, even dilapidated, it serves well—within limits. Hardware has a more critical breaking point. (If I may preach parenthetically, therein lies one of the overriding virtues of spliced standing rigging as opposed to swage fittings.)

Handsewn rings can lose more than one-third of their stitching and still be effective, as long as the stitching on the side of the strain is sound. Most often, repairs in this category will be part of routine maintenance. When in doubt, fix it.

THE REPAIR AND MAINTENANCE KIT

The tools and materials described in Chapter 1 go a long way toward furnishing a well-found seafaring sail-repair-and-maintenance kit. The following lists expand that capability within the realistic scope of the self-reliant daysailor or voyager. Note that repair cloth should be identical in weight, construction, and finish to that of each sail covered. With Dacron this is not so critical—try to come close, though.

To the basic repair kit of Chapter 1, the daysailor might add:

- sail-repair tape
- ½-inch double-sided sticky tape
- replacement sail hardware and the tools to set spur grommets
- replacement sail battens
- an electric or butane-powered hotknife
- ½-inch and 1-inch webbing
- double-braid-rope splicing tools
- extra sailcover and canvaswork fasteners

See the tools and materials section in Chapter 5, "How Sails Are Made," for insights on the items listed above and below. In addition to the basic kit and the tools and materials above, the serious voyaging sailor could also have in the bosun's locker:

- a high-quality treadle or hand-powered zigzag sewing machine
- machine sewing thread of the weight(s) found in sails aboard
- a long-jaw stapler
- replacement luff rope and boltrope
- 10 yards of each type of sailcloth aboard
- a 100-yard roll of 6-inch by 7- or 8-ounce luff tape
- extra cover and bag cloth
- extra D-rings and round thimbles
- extra three-strand line
- awning fabric and hardware
- extra canvas fasteners and tools
- replacement hardware for large corner rings with liner-setting tools

MAKING REPAIRS

Repairing synthetic- or natural-fiber fabrics is like *making* sails in those respective materials in that, while Dacron is less demanding to work with than cotton, it is also less forgiving, so that a poorly done repair will remain a flaw and a weak spot. With cotton, allowances must be made for stretch and shrinkage, and the use of similar materials is more critical, but any flaw stands a great chance of working itself out, even in grossly bungled repairs. Elasticity is a wonderful thing. In fact, cotton is so forgiving that it is possible to merely round-stitch a tear together, with fair likelihood that the puckering will eventually work out. This is not just an aesthetic accomplishment; it means that the cloth will have stabilized itself so that once again the strain is evenly distributed—somewhat like suturing one's skin.

In any event, it should be noted that while the repairs are the same for natural and synthetic

fibers, some adjustments must be made for cotton. Preferably, patches are made of the same material in the same condition as the sail, but unused patch material is often applied to a well-used sail. In that event, it can be expected that a cotton patch, if it is not a preshrunk cloth such as Vivatex, will shrink after it is applied, and so must be somewhat larger than the hole it is covering—about 6 percent longer on each side. This extra is taken up evenly around the patch during the sewing.

When it comes to installing large pieces of full cloth width or replacing an entire panel in cotton, the problem is stretch, which the new cloth has not done and the used sail has done considerably, especially in areas of great strain. In this instance, the replacement piece must be *smaller* than the area it is covering. There is some guesswork involved here, as the amount of stretch depends on cotton type, location in the sail, and amount of cloth being replaced—there being less strain on a partial cloth. The length of a full cloth might want to be reduced as much as 3 percent, while a half cloth would have a proportionately smaller allowance of 1 percent or so. Smaller replacement sizes would need lesser allowances.

To make the whole process less of a shot in the dark, you could consult a sailmaker or the cloth manufacturer concerning the stretch and shrinkage characteristics of the fabric you're using. Alternatively, you could conduct your own test, wetting and preshrinking a small patch. By the way, it is obviously undesirable to attempt repairs on a wet cotton sail, except in emergencies. Emergencies—sounds grim, but occasions arise at sea where the time and care for proper repairs are unavailable. Just as circumstances may call for hacking off the lower section of a sail with a rigging knife to effect a reef, it may be all one can do to lash, wire, or tape a wounded sail together. This is the stuff of survival at sea.

A slightly less precarious situation, but one still not conducive to a full repair, may call for a "homeward-bounder," a temporary lash-up to see the sail through to the next opportunity to take it all apart and mend it correctly. Bear in mind that when you do one of those non-sail-material home-ward-bounders using something like duct tape or glue, you—or someone else—is later going to have to deal with the mess. Tire cement, duct tape, and epoxy glue are poor substitutes for a well-found sail-repair kit in a bosun's locker or for homeward-bounding herringbone stitches—but they can get you home.

Herringboning

Now and then a sailor will fetch up on a small nee-dle-and-palm job for which a quick but reliable stitch is required. Perhaps it might be the seagoing necessity of sewing a corpse's nose to the canvas shroud to prevent his spirit from returning to haunt the ship. More often, though, the job might be a small sail repair—a tear large enough to demand fixing but not so large as to require a patch. For such small repairwork, but not for ship-board funerary preparations, the herringbone stitch is well suited.

Some study must be made of the damage to determine whether herringboning is the best pro-cedure to make the repair—and if so, no two tears being alike, how the stitch can be most effectively used. How big is the tear? How much strain will the repair later receive? Is it a clean hole, such as a knife slit, or a ragged, gaping wound? In what con-dition is the surrounding cloth?

The herringbone stitch works best on small, straight, clean tears in sound cloth. To herringbone any other sort of damage may be acceptable in an emergency, or as a homeward-bounder, but the correct way would be to replace the damaged area with a well-sewn patch.

There are several types of herringbone stitch. The following general remarks apply to the two that I've selected as being the strongest and most useful.

Herringboning is done with as small a needle and twine as is consistent with the nature of the sail. An arm's span of twine should be doubled through a needle and waxed. A tear requiring more twine than that is probably too large to be safely herringboned to begin with.

Note any irregularities in the hole and check to see how far out laterally from the tear the stitches must be taken so that they are in firm cloth. The stitches may be sewn in either direction, and there are a number of ways to begin. The twine can be simply knotted and the stitching commenced. Another method, as in other types of stitching, is to oversew the tail end of the twine with the subse-quent stitching. But if there's any question about how much strain the repair must withstand, by far the best way to begin a herringbone repair is to take two half hitches in the form of a clove hitch about the first stitch and oversew the tail. To finish, a clove hitch is taken on the last stitch and the twine passed under the last three or four stitches before being cut off. But I'm getting ahead of myself.

Although there is no slit to pass the needle through, I begin herringboning somewhat before the actual tear and continue a way after the break has been stitched up. It's a stronger job. As you work along the tear, the stitches must be neither too close together nor too far apart. Alternating short and long stitches will help distribute the strain.

Stitch tension is important. With too little ten-sion, the tear won't be closed up, the strain will be uneven, and the ends may tear further. With too much tension, the result will be puckered and dis-torted cloth, particularly with synthetic sailcloth where all the strain falls on the stitching. Draw your stitches up evenly and sufficiently to close the tear, but disturb the surrounding cloth as little as possible.

The Herringbone Stitch Starting in sound cloth before the tear, pass the needle down and up again, as if you were going through the torn hole and up through the cloth on the far side (Figure 9-1(1)). Now take a stitch on the near side of the hole—down and up, with the needle coming out about where it first entered but just outside the stitch thus formed across the tear line.

Take a clove hitch, as shown in Figure 9-1(2), about that first stitch, and then continue the stitch-ing sequence as you oversew the tail of the twine and progress toward the tear.

On reaching the actual hole, continue the

stitching. Sew down through the tear and up from beneath on the far side, then down through the near side, up through the hole, and cross over the stitch, repeating the sequence slightly farther along (Figure 9-1(3)).

The herringbone is finished in good cloth beyond the end of the tear, in the same way the stitching was begun, clove-hitched on the last stitch and the twine passed under the preceding stitches (Figure 9-1(4)). The twine is then cut off.

The Sailmaker's Herringbone The second form of herringbone, known variously as the *sailmaker's herringbone, stitch* or *darn,* or sometimes the *locked,* or *racked, herringbone,* is different in that each time a stitch is taken, the needle enters

from the upper side of the cloth, down, then up through the tear. Furthermore, due to the way in which each stitch is locked along the centerline, each successive stitch from one side of the tear to the other is slightly advanced.

I prefer the sailmaker's herringbone, as it seems to be stronger and the locking stitch helps fill the gap in the tear when the two edges are drawn together. This stitch is perhaps more time-consuming, and using it takes some practice in heaving the locking stitch to just the right amount of tension and correctly placing the stitching along the centerline of the repair.

Somewhat in advance of the torn hole, begin by passing the needle down through the near side and up from below, coming out along the centerline of

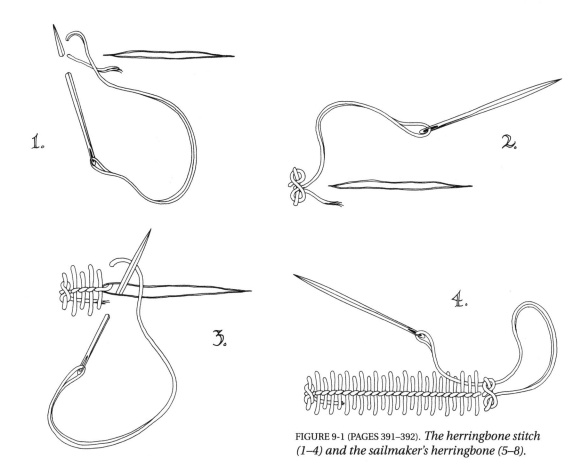

FIGURE 9-1 (PAGES 391–392). *The herringbone stitch (1–4) and the sailmaker's herringbone (5–8).*

the tear, as shown in Figure 9-1(5). Then, from the other direction, pass the needle down and up from below again, this time exiting slightly outside the first point of entry.

As in the first method, a clove hitch is taken around the stitch just formed and the tail is covered by the succeeding stitches. With each stitch, the needle comes out on the centerline, and you must be sure that the needle passes through the loop of the stitch so that the locking stitch is formed as the twine is hove home (Figure 9-1(6)). The same method is continued on both sides of the tear, except that when the tear itself is reached, the needle comes up through the

tear hole on each pass (Figure 9-1(8)).

Carried beyond the tear, this herringbone, like the others, is finished with a clove hitch taken around the last stitch, and the twine is cut off after having been passed under the last few stitches on the far side.

In order to be bedded and smoothed out well, herringboning, like other stitching, does well to be given a good rubbing down with a seam rubber. This leaves the repair more evenly tensioned and less susceptible to chafe. That's sound herringboning.

Now what kind of stitch do you use to keep the sailor's ghost from coming back and haunting the ship? Not the goblin stitch.

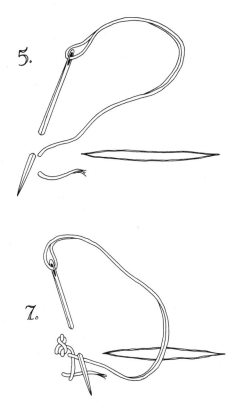

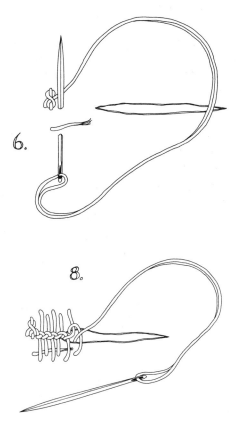

FIGURE 9-1. (*cont.*)

Sewing a Patch

It should be kept in mind that a sail is neither a sock, an inner tube, nor an elbow. A sail damaged to the extent of needing to be patched shouldn't be darned, glued, or bandaged, then left to heal itself. While even a properly repaired sail has been weakened to some extent, Band-Aid coverup techniques don't result in a sound, reliable, or permanent repair.

No two repairs are exactly alike, and it would be an endless task to cover all possible techniques in the art of sail repair, so much of which is at the discretion of the repairer. Many aspects of sail repair are quite simple, though, and can be easily and successfully accomplished by the sailor. Patching is just such a repair.

The overall objective in sail repairwork is to put the sail back together as closely as possible to the way it was originally. This means using cloth identical in weight and finish to that of which the sail is made; keeping the cloth direction or weave of the patch cloth consistent with that of the sail; using the correct-size twine; allowing adequate-size seams; and removing old or defective cloth. Every attempt should be made to restore the sail to its former strength and shape.

The folding, striking-up, and sewing techniques for reinforcement patches presented in Chapter 1 are the same techniques employed in sewing a repair patch. The primary differences, however, are the formation of a flat seam around the damaged area and the removal of the damaged cloth.

Patchable tears come in all shapes and sizes. Patches can too, if you want your sail to look like an old pair of mended trousers. For appearance sake and a stronger patch, no matter what the form of tear, I try to make the patch square or rectangular with its edges square to the weave of the cloth in the sail. Occasionally there are exceptions to this rule, such as when a tear has occurred at the meeting of two seams or is close enough to a seam running diagonally to the weave that the seam is part of the patch. But then the other edges of the patch will be square, and the principle is the same.

The Job   With the damaged part of the sail pinned out flat and undistorted, determine the size patch required to cover the torn area and remove the cloth that is weak and damaged. Allow for a seam as wide as those in the sail, a ¼-inch hem on the patch, and sufficient cloth around the tear to permit a ¼-inch hemming-under of the sail in the patch seam.

If you are working with synthetic sailcloth and have a hotknife or are careful with a match, the sail and patch edges can be melted, the hemming dispensed with, and the size of the patch adjusted accordingly.

Heat sealing the cut edges in the patching of synthetic sailcloth is expeditious, but it is a technique better suited to machine sewing. Hand stitching a hotknifed edge tends to fracture the seal and, moreover, the sharpness of the melted edge chafes the twine. So, even if it's synthetic sailcloth, if you are going to sew it by hand, best hem the cut edges. I might add that if you are patching that ultralight synthetic stuff, it ought to be machine sewn with light stitch tension or it's sure to come out a rumpled mess.

After figuring the size and cloth direction, cut out the patch. Fold the patch edges under, pin it out flat over the tear, and draw the sew-to line and strike-up marks.

The sail under the patch can be cut and folded now or later, after the first sewing of the patch. If you are hotknifing, the struck-up patch must be lifted now, the seam width drawn in, and the bad cloth cut away. Likewise if you want to do the hemming method now, prior to sewing the patch. If you are waiting until after you've sewn the patch on to cut and fold, this step can be ignored.

For ease of sewing, pin, staple, or temporarily stitch the patch corners in place prior to the initial sewing, then remove the fixings as you go.

Flat stitch the patch all the way around the outer edge. Now turn the sail over. If you've pre-cut the sail, either hemmed or hotknifed, there's nothing more to do but flat stitch the inner edge of the seam to the patch. On the other hand, if the trimming and hemming have been left until

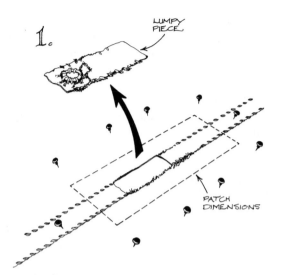

Cut out the lumpy portion of the damaged area, pin out the sail, and measure the patch dimensions.

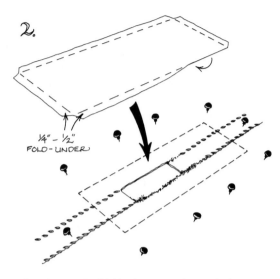

Cut the patch, fold its hems under, and place it over the damaged area.

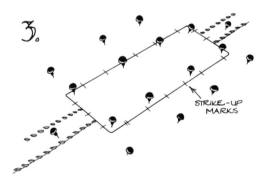

Pin the patch, make the strike-up marks, and draw the sew-to line around the patch.

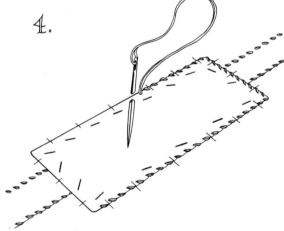

Staple the patch, pull the pins, and flat stitch the outer edge of the patch to the sail, maintaining alignment of strike-up marks.

FIGURE 9-2. *Sewing a patch.*

5.

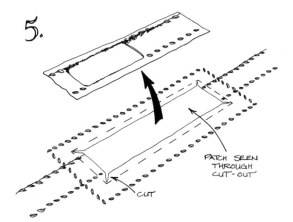

Turn the sail over and remove the remainder of the damaged cloth. Leave enough cloth for a seam and hem.

6.

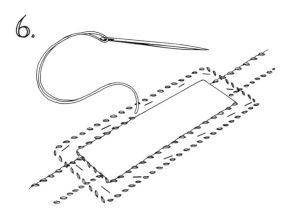

Fold the hems under, staple, and sew.

now, cut out the tear squarely and cleanly. Then cut a slit in each corner of the hole to allow a ¼-inch fold-under. Be careful not to cut the patch underneath. With a uniform seam width and all frayed edges tucked under, flat stitch around the inner edge of the seam. Finally, take a seam rubber and rub the whole job down on both sides of the sail.

You'd think that a patch would spoil the appearance of a sail and make a sailor seem lubberly indeed. On the contrary, a well-sewn patch can show assurance, care, and seafarerlike self-reliance.

Major Repairs

The principles of major repairs on a sail are the same as those for small repairs and patching. It is a matter of extent and greater difficulty in putting the sail back together as closely as possible to its original form. When one is fixing a tear more extensive than a simple patch can remedy,

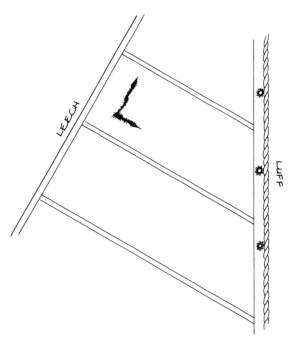

FIGURE 9-3 (PAGES 395–396). *An L-shaped rip within a panel, and the possible repairs.*

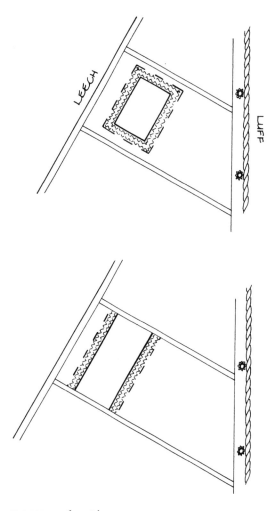

FIGURE 9-3. *(cont.)*

there are four complications that require major work:

1. a lengthy L-shaped rip
2. a long tear that crosses one or more cloths
3. a long tear that transits from 1 to 3 feet, or the whole length of a panel
4. the obliteration of a seam

L-SHAPED RIP.   In most cases, whether the tear crosses a seam onto another panel or is entirely within one panel, it is best (strongest) to repair the

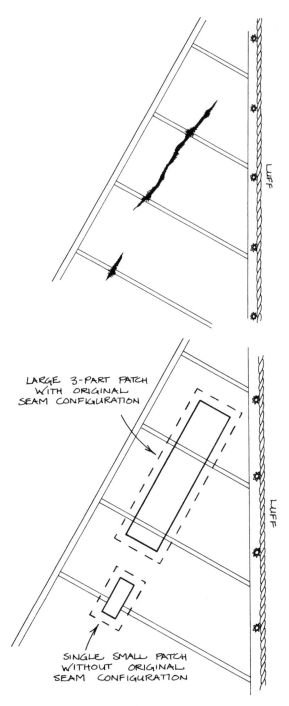

LARGE 3-PART PATCH WITH ORIGINAL SEAM CONFIGURATION

SINGLE SMALL PATCH WITHOUT ORIGINAL SEAM CONFIGURATION

FIGURE 9-4. *A tear that crosses a seam, and the possible repairs.*

full length and width in the form of a square or rectangular patch. The exception would be when the proximity of hardware or cloth reinforcements dictates an L-shaped or irregular patch. On the other hand, depending on the amount of cloth available, the dimensions of the tear, and the proximity to a seam, it may be better to replace the full panel width for as much length as the damage occupies.

TEARS THAT CROSS A SEAM.   When a tear crosses a seam into other cloths, you will want to maintain the integrity of the original panel seams, but this conflicts with the desire to simplify the job by using an uninterrupted patch. Furthermore, if the tear is more than a cloth's width in length, cloth direction could be a problem. When the patch is narrow (say, under 6 inches wide) and less than a cloth's width long, it is acceptable to cross a seam. Otherwise, you should reconstruct seams in the patch in alignment with the seams in the sail. Dou-

ble-sided sticky tape greatly eases this process, which can involve several pieces. Though you could sew a multipiece repair section by section to the sail, it is better to presew the replacement pieces together, then install the whole ensemble. The same should be done if the pieces are preassembled with sticky tape.

LONG TEARS.   The restoration of a sail with a long tear down the panel depends on how close the tear is to a seam and the availability of materials. In Dacron, it is relatively simple to replace the section with a length of Dacron luff tape; in many cases this is perfectly acceptable, but it does add more seams. Replacing the full cloth width for the length of the tear leaves just two seams across the panel, while replacing the entire panel leaves no new seams at all and is, of course, the most thorough restoration.

Full cloth replacement entails two difficulties

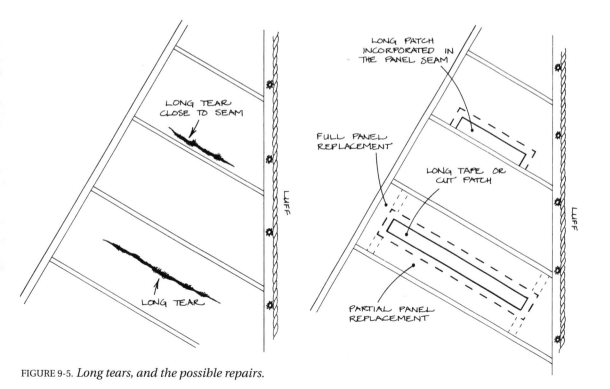

FIGURE 9-5. *Long tears, and the possible repairs.*

apart from the previously mentioned complications of natural fibers. First, when dealing with major rips it is difficult to realign the sail halves and get everything pinned out flat. Second, the chances are good of fetching up on or having to recreate broadseaming, and how much to add and where is a difficult guess on a computer-designed, laser-cut sail.

Before unpicking the old seams (i.e., pulling out the stitches), draw the sew-to line on the lower cloth and the one being replaced. Measure the cloth width to determine the form of the broadseam, if not already visible. This, combined with prior knowledge of the sail's shape and the principles of sail shaping, should offer a basis for fitting the new cloth.

Of course, replacing a full panel on a crosscut or vertically cut sail means recreating portions of edge curves as well as replacing or reusing the tablings and reinforcements at each end. This part is relatively easy, although edge tapes have to be tensioned before stitching over the new cloth. Stretch the whole tape so that the wrinkles in the rest of the tape are gone, then strike up, staple, or sticky-tape the tape in place.

OBLITERATION OF A SEAM.   The failed seam is perhaps the most common of all mishaps, as seams become increasingly weaker links in a sail's chain of integrity as time goes on. Sometimes if the seam lets go due to poor-quality or rotten

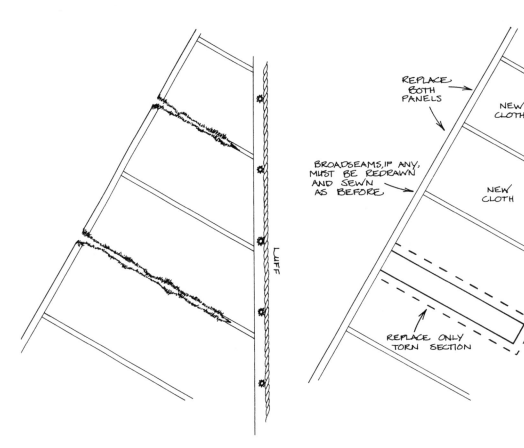

FIGURE 9-6. *Obliterated seams, and the possible repairs.*

thread, the stronger cloth of the selvage remains intact and, if not too distorted, is easily restuck and resewn. The old stitch holes can even be lined up—sometimes the only reference one has for reuniting the cloths accurately. But, if the thread was as good as or stronger than the cloth, the brute force of tearing it asunder will likely have left the selvages of the cloth and seam a line of unsalvageable shredded wheat. In this instance, one could wholly replace both cloths involved—a big job, perhaps justified in a new sail, especially if the cloths are short. Otherwise, it is simplest and satisfactory to run a tape or narrow, long patch over the shattered seam and make two seams in that section. This band should allow a minimum of 2 inches between the seams.

Finding a Professional Sail Repairer

A sewing machine alone does not a competent sail doctor make. I see many sails that have been mangled by backwater cobblers, the cruising yacht next door with a portable machine, the local canvas-repair shop, or even a sail loft. Not that any of these well-meaning people couldn't ever competently repair a sail; but the person most likely to properly repair, restore, or rebuild a sail is the person who makes sails—more specifically, makes sails like yours with the same kinds of tools, techniques, and materials (see Chapter 10 in regard to selecting a sailmaker). If you are prepared and self-reliant, you can always buy time to get a badly damaged sail to a competent professional sail doctor, even if the damage occurs off some remote atoll.

10

Buying New or Used Sails

"NEVER GIVE A SUCKER an even break!"
Though few sailmakers are solely sale makers, you are certainly at their mercy as a consumer if you arrive uninformed and leave the nature of your sails entirely to their discretion. Be prepared with a thorough explanation of what kind of sail(s) you desire as well as their intended uses and any qualifying special characteristics of the boat, rig, sailors, sailing conditions, etc. If you are in doubt about an appropriate sail type, ask, and make comparisons with similar boats. Be quite specific about sail design and cut. At least have a general expectation of camber and draft placement, number of reefs, expected wind-range applications, and points of sail.

With some understanding of sailcloth and sail construction, a buyer can discuss and express a preference for a particular cloth type, cut of sail, stitching, and reinforcement techniques. And one must not overlook the details of finishing and hardware as well as means of attachment. These are the very aspects of a sail that have the most effect on its longevity.

The price of sails, new or used, is a serious consideration and, as it turns out, you don't always get what you pay for in terms of quality. It is probably safe to assume that for a high-priced sail you are getting a lot of *something* for the money—if not

quality of material and construction, then maybe reputation and short-term performance. Where high-quality construction and materials with good performance are concerned, there are no bargains—not anymore—not even from slave labor in the Orient.

BUYING NEW SAILS

Selecting a Loft and Sailmakers

One of the best indications of an appropriate loft for your sails is that the people building the sails do or have done your kind of sailing. Maybe they've even sailed an identical boat. What are their philosophies of design and construction? Do they make their sails with the same tools you have on hand for repairing them?

A small loft is more likely to give you personal attention and follow through to your satisfaction. Lower overhead means more in the sails and less in promotion and upkeep. A smaller work crew has greater overall familiarity with your sails. A small loft buying materials in "small" quantities does not get the price breaks granted to a loft buying in large production quantities, but a low-production outfit can take the time to customize your order with unusual materials and more labor-intensive construction methods as well as handsome and artistic ornamentation.

The ads in your favorite sailing magazine are one place to look, since it is unlikely that any sailmaker would advertise in a magazine that did not concern itself with the kinds of boats and sails in which it specializes. The problem is that the mainstream cruising market is dominated by the same lofts that make racing sails, so that often their ads are the most prominent in the cruising periodicals. Naturally, a small enterprise hasn't the budget for mass advertising and relies primarily on word of mouth, which is likely how you'll hear of a good candidate and is also a good way of seeking one out. Rather than taking an ad on faith, find a boat like yours with successful sails and find out who the sailmaker was. Sailors will be the first to let you know if they have been duped or delighted.

Let's say you have found a prospective sailmaker and you know what you want—or at least you know what to ask about—and there you are standing at the entrance: Is it the sailmaker or a PR person you must talk to? Talk to the sailmaker! Does the sailmaker listen to you, hear you? Respect you and your needs? Not all artists or craftspeople are charmingly personable, but if you can't communicate with them, give them the air! Listen to the voice of experience, but it's your boat and life—get the sails *you* want.

Be specific about your expectations and require a detailed estimate with all construction aspects, price, deposits, time frames, follow-up plans, and extras, such as bags, covers, running rigging, and pendants. And make clear what you expect the sail to do.

Now you can do some comparison shopping. You will find that production lofts have reduced their quotes to dollar-per-square-foot formulas, with the price fluctuating according to cloth type, weight, and construction techniques. Options, such as full battens, are added on. Often, things like sailbags are included and *seem* to be freebies.

On the other hand, no sail loft doing the kind of refined work presented in this book can estimate strictly by formula. There are too many individual and differing details that require their own estimations of cost. It does not necessarily follow that a large sail will cost more than a smaller one, nor that a heavier sail will be more expensive per square foot than a lightweight one. It depends on the cost of the materials and the labor involved. A 10.5-ounce Dacron storm trysail could easily cost more than a 6-ounce genoa three times as large, and a 250-square-foot 7.25-ounce Dacron mainsail might not cost as much as a hand-finished and dyed cotton sail half the size.

So, if you catch my drift, by being specific about your needs you encourage a custom sailmaker to be specific concerning the details of your sails and the respective costs.

Mail-Order Sails

Buying sails from a sailmaker through the mail is a chancy undertaking, but it may be your only alternative if there are no appropriate sailmakers close at hand. Clearly, you can't go to the shop and check them out, so you do the best you can by telephone and letter to inform and be informed—this is not Little Lima Bean's "you take what you get" mail-order house.

If it is a "sail-order" house—and there are several in the Far East that maintain North American offices—you do take what you get. In those instances, money "saved" initially through import firms may be spent subsequently on recuts for measurement errors and early replacement of poor-quality materials and construction.

It is easy to shop around by mail and telephone. The problem is that the price-per-square-foot quotations you get on that route tell you little about the sails. Perhaps the biggest drawback to grab-bag sail buying is that there is generally no follow-through or accountability. The sailmaker cannot visit your boat, bend sail, and check out the work to your satisfaction.

When buying sails by mail, it is extremely important to establish exactly what you want and provide measurements and a corrected sail plan. If you study the procedure for designing the sails you wish to buy (see Chapter 6), it will be clear just what information a professional will need to build your sails at a distance with minimal guesswork. Often sails are ordered in advance of a new boat's completion, but this is a situation to be avoided. Even with the great precision and specificity of design in high-tech boats, there are substitutions and deviations from the plans that, if unknown to the sailmaker, result in an ill-fitting suit of sails.

On small, traditionally rigged craft there is considerable room for adjustment, and the rig can be built around the sails, so to speak, with little difficulty. But this catch-up method is no substitute for a completed boat from which measurements and hardware specs can be taken—or a current and final sail plan that indicates all the ultimate details of the rig and spars.

Deposits and Estimates

Whether you purchase sails by telephone or in person, you will likely be asked for a deposit. A large loft with a substantial cash flow and inventory, where you have established yourself as a reliable client, might not find it necessary, but a small loft may have to order the materials and pay the rent with the deposit while the sails are under construction. It is not unusual for a loft to require as much as 50 percent of the estimate up front. A deposit can be a good thing. It establishes your sincerity and ensures that if the sailmaker is left holding the bag (so to speak), at least the cost of the materials isn't lost.

The deposit should be preceded by a detailed estimate or quotation. There is a difference, by the way, between the two, and it should be clear whether you are making a deposit on the ultimate final price less tax (quotation) or on a rough guess that could increase (estimate). Incidentally, "Just give me a ballpark figure" is perhaps the most often heard line from prospective sail buyers. This approach inevitably makes for confusion. If off the top of my head I give you a low price, and the sail ends up costing more, you'll feel deceived. If, on the other hand, you still don't get a true read on anticipated expense you may take your business to someone who guesses low. You can see how

the dollar-per-square-foot estimates and the ballpark inquiries go hand in hand.

I believe that the final payment on a sail should be made when the sail has been delivered and is working to the satisfaction of the client—either that, or the sail should come under some sort of warranty. This arrangement requires considerable faith and responsibility from both sailor and sailmaker.

By the by, it should be apparent how important communication and presentation are in a sailmaker's relationship to clientele. If you have any interest in becoming a sailmaker, you might pause to consider what, as a client, would make you feel comfortable about writing an $8,000 deposit check—on faith. What sort of people and places foster that kind of trust?

Warranties

The best warranties are the standards and integrity of the sailmaker. Some lofts issue written warranties that provide a time frame during which they'll make good on construction faults, but there are too many variables beyond the control of the sailmaker to make any blanket guarantees for an extended period. Performance is subjective, and a sail is only as good as the sailor. Moreover, you cannot count on appropriate use of the sail in appropriate weather conditions. More basic than that, none of the components of the sail—cloth, hardware, etc.—are guaranteed by the original manufacturers. They don't know what some dimwit is likely to make out of their stuff, and they don't want to be sued.

Having specified what you want in a sail, it is certainly possible to ascertain whether that is what you've received. The procedural steps in making a sail are a guide to what to look for—everything from its shape to whether the numbers fall off. Given routine care and maintenance and barring some catastrophe, it is reasonable to expect a sail to retain its shape and integrity for several years.

Testing Sails

Sometimes a sailmaker will accompany the client out on the water and adjust the sails. But if that is not feasible, there is much a sailor can do to scrutinize new sails and communicate the successes and failures back to the sailmaker. (The chances are slim that the sailmaker will be on board when a new stormsail is tested under heavy-weather conditions, but it can at least be set up and studied.)

Naturally, new sails must fit the boat. They must fit the spars and wires with enough room left over to stretch, and they must align properly with hardware fittings. The force required to tension the sail's edges should be in balance with the power of the halyard, outhaul, etc. Hardware placement (slides, hanks, and corner rings) should be compatible in size and position with the rig.

The best way to record and communicate sail shape is with a camera. Here are some hints from Wally Ross's *Sail Power* to help you get the best photographs of the amount and location of draft in your sail:

- Use black-and-white film—not color.
- Face the windward side of the sail, just aft of the midpoint of the foot.
- Be sure that the light on the sails is such that the seams show up well.
- Shoot upward, from below the foot if you can.
- Get at least the entire upper half of the sail in the picture, from luff to leech. The more you can get in, the better.
- Photograph the main and jib or genoa, or whatever sail, separately.
- Make pictures under various wind conditions: for a medium-weather sail, you can take one set at 6 to 10 knots, one at 12 to 15 knots, and one at 20 knots. For sails with less specificity, pictures can be taken in all wind ranges.
- Mark each set with all pertinent information, including approximate wind velocity, mainsheet traveler setting or boom angle, the position of draft-control mechanisms (sheet cunningham hole, etc.), and other sails in use at the time.

From these photographs, a sailmaker should have enough information to analyze a problem. However, for your own information, you may want to carry this procedure a step further and plot the draft onto the photographs yourself.

Plotting Draft Draft should be calculated at a minimum of three heights: one-quarter, one-half, and three-quarters of the way up the sail. If you're working on a photograph, however, you may only be able to plot a couple of sections because of the limited range of the camera.

First, outline the seam from luff to leech at each height. Then, draw the chord from luff to leech at the points where the seam begins and ends. Now you have established a sail section at each height. The next step is to take four depth readings for each section: at one-quarter, one-half, and three-quarters of the way aft, and at the point of maximum draft. Now you can see with some exactitude where the draft is located at each height in the sail.

To get the camber ratio, measure the depth of the section and the length of its chord with a ruler and divide the depth by the chord. Even though you will be working at a greatly reduced scale, the result will be the same as if you had actually measured the sail itself.

Using photographs of your sails and plotting draft on them in this manner can be a very valuable tool for most sailors, particularly in analyzing your draft setting in different conditions. It is a procedure worth mastering.

A similar photographic approach can be applied to flaws in the set of the sail (e.g., wrinkles and hardspots). Very often such problems are the result of improper bending, setting, or tensioning of the sail. But there can also be design problems that a sailmaker can rectify once having seen the photographs. (See Table 10-1, The Sail Survey Checklist, page 409.)

Frequently a sailor acquires new sails as part of a package deal with a boat. A mass-production boatbuilder will likely be allied with a mass-production sailmaker, and low pricing is the dominant consideration—low pricing to the boatbuilder,

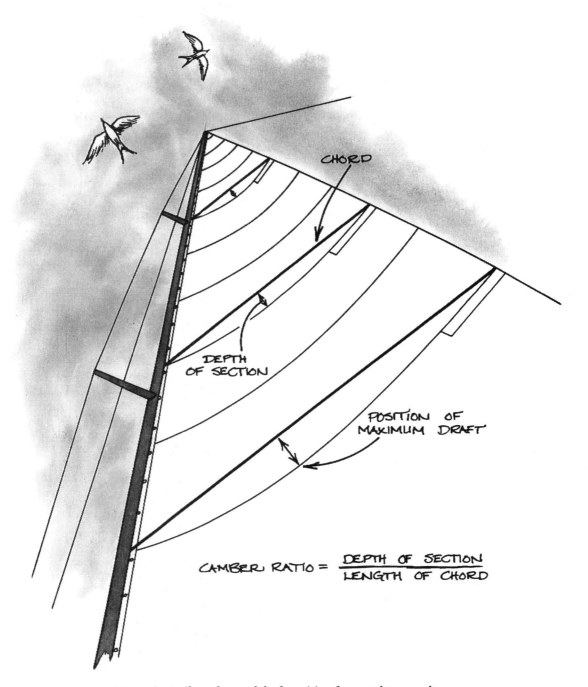

CHORD

DEPTH
OF SECTION

POSITION OF
MAXIMUM DRAFT

$$\text{CAMBER RATIO} = \frac{\text{DEPTH OF SECTION}}{\text{LENGTH OF CHORD}}$$

FIGURE 10-1. *Measuring sail camber and draft position from a photograph.*

not necessarily to the sailor. It is not unusual for a fairly well made boat to come with cheesy sails, partly to keep costs down and often because many boatbuilders don't know a good sail from a bale of hay. It is better, if you care, to specify your sail expectations to the boatbuilder and have the boatbuilder find the right sailmaker—and you pay the fare. Or, better yet, dump the complete sailaway package and go out and find your own sailmaker. In that event, the boatbuilder or distributor's markup can go toward a higher-quality suit of sails.

Boat Shows

Boat shows are grand marketplaces for new sails, including those you see on boats and those you hear about from sales representatives of sail lofts. These shows provide an opportunity to see what's available, but they are a poor environment in which to undertake an in-depth inquiry and individualized relationship with a sailmaker. Boatshow space is expensive, and it is hard for a small shop to justify the expense of sitting for three days talking constantly to endless looky-loos. But reputable sailmakers and boatbuilders do attend shows and will conduct a no-nonsense, hype-free discussion about their products. Here you can engage them in a preliminary discussion about your needs, ask about their work and pricing, and see photos and actual samples of work. (For a sailmaker who is normally an artist, being a show person and salesperson can be a grueling ordeal. The irritable, uncommunicative sailmaker you're talking to at a show may be just who you want, but it's hard to tell when you receive the brunt of his or her boat-show burnout.)

Rarely have I found the sales reps at boat shows to know anything substantial about the sails supplied with their boats. Frequently, what information they did offer was mistaken. Ask boatbuilders and representatives who makes their sails; look at samples. Are they warranted? How much off the boat if you don't want the sails in a package deal?

Boat shows have too many inherent problems to be a safe place to purchase sails, whether with the boat or from a sail loft. But they are a good place—if you are at the right show, one where sailmakers and boatbuilders of custom-made products are represented—to nose around, meet people, see some products, and ask questions.

BUYING USED SAILS

Buying pre-owned sails is more difficult in many ways than buying new sails—but there is money to be saved, and the recycling is a virtuous act.

There is an eternal discrepancy between your needs and the used sails available out there; the sails are rarely precisely what you want. Furthermore, you want to save money yet end up with a sail that, except for some age, is as good in quality as what you might have bought new.

Thus there are two basic considerations: (1) the appropriateness and quality of design, materials, and construction of the sail; (2) and its present condition. There is no money to be saved in the long run by purchasing used throwaway-quality sails. There may be some logic, however, in acquiring inferior sails for temporary use until funds are available for better ones. And such sails might be purchased for their parts, particularly the cloth. If a usable sail of inferior or poor-quality finishing is available at a reasonable price, then it could be a good investment for the sailor who will refinish it or just utilize the cloth in a recut.

Sources of Used Sails

The greatest source of used sails is the used boats they come with. Here a sailor hasn't sought out second-, third-, or fourth-hand sails—*they are there.* Obviously, when purchasing a used sailboat, the sails that come with it are major considerations. First, is there a full or partial inventory? Then, what about the quality and the condition? Who made the sails, how old are they, what kind of use have they seen, and have they been kept covered? Knowing these four things will tell you a great deal about the sails without your even looking in the bag.

Often sailmakers keep sufficient records to be able to tell you more details about particular sails.

Beyond that there are three other avenues of insight:

1. Interview the former owners about specific sail concerns.
2. Survey the sails yourself or have a respected surveyor do it.
3. Go sailing, try all the sails, and study their shape, shape retention, and set.

One would think twice about purchasing a boat with a dead or dying auxiliary motor; the sails, which could cost much more, are worthy of the same consideration and scrutiny. A good set of recent photographs will show gross problems. There is no way of knowing for sure how the sails have been treated, but it should be expected that unless the used sails that come with the boat are of the highest quality, seldom used, and well cared for, they will undoubtedly be in need of restoration or repair. There comes a point in the deterioration of a sail beyond which it is more prudent to replace it than throw good money after bad in patch-ups.

Other Sailors—Swaps and Purchases   Sailors sometimes sell their own sails for one reason or another. Buying a bulletin-board special requires the same study as when you're acquiring sails from a used boat. It may even be easier, since the owner is right there to gam with. After the gamming and the survey, try it out. Finding a sail that actually fits and still has some life to it is a stroke of good fortune indeed! Unless it is a brand-new and perfect sail in every way, you should not pay any more than 50 to 60 percent of the new replacement cost.

Sail lofts occasionally offer sensational deals on used or even new sails, sometimes because a client fails to pick up an order. Check first the lofts that make the kind of sails you're after. Though in many ways it is not in a loft's interest to have sailors dickering over used sails instead of ordering new ones, there is some money to be made as a middle person, and subsequently in the restoration of the sails. It is quite possible that the tight-budgeted sailor couldn't have afforded a new sail anyway. Not only that, but a thriving exchange keeps sailors in the neighborhood buying supplies, if nothing else, and attracting other sailors who will buy new sails. The loft, of course, is in a position to make a knowledgeable survey. If it is one of their own sails, they'll know every detail.

If you are in the market, it is worth posting your needs on a sail-loft bulletin board—or advertising in sailing publications. The former is a long shot unless you have a class boat or a popular design.

Brokers   There are also brokers of new and used sails who acquire their stock through trades and purchases. Sail brokers buy anyone's old sails as well as production-loft overruns. They'll also sell your sails for a commission.

The sails that fall into the broker's hands tend to be racing or mass-production oriented. Brokerages have guidelines and acceptable standards such that no sail they carry is likely to be worthless.

Bacon & Associates, a sail brokerage, is often asked where they get all their used sails, and how. The stories they hear would fill a book of many volumes; they could write their own version of *Ripley's Believe It or Not*. Here are some of the common reasons they give:

- Owner bought demo boat with complete set of sails, wants to race and does not like Brand X sails as selected by the dealer, sends us these "used" sails and buys a set of Brand Y sails.
- Dealer and builder promotions—we often get sails from dealers or builders when boat sales did not meet expectations.
- Boat destroyed in boatyard fire, hurricane, or trailer accident; in many cases, sails were stored elsewhere and are still usable.
- Boat changes hands; new owner is a cruiser and does not know how he will ever use all these "racing sails."
- New sail order never picked up at sailmaker; sailmaker sends us sails to recoup his working capital.
- Sail is miscut; sail cutter thought boat was a Cal 27 and, on delivery, found boat was a Cal 2-27.

LOOSE-FOOTED FEASIBILITY

Q: *A broker of used sails is sending me a used mainsail that is roped for a slotted mast and boom. However, I intend to set the sail loose-footed. Can this be rigged without any big alterations to the clew?*

A: Though the sail's not designed or constructed to be set loose-footed, it can be made to work, and no recutting is necessary. The clew must be lashed or attached to an outhaul car high enough above the boom to allow the foot roping to pass from one side of the boom to the other when you change tacks. (See Figure 12-1, page 440.)

The sail you describe could even be flown boomless, though the foot would not set or function as well as a sail made for that purpose. Ideally, for your needs, the foot of the sail you are considering will have only a small amount of tension in the foot roping and little if any shelf or pocket built into the foot. Brokers generally permit a limited trial period in which to test a sail.

If you inquire of a sail brokerage such as Bacon & Associates, they will send you a list of all the sails that fulfill your specifications. The clearer and more specific you are about the sails you need, the better a broker will be able to help you.

Here are two examples of the manner in which sails may be described by a broker:

- Luff, 24 feet, 4 inches; leech, 24 feet, 9 inches; foot, 7 feet, 10 inches. South Coast 26A main, 6-ounce Dacron, triple stitched. Half-inch slugs on shackles with guards on covered rope luff. Covered rope foot for slot. Row of reefs up 3 feet, 9 inches. Sewn insignia. Minor soil. No bag. New-used. Catalog Number 278-YH-3834. Price, $195.
- Luff, 31 feet, 5 inches; leech, 28 feet, 0 inches; foot, 12 feet, 8 inches. Jib, 6-ounce Dacron. Bronze 2-inch piston hanks on covered wire luff. Mitered. Leech line. Takes three battens. Batten pockets have been patched and need patching. Has a few 2-inch-by-2-inch patches. Needs restitching. Few snags, needs darns. Rail marked. Soiled. Stained. In bag. Fair-good. Catalog Number 25-BRO-101. Price, $150.

Once you have expressed a preference and made a deposit, the sail(s) will be shipped to you

C.O.D., whereupon you have a trial period in which to inspect but not use the sail. If you are dissatisfied, you can return the sail at your own expense for a full refund, if the sail is in the same condition in which it left the brokerage. It is permitted that you hoist the sail, but it is not to be used until purchased. This is a definite disadvantage!

It is difficult to say how much can be saved by going through a broker; with luck, 40 to 50 percent. I have had clients who purchased sails through a broker only for the cloth, had them recut, and still saved money!

Brokers generally have no information pertaining to a sail's aerodynamic shape, so in that regard you take what you get and hope it's not so inappropriate that the sail must be returned. A renowned loft with a reputation for performance in a particular boat type will likely have made a sail with good shape. Naturally, unless known already, inquire as to the sailmaker before having it delivered.

If you are buying a used sail for its cloth, it is important to consider whether the sail has been constructed with shaped panels that, unless you can incorporate that built-in shape, will render the sail unsuited to recutting.

SURVEYING USED SAILS

The first step in assessing a sail for purchase (or a sail you already own) is to know the boat and what kind of sailing you'll be doing. The demands placed on a sail for daysailing are far less than those on a cruising sail. Though commercial sail has different goals, for our purposes in surveying, we'll lump voyaging and workboat sails together as if the sailor's life depended on them.

I recommend that you do your own survey. Not only will this save money in the short term, it leads to sails that need fewer repairs and last longer.

When considering what action to take as a result of the survey, a threefold distinction is helpful:

1. *The repair route:* This signifies that only minimal maintenance and fixing is needed by an otherwise seaworthy sail.
2. *Restoration:* The sail is basically sound but in need of a major overhaul, recut, or repair. This work will reclaim a sail that, had it been in new condition, would have been immediately appropriate for the sailor's needs.
3. *Rebuilding:* This entails more or less replacement, recutting, and alteration in order to create an appropriate sail out of one that originally, even new, would not have made the grade. Something significant about the sail makes this major work economically viable.

The Survey Procedure

A complete sail survey is actually conducted in three separate, distinct phases and is most easily and rapidly done with two people. A clipboard with paper and pencil for notations, and a tape measure of sufficient length, are required. For sophisticated assessment in the latter phase, a good camera will be required. The accompanying sail survey checklist will be of immeasurable aid in noting sail details and later in formulating a conclusion. Following is a brief description of the three phases, after which is a detailed account of each.

Phase 1: This initial measurement and inspection of the sail structure and material is best done indoors on a flat surface in a clean, well-lighted space large enough to accommodate the sail fully laid out. A smaller space can be workable if the sail is methodically scrutinized section by section. Sails can be laid out and inspected outdoors on a fair, windless day, but glare and layout surface can be problems. Grass easily stains and grit can harm the fabric. Inevitably you entomb a host of insects when refolding the sail.

To thoroughly inspect sails, indoors or out, it is necessary to remove your shoes and go over every inch, stooping low or dropping down on hands and knees. On a large sail, this may take some time.

TABLE 10-1.
SAIL SURVEY CHECKLIST

TYPE OF SAIL: _____ TYPE OF CLOTH: _____

MEASUREMENTS — LUFF: _____	GIRTH: _____	REEF SAIL AREA:	DEPTH OF REEF:
FOOT: _____	LP/DIAG: _____	#1 _____	#1 _____
LEECH: _____	AREA: _____	#2 _____	#2 _____
HEAD: _____		#3 _____	#3 _____

SOURCE OF SAIL:
ASKING PRICE: _____ SHIPPING COST: _____ NEW REPLACEMENT COST: _____

INSPECTION

ITEM	APPROPRIATENESS AND QUALITY OF MATERIAL	QUALITY OF CONSTRUCTION	CONDITION OF MATERIAL	NUMBER OF REPAIRS	RESTORE	REPLACE OR REBUILD	EST. $	NOTES: (LOCATION)
SAILCLOTH								
STITCHING AND SEAMS								
OLD REPAIRS								
RINGS AND EYELETS								
CLOTH REINFORCEMENTS								
BOLTROPE/ LUFFROPE								
WIRE ROPE								
HEADBOARD								
BATTENS								
BATTEN POCKETS								
SLIDES								
HANKS								
SEIZINGS								
LEECHCORD								
FOOTCORD								
ROLLER FURLING EDGECOVERS								
PERIPHERAL HARDWARE								
CHAFING GEAR								
REEF POINTS								
(OTHER)								
GENERAL SUMMATION AND TOTALS				TOTAL #	TOTAL #	TOTAL #	TOTAL	

OBSERVATIONS ON BOARD

CONCERN	YES	NO	FAULT DESCRIPTION	DESCRIPTION OF CORRECTION	COST
SAIL COMPATIBLE WITH SPAR AND STAY LENGTHS?					
REEF POSITIONS MATCH REEF HARDWARE?					
LUFF COMPATIBLE WITH HALYARD POWER?					
HEAD AND/OR FOOT COMPATIBLE WITH OUTHAUL POWER?					

(CONT. NEXT PAGE)

Observations on Board (cont. from previous page)

Concern	Yes	No	Fault Description	Description of Correction	Cost
Sail hardware compatible with spar hardware?					
Ease of furling and rigging?					
Topping lift chafe?					
Lower shroud chafe?					
Pulpit and lifeline chafe?					
Jamming slides and hanks?					
(Other)					
General Overview					

Observations Under Sail

Full Sail Shape	High	Middle	Low	Point of Sail	True Wind Speed	Fault Description	Correction	Cost
Camber (ratio)								
Draft position (%)								
Shape of entry								
Shape of exit								
Overview								

Sail Faults	Fault Description	Correction	Cost
Corner wrinkles			
Wrinkles in body of sail			
Hooked or fluttering leech			
Hooked or fluttering foot			
Hinged leech with battens			
Edge pocket or wrinkles			
Hardspots			
Backwinding			

Full Sail Performance

Point of sail: _____ Boat speed: _____ Sail's effective wind range: (—)
Shape retention: _____ Helm: weather ( ) lee ( ) balanced ( )
Other observations and variables: _____

Effectiveness of Draft Controls	Item	Pos.	Neg.	Fault Description	Correction	Cost
	Leechcord					
	Footcord					
	Halyard and Cunningham					
	Outhauls					
	Notes					

Reefed Sail Observations

Reef in use: #1 ( ) #2 ( ) #3 ( ) Point of sail: _____ Boat speed: _____
Effective wind range: (—) Helm: weather ( ) lee ( ) balanced ( )
General ease of handling and sail shape: _____

Effectiveness of Gear	Item	Pos.	Neg.	Fault Description	Correction	Cost
	Leechcord					
	Reef points					
	Reef tackle and hardware					
	Notes:					

CONCLUSIONS OF SURVEY

```
┌────────────────────────────────────────────────────────────────────────────────┐
│ SAIL IS ACCEPTABLE: YES (  ) NO (  )                                             │
│ SAIL IS SAFE, FUNCTIONAL, AND APPROPRIATE AT PRESENT? YES (  ) NO (  )           │
│ SAIL WILL BE SAFE, FUNCTIONAL, AND APPROPRIATE WITH:  REPAIRS (  )               │
│                                                       RESTORATION (  )           │
│                                                       REBUILDING (  )            │
│                                                       CLEANING (  )              │
├────────────────────────────────────┬─────────────────────────────────────────┤
│ WORK TO BE DONE BY SELF: YES ( ) NO ( ) │ WORK TO BE DONE BY OTHER: YES ( ) NO ( ) │
│    TIME  ESTIMATE :                 │    TIME  ESTIMATE:                         │
│    COST  ESTIMATE :                 │    COST  ESTIMATE:                         │
├────────────────────────────────────┴─────────────────────────────────────────┤
│ DELIVERY DATE:                                                                  │
└────────────────────────────────────────────────────────────────────────────────┘
```

Remember, you must check both sides of the sail! If you don't have a thorough knowledge of sail terminology as a means of specifying areas in need of attention, a rough sketch can be made of the sail, with circles and arrows.

Phase 2: The sail may look great on the floor and even measure out satisfactorily, but that doesn't mean it will fit your boat. The second phase is to take the sail to the boat at the dock or in the yard and bend it on. Unless you intend to combine this and the third phase, a windless period is best, with relatively subdued light—early morning or a calm, overcast day. In bending sail, you are checking for a sail's fully tensioned compatibility with spar or stay lengths, and compatibility and alignment between spar and sail hardware. You are also checking for compatibility of sail edge tension and hauling power on halyards and outhauls. Last, the sail's two-dimensional compatibility with rig and deck hardware can be determined, and problem areas of chafe and misfit designated.

Phase 3: If there is a light breeze, one can get some indication of a sail's shape during the pre-sailing phase, but it is a poor substitute for the actual step of studying the sail under its intended and designed working conditions. If it is a multi-purpose sail, this means testing it in a wide range of wind strengths, points of sail, and sea conditions—zephyrs to gale, reefed, and full sail. If it is an as-yet-unpurchased, used sail you are taking for a test run, you are taking your chances if you take it out in a snorter. Wreck the sail, and you're probably responsible for it. You can judge fairly well from the initial phases of inspection whether a sail will stand up to heavy-weather use. There is no harm in tucking in a deeper reef than necessary just to see how she sets and how the boat handles. In this last phase, you are looking for sail shape, shape retention, function of draft controls, ease of handling, performance, and compatible interaction with other sails. One would never buy a used car without at least taking it for a drive, and the same should ideally apply to the purchase of a used sail (which is why buying a used sail from a broker can be chancy).

Phase 1: Inspecting the Sail Up Close

Obviously, if the sail you are surveying is one of your own, there is no need to take the preliminary step of measuring it. Otherwise, it is wise to eliminate further wasted effort by making sure at this point that the sail is of the correct proportions, either for immediate use or with recut. This, of course, presupposes that the measurements you need are known from having measured the boat, from an old sail, or from an accurate sail plan. This is only a rough guide to sail applicability, but it will weed out the gross misfit.

The straight-line edges of the sail should be measured under firm tension. On an appropriate floor, spikes or nails hold the sail in a stretched-out position. These measurements tell you compatibility with spar and stay length. It may also be advantageous to make other measurements in order to determine sail area, headsail overlap, sheeting angle, reef depth and areas, and trim points.

Lacking sufficient space to tack out the sail, you can measure edge by edge or even edge section by edge section, though accuracy may suffer.

We can now proceed to examine the sail in detail:

THE CLOTH.   In woven synthetics, the first thing to look for is sun damage, indicated by powdery fading or a squeaky feel to the cloth. The most exposure is at the leeches and corners as well as along the head in a gaff sail and along the foot in a Bermudan. If it looks tired, it is. When in doubt, attempt to tear the cloth with your bare hands, with and across the weave.

During the layout you will have gotten some feel for the thickness (weight) and *hand* (flexibility) of the cloth. Is the material of the desired weight and softness? A soft material can indicate an aged fabric or one that is new and intended to be soft. One loses competitive performance in the interest of durability and ease of handling when opting for a softer cloth, so it depends on the kind of sailing you do.

A relatively tired, formerly firm racing fabric could be just the thing for an easygoing cruiser or daysailer. Naturally, check the entire sail for stains, mildew, salt saturation, repairs, past recuts, unrepaired damages, and chafe spots. Most stains on synthetics, even mildew, unless they have caused deterioration of the cloth, are only of cosmetic concern. However, at current sail-cleaning prices of $1.50 or $2.00 per pound and up, the cost of thoroughly cleaning the sail has some bearing. Likewise with excessive salt buildup, which may warn of hardware corrosion—but this can easily be rinsed by the sailor.

Past damages are mainly a concern if they have been left unattended or were improperly repaired. Methods of repair come in as many variations as there are ways to harm a sail. One must look to see that the sail is put back together as closely as possible to the way it was originally: same cloth type, stitching, reinforcements, and hardware—whatever was involved in the replacement. This course is advisable if the damage resulted from accident or abuse—say, an untaped cotter pin. But if the damage is the result of poor construction, the remedy is then a rebuild; a repair or restoration would only be inviting repetition of the same mishap. To improve one aspect of a generally poor-quality sail is to put a strong link in a weak chain. A sail is an interdependent assembly of parts, and a repair must be compatible with the rest of the sail. A weak, inadequate repair leaves an Achilles' heel, whereas an overbuilt repair can result in the failure of surrounding parts of the sail due to discontinuity and unbalanced distribution of strain.

Note all unrepaired damages—slits, tears, thin spots. The following areas come in for a lot of abuse:

1. *On headsails:* the leeches from flutter and spreader ends, and from tacking across shrouds, stays, and mast; the forward foot portion of the foot rubbing on lifelines and bow pulpit; along the luff at each hank from insufficient halyard tension or sliding across the hanks.
2. *On boomed sails:* batten pockets; the seams from shroud and lazyjack chafe; along the leech from flutter and topping lift chafe; along the foot from chafe while reefed down; and leech-cord chafe.

If there is already a tear in the sail, this is an opportunity to conduct another little tear-strength test. Try with some deliberateness to tear the spot a little farther. If it goes with all the resistance of a piece of newspaper, the area may be rotten—a condition generally indicated by other symptoms as well. If an otherwise good cloth should tear that easily, it is of inferior quality and perhaps should be rejected.

STITCHING.   Check all seam stitching on both sides of the sail. Machine-sewn thread will show signs of age and deterioration before the sailcloth will, and it will fail sooner. Vigorous scraping with your fingernail will reveal weak or poorly sewn thread. Is the rotten thread in an isolated location—that is, frequently hit by sun or chafe—or is the whole sail weakly held together?

Study the quality and quantity of stitching. The thread should match the sail material and type of sail in weight. Contrary to what one might expect, too much stitching—either crowded stitches or repeated restitchings—weakens the sail (see Chapter 5). Voyaging sails should have three clean rows of zigzag stitching in the seams. A double-stitched seam can be strengthened, if wide enough, by a third row of stitching, but this process of triple stitching or restitching a large, heavy sail can be arduous and expensive.

RINGS AND EYELETS.   Most production sails are now finished with spur grommets and hydraulically pressed rings, which, in terms of voyaging, is an expediency lacking in strength and ease of replacement. The principal things to check for in these ring types are appropriateness for future sailing, corrosion, and the condition of the surrounding cloth, which tends to suffer from ring corrosion, chafe, and flexion.

Handsewn rings, the seafarer's method, should be assessed as to quality and condition of stitching, especially on the side of strain. And all rings and eyelets must be hefty enough to withstand the strain and large enough to take whatever line or hardware is to be attached. Replacing spur grommets with handsewn rings is easily done; the replacement of hydraulic rings, on the other hand, is a major undertaking.

Clew and head rings come in for the most strain and chafe, but reef-corner rings and reef-point eyelets should not be neglected. Hand sewing eyelets and corner rings is a technique easily performed by a sailor, both in upgrading a sail or in effecting repairs at sea. A ring or eyelet is only as strong as its compatibility with the underlying and surrounding materials.

REINFORCEMENTS AND TAPE.   A single layer of sailcloth is not sufficiently strong in itself to withstand the strain and tension placed on the edges and stress points of the sail. Hence, multiple layers are built up so as to distribute the load and provide heavy areas of reinforcement in which to place rings and eyelets. It is important to determine whether, for your purposes, the cloth reinforcements in the form of tablings and corner patches are sufficiently heavy (number of layers) and wide enough, and whether they distribute strain in the correct directions.

A light patch with abrupt strain transition places enormous stress on the very edge of the reinforcement and on that last outer row of stitching. Consequently, the sail's corner patch splits away. This can happen anywhere in the sail, but check in particular the clews, the luff tape at hank or slide positions, and the reef-point patches.

ROPE AND WIRE REINFORCEMENT.   Most sails that are set on a stay or set flying are further reinforced along tensioned edges with sailcloth tape. But it is not rare, and it is often advisable, to have a sail with edges reinforced by rope or wire. There are two major considerations when assessing such reinforcement: the condition of the material, and whether the rope or wire is functioning correctly. Its purpose is to limit the extent to which a sail's edge can be stretched in proportion to the outhaul or halyard-tensioning power of the sailor and rig. If the reinforcement is too light, elastic, or long, the sail will be pulled apart or distorted out of shape. If the rope or wire is too strong or short, you will never be able to tension and set the sail properly; it will always remain a puckered bag.

Moreover, in a stretchy, elastic luff arrangement, there is a governing and stretch-limiting function as well as a *controlled* amount of elasticity with which to influence luff tension and sail shape. Wire, of course, has none of this elasticity. Thus, the principal concern is whether the wire is too short. On larger sails it is not possible to fully test wire and rope function indoors without a handy billy and strong fixtures in the room for attachment. Adjustments and corrections are far more easily made for a rope or wire that is too long.

The condition of a rope or wire that is enclosed within a sail can be difficult to judge. Check for wear at the hanks, signs of wire corrosion bleeding through the cloth, and wear and deterioration at

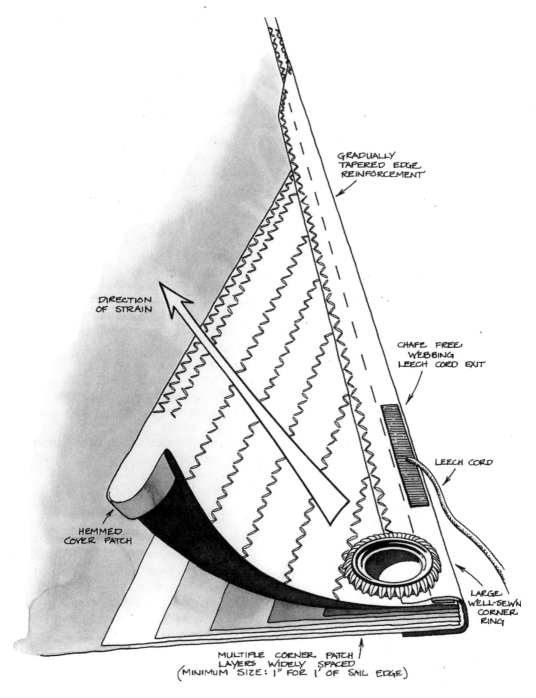

GRADUALLY
TAPERED EDGE
REINFORCEMENT

CHAFE FREE
WEBBING
LEECH CORD EXIT

LEECH CORD

DIRECTION
OF STRAIN

HEMMED
COVER PATCH

LARGE
WELL-SEWN
CORNER
RING

MULTIPLE CORNER PATCH
LAYERS WIDELY SPACED
(MINIMUM SIZE: 1" FOR 1' OF SAIL EDGE)

FIGURE 10-2. *Seaworthy sail-corner construction. (Leather chafing pieces omitted for clarity.)*

tack and head. It is worth noting that perhaps you'd prefer a different form of reinforcement than the one presently found in the sail—say, rope instead of wire, even if the wire appears sound.

External hand- or machine-sewn roping clearly reveals any problems: Is the stitching sound and even? Are there chafe spots? Is there sign of fatigue or deterioration? Metal shackles and slides and squeeze-on-type hanks are merciless to sail edges and roping and ought to be replaced with kinder fittings.

If roping is not to a certain extent shorter than the actual straight-line edge of the sail, the sail will be hoisted or tensioned by its cloth rather than by the rope that is intended to take the strain.

LEECH CORDS.   To stabilize and support as well as to alter sail shape, the leech and—if boomless—the foot of a sail will have a light line running within the tabling. These cords, used judiciously, are an important sail-handling device. First, note the presence or absence of leech and foot cords. If you find them, check for wear and chafe, particularly at the cleats, rings, and buttons to which the cords are belayed. Is the dead end of the cord securely anchored, and is the size of the line appropriate for the sail type and use? Many newer mainsails have the leech-cord dead-end at the clew, passing over sheaves and headboard and running externally down the luff. Try all leech and foot cords under sail to be assured of their functionality and to study their effect on the sail.

HEADBOARDS.   The usual difficulties with headboards, both the internally and the externally riveted types, are corrosion, halyard-shackle chafe, and cloth damage just below the headboard. Even with thick reinforcement, the flex point in the cloth along the hard metal edge of the headboard fatigues and breaks. This is the most serious concern and one that, if left unrectified, will result in the sail's literally losing its head.

Once having encountered such horrors, a cruising sailor surveying a mainsail might reconsider whether headboard, battens, and leech roach are appropriate at all, and contemplate a recut to eliminate those features.

SLIDES AND HANKS.   Inspect all hardware used to bend the sail to spar or wire. It should fit the rig and be strong and in good working condition. Note headsail hank wear, corrosion, and freeze-up. (Squeeze-on hanks are not seaworthy gear and should be replaced with handsewn hanks.)

There are many types of sail slides, and a sailor should be concerned about their strength, design, condition, and how smoothly they'll travel in or on the spar. Slug-type slides with light, plastic bails are good for fair-weather daysailing. The most important aspect of slides and hanks is the way in which they are attached to the sail. Shackles cause extensive damage to both sail and slide, and should be replaced by a seizing of webbing or twine.

REEFS.   Reefs are survival gear, and to neglect them in a sail survey would be like test-driving a car and failing to see if the brakes worked. First, are there any reefs at all? How many? Do they reduce the sail area to a degree appropriate for the sail configurations, helm balance, and handling of the boat? Your benchmarks are the boat's former sail or a sail plan and, of course, test-sailing.

The condition and scantlings of reef hardware and reinforcements are part of the earlier general study. Now it is time to check the alignment of reef rows. On boomed sails, the reef clew should be higher than the reef tack, and the big corner rings must be somewhat above the straight line of the reef points. Check reef-point spacing. A well-tucked reef requires close spacing—every 2 feet or so—with easily tied reef points of sufficient length. For the best distribution of strain, the reef points are sewn to the sail rather than merely knotted on either side of the eyelet. Furthermore, all reef points should be installed, even the deepest row. It is important to incorporate the addition or enhancement of reefs into any assessment of a sail.

ROLLER-FURLING SAILS.   Roller-furling sails are a breed with special considerations. Sun rot, par-

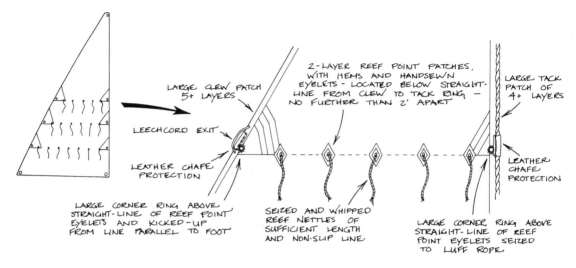

FIGURE 10-3. *Seaworthy reef placement and construction details.*

ticularly at the corners and leech and foot edges, is the biggest concern. Second, despite various contrivances, sails of this type become deformed during the rolling process and when there is a lack of reinforcement in partially rolled positions.

If the used sail has had no edge cover or sock, you'll probably have to reject it. But if it is sound and has none already, then edge covers are essential.

In the slotted extrusion-type furling gear, the sail is retained by means of a luff tape containing a small rope that runs in the slot. Note the condition of the tape at the head and tack of the sail, which is where the tape tends to pull apart.

Phase 2: The Sail Survey Continues on Board
When bending and checking a sail on board, keep in mind that in some instances conflicts between sail and spar hardware may be more easily and less expensively resolved by changing the gear on the boat than by rejecting or altering the sail. Here are some frequently encountered problems:

- nonalignment of end fittings (outhaul cars, gooseneck fittings, tack padeyes, throat and peak fittings, etc.) with sail corner rings

- incorrect slide or hank placement
- halyard and outhaul power mismatched to sail construction
- incorrect head or tack pendant length and stationary deck block placement in relation to best sheeting angles
- discrepancy between reef hardware placement and reef locations in the sail

Try stowing the sail: This is not technically part of surveying the sail, but it has some bearing on whether the sail is generally desirable. A very stiff sail will take up much more space. Does the sail work with the present sailcover and bag, or are new ones needed?

Phase 3: Put Wind in It
Judging sail shape and boat performance is, of course, a complex subject. However, some basic discernments can be made in order to eliminate a hopelessly dysfunctional sail or to identify areas in need of alteration and improvement. A sail's shape depends on many factors, and no matter how well the sail has been designed and constructed, improper attachment, setting, and trimming will show up as poor shape and performance. In addition, a sail's designed fly-

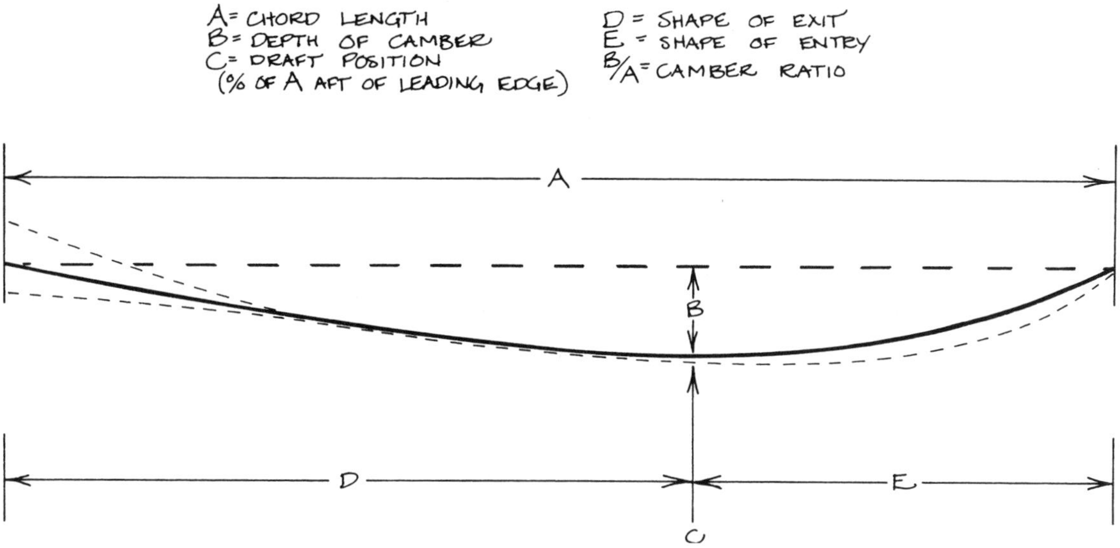

A= CHORD LENGTH
B= DEPTH OF CAMBER
C= DRAFT POSITION
(% OF A AFT OF LEADING EDGE)

D = SHAPE OF EXIT
E = SHAPE OF ENTRY
B/A= CAMBER RATIO

FIGURE 10-4. *Sail shape characteristics.*

ing shape is adjustable within limits. Therefore, the shape should be studied throughout a range of settings. In a well-set and correctly trimmed sail, there are four basic interrelated aspects to observe when sailing upwind:

1. *Sail camber* (belly, draft, fullness, amount of curvature) can be expressed in a ratio of maximum depth per width, or chord length, at any particular height in the sail. Study the relative sail cambers at various heights in the sail.
2. *Draft position:* Where is the point of maximum draft located? The location is expressed by the percentage of the chord length abaft the leading edge of the sail. For example: 50 percent or 45 percent aft.
3. *Shape of entry:* Several sails could be similar in terms of camber and draft placement, but differ radically in the shape of the leading edge of the sail. Greater curvature affords more leeway in trim angle but hurts pointing ability. A flatter entry will point higher but is less forgiving to trim. A full entry in a lapped sail is more subject to backwinding.

4. *Shape of exit:* The leech and after portion of the sail is the easiest to observe. It should be flat and smooth without hooking, fluttering, or sagging.

These shape observations are first applied to upwind sails and sailing. Sails in use offwind, of course, have different aerodynamic requirements—primarily that of creating as much wind resistance as possible—but the principles of study and shape description remain the same. The sail you are testing may be intended for all points of sail, and as you put it through its paces you can identify and record its many forms. Then you can correlate those shapes with adjustment procedures and boat performance. This is where a camera is a valuable tool for revealing sail shape while looking up from the foot of the sail, as described earlier in the chapter.

The aerodynamic form of a voyaging sail is perhaps not as critical as that of a racing sail—in a cruising sail, compromises have already been made in the interest of longevity and ease of handling—but even laid-back cruisers must weed out sluggardly sails in the pursuit of safe and enjoyable passages.

Excessive fullness hinders windward performance and demands early reefing. Too flat a sail might be fast and weatherly but lacks power to drive the boat in a lumpy sea. Draft in the after third of a working sail (unless intentionally induced) indicates big cloth and leech problems.

There must be a sail shape compromise that works well for your boat and its sail combinations. Even if you can't fathom all the principles and variables of sail dynamics, your ability to methodically observe and describe the elementary aspects of sail shape will enable a sailmaker to better advise you as to a sail's functional value and ease of alteration.

In summation, what are the chances of fetching up on a secondhand, well-made, sound, seaworthy sail, perfectly suited to your boat and needs, and available at a price less than what you'd expect to pay for the new custom-made article? Dang slim! If your standards are too high, you will never leave the dock. But a resourceful and self-reliant sailor can make discerning and informed judgments, thereby coming as close as possible to obtaining the best sail at the outset, proceeding from there to make adjustments and alterations that result in the safe, durable, functional, and economical sail that was required. It all begins with having a sail and the time and patience necessary to make a thorough survey.

11

Sailbags and Sailcovers

S OMETIMES SAILS are called "canvas," and sometimes they truly are made of flax or cotton canvas. Moreover, there was a time when there was no distinction—natural-fiber canvas was used for sails and for the myriad cloth covers and other objects aboard ship. A sail loft then was likely engaged in the making of all these items, employing the same tools and materials for all.

With the advent of synthetic materials, a sharp delineation was drawn between competitive-sail fabrics and marine utility cloths. Sails can still be flax or cotton canvas, and utility fabrics for awnings, covers, and bags can be synthetic, but generally there is a marked distinction between cloths best suited for these respective uses, particularly when it comes to high-performance sailing. But as the sailing more nearly approximates traditional modes, the cloths become less specific and more versatile—canvas for everything, if you want.

In any event, with use-specific fabrics have come specialists, and a division between canvaswork and sailwork. Some sail lofts do canvaswork as a sideline, or at least produce bags with their sails. But canvaswork, with its contemporary materials, has become an independent and perhaps more universal field, since both sail- and powerboats have need of canvas items. All this specificity notwithstanding, for the self-reliant sailor there is

little difference between the tools and materials of sailmaking and those of canvaswork. The tools and techniques used in making the ditty bag described in Chapter 1 can produce a bag, hammock, or sail-cover as well as a sail.

There are a great number of specialized tools for canvaswork, but many of these are for installing hardware and fasteners. These tools are not essential for a limited job (some are quite expensive), but for production work they save much time as well as make a neat job of it.

The sewing machines described in Chapter 5 are very versatile and suitable for canvaswork in general. There are, of course, specialized marine canvasworking machines that do specific jobs more efficiently but have little, if any, application in sailmaking. Industrial or even home-use straight-stitch sewing machines, though inappropriate for sails, may be fine for general canvaswork if they'll accommodate a large enough needle and thread. I wouldn't seek out a straight-stitch machine as an all-purpose home-and-boat, sail-and-canvas tool, but if you have one already, it could be fine for canvas projects. Certainly if canvas projects are the limit of your work, adequate straight-stitch machines can be readily and inexpensively obtained, especially older models.

Doing your own canvaswork vastly extends a

sailor's self-reliance. There are so many items aboard that are cloth, including awnings, dodgers, weather cloths, flags, windscoops, bosun's chairs, and others. Some are covers, some are containers, and some (such as flags) are independently functional items. In this chapter we consider sailbags and sailcovers. Once you've made a few of these you'll be well advanced in your canvasworking apprenticeship.

No seafarer can fail to consider sailbags and sailcovers a high priority. These two items are major factors in the condition and useful lifespan of a sail. Make yourself a sail—you'll see—after all

that work, you'll want to store and protect it properly. If instead of making the sail yourself you've paid the going rate for high-quality voyaging sails, you'll be similarly motivated to take care of your investment. Additionally, these utilitarian articles can go a long way, practically and aesthetically, in making a boat organized and handsome.

Sailbags

Desirable qualities in a sailbag include the following:

- *Size:* A sailbag as a container is intended to hold a specific sail. Snug fits are

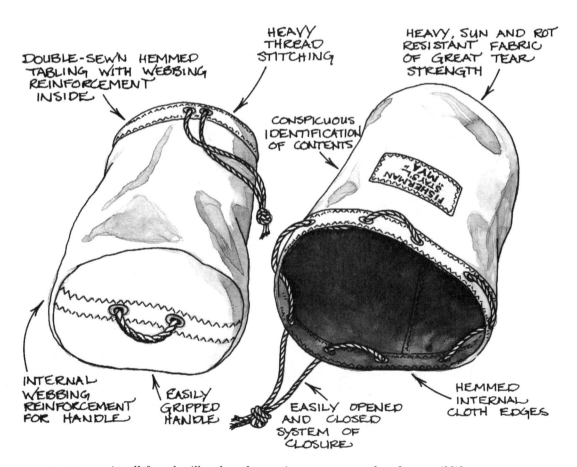

HEAVY THREAD STITCHING

HEAVY, SUN AND ROT RESISTANT FABRIC OF GREAT TEAR STRENGTH

DOUBLE-SEWN HEMMED TABLING WITH WEBBING REINFORCEMENT INSIDE

CONSPICUOUS IDENTIFICATION OF CONTENTS

FISHERMAN STAYS'L MYA

INTERNAL WEBBING REINFORCEMENT FOR HANDLE

EASILY GRIPPED HANDLE

EASILY OPENED AND CLOSED SYSTEM OF CLOSURE

HEMMED INTERNAL CLOTH EDGES

FIGURE 11-1. *A well-found sailbag lasts longer, is easy to use, and prolongs sail life.*

dysfunctional. If the sail will only be inserted when folded, then the bag need not be any larger than necessary to generously hold a well-folded sail; for example, a mainsail, usually left bent on the spars and removed only for off-season storage. A sailbag used for stuffing a sail must be several times larger. A bag with dimensions sufficient for a stuffed sail, of course, can be used as well for folded-sail storage, but never the reverse. When in doubt, make the bag bigger, especially if it will be holding sheets and other paraphernalia as well.

- *Strength:* A sailbag often sustains violent movement and tension. Tossed, heaved, and yanked by a corner with much weight and sharp hardware inside, the material must have great tear strength, and the construction must be stout. Hemmed and double-sewn seams are stronger and don't fray.
- *Protection:* Sailbags serve as covers to protect sails from chafe, sun, and dirt; therefore, they must be resistant themselves, and relatively impermeable.
- *Ease of handling:* Sails may have to be bagged or hauled out in great haste, and even if there is all the time in the world it is a miserable task trying to insert or extricate a sail from a bag with a clumsy or restrictive system of closure. A large sail in a bag can be a cumbersome article, difficult to lug around or haul out of a forepeak if you have only a fistful of bag cloth to grasp. There should be reinforced handles or grips at each end. These are useful, too, in hanging or lashing or in joint carrying efforts. In the immortal words of sailmaker Robin Lincoln, "A sailbag with no handle on the bottom is no more than a laundry bag!"
- *Identification:* A sailbag should clearly identify its contents. A color scheme could work for the initiated, but it is best to distinctly, legibly, and conspicuously label

a bag on the cloth itself with the type of sail within and the name of the boat. Additionally, the label might declare the owner's name, the sail area, and the use of the sail—and even the cloth weight. If you are in the business, of course, sailbags are an important advertising vehicle.

Size   Bag sizes vary not just with the size but also with the age, cloth weight, cloth type, and finish of a sail. A hundred square feet of 18-ounce Duradon can be folded and packed into much less space than the same area of medium-firm 9-ounce Dacron. To be most precise about the minimum-size bag required for a folded sail, simply measure the folded sail. For a stuffed sail, lash the sail or one like it into a tightly packed cylindrical form and take measurements.

For some strange reason I always assumed that I had to custom-make sailbags to fit each sail as it left the shop. It never occurred to me to systematize bagmaking, as Grant Gambell of Gambell and Hunter Sailmakers—and probably most other sailmakers with any business sense—have done, by coming up with a few standard sizes. G & H has three sizes that cover all its needs:

Size	Diameter	Height
Small	10 inches	24 inches
Medium	18 inches	36 inches
Large	26 inches	60 inches

Materials   Sailcloth itself, other than light auxiliary-sail nylons and Dacrons, makes a strong bag. Cotton Vivatex is strong and handsome, and coated bag nylons serve well if not left in the sun. The best combination of qualities can be found in the acrylic-fiber cover cloths, which are strong, protective, colorful, mildew resistant, water repellent, and sun resistant (although the colors do fade in time).

System of Closure   Snaps, twist fasteners, and Velcro are all workable alternatives. The best combination for economy, simplicity, and strength is laceline and eyelets. There are two forms, with something to be said in favor of each:

1. External line rove off through eyelets is the most durable, is easy to grab and install, and works smoothly with a free-running laceline;

the line, however, can snag hanks and hardware.

2. Internal line run through the tabling of the bag and exiting through one or two eyelets is fast; uses fewer eyelets; is smooth-running with a light, slippery line; and will not snag the

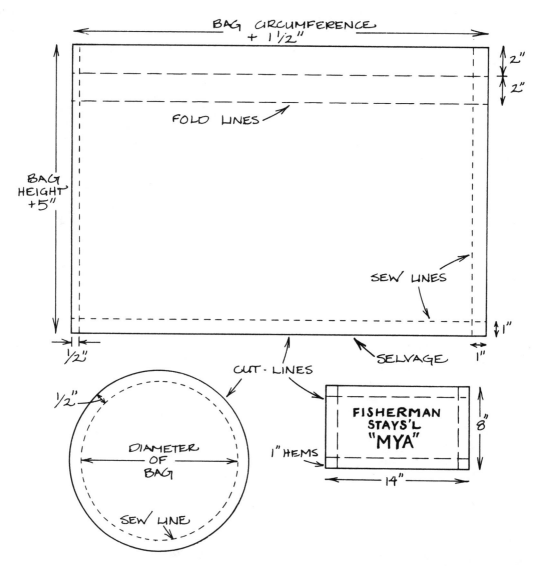

FIGURE 11-2. *Plan of basic sailbag pieces: sides, bottom, and label. A label can be stenciled directly on the outside of the bag before or after sewing.*

sail. On the other hand, an internal drawstring chafes the tabling from within, is slow when wet, and is not easy to grab.

Identification   Identification can be achieved with anything from a laundry marker to embroidery. A plush job can be made of a dark-colored acrylic bag by taking a sufficient-size piece of vanilla-colored (buff) acrylic to an embroidery shop—or embroidering the information yourself in the appropriate thread colors—and then sewing the whole piece to the bag. Otherwise, a nonbleeding laundry marker or felt-tip marker can be used on light-colored cloth, in combination with the stencils available at any stationery store. The letters can be applied directly to the bag or to a label that can be sewn later. The label method allows for error and choice of complementary colors. Test the markers first on a sample to see if the ink bleeds.

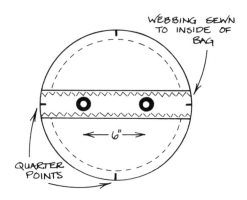

FIGURE 11-4. *Prepare the bottom of the bag by installing webbing and spur grommets and marking the quarter points. Align the handle reinforcement and quarter points with the weave of the cloth.*

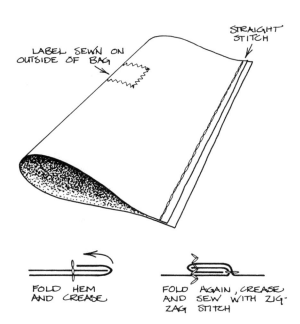

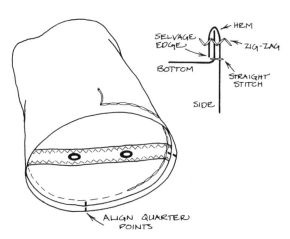

FIGURE 11-5. *Turn the bag sides inside out again, mark the quarter points, and pin or staple the bottom to the sides with the quarter points aligned. Straight stitch bottom to sides, then fold hem and zigzag stitch the folded hem.*

Parts List

- cloth (2 pieces): 1 rectangle with a height equal to the height of the bag plus hems, and length equal to bag circumference plus hems; 1 circle of the bag diameter plus hem

FIGURE 11-3. *After the label has been sewn to the outside of the bag, straight stitch the side seam together, hem over, then sew the hem down with a zigzag stitch. It will be necessary to turn the bag right side out for this second step.*

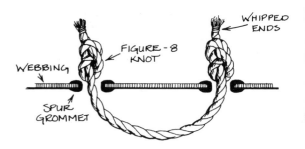

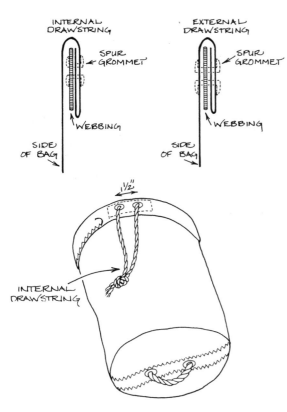

FIGURE 11-7. *Install a handle of appropriate sized and whipped line, ⅜ to ⁵⁄₁₆ inch. Secure with figure-eight knots, with enough clearance for a comfortable handhold.*

FIGURE 11-6. *Fold the hem of the bag mouth to the outside of the bag. Insert webbing into hem in way of all spur grommets. The two spur grommets of internal drawstring-type bags must be installed and the drawstring rove off prior to sewing the zigzag stitch hem. Install spur grommets for the external drawstring by subdividing the circumference to approximately 4-inch spacing.*

Sailcovers

These are the purposes and desirable qualities of a sailcover as protection, containment, and aesthetic object:

- *Complete coverage:* A sailcover is a waste of time if it doesn't cover the whole sail. In addition, a cover should protect the sail's means of attachment. Most often, it is a sail corner, a place of great stress, that doesn't receive adequate protection. A well-designed sailcover can simultaneously cover all or most of a spar as well, and this reduces hardware and spar maintenance. A cover is a poor investment if it deteriorates or becomes an unsightly embarrassment overnight. A water-repellent cover of cloth that does not breathe will keep a dry sail dry, but it will also keep a wet sail wet. Choose a fabric that breathes.
- *Protection:* Needed mostly from ultraviolet light from all sides, while permitting air flow. Clearly, a sailcover that passes ultraviolet light or encourages mildew is no protection.
- *Ease of installation:* This pertains to the system of closure and the fit of the cover. A difficult, time-consuming system discourages use of the cover when it should be on, and discourages removal when it should be

- webbing to reinforce bottom handle and tabling—1½-inch width
- spur grommets for handle and laceline
- laceline: a length 1½ times the bag circumference of ¼-inch three-strand line
- handle line: 2 feet of ⅜- to ½-inch three-strand line
- sail twine or machine thread

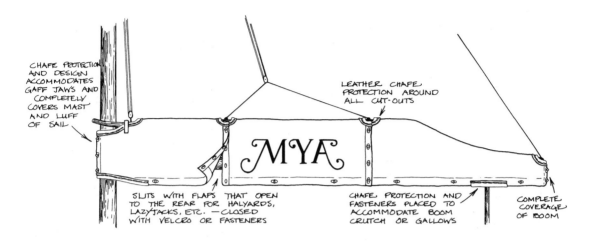

CHAFE PROTECTION AND DESIGN ACCOMMODATES GAFF JAWS AND COMPLETELY COVERS MAST AND LUFF OF SAIL

LEATHER CHAFE PROTECTION AROUND ALL CUT-OUTS

SLITS WITH FLAPS THAT OPEN TO THE REAR FOR HALYARDS, LAZYJACKS, ETC. — CLOSED WITH VELCRO OR FASTENERS

CHAFE PROTECTION AND FASTENERS PLACED TO ACCOMMODATE BOOM CRUTCH OR GALLOWS

COMPLETE COVERAGE OF BOOM

FIGURE 11-8. *A well-made gaff sailcover is as easy to use as a Bermudan mainsail cover and protects the spars as well. The boat's name is a handsome addition. In this case,* Mya *was named in honor of the steamer clam.*

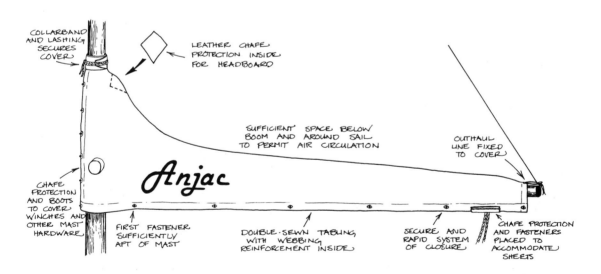

COLLARBAND AND LASHING SECURES COVER

LEATHER CHAFE PROTECTION INSIDE FOR HEADBOARD

SUFFICIENT SPACE BELOW BOOM AND AROUND SAIL TO PERMIT AIR CIRCULATION

OUTHAUL LINE FIXED TO COVER

CHAFE PROTECTION AND BOOTS TO COVER WINCHES AND OTHER MAST HARDWARE

FIRST FASTENER SUFFICIENTLY AFT OF MAST

DOUBLE-SEWN TABLING WITH WEBBING REINFORCEMENT INSIDE

SECURE AND RAPID SYSTEM OF CLOSURE

CHAFE PROTECTION AND FASTENERS PLACED TO ACCOMMODATE SHEETS

FIGURE 11-9. *Bermudan sailcover. A well-found sailcover affords sail protection and enhances a boat's appearance. Ease of installation encourages its use, and ease of removal encourages its being taken off whenever the boat is solely under power, so that in the event of engine failure the crew can hastily make sail.*

off, such as when the boat should be in a state of readiness to make sail when motoring. The necessity for quick removal of a sailcover could arise in an emergency situation. An overly large sailcover is nearly as inappropriate as one that is too small or produces a tight fit. A baggy cover slats and chafes itself, while looking ghastly. A snug cover doesn't pass air, and is difficult to install. A well-fitting cover is effortless to install or remove and large enough to comfortably contain the sail as it is customarily furled, while also accommodating winches and spar hardware.

- *Appearance:* The color of a sailcover can enhance a boat's appearance as part of a coordinated ensemble of the boat deck and general canvaswork colors. They needn't all be the same, but they'd best complement one another.

Sailcovers are supposed to keep sails clean to a certain extent, but as showpieces themselves they rapidly look pretty grungy unless washed regularly and stored in a bag themselves when not in use. A bag of the side-open type makes a dandy storage bag for sailcovers, or you could use the sail's own bag, though the label could be confusing.

- *Identification:* Usually there aren't so many sailcovers on a boat that you can't tell at a glance which sailcover is in hand, but labeling them with the sail and boat name will avoid any quandary. Additionally, sailcovers are a grand opportunity for prominently displaying the boat's name. This may or may not be a desirable function but, if it is, the graphic design, calligraphy, and installation of the name are of critical importance to the success of the sign.
- *Chafe protection:* Sailcovers come in contact with hardware, spars, rigging, and especially halyards. Leather chafe patches are essential, especially with acrylic cloth, which has poor chafe resistance.

Materials   Sailcovers can certainly be made of mildewproof, preshrunk cotton, such as Vivatex, and they do look handsome, but the best cover cloths are acrylic. The material's primary shortcoming is its lack of chafe resistance; otherwise, it has all the laudable qualities mentioned in regard to sailbags and is available in an incredible variety of colors. Acrylic cover cloth, until recently, had the annoying habit of gathering and puckering considerably when sewed, thereby making calculations and fitting difficult. New finishing processes have minimized this problem. A dyed cover or awning fabric will break down more slowly in ultraviolet light than an undyed material. I have seen blue-and-white striped covers in the tropics with the white in tatters but the blue still intact. The reason you see so many blue covers out there, by the way, is that manufacturers selected that color for mass production at the lowest price.

Systems of Closure   By far the cheapest means of closing a sailcover is with string or webbing ties. Other systems abound—zippers, lacing, hooks, and various fasteners. The ease and reliability of twist or

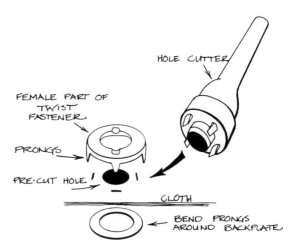

FIGURE 11-10. *The installation of the female part of a twist fastener. If the material is too thick, the prongs will not clinch the backplate.*

turnbutton fasteners more than justify their expense. (The Common Sense fasteners made by Dot Fasteners are the most common brand.) Permanently and most handsomely installed, the male twist part of the fastener is of the type riveted to the sailcover, as shown in the accompanying illustration.

For infrequent projects, an inexpensive setting die is available in a hardware store snap-fastener kit. Two nonessential but valuable specialized tools make faster work of installing twist fasteners: a hole cutter for the tangs of the female portion, and a Durable-Dot fastener-setting tool for the buttons of the male part. In another form of the male part, the same shank and twister is held to the cloth by means of prongs and a backplate instead of being riveted. This type can be installed with a special cutting tool or merely a pointed knife, but they are easily pulled out, and the button-fastened type are more handsome.

Common Sense fasteners are available in two shank lengths: $\frac{3}{16}$ inch and $\frac{5}{16}$ inch. Only in the multilayered, folded corners of a sailcover are the longer-shank fasteners possibly needed. The biggest problem with thick material is that the prongs of the female part aren't long enough to reach through to clinch the backplate. The same problem arises with the buttons holding the male part; therefore, it is important to minimize corner thickness. Right about now, the simplicity of those string ties sounds mighty appealing. Anyway, the alignment of twist fasteners is important, like buttons and buttonholes on shirts; if they are not aligned, there are bloops. I generally mark and install the female part on the sewn cover, then use those as a guide for the placement of the male part by tracing inside each hole. The alignment is perfect, and you are assured of having the two parts correctly fitting together.

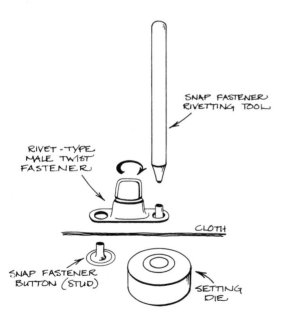

FIGURE 11-11. *Installation of the stud-mounted male part of a twist fastener. This system is strong and handsome. Check for correct alignment with the female part.*

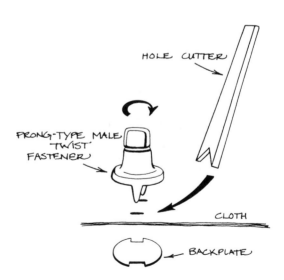

FIGURE 11-12. *The hang-and-backplate system of male twist fastener installation is less expensive but weaker than the stud-mounted type, and less attractive from the back side.*

Thread   Sailcovers should be sewn with #92 (or #16) polyester thread. This weight may be stronger than necessary, but it is consistent with typical cover cloths and will last longer in the sun than a lighter gauge. The stitching is really the weak link in an acrylic cover, even with ultraviolet-resistant thread, since the acrylic will hold up so much longer in the sun. A colored thread will last somewhat longer than an undyed filament. An acrylic cover in the tropics may last two or three restitchings.

A cotton cover can be sewn with polyester thread. If cotton thread—even a colored one—is used, the cover should be given a preservative treatment such as Canvac (see Chapter 8). The cloth may not need a treatment, but the thread does, and there is no harm in doing both simultaneously before fading or mildew sets in to weaken or mar the cover.

Taking Measurements   In general, the considerations when measuring a boat for a sailcover are the same as when measuring for a sail (see Chapter 6). And, by the way, there is no accurate alternative to measuring the boat itself. Tools needed: string, 50-foot tape measure, 12-foot tape measure, clipboard, and prepared sailcover diagram.

The rigging, spars, and sail should be set up as they customarily and normally are put away. This poses a dilemma for the professional covermaker, who knows that a well-furled sail and properly stowed lines will result in a handsomer, less expensive, and longer-lasting cover. But to set up a boat and make a cover for an owner who is not so conscientious is to invite later complaints about ill fit and chafe spots. So you must use discretion. Furthermore, sailors stow lines in their own way—for instance, bringing the several parts of a peak halyard forward and lashing them to the mast rather than leaving them standing.

In making your own cover, you can choose what manner of stowage will be compatible with the cover. In the end it's better to have a cover too big

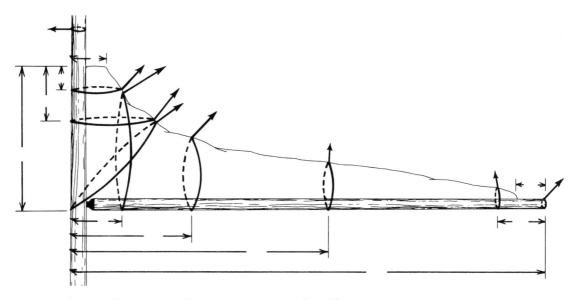

FIGURE 11-13. *Bermudan sailcover measurement plan. The minimum measurements required for making a Bermudan sailcover, if the cover is to be returned for fitting. Enlarge this plan. Add measurements for slits and fastener placement if the cover is not to be fitted. Be sure when measuring and fitting that the sail and rig are stowed as they will be when the cover is in use.*

than too small. The most recommendable way to achieve a good fit is to bring the partially completed cover back to the boat for a fitting; all guesswork is thus eliminated. This does not permit a lax attitude during the initial measuring and layout, but it does take off a good deal of pressure.

Sailcover for a Bermudan Sail

Furl the sail, belay the halyards (*cat-harping*, or tying off, external halyards to the shrouds cuts noise and chafe), and set up the boom at the desired height at the gooseneck (if adjustable), with the boom topped up in crutch or gallows and located in the usual athwartship position (i.e., centerline or clear of companionway). Set and belay as desired the auxiliary lines, lazyjacks, topping lifts, furling systems, etc. On your diagram, make note of several obstructions:

- *Sheets and blocks, gallows or crutch, vangs, dodgers:* These are areas where fasteners should not be placed, especially if the cover is not being returned for a fitting.
- *Winches, cleats, lines, and hardware:* Chafe patches will be needed in these areas. It is necessary to decide in advance of measuring the boat whether to measure *around* winches and protruding hardware and make allowances in the size of the cover, or to cut holes for the hardware and build separate socks or pockets into the cover to accommodate the hardware. Either approach is acceptable.

A boom-to-mast angle of 90 degrees is the easiest configuration to cover. Often, however, between mast rake and the topped-up angle of the boom—and invariably on a club-footed staysail—there is an angle of markedly less than 90 degrees. It is important to record this angle, especially if the cover will not be brought back for a fitting. Two straightedges and a C-clamp work well as a protractor, or you can cut a pattern from a piece of paper or merely stand back and sketch the angle of intersection. There is some latitude for error

here, but the front of the cover will not fit or close correctly if the cover does not fairly well match the spar angles.

Determining Cloth Measurements

1. The measurements taken on the boat were circumferences, which must now be halved in order to lay out a pattern for the longitudinal halves of the cover.
2. Add 4 to 6 inches to each of the half-circumference measurements that were taken around the boom, so that the completed cover will hang below the boom. (Do not add to the half-circumference measurements taken around the mast.)
3. Add 4 inches to the overall length of the cover to compensate for contraction of the cloth while sewing. (Yes, the seam really does shrink when you sew it.)
4. Measurements for the forward end of the cover are taken from the forward centerline of the mast; add 1 inch for overlap of the edges that meet in front of the mast, and 2 inches for the additional cloth in the hems.
5. Additional cloth must be allowed for the 2-inch hem along the bottom of the cover.
6. Additional cloth must also be allowed for hemming the aft end of the cover, or for whatever style of cover end is to be built.

LAYOUT AND INITIAL SEWING

1. Lay out two pieces of cloth, one on top of the other, with the selvages along the bottom edge of the cover.
2. The hems of the bottom edge of the cover are drawn parallel to the selvages.
3. Often one cloth width is not sufficient to fill the plan of a large sailcover, particularly at the mast of a Bermudan sailcover, and an extra piece(s) must be added before the ridge seam is basted together.
4. Draw the hems of the forward-end opening. Make sure to incorporate the correct angle of

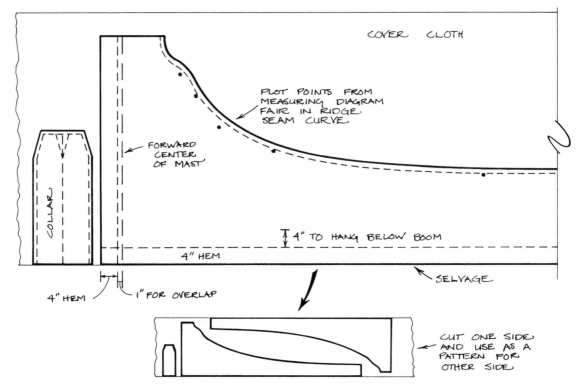

FIGURE 11-14. *Lofting the full-size Bermudan sailcover on the rolled-out cloth. When in doubt about measurements, make it bigger rather than smaller.*

intersection—bottom edge of cover to forward edge of cover—as taken from the intersection of boom and mast or stay.

5. Measuring up from the bottom finished edge and aft from the forward finished edge, plot the curve of the ridge seam of the cover. The fair curve near the forward end should become a straight taper near the aft end. A very flexible batten will help make the rather abrupt curves that occur near the mast and around the headboard. Remember that, up to this point, you are working on what will be the *inside* of the cover.

The curve on a Bermudan sailcover must extend up over the headboard, come to the mast, and then turn up abruptly parallel to the mast or leading edge of the cover, in order to conform to the shape of the contents and

also to allow sufficient material to which the collar can be sewn.

With the ridge-seam curve drawn and the cloths (one on top of the other) firmly pinned down, trim off grossly excess cloth above the ridge, allowing sufficient material to fashion a flat-felled seam. (You'll need ½ inch extra on the top cloth and 1 inch on the bottom cloth to make the flat-felled seam, which is illustrated in the "Sailbags" section earlier in this chapter.) That is all that is necessary if the cover is not to be taken to the boat for final fitting. For a fitted cover, it is best to leave 2 to 3 inches of extra cloth along the ridge, in case the cover needs to be expanded.

6. Sew the bottom and forward hems with webbing inside the rolled-tabling-type hem. Webbing contracts radically when sewn. To

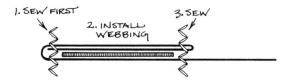

FIGURE 11-15. *The folding, reinforcement, and stitching of the lower hems of the sailcover.*

avoid this, select a webbing slightly narrower than the hem or make the hem slightly wider than whatever webbing you've got. Then, with a zigzag stitch, first sew the outer edge of the

hem, next lay in the webbing, and then sew down the inner edge of the hem without actually sewing the webbing within.

7. Staple, pin, or strike up the two halves of the cover and either pin or baste them together along the finished edge of the ridge seam with a long straight stitch.

FITTING THE COVER. T-pins, a stapler, scissors, and a marking pencil will be needed to fit the cover. If you are doing this step (and I hope you are), make sure that the boat is put away, sails furled, etc., as it was when you first measured.

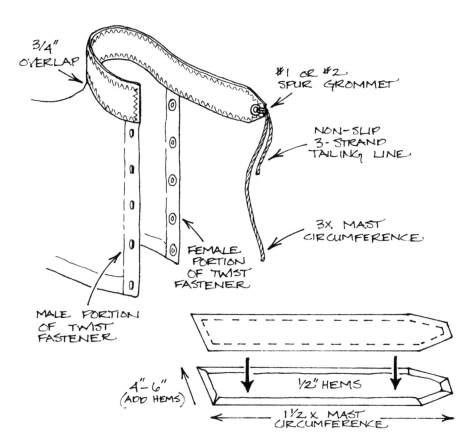

FIGURE 11-16. *Adding a collar to a Bermudan sailcover. Two identical pieces of collar are cut, hemmed under, then sewn to each other except at the edge joining the cover. The collar is then placed on* both *sides of the cut portion of the cover, overlapping ¾ inch, and sewn.*

1. Pin the cover inside out in place. To do so may require cutting slits in the cloth at places where the lines, lazyjacks, etc., will come through, and at gallows, etc. This technique of fitting the cover with its two halves pinned or basted together inside out only works if the cover is completely symmetrical. If there is a winch on only one side of the mast for which the cover is to be cut, then the cover must be pinned together and fitted right-side out. (A gaff cover invariably has asymmetrically distributed cutouts that require fitting on the boat with the cover right-side out.)

There is no great problem in this, except that it is not as easy and convenient to mark the revised ridge-seam location. You will have

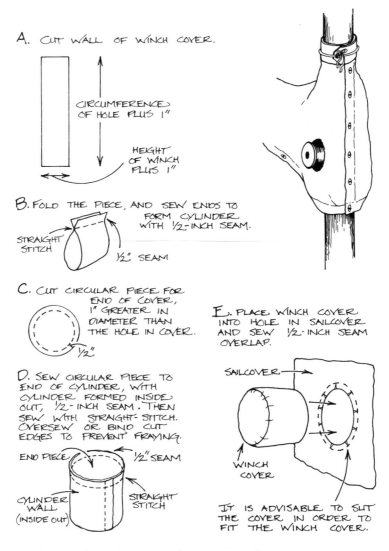

A. CUT WALL OF WINCH COVER.

CIRCUMFERENCE OF HOLE PLUS 1"

HEIGHT OF WINCH PLUS 1"

B. FOLD THE PIECE, AND SEW ENDS TO FORM CYLINDER WITH 1/2-INCH SEAM.

STRAIGHT STITCH

1/2" SEAM

C. CUT CIRCULAR PIECE FOR END OF COVER, 1" GREATER IN DIAMETER THAN THE HOLE IN COVER.

1/2"

D. SEW CIRCULAR PIECE TO END OF CYLINDER, WITH CYLINDER FORMED INSIDE OUT, 1/2-INCH SEAM. THEN SEW WITH STRAIGHT STITCH. OVERSEW OR BIND CUT EDGES TO PREVENT FRAYING.

END PIECE

1/2" SEAM

CYLINDER WALL (INSIDE OUT)

STRAIGHT STITCH

E. PLACE WINCH COVER INTO HOLE IN SAILCOVER AND SEW 1/2-INCH SEAM OVERLAP.

SAILCOVER

WINCH COVER

IT IS ADVISABLE TO SLIT THE COVER IN ORDER TO FIT THE WINCH COVER.

FIGURE 11-17. *Making and attaching a winch cover to a sailcover.*

to spot the ridge seam with occasional pins or pencil marks on the outside of the cloth; then, when you get back to the shop, redraw, cut, and sew the seam with the cover turned inside out again.

Why dink around like this? Couldn't the ridge seam be sewn up permanently and the lower-edge hems be left for adjustment after the fitting? Yes, you can do it that way—especially if the cover is not going to be brought back for a fitting. But a few things make the initial method advisable: If there is webbing sewn into the hems as a reinforcement, the webbing shrinks up quite a bit as it is sewn; to save the lower-edge hems for later would mess up the fit. If anything needs changing, it is much easier to recut and alter the ridge seam than to redraw, cut, fold, and sew the hems. Last, you get a more accurate placement of the ridge seam and front opening of the cover when you can staple or pin the finished lower-edge hems together; this also gives you a more accurate accommodation of sheets, gallows, and other obstructions.

2. Determine a comfortable hem location along the underside of the boom, 4 to 6 inches below it. Staple together the two lower-edge hems, then pull up and pin the cloth along the ridge.

3. Make all necessary marks, guidelines, and references for hardware, chafing gear, and location of fasteners.

4. Radically protruding winches are best accommodated by building socks into the cover; therefore, holes have to be cut in way of winches in order to fit the cover. Otherwise, darts can be taken to mold the cover around mast hardware.

5. Determine a comfortable front-opening position on the forward side of the mast (allowing for halyards, winches, etc.), with a 2-inch overlap. Trim, fold, staple, and pin.

6. Boom end—*wraparound style:* Set up to fit and trim around topping lift. Cut, fold, and

staple. *Open-end type:* Fold right at topping lift, mark. *Sock end* (no topping lift): Fold 2 inches beyond boom end. Mark and staple.

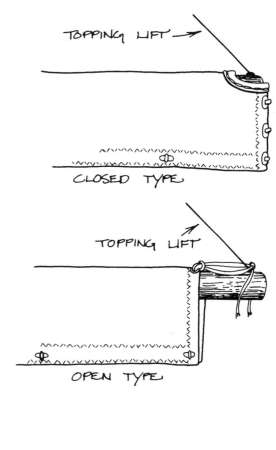

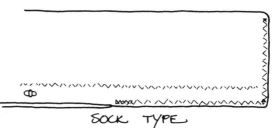

FIGURE 11-18. *Three methods of finishing the aft end of a sailcover. The open type is simple and offers the greatest margin for error in measurement, but does not protect the spar end.*

FINISH SEWING

1. Resew the adjusted ridge seam, if necessary; otherwise, trim the ridge-seam cloth in preparation for sewing a flat-felled seam. It will be necessary to clip the seam slightly along very abrupt curves, such as around a headboard or where the ridge meets the mast, so that the cloth will conform to the bend. Sew the ridge seam with one row of zigzag stitching.
2. Fashion the collar and install it.
3. Fashion and install the aft-end closure—hem, sock, etc.
4. Fashion and install all the overlapping flaps for lazyjack openings, etc. Have them open to the stern so that a headwind will not tear the cover open.
5. Fashion and install any winch or hardware socks.
6. Sew on all chafe protection, especially inside a Bermudan cover in way of a headboard, where a diamond-shaped leather patch on the inside will serve as protection.

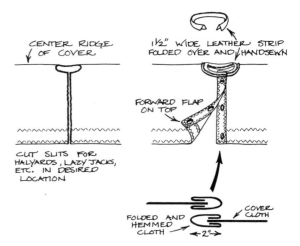

FIGURE 11-20. *A slit in a sailcover may be reinforced by webbing in the facing pieces. Though not shown here, it may be necessary to sew leather over the corners of the bottom of the facing pieces to prevent fraying.*

7. Sew on graphics if not already done.
8. Install fasteners and collar lanyard.
9. Run back to the boat, put the cover on, and use it religiously.

Sailcovers for Gaff Sails and Fore-and-Aft Sails with Yards

Making a gaff sailcover is basically the same as making a Bermudan sailcover, but the overall form has several distinct features. There is no curve to the ridge seam, and where there may have been a headboard to build around, now there is a throat halyard. If the peak halyards are left standing, the cover must be slit to fit. Additionally, gaff jaws pose a challenge in fitting.

The tools, setup, and initial measuring procedure are the same as described for the Bermudan sailcover. However, additional measurements are taken for gaff-related rigging. Lugsails are very simple to cover in that the cover is straight and open-ended, with a slit and opening required for the mast.

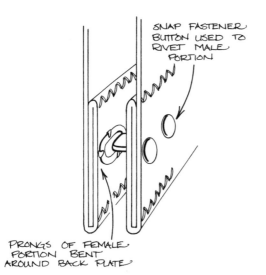

FIGURE 11-19. *The completed installation of male and female parts of a twist fastener in the hems along the bottom of a sailcover. Webbing inside the hem is optional.*

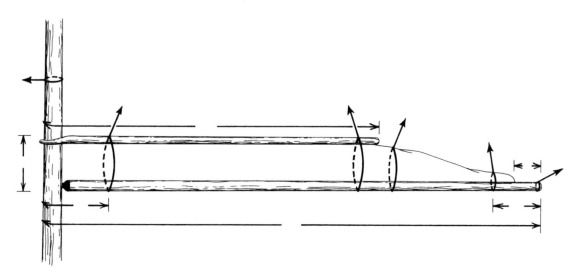

FIGURE 11-21. *Gaff sailcover measurement plan, showing basic measurements if the cover is to be returned for a fitting. Enlarge this plan, and add measurements for slits and fastener placement if cover is not to be fitted. Brailing the peak halyard forward to the mast eliminates the need for halyard and span-wire slits. Be sure when measuring and fitting that the sail and rig are stowed as they will be when the cover is in use.*

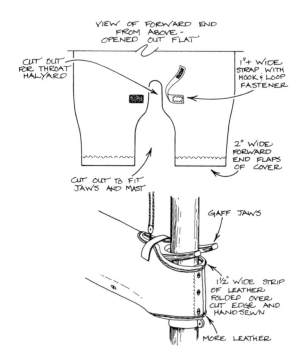

FIGURE 11-22. *Finishing the forward end of a gaff sailcover. The method shown provides a clean solution to the problem of building a cover around the protruding horns of gaff jaws while still maximizing sail coverage at the throat, luff, and tack.*

Headsail Covers

Very often, owners of boats with several headsails, or even a single sail, unbend sails for storage, but it is common and convenient to leave a headsail hanked on, especially on a boat that uses the same headsails repeatedly. There are two types of covers that facilitate this sort of headsail storage: the *staybag* and the *genoa staybag*. The staybag is really no more than a side-open sailbag designed to accommodate the stay and hanks, as well as the sail, with additional means of supporting and tying down the bag for foredeck clearance and restraint.

Elongating the staybag into a form much like that of a Bermudan sailcover produces the genoa

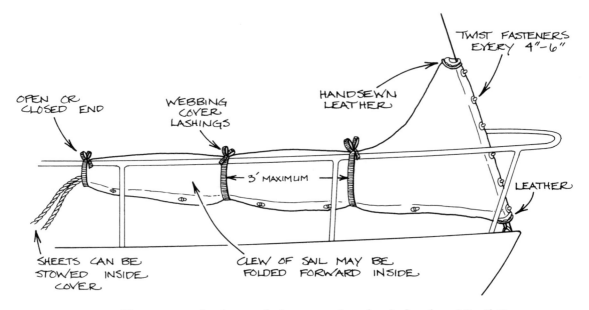

OPEN OR CLOSED END

WEBBING COVER LASHINGS

HANDSEWN LEATHER

TWIST FASTENERS EVERY 4"-6"

3' MAXIMUM

LEATHER

SHEETS CAN BE STOWED INSIDE COVER

CLEW OF SAIL MAY BE FOLDED FORWARD INSIDE

FIGURE 11-23. *The genoa staybag is one solution to stowing a hanked-on long-LP sail. To measure, gasket and lash sail in stowed position off deck and along lifelines, and proceed as for Bermudan mainsail cover. Cover lashings may be permanently attached to cover. Remove halyard when stowing sail.*

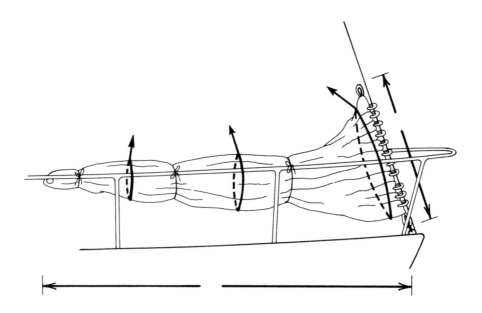

FIGURE 11-24. *Measurement plan for a genoa staybag. Enlarge this plan. Be careful to record the angle at which foot of cover meets stay. Develop a repeatable manner of stowing the sail before measuring.*

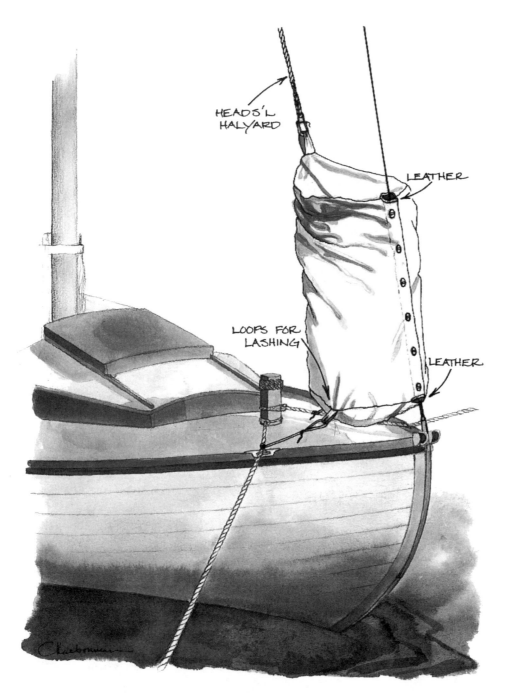

FIGURE 11-25. *The staybag is basically a side-opening cylindrical sailbag with leathered cutouts for the stay and loops for halyard and tiedowns. The halyard is to keep the bag off the deck; the lashings minimize its gyrations.*

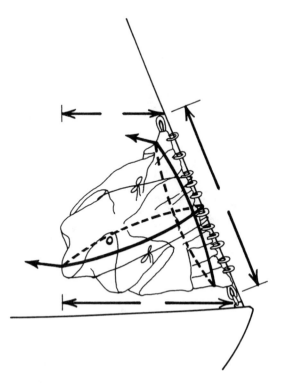

A CUT OUT HERE AND AT THE OTHER END WOULD MAKE THIS BAG DOUBLE AS A STAY BAG

HANDLE AT THIS END TOO!

"MYA" FOUL WEATHER GEAR

LABEL OF CONTENTS

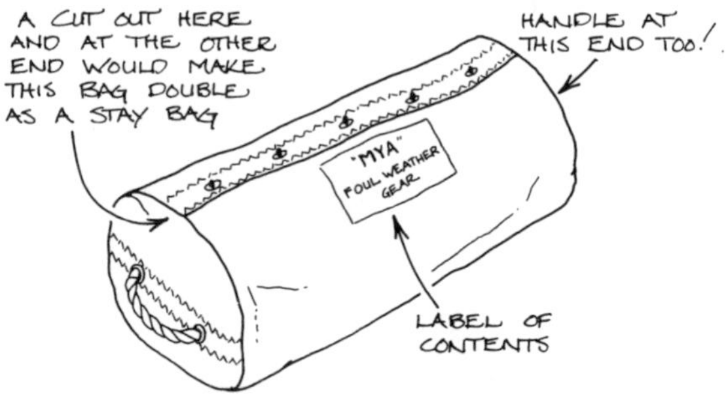

FIGURE 11-27. *The handsome and versatile side-opening sailbag is simply the conventional sailbag already described but with a "bottom" at each end and no side seam. Instead, extra cloth is allowed (as in sailcovers) for 2-inch hems that overlap and are closed with twist fasteners every 6 inches or so. Unless a full cloth width is used in the length of the bag, it is necessary to double-fold the hem on the inside of the ends to prevent fraying.*

FIGURE 11-26. *Measurement plan for the staybag. Most simply the staybag is a cylinder, but it can be flat, conical, or asymmetrical. Enlarge this plan. Lift sail up into stowed position for measuring. The majority of hanks will be above a turnbuckle.*

staybag, which is designed to contain a sail with a long luff perpendicular, lashed to the lifelines. The genoa staybag is not just for genoas, and it is a style that leaves the deck freer, but it does not double as a conventional sailbag as well as does a standard staybag.

Why not just tie a regular drawstring sailbag around the headsail? This common mispractice leaves the hanks and the luff of the sail unprotected. Unless lashed down, the bulk is free to blow and roll around.

Merely by using staybag-type construction, eliminating stay cutouts and tabs but adding end handles, results in a snazzy side-open–type sail (or anything) bag. For that matter, you could put end handles on a staybag and have quite a versatile storage container, as long as you weren't trying to hold items small enough to fall out of the stay cutouts.

If by chance you wish to have covers or bags made for you, specify the materials and constructions described in this chapter. The small custom canvas shop or sail loft is the most likely place to have quality work of this sort done. A good canvas-worker can make a fine cover. A good sailmaker can also make a fine cover, with the added advantages of knowing what it does and the importance of protecting a well-made sail. Beware of production sail lofts and mail-order covers that are generally of inferior quality and are mass produced to commercially determined sizes. A canvasworker or sailmaker with artistic skill can create canvas goods with adornments and lettering that will make your boat fairly glow with color and functional distinction.

12

Sail Handling, Trim, and Adjustment

THE BEST-MADE SAIL is of little benefit without skilled, resourceful, practical use of the basic techniques of bending, trimming, shaping, reefing, furling, and stowing. A comprehension of forces, faults, and corrections is the key to safe, efficient, and enjoyable sailing. Sail trim and fault correction on boats with high-aspect Bermudan sail plans are well covered in other books. In this chapter, the primary emphasis is on applying the same principles to traditional and voyaging rigs. Too many seafaring boats are needlessly slow and inefficient because their owners lack information on how to get the best out of the sails. What follows can help.

BENDING A SAIL

To *bend on* a sail means to affix it to the rig (stay or spar) in some fashion in preparation for setting sail. Twentieth-century yachting has seen a plethora of systems and hardware for this purpose—hanks, slides, etc.—the seizing and use of which are described elsewhere in this book. When bending sail to a stay, there are only two really seawor-

thy alternatives: conventional seafaring hanks, or the popular luff-rope-and-tape method of slotted roller-furling systems.

In contrast, there are many seaworthy ways to attach sails to spars, most of which involve hardware and are described in earlier chapters, but the most versatile and least expensive still use plain old line: lacing, robands, jackstays, parrels, or lashings. The corners of a sail are lashed for strength and alignment with the spar. The lashing may be fixed, as in a tack lashing, or movable, as in an outhaul clew lashing. The spar-bent edges of a sail can be fixed, as in marline hitching, or movable, as in the luff lacing of a sail to be raised and lowered.

Using line to bend sail to a mast works only if the sail is permanently hoisted along the luff—small spritsails, for example—or if the majority of the mast along the luff of a hoisted sail is clear of any other rigging or gear. Three-strand line is easier to splice than yacht braid, holds a knot, and is best for rope grommets, but lacing, lashings, and robands can be made of braided line—even Kevlar braid—in order to maximize strength and minimize stretch. It ain't so salty, but it sure can be

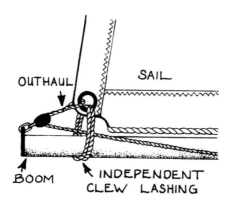

FIGURE 12-1. *An adjustable outhaul clew lashing.*

colorful! See Chapter 7 and Figure 6-86 for a few ideas and configurations.

There are five basic principles to observe when bending sail:

1. *Fair leads:* The pull of halyards, outhauls, and tack pendants should be in line with the corresponding edge of the sail. In addition, the corners of a bent-on sail should all be attached in some manner to assure alignment—for example, spritsail throat, jib tack, fisherman tack, jib head.
2. *Alignment of end lashings and intermediate attachments:* The whole edge of the sail should be equidistant from the spar or stay.
3. *No chafe:* The sail should be isolated from hardware and rig by seizings or lashings, and positioned so as not to chafe on rig or deck gear. The sail is protected by chafing leather where appropriate, and metal ring liners. Lacing and seizings are sacrificial.
4. *Hoisted or adjustable sail edges are free to run smoothly in both directions.*
5. *Fixed sail edges must have sufficient edge tension.*

It is very common to see the clew of a loose-footed sail restrained only by an outhaul. This not only puts all the strain on the outhaul line, but also undermines the effects of sheeting, lowers the boom end, and defeats the purposes of having a loose foot in the first place. A simple clew lashing will rectify all that. See Figure 12-1.

Bending on a Chinese lugsail of the voyaging type involves special considerations, as the sail must first be lashed and bent to the battens—which are really spars—then to the yard and boom before being parreled to the mast. See Figure 12-2.

SETTING A SAIL

Haul it up, yank it down, roll it down, roll it in, or, as in a squaresail, let it loose and drop! Just a small word here about making sail that can add years to the life of the canvas. Halyards and sheets cause long-term chafe and wear on a sail. Protect the sail with chafing gear, and remember to unbend halyards from jibheaded sails when not in use.

The key in setting sail is control. Much grief comes to sails raised while motoring to weather or headed downwind. Swaying up a sail only goes smoothly if all hardware, slides, etc. run freely. Enormous strain may fall on a small luff eyelet, the slide of which has jammed en route aloft. If a sailor is actually *yanking* a sail down, there is something amiss in the system. Moreover, the violence of yanking is hard on a sail. A seaworthy sail system almost hands itself by allowing the sail to fall freely and speedily where desired. Don't forget the boom topping lift! Spare the sail and the halyard the job of raising the boom too, especially when reefed down.

Sending boomless or certain types of loose-footed sails up in stops is not just a racing convention, nor is it only applicable to spinnaker use. Many auxiliary sails and some working sails can be raised in this manner, which assures control on all points of sail. Old twine, rubber bands, rotten cloth—the important thing is that the material used to stop up the sail is strong enough not to let go prematurely, but will break when desired without cutting into the sail.

(text continued on page 447)

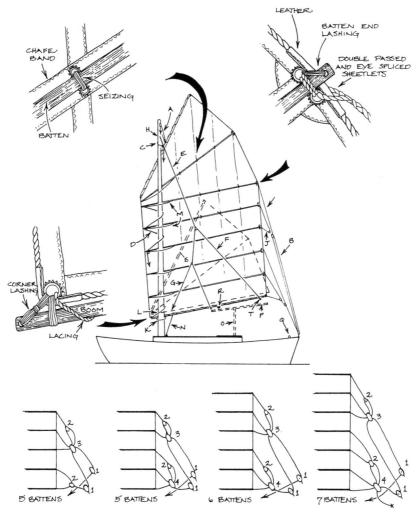

A	Halyard. Fall passes down inside E, outside C and M.
B	Sheet.
C	Yard hauling parrel. Fall passes inside E and G, outside M.
D	Luff hauling parrel. Fall passes down inside the bottom two batten parrels.
E	Topping lift upper spans.*
F	Topping lift after spans.*
G	Topping lift hauling part, outside everything except H.*
H	Burgee halyard, outside everything.
I	Upper sheet spans.
J	Lower sheet spans.
K	Mast lift.
L	Standing lower luff parrel.
M	Batten parrels.

N	Tackline.
O	Boom gallows.
P	Furled sail lowered onto gallows.
Q	Bullseye fairleads.
R	Lowest position of yard sling plate.
S	Yard sling plate.
T	Saddle eyes.
*	Duplicated on part side of sail.
1.	Deckblocks.
2.	Thimble.
3.	Sheaved euphroe.
4.	Plain euphroe.

FIGURE 12-2. *Details of the modern Chinese lug rig, as adapted from* Practical Junk Rig, *by H. G. Hasler and J. K. McLeod. See also the batten detail in Figure 6-10, page 234.*

TABLE 12-1.
THE SAIL DOCTOR'S CHART OF
SYMPTOMS, DIAGNOSES, AND REMEDIES

SYMPTOM	DIAGNOSIS	POSSIBLE REMEDIES
SCALLOPING OF SAIL LUFF WITH CROW'S FEET AT POINTS OF ATTACHMENT	• TACK OR PEAK PENDANTS OF INCORRECT LENGTH	• CHANGE PENDANT LENGTH
	• LUFF TOO LONG	• RECUT SAIL
	• INSUFFICIENT LUFF TENSION	• INCREASE HALYARD TENSION • INCREASE DOWNHAUL TENSION • CUNNINGHAM HOLE
	• LUFF ROPE/WIRE/TAPE TOO SHORT OR TOO STRONG	• LENGTHEN ROPE WIRE • REPLACE REINFORCEMENT (TAPE) • INCREASE HALYARD POWER
	• MEANS OF ATTACHMENT ALONG LUFF OF UNEQUAL LENGTH	• ADJUST LACING, ROBANDS, OR REPLACE SLIDE SEIZINGS
SCALLOPING ALONG FOOT OF BOOMED FIXED-FOOTED SAIL WITH CROW'S FEET AT POINTS OF ATTACHMENT	• FOOT TOO LONG	• RELOCATE/REPLACE TACK AND CLEW HARDWARE • LENGTHEN BOOM • RECUT SAIL
	• INSUFFICIENT EDGE TENSION	• READJUST LASHINGS • INCREASE OUTHAUL TENSIONS
	• FOOTROPE/TAPE TOO TIGHT OR TOO STRONG	• LENGTHEN ROPE/TAPE • REPLACE ROPE/TAPE • INCREASE OUTHAUL POWER
	• MEANS OF ATTACHMENT ALONG FOOT OF UNEQUAL LENGTH	• ADJUST LACING, ROBANDS, OR REPLACE SLIDE SEIZINGS
SCALLOPING ALONG HEAD OF 4-SIDED SAIL WITH CROW'S FEET AT POINTS OF ATTACHMENT (GAFF, LUG, ETC.)	• HEAD TOO LONG	• RELOCATE/REPLACE PEAK AND THROAT HARDWARE • LENGTHEN YARD/GAFF/TOPMAST • RECUT SAIL
	• INSUFFICIENT EDGE TENSION	• READJUST LASHINGS • INCREASE OUTHAUL TENSION • PEAK GAFF UP HIGHER
	• HEADROPE/TAPE TOO TIGHT OR TOO STRONG	• LENGTHEN ROPE/TAPE • REPLACE ROPE/TAPE • INCREASE OUTHAUL POWER
	• MEANS OF ATTACHMENT ALONG HEAD ARE OF UNEQUAL LENGTH	• READJUST LACING, ROBANDS, OR REPLACE SLIDE SEIZINGS

(CONT. NEXT PAGE)

THE SAIL DOCTOR'S CHART (CONT. FROM PREVIOUS PAGE)

SYMPTOM	DIAGNOSIS	POSSIBLE REMEDIES
BIG WRINKLY POCKET ALONG LUFF	• EXCESSIVE LUFF-TENSION	• EASE HALYARD • EASE DOWNHAUL • EASE CUNNINGHAM HOLE
	• LUFFROPE/WIRE/TAPE TOO LONG OR WEAK	• LENGTHEN ROPE/TAPE, ADJUST SEIZING TO WIRE HEAD THIMBLE • REPLACE ROPE/WIRE/TAPE • DIMINISH HALYARD POWER
	• INSUFFICIENT MAST BEND	• INCREASE SHEET TENSION • INCREASE BACKSTAY TENSION • ADJUST RUNNING BACKSTAYS • ADJUST SPRIT OR WISH-BONE CLEW TENSION • INCREASE BOOM VANG TENSION
	• TOO MUCH ROUND IN LUFF CURVE	• RECUT LUFF CURVE WITH LESS ROUND
BIG WRINKLY POCKET ALONG FOOT OF BOOMED OR CLUB-FOOTED SAIL WITH FIXED FOOT	• EXCESSIVE FOOT TENSION	• READJUST CLEW AND TACK LASHINGS • EASE OUTHAUL TENSION
	• FOOTROPE/TAPE/TABLING TOO LONG OR WEAK	• LENGTHEN ROPE/TAPE/TABLING • REPLACE ROPE/TAPE/TABLING
	• INSUFFICIENT BOOM BEND	• INCREASE MID-BOOM SHEET TENSION • MID-BOOM VANG/TOPPING LIFT
	• TOO MUCH ROUND IN FOOT EDGE CURVE	• RECUT FOOT CURVE WITH LESS ROUND
	• FOOTCORD OF LOOSEFOOTED OR BOOMLESS SAIL TOO TIGHT	• EASE FOOTCORD TENSION
	• FOOT TAPERS TOO NUMEROUS OR TIGHT	• EASE OR ELIMINATE TAPERS
NASTY WRINKLES RUNNING PARALLEL TO LEECH	• POOR SEAMING	• RESEW OFFENDING SEAMS
	• IMPROPERLY DRAWN AND SEWN LEECH TAPERS	• REDRAW AND RESEW TAPERS
	• BATTENS TOO SHORT FOR POCKETS	• REPLACE BATTENS
	• POORLY SEWN BATTEN POCKETS	• RESEW POCKETS

(CONT. NEXT PAGE)

THE SAIL DOCTOR'S CHART (CONT. FROM PREVIOUS PAGE)

SYMPTOM	DIAGNOSIS	POSSIBLE REMEDIES
BIG WRINKLY POCKET ALONG HEAD OF FOUR-SIDED SAIL	• EXCESSIVE HEAD TENSION	• READJUST PEAK AND THROAT LASHINGS • EASE PEAK OUTHAUL • EASE PEAK HALYARD OR SNOTTER
	• HEADROPE/TAPE TOO LONG OR WEAK	• LENGTHEN ROPE OR TAPE • REPLACE ROPE OR TAPE
	• INSUFFICIENT SPAR BEND	• INCREASE LEECH TENSION WITH SHEET OR VANG • INCREASE MID-SPAR HALYARD TENSION • MAKE SPAR MORE FLEXIBLE
	• TOO MUCH ROUND IN HEAD EDGE CURVE	• RECUT HEAD CURVE WITH LESS ROUND
	• BROADSEAMING TOO NUMEROUS OR ABRUPT	• EASE OR ELIMINATE BROADSEAMS
HINGED LEECH OR SLACK, FLAPPING LEECH	• INSUFFICIENT LUFF TENSION	• INCREASE LUFF HALYARD, DOWNHAUL OR CUNNINGHAM TENSION
	• INSUFFICIENT LEECH TENSION	• INCREASE OUTBOARD SHEET TENSION • INCREASE BOOM VANG TENSION • INCREASE WEIGHT OF BOOM • TIGHTEN LEECHCORD • TIGHTEN LEECH TAPERS • TIGHTEN TABLING • RELEASE TOPPING LIFT
	• TOO MUCH WEIGHT IN LEECH	• REPLACE WITH LIGHTWEIGHT BATTENS • REPLACE REEF CLEW HARDWARE • LIGHTER LEECHCORD
	• REEF TACKLE OR FLAGS DISTORTING LEECH	• ADJUST • LIGHTEN
	• EXCESSIVE ROACH FOR BATTEN TYPE OR CLOTH FINISH	• REPLACE BATTENS • RECUT LEECH WITH LESS ROACH
	• CLOTH DIRECTION NOT ALIGNED WITH STRAIN	• RECUT LEECH
	• CLOTH STRETCHED OR AGED	• RECUT LEECH, REPLACE SAIL
	• OMISSION OF BATTENS	• PUT 'EM IN! • DUMP THE HUMP
	• EXCESSIVE STAY SAG	• ADJUST TURNBUCKLES, BACKSTAY, RUNNING BACKS

(CONT. NEXT PAGE)

The Sail Doctor's Chart (cont. from previous page)

Symptom	Diagnosis	Possible Remedies
Tight or Hooking Leech	• Excessive leech tension	• Ease and move inboard sheet tension • Ease boom vang tension • Decrease boom weight/top up boom • Ease leechcord • Ease or lighten leech tabling • Ease leech tapers
	• Battens too long for pocket	• Replace battens or pockets
	• Leech tapers curve or too tight	• Redraw/ease tapers
	• Cloth direction not aligned with strain	• Recut leech
	• Tension on reef clew pendant when not in use	• Ease or lighten pendants
	• Excessive hollow in edge curve and rolled tabling	• Change tabling to cut-tabling/tape • Recut leech
Fluttering Leech	• Insufficient leech edge tension	• Tighten leechcord • Increase sheet and or boom vang tension • Tighten seam ends in flutter location • Replace tabling with lighter, less bulky type
	• Aged cloth	• Recut leech/replace sail
	• Insufficient leech hollow	• Recut
	• Omission of battens	• Put 'em in!
Fluttering Foot Flapping edge of Boomless or Loose-footed sail	• Insufficient foot edge tension	• Tighten footcord • Increase outhaul tension (boom/club) • Move sheet lead aft (boomless) • Tighten foot taper ends • Tighten tabling or replace with lighter type • Eliminate rolled tabling
	• Excessive round to foot curve	• Add battens !?! • Recut foot with less round
	• Aged cloth	• Recut foot / replace sail
	• Cloth direction not aligned with strain	• Recut foot

(cont. next page)

THE SAIL DOCTOR'S CHART (CONT. FROM PREVIOUS PAGE)

SYMPTOM	DIAGNOSIS	POSSIBLE REMEDIES
HOOKED FOOT OF BOOMLESS OR LOOSEFOOTED SAIL	• EXCESSIVE EDGE TENSION	• EASE FOOTCORD • EASE OUTHAUL TENSION (BOOM/CLUB) • MOVE SHEET LEAD FORWARD (BOOMLESS) • EASE FOOT TAPERS • EASE TABLINGS • REROPE OR REPLACE TABLING WITH GREATER LENGTH
	• FOOT TAPERS EXCESSIVELY HOOKED	• REDRAW AND STRAIGHTEN TAPERS
	• CLOTH DIRECTION NOT ALIGNED WITH STRAIN	• RECUT FOOT
DRAFT POSITION TOO FAR AFT ON SPAR-BENT SAIL	• INSUFFICIENT LUFF TENSION	• SEE 'SCALLOPING OF LUFF' ABOVE
	• EXCESSIVE LEECH TENSION	• SEE 'TIGHT LEECH' ABOVE
	• MISCUT OF SAIL	• RECUT/REPLACE SAIL
	• AGED CLOTH	• REPLACE SAIL
	• INSUFFICIENT PEAK/TACK DIAGONAL TENSION IN FOUR-SIDED SAIL (GAFF/LUG/SPRIT)	• INCREASE PEAK HALYARD TENSION (GAFF) • INCREASE DOWNHAUL TENSION • INCREASE HALYARD TENSION (LUG) • INCREASE SPRIT SNOTTER TENSION (SPRIT)
DRAFT POSITION TOO FAR AFT ON STAY-BENT SAIL OR SAIL SET FLYING	• INSUFFICIENT LUFF TENSION	• SEE 'SCALLOPING OF LUFF' ABOVE
	• EXCESSIVE STAY OF LUFF SAG	• TIGHTEN TURNBUCKLES, BACKSTAY, RUNNING BACKSTAYS, MAINSHEET, VANG
	• EXCESSIVE LEECH TENSION	• SEE 'TIGHT LEECH' ABOVE
	• AGED CLOTH	• REPLACE SAIL
	• MISCUT SAIL	• RECUT/REPLACE SAIL
	• INSUFFICIENT PEAK/TACK DIAGONAL TENSION IN FOUR-SIDED SAIL (FISHERMAN, GOLLYWOBBLER, ETC.)	• INCREASE PEAK HALYARD TENSION
HORRENDOUS WRINKLE FROM THROAT TO CLEW OF FOUR-SIDED FORE AND AFT SAIL	• INSUFFICIENT TENSION ON DIAGONAL FROM PEAK TO TACK	• INCREASE PEAK HALYARD TENSION (GAFF, FISHERMAN) • INCREASE SNOTTER TENSION (SPRIT) • INCREASE HALYARD TENSION OR DOWNHAUL TENSION (LUG)

(CONT. NEXT PAGE)

The Sail Doctor's Chart (cont. from previous page)

Symptom	Diagnosis	Possible Remedies
Nasty wrinkles radiating from a point of attachment closest to corner of sail	• Misalignment of corner with sail edge such that the corner has an unfair lead and closest means of attachment receives too much strain	• Check lead of halyard, lashing, pendant or hardware to corner • Attach corner itself to wire or spar • Alter corner hardware to create alignment • Alter sail edge hardware and attachment to create alignment
Painful wrinkles emanating from reef points when a reef has been taken on a boomed sail	• Insufficient reef clew outhaul tension	• Increase tension/greater power • Outhaul cheek-block too far forward • Nettles tied before outhaul tension was applied/ retuck reef
	• Nettles tied with varying amounts of tension	• Ease tight nettles /retie all
	• Reef corner ring(s) too low in relation to nettles	• Reinstall corner rings above straight line of reef nettles

SAIL TRIM

Once a sail is set, one then adjusts its attitude and relationship to the apparent wind. This angle is selected to best utilize the aerodynamic force or else the resistance drag forces of the sail. Sometimes the trim is adjusted not to propel the boat so much as to balance helm, or stabilize rolling motion, or maneuver (as in backing and filling), or even to limit the travel of the hull, as when heaving to. It is the braces and sheeting that control a squaresail's trim angle; on a fore-and-aft sail, it is of course the sheeting. One of the wonderful things about sails is that for better or worse, they do not function in one plane. The apparent wind alow may not be the same as the apparent wind aloft, and if not the sail must be adjusted, or trimmed, for the two different angles at different heights. Sheet leads (both fore-and-aft and athwartships), sheet tension, boom vang tension,

and aft turning block placement on boomless sails provide the leech tension that regulates twist for trim angles up and down the sail. A gaffer has the added luxuries of a peak halyard and a gaff vang with which to further tension the leech and completely control the athwartship trim of the head of the sail.

Wind and gravity are always trying to twist a sail's leech off, and would do so excessively without these controls. Sometimes, though, sail twist is valuable, not only for aerodynamic lift but to influence the flow of air over succeeding sails, and in turn their apparent wind angles. Then too, a sail may be intentionally twisted to lose force—that is, to spill air, thus reducing heel, helm, and rig strain. The butterfly wing–shaped boardsail, with its high topsail-like upper sail sections, is designed with those features in mind. It is intended to twist off automatically in a puff that would otherwise dump the sailor. With this in mind, I return to my pet rig,

LUGSAIL SHEETING POSITION

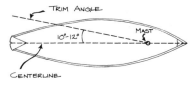

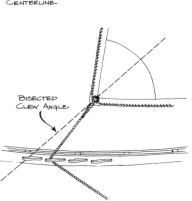

Q: *My 19-foot dory carries a 125-square-foot boom-less standing lugsail with a single sheet. What is the best sheeting position, and will it move in stronger winds?*

A: With a boomless lugs'l or sprits'l, sheeting position is a major factor in performance. Aim for a 10- to 12-degree angle from the centerline. The fore-and-aft position is affected by the relative proportions of leech and foot, the wind strength, and the point of sail. Start by bisecting the straight-line clew angle and lead the sheet to the rail. In a moderate breeze, the close-hauled position will usually be somewhat forward of this point of reference as the leech will require more sheet tension. Install additional thumb-cleats forward and aft for varied conditions.

the Chinese lug, which, in its traditional form, maintains complete control of the leech by a sheeting system of euphroe and sheetlets to restrain the boom and most, if not all, the battens. With variations in the configuration and tension of these lines, the leech is infinitely adjustable, and a change in primary sheet tension will vary the form up high, both in appearance and rate of change. It's a lot of string to fuss with—even moreso with a double set of sheets permitting large sail area on a short hull—but there's much less strain on the sail and rig with leech control divided among all those sheets and battens.

Telltales

Telltales are an indispensable aid in seeing the wind and judging sail trim in terms of airflow over the sail. The effects of sail-shaping controls, edge tension adjustments, sheeting, and sail interaction will all be revealed as those little streamers either stream out, droop, or jump about. Any sail can have telltales.

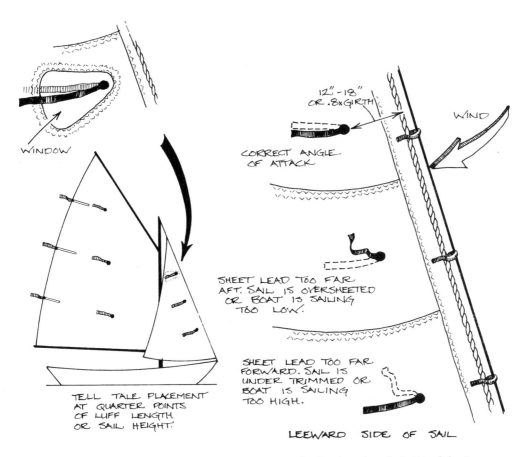

FIGURE 12-3. *Standard telltale configurations. Pieces of red spinnaker cloth, ½ inch by 6 inches, make good telltales; these are easily affixed with quarter-size discs of adhesive-backed insignia cloth.*

SAIL SHAPE

The three-dimensional form of a sail—its camber—is what generates lift and propulsion upwind, and drag, or resistance, downwind. The amount of curvature (camber ratio) and its distribution (draft position) should be altered according to sea conditions, wind speed, and point of sail for the best performance with the sails properly trimmed.

The Chinese lugsail—and other flat sails such as

the traditional batwing and the crab claw—do not make use of these adjustments. But all other cloth sails, including squaresails, do—some more than others. Chapters 4, 5, and 6 discuss how the sailmaker puts shape in a sail. The sailor can put shape in a sail, too, employing the methods the sailmaker has anticipated in the design and fabrication—notably, spar bend and bias elongation (edge tension). There may be other built-in techniques, too, such as zipper feet or flattening roach reefs. Other than adding camber, what a sailor does is alter the form of a sail by changing its draft position and its shapes of luff entry and leech exit. All these changes are made high, low, and in between.

Seeing sail shape can be difficult. Chapter 10 discusses photographing sail camber (Figure 10-1), but for judging sail shape on the fly, North Sails carries little hand-held gauges, and there are draft stripes, another racing convention (like telltales) that can be installed in any sail and would be a great benefit to a performance-conscious sailor. Horizontal seams sewn with color-contrasted thread to reveal shape will do well, as do full-length batten pockets.

Although different sail types may be shaped in different ways by the sailor, the following techniques are common.

Pulling on the Corners

Pulling on the corners of a sail—away from its center—tends to draw and flatten the whole sail in the direction of pull and, with sufficient tension not balanced by any tension at right angles, creates a great bellying wrinkle on the diagonal as the cloth weave is elongated on the bias. The sailmaker has anticipated this shaping option by laying the cloths in a conducive direction. One has only to tug on

TABLE 12-2.
DEVICES THAT INFLUENCE SAIL SHAPE THROUGH CORNER TENSION

DEVICE	CORNER	SAILS	AREA OF DIRECT EFFECT	RESULT*
SHEETS	CLEW	BOOMLESS	EDGE	CAMBER
		FOUR-SIDED SAILS	INTERIOR	CAMBER AND DRAFT POSITION
DOWNHAUL	TACK	STANDING LUGS'L, SPRITS'L	INTERIOR	CAMBER AND DRAFT POSITION
SPRIT SNOTTER	PEAK	SPRITS'L	INTERIOR	CAMBER AND DRAFT POSITION
BOOM SNOTTER	CLEW	SPRIT-BOOMED SAILS	EDGE	CAMBER
OUTHAUL	CLEW	WISHBONE-BOOMED SAILS	EDGE	CAMBER
		LOOSE-FOOTED, BOOMED, OR CLUB-FOOTED SAILS	EDGE	CAMBER
PEAK HALYARD	PEAK	FOUR-SIDED SAILS WITHOUT SPARS (FISHERMAN STAYS'LS, GOLLYWOBBLERS, ETC.) GAFF-HEADED SAILS	INTERIOR	CAMBER AND DRAFT POSITION
SELF-ADJUSTING AND PEDESTAL-MOUNTED CLUBS	CLEW	CLUB-FOOTED SAILS— WHERE CAMBER INCREASES WHEN SHEETS ARE EASED	EDGE	CAMBER

* CAMBER = DEGREE OF CURVATURE. DRAFT POSITION = LOCATION OF DEEPEST DRAFT.

TABLE 12-3.

DEVICES THAT INFLUENCE SAIL SHAPE BY PUSHING CLOTH INTO A SAIL OR PULLING IT OUT

DEVICE	SAIL OR RIG TYPE	GENERAL EFFECT	SAIL EDGE AFFECTED	NATURE OF INFLUENCE
ADJUSTABLE MASTHEAD BACKSTAY	BERMUDAN RIG	MASTBEND	LUFF	CAMBER, DRAFT POSITION, AND SHAPE OF ENTRY
RUNNING BACKSTAY'S	GAFF AND BERMUDAN RIGS			
SHEETING	BOOMED SAILS-DEPENDING ON BLOCK LOCATION			
BOOM VANG				
OUTHAUL	WISHBONE BOOMS			
SNOTTER	SPRIT-BOOMED SAILS — e.g. SHARPIE RIG			
PEAK HALYARD	GAFF-HEADED SAILS, DEPENDING ON BRIDLE AND BLOCK POSITION	GAFF BEND	HEAD	UPPER SAIL CAMBER, DRAFT POSITION, AND SHAPE OF ENTRY
HALYARD	LUG AND LATEEN SAILS	YARD BEND	HEAD/LUFF	SHAPE OF ENTRY, CAMBER, AND DRAFT POSITION
ADJUSTABLE BACKSTAY	JIBS (BERMUDAN RIG)	STAY SAG	LUFF	CAMBER AND DRAFT POSITION
RUNNING BACKSTAYS	HEADS'LS (BERMUDAN AND GAFF RIG)			
TURNBUCKLE ADJUSTMENT	STAYSET SAILS — JACKSTAYS, FORE, HEAD, AND MAIN STAYS			
SPRUNG TOPMAST OR BOWSPRIT	TOPMAST OR BOWSPRIT RIGS			
MAINSHEETS, BOOM VANG	BOOMED MAINS AND MIZZENS			
HALYARD	SAILS SET FLYING SAILS SET ON HALYARD	EDGE SAG		
LEECHCORDS	FORE-AND-AFT SAILS	TIGHTENS AND GATHERS EDGE	LEECH	CAMBER, DRAFT POSITION, AND SHAPE OF EXIT
FOOTCORDS	BOOMLESS, LOOSE-FOOTED SAILS	TIGHTENS AND GATHERS EDGE	FOOT	LOWER SAIL CAMBER AND SHELF
BOWLINES	SQUARES'LS AND UNSUPPORTED LUFF SAILS — e.g. LUGSAILS	PULLS EDGE	WEATHER LEECH/LUFF	SHAPE OF ENTRY
LACING AND ROBANDS	SPAR-BENT SAILS WITH FIXED CORNERS	PULLS OR ALLOWS EDGE TO SAG	EDGE(S) BENT TO SPAR	CAMBER, DRAFT POSITION, AND SAIL SHAPE ALONG SPAR
JACKLINE	LOWER LUFFS OF BOOMED AND CLUB-FOOTED SAILS	EDGE SAG	LOWER LUFF	CAMBER, DRAFT POSITION AND SHAPE OF ENTRY
	THROAT OF GAFFS'L	EDGE SAG	UPPER LUFF	SHAPE OF ENTRY, CAMBER
	FOOT OF BOOMED SAIL	EDGE SAG	FOOT	SHELF, LOWER SAIL CAMBER

the opposite corners of a handkerchief to observe this effect. A radially cut sail, with fabric running parallel to the tension in this direction, is intended to *prevent* distortion and sail alteration.

Think of a piece of flat sheetmetal; we could lay it over a sandbag and mold it into a rounded shape while leaving its perimeter relatively undisturbed. This is the sort of shaping done *inside* the sail's edges.

Alternatively, and often simultaneously, sails can be relatively flat within, but are encouraged to bend along one or more edges—thus forming a curvature much as though you were to take that sheetmetal and merely bend it like a musical saw. There is little control of draft position when this method is used exclusively. Many sails develop curvature in this manner, pulling and easing the clew—sprit- and wishbone-boomed sails, loose-footed boomed sails, and boomless sails. These effects are summarized in Table 12-2.

Pulling Along the Edges

This often occurs simultaneously with pulling on the corners. Depending on the angle of pull, it affects edges unequally. But in isolation, say just bowsing down on the outhaul of a boomed main, the effect is twofold—a pocket is formed along the foot by elongation of the round built into the edge and/or elongation along the bias, and the lower part of the sail is flattened as cloth is drawn toward the foot. Easing tension does the opposite in the extreme, adding great fullness as the gathered and scalloping edges billow out. This technique can be employed on any edge of a sail that is adjustable and is constructed (in terms of cloth direction and edge curve) to permit such methods. All the devices listed in Table 12-2 affect edge tension as they affect corner tension. In addition, luff tension is affected by the throat halyard of a gaff sail or the cunningham on a Bermudan sail, and leech tension is affected by a boom vang.

Edge-tension adjustment affects every aspect of three-dimensional sail shape. Further, pulling on one edge of a sail generally affects the shape of the edge opposite, as cloth is drawn away from or allowed to move toward the influenced edge. Noth-

ing messes up a well-cut leech like an improperly tensioned luff. There is more detail on these effects in Chapters 4 and 5.

Push Me, Pull You Methods

A sailmaker builds shape into a sail by cutting the edge curves. When gathered, tensioned, or placed against a spar or wire, these curves push belly-creating cloth into the body of the sail. The sailor has several means of pushing or pulling the middle of a sail edge in order to affect sail shape: spar bend, stay sag, stay tension, or hauling directly on the middle of the edge are the primary ones. These are summarized in Table 12-3.

Diehard natural-rag sailors have at their disposal one additional means of altering sail shape and cloth porosity. They can use a water scoop known as the "skeet" to fling water on the sail, thereby shrinking selected portions as the soaked fibers swell.

GETTING THE MOST OUT OF A GAFF RIG

The gaff-headed rig endures not only in classic boats, but in venerable one-design classes and even contemporary production designs. The Ancient Mariner's Association, the Friendship Sloop Society, the Catboat Association, schooner races, Beetle Cats, Wianno Seniors, and Marshall 18's represent just some of the gaffers sailing today. When these boats convene for a celebration or meet on the race course, their skippers all want to enhance speed and performance.

Gaff sailcloth is special. It should be firm and stable enough to hold a designed shape, but soft and yielding enough to give with adjustments and tolerate varying tensions in a number of directions.

One of the virtues of the four-sided sail is that it *is* so wonderfully adjustable! One of the *drawbacks* of the gaff sail is that going to weather is not its forte; the lower the peak and the less control of the gaff, the worse the upwind performance will be. In addition to the upwind shortcomings of its low

FIGURE 12-4. *Scalloping along the foot of a sail due to lack of outhaul tension.*

aspect ratio, the gaff sail's weather performance is hampered by excessive twist from the sagging off of its heavy gaff. Indeed, too much gaff sag can hinder performance on any point of sail, and, when combined with a lifting boom, can cause a whacking jibe of calamitous proportions.

The sag is more pronounced with a lower peak and is exacerbated by the general lack of controls in traditional rigs and hardware. Aesthetics, classic appearance, and class rules often put the kibosh on effective countermeasures.

This is not to say that sail twist and gaff sag should be eliminated. A certain amount is necessary, because the apparent wind angle is wider aloft (see Chapter 4). Telltales, wind indicators, and the break of the sail's leading edges are the best guides for judging proper high and low sail trim.

Trim angle, gaff sag, sail twist, and leech sag are not to be confused with one another. The last three must be controlled in order that the first may be optimized. Gaff sag is the tendency—due to gravity and wind pressure—of the spar to fall away to leeward. Sail twist is the helical configuration the sail assumes under the influence of wind pressure and differing apparent wind angles aloft and alow. Leech sag is the falling off of the roach under pressure of the wind.

The camber ratio and draft position are both

important in a fast gaff sail. Sail shape also plays a distinct roll in helm balance.

Rarely does one see draft stripes on a gaff sail. They might blemish a classic appearance, but even temporary stripes can be an invaluable aid to judging sail shape. The more vertical the leech, the more horizontal the cloths in a crosscut gaff sail. If such panels were to be sewn with thread of a contrasting color, the seams would offer an easily read indication of sail shape. Draft stripes, however, are better.

The best draft positions and camber ratios for a gaff sail under particular circumstances are impossible to generalize. A fast sail on a cat rig would not be so on a sloop, and one sloop or cutter mainsail will differ from another depending on the hulls and headsails. The available sail-adjusting gear, not to mention spar types and rigging configuration, are also major factors when determining a designed sail shape.

So how do you discover what designed shape your sail should have? A sailmaker or another sailor may already have determined the optimum shapes for your boat, and you may be able to find out from them. If not, you'll have no alternative but to find out for yourself—through a meticulous process of trial and error—what works and what does not.

Here are some basic guidelines:

- With its more vertical leading edge and reduced gaff sag, a higher aspect ratio (higher peak in particular, and a shorter boom) will yield better upwind performance. The gaff might parallel the forestay. On a split rig, a gaff vang is the best compensation for a low peak.
- The most suitable sailcloth is a woven fabric of balanced or slightly fill-oriented construction, with some but not too much bias elongation control. In contemporary terms, it is a soft cloth. Narrow panels are appropriate for smaller sails.
- Because the cloth is so giving, the initial draft position should be somewhat forward in anticipation of the wind's blowing it aft.

Starting about 40 percent of the chord length aft in a catboat sail, the draft should ultimately settle in a 45- to 50-percent position. In a sloop or split rig the draft position might start farther aft, depending on the sail ahead of it, the sail overlap, and the boat's beam; the idea is to create a good slot and maximize the flow of air over the leeward side of the sail.

- A gaff sail wants to be flattest in its upper sections, which sag off with the gaff, particularly when no gaff vang is used. The midsections are fullest, and the lower areas are moderately full. Too full a sail will be detrimental to sail interaction and pointing ability, and will overpower the hull too soon when the wind breezes on.
- A moderately full and rounded entry in a cat-rig gaff sail makes a more forgiving sail in terms of sheeting angle and compensates for gaff bend aloft. Gaff sails in general should have a slightly flatter entry along the head than the luff. Of course, too full an entry will hamper pointing ability, and on a sloop will crowd the slot and invite backwinding of the mainsail.
- A centrally distributed roach in the leech should be maximized, but not so excessively as to be unsupportable with the available leech control techniques. If appropriate, say, to fill a space in a split rig, the roach could be distributed higher, but never lower, than midleech. The fewer controls you have, the more moderate the roach should be.

All of the preceding generalizations are affected to some extent by what sail controls you have: particularly the ability to control sail twist and gaff sag by sheeting, vanging, and peak halyard tension. What follows is a description of the possible controls at your disposal. If any are unavailable to you because of class rules or any other reason, you should learn what they do anyway. Then, if possible, contrive alternative means to accomplish the same ends.

FIGURE 12-5. *Gaff-rig adjustments: (1) peak halyard; (2) sheet; (3) throat halyard; (4) horse and traveler; (5) boom vang; (6) gaff vang; (7) peak outhaul; (8) clew outhaul; (9) downhaul and/or cunningham; (10) leech cord; (11a) gaff bend; (11b) mast bend; (11c) boom bend; (12) running backstay.*

- *Peak halyard:* Along with sheeting, one of the most useful and versatile controls. Greater peak halyard tension serves to pull the draft forward through bias elongation as the length between peak and tack increases. Simultaneously, depending on the type of throat hardware, the head of the sail would also be elongated.

  Peaking up also tightens the leech and reduces gaff sag. The peak halyard demands constant adjustment for optimum sailing. Easing the peak in a blow spills wind and lowers the center of effort, which reduces heeling and eases helm.
- *Sheet:* Sheet tension controls trim angle, leech tension, and gaff sag, and may induce boom bend. Any tightening of the leech and hooking it to weather makes the sail fuller and moves the draft position farther aft.
- *Throat halyard:* Affects luff tension and thus influences lower and midsail draft placement through bias elongation. Varying the luff tension can also radically alter the shape of the sail's entry.
- *Horse and traveler:* This hardware provides the means by which the athwartship lead of the sheet, and thus the sheet's direction of pull, may be controlled. A downward pull on the boom reduces leech twist and gaff sag. An adjustable traveler position also provides the means of sheeting closer to the centerline, and can compensate for the lack of a boom vang when close-hauled in a light breeze.
- *Boom vang:* Set up to work in conjunction with the sheet, a vang offers even better leech and gaff control. Using the vang in conjunction with the peak halyard can bring the gaff well inboard and tighten a forestay. This handy device may also be used to flatten a sail through mast, gaff, and boom bend.
- *Boom bend:* Influenced by sheet block configuration, vang placement, and spar material and construction. Induced bend flattens the lower sail.

- *Running backstays:* These stays provide aft support to the mast while regulating forestay tension and mast bend. They are also a safety feature in a boat without a standing backstay.
- *Gaff vang:* Permits complete athwartship trim of the gaff and thus the head of the sail.
- *Peak outhaul:* Adjusting the outhaul influences fullness, draft position, and the shape of entry in the head of the sail. As with the luff, more tension flattens the upper sail while pulling the draft forward and rounding the entry. It is usually not adjustable underway, and must be set up in anticipation of the conditions to be met, and to allow for the strain imposed by the peaking of the gaff.
- *Clew outhaul:* Similar to the peak outhaul, but governs foot tension and influences the lower sail fullness and the shape of the shelf above the boom. The outhaul has a profound effect on the camber of a loose-footed sail.
- *Downhaul and cunningham:* Like the throat halyard, these control luff tension but are more easily tightened while the sail is full and drawing. Both permit greater tension within a fixed luff length.
- *Leech cord:* The small line running from peak to clew inside the leech tabling provides leech support on any point of sail. A tight leech means more draft aft. To be used sparingly; it is not a substitute for sheeting, vanging, or peaking.
- *Gaff bend:* Fostered by peak halyard configuration, leech tension, and spar material, gaff bend flattens the head of the sail.
- *Mast bend:* Governed by sheeting and running backstays, greater bend flattens the sail. A useful technique depending on mast material and construction.

Which of these strings and doodads do you adjust first? Table 12-4, adapted from Wallace Ross's

TABLE 12-4.

GAFF RIG SAIL ADJUSTMENTS

SAIL HANDLING CATEGORIES AND SEQUENCE	SEQUENCE OF SAIL AND HULL DIVISIONS	PRIMARY ADJUSTMENTS	SECONDARY ADJUSTMENTS	TERTIARY ADJUSTMENTS
SAIL TWIST	HEADSAIL | SLOT |	A. JIB SHEET TENSION B. SHEET LEAD FORE AND AFT	A. MAST RAKE B. HALYARD TENSION C. CUNNINGHAM TENSION	
	GAFF SAIL	A. SHEET TENSION B. TRAVELER POSITION C. PEAK HALYARD TENSION	A. BOOM VANG TENSION B. GAFF VANG TENSION	
TRIM ANGLE	HEADSAIL | SLOT	A. FAIRLEAD POSITION (ATHWARTSHIPS)	A. SHEET TENSION	
	GAFF SAIL	A. TRAVELER POSITION	A. SHEET TENSION B. BOOM VANG C. GAFF VANG	
HELM BALANCE	CENTERBOARD BOAT	A. CENTERBOARD POSITION FORE AND AFT B. FORE AND AFT HULL TRIM	A. TRIM ANGLE OF SAILS B. DRAFT AMOUNT AND POSITION C. SAIL TWIST D. REEFING	A. MAST RAKE B. FORE AND AFT RIG POSITION
	KEEL BOAT	A. TRIM TAB B. FORE AND AFT HULL TRIM	A. TRIM ANGLE OF SAILS B. DRAFT AMOUNT AND POSITION C. SAIL TWIST D. REEFING	A. MAST RAKE B. FORE AND AFT RIG POSITION
SAIL CAMBER	HEADSAIL - AMOUNT HIGH	A. SHEET TENSION	A. STAY SAG B. FAIRLEAD POSITION FORE AND AFT C. LUFF TENSION	
	HEADSAIL - AMOUNT LOW	A. FAIRLEAD POSITION FORE AND AFT	A. SHEET TENSION B. STAY SAG C. LUFF TENSION	
	HEADSAIL - FORE AND AFT POSITION OF MAXIMUM DRAFT	A. LUFF TENSION (HALYARD AND CUNNINGHAM TENSION)	A. SHEET TENSION B. FAIRLEAD POSITION FORE AND AFT C. STAY SAG	
			(RUNNING BACKSTAYS AND MAINSHEET TENSION)	
	GAFF SAIL - AMOUNT HIGH	A. PEAK OUTHAUL TENSION B. PEAK HALYARD TENSION	A. SHEET AND VANG TENSION B. GAFF BEND C. LEECH CORD	
	GAFF SAIL - AMOUNT LOW	A. CLEW OUTHAUL B. ZIPPER FOOT	A. CUNNINGHAM AND DOWNHAUL B. MAST BEND	
	GAFF SAIL - FORE AND AFT POSITION OF MAXIMUM DRAFT - HIGH	A. PEAK OUTHAUL B. PEAK HALYARD	A. SHEET AND VANG TENSION B. GAFF BEND C. LEECH CORD	
	GAFF SAIL - FORE AND AFT POSITION OF MAXIMUM DRAFT - LOW	A. PEAK HALYARD TENSION B. SHEET TENSION C. CUNNINGHAM & DOWNHAUL TENSION	A. MAST BEND B. BOOM VANG C. LEECH CORD	

Sail Power (Knopf, 1984), provides a sequential plan of attack. The program is most applicable on the wind. Generalizations, however, can be deduced for other points of sail.

Even with a lack of any profound knowledge of sail theory and principles, you can derive great benefit from this table (I recommend copying and plasticizing it) and referring to it while making adjustments as you sail.

The effects and success of your adjustments will have to be judged by observing the sail and the boat's performance. The sail will inform you of any gross tensioning errors by displaying obvious wrinkles and girts. The most glaring and detrimental adjustment, indicated by a big wrinkle running from throat to clew, is that of insufficient peak halyard tension for the wind velocity.

Plainly, you can't mess with one adjustment without affecting another. Eventually, you find yourself back at the beginning of the sequence. So, round you go again, constantly and methodically readjusting and making refinements in an ongoing quest for an efficient balance and the intuitive sensation that everything is going just right (not to mention the tangible evidence indicated by flashing your transom to the rest of the fleet). Herein lies a significant portion of the art of sailing, and there is no more exciting, responsive, demanding, and fulfilling medium of the art than the gaff rig.

SAIL REDUCTION

Anyone with any question concerning what reefing is all about should take a gander at a Block Island cowhorn's foresail. Four rows of reefs—now that is how to make use of one sail! Safe, reliable, and expeditious reduction of sail area is essential in all offshore sailers, and is advisable for many inshore sailers and daysailers as well. In the absence of alternative, smaller sails, there should be correctly placed and constructed reefs. Systems for tucking, rolling, or folding in a reef must be effective.

Motordom has deemphasized this aspect of seaworthiness, as have the plethora of mechanical stowing and furling devices. Briefly, here is why a sailor may reef or reduce a sail (sometimes before the fact in anticipation of the necessity): to slow the boat, to balance helm, to reduce heel, to heave-to, to reduce sail and rig strain, to relax, to clear the deck, because the sailcloth is unable to hold an efficient shape under full sail, to utilize an undamaged portion of a sail, to remove camber from the foot of a sail (as in a flattening reef), or to keep the boom end from striking the water in a seaway (as in a trip reef).

Roller Reefing

There is nothing new about the rolling technique of shortening sail. Colling and Pinkney patented such a system for the squaretopsails of ocean carriers in the 19th century. The principle, to quote Harold Underhill, "is extremely simple and may be seen in a large number of domestic window blinds." The Colling and Pinkney system had a feature not found in any modern counterparts—a reef band in the close reef position for the purpose of tying a conventional reef as a reinforcement in heavy weather; it was there also as an alternative if the rolling mechanism should fail. There was the added possibility of lowering the yard, thereby dousing the whole sail.

Anyhow, there are two forms of contemporary rolling on a spar: around a round mast or boom, and on a wire, or an extrusion rotating about a wire.

I have met only one voyaging or yacht sailor who actually *liked* his rolling boom, though they have been used extensively in both jibheaded and gaff-headed workboats and racers. Mechanically cranked or hand twisted, the system, if it works at all, is hard on the sail, and the sail does not set well. There is the inherent tendency, without *whelps* (tapered battens on the spar), for the boom end to droop, and the sail must be raised to roll in a reef.

Rolling a sail about a mast is a small-production-boat technique contrived to lure lazy sailors into buying throwaway boats. It is not a practical or safe reefing system. It only works with jibheaded sails, which, in order to keep the center of effort low, must be on a low, undercanvased rig—which is a good thing, since you won't have to mess so often with the ridiculous wrap-around-the-mast reefing system! Please don't confuse these antirolling rantings with sentiments about stowing sails in this manner. Therein we'll find some redeeming qualities (see page 464).

For similar reasons, I don't regard wire-oriented rolling on the stay, or within mast or boom, to be seaworthy reefing systems for certain types of sailing. They are useful when furling but not efficient when reefing, and sometimes not even when furling. These systems enable a small or unskilled crew to seemingly handle an immense boat and sail area. It's similar to a total reliance on GPS. Push-buttons do not a navigator or sailor make. The trend encourages people who can afford it to depend on systems that, should they fail, leave them literally at sea in catastrophic situations. A critical malfunction can be as simple as overlooking the fact that different-size sails require different-length furling drum lines; if you change to a large sail but fail to set up a sufficient length of line, the new big sail won't roll up all the way. Recent development of a continuous-type furling spool line does, however, offer a solution to this problem. I find headsail furling systems that provide the only forward support for the mast to be downright terrifying. But it is true—who wants to go out on a bucking bowsprit to hand a sail? The joy and exhilaration of sail handling aside, roller systems are deservedly popular and have vastly improved in recent years in terms of reliability and functionality. We shall examine their undeniable advantages for sail furling and stowage later in this chapter.

Slab Reefing on Boomed Sails

The term originated, I suppose, when some shrewd sailor thought it was possible with tack and clew reef pendants, and some form of boom support, to eliminate a whole slablike section of sail merely by pulling a couple of lines or even just one. Somehow, this has fairly recently come to be known as "jiffy reefing," a term I personally associate with high-cholesterol aluminum-fried popcorn. But no matter, it's the same thing: pull a string and you get a fast reduction in sail area, as illustrated on page 460. Even if the system is of the type where the clew pendant is hauled and the tack is brought down to a hook or lashing, it is better than setting up a reef clew lashing, especially at sea in a squall.

The next step is the salty practice of tucking and tying up the reefed portion of the sail (sometimes known as the "dog's lug") with reef points or nettles.

There is also the continuous laceline method of tucking in a reef by hauling on one line. This technique works marginally well for one row of reef-point eyelets.

It is important for the set of the sail and the sail's integrity at the reef points that the reef clew be firmly outhauled and that the topping lift, lazylifts, or whatever is supporting the boom be used during the reefing process and afterward to avoid undue strain on the leech of the sail, particularly a large Bermudan main with a heavy boom. There is much less strain on reef-point eyelets, and a neater tuck to the reef, if reef nettles are not tied around the boom, but around the foot of the reefed sail. This, of course, is not possible with boltrope, slot-bent sails. All this applies as well to taking a reef with lashings at reef tack and clew. And incidentally, it could be helpful in distinguishing one reef row from another—or rather one row that's been tied in from another—if the nettles were of different color and material. Furthermore, successive reefs are tied in on opposite sides of the sail.

The sharpie rig was jiffy reefing back when nobody had even heard of cholesterol; in this case the slab is taken from the luff. This is an easy pull-the-reefing-line-ease-the snotter operation, which has the disadvantages of leaving weight and windage aloft and a great wudge of cloth along the leading edge. Unless there is adequate reefed luff tension, the sail will set poorly and it will go hard on the reef-band eyelets. Alternatively, the sharpie reef can be tied in with the sail lowered, with a tighter, less bulky tuck to the sail, but it takes more time. It is a valuable yachting variation.

It is the weight of the sail and battens and sheet tension in the most ancient of balanced lug-sails, the Chinese lug rig, that reduces sail section by section merely by easing the halyard. The

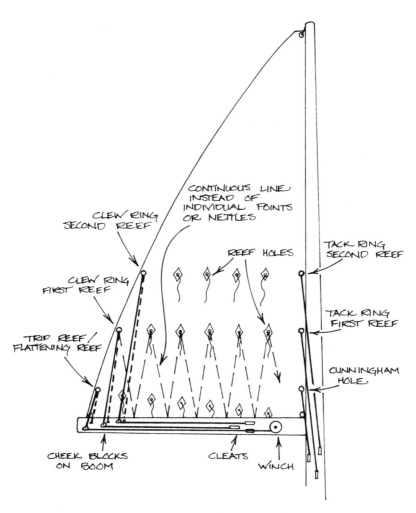

FIGURE 12-6. *Slab-reefing setup on a Bermudan mainsail.*

boom, sail, and battens and sheet tension are contained in the topping lift/lazyjacks. This may be done on any point of sail but is most effective when the sail is luffing. The lowered battens can then be lashed together, if necessary, for control, or can be restrained with batten downhauls. All this can be done from the cockpit. Contemporary full-batten sails do not have the weight or sheeting to be lowered into their lazyjacks while the sail

is drawing, and reef best when set up with the conventional slab reefing system of continuous or separate reef clew and tack pendants and reef nettles.

There can be "jiffiness" also to the reefing of a boomless sail with conventional reef points. The biggest obstacle in reefing such a sail while hoisted is getting sheets bent on the reef clew. Alternative sheets can be available and may be necessary for a change in sheet lead anyway. In that event, a slab reefing procedure can be employed with a reef tack pendant. Otherwise, the greatest control is afforded by dousing the sail, lashing the reef tack, transferring the sheet to the reef clew, and tucking and tying the dog's lug then or after the sail has been set again. Regardless of the method, it is very important to have a sufficient number of well-tied reef points, particularly at the clew, where there is much cloth to be tied up. Otherwise, the slatting about will shake out the reef.

It would be a scandal if I failed to mentioned scandalizing as a means of reducing sail area. Scandalizing is one of the virtues of the four-sided sail. It is truly amazing how much relief there is to be gained in a squall just by tensioning and making fast the boom support (topping lift, lazylifts), then dipping the peak of a gaff-headed sail. Depending on how low the peak is dropped, much more or less wind is spilled.

A Bermudan sail is said to be *scandalized* when the boom is topped up, permitting the leech to go slack, twist off, and spill wind. At the same time the sail loses power due to reduced camber.

The sprit rig offers scandalizing in the extreme. Unship the sprit and immediately the sail is reduced by half or so into a handy offwind storm trysail. In terms of sail life, the flogging involved in scandalizing is not desirable. But it is preferable to the alternatives when caught out in a blow, unable to reef, but having to carry sail.

SAIL CONTROL AND MANAGEMENT

The price of sail control and management is increased windage and chafe—there are no free lunches in sailorizing. All the devices and systems that serve to tame, confine, guide, and gather sails employ lines—sometimes many of them. These lines make for a truly seaworthy, handy rig, offering maximum effect and safety with minimum effort. Even when using no more and no larger lines than necessary, windage is an unavoidable trade-off.

Chafe cannot be eliminated either, but chafing gear applied to line and/or sail will prolong sail life sufficiently. As for chafe to the line itself, its lifespan is maximized by fair leads and smooth-running sheaves of the correct size.

Downhauls, Inhauls, and Outhauls

The dousing of both stay- and spar-bent fore-and-aft sails can be greatly eased for the shorthanded sailor with the use of downhauls. The downhaul, which could be a continuous halyard or a separate line, ensures that a sail will not only come down but stay down. In conjunction with lazyjacks, it will keep a sail well handed—all with no hands except on the halyard and the downhaul! If possible, it is best to attach the downhaul's fitting to the same piece of sail hardware to which the halyard is bent (thimble, corner ring, or headboard), or to the halyard shackle itself. It is appropriate to use the same sort of fitting with which the rest of the luff is bent, or perhaps a shackle. To this is bent the downhaul. This way there is no chance of twisting the head of the sail, damaging the sail, or causing the head to slide or the hank to jam, and no strain is placed upon the sail if tension is put on the downhaul to keep it from slatting about when the sail is set.

A voyager's course or squares'l can be set and handed with a system of outhauls and inhauls. I have seen this technique in use with track and slides and also know it to work quite well with a wire jackstay set up on the yard and conventional jib hanks along the head of the sail. The outhaul is bent to the earing and the inhaul is bent to a shackle, hank, or slide affixed to the earing. This is important not only for the reasons mentioned concerning downhauls, but also because there is no earing lashing to maintain alignment of the earing and the head of the sail. When not in use the sail is brailed or furled and lashed to the mast.

Brailing

Once so common with the square rig, *brailing* can be adapted to fore-and-aft sails. Any loose-footed fore-and-aft sail will do, but the standing gaff-headed spankers made a regular curtain out of it with outhauls and inhauls at clew and peak and brailing lines along the leech. Thames spritsail barges, with their monstrous, chain-supported sprits, utilize multiple brailing lines to corral a rarely lowered mainsail. The usual 60- to 100-square-foot small-craft boomless spritsail makes ideal use of a single brailing line (see Figure 3-6B), which gathers both sail and sprit up into a bundle. A brailing line can be effective, too, on a boomless standing lugsail or lateen sail.

Tricing Line

Brailing pertains to any gathering of a fore-and-aft sail by drawing the leech forward. Lifting the foot of a fore-and-aft sail with similar lines is called *tricing*. For a sail to be triced up, it must be loose-footed or boomless. Release the tack and haul the tricing line to clear the deck, gain visibility, or kill some of the sail's power.

Lazyjacks

Lazyjacks and their derivations, to the extent that they gather and contain the lowered, boomed sail, do so passively. How is it that such a marvelously simple piece of gear, of such virtue, could have lapsed into obscurity—this piece of rigging with such universal application as to make almost any boat, large or small, safer and easier to handle? I imagine that lazyjacks were assumed to be appropriate only for the gaff rig, which took them along to its forced obsolescence. But now the jacks are back! Full-batten contemporary Bermudan sails reef and drop sail with the greatest of ease, thanks to a simple basket of lines. Any boomed sail, loose- or fixed-footed—even club-footed—can employ lazyjacks.

One tends to think of ease of dropping sail when considering lazyjacks, but they also facilitate making sail, and in particular, they offer the means of raising just the head or the peak of a sail offwind for a short period, with topping lift supporting the boom as the lazyjacks hold the rest of the sail. Any other sail would be all over the deck and in the water, with no sheeting possible. It is the topping

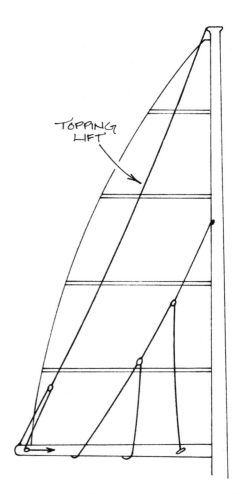

FIGURE 12-7. *Lazyjacks and topping lift on a fully battened Bermudan mainsail.*

lift function of the rig's lazylifts that makes the Chinese lug the reefer's dream. There is no need to top up the boom in the conventional slab-reefing manner—the sail sections fall neatly into the cradle. The Chesapeake Bay oyster boats and the Hudson River sloops carried lazyjacks on their headsails as well. Lazyjacks, as purely a sail-gathering mechanism, are relatively light and simple, and must be able to be slacked off when sail is set to minimize chafe and permit the sail to set correctly. Often they are used in combination with a separate topping lift,

LAZYJACKS

Q: *I recently purchased a Herreshoff America catboat and want to rig lazyjacks. Should they be adjustable? I would prefer not to have any more lines to the deck in way of the mast.*

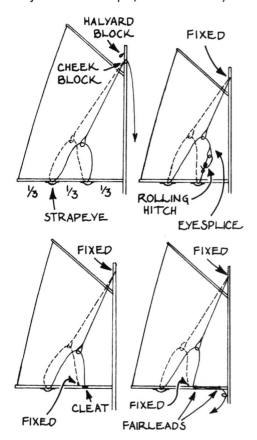

A: For a gaff-headed sail, the simplest two-legged lazyjack arrangement should divide the boom roughly into thirds. The lazyjacks are carried in pairs so that one set runs to each side of the boom. The upper ends should meet the mast somewhere in the vicinity of the throat halyard block.

To minimize chafe and avoid impeding the set of the sail, it is important that lazyjacks can be slacked off. *Lazylifts* (not illustrated here), a variation on lazyjacks, both gather the sail and act as a topping lift. Lazylifts and jacks are often set up with lines running down the mast.

If you wish to avoid adjusting these lines and don't want the topping function of lazylifts, the legs of the lazyjacks—rather than being one continuous loop—can be broken with an eyesplice and made adjustable with a rolling hitch. The upper ends would then be deadended on the mast. Alternatively, the lower legs of the lazyjacks could have one end fixed to one side of the boom, and the other end made off to a cleat on the other side of the boom. With some fairleads along the boom to the gooseneck, that arrangement could be made to permit adjustment from the cockpit on any point of sail.

which is a necessity, really, on all but the smallest of the boomed Western rigs.

It is when the functions of lazyjacks and topping lifts are combined that the more complex gear—*lazylifts* and *quarter lifts*—are used. Lazy- and quarter lifts perform the offwind partial sail-raising maneuver just described even better than lazyjacks. The thing to avoid when raising sail is catching batten ends or gaff peak under the diagonal lines as you hoist. Even though lazy- and quarter lifts are slacked off when sail is set, there is still much chafe to the sail; for this reason, on any sort of voyaging, charter, or commercial vessel, there is extensive use of baggywrinkle on the diagonal lift portion of the gear.

The "Dutchman" System

In a recently patented alternative to lazyjacks, a Bermudan boomed sail is guided in its descent by two vertical lines rove through a series of vertically placed eyelets in the sail. The sail tends to fold itself in the process. In theory and under ideal conditions, this looks good, but in practice there is likely to be much chafe and difficulty dousing a sail when it is drawing. I wonder, too, how much the guidelines hamper sail set and trim.

Pull-the-Sock Systems

This is a spinnaker and auxiliary spinnaker-drifter dousing system that works wonderfully on kayak spinnakers. Sending any size sail up in a sock works, and greatly eases the setting. It's the process of trying to haul the hoop and sock back down over a voluminous sail that can be difficult. All in all, it's an effort to make fairly uncontrollable sails acceptable to a cruising clientele who would be better off with drifters and hanked-on auxiliary sails. When not in use, the sock and hoop remain scrunched up aloft at the head of the sail—looking unsightly and adding weight and windage.

Furling and Storage on Spar or Wire

Here is where the roller stay systems get the award for convenience, despite their many drawbacks: expense, sail life, sail shape, windage, reefing, and gear failure. I don't begrudge people who are unable to handle conventional sails the opportunity to enjoy sailing aided by mechanical devices, as long as they are aware that if the devices fail, they will be doubly handicapped. The best one can do to enhance the reliability and sail life of these systems is: (1) buy high-quality gear; (2) service it regularly; (3) install edge covers on the sail, with complete coverage; and (4) roll up the sail completely so as not to leave the clew exposed. On this type of sail, by the way, a hydraulically pressed clew ring makes sense. There is no way to protect the stitching of a handsewn ring from the sun, and all in all, the hydraulic ring is consistent and compatible with the rest of the sail and gear of this type. Internal (boom or mast) roller-furling gear does not need edge covers, but does require protection on the corner of the sail that protrudes from the spar in the furled position.

If you add to a set of lazyjacks a large peapod of canvas above the boom of a Bermudan mainsail, you have a currently popular, commercially made, zip-up sail catchment and covering system. The lazyjacks guide the descending sail into the pod; you tamp it in, then pull the zipper shut, and go below for a cup of tea. It's an appealing idea if you like how the conspicuous pod looks, and if it doesn't hinder reefing. The pod doesn't always cover the sail's corners completely, and the zipper is not always easy to pull. I venture to say that a nimble sailor with a good conventional sailcover and lazyjacks could be down below sipping tea in less time than the pod packer, if sail coverage and a neat job are scored. The pod does nothing, of course, to protect spar or hardware.

The big daddy of zippered furling systems is the vertical mast-fitted stringbean pod–type with which you try to corral a fully set Bermudan sail by hauling the zipper down. As it rasps its way along the leech of the sail and the clew outhaul is eased, the zipper is supposed to force the sail into the pod. I have never had the occasion to heave on one of these pod packers, but I have inspected the system aboard a 60-foot ketch-rigged charter vessel. The professional skipper, without hesitation, roundly cursed the pod and zipper, saying it was useless for getting in sail when drawing at all, or really at any time but a light breeze on the nose. Consequently, they had to motor to get in sail. Finally, a great wudge of sail remained uncovered at the foot and clew. Like the spinnaker sock, these items strike me as being fads, which is okay for variety's sake if they work, but seem to endure about as long as flashy flavors of supermarket breakfast cereal. It's just hard to take them seriously.

APPENDIX A

Glossary

WHAT TO PUT IN A GLOSSARY when the subject of a book such as this is so expansive and technical? To solve this mind-boggler, a random selection of hapless individuals was abducted from among the motley riffraff that may be found at any given time loitering along the Camden Harbor waterfront. In exchange for food, freedom, and anonymity, these enthusiastic volunteers—ranging in nautical know-how from nozzer to salty as an oyster—were obliged to read this entire book and reveal their savvy and prejudice by disclosing the words and phrases they found to be the most mysterious and unfathomable. Here are the results of that scientific and impartial study.

aback   When the clew of a sail is to windward or pressed back against the mast with the wind on the forward side of the sail, tending to give the vessel sternway or drive her to leeward. Not to be confused with backwinding. A sail may be backed intentionally; for example, to back a jib in order to bring the bow through the eye of the wind when tacking a boat that is slow in stays.

angel's footstool   Another name for the skysail of a square-rigger.

angle of attack   The angle of a sail's chord to the apparent wind.

apparent wind   The vector combination of the true wind and the wind developed by the boat speed.

backwind   Wind deflected from a forward sail onto the sail abaft it.

bag reef   See **flattening reef.**

balance reef   A deep diagonal reef running from the leech to the throat of a gaff-headed sail for heavy-weather purposes.

baldheaded rig   A schooner with gaff-headed sails but no topsails.

balloon sails   Extra-large sails of light materials, used as large jibs or spinnakers.

bend   (1) To tie two ropes together. (2) To tie to an anchor. (3) To tie a rope to a spar. (4) To secure a sail to a spar or wire.

bias   Indicates the direction that is 45 degrees to the warp and fill of a fabric. This is always the stretchiest direction of any woven material.

blade cloth   Material used in #3 jibs, or "blades," and low-aspect mainsails. It has a high fill orientation but, because it needs enhanced bias strength and there is greater crimp in the warp, warp strength is sacrificed slightly.

calendering   A process in which a finished sail-cloth is run between hot steel rollers to flatten it, shrink it, stabilize it, and make it thinner and less porous.

canvas   Originally a coarse fabric made of flax, obtainable from heavy (#00) to very fine (#10) and supplied in bolts (rolls); used for making sails and awnings. Now a general term used to indicate a sailcloth or marine fabric or, collectively, all of a vessel's sails.

center of effort   The point at which the sum total of the forces of the sails is focused.

center of lateral resistance (CLR)   The focal point (on the vertical plane at the centerline of the hull) of the total hydrodynamic force that resists leeward movement of the hull. The CLR noted on a sail plan drawing is actually the **center of lateral plane (CLP),** which is a constant, whereas the CLR constantly shifts, especially with a centerboard.

chafing gear   Mats, baggywrinkle, Scotchmen (rollers), leather, or lamb's wool for protecting rigging, spars, and sails from wear of different sorts.

chord   A hypothetical straight horizontal line from the luff to the leech of a sail; the baseline of an aerodynamic shape.

cloth direction   The "weave" or "grain" of a fabric formed by the perpendicular crossing of warp and weft threads.

crimp   The "unstraightness" of a fiber that may be generated, for example, as it goes under and over the perpendicular fibers in a weave. The amount of crimp affects the strength of the fabric; the straighter a fiber is, the stronger it is.

crow's feet   Wrinkles radiating from a luff or foot eyelets, indicating insufficient halyard or outhaul tension.

cunningham hole   A ring a short distance up from the tack of a sail, used for tensioning the luff.

denier   A unit measure of weight of a fiber bundle, or yarn. The denier of a yarn is how many grams a piece 9,000 meters long would weigh. A 200-denier yarn, then, is a yarn that weighs 200 grams at a length of 9,000 meters.

dog's lug   The idled, projecting portion of a reefed sail; that is, the portion between the corner ring and the reef ring.

douse   To lower and stow a sail hastily.

dressing sails   The treatment of sails by the application of any of several preservative formulas to render them waterproof and resistant to mildew.

duck   Derived from the Dutch word *doek*. Originally an untwilled flaxen material, thicker than calico, lighter than working-sail canvas, used for auxiliary sails and tropical clothing. Now a collective term for cotton fabric of various uses.

Duradon   Originally a truck tarp fabric, a soft, loosely woven, synthetic sailcloth that resembles natural-fiber sailcloth. Available in weights appropriate for larger voyaging and classic boats.

dyeing   A process that changes the natural color of a material. Dyeing can have an adverse affect on the properties of many materials. Nylon, for example, suffers very little degradation when it is dyed, whereas Dacron, or polyester, suffers considerably. This is because there is nothing for the color molecules to adhere to; in order to color them, you must treat the fibers with harsh chemicals that etch their surfaces. This treatment reduces the strength of the fibers and also increases the stretch.

edge curve   The form of a sail edge (convex, straight, concave, or some combination of these) that is cut into the sail prior to finishing.

elastic limit   The extent to which you can stretch a material before it cannot recover its original shape.

fid out   To ream or round out an eyesplice, cringle, clew, eyelet hole, grommet, etc., prior to inserting a thimble or liner or otherwise finishing off.

fill   The threads that run across the bolt from edge to edge. Also known as **weft, woof,** or **picks.**

fill-oriented   When the strength of the material is mainly across the roll, or in the fill direction.

film   A thin sheet of plastic.

finish   (1) A process or processes that convert a material from greige goods, or loom-state fabric, to its final form. This may involve scouring, rinsing, dyeing, calendering, resin coating or impregnating, heat trimming, and drawing the sew-to line on the selvage edge. (2) The resin applied to a sailcloth (i.e., a hard finish for racing material or a soft finish for cruising), the purpose being to stabilize the yarns and improve bias strength.

flake a sail   To furl a sail by folding it in bights on the boom.

flattening reef, or **bag reef**   A small arced or diagonal reef along the foot of a fixed-footed boomed sail to reduce camber in higher wind velocities.

furl   To gather and secure sails with stops, gaskets, etc.

gaskets   Pieces of webbing or line used to tie up a sail when it is furled; also called **stops.**

genoa cloth   Material used in a genoa. It has a balanced weave to carry the evenly distributed loads it must withstand and has good strength in all directions.

girts   Creases or wrinkles in a sail due to cloth distortion under localized strain.

greige goods   Woven but unfinished material that still contains the lubricants added to the yarn to reduce damage during weaving. From this stage, depending on the finish applied, a material could become a fine, hard racing cloth or a soft, dyed cruising material.

half-hand sail   A sail sewn with machine stitching on one edge of the seams and hand stitching on the other edge of the seams, for extra strength.

hand   (1) To gather and furl a sail. (2) The "feel" of a fabric or rope in reference to how hard or soft it is. For example, "firm hand" refers to a sailcloth with a hard finish or a rope that is stiff.

handy billy   A small tackle used for odd jobs; also used to tension the luff rope of a sail.

hank   (1) The spring-loaded snap used to secure a sail to a stay (also called a **jib hank**). (2) A metal fitting seized to the luff of the sail. Traditionally hanks are of rope, wood, or iron, remaining on the stay, to which the sail is then seized.

heat set   Process of running woven material between hot steel rollers. This shrinks the fibers and draws them closer together. It is similar to calendering, but not as much pressure is applied by the rollers. Heat setting increases a fabric's bias strength but can degrade the strength of the material slightly and increase fiber crimp.

hoist   The forward edge of a sail or flag that is against a mast or stay.

impregnation   The process of saturating a fabric with resin and then squeezing out the excess. It leaves just enough resin to bond the fiber bundles together.

jackstay(s)   (1) Ropes, wooden battens, or iron bars stretched along the yards to which squaresails are bent. (2) A wire set up either vertically or horizontally but running parallel to a spar, to which a sail is bent on with hanks.

Jamie Green   A sail set under the jibboom, to the dolphin striker.

jib hank   See **hank.**

Kevlar   An aramid fiber made by Du Pont, characterized by high tensile strength and modulus of elasticity. It is more brittle than Dacron and will degrade slightly in sunlight. Two types of Kevlar are commonly used: type 49 in structural laminates; and type 29 in sailcloth. Because of its brittleness, sails made out of

Kevlar should be folded as loosely as possible or rolled.

knock   Another name for the upper forward corner of a four-cornered sail, alternative to **throat**.

lacing, or **laceline**   A long line used in bending and reefing sail.

laminate   In sailcloth this refers to the application of a film to a network of reinforcing fibers.

lash   (1) To bind two or more objects together. (2) To wrap a single object with a series of turns or hitches. (3) To secure any movable object on shipboard to prevent its shifting.

last seam   The miter seam of a miter-cut sail, so called because it is the last seam to be seamed up.

lay   (1)The direction of twist in a rope. (2) The lead of the strands. (3) The nature of the twist, as in hard, soft, left, right, long, or short.

leech   (1) The side edges of a squaresail or spinnaker and the after edge of a fore-and-aft sail. (2) Contraction of the "lee edge."

loose   To unfurl a sail.

mainsail cloth   A highly fill-oriented material that, due to the unbalanced weave, will tend to have relatively poor warp and bias strength. It frequently will have a "soft" finish even on racing sails. It is typically used in high-aspect mainsails and sometimes in high-aspect jibs.

make sail   (1) To set sail and get underway. (2) To set an additional sail.

melamine resin   A resin that is similar in composition to polyester resin but is normally used to impregnate greige goods to stabilize woven polyester sailcloth.

middle stitching   Reinforcing a seam by stitching along its center; also called **triple stitching.**

modulus of elasticity   The ratio of stress to strain of a material, or the amount a material stretches if a load is applied. A material with a high modulus of elasticity will stretch less than a material with a lower one.

monkey seam, or **monk's seam**   A flat seam made by overlapping two hemmed edges, as in the miter seam or "last seam" of a mitered natural-fiber sail.

motorsailer   A boat especially designed—in hull form and rig—to use motor or sails or both.

Mylar   Trade name for a polyester film developed and marketed by the Du Pont Corporation. It is very stiff, strong, and stable and is entirely nonporous, but it has low tear strength. In sailcloth it is used to control bias stretch.

offset, or **cutback**   A shift in position of sail corner placement in order to accommodate spar fittings; e.g., positioning the tack ring of a mainsail aft and out of alignment with the luff in order to attach to a tack fitting aft of a gooseneck.

panel   Also known as a **cloth.** Typically, several cloths or panels must be stitched together to make a sail.

radial   A triangular panel in a sail that radiates out from the area of stress. This gives the lowest bias load on the sail fabric of any kind of construction and is especially effective for sail construction when made out of Kevlar or Spectra 1000.

reeve   To pass the end of a rope or twine through any hole, opening, or sleeve.

resin-coating   Finishing process in which resin, usually urethane, is applied heavily to a cloth and a minimal amount of excess resin is wiped off. This leaves an extremely hard, crisp finish that is heavier but much more stable than a resin-impregnated finish.

roping   Rope sewn to the edge of a sail for strength and gathering of edge curves. Squaresails are roped on the after side and fore-and-aft sails are roped on the port side.

sail design   The scaled-down construction plan of a particular sail.

sailmaker's yard   The weight of a piece of material that measures 36 by 28½ inches, which is about 80 percent of a square yard. It is used only in the United States and, the story goes, the Americans started using this as a unit of measure during the Revolutionary War just to be different from the British! More likely it reflects the width of the looms.

sail plan   The drawn profile of a sailboat—its hull, rig, and sails—above the waterline.

sail shape   The three-dimensional form or curvature of a sail commonly referred to as draft, belly, or flow. Technically designated as camber and characterized by depth, position fore and aft of maximum depth, and the relationship between depth and chord length.

scrim   A very loose, open weave that in sailcloth applications is only used between laminated films. The main advantage to a scrim is that thread crimp is minimized; however, most scrims have very wavy yarns. Orcon's Aeroform is a scrim, but the fibers are all pretensioned and absolutely straight, so there is no crimp.

seizing   A lashing of twine, small stuff, or marline with or without riding turns.

serve   To wrap a rope or wire very tightly with multiple close-fitting turns of twine, marline, or other small stuff, which is called **service** when used for this purpose.

set flying   A sail hoisted taut on its luff and not hanked to a stay; e.g., a jib.

shake out (a reef)   To remove the gaskets or untie the reef points and loosen the sail.

sheeting angle   The vertical angle of a sheet made fast to the clew of a boomless sail. A horizontal sheet lead would give a sheeting angle of 0 degrees and would tension the foot but not the leech. A vertical lead would give a sheeting angle of 90 degrees, tensioning the leech but not the foot. Real-world sheeting angles are typically near 45 degrees.

sick seams   Seams that are weak due to worn, aged, or sunrotten stitching.

sizing   A substance, usually linseed oil and

starch, added to yarn to lubricate it during weaving or handling.

slat   The flapping of a sail when in the wind.

Spectra 900 or 1000   A polyethylene fiber developed by the Allied Corporation. As do all polyethylene fibers, Spectra yarn floats, but because of its extremely long, straight molecules it is a very strong fiber with very low stretch. This material is still under development but is sure to achieve a prominent position in marine applications.

stabilize   To add resin in either an impregnation or saturation coating to a woven material in order to make it more resistant to stretch, primarily on the bias.

strain   The deformation of a material that is being subjected to a load, or stress.

stress   A load that is applied to a material, divided by the cross-sectional area of the material.

substrate   Any woven, knit, or scrim material attached to a film. Its function is to reduce tearing, increase seamability, and give orientation to the cloth, which makes it more weight efficient than an unreinforced film.

sunrotten   Said of sailcloth or marine fabric that has suffered deterioration due to prolonged exposure to ultraviolet rays.

tabling   The folded hem, cut, or taped reinforcement along the edge of a sail.

tensile strength   The stress level that breaks a material.

throat   See **knock.**

triaxial   A material woven in an advanced loom that has yarns in three directions. This gives a material the unique property of having three strong, low-stretch orientations.

trim angle   The athwartship relationship of a sail or section of a sail to the centerline of the hull.

trip reef   A small diagonal reef running from the tack to a short way up the leech to lift the boom and prevent it from hitting the water in a seaway as the boat rolls.

unbalanced weave   A form of cloth construction

that has a heavier orientation in one direction than in the other. It is created by using a heavier denier, higher count, or different fiber in that direction.

up-and-down cut   A panel configuration in which the cloths are laid parallel to the leech; **vertically cut.**

urethane resin   A finishing resin used the same way as polyester or epoxy in boatbuilding, but to stabilize woven sailcloth.

vang (boom)   A tackle or mechanical contrivance to exert downward pressure on the boom, thus affecting leech tension and shape.

vang (gaff)   A line or lines rigged to the peak of a gaff in order to control the extent to which the spar sags off to leeward.

warp   (1) The yarns that run lengthwise in the cloth. (2) The lengthwise direction of a bolt of cloth.

warp-oriented   Indicates that the cloth is strongest in the warp direction.

weave   The exact pattern in which yarns go over and under each other in a given fabric. In some aerospace applications, a yarn will go over as many as eight other yarns before it goes under one. This reduces the crimp and improves strength and modulus.

wind gradient   The variation in wind velocity at different heights above the water.

yarn   Discrete bundles of filaments of a material. These may be combined by twisting to form a plied yarn. Yarn is the longitudinal and transverse element of a weave.

yield   The point at which a material has exceeded its elastic limit and is permanently distorted. It is the point on a stress-strain graph where the curve becomes linear.

zoli   The toilet box slung over the side of an Arabian dhow. (I include this word of no great sailmaking relevance just so's you get an entry that begins with the last letter of the alphabet.)

APPENDIX B

Sailmakers, Riggers, Brokers, and Cleaners

SAILMAKERS WHO SPECIALIZE IN SAILMAKING TO THE STANDARDS AND PRINCIPLES ESPOUSED IN THIS BOOK:

Balogh Sail Designs
  Star Route, Box 795
  Cedar Island, NC 28520
  919-225-6631

David Bierig Sailmakers
  11092 Freeport Lane
  North East, PA 16428
  814-459-8001

Frøde Bjoru
  Joa 7815
  Seierstad, Norway
  077-869-44

Center Harbor Sails
  Robin Lincoln, Sailmaker
  Box 32
  Brooklin, ME 04616
  207-359-2003

Thomas Clark & Company Sailmakers, Inc.
  37 Pratt Street
  Essex, CT 06426
  203-767-8278

Gambell and Hunter Sailmakers
  Grant Gambell, Brad Hunter
  16 Limerock Street
  Camden, ME 04843
  207-236-3561

Bob Henderson Sailmakers
  San Diego, CA
  619-544-9757

Glenn Housley Sails
  1810 Virginia Avenue
  Annapolis, MD 21401
  301-263-4913

Emiliano Marino
  c/o International Marine
  P.O. Box 220
  Camden, ME 04843
  207-236-4837

Hasse and Comapny
    Port Townsend Sails
    315 Jackson Street
    Port Townsend, WA 98368
    360-385-1640

Sailmaker's Loft
    12306 East 48th Street
    Sumner, WA 98390
    360-863-4381

Schattauer Sails, Inc.
    6010 Seaview Avenue
    Seattle, WA 98107
    206-783-2400

Sound Sails
    Ellen Falconer
    311A Haines Place
    Port Townsend, WA 98368
    360-385-3881

E. W. Smith Company
    10 Union Wharf
    Fairhaven, MA 02719
    508-993-2700

Nathaniel S. Wilson Sailmakers
    P.O. Box 71
    Lincoln Street
    East Boothbay, ME 04544
    207-633-5071

Note: Small lofts such as these are not high-profile advertisers, and I might have overlooked some-one. Further, names, addresses, and circumstances change. Please let me know of errors or omissions so that these may be corrected in a future edition.

SAIL-CLEANING SPECIALISTS

Manchester Sails
    South Dartmouth, MA 02748
    508-992-6322

Sail Care, Inc.
    Ford City, PA 16226
    800-433-7245/412-264-5009

SAIL BROKERS

Atlantic Sail Traders
    Sarasota, FL
    813-351-6023

Bacon and Associates
    Annapolis, MD
    301-263-4880

The Sail Exchange
    Newport Beach, CA
    714-631-0184

RIGGERS SPECIALIZING IN RIGGING AND MARLIN-SPIKE WORK CONSISTENT WITH THE PRINCIPLES AND STANDARDS ESPOUSED IN THIS BOOK:

Gary Adair, Rigger
    Box 6000
    Mystic Seaport Museum
    Mystic, CT 06355
    203-572-0711

Kit Africa
    1612 Rosewood
    Port Townsend, WA 98368
    206-385-5342

Center Harbor Rigging
    Brion Toss, Rigger
    311 Jackson Street
    Port Townsend, WA 98368
    800-488-0855/206-385-1640

Joe Mello, Rigger
    The Rigging Loft
    South Dartmouth, MA 02748
    508-992-0434

APPENDIX C

Sources of Materials

WHOLESALE SOURCES OF SYNTHETIC SAILCLOTH

Note: These will not sell directly to consumers.

Bainbridge/Aquabatten, Inc.
   252 Revere Street
   Canton, MA 02021
   800-422-5684

Challenge Sailcloth, Inc.
   104 East Main Street
   P. O. Box 716
   Rockville, CT 06066
   800-962-4499

Dimension Sailcloth
   Moosup, CT 06354
   800-441-2424/203-564-2785

SATI/USA Sailcloth
   Annapolis, MD (Tanbark Dacron)
   301-224-2343

Texlon Corporation
   Torrance, CA
   800-624-3999

RETAIL SOURCES OF SYNTHETIC SAILCLOTH

Sailrite Kits
   305 West Van Buren Street
   P.O. Box 987
   Columbia City, IN 46725
   800-348-2769

Also, most any sail loft, including the ones listed in Appendix B.

SOURCES OF DURADON AND/OR NATURAL-FIBER SAILCLOTH

British Millerain Company, Ltd. (wholesaler; Duradon, cotton, and flax)
   92/2 High Street
   Arbroath, Scotland DD11 1HL
   Tel: 0241-431 054
   Fax: 0241-431 657

Test Fabrics (retailer; untreated Egyptian cotton and cotton duck)
   Middlesex, NJ 08846
   201-469-6446

(See list of marine fabric sources for cotton fabric that can be used as sailcloth.)

Nathaniel S. Wilson Sailmakers (retailer; Duradon and cotton)
P.O. Box 71
Lincoln Street
East Boothbay, ME 04544
207-633-5071

SOURCES OF SYNTHETIC CORDAGE FOR SAIL-MAKING AND RIGGING

Bainbridge/Aquabatten, Inc. (wholesaler)
252 Revere Street
Canton, MA 02021
800-422-5684

New England Ropes (wholesaler)
Pope's Island
New Bedford, MA 02740
617-999-2351

West Marine Products (retailer)
2450 17th Avenue
Santa Cruz, CA 95062
408-476-1900

SOURCES OF NATURAL-FIBER AND PSEUDO-NATURAL-FIBER CORDAGE FOR SAILMAKING AND RIGGING

Fur Rebslåeri (tarred and untarred hemp, tarred marline)
Skivevej 57
7870 Roslev
Denmark
07-59-7101

Halls Barton Ropery Company, Ltd. (lightly tarred flax, hemp)
New Cleveland Street
Hull, HU8 7HD
England
0482-23028

Ludlow Textiles Company, Inc. (waxed linen twine)
P.O. Box I
Ludlow, MA 01056
800-628-9048

The Wooden Boat Shop (retailer; manila, Hardy Hemp, Roblon-Spunflex, gold nylon)
1007 NE Boat Street
Seattle, WA 98145
206-634-3600

WHOLESALE SOURCES OF MARINE FABRICS AND CANVASWORK TOOLS, SUPPLIES, AND HARDWARE

Note: These will not sell directly to consumers.

Astrup Company (cotton and synthetics)
2937 West 25th Street
Cleveland, OH 44113
216-696-2820

Bainbridge/Aquabatten, Inc. (synthetics)
252 Revere Street
Canton, MA 02021
800-422-5684

John Boyle & Company, Inc. (cotton and synthetics)
P.O. Drawer 672
Statesville, NC 28677
800-221-5875/704-872-6303

Redrum Fabrics, Inc. (cotton and synthetics)
Endicott Street, Building 26
Norwood, MA 02062-0917
800-225-9834

Unitex West (cotton and synthetics)
5175 Commerce Drive
Baldwin Park, CA 91706
800-456-6282/818-962-6282

SOURCES OF SAILMAKING TOOLS, SUPPLIES, AND HARDWARE

Bainbridge/AquaBatten, Inc. (wholesaler)
   252 Revere Street
   Canton, MA 02021
   800-422-5684

Challenge Sailcloth, Inc. (wholesaler; also canvaswork tools and hardware)
   104 East Main Street
   P.O. Box 716
   Rockville, CT 06066
   800-962-4499

Sailrite Kits (retailer)
   305 West Van Buren Street
   P.O. Box 987
   Columbia City, IN 46725
   800-348-2769

SOURCES OF LEATHER FOR SAILMAKING AND RIGGING

Berman Leathercraft, Inc.
   Boston, MA
   617-426-0870

Macpherson Leather Supply
   Seattle, WA
   206-328-0855

SOURCES OF SAIL KITS

Sailrite Kits
   305 West Van Buren Street
   P.O. Box 987
   Columbia City, IN 46725
   800-348-2769

Sailmaker's Loft
   12306 East 48th street
   Sumner, WA 98390
   206-863-4381

APPENDIX D

Bibliography

Note: Some of these books are out of print.

SAILS, SAIL THEORY, RIGGING PRINCIPLES, AND SAILING

Andersen, Bent & Eric. *Rasejlet-Darjens Vinge.* Denmark: Vinkingeskibshallen Roskilde, 1989.

Baader, Juan. *The Sailing Yacht.* London: Adlard Coles, Ltd., 1965.

Bray, Maynard. *Mystic Seaport Museum Watercraft.* Mystic, Conn.: Mystic Seaport Museum, 1979.

Brewer, Ted. *Understanding Boat Design,* 4th ed. Camden, Maine: International Marine, 1994.

Burgess, F. H. *Dictionary of Sailing.* London: Penguin Books, Ltd., 1961.

Cambell, John. *Easier Rigs for Safer Cruising.* London: Hollis and Carter, 1986.

Carr, Frank G. G., et al. *The Medley of Mast and Sail: A Camera Record.* Brighton, England: Teredo Books, Ltd., 1976.

Carrick, Robert W., and Richard Henderson. *John G. Alden and His Yacht Designs.* Camden, Maine: International Marine, 1983.

Chapelle, Howard I. *American Small Sailing Craft.* New York: W. W. Norton and Company, Inc., 1951.

Colvin, Thomas E. *Coastwise & Offshore Cruising Wrinkles.* Camden, Maine: International Marine, 1972.

Colvin, Thomas E. *Cruising Designs from the Board of T.E.C.* Camden, Maine: International Marine, 1977.

Culler, R. D. *Skiffs and Schooners.* Camden, Maine: International Marine, 1974, 1990.

Faerøyvik, Bernard and Oystein. *Inshore Craft of Norway.* London: Conway Maritime Press, Ltd., 1979.

Godal, Jon. *Nordlandsbåten Og Åfjordsbåten.* 4 vols. Lesja, Norway: Gunnar Eldjarn–A. Kjellands Forlag A.S., 1988.

Hasler, H. G., and J. K. McLeod. *The Practical Junk Rig*. Camden, Maine: International Marine, 1988.

Kenny, Dick. *Looking at Sails*. Camden, Maine: International Marine, 1988.

Leather, John. *Gaff Rig*. Camden, Maine: International Marine, 1982, 1989.

Leather, John. *Spritsails and Lugsails*. Camden, Maine: International Marine, 1989.

Marchaj, C. A. *Sailing Theory and Practice*. New York: Dodd, Mead & Company, 1962.

Ross, Wallace. *Sail Power*. New York: Alfred A. Knopf, 1975.

Schult, Joachim. *Curious Yachting Inventions*. New York: Taplinger Publishing Company, 1974.

Svensson, Sam. *Sails Through the Centuries*. New York: Macmillan, n.d.

Taylor, Roger C. *Thirty Classic Boat Designs*. Camden, Maine: International Marine, 1992.

Underhill, Harold. *Masting and Rigging the Clipper Ship and Ocean Carrier*. Brown, Son and Ferguson; Dobbs Ferry, N.Y.: Sheridan House, 1946.

Worcester, G. R. G. *Junks and Sampans of the Yangtze*. Annapolis, Md.: Naval Institute Press, 1971.

Worcester, G. R. G. *Sail & Sweep in China: The History and Development of the Chinese Junk as Illustrated by the Collection of Chinese Junk Models in the Science Museum*. London: Her Majesty's Stationery Office, 1966.

CANVASWORK, MARLINSPIKEWORK, KNOTWORK, RIGGINGWORK

Ashley, Clifford W. *The Ashley Book of Knots*. New York: Doubleday and Company, Inc., 1944.

Blanford, P. W. *Working in Canvas*. Brown, Son and Ferguson; Dobbs Ferry, N.Y.: Sheridan House, 1965.

Grant, Jim. *The Complete Canvasworker's Guide*. 2d ed. Camden, Maine: International Marine, 1992.

Graumont, Raoul, and John Hensel. *Splicing Wire and Fiber Rope*. Centreville, Md.: Cornell Maritime Press, 1945.

Jarman, Colin. *The Essential Knot Book*. Camden, Maine: International Marine, 1984.

Lipe, Karen. *The Big Book of Boat Canvas*. Camden, Maine: International Marine, 1988.

Merry, Barbara. *The Splicing Handbook*. Camden, Maine: International Marine, 1987.

Smith, Hervey Garrett. *The Marlinspike Sailor*. Camden, Maine: International Marine, 1960, 1971, 1993.

Taylor, Roger C. *Knowing the Ropes*. 2d ed. Camden, Maine: International Marine, 1993.

Toss, Brion. *The Rigger's Apprentice*. Camden, Maine: International Marine, 1985, 1992.

Toss, Brion. *The Rigger's Locker*. Camden, Maine: International Marine, 1992.

SAILMAKING

Bowker, R. M., and S. A. Budd. *Make Your Own Sails*. London: Macmillan, 1957.

Devillers, D. *Manuel de Matelotage & de Voilerie.* Editions Maritimes et de Outre Mer, 1971.

Grant, James Lowell. *The Sailmaker's Library.* Columbia City, Ind.: Sailrite Enterprises, 1984.

Gray, Alan. *Sailmaking Simplified.* New York: The Rudder Publishing Company, 1940.

Gutelle, Pierre. *Voiles et Gréements.* Editions Maritimes et de Outre Mer, 1968.

Howard-Williams, Jeremy. *The Care and Repair of Sails.* London: Adlard Coles, Ltd., 1976.

Howard-Williams, Jeremy. *Sails.* London: Adlard Coles, Ltd., 1976.

Howard-Williams, Jeremy. *Small Boat Sails.* Camden, Maine: International Marine, 1987.

Kipping, Robert. *Sails and Sailmaking.* London: London Technical Press, 1847.

Ratsey, Ernest A., and W. H. de Fontaine. *Yacht Sails: Their Care and Handling.* New York: W. W. Norton and Company, 1957.

Steel. *Steel's Elements of Mastmaking, Sailmaking, and Rigging.* New York: Edward Sweetman, 1932.

Whidden, Tom. *The Art and Science of Sails. A Guide to Modern Materials, Construction, Aerodynamics, Upkeep. . . .* New York: St. Martins Press, 1990.

PERIODICALS

Classic Boat, Boating Publications Ltd. Link House, Dingwall Avenue, Croydon, Surrey, England CR92TA; Tel: 0181-646-6672 (subscriptions); Fax: 0181-781-6535.

Cruising World magazine, 524 Thames Street, Newport, R.I. 02840.

Messing About in Boats, 29 Burley Street, Wenham, Mass. 01984.

National Fisherman, 120 Tillson Avenue, Rockland, Maine 04841.

Rudder magazine (discontinued, but back issues available in libraries).

SAIL, Charlestown Naval Yard, 100 First Avenue, Charlestown, Mass. 02129.

SAILING, Inland & Offshore, P.O. Box 3324, Durban 4000, Durban 4001, South Africa.

SmallBoat Journal (discontinued, but back issues available in libraries).

WoodenBoat magazine, P.O. Box 78, Brooklin, Maine 04616.

Yachting, 5 River Road, Cos Cob, Conn. 06807.

Other Sources of Information

The American Schooner Association
P.O. Box 484
Mystic, CT 06355

The Ancient Mariner's Association
P.O. Box 6484
San Diego, CA 92166

The Catboat Association
Max Fife
P.O. Box 427
Stockton Springs, ME 04981
207-567-3391

Industrial Fabrics Association International
345 Cedar Street, Suite 800
St. Paul, MN 55101
612-222-2508

Maine Maritime Museum
963 Washington Street
Bath, ME 04530
207-442-7401

Mystic Seaport Museum
Box 6000
Mystic, CT 06355
203-572-0711

Northwest School of Wooden Boatbuilding
251 Otto Street
Port Townsend, WA 98368
206-385-4948

The Old Gaffers Association
Portview, New Road
Mistley Essex CO11 2AE
England
0206 393537

The Seven Seas Cruising Association
521 South Andrews Avenue
Fort Lauderdale, FL 33301
305-463-2431

The Smithsonian Institution
Division of Transportation
MNAH 5010/MRC 628
Washington, DC 20560
202-357-2025

The Society of Workers in Early Arts and Trades
(SWEAT)
606 Lake Lena Boulevard
Auburndale, FL 33823
813-967-3262

South Street Seaport Museum and Library
  207 Front Street
  New York, NY 10038
  212-669-9400

The WoodenBoat Publications Library
  Naskeag Road
  P.O. Box 78
  Brooklin, ME 04616
  207-359-4651

The WoodenBoat School
  P.O. Box 78
  Naskeag Road
  Brooklin, ME 04616
  207-359-4651

Index